W9-BYU-606

Reading and Writing About Contemporary Issues

Third Edition

Kathleen T. McWhorter
Niagara County Community College

 Pearson

Executive Portfolio Manager: Chris Hoag
Portfolio Manager: Matt Summers
Content Producer: Katharine Glynn
Managing Producer: Alex Brown
Content Developer: Janice Wiggins
Portfolio Manager Assistant: Andres Maldonado
Product Marketer: Erin Rush
Field Marketer: Michael Coons
Content Producer Manager: Ken Volcjak

Content Development Manager: Joanne Dauskewicz
Art/Designer: iEnergizer Aptara®, Ltd.
Course Producer: Jessica Kajkowski
Full-Service Project Manager: iEnergizer Aptara®, Ltd.
Compositor: iEnergizer Aptara®, Ltd.
Printer/Binder: LSC Communications, Inc.
Cover Printer: Phoenix Color/Hagerstown
Cover Design: Wing Ngan, Ink design, inc.
Cover Art Direction: Cate Rickard Barr

Credit for Making Connections feature photo: lightwise/123rf.com.

Acknowledgements of third party content appear within the text or on pages 661–664, which constitutes an extension of this copyright page.

Copyright © 2020, 2017, 2015 by Pearson Education, Inc. 221 River Street, Hoboken, NJ 07030 or its affiliates. All Rights Reserved. Printed in the United States of America. This publication is protected by copyright, and permission should be obtained from the publisher prior to any prohibited reproduction, storage in a retrieval system, or transmission in any form or by any means, electronic, mechanical, photocopying, recording, or otherwise. For information regarding permissions, request forms and the appropriate contacts within the Pearson Education Global Rights & Permissions department, please visit www.pearsoned.com/permissions/.

PEARSON, ALWAYS LEARNING, and MYLAB READING AND WRITING SKILLS are exclusive trademarks owned by Pearson Education, Inc. or its affiliates, in the U.S., and/or other countries.

Unless otherwise indicated herein, any third-party trademarks that may appear in this work are the property of their respective owners and any references to third-party trademarks, logos, or other trade dress are for demonstrative or descriptive purposes only. Such references are not intended to imply any sponsorship, endorsement, authorization, or promotion of Pearson's products by the owners of such marks, or any relationship between the owner and Pearson Education, Inc. or its affiliates, authors, licensees, or distributors.

Library of Congress Cataloging-in-Publication Data

Names: McWhorter, Kathleen T., author.
Title: Reading and writing about contemporary issues / Kathleen T. McWhorter.
Description: Third edition. | [New York, New York] : Pearson Education, Inc., [2020] | Includes bibliographical references and index.
Identifiers: LCCN 2018051783 | ISBN 0134996305 (Student Edition : alk. paper) | ISBN 9780134996301 (Student Edition : alk. paper) | ISBN 0135228875 (Loose-Leaf Edition : alk. paper) | ISBN 9780135228876 (Loose-Leaf Edition : alk. paper)
Subjects: LCSH: College readers. | English language—Rhetoric—Problems, exercises, etc. | Report writing—Problems, exercises, etc. | Current events—Problems, exercises, etc.
Classification: LCC PE1417 .M45653 2020 | DDC 808/.0427—dc23 LC record available at https://lccn.loc.gov/2018051783

MyLab Access Code Card
ISBN-10: 0-13-530513-6
ISBN-13: 978-0-13-530513-3

Student Edition
ISBN-10: 0-13-499630-5
ISBN-13: 978-0-13-499630-1

Loose-leaf Edition
ISBN-10: 0-13-522887-5
ISBN-13: 978-0-13-522887-6

Brief Contents

Detailed Contents

Preface

The third edition of *Reading and Writing About Contemporary Issues* offers an integrated approach to reading and writing, using a handbook for reference and instruction followed by readings for analysis and writing. The nonfiction readings are organized into units that focus on contemporary issues. Chosen to interest and motivate students, they are drawn from books, textbooks, periodicals, popular magazines, newspapers, Web sites, and internet sources with the objective of providing stimulating and challenging readings that enable students to apply reading and critical-thinking skills and respond to text through writing. The book also offers a multi-disciplinary casebook of readings on the topic of globalization and a brief skill refresher review of grammar and correctness.

Addressing Changing Needs of Readers and Writers

College readers and writers continue to face new challenges. Increasingly more reading is being done online. Online reading requires modification and adaption of skills to suit the digital delivery mode. Online reading also demands an increased vigilance for unreliable or inaccurate sources. The third edition of *Reading and Writing About Contemporary Issues* addresses these concerns through new instructional material in Part One on developing digital reading skills and on recognizing fake news. The society in which we live is rapidly changing; it presents us with new opportunities and technologies previously never thought possible. However, our society also presents us with risks and dangers. Several new readings in Part Two address both technological innovations and possible threats to personal safety and security.

Re-Visioning *Reading and Writing About Contemporary Issues* for the Third Edition for Course Redesign

The third edition of *Reading and Writing About Contemporary Issues* was written in response to the continuing changes in the fields of reading, writing, and composition. Course redesign is occurring within both developmental writing and first-year composition classes. The ALP (Accelerated Learning Program) co-requisite model is being widely adopted due to state mandates, institutional or departmental policies, and individual instructor choice. Fewer classes are being offered in developmental reading and writing, and students who formerly were enrolled in those developmental classes are now placed in first-year composition classes while enrolling simultaneously in an additional instructional support course.

In the ALP model, instructors of the co-requisite sections have found that they must provide supplemental instruction in reading and writing skills to enable students to handle the demands of the first-year composition classes. *Reading and Writing About Contemporary Issues* guides instructors in providing the extra reading and writing skills that students are lacking. The handbook in Part One provides concise review of essential reading and writing skills, and the apparatus preceding and following each of the readings in Part Two offers guided reading and writing instructional support. Part Three, A Multi-Disciplinary Casebook on Globalization, enables instructors to focus on comparison, synthesis, and evaluation of ideas using a set of closely related readings. Part Four, a set of skill refreshers, offers writers a review of essential points of grammar and correctness.

Developmental reading and writing courses continue to evolve as well, more strongly emphasizing the integration of reading and writing. These courses are also moving away from drill and practice instruction, instead embracing a readings-based model that emphasizes contextualized learning. *Reading and Writing About Contemporary Issues* is well-suited to both integration and a readings-based approach, with the largest portion of the book devoted to themed readings that teach both reading and writing skills through pre- and post-reading activities and questions.

NEW TO THE THIRD EDITION

Significant changes have been made throughout the book.

Changes to Part One: A Handbook for Reading and Writing in College

- **NEW Coverage of Digital Reading Skills.** Because students are asked to read both academic and everyday sources online, digital reading skills are essential to today's college students. A new section in Chapter 1 examines the differences between reading print and digital text and offers numerous strategies for adapting reading skills to accommodate the characteristics of digital text.
- **NEW Coverage of Fake News.** Because Internet postings are seldom monitored or screened for reliability or accuracy, fake news has become an issue of growing concern. In fact, fake news has become a current topic of discussion and debate in many academic communities. A new section in Chapter 9 defines fake news, offers examples, and suggests strategies for identifying fake news.
- **NEW Self-Test End-of-Chapter Summaries.** The chapter summaries in Part One have been revised to facilitate interactive self-testing. Key points of chapter content are presented in question form. Students are encouraged to cover the column that contains the answers, answer each question, and then check to verify that their recall is accurate and complete. Self-testing provides a form of review and rehearsal, both of which enhance recall and retention.

- **NEW Shared Writing Coverage.** A new section in Chapter 2 describes how to use Google Docs to create and share word processed documents and discusses its use in a writing class.
- **Updated passages.** Numerous textbook practice excerpts and passages have been changed to reflect more contemporary issues.

Changes to Part Two: Reading and Writing About Contemporary Issues

- **NEW Chapter 11 Marginal Commentary.** Each of the three readings in Chapter 11 contain marginal commentary that demonstrate to students the kinds of thinking that should occur as they read. Using both statements and questions, these prompts model the kinds of thinking that should occur while reading. The marginal commentary is focused as follows:
  - **Reading 1 Essential Literal Comprehension Skills.** The first reading demonstrates the thinking that occurs in applying essential literal comprehension skills, including paragraph and essay organization. Specifically, students learn the function of headings, examine word meaning, identify topics, details, transitions, and theses, and consider what is important to learn.
  - **Reading 2 Analyzing Author's Techniques.** The second reading models the critical thinking skills involved in examining the author's techniques, including the function of the title and quotations, use of types of evidence, word choice, and use of generalizations.
  - **Reading 3 Evaluating Author's Ideas.** The third reading presents examples of critical thinking skills involved in examining the author's ideas. Skills include assessing the author's attitude toward the subject and his or her credibility, evaluating relevancy and sufficiency of information, and identifying emotional appeals.
  - In Chapters 12–17, students are encouraged to write their own marginal commentary that reflects their thinking and records their ideas for written response.

- **NEW Contemporary Issue Chapter 15: Personal Safety and Security.** One of the biggest changes in the past decade is the growing threat to our safety and security in the classroom, the workplace, and other public places. Numerous tragic events pervade our consciousness as never before. Also, many people no longer feel secure using computer-related technology. Identify theft, facial recognition technology, and theft of financial records are now serious threats. Chapter 15 explores the theme of personal safety and security through readings on mass shootings, China's government espionage of its own citizens, and a textbook excerpt overview of crime fighting technologies designed to keep us safe and thwart criminal behavior.
- **NEW Nine Professional Readings.** New topics include the long-term effects of megastorms, BPA in water bottles, phubbing, falling in love

online, ethical issues in medicine, surviving a mass shooting, surveillance in China, crime fighting technology, and hate speech on campus.

- **REFOCUSED Chapter 14.** The previous chapter broadly focused on ethical issues in science. The revised chapter is now limited to medical ethics, providing a tighter thematic unit.
- **NEW and Reorganized Apparatus Accompanying Each Reading.** The apparatus that accompanies each reading mirrors the organization of Part One, offering pre-reading strategies, during reading strategies, and post-reading strategies. To better enable instructors to teach both reading and writing via the reading selections, new activities have been added and existing ones revised. The pre-reading section of the apparatus now includes the following features:
  - **Preview It.** The section asks students to preview the reading and answer questions, often open-ended, about what they anticipate the reading will cover.
  - **Look It Up.** Because activation or acquisition of background knowledge contributes to both comprehension and retention, students are encouraged to use an electronic device (laptop, tablet, smart phone, etc.) to research an aspect of the topic covered in the reading. This activity builds interest and serves as a starting point for class discussion prior to reading.
  - **Discuss It.** Using what they learned from the above Look It Up feature, students have an opportunity to talk about the topic before reading the chapter essay. This activity activates existing schema and allows students to fill in gaps in their knowledge and experience related to the topic before reading.
  - **Write About It.** This activity asks students to write a paragraph in response to a prompt related to the topic of the reading. This feature enables students to begin to formulate and verbalize ideas about the reading and explore their own thoughts and experiences related to the reading.
  - **Read It.** This section offers a specific reading strategy for each reading, addressing particular characteristics of the reading or alerting students to potential pitfalls.
- **NEW Open-ended Critical Thinking Questions.** Section F of the apparatus following each reading in Part Two now includes four to five open-ended critical thinking questions. These questions demand detailed and examined responses and encourage written response.

NEW Part Three: Multi-Disciplinary Casebook on Globalization

The casebook allows students to examine a topic in depth and encourages comparison and synthesis of ideas. The casebook models the cross-disciplinary exploration of a topic by considering its implications within a variety of academic disciplines. The new casebook on globalization replaces the previous one on climate change. Globalization, the integration and interaction of people, companies, nations, and cultures, is a topic of concern in many fields of study. The casebook examines how members of the world community interact from the perspective of six academic disciplines—geography, biology, business/marketing, cultural anthropology, communication, and economics. The casebook opens with a reading that introduces the concept of globalization and makes it accessible to students by examining its impact on three items of everyday life. The remainder of the readings explore world overpopulation, global marketing, healthcare, intercultural communication, and the global economy.

NEW Part Four: Grammar and Correctness Skill Refresher

Because students need immediate and frequent reminders about the importance of grammar and correctness, a new Part Four has been added that provides a brief review of ten common errors. Each refresher concisely explains the topic and offers examples of errors and their correction.

CONTENT AND FORMAT OVERVIEW

Reading and Writing About Contemporary Issues guides students in developing basic vocabulary and comprehension skills, as well as inferential and critical-reading and thinking skills. Writing skills are cultivated through skill review, activities, and writing prompts that require students to write in response to the articles and essays they read. The text is organized into four parts:

- **Part One, A Handbook for Reading and Writing in College,** presents a concise introduction to reading and writing skills. Written in handbook format (1a, 1b, etc.), this part serves as a guide and reference tool for the skills students need to read and write about the readings in Part Two.
- **Part Two, Reading and Writing About Contemporary Issues,** consists of seven chapters, each containing three reading selections on a contemporary issue for reading and response.
- **Part Three, A Multi-Disciplinary Casebook on Globalization,** contains six readings that offer a focused, in-depth examination of a single contemporary issue.
- **Part Four, Grammar and Correctness Skill Refreshers,** reviews ten common grammatical errors and explains how to correct them.

Format of Part One: A Handbook for Critical Reading and Writing in College

The handbook guides students in learning the reading, critical-thinking, and writing skills essential for college success. It contains the following features:

- **Integrated approach to reading and writing.** Reading and writing are approached as complementary processes that are best learned together. Most college reading assignments require written responses of some sort—essay exams, papers, or research projects. This text shows students how to analyze reading and writing assignments; teaches them the important skills of annotating, paraphrasing, outlining, and mapping, which enable and prepare them to write response papers; and provides guidance and instruction on how to write and revise paragraphs, essays, and documented papers.

- **Students approach reading and writing as thinking.** Reading and writing are approached as thinking processes involving interaction with textual material and sorting, evaluating, and responding to its organization and content. The apparatus preceding and following each reading focuses, guides, and shapes the students' thought processes and encourages thoughtful and reasoned responses.
- **Students develop a wide range of critical-reading and -thinking skills.** Because simply understanding what a writer says is seldom sufficient in college courses, this handbook teaches students to examine, interpret, analyze, and evaluate ideas. Students learn to make inferences, consider an author's techniques, and identify his or her biases in relation to the message presented and then apply this knowledge to their own writing.
- **Students learn to analyze and write arguments.** Because argumentation is an important part of both academic discourse and workplace and everyday communication, students learn to read and analyze arguments and to plan, develop, organize, write, and revise effective written arguments.
- **Students learn to write a documented paper.** Writing a documented paper is required in many college courses. Students learn to identify trustworthy sources, extract information from them so as to avoid plagiarism, integrate information from sources into essays, incorporate quotations, and use the MLA and APA documentation systems.

Format of Part Two: Reading and Writing About Contemporary Issues

Each chapter in Part Two begins with an introduction that focuses students' attention on the issue, provides context and background information, discusses its importance and relevance to college coursework, and includes tips for reading about the issue. Each chapter contains three readings, each of which is preceded by before reading activities and followed by exercises that allow students to practice and apply the reading and writing strategies covered in Part One. A section of activities titled "Making Connections: Thinking Within the Issues" ends each chapter and encourages students to synthesize ideas related to two or more readings in the chapter, and a final section titled "Making Connections: Thinking Across the Issues" ends Part Two with activities that encourage students to think about ideas from readings across the chapters.

- **Choice of readings.** Nonfiction readings were chosen to be interesting and engaging and to serve as good models of writing. These readings are taken from a variety of sources including textbooks, digital sources, online sites, and periodicals. Issues include surviving a mass shooting, e-waste, the right to die movement, human trafficking, and group conformity.

- **Lexile levels for all readings.** Lexile® measure—the most widely used reading metric in U.S. schools—provides valuable information about a student's reading ability and the complexity of text. It helps match students with reading resources and activities that are targeted to their ability level.
- **Pre-reading exercises.** Students learn to focus their attention and prepare to read by learning about the source and context of the reading provided in a headnote and by previewing the reading, researching, discussing, writing about the topic, and considering specific strategies for reading the article. These exercises encourage them to activate their prior knowledge and experience about the topic.
- **Post-reading exercises.** Post-reading exercises mirror the organization of Part One, providing students practice in checking their comprehension, analyzing the reading, and writing in response to it. Students progress through vocabulary skills, recognition of thesis and main ideas, identifying details, recognizing methods of organization and transitions, analyzing visuals, figuring out implied meanings, thinking critically, reviewing and organizing a reading using paraphrases, maps, outlines, or summaries, and analyzing arguments. Students also write in response to the reading using paragraph and essay prompts.
- **End-of-chapter and end-of-part synthesis activities.** Each chapter concludes with a section titled "Making Connections: Thinking Within the Issues" that encourages students to draw connections between and among the chapter readings, extend their critical-reading and -thinking skills, and explore the issue further through discussion and writing. Part Two concludes with a set of activities, "Making Connections: Thinking Across the Issues," that requires students to see relationships among the various issues presented in Part Two.

Format of Part Three: A Multi-Disciplinary Casebook on Globalization

The casebook contains six readings from a variety of academic disciplines that provide different perspectives on the issue of globalization, demonstrating the far-reaching environmental, cultural, economic, and geographic implications of a single contemporary issue. The introduction provides tips for reading about the issue, synthesizing sources, and previewing. Each selection is followed by activities that ask students to apply reading and writing skills presented earlier in the book and critical-thinking questions. The "Synthesis and Integration Questions and Activities" section at the end of the casebook encourages students to synthesize the information in the readings. A final section offers students opportunities to write about the readings in the casebook.

Format of Part Four Grammar and Correctness Skill Refresher

This collection of skill refreshers addresses ten common problems students experience with grammar and correctness. Each topic identifies the error and shows how to correct it.

MYLAB READING & WRITING SKILLS WWW.MYSKILLSLAB.COM

Reach Every Student by Pairing This Text with MyLab Reading & Writing Skills

MyLab™ is the teaching and learning platform that empowers you to reach *every* student. By combining trusted content with digital tools and a flexible platform, MyLab personalizes the learning experience and improves results for each student. When students enter the classroom with varying skill levels, MyLab can help instructors identify which students need extra support and provide them targeted practice and instruction outside of class. Learn more at www.pearson.com/mylab/reading-and-writing-skills.

- **Empower each learner:** Each student learns at a different pace. Personalized learning pinpoints the precise areas where each student needs practice, giving all students the support they need—when and where they need it—to be successful.
  - MyLab diagnoses students' strengths and weaknesses through a pre-assessment known as the **Path Builder**, and offers up a personalized Learning Path. Students then receive targeted practice and multimodal activities to help them improve over time.
  - MyLab Reading & Writing Skills uses **The Lexile® Framework for Reading** to diagnose a student's reading ability. After an initial Locator Test, students receive readings and practice at their estimated reading level. Throughout the course, periodic diagnostic tests incrementally adjust their level with increasing precision.
- **Instructors can teach the course in their own ways.** Each course is unique. So whether an instructor prefers to build his or her own assignments, teach multiple sections, or set prerequisites, MyLab gives instructors the flexibility to easily create a course to fit their needs.
- **Improve student results:** When instructors teach with MyLab, student performance improves. That's why instructors have chosen MyLab for over 15 years, touching the lives of over 50 million students.

TEXT-SPECIFIC ANCILLARIES

Annotated Instructor's Edition for *Reading and Writing About Contemporary Issues* **(ISBN 0135228816/9780135228814)** The Annotated Instructor's Edition is identical to the student text but includes all the answers printed directly on the pages where questions, exercises, or activities appear.

Instructor's Resource Manual and Test Bank for *Reading and Writing About Contemporary Issues 2e* **(ISBN 0135228832/9780135228838)** The online Instructor's Resource Manual contains general information on how to teach an integrated course, plus a teaching tip sheet, sample pacing guide, syllabus, and other useful handouts. It includes teaching suggestions and handouts for

Part One (Chapters 1–10), provides collaborative activities that complement the readings, and offers students opportunities to think critically and solve problems in a group setting for Part Two. In addition, it contains tips for teaching the Part Three Casebook and suggested writing activities and topics for each reading. The Test Bank contains a set of multiple-choice content review quizzes for Chapters 1–10 formatted for easy distribution and scoring.

PowerPoint Presentation (Download Only) for *Reading and Writing About Contemporary Issues* **(ISBN 0135228824/9780135228821)** PowerPoint presentations to accompany each chapter consist of classroom-ready lecture outline slides, lecture tips, classroom activities, and review questions. Available for download from the Instructor Resource Center.

Answer Key for *Reading and Writing About Contemporary Issues* **(ISBN 0135228905 9780135228906)** The Answer Key contains the solutions to the exercises in the student edition of the text. Available for download from the Instructor Resource Center.

Pearson MyTest for *Reading and Writing About Contemporary Issues* **(ISBN 0135228891/9780135228890)** This supplement is created from the Test Bank and is a powerful assessment generation program that helps instructors easily create and print quizzes, study guides, and exams. Select Pearson's questions and supplement them with your own questions. Available at www.pearsonmytest.com.

ACKNOWLEDGMENTS

I would like to express my gratitude to my reviewers for their excellent ideas, suggestions, and advice on the preparation and revision of this text:

Wes Anthony, *Cleveland Community College*; Andrea Berta, *University of Texas–El Paso*; Christi BlueFeather, *Tarrant County College*; Frances Boffo, *St. Phillip's College*; Elizabeth Braun, *Catawba Valley Community College*; Louise Brown, *Salt Lake Community College*; Sandra Christensen, *Camosun College*; Lyam Christopher, *Palm Beach State College*; Louise Clark, *Austin Community College*; Yanely Cordero, *Miami Dade, Homestead*; Cynthia Crable, *Allegany College of Maryland*; Kathy Daily, *Tulsa Community College*; Crystal Edmonds, *Robeson Community College*; Scott Empric, *Housatonic Community College*; Kelley Evans, *Brunswick Community College*; Marsi Franceschini, *Central Piedmont Community College*; Sally Gearhart, *Santa Rosa Junior College*; Betty Gray, *Southeastern Community College*; Brent Green, *Salt Lake Community College*; Elizabeth Hall, *Rockland Community College*; Caroline Helsabeck, *Forsyth Technical Community College*; Eric Hibbison, *J. Sargeant Reynolds Community College*; Elizabeth High, *Southeastern Community College*; Suzanne Hughes, *Florida State College at Jacksonville*; Jennifer Johnson, *Vance-Granville Community College*; Patty Kunkel, *Santa Fe College*; James Landers, *Community College of Philadelphia*; Dawn Langley, *Piedmont Community College*; Joy Lester, *Forsyth Technical Community College*; Desmond Lewis, *Houston Community College*; Nancy Marguardt, *Gaston College*; Barbara Marshall, *Rockingham Community College*;

Kerry McShane-Moley, *Cape Fear Community College*; Susan Monroe, *Housatonic Community College*; Emily Chevalier Moore, *Wake Technical Community College*; Laura Corso Moore, *Cape Fear Community College*; Arlene Neal, *Catawba Valley Community College*; Karen Nelson, *Craven Community College*; Mary Nielson, *Dalton State College*; Elizabeth A. O'Scanlon, *Santa Barbara Community College*; Gloria Rabun, *Caldwell Community College*; Adalia Reyna, *South Texas College*; Nancy M. Risch, *Caldwell Community College and Technical Institute*; Jason Roberts, *Salt Lake Community College*; Amy Rule, *Collin College*; Jamie Sadler, *Richmond Community College*; Mike Sfiropoilos, *Palm Beach State College*; Susan Swan, *Glendale Community College*; Stacey Synol, *Glendale Community College*; Kelly Terzaken, *Coastal Carolina Community College*; Jeanine Williams, *The Community College of Baltimore County*; Chris Yockey, *Mitchell Community College*; B. J. Zamora, *Cleveland Community College*.

I wish to thank Janice Wiggins, Executive Development Editor, for her creative vision of the project, her helpful suggestions, her careful editing, and her overall assistance. I also thank Chris Hoag, Vice President and Portfolio Manager, for her support of the project, and Phoebe Mathews for her assistance in copyediting the manuscript. Additionally, I thank Joanne Dauksewicz, Managing Editor, and Erin Bosco, Program Manager, at Ohlinger Studios for managing the production of the book.

Finally, I owe a debt of gratitude to Kathryn Tyndall, retired department head of the Pre-Curriculum Department at Wake Technical Community College, for consulting with me about the project.

Kathleen T. McWhorter

A Handbook
for Reading
and Writing
in College

wavebreakmedia/Shutterstock

bikeriderlondon/Shutterstock

The Reading Process

What does it take to do well in college? In answer to this question, many college students are likely to say

- "Knowing how to study."
- "You have to like the course."
- "Hard work!"
- "Background in the subject area."
- "A good teacher!"

Students seldom mention reading college textbooks and writing in response to reading as essential skills. When you think about college, you think of attending classes and labs, completing assignments, studying for and taking exams, doing research in the library or on the Internet, and writing papers. A closer look at these activities, however, reveals that reading and writing are important parts of each.

Throughout this handbook, you will learn numerous ways to use reading and writing as tools for college success. You will improve your basic comprehension skills and learn to think critically about the materials you read. You will also learn to write effective paragraphs and essays and use your skills to respond to articles, essays, and textbook excerpts that you read. Finally, you will also learn to handle high-stakes writing assignments that involve using sources to explain and support your own ideas.

In this chapter, you will learn the basics of college textbook reading and then develop specific strategies to use before, during, and after reading. These strategies will enable you to understand and remember more of what you read and be prepared to write about what you have read.

The readings that appear in Part Two of this book will help you apply before, during, and after reading and writing strategies to both textbook and non-textbook readings.

1a   ACTIVE READING: THE KEY TO ACADEMIC SUCCESS

LEARNING OBJECTIVE 1
Read and think actively

Reading involves much more than moving your eyes across lines of print, more than recognizing words, and more than reading sentences. Reading is *thinking*. It is an active process of identifying important ideas and comparing, evaluating, and applying them.

Have you ever gone to a ball game and watched the fans? Most do not sit and watch passively. Instead, they direct the plays, criticize the calls, encourage the players, and reprimand the coach. They care enough to get actively involved in the game. Just like interested fans, active readers get involved. They question, challenge, and criticize, as well as understand. Table 1-1 contrasts the active strategies of successful readers with the passive strategies of less successful readers. Not all strategies will work for everyone. Experiment to discover those that work particularly well for you.

EXERCISE 1-1 . . . ACTIVE READING

Consider each of the following reading assignments. Discuss ways to get actively involved in each assignment.

1. Reading two poems by Maya Angelou for an American literature class

   _____

   _____

2. Reading the procedures for your next chemistry lab

   _____

3. Reading an article in *Time* magazine, or on the *Time* magazine Web site, assigned by your political science instructor in preparation for a class discussion

   _____

   _____

TABLE 1-1 ACTIVE VERSUS PASSIVE READING

ACTIVE READERS . . .	PASSIVE READERS . . .
Tailor their reading to suit each assignment.	Read all assignments the same way.
Analyze the purpose of an assignment.	Read an assignment because it was assigned.
Adjust their speed to suit their purpose.	Read everything at the same speed.
Question ideas in the assignment.	Accept whatever is in print as true.
Compare and connect textbook material with lecture content.	Study lecture notes and the textbook separately.
Skim headings to find out what an assignment is about before beginning to read.	Check the length of an assignment and then begin reading.
Make sure they understand what they are reading as they go along.	Read until the assignment is completed.
Read with pencil in hand, highlighting, jotting notes, and marking key vocabulary.	Read.
Develop personalized strategies that are particularly effective.	Follow routine, standard methods. Read all assignments the same way.
Look for the relevance of the assignment to their own lives.	Fixate on memorizing terms and definitions solely to pass the exam or get a good grade.
Engage with the contemporary issues under discussion with an open mind.	React emotionally to reading assignments without taking the time to carefully consider the author's key points.

1b   READING TEXTBOOKS

LEARNING OBJECTIVE 2
Read textbooks effectively

In most college courses, textbooks are the primary source of reading material. They are almost always written by college teachers who know what students are likely to need to help them understand the material and participate in classroom lectures and discussions. As you read your textbook assignments in preparation for class, be sure to take advantage of the valuable learning aids built into each chapter.

Guidelines for Reading Textbooks

Use the following guidelines to get the most from your textbooks.

1. **Use the textbook's learning aids.** Textbooks provide many features designed to help you learn and remember the content. Table 1-2 summarizes these features and explains how to use each.

2. **Pay close attention to the examples.** If your textbook does not provide an example of an important concept, ask your instructor for one.

3. **Be patient and reward yourself when you have reached key milestones in the assignment.** Take occasional short breaks from reading, and reward yourself with a snack or something that motivates you to complete the assignment with a high level of comprehension.

4. **Look for relevance to your own life.** For instance, a business textbook discussion about the price of generic equivalents versus expensive brand names might help you the next time you need to buy aspirin.

5. **Use additional print-based or online resources.** In many disciplines, online labs provide additional practice opportunities; check your textbook to find out what is available.

6. **Read with a highlighter or pen in hand.** Highlighting (see Section 1f) and annotating (see Section 1g) are particularly helpful for marking key points in the textbook. Studies have proven that students learn better when they write, annotate, and take notes as they read.

TABLE 1-2 TEXTBOOK AIDS TO LEARNING

FEATURE	HOW TO USE IT
Preface or "To the Student"	• Read it to find out how the book is organized, what topics it covers, and what learning features it contains.
Chapter Opener (may include chapter objectives, photographs, and chapter outlines)	• Read it to find out what the chapter is about. • Use it to test yourself later to see whether you can recall the main points.
Marginal Vocabulary Definitions	• Learn the definition of each term. • Create a vocabulary log (in a notebook or computer file) and enter words you need to learn.
Photographs and Graphics	• Determine their purpose: what important information do they illustrate? • For diagrams, charts, and tables, note the process or trend they illustrate. Make marginal notes. • Practice redrawing diagrams without referring to the originals.
Test Yourself Questions (after sections within the chapter)	• Always check to see whether you can answer them before going on to the next section. • Use them to check your recall of chapter content when studying for an exam.
Special Interest Inserts (can include profiles of people, coverage of related issues, critical thinking topics, etc.)	• Discover how the inserts are related to the chapter content: what key concepts do they illustrate?
Review Questions/Problems/Discussion Questions	• Read them over once before you read the chapter to discover what you are expected to learn. • Use them to test your recall after you have read the chapter.
Chapter Summary	• Test yourself by converting summary statements into questions using the words Who? Why? When? How? and So what?
Chapter Review Quiz	• Use this to prepare for an exam. Pay extra attention to items you get wrong.

EXERCISE 1–2 . . . READING COLLEGE TEXTBOOKS

Using a textbook from one of your other courses, make a list of the learning aids it contains. Then briefly indicate how you can use each to study.

PRE-READING STRATEGIES

1c   PREVIEWING, PREDICTING, AND ASKING QUESTIONS

LEARNING OBJECTIVE 3
Preview, predict, and ask questions

Before you read an assignment, you should preview it, make predictions about the material, and develop questions that you expect the material to address.

Previewing

Previewing is a means of familiarizing yourself with the content and organization of an assignment *before* you read it. Think of previewing as getting a "sneak preview" of what a chapter or reading will be about. You can then read the material more easily and more rapidly.

How to Preview Reading Assignments

Use the following steps to become familiar with the content and organization of a chapter, essay, or article, either print or online.

1. **Read the title and subtitle.** The title indicates the topic of the article or chapter; the subtitle suggests the specific focus of, or approach to, the topic.

2. **Check the author and source of an article or essay.** This information may provide clues about the article's content or focus. If you are reading a collection of essays, there may be a **head note** before each essay that provides concise background information about the author and the essay.

3. **Read the introduction or the first paragraph.** The introduction or first paragraph serves as a lead-in, establishing the overall subject and suggesting how it will be developed.

4. **Read each boldfaced (dark black print) or colored heading.** Headings label the contents of each section and announce the major topic covered.

5. **Read the first sentence under each heading.** The first sentence often states the main point of the section. If the first sentence seems introductory, read the last sentence; often this sentence states or restates the main point.

6. **If headings are not provided, read the first sentence of several paragraphs per page.** This sentence is often the topic sentence, which states the main idea of the paragraph. By reading first sentences, you will encounter most of the key ideas in the article.

7. **Note any typographical aids and information presented in list format.** Colored print, **boldface**, and *italics* are often used to emphasize important terminology and definitions, distinguishing them from the rest of a passage. Material that is numbered 1, 2, 3; lettered a, b, c; or presented in list form is also of special importance.

8. **Read the first sentence of each item presented as a list.**

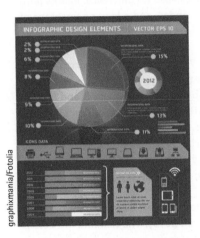

graphixmania/Fotolia

9. **Note any graphic aids.** Graphs, charts, photographs, and tables often suggest what is important. As part of your preview, read the captions of photographs and the legends on graphs, charts, and tables.

10. **Read the last paragraph or summary.** This provides a condensed view of the article or chapter, often outlining the key points.

11. **Read quickly any end-of-article or end-of-chapter material.** This material might include references, study questions, discussion questions, chapter outlines, or vocabulary lists. If study questions are included, read them through quickly because they tell you what to look for in the chapter. If a vocabulary list is included, rapidly skim through it to identify the terms you will be learning as you read.

EXAMINING PROFESSIONAL WRITING

The following textbook excerpt is taken from *Sociology: A Down-to-Earth Approach*, 13e, by James Henslin. This excerpt will be used throughout this chapter to demonstrate techniques and give you practice in reading and learning from college textbooks. The following section, discussing social class, illustrates how previewing is done. The portions to focus on when previewing are shaded. Read only those portions. After you have finished, test how well your previewing worked by completing Exercise 1-3, "What Did You Learn from Previewing?"

Issue: Wealth and Poverty

Consequences of Social Class

James Henslin

1   Does social class matter? And how! Think of each social class (whether upper-class, middle-class, working-class, or poor/underclass) as a broad subculture with distinct approaches to life, so significant that it affects our health, family life, education, religion, politics, and even our experiences with crime and the criminal justice system. Let's look at how social class affects our lives.

Physical Health

2   The principle is simple: As you go up the social-class ladder, health increases. As you go down the ladder, health decreases (Hout 2008). Age makes no difference. Infants born to the poor are more likely to die before their first birthday, and a larger percentage of poor people in their old age—whether 75 or 95—die each year than do the elderly who are wealthy.

3   How can social class have such dramatic effects? While there are many reasons, here are three. First, social class opens and closes doors to medical care. People with good incomes or with good medical insurance are able to choose their doctors and pay for whatever treatment and medications are prescribed. The poor, in contrast, don't have the money or insurance to afford this type of medical care.

4   A second reason is lifestyle, which is shaped by social class. People in the lower classes are more likely to smoke, eat a lot of fats, be overweight, abuse drugs and alcohol, get little exercise, and practice unsafe sex (Chin et al. 2000; Dolnick 2010). This, to understate the matter, does not improve people's health.

5   There is a third reason, too. Life is hard on the poor. The persistent stresses they face cause their bodies to wear out faster (Geronimus et al. 2010). The rich find life better. They have fewer problems and more resources to deal with the ones they have. This gives them a sense of control over their lives, a source of both physical and mental health.

Mental Health

6   Sociological research from as far back as the 1930s has found that the mental health of the lower classes is worse than that of the higher classes (Faris and Dunham 1939; Srole et al. 1978; Peltham 2009). Greater mental problems are part of the higher stress that accompanies poverty. Compared with middle- and upper-class Americans, the poor have less job security and lower wages. They are more likely to divorce, to be the victims of crime, and to have more physical illnesses. Couple these conditions with bill collectors and the threat of eviction, and you can see how they can deal severe blows to people's emotional well-being.

7   People higher up the social class ladder experience stress in daily life, of course, but their stress is generally less, and their coping resources are greater. Not only can they afford vacations, psychiatrists, and counselors, but *their class position also gives them greater control over their lives, a key to good mental health.*

Family Life

8   Social class also makes a significant difference in our choice of spouse, our chances of getting divorced, and how we rear our children.

9   **Choice of Husband or Wife.** Members of the upper class place strong emphasis on family tradition. They stress the family's history, even a sense of purpose or destiny in life (Baltzell 1979; Aldrich 1989). Children of this class learn that their choice of husband or wife affects not just them, but the entire family, that it will have an impact on the "family line." These background expectations shrink the field of "eligible" marriage partners, making it narrower than it is for the children of any other social class. As a result, parents in this class play a strong role in their children's mate selection.

10   **Divorce.** The more difficult life of the lower social classes, especially the many tensions that come from insecure jobs and inadequate incomes, leads to higher marital friction and a greater likelihood of divorce. Consequently, children of the poor are more likely to grow up in broken homes.

11   **Child Rearing.** Lower-class parents focus more on getting their children to follow rules and obey authority, while middle-class parents focus more on developing their children's creative and leadership skills (Lareau and Weininger 1977). Sociologists have traced this difference to the parents' occupations (Kohn 1977). Lower-class parents are closely supervised at work, and they anticipate that their children will have similar jobs. Consequently, they try to teach their children to defer to authority. Middle-class parents, in contrast, enjoy greater independence at work. Anticipating similar jobs for their children, they encourage them to be more creative. Out of these contrasting orientations arise different ways of disciplining children; lower-class parents are more likely to use physical punishment, while the middle classes rely more on verbal persuasion.

Education

12   Education increases as one goes up the social class ladder. It is not just the amount of education that changes, but also the type of education. Children of the upper class bypass public schools. They attend exclusive private schools where they are trained to take a commanding role in society. These schools teach upper-class values and prepare their students for prestigious universities (Beeghley 2008; Stevens 2009).

13   Keenly aware that private schools can be a key to upward social mobility, some upper-middle-class parents make every effort to get their children into the prestigious preschools that feed into these exclusive prep schools. Although some preschools cost $23,000 a year, they have a waiting list (Rohwedder 2007). Not able to afford this kind of tuition, some parents hire tutors to train their 4-year-olds in test-taking skills, so they can get into public kindergartens for gifted students. They even hire experts to teach these preschoolers to look adults in the eye while they are being interviewed for these limited positions (Banjo 2010). You can see how such parental involvement and resources make it more likely that children from the more privileged classes go to college—and graduate.

Religion

14   One area of social life that we might think would not be affected by social class is religion. ("People are just religious, or they are not. What does social class have to do with

This young woman is being "introduced" to society at a debutante ball in Laredo, Texas. Like you, she has learned from her parents, peers, and education a view of where she belongs in life. How do you think her view is different from yours?

Dm Cherry/Shutterstock

it?") However, the classes tend to cluster in different religious denominations. Episcopalians, for example, are more likely to attract the middle and upper classes, while Baptists draw heavily from the lower classes. Patterns of worship also follow class lines: The lower classes are attracted to more expressive worship services and louder music, while the middle and upper classes prefer more "subdued" worship.

Politics

15   The rich and poor walk different political paths. The higher that people are on the social class ladder, the more likely they are to vote for Republicans (Hout 2008). In contrast, most members of the working class believe that the government should intervene in the economy to provide jobs and to make citizens financially secure. They are more likely to vote for Democrats. Although the working class is more liberal on *economic issues* (policies that increase government spending), it is more conservative on *social issues* (such as opposing the Equal Rights Amendment) (Houtman 1995; Hout 2008). People toward the bottom of the class structure are also less likely to be politically active—to campaign for candidates or even to vote (Gilbert 2003; Beeghley 2008).

Crime and Criminal Justice

16   If justice is supposed to be blind, it certainly is not when it comes to one's chances of being arrested (Henslin 2012). Social classes commit different types of crime. The white-collar crimes of the more privileged classes are more likely to be dealt with outside the criminal justice system, while the police and courts deal with the street crimes of the lower classes. One consequence of this class standard is that members of the lower classes are more likely to be in prison, on probation, or on parole. In addition, since those who commit street crimes tend to do so in or near their own neighborhoods, the lower classes are more likely to be robbed, burglarized, or murdered.

—adapted from Henslin, *Sociology*, pp. 275–278

EXERCISE 1-3 . . . WHAT DID YOU LEARN FROM PREVIEWING?

Without referring to the passage, answer each of the following questions.

1. What is the overall subject of this passage?

_____

2. What happens to physical health as you go up the social class ladder?

   _____

3. In addition to choice of spouse, what other two aspects of family life are significantly affected by social class?

   _____

4. Who is the young woman in the photograph and to what class does she probably belong?

   _____

5. On a scale of 1 to 5 (1=easy, 5=very difficult), how difficult do you expect the passage to be?

   _____

You probably were able to answer all (or most) of the questions correctly. Previewing, then, does provide you with a great deal of information. If you were to return to the passage from the textbook and read the entire section, you would find it easier to do than if you hadn't previewed it.

Why Previewing Is Effective

Previewing is effective for several reasons:

- Previewing helps you decide what reading and study strategies to use as you read.
- Previewing puts your mind in gear and helps you start thinking about the subject.
- Previewing enables you to see connections and create a mental outline of the content, which will make your reading easier. However, previewing is never a substitute for careful, thorough reading.

Making Predictions

We make predictions about many tasks before we undertake them. We predict how long it will take to drive to a shopping mall, how much dinner will cost at a new restaurant, how long a party will last, or how difficult an exam will be. Prediction helps us organize our time and cope with new situations.

Prediction is an important part of active reading as well; it enables you to approach the material systematically and read actively because you continually accept or reject your predictions. As you preview, you can predict the development of ideas, the organization of the material, and the author's conclusions. For example, for her philosophy class, a student began to preview an essay titled "Do Computers Have a Right to Life?" From the title, she predicted that the essay would discuss the topic of artificial intelligence: whether computers can "think." Then, as she read the essay, she discovered that this prediction was correct.

In textbook chapters, boldfaced headings serve as section "titles" and also are helpful in predicting content and organization. Considered together, chapter headings often suggest the development of ideas through the chapter. For instance, the following headings appear in "Liking and Loving: Interpersonal Attraction":

> The Rules of Attraction
> Love Is a Triangle—Robert Sternberg's Triangular Theory of Love

These headings reveal the authors' approach to love and attraction. We can predict that the chapter will discuss factors that are involved in interpersonal attraction and describe three different kinds of love.

EXERCISE 1-4 . . . MAKING PREDICTIONS

Predict the subject and/or point of view of each of the following essays or articles.

1. "The Nuclear Test-Ban Treaty: It's Time to Sign"

   _____

2. "Flunking Lunch: The Search for Nutrition in School Cafeterias"

   _____

3. "Professional Sports: Necessary Violence"

   _____

Forming Guide Questions

Did you ever read an entire page or more and not remember anything you read? Guide questions can help you overcome this problem. **Guide questions** are questions you expect to be able to answer while or after you read. Most students form them mentally, but you can jot them in the margin if you prefer.

The following tips can help you form questions you can use to guide your reading. It is best to develop guide questions *after* you preview but *before* you read.

1. **Turn each major heading into a series of questions.** The questions should ask something that you feel is important to know.

2. **As you read a section, look for the answers to your questions.** Highlight the answers as you find them.

3. **When you finish reading a section, stop and check to see whether you can recall the answers.** Place check marks by those you cannot recall. Then reread.

4. **Avoid asking questions that have one-word answers, like *yes* or *no*.** Questions that begin with *what, why,* or *how* are more useful.

Here are a few textbook headings and some examples of questions you might ask about them:

HEADING	QUESTIONS
Managing Interpersonal Conflict	What is interpersonal conflict?
	What are strategies for managing conflict?
Paralegals at Work	What is a paralegal?
	What do paralegals do?
Kohlberg's Theory of Moral Development	Who was Kohlberg?
	How did Kohlberg explain moral development?

EXERCISE 1-5 . . . FORMING GUIDE QUESTIONS

Select the guide question that would be most helpful in improving your understanding of the textbook chapter sections that begin with the following headings:

_____ 1. Defining Loneliness
    a. Is loneliness unusual?
    b. What does loneliness mean?
    c. Are adults lonelier than children?
    d. Can loneliness ever be positive?

_____ 2. The Four Basic Functions of Management
    a. How important is management?
    b. Are there other functions of management?
    c. What are management's four basic functions?
    d. Do poor managers cause serious problems?

_____ 3. Surface Versus Depth Listening
    a. Is surface listening difficult?
    b. What is listening?
    c. How do surface and depth listening differ?
    d. Is depth listening important?

_____   4. The Origins of the Cold War

        a. How did the Cold War start?

        b. Is the Cold War still going on?

        c. How did the United States deal with the Cold War?

        d. Did the Cold War end through compromise?

_____   5. Some People Are More Powerful than Others

        a. Does power affect relationships?

        b. Why are some people more powerful than others?

        c. What is power?

        d. Can people learn to become more powerful?

1d   ACTIVATING PRIOR KNOWLEDGE

LEARNING OBJECTIVE 4
Activate your prior knowledge

After previewing your assignment, you already know *something* about the topic. This is your **prior knowledge**. For example, when asked to read an article titled "Growing Urban Problems" for a government class, a student who lived in a rural area first thought that he knew very little about the topic. But when he thought of a recent trip to a nearby city, he remembered seeing the homeless people and crowded conditions, and he remembered reading about drug problems, drive-by shootings, and muggings.

Activating your prior knowledge aids your reading in three ways. First, it makes reading easier because you have already thought about the topic. Second, the material is easier to remember because you can connect the new information with what you already know. Third, topics become more interesting if you can link them to your own experiences.

How to Activate Your Prior Knowledge

Here are some techniques to help you activate your background knowledge.

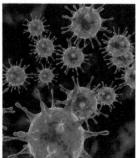

ralwel/Fotolia

Virus cells, bacteria.
Microscopic view.

- **Ask questions and try to answer them.** If a chapter in your biology textbook titled "Human Diseases" contains headings such as "Infectious Diseases," "Cancer," and "Vascular Diseases," you might ask and try to answer such questions as the following: What kinds of infectious diseases have I seen? What causes them? What do I know about preventing cancer and other diseases?

- **Draw on your own experience.** If a chapter in your business textbook is titled "Advertising: Its Purpose and Design," you might think of several ads you have seen and analyze the images used in each, as well as the purpose of each ad.

- **Brainstorm.** Write down everything that comes to mind about the topic. Suppose you're about to read a chapter in your psychology textbook on domestic violence. You might list types of violence—child abuse, spousal abuse, and so on. You might write questions such as "What causes child abuse?" and "How can it be prevented?" Alternatively, you might list incidents of domestic violence you have heard or read about. Any of these approaches will help make the topic interesting and relevant.

EXERCISE 1-6 . . . ACTIVATING PRIOR KNOWLEDGE

Use one of the three strategies listed above to discover what you already know about how social class affects our lives.

Researching, Discussing, and Writing

On occasion, based on your preview, prediction, and activation of prior knowledge, you may realize that the topic is unfamiliar or that your background knowledge is lacking or incomplete. In these cases, take a moment to look up background information online. Taking a few notes may be helpful. Discussing the topic with a classmate before reading may also broaden your knowledge or experience with the topic. In addition, writing a few sentences about the topic may serve to focus your attention.

DURING READING STRATEGIES

1e   CHECKING AND STRENGTHENING YOUR COMPREHENSION

LEARNING OBJECTIVE 5
Check and strengthen your comprehension

What happens when you read material you can understand easily? Does it seem that everything "clicks"? Do ideas seem to fit together and make sense? Is that "click" noticeably absent at other times? What should you do when this happens?

Monitoring Your Comprehension

Table 1-3 lists and compares common signals to assist you in checking your comprehension. Not all the signals appear at the same time, and not all the signals work for everyone. But becoming aware of these positive and negative signals will help you gain more control over your reading.

TABLE 1-3   COMPREHENSION SIGNALS

POSITIVE SIGNALS	NEGATIVE SIGNALS
You feel comfortable and have some knowledge about the topic.	The topic is unfamiliar, yet the author assumes you understand it.
You recognize most words or can figure them out from context.	Many words are unfamiliar.
You can express the main ideas in your own words.	You must reread the main ideas and use the author's language to explain them.
You understand why the material was assigned.	You do not know why the material was assigned and cannot explain why it is important.
You read at a regular, comfortable pace.	You often slow down or reread.
You are able to make connections among ideas.	You are unable to detect relationships; the organization is not apparent.
You are able to see where the author is heading.	You feel as if you are struggling to stay with the author and are unable to predict what will follow.
You understand what is important.	Nothing (or everything) seems important.
You read calmly and try to assess the author's points without becoming too emotionally involved.	When you encounter a controversial topic, you close your mind to alternative viewpoints or opinions.

EXERCISE 1–7 . . . CHECKING YOUR COMPREHENSION

Read the passage titled "Consequences of Social Class" that appears on pages 8–10. Be alert for positive and negative comprehension signals as you read. After reading the passage, answer the following questions on your own sheet of paper.

1. On a scale of 1 to 5 (1=very poor, 5=excellent), how would you rate your overall comprehension? _____

2. What positive signals did you sense? List them.

   _____

   _____

   _____

3. What negative signals did you experience, if any? List them.

   _____

   _____

   _____

4. In which sections was your comprehension strongest? List the paragraph numbers. _____

5. Did you feel at any time that you had lost, or were about to lose, comprehension? If so, go back to that part now. What made it difficult to read?

_____

_____

_____

Strengthening Your Comprehension Using Self-Testing

When you have finished reading, don't just close the book. Stop and assess how well you understood what you read. Test yourself. Choose a heading and turn it into a question. Cover up the text below it and see if you can answer your question. For example, convert the heading "Effects of Head Trauma" into the question "What are the effects of head trauma?" and answer your question mentally or in writing. Then check your answer by looking back at the text. This self-testing process will also help you remember more of what you read because you are reviewing what you just read.

If you are not satisfied with your self-test, or if you experienced some or all of the negative signals mentioned in Table 1-3, be sure to take action to strengthen your comprehension. Chapters 4 and 5 present basic comprehension strategies for reading paragraphs, including identifying main ideas, details, and signal words. Using context clues to figure out words you don't know is covered in Chapter 3. Here are some immediate things you can do when you realize you need to strengthen your comprehension.

Tips for Strengthening Your Comprehension

phoenix021/Fotolia

1. **Analyze the time and place in which you are reading.** If you've been reading or studying for several hours, mental fatigue may be the source of the problem. If you are reading in a place with distractions or interruptions, you might not be able to concentrate on what you're reading.

2. **Reread and/or express complicated ideas in your own words.** You might need to approach complicated material sentence by sentence, determining exactly what each means (see Paraphrasing in Section 1i).

3. **Read aloud sentences or sections that are particularly difficult.** Reading out loud sometimes makes complicated material easier to understand.

4. **Slow down your reading rate.** On occasion, simply reading more slowly and carefully will provide you with the needed boost in comprehension.

5. **Determine whether you lack prior knowledge.** Comprehension is difficult, and at times impossible, if you lack essential information that the writer

assumes you have. Suppose you are reading a political science textbook section on the balance of power in the Third World. If you do not understand the concept of balance of power, your comprehension will break down. When you lack background information, take immediate steps to correct the problem:

- Consult other sections of your text, using the glossary and index.
- Obtain a more basic text that reviews fundamental principles and concepts.
- Consult reliable Web sources.

Using Review to Strengthen Your Recall

Understanding something as you read is no guarantee that you have learned it and will remember it the next day, week, or month. To be able to recall information you read, you have to review and organize it. The best time to review material is right after you read it, then periodically until you are confident you have learned it. Take a few minutes right after you finish reading an assignment to go back through the chapter and reread headings, your highlights and annotations, and the summary or conclusion.

The skills you will learn in the Post-reading Strategies section—paraphrasing, outlining, mapping, and summarizing—will also serve as forms of review and will help you organize ideas, pull them together, and see how they connect.

1f   HIGHLIGHTING TO IDENTIFY IMPORTANT INFORMATION

LEARNING OBJECTIVE 6
Highlight important information to learn and recall it

Highlighting forces you to decide what is important and distinguish key information from less important material. Sorting ideas this way improves both comprehension and recall.

Guidelines for Effective Highlighting

To highlight effectively, use these guidelines:

1. **Analyze the assignment.** Preview the assignment and define what type of learning is required. Determine how much and what type of information you need to highlight.

2. **Assess your familiarity with the subject.** Depending on your background knowledge, you may need to highlight only a little or a great deal. Do not waste time highlighting what you already know.

3. **Read first, then highlight.** Finish a paragraph or self-contained section before you highlight. As you read, look for words and phrases that signal organizational patterns (see Chapter 7). Each idea may seem important when you first encounter it, but you must see how it compares with other ideas before you can judge its relative importance.

4. **Use headings as a guide.** Headings are labels that indicate the overall topic of a section. They indicate what is important to highlight.

5. **Highlight only main ideas and key supporting details.** Avoid highlighting examples and secondary details.

6. **Avoid highlighting complete sentences.** Highlight only enough so that your highlighting makes sense when you reread it. In the following selection, note that only key words and phrases are highlighted. Now read only the highlighted words. Can you grasp the key idea of the passage?

Issue: Immigrant Families

Like multiracial families, immigrant families face myriad challenges although they differ in nature. Fathers often find that the vocational and educational skills they worked so hard to achieve in their nation of origin are not transferable to the United States; former professionals may find themselves performing unskilled labor, earning incomes too meager to adequately support a family. Financial need may require the wife, who probably did not work in the nation of origin, to find a job to supplement the family income. In the new work setting she may find that gender roles in the United States allow more freedom to women and that she has new legal rights. She may begin to challenge the gender roles of her nation of origin, leading to marital strife. Men may begin to feel a loss of power and self-esteem while the wife gains more power and authority.

—Suppes and Wells, *The Social Work Experience*, p. 148

7. **Move quickly through the document as you highlight.** If you have understood a paragraph or section, then your highlighting should be fast and efficient.

8. **Develop a consistent system of highlighting.** Decide how you will mark main ideas, how you will distinguish main ideas from details, and how you will highlight new terminology. You can also use brackets, asterisks, and circles, or different ink colors, or combinations of pens and pencils, to distinguish various types of information. (See also Section 1g on annotating.)

9. **Use the 15–25 percent rule of thumb.** Although the amount you will highlight will vary from source to source, try to highlight no more than 15 to 25 percent of any given page. If you exceed this amount, you are likely not sorting ideas as efficiently as possible. Remember: the more you highlight, the smaller your time-saving dividends when you review.

EXERCISE 1-8 . . . HIGHLIGHTING

Read the following pair of passages, which have been highlighted in two different ways. Look at each highlighted version, and then answer the questions that follow.

Issue: First Impressions

Example A

Do you care if you make a good first impression on others? You should, according to the research findings, because such impressions seem to exert strong and lasting effects on others' perceptions of us. A recent study of 10,526 participants in HurryDate sessions—in which men and women interact with each other for very short periods, usually less than three minutes, and then indicate whether they are interested in future interaction—found that individuals know almost instantly if a person appeals to them when they see them. Men and women in the study assessed potential compatibility within moments of meeting. They based their compatibility on physically observable attributes such as age, height, attractiveness, and physique, instead of hard-to-observe attributes such as education, religion, and income, which seemed to have little effect on their choices. It is clear that the way others first perceive us strongly influences their behavior toward us and whether they want to interact with us.

—Seiler, William J, Melissa Beall,and Joseph P. Mazur. "*Communication.*" p. 68.
Reprinted and electronically reproduced by permission of Pearson Education, Inc.

Example B

Do you care if you make a good first impression on others? You should, according to the research findings, because such impressions seem to exert strong and lasting effects on others' perceptions of us. A recent study of 10,526 participants in HurryDate sessions—in which men and women interact with each other for very short periods, usually less than three minutes, and then indicate whether they are interested in future interaction—found that individuals know almost instantly if a person appeals to them when they see them. Men and women in the study assessed potential compatibility within moments of meeting. They based their compatibility on physically observable attributes such as age, height, attractiveness, and physique, instead of hard-to-observe attributes such as education, religion, and income, which seemed to have little effect on their choices. It is clear that the way others first perceive us strongly influences their behavior toward us and whether they want to interact with us.

—Seiler, Beall, and Mazur, *Communication*, p. 68

1. Is Example A or Example B the better example of effective highlighting? ___

2. Why isn't the highlighting in the other example effective?

_____

_____

EXERCISE 1-9 . . . HIGHLIGHTING

Highlight an essay provided by your instructor, or choose one from Part Two of this text or from another class you are taking. Use the techniques discussed above.

1g   ANNOTATING TO RECORD YOUR IDEAS

LEARNING OBJECTIVE 7
Use annotation to record your thinking

Active readers think as they read. They summarize, react, respond, question, judge, and evaluate ideas. Be sure to record your thoughts so you can refer to them later when studying the material, preparing for a class discussion, or searching for ideas to write about. **Annotating** is a process of making marginal notes that record your thinking. Be sure to identify sections that you do not understand or need to reread later.

Figure 1-1 suggests various types of annotation that you can use and provides examples of each in relation to a political science textbook chapter. However, you should feel free to develop your own system of annotations, symbols, and abbreviations. Annotating is a very personal process; you should annotate using whatever system helps you study best.

FIGURE 1-1 SAMPLE MARGINAL ANNOTATIONS

TYPES OF ANNOTATION	EXAMPLE
Circling unknown words	... redressing the apparent (asymmetry) of their relationship
Marking definitions	*def* [To say that the balance of power favors one party over another is to introduce a disequilibrium
Marking examples	*ex* [... concessions may include negative sanctions, trade agreements ...
Numbering lists of ideas, causes, reasons, or events	components of power include ①self-image, ② population, ③ natural resources, and ④ geography
Placing asterisks next to important passages	* [Power comes from three primary sources ...
Putting question marks next to confusing passages	?→ war prevention occurs through institutionalization of mediation ...
Making notes to yourself	Check def in soc text — power is the ability of an actor on the international stage to ...
Marking possible test items	T — There are several key features in the relationship ...
Drawing arrows to show relationships	Can terrorism be prevented through similar balance? — ↗... natural resources ..., ... control of industrial ↘manufacture capacity
Writing comments, noting disagreements and similarities	war prevention through balance of power is ...
Marking summary statements	Sum [the greater the degree of conflict, the more intricate will be ...

Here is an example of the annotations one student made on an excerpt from the reading "Consequences of Social Class" on pages 8–10.

Issue: Mental Health

Any improvement/change since the '30s? How is mental health measured? What constitutes middle- and upper-class? Other effects of poverty— test question?	Sociological research from as far back as the <u>1930s</u> has found that the <u>mental health</u> of the lower classes is worse than that of the higher classes (Faris and Dunham 1939; Srole et al. 1978; Peltham 2009). Greater mental problems are part of the higher stress that accompanies poverty. Compared with <u>middle- and upper-class</u> Americans, the poor have less job security and lower wages. They are <u>more likely to divorce, to be the victims of crime, and to have more physical illnesses.</u> Couple these conditions with bill collectors and the threat of eviction, and you can see how they can deal severe blows to people's emotional well-being.
Coping resources + control = better mental health	People higher up the social class ladder experience stress in daily life, of course, but their stress is generally less, and their coping resources are greater. Not only can they afford vacations, psychiatrists, and counselors, but *their class position also gives them greater control over their lives, a key to good mental health.*

EXERCISE 1-10 . . . ANNOTATING

Review Figure 1-1 and then annotate the reading you highlighted for Exercise 1-9.

1h   READING DIGITAL TEXT

LEARNING OBJECTIVE 8
Read digital text effectively

Digital reading is becoming increasingly important because we live in a digital world. We not only read e-books, but also read text on smartphones, tablets, Kindles, and so forth. College courses, too, often require digital reading for research, online courses, and document sharing in writing classes, for example.

Reading digital material and reading print material differ in numerous ways. To read and learn effectively, you need to be aware of their differences and adapt your skills accordingly.

Layout, digital features, and your movement through the text create a unique reading and learning environment:

- **Print text is linear; readers proceed in one direction, from beginning to end.** Digital text, on the other hand, is multi-directional; readers can follow hyperlinks, research numerous sources, and then return to the original text.

- **Because readers move through digital text by scrolling, they tend to read faster.** They also tend to alternate between reading and skimming. This skimming process leads to less detailed, careful reading.
- **Reading digital text is more stimulating.** Varying colors, print sizes, numerous graphics, shifting screens, as well as the temptation to follow hyperlinks tend to draw readers' attention away from the content of the material.
- **It is easy to get lost reading digital text.** Following hyperlinks can lead you astray from the original material and lose sight of its main points.
- **Digital reading makes multitasking more tempting.** It is easy to skip over to a social media site, for example. In fact, one research study reported that 95 percent of students report multitasking while reading digital content, while only 1 percent of students reported the same while reading print text.
- **Digital readers have to make more choices and more decisions about how to proceed on the screen (whether to follow or ignore hyperlinks, graphics, etc.) than print readers do.** These decision-making tasks may divert concentration from the ideas presented in the material.

Certainly, digital reading is here to stay, so readers need to devise new and different reading strategies for reading digital text, as outlined in the box below.

STRATEGIES FOR READING DIGITAL TEXT

To maximize time spent reading online, use the following strategies:

1. **Recognize that reading online requires as much time and effort as reading print materials, perhaps even more.** At times, you may need to purposely slow down.

2. **Evaluate your sources carefully.** Not everything that appears online is accurate and reliable. Also be sure to evaluate any hyperlinks you follow.

3. **Make conscious decisions about how and what to read.** First, consider your purpose and choose strategies accordingly. Do you need an overview of the material or in-depth understanding, for example? Read and reread to suit your purpose. Decide whether to read or mentally filter out visuals, graphics, and inserts. Remember, these digital "add-ons" make reading a more complex mental process.

4. **Make deliberate decisions, in particular about hyperlinks.** For example, will you follow links on your first reading, or read the material through once and then, after completing a first reading, follow links that seem appropriate and necessary? Maybe, under some circumstances, you will not need to follow any of the links; other times you may need to be selective.

5. **Remember that, as with print materials, reading is not learning.** Choose appropriate during- and after-reading strategies, such as paraphrasing, highlighting and annotating (if the technology supports it), outlining, summarizing, and mapping.

6. **Make a deliberate effort to concentrate on basic comprehension.** Use the same strategies you use for print materials—preview, read for meaning, and review after reading. Research substantiates that stronger basic comprehension occurs when reading print materials than when reading digital materials, so additional focus and effort may be required. You may need to stop, every so often, to mentally review and test your recall of what you have read, make notes, or jot down questions.

7. **Think critically.** It is easy to glide through digital content without analyzing and evaluating the ideas presented. Be sure to make an extra effort to subject digital content to close and careful scrutiny and analysis.

EXERCISE 1-11 . . . READING DIGITAL TEXT

Conduct an Internet search for an article on digital reading. First, skim the article to get a general idea of the content of the article. Next, read the article, making a deliberate effort to comprehend the meaning of the text. Using either annotation (through the comment feature in Word) or highlighting, indicate the main ideas of the article. After you have thoroughly read and marked the article, write a paragraph summary that highlights the main ideas.

POST-READING STRATEGIES

1i   PARAPHRASING

LEARNING OBJECTIVE 9
Paraphrase ideas accurately, using your words

A **paraphrase** is a restatement of a reading selection's ideas in *your own words* that retains the author's meaning. We use paraphrasing frequently in everyday speech. For example, when you relay a message from one person to another, you convey the meaning but generally do not use the person's exact wording. A paraphrase can be used to make a reading selection more understandable. For example, you might paraphrase the steps in solving a math problem or the process by which a blood transfusion is administered. If you can express the author's ideas in your own words, you can be certain you understand them. If you find yourself at a loss for words—except for those of the author—you will know your understanding is incomplete.

Paraphrasing is also a helpful strategy when working with material that is stylistically complex, poorly written, or overly formal, awkward, or biased. Figure 1-2 is a paraphrase of a paragraph from "Consequences of Social Class."

Tips for Effective Paraphrasing

1. **Read slowly and carefully.** Read the selection through in its entirety before writing anything. As you read, pay attention to exact meanings and relationships among ideas.

2. **Paraphrase sentence by sentence.** Read each sentence and express the key idea in your own words. Reread the original sentence, then look away and write your own sentence. Finally, reread the original and add anything you missed.

3. **Work with ideas.** Don't try to paraphrase word by word. You may combine several original sentences into a more concise paraphrase.

4. **Check a dictionary to locate more familiar meanings of difficult words.**

5. **Do not plagiarize;** your paraphrase should use your own words as much as possible, and you should include source information or an in-text citation (see Chapter 8) to avoid plagiarism.

FIGURE 1-2   A SAMPLE PARAPHRASE

PARAGRAPH	PARAPHRASE
Keenly aware that private schools can be a key to upward social mobility, some upper-middle-class parents make every effort to get their children into the prestigious preschools that feed into these exclusive prep schools. Although some preschools cost $23,000 a year, they have a waiting list (Rohwedder 2007). Not able to afford this kind of tuition, some parents hire tutors to train their 4-year-olds in test-taking skills, so they can get into public kindergartens for gifted students. They even hire experts to teach these preschoolers to look adults in the eye while they are being interviewed for these limited positions (Banjo 2010). You can see how such parental involvement and resources make it more likely that children from the more privileged classes go to college—and graduate.	Upper-middle-class parents seek to move up the social ladder by enrolling their children in high-status preschools. These preschools have a waiting list, in spite of their $23,000 annual tuition (Rohwedder 2007). Some parents who can't afford that tuition pay a tutor to teach their preschoolers how to test well enough to qualify for gifted programs in public kindergartens. Experts are also hired to train preschoolers to make eye contact with adults while interviewing for these schools (Banjo 2010). Upper-middle-class children are more likely to attend college and graduate because of the involvement and resources of their parents.

EXERCISE 1-12 . . . PARAPHRASING

Read the paragraph about family trends and the paraphrases that follow. Then answer the questions about the paraphrases.

Issue: Family Trends

Today, the dominant family form in the United States is the child-free family, where a couple resides together and there are no children present in the household. With the aging of the baby boomer cohort, this family type is expected to increase over time. If current trends continue, nearly three out of four U.S. households will be childless in another decade or so.

—Thompson and Hickey, *Society in Focus*, p. 383

Paraphrase 1

A child-free family is one where two adults live together and have no children. It is the dominant family form (Thompson and Hickey 383).

Paraphrase 2

The child-free family is dominant in the United States. Baby boomers are having fewer children. Three out of four homes do not have children in them (Thompson and Hickey 383).

Paraphrase 3

The child-free family is dominant in the United States. As baby boomers get older, there will be even more of these families. If this trend continues, three-quarters of all U.S. homes will be childless ten years from now (Thompson and Hickey 383).

1. Which is the best paraphrase of the paragraph? _____

2. Why are the other paraphrases not as good?

_____

_____

1j   OUTLINING

LEARNING OBJECTIVE 10
Outline text to organize and connect information

Outlining is a writing strategy that can assist you in organizing information and pulling ideas together. It is also an effective way to pull together information from two or more sources—your textbook and class lectures, for example. Finally, outlining is a way to assess your comprehension and strengthen your recall. Use the following tips to write an effective outline.

Tips for Writing an Effective Outline

1. **Read an entire section and then jot down notes.** Do not try to outline while you are reading the material for the first time.

2. **As you read, be alert for organizational patterns** (see Chapter 7). These patterns will help you organize your notes.

3. **Record all the most important ideas in the briefest possible form.**

4. **Think of your outline as a list of the selection's main ideas and supporting details.** Organize your outline to show how the ideas are related or to reflect the organization of the selection.

5. **Write in your own words; do not copy sentences or parts of sentences from the selection.** When outlining to organize and learn information you have read, use words and short phrases to summarize ideas. Do not write in complete sentences.

6. **Keep entries parallel.** Each entry in your outline should use the same grammatical form. Express all of your ideas in words or all of them in phrases.

7. **Use an indentation system to separate main ideas and details.** As a general rule, the more important the idea, the closer it is placed to the left margin. Ideas of lesser importance are indented and appear closer to the center of the page. Your outline should follow the format pictured here, based on a portion (the first seven paragraphs) of the textbook excerpt "Consequences of Social Class" on page 8.

Topic	I. Consequences of Social Class
Main Idea	A. Physical Health
Supporting detail	1. Higher social class = better health; lower social class = worse health
Supporting detail	2. Three main reasons
Fact	a. access to medical care
Fact	b. lifestyle: diet, drugs, alcohol, exercise, sexual practices
Fact	c. persistent stresses faced by poor (not faced by rich)
Main Idea	B. Mental Health
Supporting detail	1. Higher social class = better mental health; lower social class = worse mental health
Fact	a. poor: more stress, less job security, lower wages, more likely to divorce, be victims of crime
Fact	b. higher social class: lower stress, better coping skills, afford vacations and doctors

EXERCISE 1-13 . . . OUTLINING

Read the following passage and use the headings listed to write an outline of the passage.

Issue: Business Issues and Practices

Behavior segmentation focuses on whether people buy and use a product, as well as how often and how much they use or consume. Consumers can be categorized in terms of **usage rates**: heavy, medium, light, or nonusers. Consumers can also be segmented according to **user status**: potential users, nonusers, ex-users, regulars, first-timers, or users of competitors' products. Marketers sometimes refer to the **80/20 rule** when assessing usage rates. This rule (also known as the *law of disproportionality* or *Pareto's Law*) suggests that 80 percent of a company's revenues or profits are accounted for by 20 percent of a firm's products or customers. Nine country markets generate about 80 percent of McDonald's revenues. This situation presents McDonald's executives with strategy alternatives: Should the company pursue growth in the handful of countries where it is already well known and popular? Or, should it focus on expansion and growth opportunities in the scores of countries that, as yet, contribute little to revenues and profits?

— Keegan and Green, *Global Marketing*, pp. 202, 204

Behavior Segmentation

A. _____ : how much or how often people use or consume the product

   1. _____

   2. medium

   3. _____

   4. non users

B. User status: _____

   1. potential users

   2. _____

   3. ex-users

   4. _____

   5. _____

   6. users of competitive products

C. 80/20 rule

   1. also known as _____ or _____

   2. ____ of customers or products account for ____ of revenue or profit

   3. McDonald's strategy

      a. _____

      b. option 1: pursue growth where the company is already well known and popular

      c. option 2: _____

              _____

1k   USING MAPS TO SHOW RELATIONSHIPS

LEARNING OBJECTIVE 11
Draw conceptual maps to show relationships among ideas

Maps allow you to organize text material visually. **Mapping** involves drawing a diagram to describe how a topic and its related ideas are connected and is a visual means of organizing, consolidating, and learning information. This section discusses four types of maps: *conceptual maps, process diagrams, time lines,* and *part and function diagrams.*

Conceptual Maps

A **conceptual map** is a diagram that presents ideas spatially rather than in list form. It is a "picture" of how ideas are related. Use the following steps to construct a conceptual map.

Steps for Constructing a Conceptual Map

1. Identify the topic and write it in the center of the page.
2. Identify ideas, aspects, parts, and definitions that are related to the topic. Draw each one on a line radiating from the topic.
3. As you discover details that further explain an idea already recorded, draw new lines branching from the idea and add the details to them.

   A conceptual map of this handbook is shown in Figure 1-3. This figure shows only the major topics included in the handbook. Maps can be much more detailed and include more information than the one shown.

FIGURE 1-3 A CONCEPTUAL MAP OF THIS HANDBOOK

EXERCISE 1-14 . . . DRAWING A CONCEPTUAL MAP

Create a conceptual map of the professional reading "Consequences of Social Class" on pages 8–10.

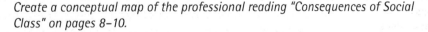

Process Diagrams

In the technologies and the natural sciences, as well as in many other courses and careers, *processes* are an important part of the course content or job. **Process diagrams** visually describe the steps, variables, or parts of a process, making learning easier. For example, the diagram in Figure 1-4 visually describes the steps that businesses follow in selecting a brand name for a new product.

FIGURE 1-4 A PROCESS DIAGRAM: SELECTING A BRAND NAME FOR A PRODUCT

Process: Selecting a Brand Name for a New Product

Identify objectives → Brainstorm possible names → Evaluate and select better names → Field test on consumers → Select brand name

Time Lines

When you are reading a selection focused on sequence or chronological order, a **time line** is a helpful way to organize the information. Time lines are especially useful in history courses. To map a sequence of events, draw a single line and mark it off in year intervals, just as a ruler is marked off in inches. Then write events next to the correct year. The time line shown in Figure 1-5 shows an effective way to organize historical events.

FIGURE 1-5 A SAMPLE TIME LINE

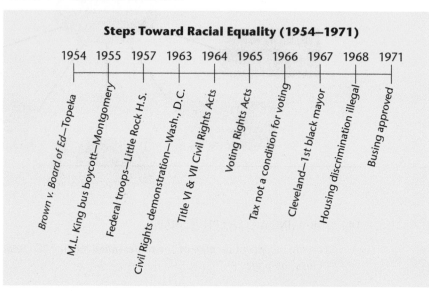

Steps Toward Racial Equality (1954–1971)

| 1954 | 1955 | 1957 | 1963 | 1964 | 1965 | 1966 | 1967 | 1968 | 1971 |

- 1954 Brown v. Board of Ed—Topeka
- 1955 M.L. King bus boycott—Montgomery
- 1957 Federal troops—Little Rock H.S.
- 1963 Civil Rights demonstration—Wash., D.C.
- 1964 Title VI & VII Civil Rights Acts
- 1965 Voting Rights Acts
- 1966 Tax not a condition for voting
- 1967 Cleveland—1st black mayor
- 1968 Housing discrimination illegal
- 1971 Busing approved

Part and Function Diagrams

In college courses that deal with the use and description or classification of physical objects, labeled drawings are an important learning tool. In a human anatomy and physiology course, for example, the easiest way to learn the parts and functions of the brain is to draw it. To study it, you would sketch the brain and test your recall of each part and its function.

1I   SUMMARIZING

LEARNING OBJECTIVE 12
Summarize text concisely and accurately

Like outlining, summarizing is an excellent way to learn from your reading and to increase recall. A **summary** is a brief statement that condenses an author's main ideas into sentences written in your own words. A summary contains only the gist of the text, with limited explanation, background information, or supporting detail. Be sure you understand the material and have identified the writer's major points before using the following suggestions to write a summary.

How to Write a Concise, Accurate Summary

1. Highlight or write brief notes on (annotate) the material.
2. Write one sentence that states the author's overall concern or most important idea. To do this, identify the topic and the point the author is trying to make about that topic. Use your answer to write a topic sentence for your summary. (You may find that the author has provided this sentence for you in the form of a thesis sentence, but *you must rewrite that thesis sentence in your own words.*)
3. Throughout the summary, be sure to paraphrase, using your own words rather than the author's.
4. Review the major supporting information that the author provides to explain the major idea or thesis.
5. The amount of detail you include, if any, depends on your purpose for writing the summary. For example, a summary of a television documentary for a research paper might be more detailed than a summary of the same program you write to jog your memory for a class discussion.
6. Present ideas in the summary in the same order in which they appear in the original material. Begin your summary by noting the title and author of the original material.
7. If the author presents a clear opinion or expresses a particular attitude toward the subject, include it in your summary.
8. Be sure to acknowledge any sources used in your summary. For more information on giving credit to sources, see Chapter 8, page 254.
9. If the summary is for your own use only and will not be submitted as an assignment, do not worry about sentence structure. Some students prefer to write summaries using words and phrases rather than complete sentences.

Figure 1-6 is a sample summary of the article "Consequences of Social Class," which appears on pages 8–10.

FIGURE 1-6 A SAMPLE SUMMARY

According to James Henslin in his book *Sociology*, social class plays an important role in most aspects of a person's life. In terms of both physical and mental health, people of the higher social classes are healthier than those of the lower classes. In terms of family life, social class affects the choice of spouse, with upper-class parents playing a larger role in maintaining the sense of family and helping choose their children's mates. Divorce is more common among the lower classes, who are more likely than the middle and upper classes to orient their children toward following the rules. The upper classes are more educated than the lower classes, and people of different classes are even drawn to different religious denominations. Politically, the upper classes tend to vote Republican, the lower classes Democrat. Members of the lower classes are more likely to be arrested and imprisoned, while the white-collar crimes committed by the upper classes don't often land the criminals in jail (pp. 261–264).

EXERCISE 1-15 . . . SUMMARIZING

Write a summary of four paragraphs of a reading assigned by your instructor.

1m   WRITING IN RESPONSE TO READING

LEARNING OBJECTIVE 13
Write in response to reading

At first, reading and writing may seem like very different, even opposite, processes. A writer starts with a blank page or computer screen and creates and develops ideas, while a reader starts with a full page and reads someone else's ideas. Although reading and writing may seem very different, they are actually parts of the same communication process. Because reading and writing work together, improving one set of skills often improves the other.

Some instructors assign a response to a reading, which requires you to read the selection, analyze it, and then write about it. The response may be somewhat informal (for example, adding an entry in your writing journal or posting a response to an electronic bulletin board), or it may be more formal (for example, a standard essay that should be drafted, revised, and proofread before being handed in).

Before responding to any reading, make sure you understand the response assignment. Ask questions if you are unclear about what is expected. For example, you may want to ask:

- How long should this response be?
- Should I include my opinion on the topic, a summary of the author's ideas, or both?

Writing an Informal Response

In an informal response, you simply write and respond without worrying about grammar, punctuation, and the other requirements of a formal paper. Suppose you have been assigned a reading titled "Adoption by Single People: Bad for the Parent, Bad for the Child." Your instructor asks you to write a journal entry responding to the reading. Here are some ways you might respond:

How to Write an Informal Response

- **Write about your opinion on the topic.** Do you think single people should be allowed to adopt? Why or why not? It is acceptable to write about your emotional response to the topic in your journal. (In more formal response assignments, emotion is discouraged, and convincing evidence and examples are encouraged.)

- **Talk about your personal experiences with the subject.** Do you know any single people who have adopted children? What have their experiences been? Would they agree or disagree with the author, and why?

- **Speculate why the author is so opposed to single people adopting children.** Is he basing his conclusions on his own experiences or on good, solid research?

- **Think about alternative scenarios.** Is a child better left in an orphanage than adopted by an unmarried person? Suppose you were an orphan. Would you rather be adopted by an unmarried person or left in a foster home or orphanage?

Here is a sample journal entry by a student writing in response to "Adoption by Single People: Bad for the Parent, Bad for the Child":

```
        I can see the writer's point even if I don't agree
with it. Of course, we all want to have both a mother
and a father. I think that's true whether you're male
or female—you always want both. But that's just not
always possible, and I personally would rather be
adopted by a loving unmarried woman, or man, than
have to live in a group home or be out there in the
world fending for myself. People who want to adopt
have a lot of love in their hearts, otherwise why
would they want someone else's child? I don't think
it should matter if the person is unmarried, but I do
think it's important that the person have the finan-
cial means to support the kid they adopt.
```

EXERCISE 1-16 . . . WRITING AN INFORMAL RESPONSE

Write an informal response (in the form of a journal entry) to "Consequences of Social Class," on pages 8–10.

Writing a Formal Response

In a formal response, you may decide to include a brief summary, but you should focus on analyzing and evaluating the reading selection. Do not discuss all of your reactions, however. Rather, select one key idea, one question the reading raises, or one issue it tackles. Then respond to that one idea, question, or issue.

For example, suppose your instructor asks you to read an article titled "Facebook: Many Friends, Few Relationships," which argues that Facebook encourages surface friendships at the expense of deeper, more lasting relationships. Your instructor asks you to write a formal one-page response paper about the article, allowing you to choose your own topic. In writing your response, you might take one of the following approaches:

- Discuss your own experiences with Facebook, as a way of confirming or refuting the author's main points.
- Evaluate the author's claim, evidence, and overall argument, either agreeing or disagreeing with her conclusions.
- Discuss some interesting aspects of Facebook that the author has not considered.
- List and discuss the author's assumptions or omissions.

Before you sit down to write, devise critical questions about the reading. Use the suggestions in Chapter 9 of this handbook to identify the author's opinions, her purpose for writing, her tone, her use of figurative language, her possible bias, and the reliability, relevance, and timeliness of her examples. Examining these aspects of the reading will likely generate many ideas to which you can choose to respond. (Of course, you will have to narrow your list and choose just one topic to write about.)

Because you will likely be graded or otherwise evaluated on your formal response, be sure to use good writing practices before you submit your formal response paper. Ask a classmate to read your first draft and offer ideas for improvement. Revise your paper to ensure it reads clearly and presents valid arguments and evidence. Before turning it in, proofread for grammar, spelling, and punctuation.

EXERCISE 1-17 . . . WRITING A FORMAL RESPONSE

Write a one-page formal response to a reading from the text assigned by your instructor.

SELF-TEST SUMMARY

To test yourself, cover the right column with a sheet of paper and answer the question in the left column. Evaluate each of your answers by sliding the paper down and comparing it with what is printed in the right column.

QUESTION	ANSWER
1 *What is active reading?*	**Active reading** is the process of identifying important ideas in a reading selection and comparing, evaluating, and applying them. **Active readers** determine the purpose of a reading assignment and then adjust their speed to suit the purpose.
2 *How do you read textbooks effectively?*	To **read a textbook selection**, use the textbook's pedagogical aids (learning objectives, headings, marginal terms, etc.); pay close attention to examples; look for relevance to your own life; use additional print-based or online resources if necessary to improve your comprehension; and read with a highlighter or pen in hand.
3 *How do you preview effectively?*	Previewing is a way to familiarize yourself with the content and organization of an assignment *before* you read it. **Effective previewing** involves using the title and subtitle, headings, the introductory and concluding paragraphs, key sentences, and typographical aids to get a "sneak preview" of what a reading selection will be about. Previewing also enables you to predict and form questions about the material.
4 *Why is activating prior knowledge important?*	**Prior knowledge** is what you already know about a topic. *Activating*—connecting to—prior knowledge makes reading easier because you have already thought about the topic. It helps with recall, as you can connect the new information to what you already know, and it makes topics become more interesting because you have linked them to your own experiences.
5 *How do you check and strengthen your comprehension?*	Active readers use **comprehension signals** while they read to determine how well they understand the material. If they experience a low level of comprehension, they adjust their reading strategy. (See Table 1-3 on p. 16.) To **strengthen comprehension**, use self-testing to make sure you understood what you just read; be sure your reading area is free of distractions; rephrase paragraphs and ideas in your own words; reread complicated sections; decrease your reading rate or read sentences aloud; create questions and outlines to engage with the reading; and assess your background knowledge and consult other sources if necessary.

QUESTION	ANSWER
6 *How do you highlight effectively?*	To **highlight** effectively, analyze the assignment, assess your familiarity with the topic, read first before highlighting, use headings as a guide, highlight main ideas and key details, avoid highlighting complete sentences, work quickly, use a highlighting system, and apply the 15–25 percent rule.
7 *How do you annotate?*	**Annotating** is a process of making marginal notes that record your thinking. Annotation is a personal process, so you should feel free to develop your own annotations, symbols, and abbreviations, using whatever system helps you study best. See Figure 1-1 (page 21) for sample marginal annotations.
8 *How is reading digital text different from reading print text?*	**Digital text** is multi-directional, contains hypertext, and is more visually stimulating. Readers tend to skim rather than read and, at times, may experience lower comprehension and retention.
9 *How do you paraphrase?*	To **paraphrase** a reading selection, rewrite the selection, keeping the author's meaning but using your own words. Paraphrase sentence by sentence, but work with ideas rather than individual words, and be sure that you credit the source that you are paraphrasing. Paraphrasing can help you check your understanding.
10 *How do you outline?*	**Outlining** helps you organize information and pull ideas together. To outline a reading selection, read the entire reading selection and jot down notes, being alert for organizational patterns. Record the most important ideas and supporting details in the briefest possible form. Use your own words, and use an indentation system to separate main ideas from details. For an outline format, see page 27.
11 *How can you use concept maps?*	**Drawing concept maps** allows you to organize material visually and involves drawing a diagram to show how a topic and its related ideas are connected. Four common types of maps are *conceptual maps*, *process diagrams*, *time lines*, and *part and function diagrams*, which allow you to see connections between ideas, steps in a process, the order in which events occurred, and the structure and function of items.

QUESTION	ANSWER
12 *How do you summarize?*	A **summary** is a brief statement that condenses an author's main ideas into sentences written in your own words and contains only the gist of the text, with limited explanation, background information, or supporting detail. To write a summary, first highlight or annotate the material; then write one sentence that states the author's overall concern or most important idea. Include the amount of detail required by the assignment, and present ideas in the same order in which they appear in the original. If the author presents a clear opinion or expresses a particular attitude toward the subject, include it in your summary. Be sure to indicate the source of the material you are summarizing.
13 *How do you write informal and formal responses?*	To write an **informal response**, you might write about your opinion on the topic, discuss your personal experience, speculate about the author's purpose, or think about other aspects of the topic. To write a **formal response**, select one key idea, one question raised by the reading, or one issue discussed in the reading. Then respond to that one idea, question, or issue in a piece of writing that you edit, improve, and proofread before you submit it to your instructor.

The Writing Process

Like any other skill (such as playing basketball, accounting, or cooking), reading and writing require both instruction and practice. Chapter 1 provided an overview of the active reading process and this chapter discusses the writing process. Reading and writing go hand in hand: readers read what writers have written, and writers write for readers.

Writing involves much more than sitting down at your computer and starting to type. It involves reading about others' ideas, generating and organizing your own ideas, and expressing your ideas in sentence, paragraph, or essay form. Writing is a *process*; it involves prewriting, drafting, revising, editing, and proofreading your work. Studying the sample student essay in this chapter (beginning on page 41) will give you a good sense of what writing involves.

2a UNDERSTANDING THE WRITING PROCESS

LEARNING OBJECTIVE 1
Understand and use the writing process

Writing, like many other skills, is not a single-step process. Think of the game of football, for instance. Football players spend a great deal of time planning and developing offensive and defensive strategies, trying out new plays, improving existing plays, training, and practicing. Writing involves similar planning and preparation. It also involves testing ideas and working out the best way to express them. Writers often explore how their ideas might "play out" in several ways before settling upon one plan of action.

Writing should always be an expression of your own ideas. Be sure that you do not use other authors' ideas or words without giving them credit through a source citation in your essay or paragraph. Using the ideas of others without giving proper acknowledgment is known as **plagiarism**, and it can result in academic penalties such as failing grades or even academic dismissal. For a more detailed explanation of plagiarism, see Chapter 8, page 242.

All writing involves four basic steps, as outlined in Table 2-1.

TABLE 2-1 STEPS IN THE WRITING PROCESS

STEP IN THE WRITING PROCESS	DESCRIPTION
1. Prewriting	Finding ideas to write about and discovering ways to arrange your ideas logically, considering audience, purpose, point of view, and tone.
2. Drafting	Expressing your ideas in sentence, paragraph, or essay form.
3. Revising	Rethinking your ideas and finding ways to make your writing clearer, more complete, and more interesting. Revising involves changing, adding, deleting, and rearranging your ideas and words to improve your writing.
4. Editing/Proofreading	Checking for errors in spelling, punctuation, capitalization, and grammar.

2b   USING TECHNOLOGY FOR WRITING

LEARNING OBJECTIVE 2
Use technology to produce correctly formatted, well-written work

Technology has much to offer writers for each step in the writing process. Technology can help you produce a well-written, correct paragraph or essay, save you time, and allow you spend more of your time on the creative task of writing and less on the mechanical details of presenting your work in a readable, visually appealing form.

Using Technology to Generate Ideas

The methods for prewriting suggested later in this chapter (Section 2c, page 42) can be done on the computer, often more easily than on paper. Try dimming your computer screen so you are not distracted by what you are typing and don't become concerned with grammar, punctuation, or typing errors. After you have finished, you can easily move and rearrange usable ideas.

You might also use social media such as Facebook or blogs to generate ideas and share them with others. Think of your page as a type of journal in which you record and exchange ideas. Your posts may feel conversational, but they will work in helping you share and explore ideas and responses. Because you can post different types of media, you might include photos and videos that stimulate your thinking, spur your creativity, and help you generate ideas. Be sure to check your privacy settings so access is restricted, and never post anything on the site that you wouldn't want everyone to see.

Using Technology for Drafting and Revising

Drafting on your computer is faster and more efficient than on paper. When drafting on a computer, be sure to do the following:

- **Format your paper before you begin,** considering font, spacing, margins, page numbering, and so forth. Check to be sure you are using a format preferred by your instructor or specified by MLA or APA style (see Chapter 8).
- **Name and store each document so you can easily retrieve it.**
- **Copy each draft and create a new file for it.** Date each draft, as you may want to go back to an earlier draft to include things from it.
- **Save your work frequently** and every time you leave your computer so you do not lose material.
- **Share your work with peers.** Many course management systems such as Blackboard make it easy to share your work with your classmates for peer review. Google Docs is also an effective tool. Check with your instructor or the computer lab for more information.

The following box contains tips that will help you use the features in your word processing program for editing and proofreading.

WORD PROCESSING FEATURES FOR WRITERS

- **Use a spell-checker to identify misspellings and typing mistakes.** However, do *not* rely on the program to catch all the errors. The checker will not flag words that you have misused (*to,* instead of *two,* for example). It may also suggest incorrect alternatives.
- **Use a grammar and style checker** to help you identify incorrect grammar or punctuation, repeated words, and awkward or wordy sentences. Do *not* rely on the checker to spot all your errors, and realize that the checker may flag things that are correct.
- **Use the Find command to locate and correct common problems or errors,** such as words you commonly misspell, overused words, or wordy phrases.

EXAMINING STUDENT WRITING

A good way to learn to read and write essays is to study the work of other student writers. Throughout this chapter, we will use the following student essay by Santiago Quintana Garcia to demonstrate techniques for reading and writing essays.

Santiago is a student at Beloit College in Wisconsin, where he majors in biochemistry and literature. He wrote this personal essay for his freshman composition class.

The Space In-Between

Santiago Quintana Garcia

Santiago Quintana Garcia

1   There are around twenty million people living in Mexico City, and this number is constantly increasing. Mexico is where I was born and grew up, before I moved to Beloit, Wisconsin, to attend Beloit College. The town of Beloit has roughly thirty thousand people. This means that about seven hundred towns the size of Beloit would fit inside Mexico City. In Mexico City, I was no more than a speck of dust in a dirty room. In Beloit, if I go have breakfast in one of three downtown cafés, I can be sure that there will be at least one person I know, probably around five or more. I live between two different worlds—Mexico and Beloit—but I call both of them "home": living between these two worlds can be difficult, but it offers many opportunities for growth.

2   Although I am at home in both Mexico and Beloit, I am also a foreigner in both. I am racially "foreign" in Mexico and culturally "foreign" in Beloit. Racially, I am Mexican. I should probably have beautiful cinnamon skin, hair black as night and falling straight like a waterfall to frame two glowing brown eyes. Many people think this is what a "true Mexican" looks like. Drawing a line between what is a true Mexican and what isn't based on looks is not a simple task. I myself think it is impossible. This stereotype has played a role in my life both in Mexico and Beloit. I have white skin, the only blue eyes in my family of brown eyes, and curly light brown hair. In Mexico City, when I went to the market to buy vegetables for the week, people didn't bother to ask my name. They called me *güerito*, blond. I got asked if I was from the United States or from another country. I was never completely a part of the nation I was born and grew up in. In Beloit, though, people are fascinated by my cultural background and ask about my customs and daily life back home. Inevitably, at some point in the conversation they tell me that I don't look Mexican.

3   Living a life in between two worlds, never completely a part of either, is a very complicated and extremely interesting place to be. Living in-between encourages growth and maturity. As a teenager, I struggled with feelings of not belonging and wanting to be a part of a group. I did not play soccer, or the guitar, and I suffered from bullying. The impact this

had on my life was emotionally wrecking. Often when people find themselves in similar situations, they turn to familiar things for comfort. Things like a group they belong to, like a culture, or a race, or a religious group. This was not accessible to me in the same way as it was to others. On the other hand, though, standing on no man's land let me observe the effects of the culture I grew up with on my way of thinking, and has greatly influenced my area of focus in my college studies. Standing in this middle ground was a vantage point from which I could analyze the opinions I held and the habits I developed and see my virtues and faults through different eyes. The hardiest weeds live where the pavement meets the prairie. I live where outsider meets insider.

4   What happens in this middle ground is that concepts such as gender, race, nationality, and other identities seem held up by pins. They are extremely volatile and impermanent, constantly changing and molding. This knowledge is present with me every time I say "I am Mexican" or "I am white." I had thought that people who fit snugly into a stereotype would never experience being an outsider. But I soon found out otherwise.

5   The first time I touched on this subject with a friend of mine, he said that he saw what I meant. I was convinced he didn't. He was the perfect example of the "Mexican" racial stereotype. He explained that he couldn't know about my situation, but that he was having a similar problem with his family. His mom had recently mentioned that he should be going to church more, instead of hanging out with his friends on Sunday mornings. That was his middle place. He identified with these two seemingly separate identities that he had created: his Catholic self and his social self. He was having trouble negotiating between the two. He stood in a place in the middle, where his church community was not understanding about his absences, and his friends made fun of his religious background. At the edges of these groups, he had thought about these two in much greater depth than I ever had, and he shared some incredible insights about the baggage associated with both identities, and how they weren't as solid as he thought; they had blurry edges and a lot of holes subject to interpretation.

6   It is the places in-between where the most potential for growth lives. All people have a place where they feel like outsiders, or not completely insiders. Realizing that this is where you are standing, and that it is perfectly fine to have one foot inside and one foot outside, will let the unique reveal itself through you. Being in-between can be difficult, but it is there that the most unexpected and wonderful things happen.

PREWRITING STRATEGIES

2c   GENERATING IDEAS

LEARNING OBJECTIVE 3
Generate ideas for your writing

Prewriting is an important first step in the writing process. Many students mistakenly believe they can just sit down at a computer and start writing a paragraph or essay. Writing requires thinking, planning, and organizing. Although these strategies take time, they pay off in the long run by saving you time later on and enabling you to produce a more effective piece of writing.

Choosing Your Topic

When your instructor gives you an assignment, you might not like the topic, but at least a good part of topic selection and narrowing has been done for you. When your instructor allows you to choose your own topic, you have to brainstorm for ideas and explore possible topics using prewriting. Use the following suggestions to help you choose an appropriate, effective, and workable topic:

Tips for Choosing an Appropriate, Effective, and Workable Topic

- **Take time to think about your choice.** Don't grab the first topic you come upon. Instead, think it through and weigh its pros and cons. It is often helpful to think of several topics and then choose the one you feel you are best prepared to write about.
- **Choose a topic that interests you.** You will feel more like writing about it and will find you have more to say.
- **Write about something familiar.** Select a topic you know a fair amount about. Otherwise, you will have to do extensive research on your topic in the library or online. Your experience and knowledge of a familiar topic will provide the content of your essay.
- **Use your writing journal as a source for ideas.**
- **Discuss possible topics with a friend or classmate.** These conversations may help you discover worthwhile topics.

Table 2-2 lists additional sources of ideas for essay topics.

TABLE 2-2 SOURCES OF IDEAS FOR TOPICS

SOURCES OF IDEAS	EXAMPLES
Your daily life. Pay attention to events you attend, activities you participate in, and routines you follow.	*Attending a sporting event may suggest topics about professional athletes' salaries, sports injuries, or violence in sports.*
Your college classes. Class lectures and discussions as well as reading assignments may give you ideas for topics.	*A class discussion in sociology about prejudice and discrimination may inspire you to write about racial or ethnic identities, stereotypes, or types of discrimination (age, gender, weight, etc.).*
Your job. Your responsibilities, your boss, your co-workers, and your customers are all sources of ideas.	*Watching a family with wild, misbehaving children throwing food and annoying other customers in a restaurant may prompt you to write about restaurant policies, child rearing, or rude and annoying behavior.*
The media. Radio, television, movies, newspapers, magazines, and online sources all contain hundreds of ideas for topics each day.	*A commercial for a weight-loss product may suggest an essay on society's emphasis on thinness or the unrealistic expectations for body image presented in commercials.*

Generating Ideas

Before you can write about a topic, you must generate ideas to write about. Three techniques are helpful in collecting ideas: *freewriting*, *brainstorming*, and *diagramming*.

Freewriting

Freewriting is writing nonstop about a topic for a specified period of time. In freewriting, you write whatever comes into your mind without worrying about punctuation, spelling, and grammatical correctness. After you have finished, you go back through your writing and pick out ideas that you might be able to use.

Here is a sample freewrite on the topic of climate change:

> It's so hard to sort out the facts about climate change. On the one hand it seems like the weather has been crazy. I'm 22 years old and I never remember summers being so hot when I was a kid. And the humidity is so bad too, it seems like summer now starts in April and goes straight through to December. We've had hurricanes, tornadoes, and unbelievable rainfall, plus high winds that have brought trees crashing down. And I keep reading that climate change is responsible for this extreme weather. But on the other hand I know that a lot of people don't believe that climate change is really happening. From what I can figure out, they think "climate change" is not really happening and that all the talk of "global warming" is greatly exaggerated. It's so hard to know who to believe, everyone seems to have an agenda and it seems like nobody reports the facts. Even when facts and figures are reported, can I really trust them? Because as soon as they come out, people start disputing them.

Brainstorming

Brainstorming involves making a list of everything you can think of that is associated with your topic. When you brainstorm, try to stretch your imagination and think of everything related to your topic: facts, ideas, examples, questions, and feelings. When you have finished, read through what you have written and highlight usable ideas.

Imagine that you have been asked to write an essay about "identity" and how you see yourself. Here is the brainstorming list that Santiago wrote about his identity.

> Identity—Mexican? White? Very arbitrary and flimsy
>
> Easily deconstructed when seen from the edges
>
> Not wrong to subscribe to a certain identity
>
> Type of clothing is one way of identifying people
>
> Everyone has their in-betweens, not all race and nationality
>
> Mexican stereotype: I don't look Mexican. I'm foreign in my own country/race
>
> Foreigners have a difficult time assimilating into a new culture

| White: Not quite. I am Mexican after all. |
| Creates a struggle between the ideal and the reality, from this comes synthesis, movement |
| All teenagers struggle with identity |
| Feelings of not belonging as a teenager. No comfort objects. No cushion to fall back to easily, BUT growth and awareness. |
| Perception is reality |
| I am Mexican. I still subscribe but with a lot more awareness of how that label is not representative and exhaustive. It is necessary; practical. |
| Living in between = energy, movement, growth |

Diagramming

Drawing diagrams or drawings is a useful way to generate ideas. Begin by drawing a 2-inch oval in the middle of a page. Write your topic in that oval. Think of the oval as a tree trunk. Next, draw lines radiating out from the trunk, as branches would. Write an idea related to your topic at the end of each branch. When you have finished, highlight the ideas you find most useful. Here is a sample branching diagram on the topic of labor unions:

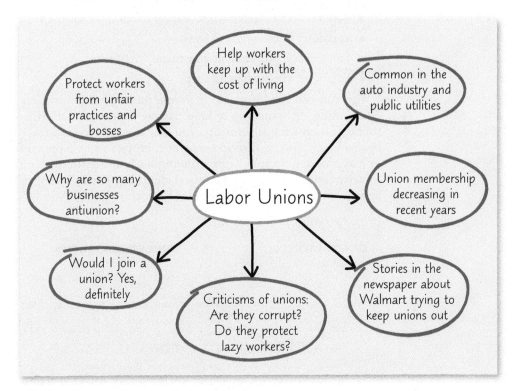

EXERCISE 2-1 . . . THE WRITING PROCESS: GENERATING IDEAS

Select two of the following topics. Then generate ideas about each one using two different idea-generation techniques.

1. Identity theft
2. Texting while driving
3. Doping in sports
4. Government spying
5. Social impacts of Snapchat

6. Same-sex marriage
7. Legalizing marijuana for medical use
8. Controlling pandemic diseases
9. Benefits of space exploration
10. Farm to table food movement

Narrowing Your Topic

Avoid working with a topic that is either too broad or too narrow. If your topic is *too narrow*, you will find you don't have enough to write about. If it is *too broad*, you will have too much to say, which will create several related problems:

- You will tend to write in generalities.
- You will not be able to explore each idea in detail.
- You will probably wander from topic to topic and become unfocused.

To discover whether your topic is too broad, look for these warning signals:

- You feel overwhelmed when you try to think about the topic.
- You don't know where to start.
- You feel as if you are going in circles with ideas.
- You don't know where to stop.

You can use the ideas you generate during brainstorming, freewriting, questioning, or branching to help narrow your topic. Often, more than one round of narrowing is necessary. You may need to reduce a topic several times by dividing it into smaller and smaller subtopics using a prewriting technique or diagram to help you. After studying his brainstorming, Santiago decided to write about his racial and cultural identities. The following diagram shows how he further narrowed the topic of his identity.

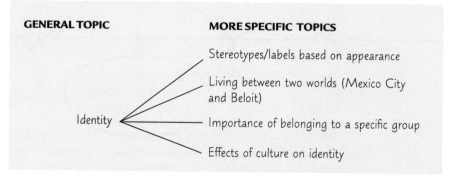

GENERAL TOPIC

MORE SPECIFIC TOPICS

Identity

Stereotypes/labels based on appearance

Living between two worlds (Mexico City and Beloit)

Importance of belonging to a specific group

Effects of culture on identity

In this way, he wound up with several manageable topics related to identity to choose from and decided to write about his experience of living between two worlds.

A question many students ask is, "How do I know when to stop narrowing?" For an essay, you will need at least three or four main points to support your thesis. Make sure that you have at least this number and that you can support each one with adequate detail. If you cannot do this, you'll know you have narrowed too far.

EXERCISE 2-2 . . . NARROWING TOPICS

Narrow one topic you chose for Exercise 2-1. Continue narrowing it until you find a topic about which you could write a five- to seven-paragraph essay.

2d   CONSIDERING AUDIENCE, PURPOSE, POINT OF VIEW, AND TONE

LEARNING OBJECTIVE 4
Consider your audience, purpose, point of view, and tone

Before you begin a draft, there are four important factors to consider: *audience, purpose, point of view,* and *tone.*

Considering Audience

Analyzing your audience is always a first step when writing any essay. It will help you decide what to say and what type of details to include. Here are some key questions to consider when you begin your analysis:

- Is my reader familiar with the topic?
- How much background or history does my reader need to understand the information?
- Do I need to define any unfamiliar terms?
- Do I need to explain any unfamiliar people, places, events, parts, or processes?

Suppose you are writing an essay on how to find an apartment to rent. Knowing how much information to present involves analyzing both your audience and your purpose. First, consider how much your audience already knows about the topic. If you think your readers know a lot about renting apartments, briefly review what they already know and then move on to a more detailed explanation of new information. However, if your topic is brand new to your readers, capture their interest without intimidating them. Relate the topic to their own experiences. Show them how renting an apartment resembles something they already know how to do; for example, by comparing renting an apartment to other types of shopping for something with certain desired features and an established price range.

If you are uncertain about your audience's background, it is safer to include information they may already know rather than to assume that they know it. Readers can skim or skip over information they know, but they cannot fill in gaps in their understanding without your help.

science photo/Fotolia

Considering Purpose

Once you have identified your audience and decided what they will need to know, you will want to identify your **purpose**, or goal, for writing. There are three main purposes for writing:

- **To express yourself.** In expressive essays, you focus on your feelings and experiences. You might, for example, write an expressive essay about the value of friendship.
- **To inform.** Informative essays are written to present information. An essay on how to set up and run a biology experiment is an informative essay.
- **To persuade.** Persuasive essays attempt to persuade readers to accept a particular viewpoint or take a particular action. A persuasive essay might attempt to convince you that zoos are inhumane.

When planning your essay, decide what you want it to accomplish, and focus on how to meet that goal.

Considering Point of View

Point of view refers to the perspective you take on your topic. Your point of view may be expressed using first, second, or third person. If you write in the first person (using words like *I* and *me*), then you are speaking personally to your reader. If you write in the second person (using words like *you* and *your*), you address your reader directly. If you write in the third person, you use nouns or pronouns to refer to a person or thing spoken about (using words like *he, she, Jody,* or *children*).

Your choice of person determines how formal or informal your essay becomes and also creates closeness or distance between the reader and writer. Most academic writing uses the third person. The second person is rarely used. Whatever person you choose to use, stay with it throughout your essay.

Considering Tone

Tone means how you sound to your readers and how you feel about your topic. An essay can have a serious, argumentative, humorous, informative, or other tone, for example. Your tone should reflect your relationship to your audience: the less familiar you are with your audience, the more formal your tone should be. (For more about tone, see Chapter 9, page 283.)

Here are a few examples of sentences in which the tone is inappropriate for most academic and career writing, and how they could be revised to be appropriate for an academic audience.

Inappropriate	That dude's swag. He's all swole up from lifting at the gym.
Revised	That man has style. He has a well-defined physical appearance from using weights at the gym.
Inappropriate	Hey dude, that jacket's dope!
Revised	I think that jacket is original and really well made.

Ways to Keep Your Tone Appropriate

Follow these suggestions to help keep your tone appropriate:

1. Avoid slang expressions.
2. Use first-person pronouns (*I*, *me*) sparingly.
3. Make your writing sound more formal than casual conversation or a letter to a close friend.
4. To achieve a more formal tone, avoid informal or everyday words. For example:

Use *met* instead of *ran into*.
Use *children* instead of *kids*.
Use *annoying* instead of *bugging*.

EXERCISE 2-3 . . . REVISING TONE

Revise each of the following statements to give it a more formal tone.

1. I used to be a dork in high school, but now I'm awesome in college.
2. Sam is the kind of guy every woman would like to sink her claws into.
3. Because Marco is one of those easygoing types, people think they can walk all over him.
4. In my talk to the group, I riffed on why scanners are a big money saver.
5. Emily Dickinson is a boring poet; some of her poems are really lame.

2e   PLANNING AND ORGANIZING

LEARNING OBJECTIVE 5
Plan and organize
your ideas

Two common methods of organizing ideas are outlining and idea mapping, the same two strategies discussed in Chapter 1 (pp. 26 and 28) for understanding and organizing ideas in the texts you read. Understanding each will help you decide how to arrange the ideas that you have identified as useful in a way that makes them accessible to your reader.

Outlining

When you create an **outline**, you list the main points you will cover, the details you will use to support your main points, and the order in which you will present them. To prepare an outline, list the most important ideas on separate lines on the left side of a sheet of paper, leaving space underneath each main idea. Then, in the space under each main idea, list the details that you will include to explain that main idea. Indent the list of details that fits under each of your main ideas.

How to Use an Outline Format

Here are a few suggestions for using the outline format:

- **Do not be overly concerned with following the outline format exactly.** As long as your outline shows the organization of your ideas, it will work for you.
- **Write complete sentences whenever possible.** When you are planning your writing, complete sentences allow for fuller expression of your ideas.
- **Pay attention to headings.** Be sure that all the information you place underneath a heading explains or supports that heading. Every heading indented the same amount on the page should be of equal importance.

Here is a sample outline for paragraph 3 of the essay that Santiago wrote about identity.

I. Living in two worlds

   A. Never completely part of either world

      1. Complicated

      2. Interesting

   B. Living in between encourages growth and maturity

      1. Nothing to hold on to

      2. Effects of culture

C. Living in between offers a vantage point

   1. Analyze opinions and habits

   2. See virtues and faults through different eyes

D. Live where outsider meets insider

Using Idea Maps

Create an **idea map** to show how your ideas are connected, organize the content of your writing, and identify which ideas are not relevant to your topic. Here is a sample idea map drawn for the topic of protecting your identity.

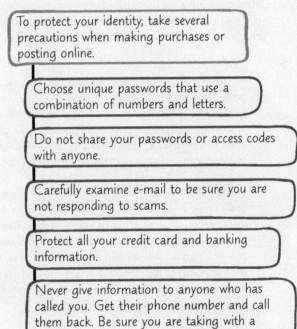

EXERCISE 2-4 ... THE WRITING PROCESS: USING OUTLINING OR MAPPING

Prepare an outline or idea map for the topic you narrowed in Exercise 2-2.

DRAFTING STRATEGIES

2f   DRAFTING AND REVISING PARAGRAPHS

LEARNING OBJECTIVE 6
Write an effective
paragraph

A **paragraph** is a group of sentences, usually at least three or four, that express one main idea. Paragraphs may stand alone to express one thought, or they may be combined into essays or longer readings. Paragraphs are one of the basic building blocks of writing.

Understanding the Structure of Paragraphs

A paragraph's one main idea is often expressed in a single sentence called the **topic sentence**. The other sentences in the paragraph, which explain or support the main idea, are called **supporting details**. (These terms are explained in more detail in Chapters 4 and 5.) An idea map can help you visualize the structure of a paragraph. Below is paragraph 2 from Santiago's essay on page 41. The two idea maps that follow are a model of paragraph structure on the left and a map of the sample paragraph on the right.

Although I am at home in both Mexico and Beloit, I am also a foreigner in both. I am racially "foreign" in Mexico and culturally "foreign" in Beloit. Racially, I am Mexican. I should probably have beautiful cinnamon skin, hair black as night and falling straight like a waterfall to frame two glowing brown eyes. Many people think this is what a "true Mexican" looks like. Drawing a line between what is a true Mexican and what isn't based on looks is not a simple task. I myself think it is impossible. This stereotype has played a role in my life both in Mexico and Beloit. I have white skin, the only blue eyes in my family of brown eyes, and curly light brown hair. In Mexico City, when I went to the market to buy vegetables for the week, people didn't bother to ask my name. They called me güerito, blond. I got asked if I was from the United States or from another country. I was never completely a part of the nation I was born and grew up in. In Beloit, though, people are fascinated by my cultural background and ask about my customs and daily life back home. Inevitably, at some point in the conversation they tell me that I don't look Mexican.

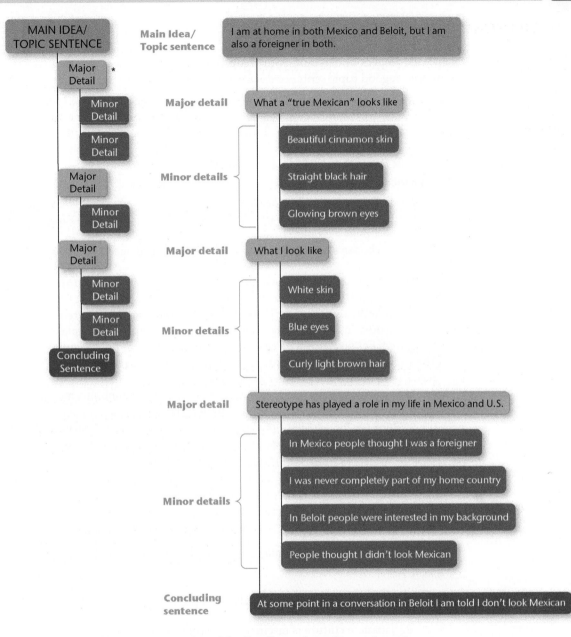

MAIN IDEA/
TOPIC SENTENCE

Major Detail *

Minor Detail

Minor Detail

Major Detail

Minor Detail

Major Detail

Minor Detail

Minor Detail

Concluding Sentence

Main Idea/ Topic sentence — I am at home in both Mexico and Beloit, but I am also a foreigner in both.

Major detail — What a "true Mexican" looks like

Minor details
- Beautiful cinnamon skin
- Straight black hair
- Glowing brown eyes

Major detail — What I look like

Minor details
- White skin
- Blue eyes
- Curly light brown hair

Major detail — Stereotype has played a role in my life in Mexico and U.S.

Minor details
- In Mexico people thought I was a foreigner
- I was never completely part of my home country
- In Beloit people were interested in my background
- People thought I didn't look Mexican

Concluding sentence — At some point in a conversation in Beloit I am told I don't look Mexican

*The number of details will vary depending on the topic.

Writing Effective Topic Sentences

As a writer, it is important to develop clear and concise topic sentences that help your readers understand your main ideas and guide them through your sentences. A good topic sentence does two things:

- It makes clear what the paragraph is about—the topic.
- It expresses a view or makes a point about the topic.

TIPS FOR WRITING EFFECTIVE TOPIC SENTENCES

Use the following suggestions to write clear topic sentences:

1. **Your topic sentence should state the main point of your paragraph.** Be sure your topic sentence has two parts. It should identify your topic and express a view toward it.
2. **Be sure to choose a manageable topic.** It should be neither too general nor too specific.
3. **Make sure your topic sentence is a complete thought.** Be sure your topic sentence is not a fragment or run-on sentence.
4. **Place your topic sentence first in the paragraph.** Topic sentences often appear in other places in paragraphs, or their controlling idea is implied, not stated. For now, it will be easier for you to put yours at the beginning. That way, as you write, you can make sure you stick to your point, and your readers will immediately be alerted to that point.
5. **Avoid announcing your topic.** Sentences that sound like announcements are usually unnecessary. Avoid such sentences as "This paragraph will discuss how to change a flat tire," or "I will explain why I object to legalized abortion." Instead, directly state your main point: "Changing a flat tire involves many steps," or "I object to abortion on religious grounds."

EXERCISE 2-5 . . . EVALUATING TOPIC SENTENCES

Evaluate each of the following topic sentences and mark them as follows:

E = effective, G = too general, A = announcement, N = not complete thought, S = too specific

_____ 1. This paper will discuss the life and politics of Simón Bolívar.

_____ 2. Japanese culture is fascinating to study because its family traditions are so different from American traditions.

_____ 3. The admission test for the police academy includes vocabulary questions.

_____ 4. The discovery of penicillin was a great step in the advancement of modern medicine.

Chuck Aghoian/Shutterstock

5. I will talk about the reasons for the popularity of reality television shows.

_____ 6. A habit leading to weight gain.

_____ 7. Each year Americans are the victims of more than 1 million auto thefts.

_____ 8. The White House has many famous rooms and an exciting history.

_____ 9. There are three factors to consider when buying a Smart TV.

_____ 10. Iraq has a long and interesting history.

Writing Effective Paragraphs

You can write an effective paragraph if you follow the organization shown in the diagram on page 53. Use the following suggestions to make sure your paragraph is clear and understandable.

1. **Choose a manageable topic.** Your topic should be broad enough to allow you to add interesting and relevant details, but specific enough to allow you to adequately cover it in approximately five to ten sentences.

2. **Write a clear topic sentence.** Your topic sentence should state the main point of your paragraph. Often it works well to place your topic sentence first in the paragraph and then go on to explain and support it in the remaining sentences. Avoid announcing your topic ("This paragraph is about...").

3. **Choose details to support your topic sentence.** Each sentence in your paragraph should explain or support your topic sentence. Be sure to include enough details to fully explain it.

4. **Organize your details in a logical manner.** Make your paragraph easy to understand by arranging your details using one of the patterns described in Chapter 7: *illustration, process, definition, classification, cause and effect,* and *comparison and contrast.*

5. **Connect your ideas using transitions.** Transitions are words and phrases that help your reader move from one detail to the next and understand the connections between and among them. See Chapter 5 (pp. 128 and 130) for lists of useful transition words.

Revising Paragraphs

Revision involves examining your ideas by rereading all the sentences you have written and making changes to them. Your goal is to examine your ideas to make sure you have explained them clearly and correctly. It is usually best to let your paragraph sit for a while before you revise it. Turn to page 65 to see how Santiago revised a couple of draft paragraphs within his essay.

If you have trouble knowing what to revise, try drawing an idea map of your ideas. An idea map will help you see exactly how much support you have for your topic sentence, how your ideas fit together, and whether a detail is off-topic.

Below is a revision checklist you can use to make sure you have done a careful and thorough revision.

PARAGRAPH REVISION CHECKLIST

Paragraph Development

1. Is the topic manageable (neither too broad nor too narrow)?
2. Is the paragraph written with the reader in mind?
3. Does the topic sentence identify the topic?
4. Does the topic sentence make a point about the topic?
5. Does each sentence support the topic sentence?
6. Is there sufficient detail?
7. Is there a sentence at the end that brings the paragraph to a close?

Sentence Development

8. Are there any sentence fragments, run-on sentences, or comma splices?
9. Are ideas combined to produce more effective sentences?
10. Are adjectives and adverbs used to make the sentences vivid and interesting?
11. Are relative clauses and prepositional phrases used to add detail?
12. Are pronouns used correctly and consistently?

EXERCISE 2-6 . . . DRAFTING AND REVISING A PARAGRAPH

Using the outline or idea map you created in Exercise 2-4, write and revise a paragraph about the topic you chose.

2g   DRAFTING ESSAYS

LEARNING OBJECTIVE 7
Draft an effective
essay
An **essay** is a group of paragraphs about one subject. It contains one key idea about the subject. This key idea is called the **thesis statement**. Each paragraph in the essay supports or explains some aspect of the thesis statement.

Understanding the Structure of Essays

An essay follows a logical and direct plan. It introduces an idea (the thesis statement), explains it, and draws a conclusion. Therefore, an essay usually has at least three paragraphs:

1. Introductory paragraph
2. Body (one or more paragraphs)
3. Concluding paragraph

The Introductory Paragraph

Your introductory paragraph should accomplish three goals:

- It should establish the topic of the essay.
- It should present your essay's thesis statement in a manner that is appropriate for your intended audience.
- It should stimulate your audience's interest. That is, it should make readers want to read your essay.

The Body

The body of your essay should accomplish three goals:

- It should provide information that supports and explains your thesis statement.
- It should present each main supporting point in a separate paragraph.
- It should contain enough detailed information to make the main point of each paragraph (that is, the topic sentence) understandable and believable.

The Concluding Paragraph

Your concluding paragraph should accomplish two goals:

- It should reemphasize but not restate your thesis statement.
- It should draw your essay to a close.

The following idea map shows the ideal organization of an essay:

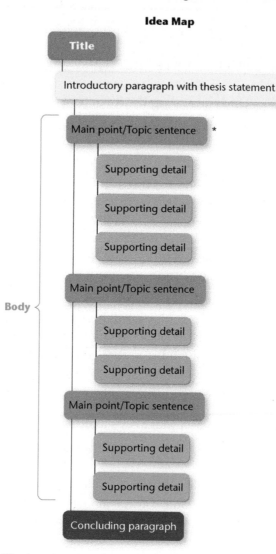

Idea Map

*Number of main points may vary. Each main point should contain a sufficient number of details.

Writing Effective Thesis Statements

A thesis statement very rarely just springs into a writer's mind: it evolves and, in fact, may change during the process of prewriting, grouping ideas, drafting, and revising.

Grouping Ideas to Discover a Thesis Statement

Once you know what you want to write about, the next step is to group or connect your ideas to form a thesis.

Santiago discovered more ideas by first brainstorming about his topic of identity. As you can see on pages 44–45, he wrote many ideas, far more than he needed, but that gave him choices.

After brainstorming, Santiago reviewed what he had written and decided to limit his essay to how his identity has been affected by living between two worlds—Mexico City and Beloit. He highlighted usable ideas and tried to group or organize them logically: (1) his life in Mexico City, (2) his life in Beloit, and (3) his perspective on living in two places. Once he had grouped his ideas into these three categories, he wrote a working thesis statement:

Working Thesis Statement	Living between two worlds can be difficult, but it offers many opportunities for growth.

This working thesis statement identifies his topic—living between two worlds—and suggests that he will examine how he has grown as a result. You can see that this thesis statement grew out of his idea groupings. Furthermore, this thesis statement gives readers clues as to how the essay will be organized; he will compare his identities in both places.

Ways to Make Connections Between Ideas

How do you know which ideas to group? Look for connections and relationships among the ideas you generate during prewriting. Here are some suggestions:

1. **Look for categories.** Try to discover ways your ideas can be classified or subdivided. Think of categories as titles or slots into which ideas can be placed. Look for a general term that is broad enough to cover several of your ideas. For example, suppose you are writing a paper on where sexual discrimination occurs. You could break down the topic by location.

Thesis Statement	Sexual discrimination exists in the workplace, in social situations, and in politics.

2. **Try organizing your ideas chronologically.** Group your ideas according to the clock or calendar.

Thesis Statement	Tracing metal working from its early beginnings in history to modern times reveals certain social and economic patterns.

3. **Look for similarities and differences.** When working with two or more topics, see whether they can be approached by looking at how similar or different they are.

Thesis Statement	Wundt and James, influential founders of psychology, advocated differing approaches to its study.

4. **Separate your ideas into causes and effects or problems and solutions.** Events and issues can often be analyzed in this way.

Thesis Statement	Both employer and employees must work together to improve low morale in an office.

5. **Divide your ideas into advantages and disadvantages or pros and cons.** When you are evaluating a proposal, product, or service, this approach may work.

Thesis Statement	Playing on a college sports team has many advantages but also several serious drawbacks.

6. **Consider several different ways to approach your topic or organize and develop your ideas.** As you consider what your thesis statement is going to be, push yourself to see your topic from a number of different angles or a fresh perspective.

For example, Santiago could have chosen to write about his experiences as a college student in Beloit, or he could have examined his brainstorming and decided to focus only on his life in Mexico City.

Drafting a Thesis Statement

Think of your thesis statement as a promise; it promises your reader what your paper will deliver. Here are some guidelines to follow for writing an effective thesis statement:

Guidelines for Writing an Effective Thesis Statement

1. **It should state the main point of your essay.** It should not focus on details; it should give an overview of your approach to your topic.

Too Detailed	A well-written business letter has no errors in spelling.
Revised	To write a grammatically correct business letter, follow three simple rules.

2. **It should assert an idea about your topic.** Your thesis should express a viewpoint or state an approach to the topic.

Lacks an Assertion	Advertising contains images of both men and women.
Revised	In general, advertising presents men more favorably than women.

3. **It should be as specific and detailed as possible.** For this reason, it is important to review and rework your thesis *after* you have written and revised drafts.

Too General	Advertisers can influence readers' attitudes toward competing products.
Revised	Athletic-shoe advertisers focus more on attitude and image than on the actual physical differences between their product and those of their competitors.

4. **It may suggest the organization of your essay.** Mentioning key points that will be discussed in the essay is one way to do this. The order in which you mention them should be the order in which you discuss them in your essay.

Does Not Suggest Organization	Public school budget cuts will negatively affect education.
Revised	Public school budget cuts will negatively affect academic achievement, student motivation, and the dropout rate.

5. **It should not be a direct announcement.** Do not begin with phrases such as "In this paper I will" or "My assignment was to discuss."

Direct Announcement	The purpose of my paper is to show that businesses lose money due to inefficiency, competition, and inflated labor costs.
Revised	Businesses lose money due to inefficiency, competition, and inflated labor costs.

6. **It should offer a fresh, interesting, and original perspective on the topic.** A thesis statement can follow the guidelines above, but if it seems dull or predictable, it needs more work.

Predictable	Circus acts fall into three categories: animal, clown, and acrobatic.
Revised	Each of the three categories of circus acts— animal, clown, and acrobatic—is exciting because of the risks it involves.

EXERCISE 2-7 . . . EVALUATING THESIS STATEMENTS

Working with a classmate, identify what is wrong with the following thesis statements, and revise each one to make it more effective:

1. Jogging has a lot of benefits.
2. Counseling can help people with problems.
3. Getting involved in campus activities has really helped me.
4. Budgeting your time is important.
5. Commuting to college presents problems.
6. The movie is about parenting.
7. Violence on television must be brought to an end.
8. Divorce laws are unfair and favor women.
9. Fad diets are losing their appeal.
10. Automobile air bags save lives.

Writing First Drafts

Once you have used prewriting to develop and organize your ideas, you are ready to write a first draft of the essay. **Drafting** is a way of trying out ideas to see whether and how they work.

To understand what drafting involves, consider the following comparison. Suppose you need to buy a car. You visit a used car lot and look at various cars that fit your requirements. After narrowing down your choices, you test drive several cars, then go home to think about how each one might suit you. You revisit the used car lot, go for another test drive, and finally decide which car to buy. Writing a draft of an essay is similar to buying a car. You have to try out different ideas through prewriting, see how they work together as you organize them, express them in different ways, and, after writing several drafts, settle on what you will include.

A first draft expresses your ideas in sentence form. Work from your list of ideas (see Section 2c), and don't be concerned with grammar, spelling, or punctuation at this point. Instead, focus on expressing and developing each idea fully. The following suggestions will help you write effective first drafts:

Tips for Writing Effective First Drafts

1. **After you have thought carefully about the ideas on your list, write one sentence that expresses the thesis statement (main point) of your essay.** See Chapter 8 for more information on thesis statements.

2. **Concentrate on explaining your thesis statement using ideas from your list.** Devote one paragraph to each main idea that supports your thesis. Focus first on the ideas that you think express your main point particularly well. The main point of each paragraph is the topic sentence. It usually appears first in the paragraph, but it can appear anywhere in the paragraph. Later in the writing process, you may find you need to add other ideas from your list.

3. **Think of a first draft as a chance to experiment with different ideas and different ways of organizing them.** While you are drafting, if you think of a better way to organize or express your ideas, or if you think of new ideas, make changes. Be flexible. Do not worry about getting your wording exact at this point.

4. **As your draft develops, feel free to change your focus or even your topic (if your instructor has not assigned a specific topic).** If your draft is not working out, don't hesitate to start over completely. Go back to generating ideas. It is always all right to go back and forth among the steps in the writing process. Many writers make a number of "false starts" before they produce a first draft that satisfies them.

5. **Don't expect immediate success.** When you finish your first draft, you should feel that you have the beginnings of a paper you will be happy with. Now ask yourself whether you have a sense of the direction your paper will take. Do you have a thesis statement for your essay? Do the paragraphs each explain or support your thesis? Does each paragraph have sufficient supporting details? Is the organization logical? If you can answer "yes" to these questions, you have something good to work with and revise.

The following first draft evolved from Santiago's brainstorming list on pages 44–45 and his outline. The highlighting indicates the main points he developed as he wrote.

First Draft of Santiago's Essay

Introductory paragraph

1   There are around twenty million people living in Mexico City, and this number is constantly increasing. Mexico is where I was born and grew up, before I moved to Beloit, Wisconsin, to attend Beloit College. The town of Beloit has roughly thirty thousand people. This means that about seven hundred towns the size of Beloit would fit inside Mexico City. In Mexico City, I was no more than a speck of dust in a dirty room. In Beloit, if I go have breakfast in one of three downtown cafés, I can be sure that there will be at

Working thesis statement

least one person I know, probably around five or more. Living between two worlds can be difficult, but it offers many opportunities for growth.

Topic sentence

2   I am Mexican. I probably have beautiful cinnamon skin, hair black as night and falling straight like a waterfall to frame two glowing brown eyes.

Many people think this is what a "true Mexican" looks like. Drawing a line between what is a true Mexican and what isn't based on looks is not a simple task. I myself think it is impossible. This stereotype has played a role in my life both in Mexico and Beloit. I have white skin, the only blue eyes in my family of brown eyes, and curly light brown hair. When I go to the market to buy vegetables for the week, people don't bother to ask my name. They call me *güerito*, blonde. I get asked if I am from the United States or from another country. I was never completely a part of the nation I was born and grew up in. In Beloit, though, people are fascinated by my cultural background and ask about my customs and daily life back home. Inevitably, at some point in the conversation they tell me that I don't look Mexican. I live between two worlds; being racially "foreign" in Mexico, and being culturally "foreign" in Beloit.

Topic sentence   3   Living a life in between two worlds, never completely a part of any, is a very complicated and extremely interesting place to be. Living in-between encourages growth and maturity. On one hand, in my teenage years, when I desperately wanted to feel I was a part of something, there wasn't anything to take refuge in and feel strongly about. On the other, though, this made me see the effects of the culture I grew up with on my way of thinking. Standing in this middle ground was a vantage point where I could analyze the opinions I held and the habits I developed and see the virtues and faults through different eyes. The hardiest weeds live where the pavement meets the prairie. I live where outsider meets insider.

Topic sentence   4   I became used to being in the middle. I discovered that most questions can have more than one answer, or no answer at all. I realized that people are a lot more complex than I thought, and you really can't stick a label to them that won't become old and fall off. I had thought that people who fit snugly into the stereotype would never experience being an outsider. But I soon found out otherwise. Some had to choose between going to the cinema with their friends and going to church with their family. Some loved playing soccer in the mornings, and then go ballroom dancing in the afternoon. Everyone had their own experience of being in-between two places they sometimes love and sometimes hate.

Topic sentence   5   It is the places in-between where the most potential for growth lives.

Concluding paragraph   Everyone has their own place where they feel like outsiders, or not completely insiders. Realizing that this is where you are standing, and that it is perfectly fine to have one foot inside and one foot outside, will let the unique reveal itself through you. Being in-between can be difficult, but it is there that the most unexpected and wonderful things happen.

EXERCISE 2-8 . . . THE WRITING PROCESS: WRITING THE FIRST DRAFT OF AN ESSAY

Choosing one of the topics you did not use in Exercise 2-1, generate ideas about it using freewriting, brainstorming, or branching. then create an outline or idea map to organize the ideas that best support your topic, and write a short essay.

REVISION STRATEGIES

2h   REVISING AN ESSAY

LEARNING OBJECTIVE 8
Revise an essay

Think again about the process of buying a car. At first you may think you have considered everything you need and are ready to make a decision. Then, a while later, you think of other features that would be good to have in your car; in fact, these features are at least as important as the ones you have already thought of. Now you have to rethink your requirements and perhaps reorganize your thoughts about what features are most important to you. You might eliminate some features, add others, and reconsider the importance of others.

A similar thing often happens as you revise your first draft. When you finish a first draft, you are more or less satisfied with it. Then you reread it later and see you have more work to do. When you revise, you have to rethink your entire paper, reexamining every part and idea.

Revising is more than changing a word or rearranging a few sentences, and it is not concerned with correcting punctuation, spelling, or grammar. (You make these proofreading changes later, after you are satisfied that you have presented your ideas in the best way. See Section 2i.) Revision is your chance to make significant improvements to your first draft. It might mean changing, adding, deleting, or rearranging whole sections of your essay.

Here is an excerpt from a later draft of Santiago's essay. In this revised draft of the third and fourth paragraphs, you can see how Santiago expands his ideas, adding words and details (underlined), and deleting others.

Santiago's Revision of Paragraphs 3 and 4

Santiago adds details to explain living in-between.

3   Living a life in-between two worlds, never completely a part of any, is a very complicated and extremely interesting place to be. Living in-between encourages growth and maturity. As a teenager, I struggled with feelings of not belonging and wanting to be a part of a group. I did not play soccer, or the guitar, and suffered from bullying. The impact this had in my life was emotionally wrecking. Often when people find themselves in similar

situations, they turn to familiar things for comfort. Things like a group they belong to, like a culture, or a race, or a religious group. This was not accessible to me in the same way as it was to others. ~~On one hand, in my teenage years, when I desperately wanted to feel I was part of something, there wasn't anything to take refuge in and feel strongly about.~~ On the other hand, though, standing on no man's land let ~~this made~~ me observe ~~see~~ the effects of the culture I grew up with on my way of thinking, and has greatly influenced my area of focus in my college studies. Standing in this middle ground was a vantage point from which I could analyze the opinions I held and the habits I developed and see my virtues and faults through different eyes. The hardiest weeds live where the pavement meets the prairie. I live where outsider meets insider.

Santiago adds mention of college

4   ~~I became used to being in the middle. I discovered that most questions can have more than one answer, or no answer at all. I realized that people are a lot more complex that I thought, and you really can't stick a label to them that won't become old and fall off.~~ What happens in this middle ground is that concepts such as gender, race, nationality, and other identities seem held up by pins. They are extremely volatile and impermanent; constantly changing and molding. This knowledge is present with me every time I say "I am Mexican" or "I am white." I had thought that people who fit snugly into a stereotype would never experience being an outsider. But I soon found out otherwise.

ESSAY REVISION CHECKLIST

Use these suggestions to revise an essay effectively.

1. **Reread the sentence that expresses your main point, the thesis statement of your essay.** It must be clear, direct, and complete. Experiment with ways to improve it.
2. **Make sure each paragraph supports your thesis statement.** Do all the paragraphs relate directly to the thesis? If not, cross out or rewrite those that do not clarify their connection to the main point.
3. **Make sure your essay has a beginning and an end.** An essay should have introductory and concluding paragraphs.
4. **Replace words that are vague or unclear with more specific or more descriptive words.**

5. **Seek advice.** If you are unsure about how to revise, visit your writing instructor during office hours and ask for advice, or try peer review (discussed below).

6. **When you have finished revising, you should feel satisfied with what you have said and with the way you have said it.** If you do not feel satisfied, revise your draft again.

Once you are satisfied, you are ready to edit and proofread.

Using Peer Review

Peer review entails asking one or more of your classmates to read and comment on your writing. It is an excellent way to discover what is good in your draft and what needs improvement. Here are some suggestions for making peer review as valuable as possible.

When You Are the Writer . . .

1. Prepare your draft in readable form. Double-space your work and print it on standard 8.5" × 11" paper.

2. When you receive your peers' comments, weigh them carefully. Keep an open mind, but do not feel that you must accept every suggestion.

3. If you have questions or are uncertain about your peers' advice, talk with your instructor.

When You Are the Reviewer . . .

1. Read the draft through at least once before making any suggestions.

2. Use the Paragraph Revision Checklist on page 56 as a guide to reviewing paragraphs and the Essay Revision Checklist on page 66 to review essays.

3. As you read, keep the writer's intended audience in mind (see Section 2d, p. 47). The draft should be appropriate for that audience.

4. Offer positive comments first. Say what the writer did well.

5. Be specific in your review, and offer suggestions for improvement.

6. Be supportive; put yourself in the place of the person whose work you are reviewing. Phrase your feedback in the way you would want to hear it!

EXERCISE 2-9 . . . THE WRITING PROCESS: REVISING A DRAFT

Revise the first draft you wrote for Exercise 2-8.

EXERCISE 2-10 . . . USING PEER REVIEW

Pair with a classmate for this exercise. Read and evaluate each other's drafts written for Exercise 2-8, using the peer review guidelines provided in this section.

Using Google Docs

Google Docs is a collection of open-source, easy-to-use tools that you can use to create and share word processed documents, spreadsheets, and presentations. Offered by Google, these apps are free to online users.

Accessing Google Docs

Accessing Google Docs is a simple process; after creating a Google account, you sign on and select the app you want to use. Then you are ready to work. Because it is a Web-based product, you can access Google Docs from any phone, tablet, or computer that has Internet capability. Also, you never have to worry about saving the document to an external drive or losing your work because it is automatically saved and stored in Google Drive, a cloud storage program. So, no matter where you are, as long as you are connected to the Internet, you can always retrieve your work.

Not only does Google Docs enable you to create documents, but it also makes it possible for you to share documents with other Google Docs users. Shared documents can be edited by multiple persons at the same time with every change saved automatically.

Using Google Docs in a Writing Class

Google Docs is a valuable resource for students in a writing class. In addition to creating and formatting documents with the word processor, you can share documents with your fellow students and your instructor. The collaborative feature makes peer revision easy and convenient. After you invite your peers to look at your document, they will log in to their Google accounts from wherever they may be and then review the document, using an appropriate peer revision checklist. Their changes, suggestions, and comments will be saved automatically and then shared with you. If your instructor so desires, you can also share documents with him or her and receive feedback on your drafts.

EXERCISE 2-11 . . . USING GOOGLE DOCS

Join with three classmates for this exercise. Using Google Docs, share, read, and evaluate each other's drafts written for Exercise 2-8, using the peer review guidelines provided in this section.

2i   EDITING AND PROOFREADING YOUR WORK

LEARNING OBJECTIVE 9
Proofread for correctness

Editing and **proofreading** require a final reading of your paper to check for errors. In this final polishing of your work, the focus is on correctness, so don't proofread until you have completed your drafting and revising. When you are ready to edit and proofread, you should check your writing for errors in

- sentences (run-ons or fragments)
- grammar

- spelling
- punctuation
- capitalization

Editing and Proofreading Checklist

The following tips will help you as you edit and proofread:

1. **Review your paper once for each type of error.** First, read it for run-on sentences or fragments. Take a short break, and then read it four more times, each time paying attention to one of the following: *grammar*, *spelling*, *punctuation*, and *capitalization*. Don't do this when you are tired; you might miss some mistakes or introduce new ones.

2. **To find spelling errors and identify fragments, read your paper from the last sentence to the first sentence and from last word to first word.** By reading this way, you will not get distracted by the flow of ideas, so you can focus on finding spelling errors. Also use the spell-checker on your computer, but be sure to proofread for the types of errors it cannot catch: missing words, errors that are themselves words (such as *of* for *or*), and homophones (for example, using *it's* for *its*).

3. **Read each sentence, slowly and deliberately.** This technique will help you catch endings that you have left off verbs or missing plurals.

4. **Check for errors one final time after you print your paper.** Ask a classmate or friend to read your paper to catch any mistakes you missed.

Here is a paragraph that shows the errors that Santiago corrected during editing and proofreading. Notice that errors in grammar, spelling, and punctuation were corrected.

It is places in-between where the most potential for growth lives. ^the all people have a place ^were they feel like outsiders, or not completely insiders. Realizing that this is where ^you are standing, and that it's ^it is perfectly fine to have one foot inside and one foot outside will let the unique reveal itself ~~though~~ ^through you. Being in-between can be difficult, but it is there that ^the most unexpected and wonderful things happen.

To view Santiago Quintana Garcia's final, proofread essay, see "The Space In-Between" on page 41 at the beginning of this chapter.

EXERCISE 2-12 . . . WRITING IN PROCESS: EDITING AND PROOFREADING

Prepare a final version of your essay by editing and proofreading the revised draft you created in Exercise 2-8.

SELF-TEST SUMMARY

To test yourself, cover the right column with a sheet of paper and answer the question in the left column. Evaluate each of your answers by sliding the paper down and comparing it with what is printed in the right column.

QUESTION	ANSWER
1 **What is the writing process?**	The **writing process** consists of *four basic steps*: prewriting to generate and organize ideas, writing a first draft, revising, and editing and proofreading.
2 **What are the benefits and drawbacks of using technology?**	**Computers** are useful at each stage of the writing process. They save you time, but be sure not to rely solely on their features to produce error-free text.
3 **What are prewriting techniques to generate ideas?**	Three techniques for generating ideas are **freewriting** (writing nonstop about a topic for a specified period without worrying about punctuation, spelling, and grammatical correctness), **brainstorming** (making a list of everything you can think of that is associated with your topic), and **diagramming** (writing your topic in a circle and drawing lines out from it to connect to related ideas).
4 **What should you consider before you write?**	To consider your **audience**, ask yourself who will be reading what you write. To consider your **purpose**, think about what you are trying to achieve through your writing. Choose a **point of view** and **tone** appropriate to your audience and purpose.
5 **How can you organize ideas?**	Two common methods of organizing ideas are **outlining** (listing main points and details in the order in which you will present them) and idea **mapping** (creating a drawing that shows the content and organization of your writing).
6 **What constitutes an effective paragraph?**	A **paragraph** is a group of sentences, usually at least three or four, that express one main idea. An **effective paragraph** contains a topic sentence that clearly states the main idea and logically organized supporting details that explain and illustrate it. Transitional words and phrases are used to connect ideas within and between paragraphs. Paragraphs may stand alone or be combined into essays or longer works.

QUESTION	ANSWER
7 *How do you structure an essay? What is involved in drafting?*	An **essay** is a group of at least three paragraphs about one subject. Essays should include an introductory paragraph, a body, and a concluding paragraph. (See the idea map for essays on page 58.) **Drafting** is a way of trying out ideas to see whether and how they work. Begin by writing one sentence expressing your main point, your thesis statement, then focus on explaining that sentence. A first draft is ideal for experimenting with different ideas and different ways of organizing them.
8 *What is revision?*	**Revision** allows you to make significant improvements to your draft by changing, adding, deleting, or rearranging words, parts, and ideas.
9 *How do you edit and proofread?*	**Edit** and **proofread** by checking for errors in sentences, grammar, spelling, punctuation, and capitalization. Read your paper once for each type of error, read your paper from the end to the beginning, read aloud, and check for errors again after you print your paper.

3 Vocabulary for Readers and Writers

LEARNING OBJECTIVES

1 Use context clues to understand unfamiliar words as you read
2 Use affixes (prefixes, roots, and suffixes) to decode meaning
3 Use a dictionary and a thesaurus when other strategies fail
4 Use language effectively when you write

Your vocabulary can be one of your strongest assets or one of your greatest liabilities. It defines and describes you by revealing a great deal about your level of education and your experience. Your vocabulary contributes to that all-important first impression people form when they meet you. A strong vocabulary provides both immediate academic benefits and long-term career effects, increasing your comprehension and critical-thinking skills. This chapter helps you to strengthen your vocabulary and use language effectively when you write.

What should you do when you are reading a passage and you come to a word you don't know? Despite what you might expect, looking up a word in a dictionary is not the first thing to do. In fact, a dictionary is your last resort—somewhere to turn when all else fails. Instead, first try to figure out the meaning of the word from its context—the words around it in the sentence, paragraph, or passage you are reading that provide clues to its meaning. These words are referred to as *context clues*. You can use four basic types of context clues in determining word meanings in textbook material: *definition*, *example*, *contrast*, and *logic of the passage*.

If a word's context does not provide clues to its meaning, you might try breaking the word into parts. Analyzing a word's parts, which may include its prefix, root, and suffix, also provides clues to its meaning. Finally, if word parts do not help, look up the word in a dictionary. Regardless of the method you use to find a word's meaning, be sure to record its meaning in the margin of the page. Later, transfer its meaning to a vocabulary log. You will learn how to use each of these strategies later in this chapter.

3a   USING CONTEXT CLUES

LEARNING OBJECTIVE 1
Use context clues to understand unfamiliar words as you read

Read the following brief paragraph in which some words are missing. Try to figure out the missing words and write them in the blanks.

> Rate refers to the _____ at which you read. If you
> read too _____, your comprehension may suffer. If you
> read too _____, you are not likely to complete your
> assignments on time.

Did you insert the word *speed* in the first blank, *fast* in the second blank, and *slowly* in the third blank? Most likely you correctly identified all three missing words. You could tell from the sentence which word to put in. The words around the missing words—the sentence **context**—provided clues as to which word would fit and make sense; such clues are called **context clues**.

While you probably won't find missing words on a printed page, you will often find words whose meaning you do not know. Context clues can help you figure out the meanings of unfamiliar words, as shown in the following example.

> Our culture devalues **stoicism** and rewards overreacting to every little thing, especially on reality TV.

From the sentence, you can tell that *stoicism* is the opposite of overreacting, so it most likely means "the state of remaining calm or showing little passion." Here's another example:

> What makes them difficult is their fierce demands **coupled** with their inability to compromise.

You can figure out that *coupled* means "paired with" or "linked together."

There are four types of context clues to look for: (1) definition, (2) example, (3) contrast, and (4) logic of the passage. Study the following chart to learn how to use each type.

TYPES OF CONTEXT CLUES

CONTEXT CLUE	HOW TO FIND MEANING	EXAMPLE
Definition	1. Look for words that announce that meanings will follow (*is, are, refers to, means*).	Broad, flat noodles that are served with sauce or butter are called **fettuccine**.
	2. Look for parentheses, dashes, or commas that set apart synonyms or brief definitions.	Psychologists often wonder whether **stereotypes**—the assumptions we make about what people are like—might be self-fulfilling.
Example	Figure out what the examples have in common. (For example, both pepper and mustard aren't eaten by themselves but are put on other foods.)	Most **condiments**, such as pepper, mustard, and ketchup, are used to improve the flavor of foods.
Contrast	Look for a word or phrase that is the opposite of a word whose meaning you don't know.	Before their classes in manners, the children were disorderly; after graduation, they acted with more **decorum**.
Logic of the Passage	Use the rest of the sentence to help you. Pretend the word is a blank line and fill in the blank with a word that makes sense.	On hot, humid afternoons, I often feel **languid**.

EXERCISE 3-1 . . . USING DEFINITION CLUES

Read the following excerpt and use definition clues to help you determine the meaning of each boldfaced word or phrase.

Issue: Cultural Similarities and Differences

Within every culture, there is an overall sense of what is beautiful and what is not beautiful, what represents good taste as opposed to tastelessness or even obscenity. Such considerations are matters of **aesthetics**. Global marketers must understand the importance of visual aesthetics embodied in the color or shape of a product, label, or package. Aesthetic elements that are attractive, appealing, and in good taste in one country may be perceived differently in another. In some cases, a **standardized color** can be used in all countries; an example is the distinctive yellow color on Caterpillar's earth-moving equipment and its licensed outdoor gear.

Music is an aesthetic component of all cultures and is accepted as a form of artistic expression and a source of entertainment. In one sense, music represents a **transculture** that is not identified with any particular nation. However, sociologists have noted that national identity derives in part from a country's **indigenous**, or native, music; a unique musical style can represent the uniqueness of the culture and the community.

—adapted from Keegan and Green, *Global Marketing*, p. 104

1. aesthetics _____

    _____

2. standardized color _____

    _____

3. transculture _____

    _____

4. indigenous _____

EXERCISE 3-2 ... USING EXAMPLE CLUES

*Read the following excerpt and use definition and example clues to help you
determine the meaning of each boldfaced word.*

Issue: Terrorism

Terrorism is the systematic use of violence by a group in order to **intimidate** a population or **coerce** a government into granting its demands. Terrorists attempt to achieve
their **objectives** through organized acts that spread fear and anxiety among the population, such as bombing, kidnapping, hijacking, taking of hostages, and **assassination**.
They consider violence necessary as a means of bringing widespread publicity to goals
and **grievances** that are not being addressed through peaceful means. Belief in their
cause is so strong that terrorists do not hesitate to strike despite knowing they will
probably die in the act.

Distinguishing terrorism from other acts of political violence can be difficult. For
example, if a Palestinian suicide bomber kills several dozen Israeli teenagers in a Jerusa-
lem restaurant, is that an act of terrorism or wartime **retaliation** against Israeli government policies and army actions? Competing arguments are made: Israel's **sympathizers**
denounce the act as a terrorist threat to the country's existence, whereas **advocates** of
the Palestinian cause argue that long-standing injustices and Israeli army attacks on
Palestinian civilians provoked the act.

—Rubenstein, *Contemporary Human Geography*, p. 190

1. terrorism _____

    _____

2. intimidate _____

3. coerce _____

4. objectives _____

5. assassination _____

6. grievances _____

7. retaliation _____

8. sympathizers _____

9. advocates _____

EXERCISE 3-3 . . . USING CONTRAST CLUES

Read the following excerpt and use contrast clues to help you determine the meaning of each boldfaced word. Consult a dictionary, if necessary.

Issue: "Dirty" Political Campaigns

The Whigs chose General William Henry Harrison to run against President Martin Van Buren in 1840, using a **specious** but effective argument: General Harrison is a plain man of the people who lives in a log cabin. Contrast him with the suave Van Buren, **luxuriating** amid "the Regal Splendor of the President's Palace." Harrison drinks ordinary hard cider with his hog meat and grits, while Van Buren **eschews** plain food in favor of expensive foreign wines and fancy French cuisine. The general's furniture is **unpretentious** and sturdy; the president dines off gold plates and treads on carpets that cost the people $5 a yard. In a country where all are equal, the people will reject an **aristocrat** like Van Buren and put their trust in General Harrison, a simple, brave, honest, public-spirited common man. (In fact, Harrison came from a distinguished family, was well educated and financially comfortable, and certainly did not live in a log cabin.)

—adapted from Carnes and Garraty, *The American Nation*, p. 267

1. specious _____

2. luxuriating _____

3. eschews _____

4. unpretentious _____

5. aristocrat _____

EXERCISE 3-4 . . . USING LOGIC OF THE PASSAGE CLUES

Read the following excerpt and use the logic of the passage clues to help you select the correct meaning of each boldfaced word or phrase.

Issue: Cultural Similarities and Differences

In 2005, while writing a children's book on the life of the **prophet** Mohammed, Danish author Klare Bluitgen searched unsuccessfully for an **illustrator**. The problem:

Many of the world's Muslims believe that it is **blasphemy** to **depict** images of the prophet. Denmark's conservative *Jyllands-Posten* newspaper picked up the story; concerned that this was a case of **self-censorship**, the paper's cultural editor challenged dozens of well-known illustrators to "draw Mohammed in the way they see him." In September 2005, *Jyllands-Posten* printed submissions from 12 illustrators **in conjunction with** articles on freedom of speech; one of the images depicted Mohammed with a bomb in his turban.

—Keegan and Green, *Global Marketing*, p. 105

1. prophet _____

2. illustrator _____

3. blasphemy _____

4. depict _____

5. self-censorship _____

6. in conjunction with _____

3b   LEARNING AFFIXES: PREFIXES, ROOTS, AND SUFFIXES

LEARNING OBJECTIVE 2
Use affixes (prefixes, roots, and suffixes) to decode meaning

Suppose you come across the following sentence in a biology textbook:

At times, fire can be an important **abiotic** factor in some ecosystems.

If you did not know the meaning of *abiotic*, how could you determine it? There are no context clues in the sentence. One solution is to look up the word in a dictionary. An easier and faster way is to break the word into parts and analyze the meaning of each part. Many words in the English language are made up of affixes called *prefixes*, *roots*, and *suffixes*. These **affixes** have specific meanings that, when added together, can help you determine the meaning of the word as a whole.

The word *abiotic* can be divided into three parts: its prefix, root, and suffix.

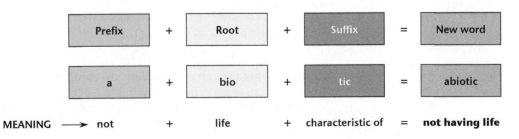

You can see from this analysis that *abiotic* means "not having life." Here are two other examples of words that you can figure out by using prefixes, roots, and suffixes:

1. I wanted to run the marathon, but after suffering from the flu for two weeks, I was a **nonstarter**.

   non- = not

   start = begin

   -er = one who does something

   nonstarter = someone who fails to take part in (or begin) a race

2. Remaining composed in the face of **unreasonableness** helps you figure out exactly what species of difficulty you're dealing with.

   un- = not

   reason = to think in a logical manner

   -able = capable of

   -ness = condition of

   unreasonableness = the condition of not being able to think in a logical manner

The first step in using the prefix–root–suffix method is to become familiar with the most commonly used affixes. The prefixes and roots listed in Tables 3-1 and 3-2 (pp. 79-80 and 82) will give you a good start in determining the meanings of thousands of words without having to look them up in the dictionary.

What You Need to Know About Affixes

Before you begin to use affixes to figure out new words, there are a few things you need to know:

1. **In most cases, a word is built upon at least one root.**
2. **Words can have more than one prefix, root, or suffix.**
   a. Words can be made up of two or more roots (*geo/logy*).
   b. Some words have two prefixes (*in/sub/ordination*).
   c. Some words have two suffixes (*beauti/ful/ly*).
3. **Words do not always have a prefix and a suffix.**
   a. Some words have neither a prefix nor a suffix (*read*).
   b. Others have a suffix but no prefix (*read/ing*).
   c. Others have a prefix but no suffix (*pre/read*).
4. **The spelling of roots may change as they are combined with suffixes.** Some common variations are included in Table 3-2 (p. 82).
5. **Different prefixes, roots, or suffixes may have the same meaning.** For example, the prefixes *bi-*, *di-*, and *duo-* all mean "two." The prefixes *un-*, *in-*, and *non-* all mean "not."

6. **Some roots, prefixes, and suffixes have different meanings in different words.** The meaning is based on whether the word part comes from Latin or Greek. For example, the biological term for mankind is *homo sapiens*. Here, *homo* means "man." In the word *homogenous*, which means "all of the same kind," *homo* means "same." Other words that use the Greek meaning of homo are *homogenize* (to make uniform or similar) and *homonym* (two words that sound the same).

7. **Sometimes you may identify a group of letters as a prefix or root but find that it does not carry the meaning of that prefix or root.** For example, the letters *mis* in the word *missile* are part of the root and are not the prefix *mis-*, which means "wrong; bad."

Prefixes

Prefixes appear at the beginning of many English words. They alter the meaning of the root to which they are connected. For example, if you add the prefix *re-* to the word *read*, the word *reread* is formed, meaning "to read again." If *pre-* is added to the word *reading*, the word *pre-reading* is formed, meaning "before reading." If the prefix *post-* is added, the word *post-reading* is formed, meaning "after reading." Table 3-1 lists common prefixes grouped according to meaning.

TABLE 3-1 COMMON PREFIXES

PREFIX	MEANING	SAMPLE WORD	MEANING OF SAMPLE WORD
Prefixes referring to amount or number			
mono-/uni-	one	monocle/unicycle	eyeglass for one eye/one-wheel vehicle
bi-/di-/duo-	two	bimonthly/ diandrous/duet	twice a month/flower with two stamens/two singers
tri-	three	triangle	a figure with three sides and three angles
quad-	four	quadrant	any of four parts into which something is divided
quint-/pent-	five	quintet/pentagon	a group of five/five-sided figure
deci-	ten	decimal	based on the number ten
centi-	hundred	centigrade	divided into 100 degrees, as a thermometer scale
milli-	thousand	milligram	one thousandth of a gram
micro-	small	microscope	an instrument used to see a magnified image of a small object
multi-/poly-	many	multipurpose/ polygon	having several purposes/figure with three or more sides
semi-	half	semicircle	half of a circle
equi-	equal	equidistant	at equal distances
Prefixes meaning "not" (negative)			
a-	not	asymmetrical	not identical on both sides of a central line
anti-	against	antiwar	against war

TABLE 3-1   COMMON PREFIXES   (*Continued*)

PREFIX	MEANING	SAMPLE WORD	MEANING OF SAMPLE WORD
contra-	against, opposite	contradict	deny by stating the opposite
dis-	apart, away, not	disagree	have a different opinion
in-/il-/ir-/im-	not	incorrect/illogical/impossible	wrong/not having sound reasoning/not possible
mis-	wrongly	misunderstand	fail to understand correctly
non-	not	nonfiction	writing that is factual, not fiction
pseudo-	false	pseudoscientific	a system of theories or methods mistakenly regarded as scientific
un-	not	unpopular	not popular
Prefixes giving direction, location, or placement			
ab-	away	absent	away or missing from a place
ad-	toward	adhesive	able to stick to a surface
ante-/pre-	before	antecedent/premarital	something that came before/before marriage
circum-/peri-	around	circumference/perimeter	the distance around something/border of an area
com-/col-/con-	with, together	compile/collide/convene	put together/come into violent contact/come together
de-	away, from	depart	leave, go away from
dia-	through	diameter	a straight line passing through the center of a circle
ex-/extra-	from, out of, former	ex-wife/extramarital	former wife/occurring outside marriage
hyper-	over, excessive	hyperactive	unusually or abnormally active
inter-	between	interpersonal	existing or occurring between people
intro-/intra-	within, into, in	introvert/intramural	turn or direct inward/involving only students within the same school
post-	after	posttest	a test given after completion of a program of course
re-	back, again	review	go over or inspect again
retro-	backward	retrospect	a survey or review of the past
sub-	under, below	submarine	a ship designed to operate under water
super-	above, extra	supercharge	increase or boost the power of something
tele-	far	telescope	an instrument for making distant objects appear nearer
trans-	across, over	transcontinental	extending across a continent

EXERCISE 3–5 . . . USING PREFIXES

Read the following paragraph and use your knowledge of prefixes to identify the meaning of each word in boldfaced type. Use a dictionary if necessary.

Issue: Mental Health Disorders

Major depression is sometimes referred to as a **unipolar** disorder because the emotional problems exist at only one end, or "pole," of the emotional range. When a person suffers from severe mood swings that go all the way from depression to manic episodes (excessive excitement, energy, and elation), that person is said to suffer from a **bipolar** disorder, meaning that emotions cycle between the two poles of possible emotions. Unlike mild or moderate mood **disorders**, there is usually no external cause for the extreme ups and downs of the bipolar person. The depressive phases of a bipolar person are **indistinguishable** from major depression but give way to manic episodes that may last from a few weeks to a few months. In these manic episodes, the person is extremely happy or **euphoric** without any real cause to be so happy.

—Ciccarelli and White, *Psychology*, p. 547

1. unipolar _____

2. bipolar _____

3. disorders _____

4. indistinguishable _____

5. euphoric _____

Roots

Roots carry the basic or core meaning of a word. Hundreds of root words are used to build words in the English language. Some of the most common and most useful are listed in Table 3-2. Knowing the meanings of these roots will help you unlock the meanings of many words. For example, if you know that the root *path* means "feeling," then you have a clue to the meanings of such words as *empathy* (the ability to understand and share another person's feelings), *pathetic* (evoking feelings of tenderness, pity, or sorrow), and *sociopath* (someone who behaves in a dangerous or violent way toward others without feelings of guilt).

TABLE 3-2   COMMON ROOTS

COMMON ROOT	MEANING	SAMPLE WORD	MEANING OF SAMPLE WORD
aster/astro	star	astronaut	a person trained to travel in space
aud/audit	hear	audible	able to be heard
bene	good, well	benefit	an advantage gained from something
bio	life	biology	the scientific study of living organisms
cap	take, seize	captive	a person who has been taken prisoner
chron/chrono	time	chronology	the order in which events occur
cog	to learn	cognitive	related to mental processes
corp	body	corpse	dead body
cred	believe	incredible	difficult/impossible to believe
dict/dic	tell, say	predict	declare something will happen in the future
duc/duct	lead	introduce	bring in or present for the first time
fact/fac	make, do	factory	a building where goods are manufactured
geo	earth	geophysics	the physics of the earth
graph	write	telegraph	a system for sending messages to a distant place
log/logo/logy	study, thought	psychology	the scientific study of the human mind
mit/miss	send	permit/dismiss	allow or make possible/send away
mort/mor	die, death	immortal	everlasting, not subject to death
path	feeling	sympathy	sharing the feelings of another
phon	sound, voice	telephone	a device used to transmit voices
photo	light	photosensitive	responding to light
port	carry	transport	carry from one place to another
scop	seeing	microscope	an instrument that magnifies small objects
scrib/script	write	inscription	a written note
sen/sent	feel	insensitive	lacking concern for others' feelings
spec/spic/spect	look, see	retrospect	a survey or review of the past
tend/tens/tent	stretch or strain	tension	mental or emotional strain
terr/terre	land, earth	territory	a geographic area, a tract of land
theo	god	theology	the study of the nature of God and religious belief
ven/vent	come	convention	a meeting or formal assembly
vert/vers	turn	invert	put upside down or in the opposite position
vis/vid	see	invisible/video	not able to be seen/related to televised images
voc	call	vocation	a person's occupation or calling

EXERCISE 3-6 . . . USING ROOTS

Read the following excerpt and choose the correct root from the box below to fill in the blank next to each boldfaced word part. One root will not be used.

osteo	phys	mort
vasc	cardio	dic

Issue: Health and Fitness

(1) _____ **respiratory** fitness reflects the heart and lungs' ability to perform exercise using large-muscle groups at moderate to high intensity for prolonged periods. Because it requires the blood vessels of the (2) **cardio** _____ **ular** system as well as respiratory systems to supply oxygen to the body during sustained physical activity, it is a good (3) **in** _____ **ator** of overall health. Low levels of fitness are associated with increased risk of premature death and disease.

A common affliction among older adults is (4)_____ **porosis**, a disease characterized by low bone mass and deterioration of bone tissue, which increase facture risk. Bone, like other human tissues, responds to the demands placed on it. Women (and men) have much to gain by remaining (5) _____ **ically** active as they age—bone mass levels are significantly higher among active than among sedentary women. Regular weight-bearing exercise, when combined with a healthy diet containing adequate calcium, helps keeps bones healthy.

—adapted from Donatelle, *Health*, pp. 329–330

Suffixes

Suffixes are word endings that often change the word's tense and/or part of speech. For example, adding the suffix *-y* to the noun *cloud* forms the adjective *cloudy*. Accompanying the change in part of speech is a shift in meaning (*cloudy* means "resembling clouds; overcast with clouds; dimmed or dulled as if by clouds").

Examples

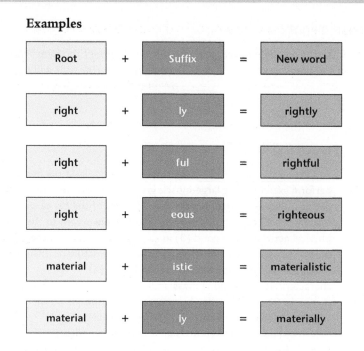

Often, several different words can be formed from a single root word with different suffixes. If you know the meaning of the root word and the ways in which different suffixes affect the meaning of the root word, you will be able to figure out a word's meaning when a suffix is added.

A list of common suffixes and their meanings appears in Table 3-3.

TABLE 3-3 COMMON SUFFIXES

SUFFIX	MEANING	SAMPLE WORD	MEANING OF SAMPLE WORD
Suffixes that refer to a state, condition, or quality			
-able	capable of	touchable	capable of being touched
-ance	characterized by	assistance	the action of helping
-ation	action or process	confrontation	an act of confronting or meeting face to face
-ence	state or condition	reference	an act or instance of referring or mentioning
-ible	capable of	tangible	capable of being felt, having substance
-ion	action or process	discussion	the act of examining in speech or writing
-ity	state or quality	superiority	the quality or condition of being higher in rank or status
-ive	performing action	permissive	characterized by freedom of behavior
-ment	action or process	amazement	a state of overwhelming surprise or astonishment
-ness	state, quality, condition	kindness	the quality of being kind
-ous	possessing, full of	jealous	envious or resentful of another

SUFFIX	MEANING	SAMPLE WORD	MEANING OF SAMPLE WORD
-ty	condition, quality characterized by	loyalty	the state of being loyal or faithful
-y		creamy	resembling or containing cream
Suffixes that mean "one who"			
-an		Italian	one who is from Italy
-ant		participant	one who participates
-ee		referee	one who enforces the rules of a game or sport
-eer		engineer	one who is trained in engineering
-ent		resident	one who lives in a place
-er		teacher	one who teaches
-ist		activist	one who takes action to promote or advocate a cause
-or		advisor	one who advises
Suffixes that mean "pertaining to or referring to"			
-al		autumnal	occurring in or pertaining to autumn
-ship		friendship	the state of being friends
-hood		brotherhood	the relationship between brothers
-ward		homeward	leading toward home

You can expand your vocabulary by learning the variations in meaning that occur when suffixes are added to words you already know. When you find a word whose meaning you do not know, look for the root. Then, using context, figure out what the word means with the suffix added. Occasionally you may find that the spelling of the root word has changed. For instance, a final *e* may be dropped, a final consonant may be doubled, or a final *y* may be changed to *i*. Consider the possibility of such changes when trying to identify the root word. Here are some examples:

1. What you might experience as a minor **frustration** is, for the neurotic, a hopeless difficulty.

   root + suffix

   frustrat(e) + -ation = the condition of being frustrated

2. Many observers find that the psychological **fragility** that underlies rejection-sensitivity is on the rise.

   root + suffix

   fragil(e) + -ity = the state or quality of being weakened or fragile

3. Plan the interaction around some kind of recreational activity or **entertainment**.

   root + suffix

   entertain + -ment = the act of amusing or entertaining people

EXERCISE 3-7 . . . USING SUFFIXES

Read the following excerpt. For each pair of words in parentheses, underline the word that correctly completes the sentence.

Issue: Business Ethics

Oil companies aren't usually known for their (environmentalism / environmentally) responsible reputations. Global energy giant BP, however, has made an effort to market an image that is Earth-friendly. For the most part, this strategy has (worked / working)—leading many to overlook the facts (suggesting / suggestion) that BP's claims are exaggerated or even completely false.

For the past several years, BP has (commitment / committed) environmental offenses almost (annually / annual). In 2000, the company was convicted of a felony for failing to report that its subcontractor was dumping (hazardously / hazardous) waste in Alaska. In 2005, BP allegedly ignored knowledge that its Texas City refinery was unsafe in a cost-cutting effort that led to an (explosive / explosion), 15 deaths, and even more injuries. The following year, BP's negligence at its Prudhoe Bay oil field (caused / causes) a 200,000-gallon oil spill and violation of the Clean Water Act. Then, in 2007, BP lobbied Indiana regulators for an (exemption / exemptive) allowing it to increase its daily release of ammonia and sludge into Lake Michigan.

—adapted from Ebert and Griffin, *Business Essentials*, p. 21

3c   USING A DICTIONARY AND A THESAURUS

LEARNING OBJECTIVE 3
Use a dictionary and a thesaurus when other strategies fail

To read and write effectively, you need resources to help you find the meanings of unfamiliar words as you read and to locate exact and precise words that convey your intended meaning when you write.

Types of Dictionaries

There are several types of dictionaries, each with its own purpose and use:

1. **Online dictionaries** are readily available. Two of the most widely used are *Merriam-Webster* (http://www.m-w.com) and *American Heritage* (http://www.ahdictionary.com/). Online dictionaries have several important advantages over print dictionaries.

   - **Audio component.** Some online dictionaries, such as *Merriam-Webster Online* and *The American Heritage Dictionary of the English Language*, feature an audio component that allows you to hear how words are pronounced.

   - **Multiple dictionary entries.** Some sites, such as Dictionary.com, display entries from several dictionaries for each word you look up.

   - **Misspellings.** If you aren't sure how a word is spelled or if you mistype it, several possible words and their meanings will be provided.

2. **A pocket or paperback dictionary** is an inexpensive, easy-to-carry, short-ened version of a standard desk dictionary.

3. **A collegiate dictionary** includes more words than a pocket dictionary and offers more complete definitions and specialized meanings.

Using a Dictionary

To use a dictionary effectively, you must become familiar with the kinds of information it provides.

Here is a brief review of the information a dictionary contains.

Pronunciation   Part of speech   Spelling of other forms of the entry word

Meanings

in·noc·u·ous (i-nä-kyə-wəs) *adj.* 1. producing no injury; harmless. 2. not likely to give offense or to arouse strong feelings or hostility; inoffensive, insipid. –**in·noc·u·ous·ly** *adv.* –**in·noc·u·ous·ness** *n.* [From Latin *innocuus*]

Etymology

EXERCISE 3–8 . . . USING A DICTIONARY

Use a dictionary to answer each of the following questions. Write your answer in the space provided.

1. What does the abbreviation *e.g.* stand for? _____

2. How is the word *deleterious* pronounced? (Record its phonetic spelling.)

   _____

3. From what languages is the word *delicatessen* taken?

   _____

4. Locate one restricted meaning for the word *configuration*.

   _____

   _____

5. What is the history of the word *mascot*?

   _____

   _____

   _____

   _____

6. What is the plural spelling of *addendum*? _____

7. What type of punctuation is a *virgule*?

_____

8. List a few words that contain the following sound: i

_____

9. Who or what is a *Semite*?

_____

10. Can the word *phrase* be used other than as a noun? If so, how?

_____

A dictionary lists all the common meanings of a word, but usually you are looking for only one definition. Meanings in an entry are grouped and numbered consecutively according to part of speech. If you are able to identify the part of speech of the word you are looking up, you can skip over all parts of the entry that do not pertain to that part of speech. If you cannot identify the part of speech of a word you are looking up, begin with the first meaning listed. Generally, the most common meaning appears first, and more specialized meanings appear toward the end of the entry. When you find a meaning that could fit into the sentence you are working with, replace the word with its definition and then read the entire sentence. If the definition makes sense in the sentence, you can be fairly certain that you have selected the appropriate meaning.

EXERCISE 3-9 . . . FINDING MEANINGS

Write an appropriate meaning for each boldfaced word in the following paragraph. Use a dictionary to help you find the meaning that makes sense in the sentence.

An all-too-common **variant** of hostility is passive aggression, in which the hostility is **covert**, expressed in nonobvious, underhanded ways—dragging one's heels on a project, failing to respond to a meaningful request. It's often difficult to pin down the hostility, but the effects are usually clear—your goals and dreams are **sabotaged**. A colleague briefs you on events but leaves out critical information you need for getting your job done. Your spouse **belittles** you in front of others—and then insists he was "just kidding" as you **seethe** with rage and humiliation.

1. variant: _____

2. covert: _____

3. sabotaged: _____

4. belittles: _____

5. seethe: _____

Using a Thesaurus

A **thesaurus**, or dictionary of synonyms, is a valuable reference for locating a precise, accurate, or descriptive word to fit a particular situation. A thesaurus lists synonyms for words and phrases, and you can choose from the list the word that most closely suggests the meaning you want to convey. The easiest way to do this is to test out, or substitute, various choices in your sentence to see which one is most appropriate; check a dictionary if you are not sure of a word's exact meaning. Here's an example:

> "Metalinguistic" abilities receive the **biggest** boost here.
>
> Biggest: *largest, greatest, heftiest, fullest, grandest, utmost, highest, bulkiest*

Try substituting several of the synonyms listed above for the word *biggest* and see how doing so changes the tone and meaning of the sentence.

Many students misuse thesauruses by choosing words that do not fit the context of their writing. *Be sure to use words only when you are familiar with all their shades of meaning.* Remember, a misused word is often a more serious error than a wordy or imprecise expression.

The most widely used print thesaurus is *Roget's Thesaurus*; it is readily available in an inexpensive paperback edition. Online thesauruses are available at the sites below; you can also pick a thesaurus from search choices.

- Thesaurus.com http://www.thesaurus.com
- Merriam-Webster http://merriam-webster.com/

EXERCISE 3-10 . . . USING A THESAURUS

Replace the boldfaced word or phrase in each sentence with a more descriptive word or phrase. Use a thesaurus to choose your replacement.

1. When Sara learned that her sister had committed a crime, she was **mad**. _____

2. Compared with earlier chapters, the last two chapters in my chemistry text are **hard**. _____

3. The instructor spent the entire class **talking about** the causes of inflation and deflation. _____

4. The main character in the film was a **thin**, talkative British soldier.

    _____

5. We went to see a **great** film that won the Academy Award for best picture. _____

3d   USING LANGUAGE EFFECTIVELY

LEARNING OBJECTIVE 4
Use language effectively when you write
Words have incredible power. On the positive side, words can inspire, comfort, and educate. At the other end of the spectrum, words can inflame, annoy, or deceive. Good writers understand that word choices greatly influence the reader, and they choose words that will help them achieve their goals. Careful readers understand the nuances of words and pay attention to how writers use them. This section describes numerous language features important to both readers and writers.

Denotation and Connotation

To understand the nuances (shades of meaning) of words, it is important to understand the difference between denotation and connotation. Which of the following would you like to be a part of: a *crowd, mob, gang, audience, congregation,* or *class*? Each of these words has the same basic meaning: "an assembled group of people." But each has a different *shade* of meaning. *Crowd* suggests a large, disorganized group. *Audience,* on the other hand, suggests a quiet, controlled group. Try to figure out the meanings suggested by each of the other words in the list.

This example shows that words have two levels of meanings—a literal meaning and an additional shade of meaning. A word's **denotation** is the meaning stated in the dictionary—its literal meaning. A word's **connotation** is the set of additional implied meanings, or nuances, that a word may take on. Often the connotation carries either a positive or negative association. The words *mob* and *gang* have a negative connotation because they imply a disorderly, disorganized group. *Congregation, audience,* and *class* have a positive connotation because they suggest an orderly, organized group.

Here are a few more examples. Would you prefer to be described as *slim* or *skinny*? As *intelligent* or *brainy*? As *heavy* or *fat*? As *frugal* or *cheap*? Notice that the words in each pair have a similar literal meaning, but that each word has a different connotation.

Depending on the words they choose, writers can suggest favorable or unfavorable impressions of the person, object, or event they are describing. For example, through the writer's choice of words, the two sentences below create two entirely different impressions. As you read them, notice the italicized words and their positive or negative connotations.

> The *unruly* crowd *forced* its way through the restraint barriers and *ruthlessly attacked* the rock star.
>
> The *enthusiastic* group of fans *burst* through the fence and *rushed* toward the rock star.

Connotations can help writers paint a picture to influence the reader's opinion. Thus a writer who wishes to be kind to an overweight politician might describe him as *pleasingly plump* (which carries an almost pleasant connotation) or even *quite overweight* (which is a statement of fact that remains mostly neutral). However, a writer who wishes to be negative about the same politician might describe him as *morbidly obese*.

When reading, pay attention to the writer's choice of words and his or her connotations. Ask yourself, "What words does the writer use, and how do they affect me?"

EXERCISE 3-11 . . . USING CONNOTATIVE LANGUAGE

For each of the following pairs of word or phrases, write two sentences. One sentence should use the word with the more positive connotation; the second should use the word with the less positive connotation.

1. request	demand
2. overlook	neglect
3. ridicule	tease
4. display	expose
5. garment	gown
6. gaudy	showy
7. artificial	fake
8. cheap	cost-effective
9. choosy	picky
10. seize	take

EXERCISE 3-12 . . . USING CONNOTATIVE LANGUAGE

For each of the following sentences, underline the word in parentheses that has the more appropriate connotative meaning. Consult a dictionary, if necessary.

1. The new superintendent spoke (extensively / enormously) about the issues facing the school system.

2. The day after we hiked ten miles, my legs felt extremely (rigid / stiff).

3. Carlos thought he could be more (productive / fruitful) if he had a home office.

4. The (stubborn / persistent) ringing of my cell phone finally woke me up.

5. The investment seemed too (perilous / risky), so we decided against it.

Synonyms and Antonyms

Synonyms are words with similar meanings: **antonyms** are words with opposite meanings. Both categories of words are useful to expand and diversify your reading and writing vocabulary. When writing, you may want to find a synonym, a word with a more exact, descriptive, or specific meaning than the one that comes to mind. For example, you might want to describe how a person walks. There are many words that mean *walk*, although each has a different connotation: *strut, meander, stroll, hike, saunter*, and *march*. A thesaurus can help you choose the word with the exact meaning you intend.

Antonyms are useful when making a contrast or explaining differences. You might be describing two different friends' styles of communication. One type is decisive. Finding antonyms for the word *decisive* may help you describe differing styles. Antonyms include *faltering, wavering*, or *hesitant*.

Slang

Most of what you read in textbooks, magazines, newspapers, and a variety of online sources is written in Standard Written English. This means it is written using a set of conventions and rules that make language clear, correct, and easy to understand by anyone who reads it. **Slang** is an informal, nonstandard form of expression used by a particular group. It is used by people who want to give themselves a unique identity, and it can be a useful in some social situations, in informal writing, and in some forms of creative writing. It is *not* appropriate to use in academic writing, so be sure to avoid using it in papers, essays, and exams.

Slang	She and her mom are *so tight*.
Standard Written English	She and her mom *have a close relationship*.

Slang	On Saturday I plan to *chill* by the pool.
Standard Written English	On Saturday I plan to *relax* by the pool.

Colloquial Language

Colloquial language refers to casual, everyday spoken language. Be sure to avoid it in most formal writing assignments. Words that fall into this category are labeled *informal* or *colloquial* in a dictionary.

| Colloquial | I almost *flunked bio* last sem. |
| **Standard Written English** | I almost *failed biology* last semester. |

| Colloquial | Janice *go* to the store. |
| **Standard Written English** | Janice *goes* to the store. |

Idioms

An **idiom** is a phrase with a meaning different from the phrase's individual words. Sometimes you can figure out an idiom's meaning from context within the sentence or paragraph, but more commonly you must simply know the idiom to understand it. Here are some examples of idiomatic speech:

He *has a short fuse* and is commonly cynical and mistrustful. (becomes angry quickly and often)

It's often difficult to *pin down* the hostility. (discover the facts or specific details about something)

An all-too-common behavior of passive aggression is *dragging one's heels* on a project. (acting with intentional slowness, deliberately delaying)

They'll find the *cloud in any silver lining*. (The idiom is "Every cloud has a silver lining," which means there is something good in every bad situation. Here it is turned around to mean someone is looking for something bad in a good situation.)

As you read, be on the lookout for phrases that use common words but do not make sense no matter how many times you reread them. When you find such a phrase, you have likely encountered an idiom. (It is estimated that English has almost 25,000 idiomatic expressions.)

EXERCISE 3–13 . . . UNDERSTANDING IDIOMS

For each sentence, write the meaning of the idiomatic expression in boldface.

1. The kidnapping of the twins from Utah in 1985 has turned into a **cold case**.

   _____

2. Jake decided to **zero in on** his goal of becoming a firefighter.

   _____

3. I am trying to make an appointment with my academic advisor, but she's been hard to **pin down**.

   _____

4. The mystery novels of P. D. James **blur the line** between popular fiction and literature.

   _____

5. Milton **saw red** when someone rear-ended his car. _____

Analogies

Analogies are abbreviated statements that express similarities between two pairs of items. You will find them on a variety of entrance and competency tests and exams. They are tests of both your thinking skills and your word knowledge. Analogies are often written in the following format:

> black : white :: dark : light

This can be read in either of two ways:

1. Black is to white as dark is to light.
2. White has the same relationship to black as light does to dark. (White is the opposite of black and light is the opposite of dark.)

In analogies the relationship between the words or phrases is critically important. Analogies become test items when one of the four items is left blank, and you are asked to supply or select the missing item.

> celery : vegetable :: orange : _____
> video : watch :: audio : _____

A variety of relationships are expressed in analogies. These include

- **Opposites** yes : no :: stop : start
- **Whole/part** year : month :: week : day
- **Synonyms** moist : damp :: happy : glad
- **Categories** dessert : cake :: meat : beef
- **Similarities** lemon : orange :: broccoli : cabbage
- **Association or action** train : conductor :: airplane : pilot
- **Knowledge** Picasso : painter :: Shakespeare : writer

EXERCISE 3-14 . . . WORKING WITH ANALOGIES

Complete each of the following analogies by supplying a word or phrase that completes it.

1. sculptor : statue :: musician : _____

2. Allah : Islam :: God : _____

3. fresh : rancid :: unique : _____

4. hasten : speed up :: outdated : _____

5. old age : geriatrics :: infancy : _____

Technical and Academic Language

Have you noticed that each sport and hobby has its own language—a specialized set of words and phrases with very specific meanings? Baseball players and fans talk about slides, home runs, errors, and runs batted in, for example. Each academic discipline also has its own language. For each course you take, you will encounter an extensive set of words and terms that have a particular, specialized meaning in that subject area. In this reading and writing course, you will learn terms such as *topic sentence, supporting details, idea map,* and *transitions.*

One of the first tasks you will face in a new college course is to learn its specialized language. This is particularly true of introductory courses in which a new discipline or field of study is explained.

It is important to learn to understand the language of a course when reading and to use the language of a course when speaking and writing.

A sample of the words introduced in economics and chemistry are given below. Some of the terms are common, everyday words that take on a specialized meaning; others are technical terms used only in that subject area.

NEW TERMS: ECONOMICS TEXT	NEW TERMS: CHEMISTRY TEXT
capital	matter
ownership	element
opportunity cost	halogen
distribution	isotope

Recognition of academic and technical terminology is only the first step in learning the language of a course. More important is the development of a systematic way of identifying, marking, recording, and learning these terms. Because new terminology is introduced in both class lectures and course textbooks, be sure to develop a procedure for handling the specialized terms in each. You might highlight them, annotate, or create a vocabulary log using computer file or notebook, for example.

SELF-TEST SUMMARY

To test yourself, cover the right column with a sheet of paper and answer the question in the left column. Evaluate each of your answers by sliding the paper down and comparing it with what is printed in the right column.

QUESTION	ANSWER
1 *What are context clues?*	**Context clues** help readers figure out the meaning of unfamiliar words. Context clues fall into four categories: (1) *definition clues*, (2) *example clues*, (3) *contrast clues*, and (4) *logic of the passage clues*.
2 *How can word parts unlock meaning?*	Many words are composed of some combination of prefix, root, and suffix. The **prefix** precedes the main part of the word; the **root** is the key part of the word that carries its core meaning; and the **suffix** appears at the end of the word. Knowing the meanings of key prefixes, roots, and suffixes will help you unlock the meaning of many unfamiliar words.
3 *How can you build vocabulary?*	To **build vocabulary**, you can use online and print dictionaries to locate the meanings of unfamiliar words. A *thesaurus*, a dictionary of synonyms, is also useful for selecting the most accurate and precise word to fit a particular situation.
4 *How can you use language effectively?*	Good writers understand that word choices greatly influence the reader, and they choose the words that will help them achieve their goals. Careful readers understand the nuances of words and pay attention to how writers use them. *Knowing about the following types of language will help you read and write more effectively*. The **denotative meaning** of a word is its stated dictionary meaning; a word's **connotation** is a set of implied meanings a word may take on. **Synonyms** are words of similar meaning; **antonyms** are words of opposite meaning. **Slang** refers to nonstandard or everyday informal language used by a particular group. **Colloquial language** refers to casual, everyday spoken language. An **idiom** is a phrase with a meaning different from the phrase's individual words. **Analogies** are abbreviated statements that express a relationship between two pairs of items. **Technical and academic language** refers to the specialized use of terms in particular academic disciplines.

4 Main Ideas and Topic Sentences

LEARNING OBJECTIVES

1 Understand the structure of a paragraph
2 Identify and select topics
3 Read and write topic sentences

Most articles, essays, and textbook chapters contain numerous ideas expressed in paragraph form. As you read, your job is to sort out the important ideas from those that are less important. As you write, you are expected to express your ideas clearly and correctly in paragraph form. In this chapter, you will learn to identify and select topics and to read and write topic sentences.

4a WHAT IS A PARAGRAPH?

LEARNING OBJECTIVE 1
Understand the structure of a paragraph

A **paragraph** is a group of related sentences that develop a main thought, or idea, about a single topic. The structure of a paragraph is not complex. There are usually four basic elements: (1) a topic, (2) a main idea, or topic sentence, (3) supporting details, and (4) transitions.

- A **topic** is the one thing a paragraph is about.
- The **topic sentence** expresses an idea about that topic. The topic sentence states the main point or controlling idea.
- The sentences that explain this main point are called **supporting details**.
- Words and phrases that connect and show relationships between and among ideas are called **transitions**.
- Stand-alone paragraphs (those not part of an essay) often include a concluding sentence that wraps up the paragraph and brings it to a close.

These elements help you know what to look for and ensure that you will understand and remember what you read. Now, read the following paragraph, noticing how all the details relate to one point, explaining the topic sentence.

Issue: Color Psychology

There is some evidence that colors affect people physiologically. For example, when subjects are exposed to red light, respiratory movements increase; exposure to blue decreases respiratory movements. Similarly, eye blinks increase in frequency when eyes are exposed to red light and decrease when exposed to blue. After changing a school's walls from orange and white to blue, the blood pressure of the students, decreased while their academic performance improved. This seems consistent with the intuitive feelings about blue being more soothing and red being more arousing.

—adapted from DeVito, *Human Communication*, p. 182

In this paragraph, the topic sentence identifies the topic as *color* and states that *colors affect people physiologically*. The remaining sentences provide further information about the effects of color. Since this paragraph first appeared in a textbook chapter, it does not have a concluding sentence. Below is a map of the paragraph on color.

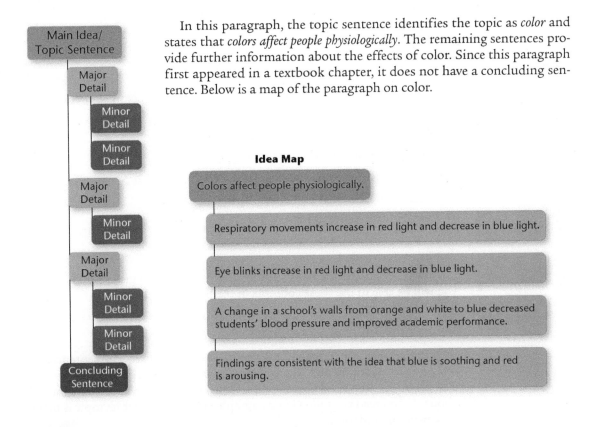

4b   IDENTIFYING AND SELECTING TOPICS

LEARNING OBJECTIVE 2
Identify and select topics

Topics are important to both readers and writers. Identifying the topic of a paragraph helps readers to understand what it is about. Choosing focused topics helps writers clarify their thinking and organize their ideas.

Distinguishing Between General and Specific Ideas

A **general idea** applies to a large number of individual items. The term *television programs* is general because it refers to a large collection of shows—soap operas, sports specials, sitcoms, and so on. A **specific idea** or term is more detailed or particular. It refers to an individual item. The term *reality TV*, for example, is more specific than the word *program*. The title "The Real Housewives of Atlanta" is even more specific. Here are some more examples:

General:	Continents	*General:*	U.S. Presidents
Specific:	Africa	*Specific:*	John F. Kennedy
	Asia		Barack Obama
	Australia		Thomas Jefferson

EXERCISE 4-1 . . . IDENTIFYING GENERAL IDEAS

For each list of items, write a word or phrase that best describes that grouping.

1. sadness, joy, anger, bereavement _____

2. Capricorn, Aquarius, Taurus, Libra _____

3. U.S. Constitution, Bill of Rights, Federalist Papers, First Amendment

    _____

4. Mars, Saturn, Jupiter, Mercury _____

Now that you are familiar with the difference between general and specific, you will be able to use these concepts in the rest of the chapter.

Finding the Topic of a Paragraph

We have defined a paragraph as a group of related ideas. The sentences are related to one another and all are about the same person, place, thing, or idea. The common subject or idea is called the *topic*—what the entire paragraph is about. As you read the following paragraph, you will see that its topic is unemployment and inflation.

Issue: The Economy

Unemployment and inflation are the economic problems that are most often discussed in the media and during political campaigns. For many people, the state of the economy can be summarized in just two measures: the unemployment rate and the inflation rate. In the 1960s, Arthur Okun, who was chairman of the Council of Economic Advisors during President Lyndon Johnson's administration, coined the term *misery index*, which adds together the inflation rate and the unemployment rate to give a rough measure of the state of the economy. Although unemployment and inflation are important problems in the short run, the long-run success of an economy is best judged by its ability to generate high levels of real GDP (gross domestic product) per person.

—adapted from Hubbard and O'Brien, *Essentials of Economics*, p. 408

Each sentence of this paragraph discusses or describes unemployment and inflation. To identify the topic of a paragraph, then, ask yourself: *"What or whom is the paragraph about?"*

EXERCISE 4-2 . . . IDENTIFYING THE TOPIC

After reading each of the following selections, select the choice that best represents the topic of the selection.

Issue: Prejudice and Stereotypes

_____ 1. Everyone is familiar with the legacy of racial prejudice in the United States. Arguments over the legitimacy of slavery are 150 years in the past and it has been decades since public schools were integrated, yet racial prejudice remains a major concern among all demographic groups in this country. The emphasis on race has also increased our awareness of other forms of stereotyping. For example, psychologists have researched stereotypes and prejudice related to weight and body size, sexual orientation, and religious affiliation. Racial, ethnic, and other outgroup stereotypes are pervasive and, unfortunately, seem to thrive in times of hardship. For example, during economic slumps, an outgroup (a collection of people who are perceived as different) is often targeted for taking jobs from the in group or for draining resources from the local economy.

—adapted from Krause and Corts, *Psychological Science*, p. 569

a. racial prejudice and forms of stereotyping
b. U.S. history
c. in groups and outgroups
d. the results of economic hardship

Issue: Personal Relationships

_____ 2. According to Bella DePaulo and Wendy Morris, one of the major disadvantages of not being married is that single adults are the targets of *singlism*, the negative stereotypes and discrimination faced by singles. Their research found that single people were viewed more negatively than married people.

Compared to married or coupled people, who are often described in very positive terms, singles are assumed to be immature, maladjusted, and self-centered. Loneliness, lack of companionship, being excluded from couples' events, or feeling uncomfortable in social settings involving mostly couples, not having children, and social disapproval of their lifestyle are among the other frequently reported disadvantages of being single. Another disadvantage of living alone is more gender-specific. Women living alone confront safety issues in deciding where to live, what mode of transportation to use, and which leisure activities to attend.

—Schwartz and Scott, *Marriages and Families*, p. 211

a. singlism
b. gender-specific perceptions
c. disadvantages of being single
d. societal perceptions of married people

Issue: Heart Health

_____ 3.   When the wall of an artery becomes weakened, as may result from disease, inflammation, injury, or a congenital defect, the pressure of the blood flowing through the weakened area may cause it to swell outward like a balloon, forming an aneurysm. Common locations for aneurysms include arteries in the brain and the aorta, the major artery leaving the left ventricle that carries blood to body cells. An aneurysm does not always cause symptoms, but it can be threatening just the same. The primary risk is that the aneurysm will burst, causing blood loss and depriving tissues of oxygen and nutrients, a situation that can be fatal. Even if it does not rupture, an aneurysm can cause life-threatening blood clots to form. An aneurysm can be detected with either an MRI or ultrasound scan. Treatment often includes surgical removal or applying support with a coil or stent.

—Goodenough and McGuire, *Biology of Humans*, p. 233

a. arteries
b. blood clots
c. aneurysms
d. blood flow

Selecting a Topic to Write About

To write a good paragraph, you need a manageable topic, one that is the right size. Your topic must be general enough to allow you to add interesting details that will engage your reader. It must also be specific or narrow enough so that you can cover it adequately in a few sentences. If your topic is too general, you'll end up with a few unrelated details that do not add up to a specific point. If your topic is too narrow, you will not have enough to say.

Suppose you have decided to write a paragraph about sports. Here is your topic.

sports as a favorite activity for many people

This topic is much *too broad* to cover in one paragraph. Think of all the different aspects you could write about. Which sports would you consider? Would you write about both playing sports and watching them? Would you write about both professional and amateur sports? Would you write about the reasons people enjoy sports? The topic must be more specific:

watching professional football on Sunday afternoons with my family

Here you have limited your topic to a specific sport (football), a specific time (Sunday afternoon), and some specific fans (your family).

Here are other examples of topics that are too general. Each has been revised to be more specific.

Too General	influence of my parents
Revised	influence of my parents on my choice of college

Too General	sex education
Revised	how sex education in high school helps students talk more openly

If your topic is *too specific* (narrow), you will not have enough details to use in a paragraph, or you may end up including details that do not relate directly to the topic. Suppose you decide to write a paragraph about the Internet and come up with this topic:

the role of the Internet in keeping me in touch with friends and family

What else would your paragraph say? You might name some specific friends and where they are, but this list would not be very interesting. This topic is too specific. It might work as a detail, but not as the main point of the paragraph. To correct the problem, ask, "What else does the Internet allow me to do?" You might say that it allows you to stay in touch with friends by e-mail, that it makes doing research for college papers easier, and that it provides information on careers and even specific job openings. Here is a possible revised topic:

the Internet as an important part of my personal, college, and work life

Here are a few other examples of topics that are too narrow, along with revisions for each one:

| Too Narrow | the 36% voting rate in the last midterm election |
| **Revised** | Americans who do not exercise their right to vote |

| Too Narrow | primary-care providers receive six weeks childcare leave |
| **Revised** | flexible child-care leave policy at Markel Carpet Company |

How can you tell if your topic is too general or too specific? Try brainstorming or branching to generate ideas. If you find you can develop the topic in many different directions, or if you have trouble choosing details from a wide range of choices, your topic is probably too general. If you cannot think of anything to explain or support it, your topic sentence is too specific.

EXERCISE 4–3 . . . WRITING: SELECTING A TOPIC

Narrow or broaden each of the following topics so that it can be developed in a single paragraph.

1. Road trips

2. Health benefits of exercise

3. Global unemployment rate for 15- to 24-year-olds

4. Beekeeping

5. Sports mascots

4c   READING AND WRITING TOPIC SENTENCES

LEARNING OBJECTIVE 3
Read and write topic sentences

Once you know how to locate and develop a topic, you can easily locate and write topic sentences.

Finding the Topic Sentence of a Paragraph

The **main idea** of a paragraph is what the author wants you to know about the topic. It is the broadest, most important idea that the writer develops throughout the paragraph. The entire paragraph explains, develops, and supports this main idea. A question that will guide you in finding the main idea is *"What key point is the author making about the topic?"* In the paragraph about unemployment and inflation on pages 100–101, the writer's main idea is that unemployment and inflation are two important measures of the economy's overall health. Often, but not always, one sentence expresses the main idea: this sentence is called the **topic sentence**.

To find the topic sentence, search for the one general sentence that explains what the writer wants you to know about the topic; the remaining sentences of the paragraph will provide details about or explain the topic sentence.

In the following paragraph, the topic is one of IKEA's marketing strategies. Read the paragraph to find out what the writer wants you to know about this topic. Look for the one sentence that states this.

Issue: Marketing

To help women who do the shopping cope with significant others who hate to come along, furniture retailer IKEA created an in-store area called Mänland. It is a kind of daycare area where retail-phobic husbands and boyfriends can hang out while the women shop. The area was actually modeled after the retailer's toddler-care area, but instead of arts and crafts, the men play pinball and video games, watch sports, and eat free hot dogs. The women are even given a buzzer to remind them to collect their significant others after 30 minutes of shopping.

—adapted from Kotler and Armstrong, *Principles of Marketing*, p. 145

The paragraph opens with a statement and then proceeds to explain it with supporting evidence. The first sentence is the topic sentence, and it states the paragraph's main point: *IKEA devised Mänland as a solution for men who hate to shop.*

TIPS FOR LOCATING TOPIC SENTENCES
1. **Identify the topic.** Figure out the general subject of the entire paragraph. In the preceding sample paragraph, "Mänland" is the topic.
2. **Locate the most general sentence (the topic sentence).** This sentence must be broad enough to include all of the other ideas in the paragraph. The topic sentence in the sample paragraph "To help women who do the shopping cope with significant others who hate to come along, furniture retailer IKEA created an in-store area called Mänland." covers all of the other details in the paragraph.

Common Positions for Topic Sentences

A writer often places the topic sentence first in the paragraph—a position that enables the writer to state his or her main idea and then move on to explain it. The topic sentence can also be placed last or in the middle. On occasion a writer may choose to state the main idea once at the beginning of the paragraph and restate it at the end or use both sentences to fully explain his or her main idea. Although a topic sentence can be located anywhere in a paragraph, it is usually *first* or *last*.

VISUAL	PLACEMENT	EXAMPLE
General — Topic Sentence / Detail / Specific — Detail / Detail	**Topic Sentence First** Here the writer defines the term "focus group" and then provides details about focus groups.	A focus group is a small group, usually consisting of about seven to ten people who are brought together to discuss a subject of interest to the researcher. Focus groups are commonly used today in business and politics; that flashy slogan you heard for a political campaign or a new toothpaste was almost certainly tested in a focus group to gauge people's reactions. Social researchers may use a focus group to help design questions or instruments for quantitative research or to study the interactions among group members on a particular subject. In most cases, researchers ask predetermined questions, but the discussion is unstructured. Focus groups are a relatively cheap method of research and can be completed quickly. They also allow for the flexible discussions and answers that are desirable in qualitative research. —Kunz, *THINK Marriages & Families*, p. 36
Specific — Detail / Detail / Detail / General — Topic Sentence	**Topic Sentence Last** Here the author reports details of a study examining jealousy in two types of cultures and then states the study's findings in the last sentence.	Is jealously universal? Surveying two centuries of anthropological reports, a study found two types of cultures: In one, jealousy was rare (for example, the Todas of southern India); in the other, jealousy was common (for example, the Apache Indians of North America). Toda culture discouraged possessiveness of material objects or people. It placed few restrictions on sexual gratification, within or outside of marriage. In contrast, Apache society prized virginity, paternity, and fidelity. While a man was away from home, for example, he had a close relative keep secret watch over his wife and report on her behavior when he returned. Based on the variations found in different cultures, the study concluded that jealousy is neither universal nor innate. —adapted from Benokraitis, *Marriages and Families*, p. 164

VISUAL	PLACEMENT	EXAMPLE
Specific · Detail / Detail · General · Topic Sentence · Specific · Detail / Detail	**Topic Sentence in Middle** Here the author first offers some basic facts about buzz marketing and then defines the term. After the definition, the author goes on to explain buzz marketing's advantages and list its specific forms.	Buzz marketing has become one of the fastest-growing areas in alternative marketing. Estimated expenditures for these programs total more than $1 billion annually. Buzz marketing, or *word-of-mouth marketing*, emphasizes consumers passing along information about a product. A recommendation by a friend, family member, or acquaintance carries higher levels of credibility than an advertisement. Buzz can be more powerful than the words of a paid spokesperson or endorser. Word-of-mouth endorsements can be supplied by consumers who like a brand and tell others, consumers who like a brand and are sponsored by a company to speak to others, or by company or agency employees who talk about the brand. —Clow and Baack, *Integrated Advertising, Promotion, and Marketing Communications*, p. 208
Topic Sentence · Detail · Detail · / · Detail · Detail · Topic Sentence	**Topic Sentence First and Last** The first and last sentences together explain that the NCI takes an aggressive strategy to finding and testing samples for cancer suppression.	The National Cancer Institute (NCI) has taken a brute-force approach to screening species for cancer-suppressing chemicals. NCI scientists receive frozen samples of organisms from around the world, chop them up, and separate them into a number of extracts, each probably containing hundreds of components. These extracts are tested against up to 60 different types of cancer cells for their efficacy in stopping or slowing growth of the cancer. Promising extracts are then further analyzed to determine their chemical nature, and chemicals in the extract are tested singly to find the effective compound. This approach is often referred to as the "grind 'em and find 'em" strategy. —Belk and Maier, *Biology*, p. 334

EXERCISE 4-4 . . . FINDING TOPIC SENTENCES

Underline the topic sentence(s) of each of the following paragraphs.

Paragraph 1

Issue: Infant-Directed Speech

Although the words themselves differ across languages, the way that words are spoken to infants is quite similar. For example, 6 out of 10 most frequent major characteristics of speech directed at infants used by native speakers of English and Spanish are common to both languages: exaggerated intonation, high pitch, lengthened vowels, repetition, lower volume, and heavy stress on certain key words (such as emphasizing the word "ball" in the sentence, "No, that's a ball"). Similarly, mothers in the United States, Sweden, and Russia all exaggerate and elongate the pronunciation of the three vowel sounds of "ee," "ah," and "oh" when speaking to infants in similar ways, despite differences in the languages in which the sounds are used. According to a growing body of research, there are basic similarities across cultures in the nature of infant-directed speech.

— Feldman, *Development Across the Life Span*, p. 173

Paragraph 2

Issue: Medical Liability and the Law

In the past, exposure to liability made many doctors, nurses, and other medical professionals reluctant to stop and render aid to victims in emergency situations, such as highway accidents. Almost all states have enacted a Good Samaritan law that relieves medical professionals from liability for injury caused by their ordinary negligence in each set of circumstances. Good Samaritan laws protect medical professionals only from liability for their *ordinary negligence*, not for injuries caused by their gross negligence or reckless or intentional conduct. Many Good Samaritan laws have protected licensed doctors and nurses and laypersons who have been certified in CPR. Good Samaritan statutes generally do not protect laypersons who are not trained in CPR—that is, they are liable for injuries caused by their ordinary negligence in rendering aid.

—Goldman and Cheeseman, *Paralegal Professional*, p. 459

Paragraph 3

Issue: Fashion

One of the best ways to analyze your wardrobe is to determine which items you already own. This requires a thorough closet cleaning, purging items that no longer fit, are out of fashion, are not appropriate for your career or leisure time, or have not been worn in a year. Trying on everything gives you the opportunity to categorize clothing into piles labeled: keepers, "iffy," resells, and purge. After this exercise, organize the garments that remain by category and color, starting with neutrals and moving to brights in this order: shirts/tops, bottoms, jackets/coats/sweaters, and, for women, dresses. Put out-of-season in another storage area. After wearing, always replace garments in their original location.

—adapted from Marshall, Jackson, and Stanley, *Individuality in Clothing Selection and Personal Appearance*, p. 293

Paragraph 4

Issue: Gender in Advertising

Women of all nationalities and ethnic groups have always been an important audience in the field of business. Indeed, Ketchum Communications makes the point, "Today's women hold an overwhelming share of consumer purchasing influence, making more than 80 percent of household purchase decisions. . . ." According to a Nielsen report in 2013, estimates on female purchasing power vary from $5 trillion to 15 trillion annually, and trends indicate that women will control two-thirds of the consumer wealth in the United States over the next decade. Given these statistics, it is no surprise that women are also emerging as "influential" in a variety of marketing campaigns for a spectrum of companies.

—adapted from Wilcox, Cameron, and Reber, *Public Relations*, p. 291

Paragraph 5

Issue: Cultural Similarities and Differences

In Japan, it's called *kuroi kiri* (black mist); in Germany, it's *schmiergeld* (grease money), whereas Mexicans refer to *la mordida* (the bite), the French say *pot-de-vin* (jug of wine), and Italians speak of the *bustarella* (little envelope). They're all talking about *bakshsheesh*, the Middle Eastern term for a "tip" to grease the wheels of a transaction. Giving "gifts" in exchange for getting business is common and acceptable in many countries, even though this may be frowned on elsewhere.

—adapted from Solomon, *Consumer Behavior*, p. 21

EXERCISE 4-5 . . . FINDING MAIN IDEAS

After reading the following passage, answer the questions that follow.

What Makes Eating So Enjoyable?

Topic: _____ 1

As much fun as it is to eat, you're not just taking in food for fun. Food satisfies a genuine physical need. Eating food and drinking fluids often begins with the sensation of either **hunger** or **thirst**. The amount of food that we eat and the timing of our meals are driven by physical needs. **Appetite** is another powerful drive, but it is often unreliable. Appetite is influenced by our food preferences and the psychological stimulation to eat. In other words, you can become interested in food, pursue food, and experience the desire to eat too much food without actually needing nourishment or being hungry.

We Develop a Taste for Certain Foods

Topic: _____ 2

Everyone enjoys eating food that tastes delicious, but what exactly is taste? There are five basic categories of taste: sweet, salty, sour, bitter, and savory ("umami"). Most taste buds are located on the tongue, but additional taste buds are found in the throat and elsewhere in the mouth. Food scientists estimate that each of us has at least 10,000 taste buds.

Topic: _____ 3

Even though we each have our own favorite foods, we share some taste traits. In general, we all have an innate preference for sweet, salty, and fatty foods. There is a scientific explanation for these preferences. Sugar seems to elicit universal pleasure (even among infants), and the brain seeks pleasure. Salt provides two important **electrolytes** (sodium and chloride) that are essential to your body and can stimulate the appetite. Your liking of both sugar and salt makes carbohydrate-rich foods appealing to you. Foods rich in carbohydrates provide the fuel that your body needs daily. High-fat foods not only have rich textures and aromas that round out the flavors of food, but also provide essential nutrients that are critical to your health. Thus while we tend to enjoy rich sauces, gravies, and salad dressings, we are, at the same time, meeting our nutritional needs.

Topic: _____ 4

Sometimes, our food preferences and our nutritional needs conflict. We may eat too much because the food is so pleasurable. When there is a reason to change our food habits, such as a need to lose weight or reduce salt or fat intake, we realize how challenging it can be to control our food choices.

Topic: 5   How does the brain recognize taste? When food is consumed, portions of the food are dissolved in saliva. These fluids then make contact with the tongue's surface. The taste (gustatory) cells send a message to the brain. The brain then translates the nerve impulses into taste sensations that you recognize.

Aromas and Flavors Enhance the Pleasure of Eating

Topic: 6   The sensing structures in the nose are also important to the ability to taste foods. The average person is capable of distinguishing 2,000 to 4,000 aromas. We detect food aroma through the nose when we smell foods and, as we eat, when food odors enter the mouth and migrate to the back of the throat and into the nasal cavities. The average person has about 10 million to 20 million olfactory cells (odor cells) in the nasal cavity. Therefore, both your mouth and your nose contribute to the tasting of foods. This explains why you lose interest in eating when you have a cold or other forms of nasal congestion. Food loses some of its appeal when you can't smell it.

Topic: 7   Both the taste and the aroma of a food contribute to its *flavor*. The term *flavor* also refers to the complete food experience. For example, when you eat a candy bar, you sense a sweet taste, but the flavor is chocolate.

Topic: 8   The presence of fat tends to enhance the flavor of foods. When the fat content increases, the intensity of the flavor also increases, as many aromatic compounds are soluble in fat. Increased fat content causes the flavor of food to last longer compared with flavor compounds dissolved in water. Flavors dissolved in water are quickly detected, but also quickly dissipated. This explains why most people prefer premium ice cream over frozen popsicles. It also explains why several low-fat foods have an acceptable flavor, but they are not as delicious as their high-fat counterparts.

—Blake, *Nutrition and You*, pp. 66–67

1. Identify the topic of each paragraph and write it on the line provided.

2. Underline the topic sentence of each paragraph.

3. Did you find any paragraphs that did not have topic sentences? If so, which were they? _____

Writing a Topic Sentence

As a writer, it is important to develop clear and concise topic sentences that help your readers understand your ideas and guide them through your paragraphs. A good topic sentence does two things:

- It makes clear what the paragraph is about—the topic.
- It expresses a viewpoint about the topic.

An effective topic sentence always expresses a viewpoint about the topic. A viewpoint is an attitude or focus about a topic. If the topic is wild game hunting, there are several viewpoints that you could express about it:

- Wild game hunting helps control overpopulation of wildlife.
- Wild game hunting involves killing animals for pleasure.
- Wild game hunting allows hunters to experience and appreciate nature.

Each of the above examples offers a different attitude toward the topic. In contrast, notice how the following sentences do *not* express a viewpoint.

- There are 2 million wild game hunters in the United States.
- Wild game hunting season often begins in the fall.

If you write a topic sentence without a viewpoint, you will find you have very little to write about in the remainder of the paragraph.

EXERCISE 4-6 . . . WRITING: EXPRESSING A VIEWPOINT ABOUT A TOPIC

For each of the following topic sentences, write a topic sentence that expresses a different viewpoint about the topic.

1. It is better to live in a city than in the country because the city offers many more activities and opportunities to its residents.

   _____

   _____

2. Because tobacco products harm people's health, all tobacco products should be banned.

   _____

   _____

3. Social networking sites like Facebook and MySpace create communities of close-knit friends.

   _____

   _____

4. *Dancing with the Stars* entertains us by allowing celebrities to exhibit their unknown dance talents.

   _____

   _____

Now that you know how to develop a manageable topic and determine your point of view, you are ready to put the two together and write topic sentences.

Writing Broad Versus Narrow Topic Sentences

A topic sentence should be neither too broad nor too narrow. Either produces an ineffective paragraph.

Topic Sentences That Are Too Narrow   If your topic sentence is too narrow, you will not have enough to write about to complete a paragraph. Topics that are too narrow often lack a viewpoint.

Too Narrow	Almost 90 percent of Americans own cell phones.
Revised	Americans own and use a wide variety of cell phones, depending on their work and personal needs.

To revise a topic sentence that is too narrow, use the following tips:

- State a clear viewpoint about your topic.
- Broaden your topic to include a wider group or range of items.
- Expand your topic to include causes and effects or comparisons or contrasts.

Topic Sentences That Are Too Broad   If your topic sentence is too broad you will have trouble covering all aspects of it in a single paragraph. Topics that are too broad often lead to rambling or disorganized writing. You will find that you have too many general statements and not enough specifics to support them.

Too Broad	Internet crime in the world today is increasing dramatically.
Revised	Phishing scams are responsible for increases in identify theft among senior citizens in our town.

To revise a topic sentence that is too broad, use the following tips:

- Narrow your topic by subdividing it.
- Rewrite your topic sentence to focus on one aspect or part of the topic.
- Apply the topic sentence to a specific time and place.
- Consider using one of your details as a topic sentence.

Tips for Writing Effective Topic Sentences

As you write your topic sentences, keep the following tips in mind:

1. **Select a manageable topic.** It should be neither too general nor too specific. Topic sentences that are too general often promise more than they can deliver in a single paragraph. They lead to writing that is vague and rambling. Topic sentences that are too specific produce weak paragraphs because there is not enough to say about them.

2. **Your topic sentence should state the main point of your paragraph.** Make sure it identifies your topic and expresses a view toward it.

3. **Make sure your topic sentence is a complete thought.** Be sure your topic sentence is not a fragment or run-on sentence.

4. **Place your topic sentence first in the paragraph.** Although topic sentences often appear in other places in paragraphs, place yours at the beginning so that you can stay focused on your main point and alert your readers to that point.

5. **Avoid announcing your topic.** Sentences that sound like announcements are usually unnecessary. Avoid such sentences as "This paragraph will discuss how to change a flat tire," or "I will explain why I do not support stricter laws governing the use of surveillance cameras." Instead, directly state your main point: "Changing a flat tire involves many steps," or "Laws that support the use of surveillance cameras limit privacy rights."

Not all expert or professional writers follow all of these suggestions. Sometimes, a writer may use one-sentence paragraphs or include topic sentences that are fragments to achieve a special effect. You will find these paragraphs in news and magazine articles and other sources. Although professional writers can use these variations effectively, you probably should not experiment with them too early. It is best while you are polishing your skills to use a more standard style of writing.

EXERCISE 4-7 . . . EVALUATING TOPIC SENTENCES

Evaluate each of the following topic sentences and mark them as follows:

E = effective   G = too general   A = announcement   N = not complete thought
S = too specific

_____ 1. An academic success course is a worthwhile course for college students.

_____ 2. This paper will discuss the various aspects of the "college experience."

_____ 3. Divorce affects not only the couple involved, but also their extended family members, friends, and children.

_____ 4. The New SAT will no longer include sentence completion questions.

_____ 5. The pneumonia vaccine has had a tremendous impact on the health of senior citizens over the age of sixty-five.

_____ 6. I will present the ethical issues associated with animal experimentation in the cosmetic industry.

_____ 7. A decline in face-to-face relationships.

_____ 8. Each year more than 1.3 million auto accidents in America involve the use of cell phones.

_____ 9. The college has many clubs and exciting athletic events.

_____ 10. There are three major advantages of attending a community college.

EXERCISE 4-8 . . . REVISING TOPIC SENTENCES

Analyze the following topic sentences. If a sentence is too general or too specific, or if it makes a direct announcement or is not a complete thought, revise it to make it more effective.

1. World hunger is a crime.

   REVISED _____

2. E-mail is used by a great many people.

   REVISED _____

3. I will point out the many ways energy can be saved in the home.

   REVISED _____

4. Because Congress is very important in the United States.

   REVISED _____

5. In 2017, over 10,000 people died in alcohol-impaired driving crashes.

   REVISED _____

SELF-TEST SUMMARY

To test yourself, cover the right column with a sheet of paper and answer the question in the left column. Evaluate each of your answers by sliding the paper down and comparing it with what is printed in the right column.

QUESTION	ANSWER
1 *What are the elements of a paragraph?*	A **paragraph** is a group of sentences about a single topic. A paragraph has four essential parts: • Topic: the subject of the paragraph • Main idea: the most important idea expressed about the topic • Details: the information that explains or supports the main idea • Transitions: words that help readers follow the writer's thought patterns
2 *How do you distinguish between general and specific ideas? How do you identify and select the topic of a paragraph?*	A **general idea** applies to a large nmber of individual items, whereas a **specific idea** or term is more detailed or particular. To identify the topic of a paragraph, ask yourself: "What or whom is the paragraph about?" To write a good paragraph, select a topic that is general enough to allow you to add interesting details that will engage your reader and specific enough that you can cover it adequately in a few sentences.
3 *How do you locate and write topic sentences?*	The **main idea** of a paragraph is what the author wants you to know about the topic; the main idea is often expressed in the **topic sentence**. To find the topic sentence, search for the one general sentence that explains what the writer wants you to know about the topic. Although a topic sentence can be located anywhere in a paragraph, it is usually *first* or *last*. To write a topic sentence, identify your topic and express a viewpoint about it. Be sure your topic sentence is neither too broad nor too narrow.

5 Supporting Details, Transitions, and Implied Main Ideas

LEARNING OBJECTIVES

1 Identify and select supporting details
2 Recognize and use transitional words and phrases
3 Find implied main ideas

In Chapter 4 you learned that a paragraph is structured around a main idea that is often expressed in a topic sentence. In this chapter you will see how the remainder of the paragraph consists of details that support the main idea and how transitional words and phrases are used to connect these details. You will also learn about paragraphs that consist only of details, leaving the main idea unstated.

5a IDENTIFYING AND SELECTING SUPPORTING DETAILS

LEARNING OBJECTIVE 1
Identify and select supporting details

Supporting details are those facts and ideas that prove or explain the main idea of a paragraph. While all the details in a paragraph support the main idea, not all details are equally important.

Recognizing Supporting Details

As you read, try to identify and pay attention to the most important details. Pay less attention to details of lesser importance. The key details directly explain the main idea. Other details may provide additional information, offer an example, or further explain one of the key details.

Figure A shows how details relate to the main idea and how details range in degree of importance. In the diagram, more important details are placed toward the left; less important details are closer to the right. Now read the following paragraph and study Figure B.

Issue: Health and Wellness

The skin of the human body has several functions. First, it serves as a protective covering. In doing so, it accounts for 17% of the body weight. Skin also protects the organs within the body from damage or harm. The skin serves as a regulator of body functions. It controls body temperature and water loss. Finally, the skin serves as a receiver. It is sensitive to touch and temperature.

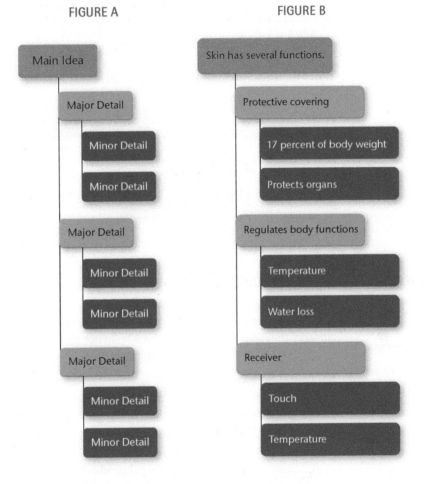

From Figure B you can see that the three functions of skin are the key details. Other details, such as "protects the organs," provide further information and are less important.

Read the following paragraph and pick out the more important details.

Issue: Cultural Similarities and Differences

Many cultures have different rules for men and women engaging in conflict. Asian cultures are more strongly prohibitive of women's conflict strategies. Asian women are expected to be exceptionally polite; this is even more important when women are in conflict with men and when the conflict is public. In the United States, there is a verbalized equality; men and women have equal rights when it comes to permissible conflict strategies. In reality, there are many who expect women to be more polite, to pursue conflict in a non-argumentative way, while men are expected to argue forcefully and logically.

This paragraph could be diagrammed as follows (key details only):

> Many cultures have different rules for men and women engaging in conflict.
>
> > Rules in Asian cultures
> >
> > Rules in the United States

EXERCISE 5-1 ... RECOGNIZING SUPPORTING DETAILS

Each of the following topic sentences states the main idea of a paragraph. After each topic sentence are five sentences containing details that may or may not support the topic sentence. Read each sentence and put an "S" beside those that contain details that support the topic sentence.

1. **Topic Sentence:** A monopoly is a company that controls the sale of a certain good and therefore is able to set high prices.

   _____ a. The automobile industry is a good example of an oligopoly, because none of the large companies (such as Ford, Toyota, and Honda) controls the industry.

   _____ b. Markets for agricultural products like cotton and wheat are considered very competitive, and farmers are often unable to set high prices for their goods.

   _____ c. Many critics have accused monopolies of unfair pricing.

   _____ d. The DeBeers Company, which mines diamonds in Africa and elsewhere, holds a monopoly in the world market for diamonds.

   _____ e. Some common examples of monopolies are public utility companies and sports franchises in major U.S. cities.

2. **Topic Sentence:** *Mens rea*, a term that refers to a person's criminal intent when committing a crime, or his or her state of mind, can be evaluated in several ways.

_____ a. Confessions by criminals are direct evidence of their criminal intent.

_____ b. Circumstantial evidence can be used to suggest mental intent.

_____ c. *Actus rea* is the set of a person's actions that make up a crime.

_____ d. People who commit crimes are often repeat offenders.

_____ e. Expert witnesses may offer an opinion about a person's criminal intent.

3. **Topic Sentence:** Food irradiation is a process in which food is treated with radiation to kill bacteria.

_____ a. Many consumers are concerned about the increasing number of genetically modified foods.

_____ b. The radioactive rays pass through the food without damaging it or changing it.

_____ c. One form of irradiation uses electricity as the energy source for irradiation.

_____ d. Irradiation increases the shelf life of food because it kills all bacteria present in the food.

_____ e. *E. coli*, salmonella, and listeria cause many illnesses each year.

4. **Topic Sentence:** The television and film industries promote unhealthy body images for both women and men.

_____ a. Many Hollywood films feature unacceptable levels of violence.

_____ b. Many TV and film stars have undergone extensive plastic surgery that makes them look not quite human.

_____ c. Movies and television programs portray the ideal female body type as slender and curvaceous.

_____ d. Television relies on advertisements to fund its programming.

_____ e. Many teenage boys are injecting themselves with illegal steroids to achieve muscular bodies like those they see on television and in the movies.

EXERCISE 5-2 . . . RECOGNIZING SUPPORTING DETAILS

Underline only the most important details in each of the following paragraphs.

Paragraph 1

Issue: Drugs and Addiction

Physiological dependence, the adaptive state that occurs with regular addictive behavior and results in withdrawal syndrome, is only one indicator of addiction. Chemicals are responsible for the most profound addictions because they cause cellular changes to which the body adapts so well that it eventually requires the chemical to function normally. Psychological dynamics, though, also play an important role. Psychological and physiological dependence are intertwined and nearly impossible to separate; all forms of addiction probably reflect dysfunction of certain biochemical systems in the brain.

—Donatelle, *My Health*, p. 122

Paragraph 2

Issue: Crime and Communities

There are four different dimensions of an arrest: legal, behavioral, subjective, and official. In legal terms, an arrest is made when someone lawfully deprives another person of liberty; in other words, that person is not free to go. The actual word *arrest* need not be uttered, but the other person must be brought under the control of the arresting individual. The behavioral element in arrests is often nothing more than the phrase "You're under arrest." However, that statement is usually backed up by a tight grip on the arm or collar, or the drawing of an officer's handgun, or the use of handcuffs. The subjective dimension of arrest refers to whenever people believe they are not free to leave; to all intents and purposes, they are under arrest. In any case, the arrest lasts only as long as the person is in custody, which might be a matter of a few minutes or many hours. Many people are briefly detained on the street and then released. Official arrests are those detentions that the police record in an administrative record. When a suspect is "booked" at the police station, a record is made of the arrest.

—Barlow, *Criminal Justice in America*, p. 238

Paragraph 3

Issue: Foods Containing Gluten

What's the big deal with eating foods that contain gluten? Gluten is a protein found in grains such as wheat, barley, and rye. Foods and beverages that may contain gluten are widespread and include beer, breads and other baked goods, cereals, soups, sauces, and many other packaged food products. Gluten consumption poses a serious health problem for people with celiac disease. This condition, caused by an abnormal immune response to gluten, can damage the lining of the intestine. This damage prevents important nutrients from being absorbed. The incidence of celiac disease is estimated as about 1 percent of the U.S. population. A small number of people who do not have celiac disease also experience an allergic reaction to gluten or have gluten sensitivity. For those with celiac disease or gluten sensitivity, consumption of gluten-free foods is essential to remain healthy. However, if you do not suffer from these conditions, is a gluten-free diet healthier than a diet that contains gluten? The short answer is no. Indeed, for people who are not allergic to gluten, a gluten-free diet has not been shown to be a healthier diet compared to diets containing gluten. A poorly balanced gluten-free diet can lack vitamins, minerals, and fiber. Therefore, unless you suffer from celiac disease or a gluten allergy problem, there is little reason to avoid gluten-rich foods.

—Powers and Dodd, *Total Fitness and Wellness*, p. 230

EXERCISE 5-3 . . . RECOGNIZING SUPPORTING DETAILS

Reread the article "Consequences of Social Class" on page 8 and underline the most important supporting details in each paragraph.

Selecting and Organizing Supporting Details

The details you choose to support your topic sentence must be both relevant and sufficient. **Relevant** means that the details directly explain and support your topic sentence. **Sufficient** means that you must provide enough information to make your topic sentence understandable and convincing. In addition to choosing relevant and sufficient details, be sure to select a variety of details, use specific words, and organize your paragraph effectively.

Selecting Relevant Details

Relevant details directly support your topic sentence. They help clarify and strengthen your ideas, whereas irrelevant details make your ideas unclear and confusing. Here is the first draft of a paragraph written by a student named Alex to explain why he decided to attend college. Can you locate the detail that is not relevant?

> [1]I decided to attend college to further my education and achieve my goals in life. [2]I am attempting to build a future for myself. [3]When I get married and have kids, I want to be able to offer them the same opportunities my parents gave me. [4]I want to have a comfortable style of living and a good job. [5]As for my wife, I don't want her to work because I believe a married woman should not work. [6]I believe college is the way to begin a successful life.

Sentence 5 does not belong in the paragraph. The fact that Alex does not want his wife to work is not a reason for attending college. Use the following simple test to be sure each detail you include belongs in your paragraph.

TEST FOR RELEVANT DETAILS

1. **Read your topic sentence in combination with each of the other sentences in your paragraph.** For example,
   - read the topic sentence + the last sentence.
   - read the topic sentence + the second-to-last sentence.
   - read topic the sentence + the third-to-last sentence.

2. **For each pair of sentences, ask yourself, "Do these two ideas fit together?"** If your answer is "No," then you have found a detail that is not relevant to your topic. Delete it from your paragraph.

Another student wrote the following paragraph on the subject of the legal drinking age. As you read it, cross out the details that are not relevant.

> ¹The legal drinking age should be raised to 25. ²Anyone who drinks should be old enough to determine whether or not it is safe to drive after drinking. ³Bartenders and others who serve drinks should also have to be 25. ⁴In general, teenagers and young adults are not responsible enough to limit how much they drink. ⁵The party atmosphere enjoyed by so many young people encourages crazy acts, so we should limit who can drink. ⁶Younger people think drinking is a game, but it is a dangerous game that affects the lives of others.

Which sentence did you delete? Why did you delete it? The third sentence does not belong in the paragraph because the age of those who bartend or serve drinks is not relevant to the topic. Sentence 5, about partying, should also be eliminated or explained because the connection between partying and drinking is not clear.

EXERCISE 5-4 . . . IDENTIFYING RELEVANT DETAILS

Place a check mark by those statements that provide relevant supporting details.

1. Sales representatives need good interpersonal skills.

_____ a. They need to be good listeners.

_____ b. They should like helping people.

_____ c. They should know their products well.

2. Water can exist in three forms, which vary with temperature.

_____ a. At a high temperature, water becomes steam; it is a gas.

_____ b. Drinking water often contains mineral traces.

_____ c. At cold temperatures, water becomes ice, a solid state.

3. Outlining is one of the easiest ways to organize facts.

_____ a. Formal outlines use Roman numerals and letters and Arabic numerals to show different levels of importance.

_____ b. Outlining emphasizes the relationships among facts.

_____ c. Outlines make it easier to focus on important points.

Including Sufficient Detail

Including **sufficient detail** means that your paragraph contains an adequate amount of specific information for your readers to understand your main idea. Your supporting details must thoroughly and clearly explain why you believe your topic sentence is true. Be sure that your details are specific; do not provide summaries or unsupported statements of opinion.

Let's look at a paragraph a student wrote on the topic of billboard advertising.

> There is a national movement to oppose billboard advertising. Many people don't like billboards and are taking action to change what products are advertised on them and which companies use them. Community activists are destroying billboard advertisements at an increasing rate. As a result of their actions, numerous changes have been made.

This paragraph is filled with general statements. It does not explain who dislikes billboards or why they dislike them. It does not say what products are advertised or name the companies that make them. No detail is given about how the billboards are destroyed, and the resulting changes are not described. There is not sufficient support for the topic sentence. Here is the revised version:

> Among residents of inner-city neighborhoods, a national movement is growing to oppose billboard advertising. Residents oppose billboards that glamorize alcohol and target people of color as its consumers. Community activists have organized and are taking action. They carry paint, rollers, shovels, and brooms to an offending billboard. Within a few minutes the billboard is painted over, covering the damaging advertisement. Results have been dramatic. Many liquor companies have reduced their inner-city billboard advertising. In place of these ads, some billboard companies have placed public-service announcements and ads to improve community health.

If you have trouble thinking of enough details to include in a paragraph, try brainstorming or one of the other techniques for generating ideas described in Chapter 2. Write your topic sentence at the top of a sheet of paper. Then list everything that comes to mind about that topic. Include examples, events, incidents, facts, and reasons. You will be surprised at how many useful details you think of. When you finish, read over your list and cross out details that are not relevant. (If you still don't have enough, your topic may be too specific. See page 112.) The section "Arranging Details Logically" on page 124 will help you decide in what order you will write about the details on your list.

Types of Supporting Details

There are many types of details you can use to explain or support a topic sentence. The most common types of supporting details are (1) examples, (2) facts or statistics, (3) reasons, (4) descriptions, and (5) steps or procedures. It is advisable to vary the types of details you use, and to choose those appropriate to your topic.

EXERCISE 5-5 . . . WRITING SUPPORTING DETAILS

Working with a classmate, for each topic sentence write at least three different types of details that could be used to support it. Label each detail as example, fact or statistic, reason, description, or steps or procedure.

1. People make inferences about you based on the way you dress.

2. Many retailers with traditional stores have decided to market their products through Web sites as well.

3. Many Americans are obsessed with losing weight.

4. Historical and cultural attractions can be found in a variety of shapes, sizes, and locations throughout the world.

5. Using a search engine is an effective, though not perfect, method of searching the Internet.

Arranging Details Logically

Nan had an assignment to write a paragraph about travel. She drafted the paragraph and then revised it. As you read each version, pay particular attention to the order in which she arranged the details.

First Draft

This summer I had the opportunity to travel extensively. Over Labor Day weekend I backpacked with a group of friends in the Allegheny Mountains. When spring semester was over, I visited my seven cousins in Florida. My friends and I went to New York City over the Fourth of July to see fireworks and explore the city. During June I worked as a wildlife-preservation volunteer in a Colorado state park. On July 15 I celebrated my twenty-fifth birthday by visiting my parents in Syracuse.

Revision

This summer I had the opportunity to travel extensively in the United States. When the spring semester ended, I went to my cousins' home in Florida to relax. When I returned, I worked during the month of June as a wildlife-preservation volunteer in a Colorado state park. Then my friends and I went to New York City to see the fireworks and look around the city over the Fourth of July weekend. On July 15th, I celebrated my twenty-fifth birthday by visiting my parents in Syracuse. Finally, over Labor Day weekend, my friends and I backpacked in the Allegheny Mountains.

Did you find Nan's revision easier to read? In the first draft, Nan recorded details as she thought of them. There is no logical arrangement to them. In the second version, she arranged the details in the order in which they happened. Nan chose this arrangement because it fit her details logically.

The three common methods for arranging details are as follows:

- Time sequence
- Spatial arrangement
- Least/most arrangement

1. **Time sequence** means the order in which things happen. For example, if you were to write about a particularly bad day, you could describe the day in the order in which everything went wrong. You might begin with waking up in the morning and end with going to bed that night. If you were describing a busy or an exciting weekend, you might begin with what you did on Friday night and end with the last activity on Sunday. Here is an example of a time sequence paragraph:

> When Su-ling gets ready to study at home, she follows a set routine. First of all, she tries to find a quiet place, far away from her kid sisters. This place might be her bedroom, the porch, or the basement, depending on the noise levels in her household. Next, she finds a snack to eat while she is studying, perhaps potato chips or a candy bar. If she is on a diet, she tries to find some healthy fruit. Finally, Su-ling tackles the most difficult assignment first because she knows her level of concentration is higher at the beginning of study sessions.

2. **Spatial arrangement** presents details as they occur in relation to each other. Suppose, for instance, you are asked to describe the room in which you are sitting. You want your reader, who has never been in the room, to visualize it, so you need to describe, in an orderly way, where items are positioned. You could describe the room from left to right, from ceiling to floor, or from door to window. In other situations, your choices might include front to back, inside to outside, near to far, east to west, and so on. How are the details arranged in the following paragraph?

> Keith's antique car was gloriously decorated for the Fourth of July parade. Red, white, and blue streamers hung in front from the headlights and bumper. The hood was covered with small American flags. The windshield had gold stars pasted on it, arranged to form an outline of our state. On the sides, the doors displayed red plastic-tape stripes. The convertible top was down, and Mary sat on the trunk dressed up like the Statue of Liberty. In the rear, a neon sign blinked "God Bless America." His car was not only a show-stopper but the highlight of the parade.

The details are arranged from front to back. The topic you are writing about will often determine the arrangement you choose. In writing about a town, you might choose to begin with the center and then move to each surrounding area. In describing a building, you might go from bottom to top.

EXERCISE 5-6 . . . USING SPATIAL ARRANGEMENT

Indicate which spatial arrangement you would use to describe the following topics. Then write a paragraph on one of the topics.

1. A local market or favorite store

2. A photograph you value

3. A prized possession

4. A building in which you work

5. Your campus cafeteria, bookstore, or lounge

3. **Least/most arrangement** presents details in order from least to most or most to least, according to some quality or characteristic. For example, you might arrange details from least to most *expensive*, least to most *serious*, or least to most *important*. The writer of the following paragraph uses a least-to-most arrangement.

> The entry-level job in many industries today is administrative assistant. Just because it's a lower-level job, don't think it's an easy job. A good administrative assistant must have good computer skills. If you aren't proficient on a computer, you won't be able to handle your supervisor's correspondence and other paperwork. Even more important, an administrative assistant must be well organized. Every little task—from answering the phone to setting up meetings to making travel arrangements—lands on the administrative assistant's desk. If you can't juggle lots of loose ends, this is not the job for you. Most important of all, though, an administrative assistant needs a sense of humor. On the busiest days, when the office is in total chaos, the only way to keep your sanity—and your temper—is to take a deep breath, smile, and say "When all this is over, I'm going to have a well-earned nervous breakdown!"

Computer skills	Important
Organizational skills	More important
Sense of humor	Most important

Notice that this writer wrote about a basic requirement for the job—computer skills—and then worked up to the most important requirement.

You can also arrange details from most to least. This structure allows you to present your strongest point first. Many writers use this method to construct a case or an argument. For example, if you were writing a business letter requesting a refund for damaged mail-order merchandise, you would want to begin with the most serious damage and put the minor complaints at the end, as follows:

> I am returning these boots, which I just received in the mail, because they are damaged. The heel is half off on the left shoe and there is a deep scratch across the toe. The right shoe has black streaks on the sides, and the buckle is tarnished. I trust you will refund my money promptly.

5b   RECOGNIZING AND USING TRANSITIONS

LEARNING OBJECTIVE 2
Recognize and use transitional words and phrases

Transitions are linking words or phrases used to lead the reader from one idea to another. If you get in the habit of recognizing transitions, you will see that they often guide you through a paragraph, helping you read it more easily. When writing, be sure to use these words to help your reader follow your train of thought and to see connections between and among your ideas.

Recognizing Transitions

Readers can use transitions to discover how details relate to one another. In the following paragraph, notice how the underlined transitions lead you from one important detail to the next.

> Kevin works as a forensic scientist. When he examines a crime scene, he follows a certain procedure. <u>First of all</u>, he puts on special gear to avoid contaminating the crime scene. <u>For example</u>, he wears gloves (so that he doesn't leave fingerprints) and a special hat (so that he does not leave hair samples). <u>Next</u>, he prepares his camera and other forensic equipment, <u>such as</u> plastic bags and glass slides. <u>Then</u>, he presses "record" on his tape recorder so that he can describe the crime scene as he examines it. <u>Finally</u>, he goes over the crime scene one square foot at a time, very slowly, so that he does not miss any evidence.

Not all paragraphs contain such obvious transitions, and not all transitions serve as such clear markers of major details. Often, however, transitions alert you to what will come next in the paragraph. If you see the phrase *for instance* at the beginning of a sentence, then you know an example will follow. When you see the phrase *on the other hand*, you can predict that a different, opposing idea will follow. Table 5-1 lists some of the most common signal words used within a paragraph and indicates what they tell you.

TABLE 5-1 COMMON TRANSITIONS

TYPES OF TRANSITIONS	EXAMPLES	WHAT THEY TELL THE READER
Time Sequence	*first, later, next, finally*	The author is arranging ideas in the order in which they happened.
Example	*for example, for instance, to illustrate, such as*	An example will follow.
Enumeration or Listing	*first, second, third, last, another, next*	The author is marking or identifying each major point (sometimes these may be used to suggest order of importance).
Continuation	*also, in addition, and, further, another*	The author is continuing with the same idea and is going to provide additional information.
Contrast	*on the other hand, in contrast, however*	The author is switching to a different, opposite, or contrasting idea than previously discussed.
Comparison	*like, likewise, similarly*	The writer will show how the previous idea is similar to what follows.
Cause and Effect	*because, thus, therefore, since, consequently*	The writer will show a connection between two or more things, how one thing caused another, or how something happened as a result of something else.

EXERCISE 5-7 . . . SELECTING APPROPRIATE TRANSITIONS

Select the signal word or phrase from the box below that best completes each of the following sentences. Two of the signal words in the box may be used more than once.

on the other hand	for example	because	in addition
similarly	after	next	however
also			

1. Typically, those suffering from post-traumatic stress disorder (PTSD) are soldiers after combat. Civilians who witnessed or lived through events such as the World Trade Center destruction can _____ experience PTSD.

2. Columbus was determined to find an oceanic passage to China _____ finding a direct route would mean increased trading and huge profits.

3. In the event of a heart attack, it is first important to identify the symptoms. _____ , call 911 or drive the victim to the nearest hospital.

4. In the 1920s, courtship between men and women changed dramatically. _____, instead of visiting the woman's home with her parents present, men began to invite women out on dates.

5. Direct exposure to sunlight is dangerous because the sun's ultraviolet rays can lead to skin cancer. _____, tanning booths emit ultraviolet rays and are as dangerous as, if not more dangerous than, exposure to sunlight.

6. Lie detector tests are often used by law enforcement to help determine guilt or innocence. _____, because these tests often have an accuracy rate of only 60 to 80 percent, the results are not admissible in court.

7. The temporal lobes of the brain process sound and comprehend language. _____, the temporal lobes are responsible for storing visual memories.

8. The theory of multiple intelligences holds that there are many different kinds of intelligence, or abilities. _____, musical ability, control of bodily movements (athletics), spatial understanding, and observational abilities are all classified as different types of intelligence.

9. During World War II, Japanese Americans were held in relocation camps. _____ the war was over, the United States paid reparations and issued an apology to those who were wrongfully detained.

10. Many believe that the United States should adopt a flat tax in which every person pays the same tax rate. _____, it is unlikely that the tax code will be overhauled any time soon.

EXERCISE 5-8 . . . RECOGNIZING THE FUNCTION OF TRANSITIONS

Each of the following beginnings of paragraphs uses a transitional word or phrase to tell the reader what will follow. Read each, paying particular attention to the italicized word or phrase. Then, in the space provided, specifically describe what you would expect to find immediately after the transitional word or phrase.

1. Proximity should not be the only factor to consider in choosing a doctor or health-care provider. Many other factors should be considered. *For instance, . . .*

   _____

   _____

2. There are a number of things you can do to manage your stress level. *First, ...*

   _____

   _____

3. Many banks have privacy policies. *However,* ...

_____

_____

4. One advantage of taking online courses is all the time you will save by not having to travel to and from campus. *Another* ...

_____

_____

5. To select the classes you will take next term, first consult with your faculty advisor about the courses you are required to take. *Next* ...

_____

_____

EXERCISE 5-9 . . . IDENTIFYING TRANSITIONAL WORDS AND THEIR FUNCTION

For each paragraph in the article "Consequences of Social Class" on page 8, highlight each transitional word and indicate what each tells the reader.

Using Transitional Words and Phrases to Connect Details

Transitional words and phrases allow readers to move easily from one detail to another; they show how details relate to one another. Use them to guide your reader through the paragraph and signal what is to follow, as shown in the sample paragraph in the Recognizing Transitions section on page 127.

Table 5-2 shows some commonly used transitional words and phrases for each method of arranging details discussed on pages 124–127. To understand how they work, review the sample paragraph for each of these arrangements and underline each transitional word or phrase.

TABLE 5-2 FREQUENTLY USED TRANSITIONAL WORDS AND PHRASES	
ARRANGEMENT	**TRANSITIONAL WORDS AND PHRASES**
Time Sequence	*first, next, during, eventually, finally, later, meanwhile, soon, when, then, suddenly, currently, after, afterward, before, now, until*
Spatial	*above, below, behind, in front of, beside, next to, inside, outside, to the west (north, etc.) of, beneath, nearby, on the other side of*
Least/Most Important	*most, above all, especially, even more*

5c   FINDING IMPLIED MAIN IDEAS

LEARNING OBJECTIVE 3
Find implied main ideas

Study the cartoon. What main point is it making? Although the cartoonist's message is not directly stated, you were able to figure it out by looking at the details in the cartoon. Just as you figured out the cartoonist's main point, you often have to figure out the implied main ideas of speakers and writers. When an idea is **implied**,

Strels/Shutterstock

it is suggested but not stated outright. Suppose your favorite shirt is missing from your closet and you know that your roommate often borrows your clothes. You might say to your roommate, "If my blue plaid shirt is back in my closet by noon, I'll forget it was missing." This statement does not directly accuse your roommate of borrowing the shirt, but your message is clear—Return my shirt! Your statement implies or suggests to your roommate that he has borrowed the shirt and should return it.

EXERCISE 5-10 . . . UNDERSTANDING IMPLIED MAIN IDEAS

For each of the following statements, select the choice that best explains what the writer is implying or suggesting.

_____ 1. You know what I like in a book? A master detective going up against a master criminal, good suspense, and plot twists that keep me guessing.

    a. I like romance novels.

    b. I like mystery novels.

    c. I prefer to read nonfiction.

    d. I am a big fan of poetry.

_____ 2. This semester, Dino is taking courses in biochemistry, human anatomy and physiology, medical lab procedures, and medical research.

    a. Dino is a senior.

    b. Dino is studying to become a doctor.

    c. Dino spends all his time studying.

    d. Dino has no interest in the social sciences or liberal arts.

_____ 3. The steak was overcooked and tough, the mashed potatoes were cold, the green beans were withered, and the chocolate pie was mushy.

a. The dinner was tasty.

b. The dinner was nutritious.

c. The dinner was prepared poorly.

d. The dinner was served carelessly.

Inferring Implied Main Ideas

When trying to figure out the implied main idea in a paragraph, it is important to remember the distinction between general and specific ideas (see p. 100). You know that a *general* idea applies to many items or ideas, while a *specific* idea refers to a particular item. The word *color*, for instance, is general because it refers to many other specific colors—purple, yellow, red, and so forth. The word *shoe* is general because it can apply to many types, such as running shoes, high heels, loafers, and slippers.

You also know that the main idea of a paragraph is not only its most important point but also its most *general* idea. *Specific* details back up or support the main idea. Although most paragraphs have a topic sentence, some do not. Instead, they contain only details or specifics that, taken together, point to the main idea. The main idea, then, is implied but not directly stated. In such paragraphs you must **infer**, or reason out, the main idea. **Inference** is a process of adding up the details and deciding what they mean together or what main idea they all support or explain.

What general idea do the following specific sentences suggest?

- The plumber made appointments he did not keep.
- The plumber exaggerated the extent of the needed repairs in order to overcharge his customers.
- The plumber did not return phone calls when people complained about his work.

You probably determined that the plumber is inconsiderate, incompetent, and unethical.

What larger, more general idea do the following specific details and the accompanying photograph point to?

- The wind began to howl at over 90 mph.
- A dark gray funnel cloud was visible in the sky.
- Severe storms had been predicted by the weather service.

Samuel Acosta/Shutterstock

Together the three details and the photograph suggest that a tornado has devastated the area.

EXERCISE 5-11 . . . WRITING GENERAL IDEAS

For each item, read the specific details. Then select the word or phrase from the box below that best completes the general idea in the sentence that follows. Make sure that each general idea fits all of its specific details. Not all words or phrases in the box will be used.

advertisers	contributes	dangerous effects
process	factors	techniques

1. a. Celebrity endorsements catch consumers' attention.

   b. Emphasizing the negative consequences of not purchasing a particular product employs fear as a motive for buying it.

   c. "Sex sells" is a common motto among those who write commercials.

   General idea: _____ use a variety of appeals to sell products.

2. a. Children who are abused are more likely to be abusers when they become parents.

   b. Abused children often suffer from low self-esteem.

   c. Those who have been abused as children often find it difficult to develop healthy romantic relationships.

   General idea: Child abuse has _____.

3. a. Many immigrants come to the United States because they cannot make enough money to feed their families in their home country.

   b. Immigrants often come to the United States in order to be closer to their families.

   c. Sometimes immigrants are forced to flee their home countries due to warfare or persecution.

   General idea: A number of different _____ contribute to people leaving their country in search of a better life.

How to Find Implied Main Ideas in Paragraphs

When a writer leaves his or her main idea unstated, it is up to you to look at the details in the paragraph and figure out the writer's main point. The details, when taken together, will all point to a general and more important idea. Use the following steps as a guide to find implied main ideas:

1. **Find the topic.** The *topic* is the general subject of the entire paragraph. Ask yourself, "What *one thing* is the author discussing throughout the paragraph?"

2. **Figure out the most important idea the writer wants you to know about that topic.** Look at each detail and decide what larger idea is being explained.

3. **Express the main idea in your own words.** Make sure that the main idea is a reasonable one. Ask yourself, "Does it apply to all of the details in the paragraph?"

Identify the main idea in the following passage.

Issue: Health and Appearance

The Romans, with their great public baths, probably did not use any sort of soap. They covered their bodies with oil, worked up a sweat in a steam bath, and then wiped off the oil. A dip in a pool of fresh water completed the "cleansing."

During the Middle Ages, bodily cleanliness was prized in some cultures, but not in others. For example, twelfth-century Paris, with a population of about 100,000, had many public bathhouses. In contrast, the Renaissance, a revival of learning and art that lasted from the fourteenth to the seventeenth centuries, was not noted for cleanliness. Queen Elizabeth I of England (1533–1603) bathed once a month, a habit that caused many to think her overly fastidious. A common remedy for unpleasant body odor back then was the liberal use of perfume.

And today? With soap, detergent, body wash, shampoo, conditioner, deodorant, antiperspirant, aftershave, cologne, and perfume, we may add more during and after a shower than we remove in the shower.

—adapted from Hill et al., *Chemistry for Changing Times*, p. 644

The topic of this passage is *personal cleanliness*. The authors' main point is that standards for bodily cleanliness have fluctuated over human history. You can figure out the writers' main idea even though no single sentence states this directly. You can visualize this paragraph as follows:

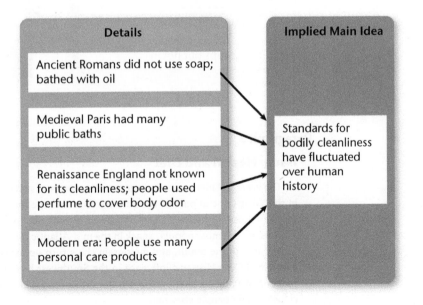

EXERCISE 5-12 . . . FINDING IMPLIED MAIN IDEAS

After reading each of the paragraphs, complete the diagram that follows by filling in the missing information.

Paragraph 1

Issue: Personal Relationships

Men's friendships are often built around shared activities—attending a ball game, playing cards, working on a project at the office. Women's friendships, on the other hand, are built more around a sharing of feelings, support, and "personalism." One study found that similarity in status, in willingness to protect one's friend in uncomfortable situations, in academic major, and even in proficiency in playing Password were significantly related to the relationship closeness of male–male friends but not of female–female or female–male friends.

—DeVito, *Messages*, p. 290

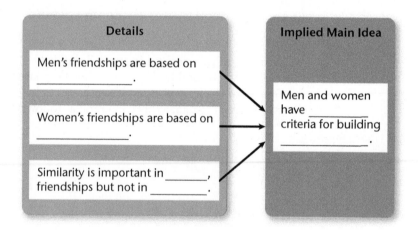

Paragraph 2

Issue: Health and Diet

The average American consumer eats 21 pounds of snack foods in a year, but people in the West Central part of the country consume the most (24 pounds per person) whereas those in the Pacific and Southeast regions eat "only" 19 pounds per person. Pretzels are the most popular snack in the mid-Atlantic area, pork rinds are most likely to be eaten in the South, and multigrain chips turn up as a favorite in the West. Not surprisingly, the Hispanic influence in the Southwest has influenced snacking preferences—consumers in that part of the United States eat about 50 percent more tortilla chips than do people elsewhere.

—adapted from Solomon, *Consumer Behavior*, p. 184

Topic _____

Details

The average consumer eats _____ of snack food in a year.

People in _____ part of the country consume the most.

People in _____ regions consume the least.

_____ are the most popular snack in the mid-Atlantic area.

Pork rinds are most likely to be eaten in _____ .

_____ are the favorite in the West.

Consumers in _____ eat more tortilla chips than do people elsewhere.

Implied Main Idea

_____ differ in their preferences for _____ _____ according to where they live.

EXERCISE 5-13 . . . FINDING IMPLIED MAIN IDEAS

After reading each of the following paragraphs, select the choice that best answers each of the questions that follow.

Paragraph A

Issue: Social Networking and Privacy

When registering for online services under a screen name, it can be tempting to think your identity is a secret to other users. Many people will say or do things on the Internet that they would never do in real life because they believe that they are acting anonymously. However, most blogs, e-mail and instant messenger services, and social networking sites are tied to your real identity in some way. While your identity may be superficially concealed by a screen name, it often takes little more than a quick Google search to uncover your name, address, and other personal and possibly sensitive information.

—Ebert and Griffin, *Business Essentials*, p. 188

_____ 1. What is the topic?

    a. online identity

    b. screen names

    c. online services

    d. Google searches

_____ 2. What is the writer saying about the topic?

    a. Google searches offer clues to your identity.

    b. People write things on the Internet they would never say face-to-face.

    c. Your identity is not secret on the Internet.

    d. Screen names help conceal your identity.

Paragraph B

Issue: Business Ethics

"Frugal engineering." "Indovation." "Reverse innovation." These are some of the terms that GE, Procter & Gamble, Siemens, and Unilever are using to describe efforts to penetrate more deeply into emerging markets. As growth in mature markets slows, executives and managers at many global companies are realizing that the ability to serve the needs of the world's poorest consumers will be a critical source of competitive advantage in the decades to come. Procter & Gamble CEO Robert McDonald has set a strategic goal of introducing 800 million new consumers to the company's brands by 2015. This will require a better understanding of what daily life is like in, say, hundreds of thousands of rural villages in Africa, South America, and China.

Consider, for example, that two-thirds of the world's population—more than 4 billion people—live on less than $2 per day. This segment is sometimes referred to as the "bottom of the pyramid" and includes an estimated 1.5 billion people who live "off the grid"; that is, they have no access to electricity to provide light or to charge their cell phones. Often, a villager must walk several miles to hire a taxi for the trip to the nearest city with electricity. Such trips are costly in terms of both time and money.

—Keegan and Green, *Global Marketing*, p. 192

_____ 3. What is the topic?

    a. global branding and income inequality

    b. life off the grid

    c. marketing strategies aimed at the poor

    d. supply and demand in developing countries

_____ 4. What main idea is the writer implying?

    a. The poor people of the world do not have access to transportation.

    b. Companies are looking for ways to make money by selling their products to the world's poor people.

    c. Procter & Gamble is the world leader in supplying inexpensive products to developing nations.

    d. Cell phones offer developing nations many opportunities for increasing the standard of living.

_____ 5. Which one of the following conclusions does not logically follow from the passage?

    a. Reverse innovation is aimed at getting more products into the hands of wealthy consumers.

    b. "Emerging markets" are home to huge numbers of poor people.

    c. The majority of the world's people live on less than $2 per day.

    d. In the world's developing countries, many residents of the countryside are poor.

Paragraph C

Issue: Family

In all societies, people have ways of organizing their relationships with other people, especially their primary relationships with kin. As children, our earliest and most influential interactions are with our parents, siblings, and other relatives. We rely on our families for all of our survival needs. Our families feed us, clothe us, and provide our shelter. They also help us adjust to the world around us, teaching us the behavior and attitudes that our culture expects, and they provide emotional support in both good times and bad.

Many of our relatives continue as important economic and emotional supports throughout our lives. Even as adults, we can turn to our kin in networks of reciprocity, asking for aid in times of need. In turn, we may be asked to respond to their requests when they are in need. We may align ourselves with our relatives when they are engaged in disputes with others. We may expect loyalty from our kin when we are in conflict with neighbors or other community members. During personal or family crises, we may expect emotional support from our relatives. Together we celebrate happy occasions such as births and marriages, and we mourn the deaths of our kin.

—Bonvillain, *Cultural Anthropology*, pp. 186–187

_____ 6. What is the topic?

    a. parents

    b. siblings

    c. family

    d. culture

_____ 7. What is the writer saying about the topic?

    a. Family is more important in some societies than in others.

    b. Regardless of culture, family is one of the most important and constant influences in our lives.

    c. Most people see their family members as their "safety net" in times of difficulty.

    d. It is impossible to define the terms *kinship* and *family* with any accuracy.

EXERCISE 5-14 ... FINDING IMPLIED MAIN IDEAS

Write a sentence that states the main idea for each of the following paragraphs.

Paragraph 1

Issue: The History of Bermuda

Although isolated in prehistory, in the historical period, Bermuda sat at the intersection of sea lanes linking Europe, the Caribbean, Africa, and North America. The first settlers, in the seventeenth century, were English, but it was not too long before there were a substantial number of Africans on the islands. There is not much evidence to suggest that they were brought directly from Africa, but rather they came irregularly from other Caribbean islands, including as captives from British privateer raids on other nations' ships. Later on, substantial numbers of Native Americans began to be taken to Bermuda. Many of these were expatriated captives from Indian wars in North America. Eventually, large numbers of Portuguese immigrants came to the islands to work in shipbuilding and other trades.

—adapted from Stanford, Allen, and Anton, *Biological Anthropology*, p. 139

Main idea: _____

_____

Paragraph 2

Issue: Women's Issues

In 1985, an anonymous group of women that called themselves the Guerrilla Girls began hanging posters in New York City. They listed the specific galleries who represented less than 1 woman out of every 10 men [artists]. Another poster asked, "How Many Women Had One-Person Exhibitions at NYC Museums Last Year?" The answer:

Guggenheim 0
Metropolitan 0
Modern 1
Whitney 1

One of the Guerrilla Girls' most daring posters was distributed in 1989. It asked, "When racism & sexism are no longer fashionable, what will your art collection be worth?" It listed 67 women artists and pointed out that a collection of works by all of them would be worth less than the art auction value of any *one* painting by a famous male artist. Its suggestion that the value of the male artists' work might be drastically inflated struck a chord with many.

—adapted from Sayre, *Discovering the Humanities*, pp. 490–491

Main idea: _____

_____

Paragraph 3

Issue: Health and Wellness

Have you ever noticed that you feel better after a belly laugh or a good cry? Humans have long recognized that smiling, laughing, singing, dancing, and other actions can elevate our moods, relieve stress, make us feel good, and help us improve our relationships. Crying can have similar positive physiological effects. Several recent articles have indicated that laughter and joy may increase endorphin levels, increase oxygen levels in the blood, decrease stress levels, relieve pain, enhance productivity, and reduce risks of chronic disease; however, the long-term effects on immune functioning and protective effects for chronic diseases are only just starting to be understood.

—Donatelle, *Health*, pp. 92–93

Main idea: _____

_____

EXERCISE 5-15 . . . FINDING STATED AND IMPLIED MAIN IDEAS

Turn to the article titled "Consequences of Social Class" on page 8. Using your own paper, number the lines from 1 to 16, to correspond to the 16 paragraphs in the article. For each paragraph number, if the main idea is stated, record the sentence number in which it appears (1, 2, etc.). If the main idea is unstated and implied, write a sentence that expresses the main idea.

Writing Implied Main Ideas

While professional writers do, on occasion, imply rather than state main ideas, it is usually best in most college papers and workplace writing to state your ideas directly using clear and effective topic sentences. If you only imply your main ideas, you run the risk that your audience may misinterpret them or even come up with ideas that you do not intend. It is also possible that inexperienced readers may think your paragraph is incomplete or confusing. If you choose to study creative writing, then you will find many interesting writing situations in which you can experiment with using implied main ideas.

SELF-TEST SUMMARY

To test yourself, cover the right column with a sheet of paper and answer the question in the left column. Evaluate each of your answers by sliding the paper down and comparing it with what is printed in the right column.

QUESTION	ANSWER
1 *What are supporting details? How do you choose and organize details to support a topic sentence?*	**Supporting details** are facts and ideas that prove or explain a paragraph's main idea. Not all details are equally important. Choose *relevant details* that directly explain and support the topic sentence. Choose *sufficient details* to make your topic sentence understandable and convincing. Choose a *variety of details* to develop the topic sentence: examples, facts or statistics, reasons, descriptions, and steps or procedures. *Organize details logically* based on the topic of the paragraph using time sequence, spatial, or least/most arrangements.
2 *What are transitions, and how do you use them?*	**Transitions** are linking words and phrases used to lead the reader from one idea to another. Use transitional words and phrases to guide the reader, signal what is to follow, and connect details. See Table 5-1 (p. 128) for a list of common transitional words and Table 5-2 (p. 130) for commonly used transitional words and phrases for each method of arranging details.
3 *How do you find implied main ideas?*	When a main idea is **implied**, it is not stated outright. To identify an implied main idea, look at the details in the paragraph and figure out the writer's main point. The details, when taken together, will point to a general and more important idea. This is the implied main idea.

6 Revising and Proofreading Paragraphs

LEARNING OBJECTIVES

1 Read carefully and critically to revise
2 Revise topic sentences and details to ensure effective paragraphs
3 Use idea maps to spot revision problems
4 Proofread to find and correct errors

Revision is a process of examining and rethinking your ideas as they appear in sentence and paragraph form. It involves finding ways to make your writing clearer, more effective, more complete, and more interesting. When revising you may change, add, delete, or rearrange your ideas and how you have expressed them to improve your writing. Revision also involves careful reading and critical thinking. You have to read closely to determine whether you have said exactly what you meant to say. Then you must be able to step back from what you have written and ask yourself the questions, *Will my readers understand what I have written?* and *Is my message clear?* Using the process of peer review, you may also find suggestions from classmates helpful.

Proofreading focuses on correctness and involves checking for errors in grammar, spelling, punctuation, and capitalization. It also involves formatting your paragraph to make it easy to read. Proofreading requires close and careful reading, working word by word and sentence by sentence, searching for and correcting errors.

6a READING CAREFULLY AND CRITICALLY FOR REVISION

LEARNING OBJECTIVE 1
Read carefully and critically to revise

The first step in preparing to revise a draft is to read it critically with the purpose of finding out what works and what does not. Use the following suggestions:

Guidelines for Reading Critically

1. **Create distance.** It is easy to like your own work and see nothing wrong with it. Mentally prepare yourself to look at your writing critically by

creating distance between yourself and your work. Try setting it aside for a day or so. Then, when you return, examine it as if someone else wrote it.

2. **Plan on and allow enough time to read your draft several times.** It is difficult to check for all aspects of writing at the same time. Each time, read it for a different purpose, using the following strategy:

   - **Step 1: Read the draft once, examining your ideas.** Have you said what you want to say? If not, make the necessary changes.
   - **Step 2: Read the draft again, evaluating how effectively you have expressed your ideas, again making changes to improve the draft.** Reread to make sure your changes work.
   - **Step 3: Read it a third time, checking for correctness.** You might want to read the draft several times, looking for one common error at a time.

3. **Print a copy of your draft.** It may be easier to see mistakes or problems if you are reading print copy rather than reading from your computer screen.

4. **Read with a pen in hand.** Mark and make notes as you read and reread. If you see something that doesn't sound right or an idea that needs further explanation, mark it so you don't overlook it as you start to rewrite.

5. **Read aloud.** When you hear your ideas, you may realize they sound choppy or that a statement seems to stand alone without adequate explanation or support.

6. **Check with classmates.** After reading the draft several times, if you are still unsure of what to revise, check with a classmate. Ask him or her to read your draft and offer comments and suggestions. For more on this process, called peer review, see Chapter 2, page 67.

Even after giving yourself some distance from your work, it may be difficult to know how to improve your own writing. Simply rereading may not help you discover flaws, weaknesses, or needed changes. This chapter offers guidelines to follow and questions to ask to help you spot problems. It also shows you how to use a revision map and includes a revision checklist to guide your revision and a proofreading checklist to guide your editing.

EXAMINING STUDENT WRITING

Claire Stroup

One of the ways you will learn about revision and proofreading is by studying a model essay. Claire Stroup's essay is used throughout this chapter to illustrate how to identify and revise ineffective paragraphs.

Claire Stroup is a student at North Carolina State University, where she is pursuing a degree in history. She submitted this essay for a sociology class assignment.

The Woes of Internet Dating

Claire Stroup

Title announces subject

1   It is easy to fall in love with an idea. The idea of a six foot tall, dark haired, mysterious, perfectly chiseled man with impeccable manners or a bombshell who can take a truck engine apart and put it back together in under an hour and rock a fussy baby to sleep the next moment are both highly appealing. On Internet dating sites, people can create an identity completely the opposite of their true selves. It is easy to lie about appearance, occupation, or income. In an environment where truth often goes untold, Internet dating creates more options for lies, deception, and heartbreak; on a very rare occasion, however, these relationships do work out.

Details provide background leading up to thesis statement

Thesis statement

Topic sentence   2   There are obviously some disturbing aspects to online dating. With technology becoming widely available, underage girls and boys have more and more access to the Internet and its terrors (and wonders). Parents probably would love to think that their children are utilizing the Internet for school research purposes, but the appeal of an idea with sweet words can be too great to resist. It is no surprise that a predator can use online dating or other communication to entice victims into his web under the disguise of being a cool teen just like his victims. First dates wind up being late night movie dates, and kids go missing. Abduction, rape, and murder become increasingly simple for creative predators when unsuspecting men, women, and children utilize Internet dating and relationships while throwing caution to the wind in the hopes of finding true love or just friendship.

Details explain topic sentence

Topic sentence   3   While not all those looking for love find themselves on the tail end of a potential romance gone bad, there is a great opportunity for dysfunctional relationships to be founded on little white lies. Even something as trivial as lying about weight because "I'm going to lose those extra twenty pounds in a month or two anyway" creates an opportunity for a painful relationship. It seems easy to slip into a comfortable relationship behind a screen where people can be slightly tweaked versions of themselves, where they might have a job online when they actually just got laid off, or their profile picture is one from a couple of years back when everything was just a little bit firmer. The fact remains that a relationship, no matter what its roots, must be built on a foundation of truth and honesty. The MTV show *Catfish* illustrates what a large problem deceiving identities have become in online interactions; even if both parties had a real connection, the relationship cannot be based on white lies. These heartbreaking deceptions have become such an issue that even MTV created a show about it. Little white lies that seem harmless can be indicators to a partner that his or her lover may have lied about far more than just love handles.

Details explain and support topic sentence

Topic sentence   4   Aside from the basic problems with lying to a lover, such as distrust and potential bodily harm, there lies a less tangible effect: heartbreak. Just because a person was not physically injured by another does not make the internal pain less significant. The emotional impact of having taken a risk on a faceless person and failing miserably is without a doubt shattering and life-altering. News media publish plenty of stories about individuals who have lost their lives because of trusting the wrong person online, but they rarely tell the stories of everyone else who got the short end of the stick and

Details support topic sentence

how that relationship changed their lives. That dishonesty will live with those victims forever, inhibiting their relationships from that point onward.

Topic sentence 5 with transition moves reader along

Writer includes examples to support the topic sentence

Of course, not all Internet dating relationships are lies, and not all online couples end up hurt and ashamed. Sometimes, a relationship works and is exactly as the two people hoped it would be. These legitimate, truthful relationships usually begin online and turn into face-to-face interactions fairly quickly. Some become long-term relationships, some friendships, some marriages. Then again, some people just hate each other when they actually speak face-to-face because the tone of the person's voice is downright obnoxious. Not all of those looking for love online are creepers, nor are all of them naïve daydreamers. Occasionally, two people looking for the right partner in life find each other online, and all is well.

Concluding 6 paragraph

Writer emphasizes the importance of building a relationship on personal, face-to-face contact

The truth of the matter is that there is no substitute for interpersonal, face-to-face relationships. It is difficult to nourish or sustain a relationship when neither party can see, hear, or touch the other. Although it seems quite simple to slip into an easy love with the idea of someone through the keys of a message board, the reality of that person often is shocking and discouraging. Each relationship is unique, so it proves difficult to generalize, but media shares more news about the online relationships that ended badly than those that end in happily ever after. Perhaps online dating is the future, but not as it exists today.

6b   REVISING INEFFECTIVE PARAGRAPHS

LEARNING OBJECTIVE 2
Revise topic sentences and details to ensure effective paragraphs

To revise a paragraph, begin by examining your topic sentence, and then, once you are satisfied with it, determine whether you have provided adequate details to support it.

Revising Ineffective Topic Sentences

Your topic sentence is the sentence around which your paragraph is built, so be sure it is strong and effective. The most common problems with topic sentences include the following:

- The topic sentence lacks a point of view.
- The topic sentence is too broad.
- The topic sentence is too narrow.

Each of these problems is addressed in Chapter 4 (pp. 110–113). Be sure to review this section.

EXERCISE 6-1 . . . WRITING A PARAGRAPH

Write a paragraph on one of the following topics. Evaluate your topic sentence to determine whether it is too broad, too narrow, or lacks a point of view.

1. A memorable vacation
2. Your dream job
3. A favorite character in a book or movie
4. A person you most admire or respect
5. An embarrassing experience

Revising Paragraphs to Add Supporting Details

The details in a paragraph should give your reader sufficient information to make your topic sentence believable. Paragraphs that lack necessary detail are called underdeveloped paragraphs. **Underdeveloped paragraphs** lack supporting sentences that prove or explain the point made in the topic sentence. As you read the following first draft of paragraph 5 from Claire's essay, keep the topic sentence in mind and consider whether the rest of the sentences support it.

First Draft of Paragraph 5

Claire Stroup

> Of course, not all Internet dating relationships are lies, and not all online couples end up hurt and ashamed. Sometimes, a relationship works and is exactly as the two people hoped it would be. Then again, some people just hate each other when they actually speak face-to-face. Not all of those looking for love online are creepers. Occasionally, two people find each other, and all is well.

This paragraph begins with a topic sentence that is focused (it is neither too broad nor too narrow) and that includes a point of view. It promises to explain how not all online relationships are dishonest and hurtful. However, the rest of the paragraph does not fulfill this promise. Instead, the writer gives two very general examples of online relationships: (1) sometimes a relationship works as the two people hoped and (2) some people hate each other when they actually speak face-to-face. The third example (not all people looking for love online are creepers) is a little more specific, but it is not developed well. The last sentence suggests, but does not explain, that people can find successful relationships online.

Taking into account the need for more supporting detail, Claire revised her paragraph as follows:

Revised Paragraph

Of course, not all Internet dating relationships are lies, and not all online couples end up hurt and ashamed. Sometimes, a relationship works and is exactly as the two people hoped it would be. These legitimate, truthful relationships usually begin online and turn into face-to-face interactions fairly quickly. Some become long-term relationships, some friendships, some marriages. Then again, some people just hate each other when they actually speak face-to-face because the tone of the person's voice is downright obnoxious. Not all of those looking for love online are creepers, nor are all of them naïve daydreamers. Occasionally, two people looking for the right partner in life find each other online, and all is well.

Did you notice that Claire became much more specific in the revised version? She gave an example of relationships that began online and became long-term friendships and marriages. The example of hating someone once they speak face-to-face was explained in more detail: the tone of the person's voice is obnoxious. Finally, Claire provided more detail about the types of people looking for love online and explained how people occasionally can find the right partner online. With the extra details and supporting examples, the paragraph is more interesting and effective.

The following suggestions will help you revise an underdeveloped paragraph:

Tips for Revising Underdeveloped Paragraphs

1. **Analyze your paragraph sentence by sentence.** If a sentence does not add new, specific information to your paragraph, delete it or add to it so that it becomes relevant.

2. **Think of specific situations, facts, or examples that illustrate or support your topic.** Often you can make a general sentence more specific.

3. **Brainstorm, freewrite, or branch.** To come up with additional details or examples to use in your paragraph, try some prewriting techniques. If necessary, start fresh with a new approach and new set of ideas.

4. **Reexamine your topic sentence.** If you are having trouble generating details, your topic sentence may be the problem. Consider changing the approach.

Example	Internet dating is tedious.
Revised	Internet dating, although tedious, is worth the effort if you take the time to write a good profile, list your criteria for a partner, and invest time in face-to-face meetings with potential partners.

5. **Consider changing your topic.** If a paragraph remains troublesome, look for a new topic and start over.

EXERCISE 6-2 . . . READING: EVALUATING A PARAGRAPH

The following paragraph is poorly developed. What suggestions would you make to the writer to improve the paragraph? Write them in the space provided. Be specific. Which sentences are weak? How could each be improved?

I am attending college to improve myself. By attending college, I am getting an education to improve the skills that I will need for a good career in broadcasting. Then, after a successful career, I'll be able to get the things that I need to be happy in my life. People will also respect me more.

_____

_____

_____

_____

_____

EXERCISE 6-3 . . . WRITING: REVISING A PARAGRAPH

Evaluate the following paragraph by answering the questions that follow it.

One of the best ways to keep people happy and occupied is to entertain them. Every day people are being entertained, whether it is by a friend for a split second or by a Broadway play for several hours. Entertainment is probably one of the nation's biggest businesses. Entertainment has come a long way from the past; it has gone from plays in the park to films in eight-screen movie theaters.

1. Evaluate the topic sentence. What is wrong with it? How could it be revised?

_____

_____

2. Write a more effective topic sentence about entertainment.

_____

3. Evaluate the supporting details. What is wrong with them?

_____

4. What should the writer do to develop her paragraph?

_____

5. Use the topic sentence you wrote in question 2 above to develop a paragraph about entertainment.

ADDING SUPPORTING DETAILS

TO REVISE AN UNDERDEVELOPED PARAGRAPH,

- analyze your paragraph sentence by sentence
- think of specific situations, facts, or examples that illustrate or support your main point
- use brainstorming, freewriting, or branching
- reexamine your topic sentence
- consider changing your topic

EXERCISE 6–4 ... WRITING: REVISING A PARAGRAPH

Revise the paragraph you wrote in Exercise 6-1, ensuring you have an effective topic sentence and sufficient details to support it.

6c   USING IDEA MAPS TO SPOT REVISION PROBLEMS

LEARNING OBJECTIVE 3
Use idea maps to spot revision problems

Some students find revision a troublesome step because it is difficult for them to see what is wrong with their own work. After working hard on a first draft, it is tempting to say to yourself that you have done a great job and think, "This is fine." Other times, you may think you have explained and supported an idea clearly when actually you have not. Almost all writing, however, needs and benefits from revision.

An idea map can help you spot weaknesses and discover what you may not have done as well as you thought. It can also show how each of your ideas fits with and relates to all of the other ideas in a paragraph or essay. In this section you will learn how to use an idea map to (1) discover problems in a paragraph and (2) guide your revision as you ask and answer the following questions.

- Does every detail belong? Have I strayed from the topic?
- Are the details arranged and developed logically?
- Is the paragraph balanced? Is it repetitious?

Does Every Detail Belong, or Have You Strayed Off Topic?

Every detail in a paragraph must directly support the topic sentence or one of the other details. To spot unrelated details, draw an idea map and ask, "Does this detail directly explain the topic sentence or one of the other details?" If meaning is lost or if confusion occurs if you omit it, the detail is important. Include it in your map. If you can make your point just as well without the detail, list it under "unrelated details." Unrelated details like these are an indication that you are straying off topic.

Here is Claire's first draft of paragraph 4.

First Draft of Paragraph 4

Claire Stroup

Aside from the basic problems with lying to a lover, such as distrust and potential bodily harm, there lies a less tangible effect: heartbreak. Just because a person was not physically injured by another does not make the internal pain less significant. And excessive crying from that heartbreak may cause actual physical damage to your eyes, blurring your vision temporarily. Tea bags containing caffeine can help reduce swelling from too much crying and improve your blurred vision. The emotional impact of having taken a risk on a faceless person and failing miserably is without a doubt shattering and life-altering. News media publish plenty of stories about individuals who have lost their lives because of trusting the wrong person online, but they rarely tell the stories of everyone else who got the short end of the stick and how that relationship changed their lives. News media try to gain readers by focusing on sensational stories involving a very small percentage of people. That dishonesty will live with those victims forever, inhibiting their relationships from that point onward.

She was concerned she had included unrelated details, so she drew the following idea map:

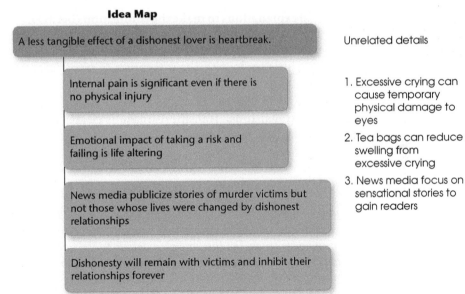

Idea Map

A less tangible effect of a dishonest lover is heartbreak.

Internal pain is significant even if there is no physical injury

Emotional impact of taking a risk and failing is life altering

News media publicize stories of murder victims but not those whose lives were changed by dishonest relationships

Dishonesty will remain with victims and inhibit their relationships forever

Unrelated details

1. Excessive crying can cause temporary physical damage to eyes

2. Tea bags can reduce swelling from excessive crying

3. News media focus on sensational stories to gain readers

Once she completed the map, she saw that the details about excessive crying and the use of teabags to reduce swelling do not directly explain the intangible effects of heartbreak. Also, the detail about the news media's focus on sensational stories to gain readers did not explain how people's lives are changed forever by dishonest online relationships. She cut these details in the final version of the paragraph.

What to Do If You Stray Off Topic

Use the following suggestions to revise your paragraph if it strays from your topic:

1. **Locate the last sentence that does relate to your topic, and begin your revision there.** What could you say next that *would* relate to the topic?
2. **Consider expanding your existing ideas.** If, after two or three details, you have strayed from your topic, consider expanding the details you have, rather than searching for additional details.
3. **Reread your brainstorming, freewriting, or branching to find more details.** Look for additional ideas that support your topic. Do more brainstorming, if necessary.
4. **Consider changing your topic.** Drifting from your topic is not always a loss. Sometimes by drifting, you discover a more interesting topic than your original one. If you decide to change topics, revise your entire paragraph. Begin by rewriting your topic sentence.

Showing How Details Belong

The following suggestions will help ensure your reader can see the relevance of your details and their connection to your topic sentence:

- **Add explanations to make the connections between your ideas clearer.** Often a detail may not seem to relate to the topic because you have not explained *how* it relates. For example, health care insurance may seem to have little to do with the prevention of breast cancer deaths until you explain that mammograms, which are paid for by some health care plans, can prevent deaths.
- **Add transitions.** Transitions make it clearer to your reader how one detail relates to another.

EXERCISE 6-5 . . . READING: IDENTIFYING UNRELATED DETAILS

Read the following first draft paragraph. Then draw an idea map that includes the topic sentence, only those details that support the topic sentence, and the concluding sentence. List the unrelated details to the side of the map, as in the example on page 151. Identify where the writer began to stray from the topic, compare your results with those of a classmate, and then decide what specific steps the writer should take to revise this paragraph.

Your credit rating is a valuable thing that you should protect and watch over. A credit rating is a record of your loans, credit card charges, and repayment history. Credit card charges can really pile up if you only pay the minimum each month, but some credit card companies will waive penalties just one time. You can try to negotiate a lower interest rate too. (No harm in asking!) If you pay a bill late or miss a payment, that information becomes part of your credit rating. It is, therefore, important to pay bills promptly. Some people just don't keep track of dates; some don't even know what date it is today. Errors can occur in your credit rating. Someone else's mistakes can be put on your record, for example. Hackers who break into credit card companies to use clients' accounts should face severe penalties once they are caught. It is a huge hassle to replace your card once your account number has been stolen. Why these credit rating companies can't take more time and become more accurate is beyond my understanding. It is worthwhile to get a copy of your credit report and check it for errors. Time spent caring for your credit rating will be time well spent.

EXERCISE 6-6 . . . WRITING: IDENTIFYING UNRELATED DETAILS IN YOUR PARAGRAPH

Draw an idea map of the paragraph you revised in Exercise 6-4. Check for unrelated details. If you find any, revise your paragraph using the suggestions given above.

Are the Details Arranged and Developed Logically?

Details in a paragraph should follow some logical order. As you write a first draft, you are often more concerned with expressing your ideas than with presenting them in the correct order. As you revise, however, you should make sure you have followed a logical arrangement. Your ideas need a logical arrangement to make them easy to follow: poor organization creates misunderstanding and confusion.

Common arrangements include time sequence, spatial order, and arranging details from least to most according to a particular quality or characteristic (see pp. 125–127). Additional methods for organizing ideas are summarized below and discussed in detail in Chapter 7.

METHODS OF ORGANIZING USING PATTERNS

METHOD	DESCRIPTION
Illustration	Explains by giving situations that illustrate a general idea or statement
Process	Arranges steps in order in which they are completed
Definition	Explains a term by giving its general class and specific characteristics
Classification	Explains a topic by identifying categories or parts
Cause and effect	Explains why something happened or what happened as a result of a particular action
Comparison and contrast	Explains an idea by comparing or contrasting it with another, usually more familiar, idea

Claire Stroup

After drafting the following paragraph, Claire drew an idea map of it, shown below.

First Draft of Paragraph 2

There are obviously some disturbing aspects to online dating. First dates wind up being late night movie dates, and kids go missing. Parents probably would love to think that their children are utilizing the Internet for school research purposes, but the appeal of an idea with sweet words can be too great to resist. With technology becoming widely available, underage girls and boys have more and more access to the Internet and its terrors (and wonders). Abduction, rape, and murder become increasingly simple for creative predators when unsuspecting men, women, and children utilize Internet dating and relationships while throwing caution to the wind in the hopes of finding true love or just friendship. It is no surprise that a predator can use online dating or other communication to entice victims into his web under the disguise of being a cool teen just like his victims.

Idea Map

There are some disturbing aspects to online dating.

First dates become late night dates and kids go missing

Parents think children use the Internet for school but kids may be responding to someone's appeal

Underage kids have more access to the Internet

Crimes are easy for predators when unsuspecting people go online for love or friendship

A predator can entice victims online by acting as a teen

An idea map lets you see quickly when a paragraph has no organization or when details are out of order. Claire's map showed that her paragraph did not present the potential results of online dating in the most logical arrangement: cause and effect. She therefore reorganized the details and revised her paragraph as follows:

Revised Paragraph

There are obviously some disturbing aspects to online dating. With technology becoming widely available, underage girls and boys have more and more access to the Internet and its terrors (and wonders). Parents probably would love to think that their children are utilizing the Internet for school research purposes, but the appeal of an idea with sweet words can be too great to resist. It is no surprise that a predator can use online dating or other communication to entice victims into his web under the disguise of being a cool teen just like his victims. First dates wind up being late night movie dates, and kids go missing. Abduction, rape, and murder become increasingly simple for creative predators when unsuspecting men, women, and children utilize Internet dating and relationships while throwing caution to the wind in the hopes of finding true love or just friendship.

Arranging and Developing Details Logically

The following suggestions will help you revise your paragraph if it lacks organization:

1. **Review the methods of arranging and developing details and of organizing and presenting material** (see Chapter 5, pp. 124–127). Will one of those arrangements work? If so, number the ideas in your idea map according to the arrangement you choose. Then begin revising your paragraph.

   If you find one or more details out of logical order in your paragraph, do the following:

   - Number the details in your idea map to indicate the correct order, and revise your paragraph accordingly.
   - Reread your revised paragraph and draw another idea map.
   - Look to see if you've omitted necessary details. After you have placed your details in a logical order, you are more likely to recognize gaps.

2. **Look at your topic sentence again.** If you are working with a revised arrangement of supporting details, you may need to revise your topic sentence to reflect that arrangement.

3. **Check whether additional details are needed.** Suppose, for example, you are writing about an exciting experience, and you decide to use the time-sequence arrangement. Once you make that decision, you may need to add details to enable your reader to understand exactly how the experience happened.

4. **Add transitions.** Transitions help make your organization obvious and easy to follow.

EXERCISE 6-7 . . . READING: EVALUATING ARRANGEMENT OF IDEAS

Read the following student paragraph, and draw an idea map of it. Evaluate the arrangement of ideas. What revisions would you suggest?

The minimum wage is not an easily resolved problem; it has both advantages and disadvantages. Its primary advantage is that it does guarantee workers a minimum wage. It prevents the economic abuse of workers. Employers cannot take advantage of workers by paying them less than the minimum. Its primary disadvantage is that the minimum wage is not sufficient for older workers with families to support. For younger workers, such as teenagers, however, this minimum is fine. It provides them with spending money and some economic freedom from their parents. Another disadvantage is that as long as people, such as teenagers, are willing to work for the minimum, employers don't need to pay a higher wage. Thus, the minimum wage prevents experienced workers from getting more money. But the minimum wage does help our economy by requiring a certain level of income per worker.

EXERCISE 6-8 . . . WRITING: EVALUATING THE ARRANGEMENT OF IDEAS IN YOUR WRITING

Review the paragraph you revised for Exercise 6-6, and use your idea map to evaluate whether your details are logically arranged. Revise if needed.

Is the Paragraph Balanced and Not Repetitious?

In a first draft, you may express the same idea more than once, each time in a slightly different way. Repetitive statements can help you stay on track and keep you writing and generating new ideas. However, it is important to eliminate repetition at the revision stage, as it adds nothing to your paragraph and detracts from its clarity.

An effective paragraph achieves a balance among its points. That is, each idea receives an appropriate amount of supporting detail and emphasis. Here is Claire's first draft of paragraph 3, followed by her idea map of it.

Claire Stroup

First Draft of Paragraph 3

While not all those looking for love find themselves on the tail end of a potential romance gone bad, there is a great opportunity for dysfunctional relationships to be founded on little white lies. Even something as trivial as lying about weight because "I'm going to lose those extra twenty pounds in a month or two anyway" creates an opportunity for a painful relationship. It seems easy to slip into a comfortable relationship behind a screen where people can be slightly tweaked versions of themselves, where they might have a job online when they actually just got laid off, or their profile picture is one from a couple of years back when everything was just a little bit firmer. It is tempting for people to present themselves using a photo from when they were younger or in better shape. It may seem trivial to some, but people really should not lie about their weight or age or job status. The fact remains that a relationship, no matter what its roots, must be built on a foundation of truth and honesty. The MTV show *Catfish* illustrates what a large problem deceiving identities have become in online interactions. Little white lies that seem harmless can be indicators to a partner that his or her lover may have lied about far more than just love handles.

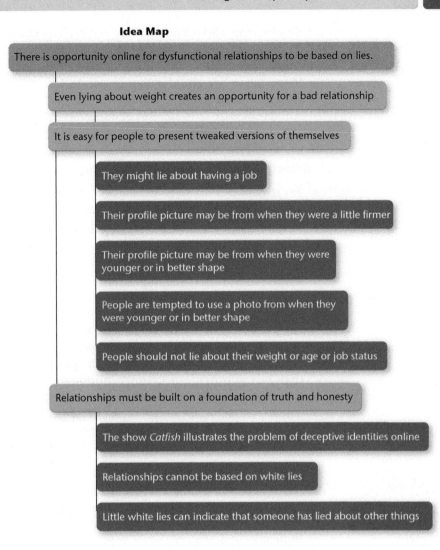

Idea Map

There is opportunity online for dysfunctional relationships to be based on lies.

Even lying about weight creates an opportunity for a bad relationship

It is easy for people to present tweaked versions of themselves

They might lie about having a job

Their profile picture may be from when they were a little firmer

Their profile picture may be from when they were younger or in better shape

People are tempted to use a photo from when they were younger or in better shape

People should not lie about their weight or age or job status

Relationships must be built on a foundation of truth and honesty

The show *Catfish* illustrates the problem of deceptive identities online

Relationships cannot be based on white lies

Little white lies can indicate that someone has lied about other things

As the idea map shows, a major portion of Claire's paragraph is devoted to how people may misrepresent their physical appearance in online descriptions. The example about MTV's show *Catfish* is not as thoroughly explained. To revise for balance, she expanded her treatment of the MTV show and eliminated some of the repetitive details about dishonest profile photos.

Making Sure Your Paragraph Is Balanced

The following suggestions will help you revise your paragraph for balance:

- **Not every point or example must have the *same* amount of explanation.** For example, more complicated ideas require more explanation than simpler, more obvious ones. When you are using a least/most arrangement, the more important details may need more coverage than the less important ones.

- **If two ideas are equally important and equally complicated, they should receive similar treatment.** For instance, if you include an example or statistic in support of one idea, you should do so for the other.

How to Avoid Repetition

The following suggestions will help you revise a paragraph with repetitive ideas:

- **Try to combine ideas.** Select the best elements and wording of each idea and use them to produce a revised sentence. Add more detail if needed.
- **Review places where you make deletions.** When you delete a repetitious statement, check to see whether the sentence before and the sentence after the deletion connect. Often a transition will be needed to help the paragraph flow easily.
- **Decide whether additional details are needed.** Often we write repetitious statements when we don't know what else to say. Thus, repetition often signals lack of development. Refer to page 148 for specific suggestions on revising underdeveloped paragraphs.
- **Watch for statements that are only slightly more general or specific than one another.** For example, although the first sentence below is general and the second is more specific, they repeat the same idea.

> Loud noises from other people's apartments can be annoying. The noises coming from my neighbor's apartment last night were very annoying.

To make the second sentence a specific example of the idea in the first sentence, rather than just a repetition of it, the writer would need to add specific details about how the noises throughout the evening were annoying.

> The sounds coming from my neighbor's apartment last night—WXKS-FM playing full blast until after 1 a.m., visitors with lead feet, and a screaming match with his girlfriend at 3 a.m.—are all examples of how annoying loud noises can be!

EXERCISE 6-9 . . . READING: REVISING REPETITION AND EVALUATING BALANCE

Read the following paragraph and delete all repetitive statements. Draw an idea map, evaluate the balance of details, and indicate where more details are needed.

Children misbehaving is an annoying problem in our society. I used to work as a waiter at Denny's, and I have seen many incidences in which parents allow their children to misbehave. I have seen many situations that you would just not believe. Once I served a table at which the parents allowed their four-year-old to make his toy spider crawl up and down my pants as I tried to serve the food. The parents just laughed. Children have grown up being rewarded for their actions, regardless of whether they are good or bad. Whether the child does something the parents approve of or whether it is something they disapprove of, they react in similar ways. This is why a lot of toddlers and children continue to misbehave. Being rewarded will cause the child to act in the same way to get the same reward.

EXERCISE 6-10 . . . WRITING: REVISING REPETITION AND EVALUATING BALANCE IN YOUR PARAGRAPH

Review the paragraph you revised for Exercise 6-8. Use your idea map to identify repetitive statements and evaluate the balance of details. Make any necessary revisions.

USING IDEA MAPS

An idea map is a visual display of the ideas in your paragraph. It allows you to see how ideas relate to one another and to identify weaknesses in your writing. You can use idea maps to answer the following five questions that will help you revise your paragraphs:

- Does the paragraph stray from the topic?
- Does every detail belong?
- Are the details arranged and developed logically?
- Is the paragraph balanced?
- Is the paragraph repetitious?

REVISION CHECKLIST
Paragraph Development

1. Is the topic manageable (neither too broad nor too narrow)?
2. Is the paragraph written with purpose and audience in mind?
3. Does the topic sentence identify the topic?
4. Does the topic sentence make a point about the topic?
5. Does each sentence support the topic sentence?
6. Is there sufficient detail?
7. Are the details arranged and developed logically?
8. Is the paragraph repetitious?
9. Is there a sentence at the end that brings the paragraph to a close?

(continued)

Sentence Development

10. Are ideas combined to produce more effective sentences?
11. Are adjectives and adverbs used to make the sentences vivid and interesting?
12. Are relative clauses and prepositional phrases like -*ing* phrases used to add detail?
13. Are pronouns used correctly and consistently?

6d   PROOFREADING FOR CORRECTNESS

LEARNING OBJECTIVE 4
Proofread to find and correct errors

Proofreading is a final reading of your paper to check for errors. In this final polishing of your work, the focus is on correctness, so don't proofread until you have done all your rethinking of ideas and revision. When you are ready to proofread your writing, you should check for errors in

- sentences (run-ons or fragments).
- grammar.
- spelling.
- punctuation.
- capitalization.

The following checklist will help you as you proofread your writing.

PROOFREADING CHECKLIST

1. Does each sentence end with an appropriate punctuation mark (period, question mark, exclamation point, or quotation mark)?
2. Is all punctuation within each sentence correct (commas, colons, semicolons, apostrophes, dashes, and quotation marks)?
3. Are there any sentence fragments, run-on sentences, or comma splices?
4. Is each word spelled correctly?
5. Are capital letters used where needed?
6. Are numbers and abbreviations used correctly?
7. Are any words left out?
8. Are all typographical errors corrected?
9. Are the pages in the correct order and numbered?

EXERCISE 6-11 . . . WRITING: PROOFREADING YOUR PARAGRAPH

Prepare and proofread the final version of the paragraph you revised for Exercise 6-10.

SELF-TEST SUMMARY

To test yourself, cover the right column with a sheet of paper and answer the question in the left column. Evaluate each of your answers by sliding the paper down and comparing it with what is printed in the right column.

QUESTION	ANSWER
1 *What strategies can you use when reading a draft for revision?*	To revise effectively, create distance, allow enough time to read your draft several times, print a copy of your draft and read it with a pen in hand, read aloud, and ask a classmate for suggestions.
2 *How do you revise ineffective paragraphs?*	Revise ineffective paragraphs by examining your topic sentence, and then determining whether you have adequate supporting details.
3 *What revision problems do idea maps help you to identify?*	Idea maps can identify where a paragraph strays from the topic, whether supporting details are relevant and logically arranged, and whether a paragraph is balanced or repetitious. Use the Revision Checklist on pages 159–160 to help you revise.
4 *What is proofreading, and how do you proofread for correctness?*	Proofreading is a final reading of your paper to check for errors. When you have done all your rethinking of ideas and revision, check for errors in sentences, punctuation, grammar, capitalization, and spelling. Use the Proofreading Checklist on page 160 to help you proofread.

7 Reading and Writing Organizational Patterns

LEARNING OBJECTIVES

1 Read and write illustration
2 Read and write process
3 Read and write definition
4 Read and write classification
5 Read and write cause and effect
6 Read and write comparison and contrast
7 Read and write mixed patterns

Most college students take courses in several different disciplines each semester. They may study psychology, anatomy and physiology, mathematics, and English composition all in one semester. Although their subject matter may differ, researchers, textbook authors, your professors, and professional writers in these fields use standard approaches, or **organizational patterns**, to express their ideas. In English composition, they are sometimes called the *rhetorical modes* or simply *modes*.

To learn what patterns of organization are and why they are useful for reading and writing, consider Lists A and B, each containing five facts. Which would be easier to learn?

List A

1. Cheeseburgers contain more calories than hamburgers.
2. Christmas cactus plants bloom once a year.
3. Many herbs have medicinal uses.
4. Many ethnic groups live in Toronto.
5. Fiction books are arranged alphabetically by author.

List B

1. Effective advertising has several characteristics.
2. An ad must be unique.
3. An ad must be believable.
4. An ad must make a lasting impression.
5. An ad must substantiate a claim.

Most likely, you chose list B. There is no connection between the facts in list A; the facts in list B, however, are related. The first sentence makes a general statement, and each remaining sentence gives a particular characteristic of effective advertising. Together they fit into a *pattern*.

The details of a paragraph, paragraphs within an essay, events within a short story, or sections within a textbook often fit a pattern. If you can recognize the pattern as you read, you will find it easier to understand and remember the content. When writing, patterns provide a framework within which to organize and develop your ideas and help you present them in a clear, logical manner. Sections of this chapter are devoted to reading and writing each of the following patterns: *illustration, process, definition, classification, cause and effect*, and *comparison and contrast*. Each of these patterns can work alone or with other patterns.

Each section of this chapter describes how to read and write using a common pattern and provides examples of its use.

7a   READING AND WRITING ILLUSTRATION

LEARNING OBJECTIVE 1
Read and write illustration

The **illustration pattern** uses examples—specific instances or situations—to explain a general idea or statement. This is especially useful when a subject is unfamiliar to the reader. Here are two general statements with specific examples that illustrate them.

GENERAL STATEMENT	EXAMPLES
I had an exhausting day.	• I had two exams. • I worked four hours. • I swam 20 laps in the pool.
Research studies demonstrate that reading aloud to children improves their reading skills.	• Whitehurst (2011) found that reading picture books to children improved their vocabulary. • Crain-Thompson and Dale (2012) reported that reading aloud to language-delayed children improved their reading ability.

Andy Dean/Fotolia

In each of these cases, the examples make the general statement clear, under-standable, and believable by giving specific illustrations or supporting details. Example paragraphs consist of examples that support the topic sentence.

Reading Illustration Paragraphs

When organizing illustration paragraphs, writers often state the main idea first and then follow it with one or more examples. In a longer piece of writing, a separate paragraph may be used for each example. Notice how the illustration pattern is developed in the following paragraph:

Issue: Popular Physics

> Static electricity is all around us. We see it in lightning. We receive electric shocks when we walk on a nylon rug on a dry day and then touch something (or someone). We can see sparks fly from a cat's fur when we pet it in the dark. We can rub a balloon on a sweater and make the balloon stick to the wall or the ceiling. Our clothes cling together when we take them from the dryer.
>
> —Newell, *Chemistry*, p. 11

Here the writer explains static electricity through the use of everyday examples. You could visualize the paragraph as follows:

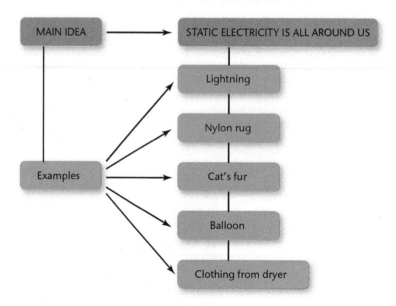

Writers often use transition words—*for example, for instance,* or *such as*—to signal the reader that an example is to follow. By using examples and transitions, the writer in the following examples explains why Shadow is Charlie's best friend.

Charlie agrees with the old saying that "a dog is a man's best friend." When he comes home from work, for instance, his dog Shadow is always happy to see him. He wags his tail, licks Charlie's hand, and leaps joyously around the room. Shadow is also good company for him. The dog is always there, for example, when Charlie is sick or lonely or just needs a pal to take for a walk. Many pets, such as cats and parakeets, provide companionship for their owners. But Charlie would put his dog Shadow at the top of any "best friend" list.

COMMON ILLUSTRATION TRANSITIONS

also	for example	in particular	to illustrate
an example is	for instance	such as	when

EXERCISE 7-1 . . . ANALYZING THE ILLUSTRATION PATTERN

The following paragraphs, all of which are about stress, use the example pattern. Read each of them and answer the questions that follow.

Issue: Stress

A.   Any single event or situation by itself may not cause stress. But, if you experience several mildly disturbing situations at the same time, you may find yourself under stress. For instance, getting a low grade on a biology lab report by itself may not be stressful, but if it occurs the same week during which your car "dies," you argue with a close friend, and you discover your checking account is overdrawn, then it may contribute to stress.

  1. Underline the transition word or phrase the writer uses to introduce the examples.

  2. Highlight the four examples the writer provides as possible causes of stress.

B.   Every time you make a major change in your life, you are susceptible to stress. Major changes include a new job or career, marriage, divorce, the birth of a child, or the death of someone close. Beginning college is a major life change. Try not to create multiple simultaneous life changes, which multiply the potential for stress.

  3. Underline the topic sentence.

  4. The writer gives six examples of major changes. Highlight each.

C.   Because you probably depend on your job to pay part or all of your college expenses, your job is important to you and you feel pressure to perform well in order to keep it. Some jobs are more stressful than others. Those, for example, in which you work under constant time pressure tend to be stressful. Jobs that must be performed in loud, noisy, crowded, or unpleasant conditions—a hot kitchen, a noisy machine shop—with co-workers who don't do their share can be stressful. Consider changing jobs if you are working in very stressful conditions.

5. Underline the topic sentence.

6. Circle the transition the writer uses to introduce the first type of job.

7. To help you understand "jobs that must be performed in loud, noisy, crowded, or unpleasant conditions," the writer provides three examples. Highlight these examples.

Writing Illustration Paragraphs

Writing paragraphs using examples involves writing a clear topic sentence, selecting appropriate and sufficient examples, arranging your details, and using transitions. When writing illustration paragraphs, be sure to use the third person in most situations (see discussion of point of view in Chapter 2, p. 48).

Writing Your Topic Sentence

You must create a topic sentence before you can generate examples to support it. Consider what you want to say about your topic and what your main point or fresh insight is. From this main idea, compose a first draft of a topic sentence. Be sure it states your topic and the point you want to make about it. You will probably want to revise your topic sentence once you've written the paragraph, but for now, use it as the basis for gathering examples.

Selecting Appropriate and Sufficient Examples

Use brainstorming to create a list of as many examples as you can think of to support your topic sentence. Suppose your topic is dog training. Your tentative topic sentence is "You must be firm and consistent when training dogs; otherwise, they will not respond to your commands." You might produce the following list of examples:

- My sister's dog jumps on people; sometimes she disciplines him and sometimes she doesn't.
- Every time I want my dog to heel, I give the same command and use a firm tone of voice.
- If my dog does not obey the command to sit, I repeat it, this time saying it firmly while pushing down on his back.
- The dog trainer at obedience class used a set of hand signals to give commands to her dog.

Then you would review your list and select between two and four examples to support your topic sentence. Here is an example of a paragraph you might write:

> When training dogs, you must be firm and consistent; otherwise, they will not respond to your commands. The dog trainer at my obedience class has a perfectly trained dog. She uses a set of hand signals to give commands to her dog, Belle. The same signal always means the same thing, it is always enforced, and Belle has learned to obey each command. On the other hand, my sister's dog is a good example of what not to do. Her dog Maggie jumps on people; sometimes she disciplines Maggie, and sometimes she doesn't. When she asks Maggie to sit, sometimes she insists Maggie obey; other times she gets discouraged and gives up. Consequently, the dog has not learned to stop jumping on people or to obey the command to sit.

Idea Map

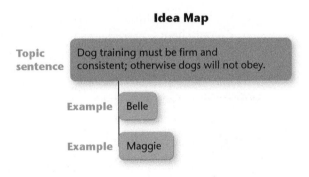

In the example paragraph, you probably noticed that some of the brainstormed examples were used; others were not. New examples were also added. Use the following guidelines in selecting details to include:

Guidelines for Selecting and Using Details

- **Each example should illustrate the idea stated in your topic sentence.** Do not choose examples that are complicated or have too many parts; your readers may not be able to see the connection to your topic sentence clearly.
- **Each example should be as specific and vivid as possible, accurately describing an incident or situation.** Suppose your topic sentence is "Celebrities are not reliable sources of information about a product because they are getting paid to praise it." Rather than follow it with a general statement like "Many sports stars are paid to appear in TV commercials," name specific athletes and products or sponsors: "Tom Brady, star quarterback for the Patriots, endorses UGG Boots and Under Armour; LeBron James, basketball superstar, endorses Nike products."

- **Choose examples that your readers are familiar with and understand.**
- **Choose a sufficient number of examples to make your point understandable.** The number you need depends on the complexity of the topic and your reader's familiarity with it. One example may be sufficient for a familiar topic, but a more difficult and unfamiliar topic may require more.
- **Vary your examples.** If you are giving several examples, choose a wide range from different times, places, people, and so on.
- **Choose typical examples.** Avoid outrageous or exaggerated examples that do not accurately represent the situation.
- **Draw the connection for your reader between your example and your main point.** If the connection is not clear, include a sentence that clarifies it. Here is the beginning of a paragraph written by a social worker. Note how the highlighted sentence makes the connection among ideas clear.

> We are continuing to see the aftereffects of last spring's tornado on our clients. In some cases, we have had to make referrals to meet our clients' needs. Several children have suffered PTSD (post traumatic stress disorder). Natoya Johns, for example, has nightmares and panic attacks . . .

Arranging Your Details

Once you have selected examples to include, arrange your ideas in a logical sequence. Here are a few possibilities:

- **Arrange the examples chronologically.** Move from older to more recent examples.
- **Arrange the examples from most to least familiar.** Place familiar examples first and then move to those that are more technical and detailed.
- **Arrange the examples from least to most important.** Begin with less convincing examples and finish with the strongest, most convincing example, thereby leaving your reader with a strong final impression.
- **Arrange the examples in the order suggested by the topic sentence.** In the earlier sample paragraph about dog training, being firm and consistent is mentioned first in the topic sentence, so an example of firm and consistent training is given first.

Using Transitions

Transition words and phrases are needed, both to signal to your reader that you are offering an example and to signal that you are moving from one example to another (see p. 165 for a list of commonly used illustration transitions). In the following paragraph, the transition words connect the examples and make them easier to follow:

Issue: Environmentally Induced Stress

For many students, where they live and the environment around them cause significant levels of stress. Although rare, natural disasters can devastate countries, cities, and communities, leaving individuals fighting for their very survival. Tsunamis, floods, earthquakes, and hurricanes, for example, wreak havoc on our lives, causing extreme levels of environmentally induced stress. In the aftermath of disasters, events can spiral out of control, leaving food, water, and other resources vulnerable indefinitely. Imagine, for instance, waking up to find that your family is missing, your home is wiped out, and you have no cell phone or other communication methods. Often as damaging as one-time disasters are background distressors in the environment, such as noise, air, and water pollution. People who cannot escape background distressors may exist in a constant stress resistance phase.

—adapted from Donatelle, *Access to Health*, p. 80

EXERCISE 7-2 . . . WRITING AN ILLUSTRATION PARAGRAPH

Select one of the topics listed below and write a paragraph that follows the guidelines presented in this section.

1. slang
2. daily hassles or aggravations
3. the needs of infants or young children
4. overcommercialization of holidays
5. growing use of blogs
6. cheap vacations
7. current fashion fad
8. dream car
9. favorite sport
10. annoying people

7b   READING AND WRITING PROCESS

LEARNING OBJECTIVE 2
Read and write process

The term *process* refers to the order in which something occurs or the order in which it is done. When writers explain how to do something or how something works, they use the **process** pattern. *Chronological order* is a variation of process that writers use to describe events in the order in which they happened. For example, a historian may discuss the sequence of events preceding the Iraq war. Another variation is *narration*, in which writers tell a story, describing events in the order in which they occurred. While this section focuses on process, you can use many of the same guidelines for reading and writing chronological order and narration as well.

Reading Process Paragraphs

Disciplines and careers that focus on procedures, steps, or stages use the process pattern. In many cases, the steps must happen in a specific order; in some cases, certain steps may happen at the same time or in no particular order. Using bulleted and numbered lists allows writers to provide clear, step-by-step explanations of processes. They also use transitions to guide the reader from one step to the next.

COMMON PROCESS TRANSITIONS

after	as soon as	finally	in addition	meanwhile	then
also	before	first	last	next	until
another	during	following	later	second	when

Note that the following selection uses numbered points to walk the reader through the process of performing mouth-to-mask ventilation in the correct, step-by-step manner. Notice that all of the steps are parallel: they begin with verbs.

Issue: Emergency Care

Mouth-to-mask ventilation is performed using a pocket face mask, which is made of soft, collapsible material and can be carried in your pocket, jacket, or purse. Many emergency medical technicians (EMTs) purchase their own pocket face masks for workplace or auto first aid kits.

To provide mouth-to-mask ventilation, follow these steps:

1. Position yourself at the patient's head and open the airway. It may be necessary to clear the airway of obstructions. If appropriate, insert an oropharyngeal airway to help keep the patient's airway open.

2. Connect oxygen to the inlet on the mask and run at 16 liters per minute. If oxygen is not immediately available, do not delay mouth-to-mask ventilations.

3. Position the mask on the patient's face so that the apex (top of the triangle) is over the bridge of the nose and the base is between the lower lip and prominence of the chin. (Center the ventilation port on the patient's mouth.)

4. Hold the mask firmly in place while maintaining head tilt.

5. Take a breath and exhale into the mask port or one-way valve at the top of the mask port. Each ventilation should be delivered over 1 second in adults, infants, and children and be of just enough volume to make the chest rise. Full expansion of the chest is undesirable; the ventilation should cease as soon as you notice the chest moving.

6. Remove your mouth from the port and allow for passive exhalation. Continue as you would for mouth-to-mouth ventilations or CPR.

—adapted from Limmer and O'Keefe, *Emergency Care*, pp. 211–212

You can visualize the process pattern as follows:

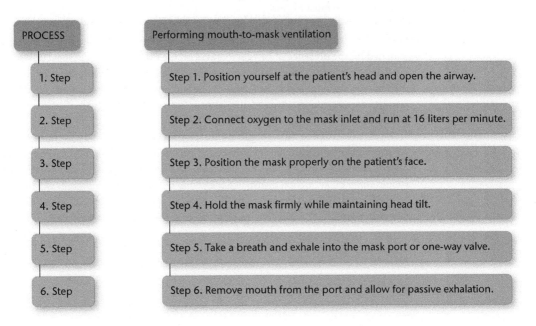

PROCESS

1. Step

2. Step

3. Step

4. Step

5. Step

6. Step

Performing mouth-to-mask ventilation

Step 1. Position yourself at the patient's head and open the airway.

Step 2. Connect oxygen to the mask inlet and run at 16 liters per minute.

Step 3. Position the mask properly on the patient's face.

Step 4. Hold the mask firmly while maintaining head tilt.

Step 5. Take a breath and exhale into the mask port or one-way valve.

Step 6. Remove mouth from the port and allow for passive exhalation.

EXERCISE 7-3 . . . USING PROCESS

Read the following selection and answer the questions that follow.

Issue: Organ Donation

The young motorcyclist was a good candidate for organ donation because he died from a brain injury. People who die from cardiac death can be tissue donors, but the lack of oxygen experienced during cardiac death causes organs to deteriorate, making such people less suitable organ donors. Since many more people will die of cardiac death than brain injury, tissues can be banked for future use, but there is a shortage of organs for use in transplant operations.

If the family agrees, the young man will be kept on a ventilator so that his organs continue to be nourished with oxygen and blood until the organs can be surgically removed. While the organs are being removed, medical personnel will attempt to find the best recipient. To select the recipient, a search of a computerized database is performed. Starting at the top of the list, medical staff will narrow down possible recipients, based in part on how long the recipient has been waiting. People at the top of the waiting list for a given organ tend to be very ill and will die if a transplant does not become available in a matter of days or weeks. These people are often hospitalized or waiting at home or in hotels near the hospital, hoping to receive a call telling them that an organ has become available. Recipients must be located close to the hospital since donor organs cannot be preserved indefinitely; they must be transplanted as soon as possible. Lungs, for instance, can be preserved for around 6 hours before the transplant operation must begin.

Organs donors and recipients must have the same blood type so that the recipient's immune system does not react against the organ. Likewise, donors and recipients are matched for the presence of certain markers on the surface of their tissues. When it has been determined that blood and marker types of donor and recipient are a close enough match, a transplant may occur. The most commonly transplanted organs are the liver, kidney, heart, and lungs. Around 10% of people on waiting lists for replacement organs will die before one becomes available.

If you would like to be an organ donor, discuss your plans with your family. Even if you carry a signed organ donor card and indicate your preference to be a donor on your driver's license, your family will need to agree to donate your tissues and organs. If you should suffer an accidental death, like the young motorcyclist, your family will be forced to make many difficult decisions quickly. Having a discussion about organ donation now will relieve them of the burden of trying to make this decision for you.

—Belk and Maier, *Biology*, pp. 435–436

1. Which processes does this passage explain?

   _____

   _____

2. Highlight each topic sentence.

3. What is the best way to ensure that someone who needs your organs receives them after you die?

   _____

   _____

4. How many steps are involved in the process? List them on your own paper.

5. Underline each of the transition words and phrases used in the passage, both those suggesting process and others, as well.

Writing Process Paragraphs

There are two types of process paragraphs—a "how-to" paragraph and a "how-it-works" paragraph. When writing process paragraphs, it is sometimes acceptable to write in the second person (you), but it is not acceptable to use the second person when writing in other patterns.

- **"How-to" paragraphs explain how something is done.** For example, they may explain how to change a flat tire, aid a choking victim, or locate a reference source in the library.

- **"How-it-works" paragraphs explain how something operates or happens.** For example, they may explain the operation of a pump, how the human body regulates temperature, or how children acquire speech.

Here are examples of both types of paragraphs. The first explains how to wash your hands in a medical environment. The second describes how hibernation works. Be sure to study the idea map for each.

"How-To" Paragraph

Washing your hands may seem a simple task, but in a medical environment it is your first defense against the spread of disease and infection, and it must be done properly. Begin by removing all jewelry. Turn on the water using a paper towel, thus avoiding contact with contaminated faucets. Next, wet your hands under running water and squirt a dollop of liquid soap in the palm of your hand. Lather the soap, and work it over your hands for two minutes. Use a circular motion, since it creates friction that removes dirt and organisms. Keep your hands pointed downward, so water will not run onto your arms, creating further contamination. Use a brush to clean under your fingernails. Then rinse your hands, reapply soap, scrub for one minute, and rinse again thoroughly. Dry your hands using a paper towel. Finally, use a new dry paper towel to turn off the faucet, protecting your hands from contamination.

Idea Map

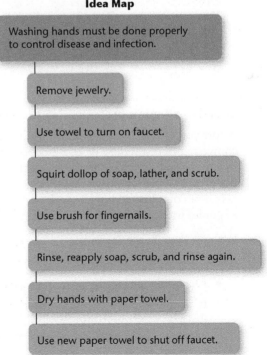

Washing hands must be done properly to control disease and infection.

Remove jewelry.

Use towel to turn on faucet.

Squirt dollop of soap, lather, and scrub.

Use brush for fingernails.

Rinse, reapply soap, scrub, and rinse again.

Dry hands with paper towel.

Use new paper towel to shut off faucet.

"How-It-Works" Paragraph

Hibernation is a biological process that occurs most frequently in small animals. The process enables animals to adjust to a diminishing food supply. When the outdoor temperature drops, the animal's internal thermostat senses the change. Then bodily changes begin to occur. First, the animal's heartbeat slows, and oxygen intake is reduced by slowed breathing. Metabolism is then reduced. Food intake becomes minimal. Finally, the animal falls into a sleeplike state during which it relies on stored body fat to support life functions.

Idea Map

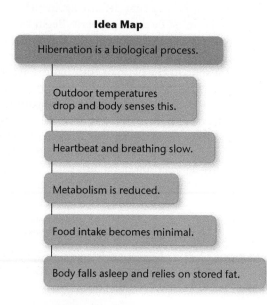

- Hibernation is a biological process.
- Outdoor temperatures drop and body senses this.
- Heartbeat and breathing slow.
- Metabolism is reduced.
- Food intake becomes minimal.
- Body falls asleep and relies on stored fat.

Selecting a Topic and Generating Ideas

Before you can describe a process, you must be very familiar with it and have a complete understanding of how it works. Begin developing your paragraph by listing the steps in the order in which they must occur. It is helpful to visualize the process. For how-to paragraphs, imagine yourself actually performing the task. For complicated how-it-works descriptions, draw diagrams and use them as guides in identifying the steps and putting them in the proper order.

Writing Your Topic Sentence

For a process paragraph, your topic sentence should accomplish two things:

- It should identify the process or procedure.
- It should explain to your reader *why* he or she should learn about the process. Your topic sentence should state a goal, offer a reason, or indicate what can be accomplished by using the process.

Here are two examples of topic sentences that contain both of these important elements.

> • Reading maps, a vital skill if you are orienteering, is a simple process, except for the final refolding.
>
> • Because leisure reading encourages a positive attitude toward reading in general, every parent should know how to select worthwhile children's books.

EXERCISE 7-4 . . . REVISING TOPIC SENTENCES

Working with a classmate, revise these topic sentences to make clear why the reader should learn the process in each.

1. Making pizza at home involves five steps.
2. Making a sales presentation requires good listening and speaking skills.
3. Most people can easily learn to perform the Heimlich Maneuver on choking victims.
4. The dental hygienist shows patients how to use dental floss.
5. Here's how to use Tumblr.

Developing and Sequencing Your Ideas

Because your readers may be unfamiliar with your topic, try to include helpful information that will enable them to understand (for how-it-works paragraphs) and follow or complete the process (for how-to paragraphs). Consider including the following:

- **Definitions.** Explain terms that may be unfamiliar. For example, explain the term *bindings* when writing about skiing.
- **Needed equipment.** For how-to paragraphs, tell your readers what tools or supplies they will need to complete the process. For a how-to paragraph on making chili, include the ingredients.
- **Pitfalls and problems.** Alert your reader about potential problems and places where confusion or error may occur. Warn your chili-making readers to add chili peppers gradually and to taste along the way so the chili doesn't get too spicy.

Use the following tips to develop an effective process paragraph:

DEVELOPING A PROCESS PARAGRAPH

1. **Place your topic sentence first.** This position provides your reader with a purpose for reading.
2. **Present the steps in a process in the order in which they happen.**
3. **Include only essential, necessary steps.** Avoid comments, opinions, or unnecessary information because they may confuse your reader.
4. **Assume that your reader is unfamiliar with your topic** (unless you know otherwise). Be sure to define unfamiliar terms and describe clearly any technical or specialized tools, procedures, or objects.
5. **Use a consistent point of view.** Use either the first person (*I*) or the second person (*you*) throughout. Don't switch between them. (Note: Process is the *only* pattern in which it is acceptable to use the second person.)

Using Transitions

Transition words in process paragraphs lead your reader from one step to the next (see p. 170 for a list of common process transitions). In the following paragraph, notice how each of the highlighted transition words announces that a new step is to follow:

Do you want to teach your children something about their background, help develop their language skills, *and* have fun at the same time? Make a family album together! First, gather the necessary supplies: family photos, sheets of colored construction paper, yarn, and glue. Next, fold four sheets of paper in half; this will give you an eight-page album. Unfold the pages and lay them flat, one on top of the other. After you've evened them up, punch holes at the top and bottom of the fold, making sure you get through all four sheets. Next, thread the yarn through the holes. Now tie the yarn securely and crease the paper along the fold. Finally, glue a photo to each page. After the glue has dried, have your child write the names of the people in the pictures on each page and decorate the cover. Remember to talk to your children about the people you are including in your album. Not only will they learn about their extended family, but they also will have great memories of doing this creative project with you.

EXERCISE 7-5 . . . WRITING A PROCESS PARAGRAPH

Think of a process or procedure you are familiar with, or select one from the following list. Using the guidelines presented in this section, write a process paragraph on the topic.

1. how to waste time
2. how to learn to like _____
3. how the NFL football draft works
4. how to protect your right to privacy
5. how to improve your skill at _____

6. how to remember names
7. how to give directions
8. how to parallel park
9. how to paint a room
10. how to deliver bad news

7c   READING AND WRITING DEFINITION

LEARNING OBJECTIVE 3
Read and write definition

Each academic discipline, field of study, and business has its own specialized vocabulary. Consequently, **definition**—providing explanations of the meaning of terms or concepts—is a commonly used pattern throughout most introductory-level college texts. Definition is also used in general-interest magazines to help readers become familiar with new ideas and concepts; for example, if *Time* publishes an article about *gerrymandering* (the process of changing boundaries of voting districts to favor a particular candidate or political party), you can expect the author to define the term early in the article.

Reading Definition Paragraphs

Definitions are generally provided using the following format.

- The first part of the definition tells what general class or group the term belongs to.
- The second part tells what distinguishes the term from other items in the same class or category.
- The third part includes further explanation, characteristics, examples, or applications.

So if a writer was asked to define the word *actuary*, she might say this:

An actuary belongs to the class of people who work with numbers (*class/group the term belongs to*). Unlike others, such as accountants, an actuary focuses on compiling and working with statistics (*distinguishes an actuary from others who work with numbers*) and works with insurance companies to help them understand risks and calculate insurance premiums (*further explanations and examples*).

See how the term *squatter settlement* is defined in the following paragraph, and notice how the term and the general class are presented. The remainder of the paragraph presents the distinguishing characteristics of squatter settlements. Sometimes writers use typographical aids, such as *italics*, **boldface**, or color to emphasize the term being defined. Here is an example.

Issue: Squatter Settlements

Term

General class

Distinguishing
characteristics
{

Overurbanization, or the too-rapid growth of cities, often results in **squatter settlements**, illegal developments of makeshift housing on land neither owned nor rented by their inhabitants. Such settlements are often built on steep hillsides or even on river floodplains that expose the occupants to the dangers of landslide and floods. Squatter settlements also are often found in the open space of public parks or along roadways, where they are regularly destroyed by government authorities, usually to be quickly rebuilt by migrants who have no other alternatives.

—Rowntree et al., *Diversity Amid Globalization*, p. 26

You can visualize the definition pattern as follows:

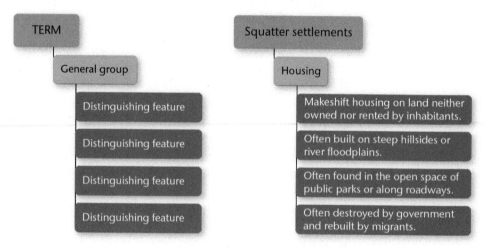

Writers often provide transitions that signal the organizational pattern being used. These transitions may occur within single sentences or as connections between sentences. (Transition words are italicized in the box below.)

COMMON DEFINITION TRANSITIONS

Genetics *is* . . .
Bureaucracy *means* . . .
Patronage *refers to* . . .

Aggression *can be defined* as . . .
Deficit is *another term* that . . .
Balance of power *also means* . . .

EXERCISE 7-6 . . . USING DEFINITION

Read each of the following paragraphs and answer the questions that follow.

A. Issue: Globalization and Cultural Diversity

A pidgin is a language that blends elements of at least two parent languages and that emerges when two different cultures with different languages come in contact and must communicate. All speakers of pidgin have their own native language(s) but learn to speak pidgin as a second, rudimentary language. Pidgins are typically limited to specific functional domains, such as trade and basic social interactions. Many pidgins of the Western Hemisphere were the result of the Atlantic slave trade and plantation slavery. Owners needed to communicate with their slaves, and slaves from various parts of Africa needed to communicate with each other. Pidgins are common throughout the South Pacific.

A pidgin often evolves into a creole, which is a language descended from a pidgin and which subsequently has its own native speakers, a richer vocabulary than a pidgin has, and a more developed grammar. Throughout the Western Hemisphere, many localized creoles have developed in areas such as Louisiana, the Caribbean, Ecuador, and Suriname. Though a living reminder of the heritage of slavery, Creole languages and associated literature and music are also evidence of resilience and creativity in the African diaspora.

—Miller, *Cultural Anthropology in a Globalizing World*, pp. 195–196

1. Highlight the terms being defined.

2. Explain the meaning of the terms in your own words.

   _____

   _____

   _____

3. Where will you find pidgin and creole languages spoken?

   _____

   _____

B. Issue: Health and Wellness

Stress can be associated with most daily activities. Generally, positive stress—stress that presents the opportunity for personal growth and satisfaction—is termed **eustress**. Getting married, successfully kayaking Class II rapids, beginning a career, and developing new friends may all give rise to eustress. **Distress**, or negative stress, is caused by events that result in debilitative stress and strain, such as financial problems, the death of a loved one, academic difficulties, and the breakup of a relationship. Prolonged distress can have negative effects on health.

—Donatelle, *Health*, p. 68

4. What terms are being defined, and what are the definitions?

_____

_____

_____

5. Highlight at least three examples that the author provides to help readers understand the definition of each term.

Writing Definition Paragraphs

Developing a definition paragraph involves writing a topic sentence and adding explanatory details. Be sure to write using the third person (*he, they, Samantha*).

Writing Your Topic Sentence

The topic sentence of a definition paragraph should accomplish two things:

1. It should identify the term you are explaining.
2. It should place the term in a general group. It may also provide one or more distinguishing characteristics.

In the topic sentence below, the term being defined is *psychiatry*, the general group is "a branch of medicine," and its distinguishing feature is that it "deals with mental and emotional disorders."

> Psychiatry is a branch of medicine that deals with mental and emotional disorders.

Adding Explanatory Details

Your topic sentence will usually *not* be sufficient to give your reader a complete understanding of the term you are defining. Explain it further in one or more of the following ways:

1. **Give examples.** Examples can make a definition more vivid and interesting to your reader.
2. **Break the term into subcategories.** Breaking your subject down into subcategories helps to organize your definition. For example, you might explain the term *discrimination* by listing some of its types: racial, gender, and age.
3. **Explain what the term is not.** To bring the meaning of a term into focus for your reader, it is sometimes helpful to give counterexamples, or to discuss in what ways the term means something different from what one might expect. Notice that this student writer does this in the following paragraph on sushi.

> Sushi is a Japanese food consisting of small cakes of cooked rice wrapped in seaweed. While it is commonly thought of as raw fish on rice, it is actually any preparation of vinegared rice. Sushi can also take the form of conical hand rolls and the more popular sushi roll. The roll is topped or stuffed with slices of raw or cooked fish, egg, or vegetables. Slices of raw fish served by themselves are commonly mistaken for sushi but are properly referred to as *sashimi*.

4. **Trace the term's meaning over time.** If the term has changed or expanded in meaning over time, it may be useful to trace this development as a way of explaining the term's current meaning.

5. **Compare an unfamiliar term with one that is familiar to your readers.** If you are writing about rugby, you might compare it to football, a more familiar sport, pointing out characteristics that the two sports share.

Organizing Your Paragraph

Distinguishing characteristics of a term should be logically arranged. You might arrange them from most to least familiar or from more to less obvious, for example. Be sure to use strong transition words and phrases to help your readers follow your presentation of ideas, guiding them from one distinguishing characteristic to another. Useful transition words and phrases are shown on page 178.

EXERCISE 7-7 . . . WRITING A DEFINITION PARAGRAPH

Write a paragraph that defines one of the following terms. Be sure to include a group and distinguishing characteristics.

1. Skype	4. gender identity	7. solar power
2. horror	5. break dancing	8. Snapchat
3. hip-hop	6. cyberattacks	9. millennials

7d   **READING AND WRITING CLASSIFICATION**

LEARNING OBJECTIVE 4
Read and write classification

Classification explains a subject by identifying and describing its types or categories. For instance, a good way to discuss medical personnel is to arrange them into categories: doctors, nurse practitioners, physician's assistants, nurses, technicians, and nurse's aides. If you wanted to explain who makes up your college faculty, you could classify the faculty members by the disciplines they teach (or, alternatively, by length of service, level of skill, or some other factor).

Reading Classification Paragraphs

Textbook writers often use the classification pattern to explain an unfamiliar or complicated topic by dividing it into more easily understood parts. These parts are selected on the basis of common characteristics. For example, a psychology textbook writer might explain human needs by classifying them into two categories, primary and secondary. Or in a chemistry textbook, various compounds may be grouped or classified according to common characteristics, such as the presence of hydrogen or oxygen.

The following paragraph explains horticulture. As you read, try to identify the categories into which the topic of horticulture is divided.

> Horticulture, the study and cultivation of garden plants, is a large industry. Recently it has become a popular area of study. The horticulture field consists of four major divisions. First, there is pomology, the science and practice of growing and handling fruit trees. Then there is olericulture, which is concerned with growing and storing vegetables. A third field, floriculture, is the science of growing, storing, and designing flowering plants. The last category, ornamental and landscape horticulture, is concerned with using grasses, plants, and shrubs in landscaping.

This paragraph approaches the topic of horticulture by describing its four areas or fields of study. You could diagram the paragraph as follows:

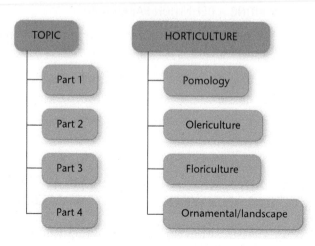

When reading textbook material, be sure you understand *how* and *why* the topic was divided as it was. This technique will help you remember the most important parts of the topic.

Here is another example of the classification pattern:

> A newspaper is published primarily to present current news and information. For large city newspapers, more than 2,000 people may be involved in the distribution of this information. The staff of a large city paper, headed by a publisher, is organized into departments: editorial, business, and mechanical. The editorial department, headed by an editor-in-chief, is responsible for the collection of news and preparation of written copy. The business department, headed by a business manager, handles circulation, sales, and advertising. The mechanical department is run by a production manager. This department deals with the actual production of the paper, including typesetting, layout, and printing.

You could diagram this paragraph as follows:

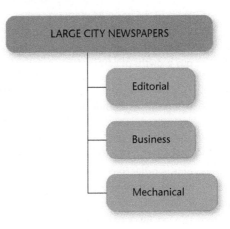

Paragraphs and passages that are organized using classification frequently use transition words and phrases to guide the reader, as shown in the following box.

COMMON CLASSIFICATION TRANSITIONS

another	different stages of	last
another kind	finally	one
classified as	first	second
comprises	include	types of
different groups that	is composed of	varieties of

EXERCISE 7-8 . . . ANALYZING CLASSIFICATION PARAGRAPHS

Read each of the following paragraphs. Then circle the topic and highlight the parts into which each topic is divided.

1.   We can separate the members of the plant kingdom into a mere four types. These are the *bryophytes*, which include mosses; the *seedless vascular plants*, which include ferns; the *gymnosperms*, which include coniferous ("cone-bearing") trees; and the *angiosperms*, a vast division of flowering plants—by far the most dominant on Earth today—that includes not only flowers such as orchids, but also oak trees, rice, and cactus.

—adapted from Krogh, *Biology*, p. 429

2.   The name of the cancer is derived from the type of tissue in which it develops. Carcinoma (carc = cancer; omo = tumor) refers to a malignant tumor consisting of epithelial cells. A tumor that develops from a gland is called an adenosarcoma (adeno = gland). Sarcoma is a general term for any cancer arising from connective tissue. Osteogenic sarcomas (osteo = bone; genic = origin), the most frequent type of childhood cancer, destroy normal bone tissue and eventually spread to other areas of the body. Myelomas (myelos = marrow) are malignant tumors, occurring in middle-aged and older people, that interfere with the blood-cell-producing function of bone marrow and cause anemia. Chondrosarcomas (chondro = cartilage) are cancerous growths of cartilage.

—Tortora, *Introduction to the Human Body*, p. 56

3.   A psychiatric study of 145 Canadian stalkers who had been referred to a forensic psychiatry center for treatment found that most were men (79%) and that many were unemployed (39%). Perhaps not surprisingly, most (52%) had never had an intimate relationship. Five types of stalkers were identified. Rejected stalkers pursue their victims in order to reverse, correct, or avenge a felt rejection (for example, divorce, separation, termination). Wanting to establish an intimate, loving relationship with the victim, intimacy-seeking stalkers may see the victim as a soul mate, someone whom they are fated to be with. Incompetent stalkers have a romantic or sexual interest in the victim despite having poor social or courting skills. Vendetta-motivated stalkers act out revenge based on a perceived wrong or grievance against the victim, and their intent is generally to frighten and distress the victim. Predatory stalkers spy on the victim in preparation for an attack, which is usually sexual in nature.

—adapted from Schmalleger, *Criminology Today*, p. 274

Writing Classification Paragraphs

Developing a classification paragraph involves deciding on a basis of classification for the subject you are discussing, writing a topic sentence, and explaining each subgroup.

Deciding on What Basis to Classify Information

To write a paper using classification, you must first decide on a basis for breaking your subject into subgroups. Suppose you are given an assignment to write about some aspect of campus life. You decide to classify the campus services into groups. You could classify them by benefit, location, or type of facility, depending on what you wanted the focus of your writing to be.

The best way to plan your classification paragraph is to find a good general topic and then brainstorm different ways to break it into subgroups or categories.

EXERCISE 7-9 . . . USING BRAINSTORMING

For three of the following topics, brainstorm to discover different ways you might classify them. Compare your work with that of a classmate and select the two or three most effective classifications.

1. crimes	5. cars	9. phones
2. movies	6. dances	10. TV shows
3. web sites	7. music	11. social media
4. books	8. jobs	12. politicians

Most topics can be classified in a number of different ways. Stores can be classified by types of merchandise, prices, size, or customer service provided, for example. Use the following tips for choosing an appropriate basis of classification:

Tips for Choosing an Appropriate Basis for Classification

- **Consider your audience.** Choose a basis of classification that will interest them. Classifying stores by size may not be as interesting as classifying them by merchandise, for example.

- **Choose a basis that is uncomplicated.** If you choose a basis that is complicated or lengthy, your topic may be difficult to write about. Categorizing stores by prices may be unwieldy, since there are thousands of products sold at various prices.

- **Choose a basis with which you are familiar.** While it is possible to classify stores by the types of customer service they provide, you may have to do some research or learn more about available services in order to write about them.

EXERCISE 7-10 . . . USING BRAINSTORMING

Choose one of the following topics. Brainstorm a list of possible ways to classify the topic.

1. professional athletes or their fans
2. bad drivers
3. diets

4. cell phone users
5. friends
6. junk food

Writing Your Topic Sentence

Once you have chosen a way to classify a topic and have identified the subgroups you will use, you are ready to write a topic sentence. Your topic sentence should accomplish two things:

1. It should identify your topic.
2. It should indicate how you will classify items within your topic.

The topic sentence may also mention the number of subgroups you will use. Here are two examples:

- Three relatively new types of family structures are single-parent families, blended families, and families without children.
- Since working as a waiter, I've discovered that there are three main types of customer complaints.

EXERCISE 7-11 . . . WRITING A TOPIC SENTENCE

For one of the topics in Exercise 7-10, write a topic sentence that identifies the topic and explains your method of classification.

Explaining Each Subgroup

The details in your paragraph should explain and provide further information about each subgroup. Depending on your topic and/or audience, it may be necessary to define each subgroup. If possible, provide an equal amount of detail for each subgroup. If you define or offer an example for one subgroup, you should do the same for each of the others.

Organizing Your Paragraph

The order in which you present your categories depends on your topic. Possible ways to organize the categories include from familiar to unfamiliar, from oldest to newest, or from simpler to more complex. Be sure to use transitions to signal your readers that you are moving from one category to another (see p. 183 for a list of commonly used classification transitions).

EXERCISE 7-12 . . . WRITING A CLASSIFICATION PARAGRAPH

For the topic sentence you wrote in Exercise 7-11, write a classification paragraph. Be sure to identify and explain each group. Use transitions as needed.

7e   READING AND WRITING CAUSE AND EFFECT

LEARNING OBJECTIVE 5
Read and write cause and effect

The **cause and effect** pattern expresses a relationship between two or more actions, events, or occurrences that are connected in time. The relationship differs, however, from chronological order. In the cause and effect pattern, one event leads to another by *causing* it. Information organized with the cause and effect pattern may

- explain causes, sources, reasons, motives, and actions.
- explain the effect, result, or consequence of a particular action.
- explain both causes and effects.

Reading Cause and Effect Paragraphs

Cause and effect is clearly illustrated by the following paragraph, which gives the reasons why fashions occur, the causes of fashion trends.

Issue: Fashions

Why do fashions occur in the first place? One reason is that some cultures, like that of the United States, *value change:* What is new is good. And so, in many modern societies, clothing styles change yearly, while people in traditional societies may wear the same style for generations. A second reason is that many industries *promote* quick changes in fashion to increase sales. A third reason is that fashions usually *trickle down from the top.* A new style may occasionally originate from lower-status groups, as blue jeans did. But most fashions come from upper-class people, who like to adopt some style or artifact as a badge of their status. They cannot monopolize most status symbols for long, however. Their style is adopted by the middle class and may be copied or modified for use by lower-status groups, offering many people the prestige of possessing a high-status symbol.

—Thio, *Sociology*, p. 409

You can visualize the cause and effect pattern as follows:

Many statements expressing cause and effect relationships appear in direct order, with the cause stated first and the effect stated second: "When demand for a product increases, prices rise." However, reverse order is sometimes used, as in the following statement: "Prices rise when a product's demand increases."

The cause and effect pattern is not limited to an expression of a simple one-cause, one-effect relationship. There may be multiple causes, or multiple effects, or both multiple causes and multiple effects. For example, both slippery road conditions and your failure to buy snow tires (causes) may contribute to your car sliding into the ditch or into another car (effects).

In other instances, a chain of causes or effects may occur. For instance, failing to set your alarm clock may force you to miss your 8:00 a.m. class, which in turn may cause you to miss a quiz, which may result in a penalty grade. This sequence is known as a causal chain. The following box lists transition words used in cause and effect writing.

COMMON CAUSE AND EFFECT TRANSITIONS

as a result	due to	for this reason	therefore
because	for	one cause is	thus
because of	hence	one reason is	
cause is	one result is	since	
consequently	results in	stems from	

EXERCISE 7-13 . . . USING CAUSE AND EFFECT

Read each of the following selections and answer the questions that follow.

A. Issue: Health and Fitness

Physical activity is one of the best things you can do for yourself. It benefits every aspect of your health, at every stage of your life. Some of these benefits are purely physical, such as producing a stronger heart and healthier lungs. But physical activity can also put you in a better mood and help you manage stress. Physical activity results in a lower risk of premature death, and as you age it will help postpone physical decline and many of the diseases that can reduce quality of life in your later years.

—adapted from Lynch, Elmore, and Morgan, *Choosing Health*, p. 92

1. What are the purely physical effects of exercise?

_____

_____

2. What are the nonphysical effects of exercise?

_____

3. Underline the transition words used in the paragraph.

B. Issue: Death Rates

Across human history and around the world, there has been a gradual decrease in death rates. In developed countries, public health practices and medical advances since the 19th century have lowered the number of deaths caused by pathogens, disease-causing organisms that enter and multiply in the body. As a result, these populations are more likely to die from noninfectious degenerative diseases that occur as the human body ages. For example, in 1900, the leading causes of death in the United States were infectious or parasitic diseases: pneumonia, tuberculosis, and diarrhea. Today, the leading causes of death are heart disease, cancer, and stroke.

Decreases in the crude rate also contribute to population growth. A lower death rate causes an increase in life expectancy, which is the average number of years that a newborn baby within a given population can expect to live. Since the 1950s, crude death rates dropped from over 20 per 1,000 to 8 per 1,000 in 2014. As a result, life expectancy increased from 48 to 68 years, increasing the number of people alive at any moment in time. The continued decrease in death rates is due to improved nutrition and access to modern medicine. Even in the world's poorest countries, infant mortality rates are dropping because antibiotics and immunizations that today help many babies survive were not available in the past. Modern medicine also keeps older people alive longer, and the combined effect of lowering infant mortalities and people living longer expands life expectancy. Today, life expectancies are lengthening fast in most of the world.

—Dahlman and Renwick, *Geography*, p. 225

4. Why are death rates declining? _____

_____

5. Why are life expectancies increasing? _____

_____

6. Underline the transition words used in the passage.

Writing Cause and Effect Paragraphs

Writing a cause and effect paragraph involves writing a clear topic sentence that indicates whether you are talking about causes, effects, or both; organizing supporting details; and using transition words.

Writing Your Topic Sentence

To write effective topic sentences for cause and effect paragraphs, do the following:

1. **Clarify the cause and effect relationship.** Before you write, carefully identify the causes and the effects. If you are uncertain, divide a sheet of paper into two columns. Label one column "Causes" and the other "Effects." Brainstorm about your topic, placing each idea in the appropriate column.

2. **Decide whether to emphasize causes or effects.** In a single paragraph, it is best to focus on either causes or effects—not both. For example, suppose you are writing about students who drop out of college. You need to decide whether to discuss why they drop out (causes) or what happens to students who drop out (effects). Your topic sentence should indicate whether you are going to emphasize causes or effects. (In essays, you may consider both causes and effects.)

3. **Determine whether the events are related or independent.** Analyze the causes or effects to discover whether they occurred as part of a chain reaction or whether they are not related to one another. Your topic sentence should suggest the type of relationship about which you are writing. If you are writing about a chain of events, your topic sentence should reflect this—for example, "A series of events led up to my sister's decision to drop out of college." If the causes or effects are not related to one another, then your sentence should indicate that—for example, "Students drop out of college for a number of different reasons."

Now read the following paragraph that a sales representative wrote to her regional manager to explain why she had failed to meet a monthly quota. Then study the diagram that accompanies it. Notice that the topic sentence makes it clear that she is focusing on the causes (circumstances) that led to her failure to make her sales quota for the month.

> In the past, I have always met or exceeded my monthly sales quota at Thompson's Office Furniture. This January I was $20,000 short, due to a set of unusual and uncontrollable circumstances in my territory. The month began with a severe snowstorm that closed most businesses in the area for most of the first week. Travel continued to be a problem the remainder of the week, and many purchasing agents did not report to work. Once they were back at their desks, they were not eager to meet with sales reps; instead, they wanted to catch up on their backlog of paperwork. Later that month, an ice storm resulted in power losses, again closing most plants for almost two days. Finally, some of our clients took extended weekends over the Martin Luther King holiday. Overall, my client contact days were reduced by more than 26%, yet my sales were only 16% below the quota.

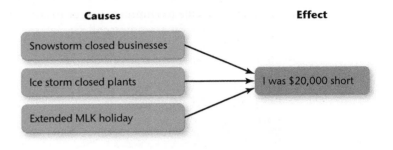

Causes		Effect
Snowstorm closed businesses		I was $20,000 short
Ice storm closed plants		
Extended MLK holiday		

EXERCISE 7-14 ... WRITING TOPIC SENTENCES

Select one of the topics below, and write a topic sentence for a paragraph that will explain either its causes or effects.

1. Spending too much time on a computer
2. Texting while driving
3. The popularity of superhero films
4. Rising cost of attending college
5. Eating locally grown food

Providing Supporting Details

Providing supporting details for cause and effect paragraphs requires careful thought and planning. Details must be relevant, sufficient, and effectively organized.

Provide Relevant and Sufficient Details

Each cause or effect you describe must be relevant to the situation introduced in your topic sentence. Suppose you are writing a paragraph explaining why you are attending college. Each sentence must explain this topic. You should not include ideas about how college is different from what you expected. If you discover you have more ideas about how college is different from what you expected than you do about your reasons for attending college, you need to revise your topic sentence in order to refocus your paragraph.

Each cause or reason requires explanation, particularly if it is *not* obvious. For example, it is not sufficient to write, "One reason I decided to attend college was to advance my position in life." This sentence needs further explanation. For example, you could discuss the types of advancement (financial, job security, job satisfaction) you hope to attain. Jot down a list of the causes or reasons you plan to include. This process may help you think of additional causes and will give you a chance to consider how to explain or support each one. You might decide to eliminate one or to combine several. Here is one student's list of reasons for attending college.

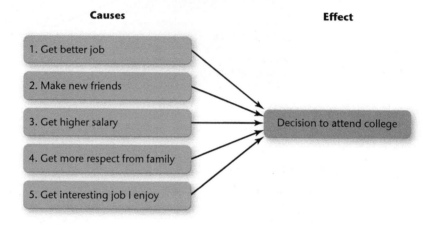

Causes

1. Get better job
2. Make new friends
3. Get higher salary
4. Get more respect from family
5. Get interesting job I enjoy

Effect

Decision to attend college

By listing his reasons, this student realized that the first one—to get a better job—was too general and was covered more specifically later in the list, so he eliminated it. He also realized that "get higher salary" and "get interesting job" could be combined. He then wrote the following paragraph:

> There are three main reasons I decided to attend Ambrose Community College. First, and most important to me, I want to get a high-paying, interesting job that I will enjoy. Right now, the only jobs I can get pay minimum wage, and as a result, I'm working in a fast food restaurant. This kind of job doesn't make me proud of myself, and I get bored with routine tasks. Second, my parents have always wanted me to have a better job than they do, and I know my father will not respect me until I do. A college degree would make them proud of me. A third reason for attending college is to make new friends. It is hard to meet people, and everyone in my neighborhood seems stuck in a rut. I want to meet other people who are interested in improving themselves like I am.

Organize Your Details

There are several ways to arrange the details in a cause and effect paragraph. The method you choose depends on your purpose, as well as your topic. To write a paragraph about the effects of a coastal hurricane, you might use one of the following arrangements:

- **Chronological.** Arrange your details in the order in which they happened.
- **Order of importance.** Arrange your details from least to most important or from most to least important. In describing the effects of the hurricane, you could discuss the most severe damage first and then describe lesser

damage. Alternatively, you could build up from the least to the most important damage for dramatic effect.

- **Spatial.** Arrange your details by physical or geographical position. In describing the hurricane damage, you could start by describing damage to the beach and work toward the center of town.

- **Categorical.** Divide your topic into parts and categories to describe hurricane damage, recounting details of what the storm did to businesses, roads, city services, and homes.

Each arrangement has a different emphasis and achieves a different purpose. Once you decide on a method of organization, study your list of effects again, make changes, eliminate or combine, and then renumber.

Using Transitions

To blend your details smoothly, use transition words and phrases. The student paragraph on page 192 is a good example of how transitional words and phrases are used to identify each separate reason. Some common transition words for the cause and effect pattern are listed on page 188.

EXERCISE 7-15 . . . WRITING A CAUSE AND EFFECT PARAGRAPH

Choose one of the following topic sentences and develop a paragraph using it. Organize your paragraph by using one of the methods described above.

1. Exercise has several positive (or negative) effects on the body.
2. Professional athletes deserve (or do not deserve) the high salaries they are paid.
3. There are several reasons why parents should reserve time each day to spend with their children.
4. Many students work two or even three part-time jobs; the results are often disastrous.

7f   READING AND WRITING COMPARISON AND CONTRAST

LEARNING OBJECTIVE 6
Read and write comparison and contrast

The **comparison organizational pattern** emphasizes or discusses similarities between or among ideas, theories, concepts, or events. The **contrast pattern** emphasizes differences. When a speaker or writer is concerned with both similarities and differences, a combination pattern called **comparison**

and contrast is used. You can visualize these three variations of the pattern as follows:

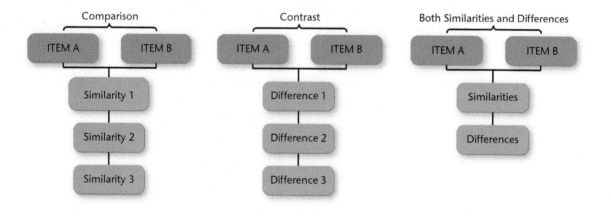

Reading Comparison and Contrast Paragraphs

A contrast is shown in the following selection, which outlines the differences between reptiles and amphibians.

Issue: Reptiles and Amphibians

Although reptiles evolved from amphibians, several things distinguish the two kinds of animals. Amphibians (such as frogs, salamanders, and newts) must live where it is moist. In contrast, reptiles (which include turtles, lizards and snakes, and crocodiles and alligators) can live away from the water. Amphibians employ external fertilization, as when the female frog lays her eggs on the water and the male spreads his sperm on top of them. By contrast, all reptiles employ internal fertilization—eggs are fertilized inside the female's body. Another difference between amphibians and reptiles is that reptiles have a tough, scaly skin that conserves water, as opposed to the thin amphibian skin that allows water to escape. Reptiles also have a stronger skeleton than amphibians, more efficient lungs, and a better-developed nervous system.

—adapted from Krogh, *Biology*, pp. 466-67, 474

A map of this passage might look like this:

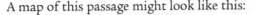

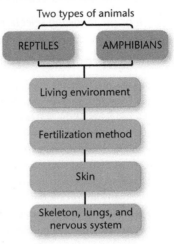

Depending on whether the speaker or writer is concerned with similarities, differences, or both similarities and differences, the pattern might be organized in different ways. To compare the work of two English poets, William Wordsworth and John Keats, each of the following assignments is possible:

1. **Compare and then contrast the two.** That is, first discuss how Wordsworth's poetry and Keats's poetry are similar, and then discuss how they are different.

2. **Discuss by author.** Discuss the characteristics of Wordsworth's poetry, then discuss the characteristics of Keats's poetry, and then summarize their similarities and differences.

3. **Discuss by characteristic.** First discuss the two poets' use of metaphor, next discuss their use of rhyme, and then discuss their common themes.

COMMON COMPARISON TRANSITIONS

Similarities between Wordsworth and Keats . . .
Wordsworth is *as* powerful *as* . . .
Like Wordsworth, Keats ...
Both Wordsworth and Keats ...
Wordsworth *resembles* Keats in that ...

Other transition words of comparison are *in a like manner, similarly, similar to, likewise, correspondingly,* and *in the same way.*

COMMON CONTRAST TRANSITIONS

Unlike Wordsworth, Keats ...
Less wordy *than* Wordsworth ...
Contrasted with Wordsworth, Keats...
Wordsworth *differs from* ...

Other transition words of contrast are *in contrast, however, on the other hand, as opposed to,* and *whereas.*

EXERCISE 7-16 ... USING COMPARISON AND CONTRAST

Read each of the following selections and answer the questions that follow.

A. Issue: Governmental Structure

Congress is bicameral, meaning that it is made up of two houses, the Senate and the House of Representatives. According to the Constitution, all members of Congress must be residents of the states that they have been elected to represent. The Constitution also specifies that representatives must be at least 25 years old and American citizens for 7 years, whereas senators must be at least 30 and American citizens for 9 years. The roles of majority and minority leaders are similar in both houses, and both use committees to review bills and to set their legislative agenda. Despite these similarities, there are many important differences between the two houses. First, the term of office is two years for representatives but six years for senators. Further, each state is guaranteed two senators, but its number of representatives is determined by the state's population; thus the House of Representatives has 435 members and the Senate has 100. Another difference involves procedure: the House places limits on debate, whereas the Senate allows unlimited debate, which sometimes leads to a filibuster.

1. Highlight the two items being discussed.

2. Does this passage mainly use comparison, contrast, or both? ____

3. Explain why the House and Senate have a different number of members.

   _____

   _____

4. List the ways in which the two houses differ.

   _____

   _____

5. Underline the transition words in the paragraph, regardless of the type of organizational pattern they signal.

B. Issue: Environmental Issues and Conservation

Local and regional variation in temperatures produces weather and climate. Climate refers to atmospheric conditions such as temperature, humidity, and rainfall that exist over large regions and relatively long periods of time. In contrast, weather refers to short-term variations in local atmospheric conditions. When we say that Los Angeles will experience a cool, foggy morning and hot afternoon, we're talking about weather. When we say that Southern California has mild, moist winters and hot, dry summers, we are describing the climate of this region.

—Christensen, *The Environment and You*, p. 86

6. Highlight the two things are being compared or contrasted.

7. Which two factors are used to define the difference between weather and climate?

_____

8. Circle the transition phrase that signals the paragraph's primary organizational pattern.

9. Which term would be used to describe a snowstorm that occurred in Chicago in November 2018?

_____

10. Which term would be used to describe the high level of heat but relatively low level of humidity found in Arizona and New Mexico?

_____

Writing Comparison and Contrast Paragraphs

Writing a comparison and contrast paragraph involves identifying similarities and differences between two items, writing a topic sentence that indicates the item you will be comparing and contrasting and your point, organizing your paragraph, developing your points, and using transition words.

Identifying Similarities and Differences

If you have two items to compare or contrast, the first step is to figure out how they are similar and how they are different. Be sure to select subjects that are neither too similar nor too different. If they are, you will have either too little or too much to say. Follow this effective two-step approach:

1. Brainstorm to produce a two-column list of characteristics.
2. Match up the items and identify points of comparison and contrast.

Brainstorm to Identify Points of Comparison and Contrast

Let's say you want to write about two friends—Maria and Vanessa. Here is how to identify their similarities and differences and develop points of comparison and contrast to write about:

1. Brainstorm and list the characteristics of each person.
2. Match up items that share the same point of comparison or contrast—age, personality type, marital status—as shown below.
3. If you list an item in a certain category for one person but not for the other, think of a corresponding detail that will balance the lists.

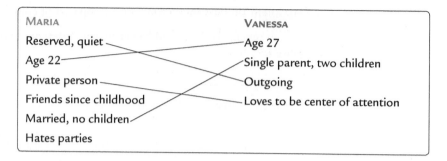

4. Identify points of comparison and contrast by reorganizing the lists so that the items you matched up *appear next to each other*. In a new column to the left of your lists, write the term that describes or categorizes each set of items in the lists. These general categories are your "points of comparison/ contrast," the characteristics you will use to examine your two subjects. As you reorganize, you may find it easier to group several items together. For example, you might group some details about Maria and Vanessa together under the category of personality.

POINTS OF COMPARISON/ CONTRAST	MARIA	VANESSA
Personality	Quiet, reserved, private person	Outgoing, loves to be center of attention
Marital/familial status	Married, no children	Single parent, two children
Length of friendship	Friends since childhood	Met at work last year
Shared activities	Go shopping	Play softball together, go to parties

This two-step process can work in reverse order as well. You can decide points of comparison/contrast first and then brainstorm characteristics for each point. For example, suppose you are comparing and contrasting two restaurants. Points of comparison/contrast might be location, price, speed of service, menu variety, and quality of food.

5. Study your list and decide whether to write about similarities or differences, or both. It is usually easier to concentrate on one or the other. If you see similarities as more significant, you might need to omit or de-emphasize differences—and vice versa if you decide to write about differences.

EXERCISE 7-17 . . . SELECTING A TOPIC AND LISTING POINTS OF COMPARISON/CONTRAST

List at least three points of comparison/contrast for each of the following topics. Then choose one topic and make a three-column list on a separate sheet of paper.

_____

1. Two films you have seen recently
   Points of comparison/contrast: _____

2. Two jobs you have held
   Points of comparison/contrast: _____

3. Baseball and football players
   Points of comparison/contrast: _____

Writing Your Topic Sentence

Your topic sentence should do two things:

- It should identify the two subjects that you will compare or contrast.
- It should state whether you will focus on similarities, differences, or both.

Suppose you are comparing two world religions—Judaism and Hinduism. Obviously, you could not cover every aspect of these religions in a single paragraph. Instead, you could limit your comparison to their size, place of worship, or the type of divine being(s) worshipped, as in the following examples.

- Judaism is one of the smallest of the world's religions; Hinduism is one of the largest.
- Neither Judaism nor Hinduism limits worship to a single location, although both hold services in temples.
- Unlike Hinduism, Judaism teaches belief in only one god.

Be sure to avoid topic sentences that announce what you plan to do such as "I'll compare network news and local news and show why I prefer local news."

Organizing Your Paragraph

Once you have identified similarities and differences and drafted a topic sentence, you are ready to organize your paragraph. There are two ways you can organize a comparison or contrast paragraph:

- Subject-by-subject
- Point-by-point

Subject-by-Subject Organization

In the **subject-by-subject** method, you write first about one of your subjects, covering it completely, and then about the other. Cover the same points of comparison and contrast for both, and in the same order so your paragraph or essay is easy to follow. If you are discussing only similarities or only differences, organize your points within each topic, using a *most-to-least* or *least-to-most* arrangement. If you are discussing both similarities and differences, you might discuss points of similarity first and then points of difference, or vice versa. Here is a sample paragraph using the subject-by-subject method and a map showing its organization:

> Two excellent teachers, Professor Meyer and Professor Rodriguez, present a study in contrasting teaching styles. Professor Meyer is extremely organized. He conducts every class the same way. He reviews the assignment, lectures on the new chapter, and explains the next assignment. He gives essay exams and they are always based on important lecture topics. Because the topics are predictable, you know you are not wasting your time when you study. Professor Meyer's grading depends half on class participation and half on the essay exams. Professor Rodriguez, on the other hand, has an easygoing style. Each class is different and emphasizes whatever she thinks will help us better understand the material. Her classes are fun because you never know what to expect. Professor Rodriguez gives both multiple-choice and essay exams. These are difficult to study for because they are unpredictable. Our final grade is based entirely on the exams, so each exam requires a lot of studying beforehand. Although each professor teaches very differently, I am figuring out how to learn from each particular style.

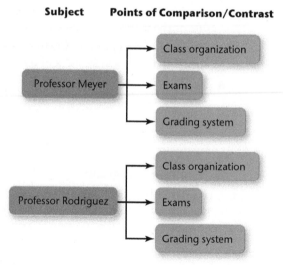

Subject   **Points of Comparison/Contrast**

Professor Meyer — Class organization, Exams, Grading system

Professor Rodriguez — Class organization, Exams, Grading system

Point-by-Point Organization

In the **point-by-point** method of organization, you discuss both of your subjects together for each point of comparison and contrast. When using this organization, maintain consistency by discussing the same subject first for each point. If your paragraph focuses only on similarities or only on differences, arrange your points in a least-to-most or most-to-least pattern. You could move from the simplest to the most complex similarity, or from the most obvious to least obvious difference, for example. Here is a sample paragraph using the point-by-point method and a map showing its organization:

Professor Meyer and Professor Rodriguez demonstrate very different teaching styles in how they operate their classes, how they give exams, and how they grade us. Professor Meyer's classes are highly organized; we work through the lesson every day in the same order. Professor Rodriguez uses an opposite approach. She creates a lesson to fit the material, which enables us to learn the most. Their exams differ too. Professor Meyer gives standard, predictable essay exams that are based on his lectures. Professor Rodriguez gives both multiple-choice and essay exams, so we never know what to expect. In addition, each professor grades differently. Professor Meyer counts class participation as half of our grade, so if you talk in class and do reasonably well on the exams, you will probably pass the course. Professor Rodriguez, on the other hand, counts the exams 100 percent, so you *have* to do well on them to pass the course. Each professor has a unique, enjoyable teaching style, and I am learning a great deal from each.

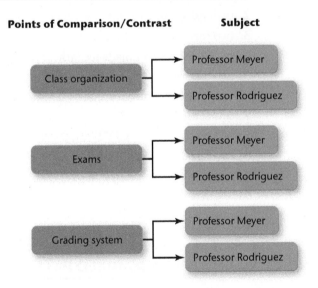

Developing Your Points of Comparison and Contrast

Don't feel as if you must compare or contrast in every sentence. Your paragraph should not just list similarities and/or differences; it should explain them. Give equal attention to each point and each subject. If you give an example for one subject, try to do so for the other as well.

Using Transitions

Transition words are particularly important in comparison and contrast writing. Because you are discussing two subjects and covering similar points for each, your readers can easily become confused, so use the list of transition words and phrases on page 195.

Note that each method of organization uses different transitions in different places. If you choose a subject-by-subject organization, you'll need the strongest transition in the middle of the paragraph, when you switch from one subject to another. You will also need a transition each time you move from one point to another while still on the same subject.

If you choose point-by-point organization, use transitions as you move from one subject to the other. On each point, your reader needs to know quickly whether the two subjects are similar or different.

EXERCISE 7–18 . . . WRITING A COMPARISON AND CONTRAST PARAGRAPH

Choose one of the following topics. Using the guidelines presented in the section, write a comparison/contrast paragraph.

1. two courses you are taking
2. two tasks (one difficult, one easy)
3. two forms of communication
4. two decisions you made recently
5. two businesses
6. two types of entertainment
7. two actors you like
8. two cars
9. two restaurants you eat at
10. two jobs you are interested in

7g   READING AND WRITING MIXED PATTERNS

LEARNING OBJECTIVE 7
Read and write mixed patterns

Organizational patterns are often combined. In describing a process, a writer may also give reasons why each step must be followed in the prescribed order. An instructor may define a concept by comparing it with something similar or familiar. Suppose a chapter in your political science textbook opens by stating, "The distinction between 'power' and 'power potential' is an important one in considering the balance of power." You might expect a definition pattern (where the two terms are defined), but you also might anticipate that the chapter would discuss the difference between the two terms (contrast pattern). The longer the reading selection, the more likely it combines multiple patterns of organization.

Reading Mixed Pattern Paragraphs

In the following paragraph, notice how the author combines two patterns: definition and contrast.

Definition
#1 →

Contrast →

Definition
#2 →

> A city's central business district, or CBD, grows around the city's most accessible point, and it typically contains a dense concentration of offices and stores. CBDs grow with the needs of the community; they expand and contract organically as the city grows and changes. In contrast, a master-planned community is a residential suburban development. In master-planned developments, houses are designed to look alike and "match," and the community also offers private recreational facilities (such as tennis courts and swimming pools) for its residents. Often, the community is gated to prevent nonresidents from entering. Weston is a master-planned community that covers 10,000 acres in Florida. In Weston, almost all aspects of the community are controlled and regulated. Shrubs are planted to shield residents from having to look at the interstate highway. Road signs have a uniform style, each in a stylish frame. Weston offers different areas to cater to different incomes and lifestyles. The houses in the Tequesta Point section come with Roman bathtubs, while an even wealthier section provides larger plots of land for people who own horses.

Look back over the examples provided in this chapter and notice that many of them combine more than one organizational pattern. The discussion of organ donation on pages 171–172, for example, combines process and cause and effect. The paragraph on dog training on page 167 uses examples, but it also explores a cause and effect relationship between consistency of commands and canine behavior.

EXERCISE 7-19 . . . USING MIXED PATTERNS

For each of the following topic sentences, anticipate what organizational pattern(s) the paragraph is likely to exhibit. Record your prediction in the space provided.

1. Many people wonder how to tell the difference between the flu and the common cold.

   Pattern: _____

2. Narcissistic personality disorder—in which the sufferer is excessively occupied with himself or herself—usually results from a number of factors working together.

   Pattern: _____

3. GDP, or gross domestic product, is the total value of goods and services produced in a country during a given year.

   Pattern: _____

4. To migrate to the United States legally, an immigrant must follow a strict set of rules.

   Pattern: _____

5. A poor diet and lack of exercise are the leading causes of obesity in the world today.

   Pattern: _____

6. Many of the contestants on *American Idol* share a number of characteristics. They are all fairly young, they are all amateurs, they all cultivate a certain image, and they all believe they are talented.

   Pattern: _____

Writing Mixed Pattern Paragraphs

Individual patterns of organization provide a clear method for organizing and presenting your thoughts. Each of these patterns allows you to focus on one important aspect of the topic. As you think about combining patterns, your paragraph should always have one primary pattern. The main pattern provides the framework for the paragraph. Additional patterns can be used to add further details and information but should not distract your reader from the main pattern.

Choosing a Primary Pattern of Organization for Your Paragraph

There are four main factors to consider when choosing a primary pattern of organization:

- The assignment
- Your purpose
- Your audience
- The complexity of your topic

The Assignment

Analyzing the assignment will help you determine the primary pattern of organization. Look in the assignment for key words and phrases that offer clues. Suppose, for example, you receive the following assignment in your hotel and restaurant management class:

> Choose one of the following beverages and write an essay describing how it is made: espresso, beer, or soda.

The assignment makes it clear that process is required. The key phrase "how it is made" is your clue. The key word *describing* also appears in the assignment, so be sure to include some description. Suppose you choose to write about soda. Your key goal, then, is to organize your essay to focus on the *process* of soda making. Your essay might also include examples of specific types of soda (cola, ginger ale, club soda) or a narrative about John Pemberton, who created Coca-Cola.

Your Purpose

All effective writing achieves a purpose. You can clarify your purpose by asking yourself the following questions:

- What am I trying to accomplish?
- What do I want my readers to understand?

Your Audience

All good writing also takes the audience into account. To help determine the primary pattern of organization for your essay, ask yourself the following questions:

- How much do my readers know about the topic?
- What can I assume about my readers' backgrounds and experiences?
- Who is most likely to read what I've written?

The Complexity of Your Topic

Some topics are simply more complex or more multifaceted than others. Consider the following topics:

- The range of human emotions
- The three branches of the U.S. government: executive, legislative, judicial
- Your bedroom

The bedroom is the simplest topic, and the range of human emotions is the most complicated. For simple topics, you could write effectively using one of the less complicated patterns, such as *description* or *example*. However, for a complicated topic such as human emotions, you choose a pattern that allows for greater depth of analysis, such as *comparison and contrast* (How do conscious feelings differ from subconscious feelings?), *classification* (What are the different kinds of emotions?), or *cause and effect* (What causes depression? What are the effects of depression?).

EXERCISE 7-20 . . . CHOOSING MULTIPLE PATTERNS OF ORGANIZATION

Choose a primary pattern of organization for each of the following writing assignments. Indicate what other patterns you might use and why.

1. Mystery novels are a popular genre and people read them for a variety of reasons. Define mystery novels and give reasons for their popularity.

_____

_____

2. Those who don't travel on airplanes are often unprepared for the demands of air travel. What steps can an inexperienced traveler take to ensure a comfortable airline flight?

_____

_____

3. Two of the most famous American poets are Emily Dickinson and T.S. Eliot. How did each poet approach the writing of poetry? In what ways are the poems of Dickinson and Eliot similar? In what ways are they different?

_____

_____

_____

EXERCISE 7-21 . . . WRITING A MIXED PATTERN PARAGRAPH

Analyze the following writing assignment and answer the questions that follow.

In your psychology class you are studying the causes and effects of stress. Your instructor has given the following writing assignment: Define stress and then choose several stress-producing incidents from your life, briefly describe each, and explain how you coped with each. You may search online to learn more about stress, if needed.

1. Describe your intended audience.

2. What is your purpose for writing?

3. Brainstorm a list of ideas your readers might find helpful or illuminating.

4. Determine a primary pattern of organization for the assignment. Which secondary patterns will you use?

5. Write the paragraph, and then share it with a classmate. Revise and finalize.

SELF-TEST SUMMARY

To test yourself, cover the right column with a sheet of paper and answer the question in the left column. Evaluate each of your answers by sliding the paper down and comparing it with what is printed in the right column.

QUESTION	ANSWER
1 *How do you read and write illustration?*	**Illustration** uses examples—specific instances or situations—to explain a general idea or statement. **As you read**, look for transitions—*for example*, *for instance*, or *such as*—that signal examples are to follow. **As you write**, use vivid, accurate, examples that are typical and familiar for readers, drawing connections between them and your main point, and organizing them logically.
2 *How do you read and write process?*	**Process** focuses on the procedures, steps, or stages by which actions are accomplished and is used to explain how things work and how to perform specific actions. **As you read**, look for numbered or bulleted lists and transitions that indicate a process is being described. **As you write**, identify the process you are describing and why it is important, provide necessary definitions, identify required equipment, provide only the essential steps in a logical order, and note possible problems.
3 *How do you read and write definition?*	In the **definition pattern**, a key word, phrase, or concept is defined and explained. **As you read**, ask what is being defined and what makes it different from other items or ideas. **As you write**, place the term in a general group, break it into categories, explain it with examples, trace its meaning over time, explain what it is not, and compare it with a familiar term.
4 *How do you read and write classification?*	The **classification pattern** explains a topic by dividing it into parts or categories. **As you read**, be sure you understand *how* and *why* the topic was divided as it was. **As you write**, decide on a basis for breaking your topic into subgroups, or categories, that is uncomplicated and with which you are familiar, and consider your audience.

QUESTION	ANSWER
5 *How do you read and write cause and effect?*	The **cause and effect pattern** expresses a relationship between two or more actions, events, or occurrences that are connected in time. One event leads to another by causing it. There may be multiple causes and/or effects. **As you read,** look for explanations of why events occurred and their results and for cause and effect transition words. **As you write,** identify the relationship you are discussing, decide on your emphasis (causes or effects), and determine whether causes and/or effects are related or independent. Provide explanations of your reasons.
6 *How do you read and write comparison and contrast?*	The **comparison pattern** emphasizes or discusses similarities among ideas, theories, concepts, or events. The **contrast pattern** emphasizes differences. Both patterns can be used together, creating the comparison and contrast pattern. **As you read,** identify whether the writer is comparing or contrasting items or doing both, and look for transitions that indicate which pattern is being used. **As you write,** identify the subjects you will compare and/or contrast, decide on what bases you will compare or contrast them, and determine your purpose for writing about them.
7 *How do you read and write mixed patterns?*	**Organizational patterns are often combined** in paragraphs, essays, and longer readings. **As you read,** look for indications (transitions, formatting, type of topic) to identify the overall pattern of a piece of writing and the additional pattern used to support it. **As you write,** use a primary pattern as a framework for your paragraph, using additional patterns to provide further details and information.

8 Writing Essays and Documented Papers

> **LEARNING OBJECTIVES**
>
> Writing Essays
> 1 Understand essay structure
> 2 Generate and organize ideas and plan your essay
> 3 Draft an essay
> 4 Revise your ideas
> 5 Edit and proofread for clarity and correctness
>
> Writing Documented Papers
> 6 Use sources to write essays
> 7 Find and record appropriate sources
> 8 Use sources to support your thesis and develop your essay
> 9 Synthesize sources
> 10 Integrate quotations into your essay
> 11 Document sources using MLA or APA styles

WRITING ESSAYS

8a THE STRUCTURE OF AN ESSAY

LEARNING OBJECTIVE 1
Understand essay structure

An **essay** introduces an idea, states it, explains it, and draws a conclusion about it. Most essays begin with an *introductory paragraph* that states the subject of the essay. It also states the key point the essay will make in the *thesis statement. Supporting paragraphs* contain ideas that explain the when, where, and how of the key point. An essay usually has two or more of these paragraphs, which are linked by transition words and sentences. The *concluding paragraph* ties all the ideas in the essay together in relation to the thesis statement. See Chapter 2, page 58, for an idea map of an essay.

EXAMINING STUDENT WRITING

David Matsui

A good way to learn to read and write essays is to study a model. In this chapter, you will follow David Matsui, a student writer, as he plans, drafts, and revises an essay. The final version of his essay, documented using APA documentation style, is shown below.

David Matsui is a student at Seattle Pacific University. He is pursuing a bachelor's degree in English and communications and hopes to pursue a career in the field of media, perhaps producing movies. He wrote the following essay for his psychology class.

The full title of the paper is centered on the title page. The title is not bolded, underlined, or italicized.

The running head is a shortened version of the title, consisting of 50 characters or fewer, including spaces and punctuation. All letters in the running head are capitalized. The words "Running head" appear only on the title page.

Running Head: THE IAM   1

The iAm: How Certain Brands Inspire the Most Loyal Consumers Ever

David Matsui

Seattle Pacific University

The author's name and university affiliation are centered under the title and double-spaced.

The running head appears flush left on every page, and the page number appears flush right on every page.

THE IAM   2

The iAm: How Certain Brands Inspire the Most Loyal Consumers Ever

Title is centered and is not in capitals, underlined, italicized, or in quotation marks.

1   Why is it that people are willing to pay ridiculous amounts of money for an

iPhone, iMac, or iPad that is functionally comparable to similar smartphones,

desktops, and tablets, and why are these consumers so devoted to them with

a "loyalty beyond reason" (Roberts, 2004)? That phrase belongs to Kevin

Roberts, CEO of advertising agency Saatchi & Saatchi Worldwide, who has

theorized that brand merits alone are an outdated model; the current way to

Set margins at 1" on all sides and double-space throughout.

consumers' wallets is through their hearts. Realizing this, Roberts created the theory of "Lovemarks." A Lovemark is a brand that inspires undying loyalty beyond any rational thinking. Researchers have further defined Lovemarks as a relationship—something to be embraced, not simply bought (Pawle & Cooper, 2006). But is this realistic? Can a company really make a product that you, the consumer, will develop a "relationship" with, and will it affect

Thesis statement ⟶ where your money goes? According to research, the answer is yes. Certain brands create an intimate connection with the consumer that inspires "loyalty beyond reason" and influences consumers' buying decisions.

Topic sentence → 2 Before getting into research results, it would be beneficial to look at how this theory of advertising evolved. The older model for advertising was described by Roberts (2004) in terms of "'ER words': whiter, brighter, cleaner, stronger, fitter"—i.e., words that describe how well a product worked and why it is better or more effective than other products. The problem nowadays is that *everything* works: generic cleaners make clothes clean, any cheap toothpaste will make your teeth cleaner, and one smartphone can call or text just as well as another.

Topic sentence → 3 Because the older model no longer worked, advertisers needed to find a new way to distinguish brands within a sea of "ER words." The solution was to create an emotional connection, something that promises that the brand is special (Roberts, 2004). Roberts offered the example of his own affinity for the Adidas brand. He once entered a store and spent upwards of eight hundred dollars without feeling guilty simply because he loved the brand. When he tried to analyze and rationalize his behavior, he could not discover any explanation other than that he felt the brand spoke strongly to him. For Roberts, his "relationship" with Adidas was intimate, but also mysterious.

THE IAM   4

Topic sentence

4   Researchers Batra, Ahuvia, and Bagozzi (2012) found that "relationship"
not mysterious but quantifiable, based on their extensive interviews with
consumers. Batra et al. (2012) identified several common features of "brand
love," including the qualities of a brand's products (such as a pleasing design
or excellent performance), consumers' use of the brand to reflect who they
are and how they want to be perceived, a sense of a "natural fit" between
consumers and the brand, and the brand's connection to consumers' core
values (p. 2). In other words, we love a brand not only because it looks great
or works well; we love a brand that seems to represent our values and reflect
our identity to the world. Batra et al. (2012) offered the example of the Apple
brand standing for "creativity and self-actualization" (p. 4); thus, consumers
who see themselves as creative connect to the Apple brand because it reflects
their values and helps present them as creative to the world. In fact, it was no
surprise when the researchers discovered that the iPod was rated the most-
loved consumer electronics brand, because it possesses several features of
brand love identified in their research. The iPod reflects a consumer's identity and values by letting consumers personalize the product through their
individual choices in music and applications; furthermore, the iPod's design
encourages "a sense of natural and intuitive fit" (p. 14).

Topic sentence

5   These features of "brand love" form the basis for people's positive attitudes toward a brand and generate strongly held beliefs that affect purchase
decisions. Research by Pawle and Cooper (2006) affirms the theory that buying decisions are based on emotions. Respondents were asked to describe
their feelings about a wide variety of brands, from cars to cereals to magazines

THE IAM   5

to financial services. Research results indicated that a sense of *intimacy* was a key factor in how respondents felt about a brand and in how they made purchasing decisions. In this context, intimacy refers to how "closely in tune" consumers felt with a brand or how meaningful the brand was to them (p. 45). Pawle and Cooper's findings support the Lovemark theory that emotions outweigh rational thinking when consumers make choices about brands, which also helps explain why people are willing to pay so much money for an iPad, iPhone, or iMac. Consumers who feel that they are "in tune" with the Apple brand are influenced by this intimate relationship with the brand when making purchase decisions.

6   That lower case letter "i" at the beginning of so many Apple products may actually represent the factors that lead people to develop brand loyalty: intimacy, individuality, and identity. As Roberts (2004) stated, "There is no reason why Apple should exist in our world, right? ... They charge a premium versus Dell, versus everybody. I mean, hell, they don't even have Microsoft Windows. But it doesn't matter; it's a Lovemark." By combining features such as excellent performance and design with values that resonate with consumers, brands like Apple are able to create a relationship with consumers and generate a consumer fan base beyond reason.

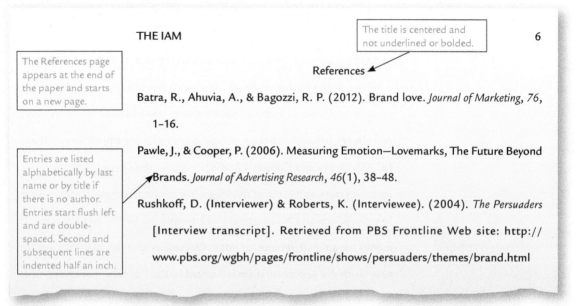

THE IAM

The title is centered and not underlined or bolded.

6

References

The References page appears at the end of the paper and starts on a new page.

Batra, R., Ahuvia, A., & Bagozzi, R. P. (2012). Brand love. *Journal of Marketing, 76,* 1–16.

Pawle, J., & Cooper, P. (2006). Measuring Emotion—Lovemarks, The Future Beyond Brands. *Journal of Advertising Research, 46*(1), 38–48.

Entries are listed alphabetically by last name or by title if there is no author. Entries start flush left and are double-spaced. Second and subsequent lines are indented half an inch.

Rushkoff, D. (Interviewer) & Roberts, K. (Interviewee). (2004). *The Persuaders* [Interview transcript]. Retrieved from PBS Frontline Web site: http:// www.pbs.org/wgbh/pages/frontline/shows/persuaders/themes/brand.html

8b   PREWRITING: GENERATING AND ORGANIZING IDEAS AND PLANNING YOUR ESSAY

LEARNING OBJECTIVE 2
Generate and organize ideas and plan your essay

Writing an effective essay requires thought and planning. Use the following prewriting strategies to help you produce a well-written essay.

Choosing Your Topic and Generating Ideas

When your instructor gives you an assignment, you might not like the topic, but at least a good part of topic selection and narrowing has been done for you. When your instructor allows you to choose your own topic, you have to brainstorm for ideas and explore possible topics using prewriting. (For a detailed discussion, see Chapter 2, page 42).

EXERCISE 8-1 . . . BRAINSTORMING TOPICS

WRITING IN PROGRESS   *Make a list of five possible topics you could use to write a two- to three-page, double-spaced essay.*

Once you have chosen a working topic, the next step is to prewrite to generate ideas about it. This step will help you determine whether the topic you have selected is usable. It will also provide you with a list of ideas you can use in planning and developing your essay. If you have trouble generating ideas about a topic, consider changing topics. Here are four methods for generating ideas. (See pp. 43–45 in Chapter 2 for a review of each.)

1. **Freewriting.** Write nonstop for a specified time, recording all the ideas that come to mind on the topic.
2. **Brainstorming.** Write a list of all ideas that come to mind about a specific topic.
3. **Questioning.** Write a list of questions about a given topic.
4. **Diagramming.** Draw a diagram showing possible subtopics into which your topic could be divided.

When David Matsui was assigned a paper on a topic of his choice, he decided to write about popular brands. To generate ideas, David used brainstorming and wrote the following list of ideas:

Sample Student Brainstorming

Popular brands

What makes a brand popular?

Some of the most popular brands today—Nike, Apple, Amazon, etc.

My favorite brands of clothes, phones, electronics, cars, fast food

What qualities do I look for in a product or brand?

Are big-name brands actually better than brands no one has heard of?

What brands are popular around campus and with my friends?

My parents' favorite brands are not the same as those of my generation—what does age have to do with it?

Advertising strategies for brands are designed to appeal to different types of people

What brands of clothes/electronics/etc. are popular in other countries or cultures?

People spend more for their favorite brands—why?

People become loyal to certain brands and won't try a new brand

Products can be practically identical so why do some brands just seem better?

EXERCISE 8-2 . . . PREWRITING

WRITING IN PROGRESS   *Select one of the topics you listed in Exercise 8-1. Use freewriting, brainstorming, questioning, or branching to generate ideas about the topic.*

Narrowing Your Topic

Avoid working with a topic that is either too broad or too narrow. If your topic is *too narrow*, you will find you don't have enough to write about. If it is *too broad*, you will have too much to say, which will create several related problems. For more information on narrowing your topic, see Chapter 2, pages 46–47.

After studying his brainstorming, David determined that his topic was too broad. The following diagram shows how he further narrowed the topic of popular brands. In this way, he ended up with several manageable topics to choose from and decided to write about what makes people prefer certain brands.

GENERAL TOPIC

MORE SPECIFIC TOPICS

Popular brands

How advertising reinforces the power of certain brands

What makes people prefer certain brands

How brand preferences are different in other cultures

How "generics" actually measure up to popular, big-name brands

---

EXERCISE 8-3 . . . NARROWING TOPICS

WRITING IN PROGRESS *Generate ideas and then narrow one topic you chose for Exercises 8-1 and 8-2. Continue narrowing each one until you find a topic about which you could write a five- to seven-paragraph essay.*

Grouping Ideas to Discover a Thesis Statement

A thesis statement very rarely just springs into a writer's mind: it evolves and, in fact, may change during the process of prewriting, grouping ideas, drafting, and revising. Once you know what you want to write about, the next step is to group or connect your ideas to form a thesis. David discovered more ideas by first freewriting about his topic of what makes people prefer certain brands. As you can see, he wrote more ideas than he needed, but that gave him choices.

Sample Student Freewriting

Why is it that people are willing to pay ridiculous amounts of money for popular "name brands" when they can find basically the same product at a much lower price? I wonder if the big names are actually superior or if it really comes down to superior marketing. I am completely satisfied with my "generic" smartphone, whereas my roommate would never consider anything but an iPhone. Furthermore, he always upgrades his phone when a new one comes on the market, whether he needs a new phone or not. His devotion to the brand means that he spends a lot of money unnecessarily. He could probably buy two new phones with basically the same features for the price of one iPhone, but there seem to be certain qualities that make him loyal to the Apple brand. What makes him, and countless other consumers, develop such a preference for certain brands and products? How does that preference or loyalty affect the way people spend their money?

Writing an Effective Thesis Statement

Think of your thesis statement as a promise; it promises your reader what your paper will deliver. Here are some guidelines to follow for writing an effective thesis statement:

Guidelines for Writing an Effective Thesis Statement

1. **It should state the main point of your essay.**

Too Detailed	A well-written business letter has no errors in spelling.
Revised	To write a grammatically correct business letter, follow three simple rules.

2. **It should assert an idea about your topic.**

Lacks an Assertion	Advertising contains images of both men and women.
Revised	In general, advertising presents men more favorably than women.

3. **It should be as specific and detailed as possible.**

Too General	Advertisers can influence readers' attitudes toward competing products.
Revised	Athletic-shoe advertisers focus more on attitude and image than on the actual physical differences between their product and those of their competitors.

4. **It may suggest the organization of your essay.**

Does Not Suggest Organization	Public school budget cuts will negatively affect education.
Revised	Public school budget cuts will negatively affect academic achievement, student motivation, and the drop-out rate.

5. **It should not be a direct announcement.**

Direct Announcement	The purpose of my paper is to show that businesses lose money due to inefficiency, competition, and inflated labor costs.
Revised	Businesses lose money due to inefficiency, competition, and inflated labor costs.

6. **It should offer a fresh, interesting, and original perspective on the topic.**

Predictable	Circus acts fall into three categories: animal, clown, and acrobatic.
Revised	Each of the three categories of circus acts—animal, clown, and acrobatic—is exciting because of the risks it involves.

After freewriting, David reviewed what he had written and decided to focus his essay on the causes and effects of brand loyalty. He highlighted usable ideas and tried to group or organize them logically: (1) what makes a consumer develop a preference for a brand, and (2) how that preference affects buying decisions. Once he had grouped his ideas into these categories, he wrote a working thesis statement:

Working Thesis Statement	Certain brands create a connection with consumers that inspires loyalty and influences buying decisions.

EXERCISE 8-4 . . . WRITING A WORKING THESIS STATEMENT

WRITING IN PROGRESS *For the topic you narrowed in Exercise 8-3, write a working thesis statement.*

Considering Purpose, Audience, Point of View, and Tone

Before you begin a draft, there are four important factors to consider: *purpose*, *audience*, *point of view*, and *tone*. First determine your purpose, or goal, for writing and focus on how to meet that goal. Then analyze your audience to decide what to say and what type of detail to include. Next decide whether you will express your point of view using first, second, or third person; be sure to stay with the same point of view throughout your essay. Finally, consider your tone and think about how to make it appropriate for your audience. (For more thorough coverage of audience, purpose, point of view, and tone, see Chapter 2, pages 47–48).

EXERCISE 8-5 . . . DEFINING PURPOSE, AUDIENCE, POINT OF VIEW, AND TONE

WRITING IN PROGRESS   *For the topic you chose in Exercise 8-3, define your purpose and audience and select a point of view. Also decide how you want to "sound" to your reader.*

Organizing Ideas Using Outlining and Mapping

Outlining is one good way to organize your ideas, discover the relationships and connections between them, and show their relative importance. The most important ideas are placed closer to the left margin. Less important ideas are indented toward the middle of the page. A quick glance at an outline shows what is most important, what is less important, and how ideas support or explain one another (see Chapter 1, p. 26, for more details).

Another way to write a solid, effective essay is to plan its development using an idea map, a list of the ideas you will discuss in the order in which you will present them. Here is a sample idea map for David's essay on brand loyalty.

Map of David's Essay on Brand Loyalty

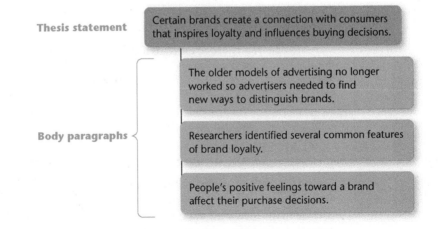

Thesis statement — Certain brands create a connection with consumers that inspires loyalty and influences buying decisions.

Body paragraphs —
- The older models of advertising no longer worked so advertisers needed to find new ways to distinguish brands.
- Researchers identified several common features of brand loyalty.
- People's positive feelings toward a brand affect their purchase decisions.

EXERCISE 8-6 . . . DRAWING A MAP OR OUTLINE

WRITING IN PROGRESS   *For the topic you chose in Exercise 8-3, draw a map or write an outline of your ideas.*

Choosing a Method of Development

Analyzing your audience and purpose will also help you choose which method or methods of development to use—*illustration, process, definition, classification, cause and effect,* or *comparison and contrast* (see Chapter 7 for details). You can select the one that suits your audience and purpose best. See Table 8-1 for a few examples.

TABLE 8-1 CHOOSING A METHOD OF DEVELOPMENT

IF YOUR PURPOSE IS TO . . .	USE . . .
Explain how something works or how to perform a specific task	Process
Explain a topic, using specific examples	Illustration
Explain what something is	Definition
Emphasize similarities or differences between two topics or explain something by comparing it to something already familiar	Comparison and Contrast
Explain why something happened	Cause and Effect

You may also use more than one of these methods of development. You might define a behavior and then offer examples to explain it. Or you might explain how a group of people are classified and argue that the classification is unfair and discriminatory. In David's essay, he decided to use specific examples to explain his topic of brand loyalty. He also used cause and effect to explain what happens as a result of consumers' loyalty toward certain brands.

EXERCISE 8-7 . . . CHOOSING A METHOD OF DEVELOPMENT

WRITING IN PROGRESS   *For the topic you chose in Exercise 8-3, choose a method of development that will best present your point.*

8c   DRAFTING AN ESSAY

LEARNING OBJECTIVE 3
Draft an essay

A **draft** is a tentative or preliminary version of an essay. Drafting involves adding, deleting, and reorganizing content to be sure your essay has a narrow focus, a clear main idea, and adequate supporting details. You should plan to write several drafts before you end up with an essay you are satisfied with. Use the following general suggestions for getting started; then work on drafting each paragraph.

Tips for Writing Essay Drafts

- **Think of drafting as a chance to experiment.** Find out what works and what does not. You might want to write your essay several different ways, trying out different approaches, content, and ways of organizing the information.
- **Focus on ideas, not correctness.** Especially for the first few drafts, concentrate on recording your ideas. Do not worry yet about grammatical errors or sentence structure, for example.
- **Be prepared to make major changes.** Often as your essay develops, you may realize that you want to change direction or that you should further limit your topic. Do not hesitate to do so.

Drafting Body Paragraphs

There are a number of different ways you can begin drafting the body paragraphs for your essay. Some students write an outline; others draw a map; still others write a list of topic sentences that support the thesis. Don't worry too much about the order of the items in your draft. At this point, it is more important to get your ideas down in writing. In later drafts, you can rearrange your ideas.

Once you have identified topics or topic sentences that support your thesis, you are ready to write first-draft paragraphs. These, too, may change, so concentrate primarily on making sure that each topic sentence supports the thesis and that each paragraph has a clear topic sentence, supporting details, and transitions (see Chapters 4 and 5).

Here is a list of topic sentences David wrote for his brand loyalty essay.

- It used to be that advertising models focused on why one product was better than others.
- Since the older advertising model no longer seemed to work, advertisers looked for a new way to distinguish brands.
- Researchers found that the connection between consumers and certain brands actually had quantifiable features.
- These features of brand loyalty form the basis for people's feelings about a brand and affect how they spend their money.
- Additional research supported the idea that buying decisions are based on emotions.

You will see that he changed, added, and expanded these topic sentences as he wrote his first draft, which appears on page 224.

Evaluating and Revising Your Thesis Statement

At various stages in the drafting process, you may decide to rewrite, revise, or completely change your thesis statement. Remember, a thesis statement should explain what your essay is about and also give your readers clues about its organization. You may not know, for example, how your essay will be organized until you have written one or more drafts. Use the following suggestions for making sure your thesis statement is clear and effective.

How to Revise Your Thesis Statement

The best time to evaluate and, if necessary, revise your thesis statement is after you have written a first draft. When evaluating your thesis statement, ask the following questions:

1. **Does my essay develop and explain my thesis statement?** As you write an essay, its focus and direction may change. Revise your thesis statement to reflect any changes. If you discover that you drifted away from your original thesis and want to maintain it, work on revising so that your paper delivers what your thesis promises.

2. **Is my thesis statement broad enough to cover all the points made in the essay?** As you develop your first draft, you may find that one idea leads naturally to another. Both must be covered by the thesis statement. For example, suppose your thesis statement is "Media coverage of national political events shapes public attitudes toward politicians." If, in your essay, you discuss media coverage of international events as well as national ones, then you need to broaden your thesis statement.

3. **Does my thesis statement use vague or unclear words that do not clearly focus the topic?** For example, in the thesis statement "The possibility of animal-organ transplants for humans is interesting," the word *interesting* is vague and does not suggest how your essay will approach the topic. Instead, if your paper discusses both the risks and benefits of these transplants, this approach should be reflected in your thesis: "Animal-organ transplants for humans offer both risks and potential benefits."

EXERCISE 8-8 . . . DRAFTING A THESIS STATEMENT

WRITING IN PROGRESS   *For the topic you chose in Exercise 8-3, draft a thesis statement.*

Supporting Your Thesis with Substantial Evidence

Every essay you write should offer substantial evidence to support the thesis statement. **Evidence** can consist of personal experience, anecdotes (stories that illustrate a point), examples, reasons, descriptions, facts, statistics, and quotations (taken from sources).

Many students have trouble locating *concrete*, specific evidence to support their thesis. Though prewriting yields plenty of good ideas and helps you focus your thesis, prewriting ideas may not always provide sufficient evidence. Often you need to brainstorm again for additional ideas. At other times, you may need to consult one or more sources to obtain further information on your topic (see Section 8f, p. 237).

David realized that he did not have enough specific evidence for his essay on brand loyalty. Table 8-2 lists ways to support and explain a thesis statement and gives an example of how David could use each in his essay. He would not need to use all of them, just those appropriate for his audience and purpose. He could also combine different types of evidence, *telling a story* that illustrates the *effects* of refusing to consider alternative brands, for instance.

TABLE 8-2 WAYS TO ADD EVIDENCE	
TOPIC: BRAND LOYALTY	
EXPLAIN YOUR THESIS BY ...	**EXAMPLE**
Telling a story	*Relate a story about a "Lovemark" relationship.*
Adding descriptive detail	*Add a description of a product that has a pleasing design.*
Explaining how something works	*Explain how a person can customize a product such as an iPod to reflect his or her personality.*
Giving an example	*Discuss specific instances of basing purchase decisions on brand loyalty.*
Giving a definition	*Explain the meaning of terms such as* brand merits *or* self-actualization.
Making distinctions	*Contrast the use of brand loyalty in purchase decisions with other factors such as price, convenience, or functionality.*
Making comparisons	*Compare two products, such as an iPhone and a generic smartphone.*
Giving reasons	*Explain why consumers want their brands to reflect their identity.*
Analyzing effects	*Explain how a consumer's brand loyalty may limit his or her product options.*

Use the following guidelines in selecting evidence to support your thesis.

Guidelines for Selecting Evidence

1. **Be sure your evidence is relevant.** That is, it must directly support or explain your thesis.

2. **Make your evidence as specific as possible.** Help your readers see the point you are making by offering detailed, concrete information. For example, if you are explaining the effects of right-to-privacy violations on individuals, include details that make the situation come alive: names of people and places, types of violations, and so forth.

3. **Be sure your information is accurate.** It may be necessary to check facts, verify stories you have heard, and ask questions of individuals who have provided information.

4. **Locate sources that provide evidence.** Because you may not know enough about your topic and lack personal experience, you may be unable to provide strong evidence. When this happens, locate several sources on your topic.

5. **Be sure to document any information that you borrow from other sources.** See Section 8g (pp. 240–244) for further information on crediting sources.

Now let's take a look at how David developed his essay on brand loyalty. As you read, notice, in particular, the types of evidence he uses and how his thesis statement promises what his essay delivers. In this first draft, he uses his free-writing from pages 216–217 and his list of topic sentences on page 221. Once David realized he needed more concrete evidence, he located several sources detailing research on the topic of brand loyalty. He was able to add specific evidence to support his thesis in later drafts, and he was careful to document the information he borrowed from these sources using APA style (see Section 8k).

Sample First Draft Essay

Why is it that people are willing to pay ridiculous amounts of money for popular "name brands" when they can find basically the same product at a much lower price? I am completely satisfied with my "generic" smartphone, whereas my roommate would never consider anything but an iPhone. As a result of his devotion to the brand, he spends a lot of money unnecessarily. He could probably buy two new phones with basically the same features for the price of an iPhone; however, there seem to be certain qualities that make him loyal to the Apple brand. What makes him, and countless other consumers, develop such a preference for certain brands and products? How does that brand loyalty affect the way people spend their money?

Before getting into research results, though, it would be beneficial to look at how this theory of advertising evolved. It used to be that advertising models focused on why one product was better or more effective than others. The problem nowadays is that everything works: generic cleaners make clothes clean, any cheap toothpaste will make your teeth cleaner, and one smartphone can call or text just as well as any another.

Since the older advertising model no longer seemed to work, advertisers looked for a new way to distinguish brands. One theory involved creating a way to reach consumers by establishing an emotional connection. In this theory, consumers see their brand as something special, maybe even mysterious.

Researchers found that the connection between consumers and certain brands actually had quantifiable features. Research showed that there were common traits (for example, a nice design or good performance) that consumers look for in a brand they love. In addition, research indicated that brands are a way for us to reflect how we perceive ourselves and how we wish to be perceived; brands connected with consumers when the brands were shown equating with similar values as that of their consumers. In other words, we love a brand not only because it looks great or works well; we love a brand that seems to represent our values and reflect our identity to the world.

These features of brand loyalty form the basis for people's feelings about a brand and affect how they spend their money. People form strongly held beliefs that affect their purchase decisions. For example, if shopper A's contract is about to renew and they have a pick of free smartphones or a big brand name that will cost them an additional two hundred dollars, which will they choose? The brand they just discovered existed or maybe the brand they have heard of? No, they will choose the expensive brand they have strong belief in. Because it is the brand that they naturally fit with, the brand they believe connects with who they want to be seen as, the brand that stands for what they believe in. These positive attitudes can also affect how we respond towards a brand, including rejecting negative information about it. In the case of the iPod, the consumer believes their values systems are similar, adapts the product into their persona and rejects any criticism of the product as a criticism of them.

Additional research supports the idea that buying decisions are based on emotions. People were asked to describe their feelings about car, cereal and magazine brands, some of the products being more popular and well known and others less so. Research showed that emotions greatly outweigh rational thinking when making choices about brands. In other words, if a consumer connects with a brand in the way described above they are a lot more likely to stick with that brand when making future purchases. That would explain why people are willing to pay lots of money for a luxury item such as an Apple product.

By establishing a brand with great performance and values that reflect a consumer's identity, Apple and other brands have created a relationship with consumers and a fan base beyond reason. Who knew that adding a lower case letter "i" before things would cause people to spend lots more money?

EXERCISE 8-9 . . . WRITING A FIRST DRAFT

WRITING IN PROGRESS *Write a first draft of an essay for the working thesis statement you wrote in Exercise 8-4 (p. 218). Support your thesis statement with at least three types of evidence.*

Using Transitions to Make Connections Among Your Ideas Clear

To produce a well-written essay, be sure to make it clear how your ideas relate to one another. There are several ways to do this:

1. **Use transitional words and phrases.** To help your essay flow smoothly and communicate clearly, use transitional words and phrases. Table 8-3 lists useful transitional words for each method of organization. Notice the use of these signal words and phrases in David's first draft: *however, though, for example, in addition, as a result.*

2. **Write a transitional sentence.** Usually the first sentence in the paragraph, the transitional sentence links the paragraph in which it appears to the previous paragraph.

3. **Repeat key words.** Repeating key words, which often appear in the thesis statement, helps your reader remember the thesis and how each idea is connected to it. You need not repeat the word or phrase exactly as long as the meaning stays the same. You could substitute "keeps your audience on target" for "enables your reader to stay on track," for example.

TABLE 8-3 USEFUL TRANSITIONAL WORDS AND PHRASES

TYPE OF CONNECTION	TRANSITIONAL WORDS AND PHRASES
Importance	*most important, above all, especially, particularly important*
Spatial relationships	*above, below, behind, beside, next to, inside, outside, to the west (north, etc.), beneath, near, nearby, next to, under, over*
Time sequences	*first, next, now, before, during, after, eventually, finally, at last, later, meanwhile, soon, then, suddenly, currently, after, afterward, after a while, as soon as, until*
Recounting events or steps	*first, second, then, later, in the beginning, when, while, after, following, next, during, again, after that, at last, finally*
Examples	*for example, for instance, to illustrate, in one case*
Types	*one, another, second, third*
Definitions	*means, can be defined as, refers to, is*
Similarities	*likewise, similarly, in the same way, too, also*
Differences	*however, on the contrary, unlike, on the other hand, although, even though, but, in contrast, yet*
Causes or results	*because, consequently, since, as a result, for this reason, therefore, thus*
Restatement	*in other words, that is*
Summary or conclusion	*finally, to sum up, all in all, evidently, in conclusion*

EXERCISE 8-10 . . . ANALYZING A DRAFT

WRITING IN PROGRESS   *Review the draft you wrote for Exercise 8-9. Analyze how effectively you have connected your ideas. Add key words or transitional words, phrases, or sentences, as needed.*

Writing the Introduction, Conclusion, and Title

The introduction, conclusion, and title each serve a specific function. Each strengthens your essay and helps your reader understand your ideas.

Writing the Introduction

An **introductory paragraph** has three main purposes:

- It presents your thesis statement.
- It interests your reader in your topic.
- It provides any necessary background information.

Although your introductory paragraph appears first in your essay, it does *not* need to be written first. In fact, it is sometimes best to write it last, after you have developed your ideas, written your thesis statement, and drafted your essay. Here are some suggestions on how to first interest your readers in your topic.

TABLE 8-4 TECHNIQUES FOR WRITING INTRODUCTIONS	
TECHNIQUE	**EXAMPLE**
Ask a provocative or controversial question.	*What would you do if you discovered that your next-door neighbor was in the witness protection program?*
State a startling fact or statistic.	*Did you know that despite the increasing risk of identity theft, the top two passwords in the world are "123456" and "password"?*
Begin with a story or an anecdote.	*When Mara Delaney decided to join the Army, little did she know it would set her on a path to becoming one of the first women to attend Ranger School.*
Use a quotation.	*As Junot Díaz wrote in* The Brief Wondrous Life of Oscar Wao, *"It's never the changes we want that change everything."*
State a little-known fact, a myth, or a misconception.	*It's hard to lose weight and even harder to keep it off. Right? Wrong! A sensible eating program will help you lose weight.*

An introduction should also provide the reader with any necessary background information. You may, for example, need to define the term *genetic engineering* for a paper on that topic. At other times, you might need to provide a brief history or give an overview of a controversial issue.

For his essay, David decided to introduce the topic of brand loyalty by asking a question: *Why is it that people are willing to pay ridiculous amounts of money for popular "name brands" when they can find basically the same product at a much lower price?* He then elaborated on his topic in the introduction with a story about his roommate's devotion to the Apple brand.

EXERCISE 8-11 . . . WRITING/REVISING THE INTRODUCTION

WRITING IN PROGRESS *Write or revise your introduction to the essay you drafted in Exercise 8-9.*

Writing the Conclusion

The final, **concluding paragraph** of your essay has two functions: it should reemphasize your thesis statement and draw the essay to a close. It should not be a direct announcement, such as "This essay has been about" or "In this paper, I hoped to show that." It's usually best to revise your essay *at least once before* working on the conclusion. During your first or second revision, you often make numerous changes in both content and organization, which may, in turn, affect your conclusion.

Ways to Write an Effective Conclusion   Here are a few effective ways to write a conclusion. Choose one that will work for your essay:

1. **Suggest a direction for further thought.** Raise a related issue that you did not address in your essay, or ask a series of questions.

2. **Look ahead.** Project into the future and consider outcomes or effects.

3. **Return to your thesis.** If your essay is written to prove a point or convince your reader of the need for action, it may be effective to end with a sentence that recalls your main point or calls for action. If you choose this way to conclude, don't merely repeat your first paragraph. Be sure to reflect on the thoughts you developed in the body of your essay.

4. **Summarize key points.** Especially for longer essays, briefly review your key supporting ideas. In shorter essays, this tends to be unnecessary.

5. **Make sure your conclusion does not contain new supporting details.** If you have trouble writing your conclusion, you may need to work further on your thesis or organization.

In the conclusion of his first draft, David decided to return to his thesis, recalling his main point about how certain brands create a relationship with consumers. For his final draft, he revised and improved the conclusion by adding a brief review of key points from his essay.

EXERCISE 8-12 . . . WRITING/REVISING THE CONCLUSION

WRITING IN PROGRESS *Write or revise a conclusion for the essay you wrote for Exercise 8-9.*

Creating a Title

Although the title appears first in your essay, it is often the last thing you should write. The **title** should identify the topic in an interesting way, and it may also suggest the focus of the paper. To select a title, reread your final draft, paying particular attention to your thesis statement and your overall method of development. Here are a few examples of effective titles:

- "Surprise in the Vegetable Bin" (for an essay on vegetables and their effects on cholesterol and cancer)
- "Denim Goes High Fashion" (for an essay describing the uses of denim for clothing other than jeans)
- "Babies Go to Work" (for an essay on corporate-sponsored day-care centers)

Tips for Writing Accurate and Interesting Titles   To write accurate and interesting titles, try the following tips:

1. **Write a question that your essay answers.** For example: "Why Change the Minimum Wage?"
2. **Use key words that appear in your thesis statement.** If your thesis statement is "The new international trade ruling threatens the safety of the dolphin, one of our most intelligent mammals," your title could be "New Threat to Dolphins."
3. **Use brainstorming techniques to generate options.** Don't necessarily use the first title that pops into your mind. If in doubt, try out some options on friends to see which is most effective.

For the title of his essay, David brainstormed several options before deciding on "The iAm: How Certain Brands Inspire the Most Loyal Consumers Ever." He created the term "The iAm" as a clever and thought-provoking reference to key ideas in his essay.

EXERCISE 8-13 . . . SELECTING A TITLE

WRITING IN PROGRESS *Come up with a good title for the essay you wrote for Exercise 8-9.*

8d   REVISING: EXAMINING YOUR IDEAS

LEARNING OBJECTIVE 4
Revise your ideas

Revising is a process of closely evaluating your draft to determine that it says what you want it to say and that it does so in a clear and effective way. Once you have revised your essay, you can move to editing to correct errors.

General Essay Revision Strategies

Here are some general suggestions for revising your final essay draft. Also refer to the Essay Revision Checklist on pages 66–67 and the Paragraph Revision Checklist on page 56.

- **Allow time between finishing your last draft and revising, until the next day, if possible.** When you return to the draft, you will have a clear mind and a new perspective.
- **Look for common problems.** If you usually have trouble, for example, with writing thesis statements or with using transitions, then evaluate these features closely each time you revise.
- **Read the draft aloud.** You may hear ideas that are unclear or realize they are not fully explained.
- **Read a print copy.** Although you may be used to writing on a computer, your essay may read differently when you see a paper copy.
- **Have a friend or classmate read your drafts.** Ask your reviewer to identify and evaluate your thesis statement. Also ask him or her to evaluate how clearly and effectively your essay supports your thesis statement.

Using Revision Maps to Revise

A revision map will help you evaluate the overall flow of ideas as well as the effectiveness of individual paragraphs. To draw an essay revision map, work through each paragraph, recording your ideas in abbreviated form. Then write the key words of your conclusion. If you find details that do not support the topic sentences, or topic sentences that do not support the thesis, record those details to the right of the map (see Chapter 6, p. 151 for more details).

When you've completed your revision map, conduct the following tests:

1. **Read your thesis statement along with your first topic sentence.** Does the topic sentence clearly support your thesis? If not, revise to make the relationship clearer. Repeat this step for each topic sentence.

2. **Read your topic sentences, one after the other, without corresponding details.** Is there a logical connection between them? Are they arranged in the most effective way? If not, revise to make the connection clearer or to improve your organization.

3. **Examine each individual paragraph.** Are there enough relevant, specific details to support the topic sentence?

4. **Read your introduction and then look at your topic sentences.** Does the essay deliver what the introduction promises?

5. **Read your thesis statement and then your conclusion.** Are they compatible and consistent? Does the conclusion agree with and support the thesis statement?

EXERCISE 8-14 . . . DRAWING A REVISION MAP

WRITING IN PROGRESS   *Draw a revision map of the essay you wrote in Exercise 8-9 and make necessary revisions.*

Revising Essay Content and Structure

When you have completed your revision map, you are ready to evaluate your essay's content and organization. If you do not ask yourself the right questions when evaluating your draft, you won't discover how to improve it. Each of the following questions and corresponding revision strategies will guide you in producing a clear and effective final essay.

1. **Does your essay accomplish your purpose?**
   If you are writing in response to an assignment, reread it and make sure you have covered all aspects of it. Delete any sentences or paragraphs that do not fulfill your assignment or stated purpose. Do you have enough ideas left? If not, do additional freewriting to discover new ideas.

2. **Is your essay appropriate for your audience?**
   Visualize your audience reading your essay. How will they respond? If you are not sure, ask a classmate or a person who is part of your audience to read your essay. Then revise your essay with your audience in mind. Add examples that may appeal to them; delete those that would not. Examine your word choice. Have you used language that is understandable and will neither confuse them nor create a negative impression?

3. **Is your thesis statement clearly expressed?**
   Highlight your thesis statement. Does it state the main point of your essay and make an assertion about your topic? If not, write one sentence stating what your essay is intended to explain or show. Use this sentence to help you revise your thesis statement. If you revise your thesis statement, be sure to revise the remainder of your essay to reflect your changes.

4. **Does each paragraph support your thesis?**
   Reread each topic sentence. Does each clearly and specifically explain some aspect of your thesis statement? If not, revise or drop the paragraph. Does

the essay contain enough information to fully explain your thesis and make it understandable to your reader? If not, do additional prewriting to help you discover more ideas. If you are stuck, your thesis statement may be too narrow, or you may need to read more about your topic. Be sure to give credit for any ideas you borrow from print or online sources. (Refer to Section 8g, pp. 240–244.)

5. **Is your essay logically organized?**
   Examine your revision map to be sure your paragraphs are in the right order. If not, rearrange them. Be sure to add sentences or transitions to connect your ideas and show your new organization. Use Table 8-1, "Choosing a Method of Development" (p. 220) to consider different ways you might rearrange your ideas.

6. **Have you used transitions to connect your ideas?**
   Circle all transitional words, phrases, and sentences. Do you use transitions to move from each main point to another? If not, add transitions, referring to Table 8-3 (page 226) as needed.

7. **Are your introduction, conclusion, and title effective?**
   Reread your introduction. If it does not lead your reader into the essay and/or does not offer needed background information, revise it by assuming your reader knows little about the topic and has shown little interest. Decide what to add to help this uninterested reader get involved with your essay. *Next, reread your conclusion.* Does it draw the essay to a close and remind the reader of your thesis statement? If not, revise it using the suggestions on page 228. *Finally, reconsider your title.* Is it an appropriate label for your essay? If it does not draw your reader into the essay, try to think of a snappier, more interesting title.

Revising Paragraphs

Once you are satisfied with the overall content and structure of your essay, next evaluate each paragraph. Ask yourself the following questions about each paragraph. For any items for which you answer *no*, refer to the pages in Chapters 4 and 5 listed below.

- Is the topic of the paragraph specific enough that it can be adequately covered in a single paragraph? (pp. 102–104)
- Does the topic sentence clearly identify the topic and express a point of view about it? (pp. 110–114)
- Are there enough relevant details to support the topic sentence? (p. 121)
- Are the details arranged in a logical order? (pp. 124–127)
- Have I used transitional words and phrases to connect my ideas? (p. 130)

Revising Sentences and Words

Once you are satisfied with your paragraphs, examine each sentence by asking the following questions:

- **Are your sentences wordy?** Do they express your meaning in as few words as possible? Here is an example of a wordy sentence, along with a possible revision. Notice that the first sentence contains empty words that do not contribute to its meaning.

Wordy	*In light of the fact* that cell phone technology changes *every year or so,* upgrading *your cell phone is what everybody has to do.*
Revised	Cell phone technology changes yearly, so regular upgrades are necessary.

- **Do your sentences repeat the same idea in slightly different words?** Here is an example of a sentence that says the same thing twice and a revised, more concise version of it.

Redundant	*My decision to choose* to attend college was the best *decision I have made in a long time.*
Revised	Choosing to attend college was one of my best decisions.

- **Do all of your sentences follow the same pattern?** That is, are they all short, or do they all start the same way? Do they seem choppy or monotonous? Sentences that are too similar make your writing seem mechanical and uninteresting.

- **Do you use strong active verbs?** These make your writing seem lively and interesting. Which of the following sentences is more interesting?

Weak Verb	The puppy *was* afraid of a laundry basket.
Revised	The puppy *whimpered, quivered,* and *scampered* away when my sister carried a laundry basket into the room.

The second sentence helps you visualize the situation, while the first is simply factual. Reread your essay, looking for verbs that seem dull or convey very little meaning. Replace them, using a dictionary or thesaurus, as needed.

- **Have you used concrete, specific language?** Your words should convey as much meaning as possible. Which phrase in each of the following pairs provides more meaning?

General	Specific
a fun vacation	*white-water rafting trip*
many flowers	*lavender petunias and white begonias*

Reread your essay and highlight words that seem dull and ordinary. Use a dictionary or thesaurus to help you find more concrete and specific replacements.

- **Have you used words with appropriate connotations?** A word's connotative meaning is the collection of feelings and attitudes that come along with it. The words *strolled*, *swaggered*, and *lumbered* all mean walked in a forward direction, but only *swaggered* would be appropriate when describing someone walking in a bold and arrogant manner. To be sure you have used words with appropriate connotations, use a dictionary to check any you are unsure of.

- **Have you avoided clichés?** A cliché is a tired, overused expression that carries little meaning. Here are a few examples.

better late than never	shoulder to cry on
ladder of success	hard as a rock
green with envy	bite the bullet

Reread your essay and replace clichés with more exact and descriptive information. You could, for example, replace *shoulder to cry on* with *sympathetic and understanding best friend* or *bite the bullet* with *accept responsibility*.

- **Have you avoided sexist language?** Sexist language expresses narrow or unfair assumptions about men's and women's roles, positions, or value. Here are a few examples of sexist language:

Sexist	A compassionate *nurse* reassures *her* patients before surgery.
Revised	Compassionate *nurses* reassure *their* patients before surgery.
Sexist	Many *policemen* hold college degrees.
Revised	Many *police officers* hold college degrees.

- **Have you used Standard American English and avoided using nonstandard dialect?** While dialects such as Black English, Spanglish, and Creole are acceptable in many situations, they are not acceptable when writing essays for college classes. If you speak a dialect of English in addition to Standard American English, be sure to reread your essay and replace any dialect words or expressions.

EXERCISE 8-15 . . . EVALUATING AND REVISING A DRAFT

WRITING IN PROGRESS *Evaluate the draft of the essay you revised in Exercise 8-14, using the questions in the preceding section. Make revisions as needed.*

| 8e | EDITING AND PROOFREADING: FOCUSING ON CLARITY AND CORRECTNESS |

LEARNING OBJECTIVE 5
Edit and proofread for clarity and correctness

Once you are satisfied that your essay expresses your ideas as you intended and is organized in a logical way, you are ready to make sure your essay is clear, error free, and presented in acceptable manuscript form. At this stage, you should try to correct errors in spelling, punctuation, and grammar, as well as typographical errors.

General Suggestions for Editing and Proofreading

Here are some general editing and proofreading suggestions:

- **Work with a double-spaced print copy of your essay.** You are likely to see more errors when working with a print copy than you do with an electronic version.
- **Create a log of common errors.** Read your paper once looking for each type of error and note them in your log.
- **Read your essay backward, starting with the last sentence and working toward the first.** Reading this way will help you focus on errors without the distraction of the flow of ideas.
- **Read your essay aloud.** You may catch errors in agreement, use of dialect, or punctuation.
- **Ask a classmate to proofread your paper.**

Using a Proofreading Checklist

Use the following proofreading checklist to remind you of the types of errors to look for when proofreading.

PROOFREADING CHECKLIST

1. Does each sentence end with an appropriate punctuation mark (period, question mark, exclamation point, or quotation mark)?
2. Is all punctuation within each sentence correct (commas, colons, semi-colons, apostrophes, dashes, and quotation marks)?

3. Are there any sentence fragments, run-on sentences, or comma splices?
4. Is each word spelled correctly?
5. Have you used capital letters where needed?
6. Are numbers and abbreviations used correctly?
7. Are any words left out?
8. Have you corrected all typographical errors?
9. Are your pages in the correct order and numbered?

Presenting Your Essay

Before your instructor even begins to read your essay, he or she forms a first impression of it. A paper that is carelessly assembled, rumpled, or has handwritten corrections creates a negative first impression. Always carefully follow any guidelines or requests that your instructor makes on format, method of submission, and so forth. Many instructors require you to use MLA format, and some require APA format. See Section 8k, page 254, for more information about each of these formats. Use the following suggestions to present your paper positively.

Tips for Presenting Your Essay

- Make sure your name, the course and section number, and the date appear at the top of your essay (unless otherwise specified by your instructor).
- Type and double-space your essay.
- Number the pages and staple or paperclip them together.
- Present a neat, clean copy. (Carry it in a manila folder or envelope until you turn it in so that it does not get rumpled or dirty.)
- If you need to make last-minute corrections, reprint your essay; do not make handwritten corrections.
- Avoid adjusting the margins to meet a page-length limit.
- If submitting your paper online, be sure to use an appropriate subject line identifying the submission.

In order to prepare his essay for publication, David made extensive revisions to his first draft (shown on p. 224) and produced the final version shown at the beginning of the chapter on page 210.

EXERCISE 8-16 . . . PROOFREADING AND PRESENTING YOUR PAPER

WRITING IN PROGRESS   *For the draft you have revised in Exercise 8-14, use the proofreading checklist to prepare your essay for final presentation.*

WRITING DOCUMENTED PAPERS

8f WHAT IS AN ESSAY THAT USES SOURCES?

LEARNING OBJECTIVE 6
Use sources to write essays

Many assignments in college require you to integrate your reading and writing skills by locating and reading several sources of information on a topic and then using them to support your ideas in an essay or report. At other times, you may be asked to integrate your skills by examining print and online sources and coming up with a new idea or thesis about them in the form of a research paper. In this part of the chapter, you will integrate your reading and writing skills by selecting and narrowing a topic, developing a thesis, using sources to find information on your topic, pulling together (synthesizing) ideas from the sources to support your thesis, writing an essay, and documenting your sources.

EXAMINING STUDENT WRITING

By examining the following documented student essay by Adam Simmons, which uses MLA documentation style, you will learn how to research a topic, synthesize information, avoid plagiarism, and write a correctly documented and formatted paper using sources. Throughout the rest of the chapter, we will use parts of Adam's essay to illustrate techniques and strategies.

Adam Simmons is a first-year student at a local state university where he is majoring in criminal justice. For his sociology class, Simmons was asked to write an essay that examined the pros and cons of a social problem or issue. We will follow Adam's progress as he selects his sources, develops a thesis statement, and writes his essay.

Student name, instructor's name, course number, and date are placed flush left.

Title is centered; is not in capitals, quotation marks, italics, or bold; and is not underlined.

Set margins at 1" at the top, bottom, and both sides of the page. Do not justify the right margin and switch off hyphenating.

Simmons 1

Student's last name and page number appear flush right on every page.

Adam Simmons

Professor Martin

Sociology 101

12 November 2015

Weighing the Consequences of Censorship in Media

1   Should music lyrics be censored if they contain violent or objectionable references? Should pornography be censored? Should media be prevented from reporting the private lives of celebrities and politicians? Should news media report events that might endanger national security? These are examples of

controversial situations about which people hold different opinions. Each side

Thesis statement

has good intentions. Those who favor censorship say it protects people or the
country while those who oppose censorship believe that censorship limits the
Constitutional right to freedom of speech, but there should be a middle ground.

2   People in favor of censorship of the media often talk about the morality of

Topic sentence states reason in support of censorship.

the content. A common argument is that some media contain inappropriate
material that could unintentionally be seen by young children. In this case,
inappropriate material is defined as pornographic, violent, vulgar, or sexual
in any way. This could lead to the loss of their innocence or even to danger.
The argument is that it could lead kids to try and repeat what they are
seeing on the television or what they are hearing about in music (Robinson
42). Censorship would protect children because they would not be exposed
to things that might not be appropriate for their age. They would also be
protected from potentially harmful people.

3   Some people also believe that censorship is important when it is used to

Topic sentence states second reason supporting censorship.

protect military information since, as President Obama was quoted as saying, "Leaks related to national security can put people at risk" (Warren).
With the government monitoring what information the media offers, it is less
likely that information the government does not want leaked out will be made
public. This could mean keeping troops safe and protecting domestic and
foreign policy, especially in wartime when enemies can track news sources
to find out about U.S. strategy. It can also help keep dangerous information,
such as details about weaponry, from getting into the wrong hands.

4   Censorship has some dangers though. It can be viewed as directly violating

Topic sentence notes censorship can be dangerous.

the First Amendment of the Constitution and taking away freedom of speech.
The amendment states "Congress shall make no law... abridging the freedom
of speech, or of the press ..." There are some who say the First Amendment

Simmons 3

acts as a "complete barrier to government censorship" (Pember and Calvert 43); since the Constitution creates this ban, censorship is in effect unlawful. However, there are Supreme Court cases that have modified the interpretation of this amendment, such as the Smith Act which makes it "a crime to advocate the violent overthrow of the government" (Pember and Calvert 52).

5   There are other reasons that people object to censorship. Some people argue that censorship can also be abused by the government and in the wrong hands it can lead to a loss of freedom of speech and halt a flow of ideas in a society, as seen under various dictatorships (Karaim 307). It can also be said that censorship stifles creativity. Saying that some works are immoral or unsuitable is making a legal statement that some art is good and some art is bad ("What Is Censorship?"). Art, in itself, is subjective and cannot really be labeled that way. If art has to be made to meet the requirements of the censors, then it will never be able to be completely creative and free.

6   Both viewpoints about censorship approach the topic with the hope of doing what is best for society but come at it from completely different angles. One hopes to make things better by removing immoral or dangerous speech, and the other seeks to let every person have the ability to say what they want regardless of whether it is seen as moral by others. Both viewpoints have merits and risks. Many cases hinge on judgment, interpretation, and opinion. What types of song lyrics are objectionable? What constitutes pornography? Who decides what events might endanger national security? What aspects of private lives of celebrities or politicians might be considered off-limits for the media? The issue of censorship is one about which many people feel strongly, but there is not an easy answer, nor is the solution clear-cut. Instead it is a matter of degree, interpretations, and definition. Let's consider situations on a case-by-case basis, and in all cases, let reason, logic, and good will prevail.

Annotations (left margin):

Topic sentence indicates there are further reasons for concern.

Adam compares the two approaches to censorship in his conclusion.

He lists questions that the two approaches raise.

He finishes with an appeal for a common sense approach.

Simmons 4

Works Cited page appears at the end of the paper and starts on a new page.

Title is centered; is not in capitals, quotation marks, italics, or bold; and is not underlined.   **Works Cited**

Karaim, Reed. "China Today." *CQ Researcher,* vol. 24, no. 13, 4 Apr. 2014,

pp. 289–312.

Entries are listed alphabetically by last name or by title if there is no author. Entries start flush left and are double-spaced. Second and subsequent lines are indented half an inch.

Pember, Don R., and Clay Calvert. *Mass Media Law.* 17th ed., McGraw-Hill, 2011.

Robinson, Kerry H. *Innocence, Knowledge and the Construction of Childhood: The*

Contradictory Nature of Sexuality and Censorship in Children's Contemporary Lives.

Taylor and Francis, 2013.

Warren, James. "President Obama Defends Aggressive Actions to Investigate

National Security Leaks, But Says Press Must Be Safeguarded Too."

NY Daily News, 16 May 2013, www.nydailynews.com/news/national/

president-promises-balance-protect-national-security-free-press-article-1.1346017.

"What Is Censorship?" American Civil Liberties Union, www.aclu.org/

what-censorship. Accessed 27 May 2014.

8g   READING: FINDING AND RECORDING APPROPRIATE SOURCES

LEARNING OBJECTIVE 7
Find and record appropriate sources

Libraries are filled with sources—print, electronic, and more. They house thousands of books, journals, videos, DVDs, pamphlets, tapes, and newspapers, as well as computers that enable you to access the World Wide Web. Yet this very abundance of sources means that one of the hardest parts of doing research is locating the sources that will be the most help to you.

Many books have been written on how to do research and how to use and document print and electronic sources. Therefore, this section gives only a brief overview of the research process and offers advice on how to get started.

For his essay, Adam found information in a variety of sources, both electronic and print. His Works Cited list includes a news magazine, a law textbook, a newspaper, and an article from the American Civil Liberties Union Web site.

Tips for Finding Appropriate Sources

Suppose you are writing an essay about differences in men's and women's communication styles. Although you will find many sources on your topic, not all will be appropriate for your particular assignment. Some sources may be too technical; others may be too sketchy. Some may be outdated, others too opinionated. Your task is to find sources that will give you good, solid, current information or points of view. Use the following tips:

1. **Consult a reference librarian.** If you are unsure of where to begin, ask a reference librarian for advice.

2. **Use a systematic approach.** Start by using general sources, either print or electronic, such as general reference books. Then, as needed, move to more specific sources such as periodicals and journals.

3. **Use current sources.** For many topics, such as scientific or medical advances, only the most up-to-date sources are useful. For other topics, such as the moral issues involved in abortion or euthanasia, older sources can be used. Before you begin, decide on a cutoff date before which you feel information will be outdated and therefore not useful to you.

4. **Sample a variety of viewpoints.** Try to find sources that present differing viewpoints on the same subject rather than counting on one source to contain everything you need. Various authors take different approaches and have different opinions on the same topic, all of which can increase your understanding of the topic.

5. **Preview articles by reading abstracts or summaries.** Many sources begin with an abstract or end with a summary, so read them to determine whether the source is going to be helpful.

6. **Read sources selectively.** Do not waste time reading an entire book or article; skim to avoid parts that are not on the subject and to locate portions that relate directly to the topic. To read selectively,

   - use indexes and tables of contents to locate the portions of books that are useful and appropriate. In articles, use abstracts or summaries as a guide to the material's organization: the order in which ideas appear in the summary or abstract is the order in which they appear in the source itself.

   - after you have identified useful sections, preview (see pp. 6–7) to get an overview of the material.

   - use headings to select sections to read thoroughly.

7. **Choose reliable, trustworthy sources.** The Internet contains a great deal of valuable information, but it also contains rumor, gossip, hoaxes, and misinformation. Before using a source, evaluate it by checking the author's credentials, considering the sponsor or publisher of the site, checking the date of posting, and verifying links. If you are uncertain about the information presented on a site, verify the information by cross-checking it with another source.

8. **Look for sources that lead to other sources.** Some sources include a bibliography, which provides leads to other works related to your topic. Follow links included in electronic sources.

Understanding Plagiarism

Plagiarism entails borrowing someone else's ideas or exact words *without giving that person credit*. Plagiarism can be intentional (submitting an essay written by someone else) or unintentional (failing to enclose another writer's words in quotation marks). Either way, it is considered a serious offense. If you plagiarize, you can fail the assignment or even the course.

Cyberplagiarism is a specific type of plagiarism. It takes two forms: (1) using information from the Internet without giving credit to the Web site that posted it, or (2) buying prewritten papers from the Internet and submitting them as your own work. For example: If you take information about Frank Lloyd Wright's architecture from a reference source (such as an encyclopedia or Web site) but do not specifically indicate where you found it, you have plagiarized. If you take the eleven-word phrase "Kelley, the lead government investigator, a fiery, temperamental, and demanding man" from a news article on the war on terrorism, you have plagiarized.

Here are some guidelines to help you understand exactly what constitutes plagiarism:

Guidelines for Understanding Plagiarism

Plagiarism occurs when you . . .

- use another person's words without crediting that person.
- use another person's theory, opinion, or idea without listing the source of that information.
- do not place another person's exact words in quotation marks.
- do not provide a citation (reference) to the original source that you are quoting.
- paraphrase (reword) another person's ideas or words without credit.
- use facts, data, graphs, and charts without stating their source(s).

Using commonly known facts or information is not plagiarism, and you need not provide a source for such information. For example, the fact that Neil Armstrong set foot on the moon in 1969 is widely known and does not require documentation.

Recording Sources to Avoid Plagiarism

Keep track of all the sources you use. There are important reasons for doing this:

- **You are more likely to avoid plagiarism if you keep accurate records of your sources.** Using an author's words or ideas without acknowledging that you have done so is a serious ethical error and legal violation. In some colleges, plagiarism is sufficient cause for failing a course or even being dismissed from the college. You can easily avoid plagiarism by properly acknowledging your sources within your paper.

- **All sources you use must be cited.** When you use sources in an essay, you must acknowledge them all at the end of your paper in a bibliography, or "Works Cited" or "References" list. Providing your reader with information on your sources is called **documentation**.

- **You may want to refer to the source again.** Be sure to record all publication information about each print and electronic source you decide to use.

- **For print sources**, record the title, author(s), other contributors such as editor(s) or translator(s), volume, edition, place and date of publication, publisher, and page number(s).

- **For online sites**, record the author, title of the work, title of the Web site, version or edition used, the publisher of the site, the date of publication, and the URL or DOI.

You may want to use index cards or a small bound notebook to record source information, using a separate card or page for each source. Other options are photocopying pages from print sources, downloading and/or printing information from Web site sources, cutting and pasting links and information into a Word document, and bookmarking sites that might be useful for future reference. Adam used a combination of these strategies: he started a Word file for listing sources and copying links into, as well as downloading and printing some of the articles he found. (You will learn how to document sources you use later in this chapter.)

Also, keep in mind that a good essay does not just consist of a series of quotations strung together. Instead, you should combine information you find in sources to come up with new ideas, perspectives, and responses to your topic. Annotating, outlining, paraphrasing, and summarizing are all important skills for doing this and are covered in Chapter 1:

annotating (p. 21)	paraphrasing (p. 24)
outlining (p. 26)	summarizing (p. 31)

EXERCISE 8-17 . . . IDENTIFYING PLAGIARISM

Read the following passage. Place a check mark next to each statement in the list that follows that is an example of plagiarism.

Issue: Brands

Brands vary in the amount of power and value they hold in the marketplace. Some brands—such as Coca-Cola, Nike, Disney, GE, McDonald's, Harley-Davidson, and others—become larger-than-life icons that maintain their power in the market for years, even generations. Other brands—such as Google, YouTube, Apple, Facebook, ESPN, and Wikipedia—create fresh consumer excitement and loyalty. These brands win in the marketplace not simply because they deliver unique benefits or reliable service. Rather, they succeed because they forge deep connections with customers. For example, to a devoted Dunkin' Donuts fan, that cup of coffee from Dunkin' isn't just coffee, it's a deeply satisfying experience that no other brand can deliver as well. Dunkin' Donuts regularly beats out Starbucks in customer loyalty ratings.

—Kotler and Armstrong, *Principles of Marketing*, 15e, p. 244

_____ 1. Brands vary in the amount of power they hold in the marketplace.

_____ 2. Brands such as Coca-Cola and Disney are "larger-than-life icons that maintain their power in the market for years" (Kotler and Armstrong, 244).

_____ 3. Other brands—such as Google, YouTube, Apple, Facebook, ESPN, and Wikipedia—create fresh consumer excitement and loyalty.

_____ 4. Both Dunkin' Donuts and Starbucks have fans among the coffee drinking population.

8h   USING SOURCES TO SUPPORT YOUR THESIS AND DEVELOP YOUR ESSAY

LEARNING OBJECTIVE 8
Use sources to support your thesis and develop your essay

Adam chose to write his assigned essay on the pros and cons of censorship. After brainstorming to generate ideas, he created a working thesis statement: "There are different viewpoints about censorship in the media." In order to present a convincing argument, he needed to find facts, statistics, and evidence to support his opinions. He realized he would need some or all of the following evidence to support his main ideas:

- definitions of terms such as *morality* and *inappropriate material*
- facts about the effects of leaks related to national security
- evidence from experts in the field of Constitutional law
- examples of the stifling effects of censorship in dictatorships

To gather this information, he went to his college library and consulted both print and online sources.

Once you decide what major idea to work with, you are ready to develop an essay. Use your newly discovered idea as your working thesis statement. Then use properly documented details from each source to develop and support your thesis statement. Follow these guidelines to properly use sources you find:

Guidelines for Proper Use of Sources

1. **Write a first draft of your essay.** Before consulting sources to support your ideas, work through the first three steps of the writing process: *prewriting*, *organizing*, and *drafting*. Decide on a working thesis statement and write down your own ideas about the topic down on paper. Once you have drafted your essay, you will be able to see what types of supporting information are

necessary. If you research first, you might get flooded with facts and with other writers' voices and viewpoints and lose your own.

2. **Analyze your draft to identify where you need additional information.** Read your draft looking for unsupported statements, underlining them as you find them. Then make a list of needed information, and form questions that need to be answered. Some students find it effective to write each question on a separate index card. For example, Adam underlined the following sentence in his second paragraph:

> A common argument is that some media contain inappropriate material that could unintentionally be seen by young children.

To support this statement, he needed to provide a definition of the term "inappropriate material" and then explain the potential effects of such material on young children, information he found in a book by Kerry Robinson.

The following types of statements benefit from supporting information:

- **Opinions**

Example	Censorship has some dangers though.
Needed Information	What evidence supports that opinion? What are the dangers?

- **Broad, general ideas**

Example	Censorship stifles creativity.
Needed Information	In what ways? Can creative works, such as art, be labeled as immoral or unsuitable?

- **Cause and effect statements**

Example	Censorship can lead to a loss of freedom of speech and halt a flow of ideas in a society.
Needed Information	In what societies has this happened?

- **Statements that assert what should be done**

Example	Censorship is important when it is used to protect military information.
Needed Information	What happens when information related to national security is leaked? What are the risks of the government monitoring what information the media offers?

3. **Record information and note sources.** As you locate needed information, make a decision about the best way to record it, using summarizing, paraphrasing, outlining, or writing annotations on photocopies of print sources. Be sure to include complete bibliographic information for each source.

   As you consult sources, you will probably discover new ideas and perhaps even a new approach to your topic. For example, as Adam read through his sources, he learned that although the Constitution establishes the right to freedom of speech, Supreme Court cases have modified the interpretation of the First Amendment; certain types of speech are subject to censorship. He recorded this new idea, along with its source, in his Word file.

4. **Revise your paper.** Begin by re-evaluating your thesis based on your research. You may need to fine-tune or revise it as a result of what you have learned. Add new supporting information (the next section of this chapter discusses how to synthesize information from other sources), and then re-evaluate your draft, eliminating statements for which you could not locate supporting information, statements you found to be inaccurate, and statements for which you found contradictory evidence.

EXERCISE 8-18 . . . DEVELOPING A THESIS STATEMENT FOR A DOCUMENTED PAPER

WRITING IN PROGRESS   *Choose one of the following broad topics. Use a prewriting strategy to narrow the topic and develop a working thesis statement (see p. 217). Locate at least three reference sources that are useful and appropriate for writing an essay of two to three pages on the topic you have developed. Be sure to record all the bibliographic information for each source.*

1. Privacy on social media sites
2. Date rape
3. Same-sex marriage
4. The evolution of rock and roll
5. The spread, control, or treatment of an infectious disease
6. Online dating
7. Controversy over college athletic scholarships
8. Legalized gambling (or lotteries)

8i   SYNTHESIZING SOURCES

LEARNING OBJECTIVE 9
Synthesize sources

Synthesis is a process of using information from two or more sources in order to develop new ideas about a topic or to draw conclusions about it. Many college assignments require you to synthesize material—that is, to locate and read several sources on a topic and use them to produce a paper. For example, in a sociology course, you may be asked to consult several sources on the topic of organized crime and then write a paper describing the relationship between organized crime and illegal-drug sales. In a marketing class, your instructor may direct you to consult several sources on advertising strategies and on the gullibility of young children, and write a paper weighing the effects of television commercials on young children.

Did you notice that, in each of the above examples, you were asked to come up with a new idea, one that did not appear in any of the sources but was *based* on *all* the sources? Creating something new from what you read is one of the most basic, important, and satisfying skills you will learn in college.

Synthesis is also often required in the workplace:

- As a sales executive for an Internet service provider company, you may be asked to synthesize what you have learned about customer hardware problems.

- As a medical office assistant, you have extensive problems with a new computer system. The office manager asks you to write a memo to the company that installed the system, categorizing the types of problems you have experienced.

- As an environmental engineer, you must synthesize years of research in order to make a proposal for local river and stream cleanup.

How to Compare Sources to Synthesize

Comparing sources is part of synthesizing. Comparing involves placing them side by side and examining how they are the same and how they are different. However, before you begin to compare two or more sources, be sure you understand each fully. Depending on how detailed and difficult each source is, use annotating, paraphrasing, and summarizing, or underline, outline, or draw idea maps to make sure that you have a good grasp of your source material (see Chapter 1 for more details on each).

Let's assume you are taking a speech course in which you are studying nonverbal communication, or body language. You have chosen to study one aspect of body language: eye contact. Among your sources are the following excerpts:

Issue: Nonverbal Communication

Source A

Eye contact, or *gaze*, is also a common form of nonverbal communication. Eyes have been called the "windows of the soul." In many cultures, people tend to assume that someone who avoids eye contact is evasive, cold, fearful, shy, or indifferent; that frequent gazing signals intimacy, sincerity, self-confidence, and respect; and that the person who stares is tense, angry, and unfriendly. Typically, however, eye contact is interpreted in light of a pre-existing relationship. If a relationship is friendly, frequent eye contact elicits a positive impression. If a relationship is not friendly, eye contact is seen in negative terms. It has been said that if two people lock eyes for more than a few seconds, they are either going to make love or kill each other (Kleinke, 1986; Patterson, 1983).

—Brehm and Kassin, *Social Psychology*, p. 322

Source B

Eye contact often indicates the nature of the relationship between two people. One research study showed that eye contact is moderate when one is addressing a very high-status person, maximized when addressing a moderately high-status person, and only minimal when talking to a low-status person. There are also predictable differences in eye contact when one person likes another or when there may be rewards involved.

Increased eye contact is also associated with increased liking between the people who are communicating. In an interview, for example, you are likely to make judgments about the interviewer's friendliness according to the amount of eye contact shown. The less eye contact, the less friendliness. In a courtship relationship, more eye contact can be observed among those seeking to develop a more intimate relationship. One research study (Saperston, 2003) suggests that the intimacy is a function of the amount of eye gazing, physical proximity, intimacy of topic, and amount of smiling. This model best relates to established relationships.

—Weaver, *Understanding Interpersonal Communication*, p. 131

To compare these sources, ask the following questions:

1. **On what do the sources agree?** Sources A and B recognize eye contact as an important communication tool. Both agree that there is a connection between eye contact and the relationship between the people involved. Both also agree that more frequent eye contact occurs among people who are friendly or intimate.

2. **On what do the sources disagree?** Sources A and B do not disagree, though they do present different information about eye contact (see the next item).

3. **How do they differ?** Sources A and B differ in the information they present. Source A states that in some cultures the frequency of eye contact suggests certain personality traits (someone who avoids eye contact is considered to be cold, for example), but Source B does not discuss cultural interpretations. Source B discusses how eye contact is related to status—the level of importance of the person being addressed—while Source A does not.

4. **Are the viewpoints toward the subject similar or different?** Both Sources A and B take a serious approach to the subject of eye contact.

5. **Does each source provide supporting evidence for major points?** Source A cites two references. Source B cites a research study.

After comparing your sources, the next step is to form your own ideas based on what you have discovered.

How to Develop Ideas About Sources

Developing your own ideas is a process of drawing conclusions. Your goal is to decide what both sources, taken together, suggest. Together, Sources A and B recognize that eye contact is an important part of body language. However, they focus on different aspects of how eye contact can be interpreted. You can conclude that studying eye contact can be useful in understanding the relationship between two individuals: you can judge the relative status, the degree of friendship, and the level of intimacy between the people. After reading and thinking about his sources, Adam realized that there were quite different, even opposite, points of view on the topic of censorship. He decided to outline the pros and cons in his essay and then provide his opinion on the topic, based on a synthesis of what he had learned. Based on this decision, he revised his thesis statement to more accurately reflect his point:

> Those who favor censorship say it protects people or the country while those who oppose censorship believe that censorship limits the Constitutional right to freedom of speech, but there should be a middle ground.

EXERCISE 8-19 . . . SYNTHESIZING SOURCES

Read each of the following excerpts from sources on the topic of lost and endangered species. Synthesize these two sources, using the steps listed above, and develop a thesis statement about the causes of the decline and loss of plant and animal species.

Issue: Species Extinction

Source A: What Causes Extinction?

Every living organism must eventually die, and the same is true of species. Just like individuals, species are "born" (through the process of speciation), persist for some period of time, and then perish. The ultimate fate of any species is extinction, the death of the last of its members. In fact, at least 99.9% of all the species that have ever existed are now extinct. The natural course of evolution, as revealed by fossils, is continual turnover of species as new ones arise and old ones become extinct.

The immediate cause of extinction is probably always environmental change, in either the living or the nonliving parts of the environment. Two major environmental factors that may drive a species to extinction are competition among species and habitat destruction.

Interactions with Other Species May Drive a Species to Extinction

Interactions such as competition and predation serve as agents of natural selection. In some cases, these same interactions can lead to extinction rather than to adaptation. Organisms compete for limited resources in all environments. If a species' competitors evolve superior adaptations and the species doesn't evolve fast enough to keep up, it may become extinct.

Habitat Change and Destruction Are the Leading Causes of Extinction

Habitat change, both contemporary and prehistoric, is the single greatest cause of extinctions. Present-day habitat destruction due to human activities is proceeding at a rapid pace. Many biologists believe that we are presently in the midst of the fastest-paced and most widespread episode of species extinction in the history of life on Earth. Loss of tropical forests is especially devastating to species diversity. As many as half the species presently on Earth may be lost during the next 50 years as the tropical forests that contain them are cut for timber and to clear land for cattle and crops.

—Audesirk, Audesirk, and Byers, *Life on Earth*, pp. 249–251

Source B: Reasons for the Decline of Species

Extinctions of the distant past were caused largely by processes of climate change, plate tectonics, and even asteroid impacts. Current threats to biodiversity include habitat destruction, pollution, invasive species population, and overexploitation. The losses in the future will be greatest in the developing world, where biodiversity is greatest and human population growth is highest. Africa and Asia have lost almost two-thirds of their original natural habitat.

Habitat Change

By far the greatest source of biodiversity loss is the physical alteration of habitats through the processes of conversion, fragmentation, simplification, and intrusion. Habitat destruction has already been responsible for 36% of the known extinctions and is the key factor in the currently observed population declines. Natural species are adapted to specific habitats, so if the habitat changes or is eliminated, the species go with it.

Pollution

Another factor that decreases biodiversity is pollution, which can directly kill many kinds of plants and animals, seriously reducing their populations. For example, nutrients (such as phosphorus and nitrogen) that travel down the Mississippi River from the agricultural heartland of the United States have created a "dead zone" in the Gulf of Mexico, an area of more than 10,000 square miles (as of 2008) where oxygen completely disappears from depths below 20 meters every summer. Shrimp, fish, crabs, and other commercially valuable sea life are either killed or forced to migrate away from this huge area along the Mississippi and Louisiana coastline. Pollution destroys or alters habitats, with consequences just as severe as those caused by deliberate conversions. Every oil spill kills seabirds and often sea mammals, sometimes by the thousands.

—adapted from Wright and Boorse, *Environmental Science*, pp. 140 and 144

EXERCISE 8-20 . . . SYNTHESIZING SOURCES AND WRITING A FIRST DRAFT

WRITING IN PROGRESS *Using the questions listed on page 248, synthesize the three reference sources you gathered for Exercise 8-18. Then write a first draft of the essay on the topic you chose. If any of these sources are dated or not focused enough for your thesis, you may need to locate additional ones.*

EXERCISE 8-21 . . . RECORDING SOURCES

WRITING IN PROGRESS *List source information for the essay you drafted in Exercise 8-20 to use in your Works Cited or References list. See page 243 for tips on what information to include.*

8j   INTEGRATING QUOTATIONS INTO AN ESSAY

LEARNING OBJECTIVE 10
Integrate quotations into your essay

Whenever you use information from a source, either in your own words or as a direct quotation, you must give credit to the source by providing an in-text citation that briefly identifies the source and references detailed source information listed at the end of your paper. This list is called a "Works Cited List" when you are using MLA style, and "References" when you are using APA style. See Section 8k (pp. 254 and 259) for more details on in-text citation.

Integrating Quotations

Quotations can lend interest, accuracy, and reliability to your essay, but they should be used sparingly. Use quotations in the following situations:

- The quotation expresses the exact idea you want to convey, and paraphrasing might alter the meaning of the quotation.
- The quotation is striking, unusual, or noteworthy. In this situation the quotation will be more effective than a paraphrase.
- The quotation expresses a strong opinion or exaggeration or other unreliable information that you want to distinguish from your own ideas.

Inserting Short Quotations

Short quotations (less than four typed lines for MLA style and less than 40 words for APA style), should be built right into your sentence and the quoted material placed within double quotation marks. The page number and author's name should be included in MLA style.

> **MLA**   As defined by James Fagin, a tort is "a private wrong that causes physical harm to another" (152).

The page number, date of publication, and author's name should be included in APA style.

> **APA**   As defined by Fagin (2012) a tort is "a private wrong that causes physical harm to another" (p. 152).

When you are quoting material from books, journal articles, magazines or newspapers, use a word or phrase to signal that you are about to include the ideas of an outside source. This **signal phrase** introduces the material by giving the author's name and/or providing the title or other background information about the source, especially if it is the first time it is used in the essay. In the following example, the writer uses the phrase "James Fagin, a professor of criminal justice and author of *CJ2014*, states that" to signal the reader that he is introducing a quotation.

> **MLA**   James Fagin, a professor of criminal justice and author of *CJ2014*, states that "sentencing procedure for capital offenses differs from that of noncapital cases" (11).

If the writer had already used this source in his paper, he might have written his sentence as follows. In this example, the word *observes* acts as a signal that information from another source is about to be provided. Other commonly used signal words are *states, explains, maintains, argues, asserts, believes, points out,* and *suggests*.

> **MLA**   He observes that "sentencing procedure for capital offenses differs from that of non-capital cases" (Fagin 11).
>
> **APA**   He observes that "sentencing procedure for capital offenses differs from that of non-capital cases" (Fagin, 2012, p. 11).

Inserting Long (Block) Quotations

In both MLA and APA style, lengthy quotations are indented in a block, one-half inch from the left margin. In MLA style, this includes quotations of more than four typed lines, while in APA style, quotations of more than 40 words are indented. **In both styles**, quotation marks are NOT used, the quotations are double-spaced, and the parenthetical citation appears after the closing punctuation mark. Here is a sample using MLA style. Notice that the quote is preceded by a colon and the parenthetical citation appears after the end punctuation.

> **MLA**   In discussing the challenges of community policing, Fagin makes the following observations:
>
>   Community policing requires more educated officers and officers with creative problem-solving abilities. Police officers

> must view members of the public as a potential resource in crime fighting rather than potential criminals. Some argue that the police officer's separation or isolation from the community makes it possible for him or her to engage in grisly interactions such as assaults, accident victims, and shootings as duty demands without becoming impaired by emotional overload. (116)

Punctuating Quotations

Use the following rules and guidelines to punctuate quotations:

1. Use a comma after a verb that introduces a quotation. Begin the first word of the quotation with a capital letter. If a verb is not used, a comma is not needed, and capitalization of the first word is not needed.

> As Fagin notes, "There are numerous . . .
> According to Fagin "there are numerous . . .

2. Place commas that follow quotations inside the quotation marks.

> "The police are the gateway linking enforcement and prosecution," according to Fagin.

3. Place question marks and exclamation points within the quotation marks when they are part of the original quotation and outside them if they punctuate your sentence.

> **Question mark as part of original material**
> Fagin asks, "Why are police arrest reports essential to a successful prosecution case?"
>
> **Question mark as part of your sentence**
> Can you imagine that the prosecution, in investigating the Casey Anthony case, "failed to search for Internet inquiries made using Mozilla Firefox browser"?

4. Do not add an additional period if a quotation ends your sentence.

> According to Fagin, "the career path of a law enforcement officer is unlike that of a person in private business."

Adapting Quotations

Quotations must grammatically fit within your own sentences. Use the following guidelines for adapting quotations:

1. Include spelling, punctuation, and capitalization exactly as they appear in the original. If there is an error in the original material, place the word *sic* in brackets immediately after it. (According to the online report, the getaway vehicle "blasted thru [sic] the barrier and burst into flames.")

2. You can leave out a portion of a quotation, but you need to add an ellipsis—three spaced periods (. . .)—to indicate material has been omitted. Be sure not to distort the author's meaning.

3. You can change the first word of a quotation to a capital letter or to a lowercase letter to fit within your sentence.

8k   DOCUMENTING SOURCES USING MLA OR APA STYLES

LEARNING OBJECTIVE 11
Document sources using MLA or APA styles

There are a number of different documentation formats (these are often called *styles*) that are used by scholars and researchers. Members of a particular academic discipline usually use the same format. For example, biologists follow a format described in *Scientific Style and Format: A Manual for Authors, Editors, and Publishers*.

Two of the most common methods of documenting and citing sources are those used by the Modern Language Association (MLA) and the American Psychological Association (APA). Both use a system of in-text citation: a brief note in the body of the text that refers to a source that is fully described in the Works Cited list (MLA) or References (APA) at the end of the paper, where sources are listed in alphabetical order.

The MLA format is typically used in English and humanities papers, while the APA format is commonly used in social science papers. In the student essay on pages 210–214, you can see how David Matsui used APA in-text citations and listed his sources on a References page. In Adam Simmons's essay on pages 237–240, you can see how he used MLA in-text citations and listed his sources on a Works Cited page. Use the following guidelines for providing correct in-text citations using the MLA and APA documentation styles.

An Overview of the MLA Style

The Modern Language Association (MLA) uses a system of in-text citation: a brief note in the body of the text that refers to a source that is fully described in the alphabetized "Works Cited" list at the end of the paper. New guidelines focus on citing sources based on a series of simple principles and elements that can be applied to a wide variety of source types and formats. For a comprehensive review of the new system, consult the *MLA Handbook,* 8th edition, or access the MLA Web site at www.mla.org.

When you refer to, summarize, paraphrase, quote, or in any way use an author's words or ideas, you must indicate their original source by inserting an in-text citation that refers your reader to the "Works Cited" list. If you name the author in your sentence, only include the page number in the citation; if you do not name the author, include both the author's name and page number in the citation. When you include a quotation, use an introductory phrase to signal that the quotation is to follow.

> Miller poses the idea that if a good story is supposed to be a condensed version of life, then life should be lived like a good story in the first place (39).
>
> If a good story is supposed to be a condensed version of life, then life should be lived like a good story in the first place (Miller 39).
>
> According to Miller, "[quotation]." As Miller notes, "[quotation]." In the words of Miller, "[quotation]."

When citing a source, use the Elements Diagram on the next page to select and organize relevant information. Note that Container 1 provides primary source information for the author and/or title in elements 1 or 2, so include all relevant information for elements 3–9 in the order shown. As the primary source may appear within a second container (e.g., a journal article may be found on a Web site or in a database), you also need to document information relevant to this second container, repeating, as needed, elements 3–9.

Elements Diagram	Core Elements	Description of Elements	Examples
1. Author. 2. Title of source. **Container 1 (primary source information)**	1. Author.	• Last name, first name • Second author's name written first name, last name • Three or more authors, reverse first name and follow with comma and "et al." • For non-author creators, add labels and spell them out • Treat pseudonyms as author names	• Carr, James I. • Carr, James I., and Martha Hopkins. • Fuentes, José, et al. • García, Emma, editor. • Cook, Douglas, translator. • @Cmdr_Hadfield.
3. Title of container,	2. Title of source.	• Place title in quotation marks if it is part of larger source (e.g., a poem, essay, TV episode, blog post, or tweet), followed by a period.	• "The Bee." (poem); "Everybody Dies." (TV episode); "On Noise." (essay); "Inside the Collapse of The New Republic." (blog post)
4. Other contributors, 5. Version,		• Place title in italics if it is self-contained (e.g., a book, play, TV series, Web site, or album), followed by a period.	• *Florence Gordon.* (novel); *King Lear.* (play); *House.* (TV series); *The New Yorker.* (Web site); *Cool It.* (album)
6. Number,	3. Title of container,	• If the source is part of a larger whole, that whole is considered a container; it is italicized and followed by a comma.	• Ronnie Corbett, performer. "We Love British Comedy." *Facebook,*
7. Publisher,		• If the title of the source is the whole, it appears as element 2, and there may be no entry for element 3.	• Maugham, W. Somerset. *Of Human Bondage.* Viking Penguin, 1963.
8. Publication date,		• A container can be nested in a second container (see diagram on left).	• Barnard, Neal D., et al. "Vegetarian and Vegan Diets in Type 2 Diabetes Management." *Nutrition Reviews,* vol. 67, no. 5, pp. 255–263. *NCBI,* doi:10.1111/j.1753-4887.2009.00198.x.
9. Location. **Container 2 (where you found the primary source, e.g., database, Web site, online archive)**	4. Other contributors,	• Place other important contributors to a work after the title of the container, preceded by a descriptor: *adapted by, performed by, directed by* or *general editor* or *guest editors,* and followed by a comma.	• Dickinson, Emily. "Griefs." *Emily Dickinson: Selected Poems,* edited by Stanley Applebaum, Dover Thrift Editions, 1990, p. 25.
	5. Version,	• Indicate if there is more than one version of the source: *Updated ed., Expanded ed., 13th ed., director's cut,*	• McWhorter, Kathleen. *In Concert: Reading and Writing.* 2nd ed., Pearson, 2016.

Elements Diagram	Core Elements	Description of Elements	Examples
3. Title of container,	6. Number,	• Use abbreviations "vol." and "no." for volume and issue number, separated by a comma.	• Bivins, Corey. "A Soy-free, Nut-free Vegan Meal Plan." *Vegetarian Journal*, vol. 30, no. 1, pp. 14–17.
4. Other contributors,	7. Publisher,	• Name of organization primarily responsible for producing source, followed by a comma.	• Pearson, Penguin, Netflix, Twentieth Century Fox,
5. Version,		• If two or more organizations are equally responsible, cite both with forward slash between them.	• Lee, Malcolm D., director. *Barbershop: The Next Cut*. Performance by Ice Cube, MGM / New Line Cinema, 2016.
6. Number,		• Use "U" for university and "P" for Press.	• Oxford UP, (abbreviation for Oxford University Press)
7. Publisher,	8. Publication date,	• Cite the most relevant date, followed by a comma. If you are citing a print work found online, use the date of the online posting.	• Lilla, Mark. "The President and the Passions." *The New York Times Magazine,* 19 Dec. 2010, p. MM 13.
8. Publication date,	9. Location.	• For print sources, provide page numbers preceded by p. or pp. and followed by a period.	• Maugham, W. Somerset. *Of Human Bondage*. Viking Penguin, 1963, p. 211.
9. Location.		• For online sites, MLA recommends providing a URL (check with your professor) or DOI (preferred), followed by a period. Drop "http://" if it appears in a URL.	• Woolf, Virginia. "A Haunted House." *Monday or Tuesday*, Harcourt Brace, 1921. Bartleby.com, www.bartleby.com/85/.

An Overview of the APA Style

The table below presents representative samples of APA in-text citation, References documentation, and Internet source citation. For a comprehensive overview of APA style, refer to the *Publication Manual of the American Psychological Association* (6th ed.), access the APA site at www.apastyle.org, or visit the Purdue University Online Writing Lab (OWL) at http://owl.english.purdue.edu.

You can also use an online site like http://easy.bib.com to generate citations. **HOWEVER**, these sites are only as good as the information you type into them; if you do not include all the required information, the citation will not be correct.

APA In-Text Citations

APA uses an author–date citation method, which means that when you refer to, summarize, paraphrase, quote, or in any way use another author's words or ideas, the author's last name and the year of publication the information comes from must be provided in the body of your essay as an **in-text citation** that refers your reader to your **References list**, which is a complete alphabetized list of all the sources you have used. The examples below are representative of some common in-text citation uses.

1. **When the author is named in the sentence or phrase, insert the publication date in parentheses after the author's name.**

   In his book *A Million Miles in a Thousand Years: What I Learned While Editing My Life*, Donald Miller (2009) poses the idea that if a good story is supposed to be a condensed version of life, then life should be lived like a good story in the first place (p. 39).

2. **If the author is not named in the sentence, then include both the author's name and the publication date in the citation.**

   If a good story is supposed to be a condensed version of life, then life should be lived like a good story in the first place (Miller, 2009, p. 39).

3. **When you include a quotation in your paper, you should use an introductory phrase that includes the author's last name followed by the date of publication in parentheses.**

   Miller (2009) comments that he "wondered whether a person could plan a story for his life and live it intentionally" (p. 39).

APA References List

Your list of works cited should include all the sources you referred to, summarized, paraphrased, or quoted in your paper. Start the list on a separate page at the end of your paper and title it "References." Arrange the entries alphabetically by each author's last name. If an author is not named (as in an editorial), then alphabetize the item by title. Double-space between and within entries. Start entries flush left, and if they run more than one line, indent subsequent lines half an inch.

1. **The basic format for a book can be illustrated as follows:**

Author	Year	Title	Place of Publication	Publisher
Lin, M.	(2011).	*Kid A.*	New York:	Continuum.

2. The basic format for a periodical can be illustrated as follows:

| Author | Date | Title | Publication | Volume | Page number |

Harvey, G. (2010). Bob Dylan in America. *The New York Review of Books, 57* (18), 34.

Internet Sources

Most electronic references are formatted the same as print ones, starting with the author name, date, and title. These are followed by either a Digital Object Identifier (DOI) or URL. In addition, APA does not require an access date if there is a publication date or edition or version number or if the source is stable. If you have to break a URL or DOI, do so before a period or slash and do not use a hyphen.

1. The format for an article from an online periodical is as follows:

| Author | Date | Title | Publication |

Sifton, S. (2011). Crosstown tour of India. *The New York Times.* Retrieved from:
http://www.nytimes.com

URL

2. The basic format for a government publication found on the Internet is as follows:

| Government entity | Date | Publication |

U.S. Financial Inquiry Commission. (2010). *The financial crisis inquiry report: Final report of the National Commission on the Causes of the Financial and Economic Crisis in the United States.*

Retrieved from http://www.fdlp.gov

URL

EXERCISE 8-22 . . . REVISING A DRAFT

WRITING IN PROGRESS   *Using the checklist below, revise the first draft of the essay you wrote in Exercise 8-20.*

REVISION CHECKLIST

1. Does your paragraph or essay accomplish your purpose?
2. Does your paragraph or essay provide your audience with the background information they need?
3. Is your main point clearly expressed?
4. Have you supported your main point with sufficient detail from sources to make it understandable and believable?
5. Is each detail relevant? Does each one explain or support your main point?
6. Is your paragraph or essay logically arranged?
7. Have you used transitions to connect your ideas within and between paragraphs?
8. Have you credited each source from which you paraphrased, summarized, or directly quoted?
9. Have you used an appropriate documentation style?
10. Does your concluding sentence or paragraph reemphasize your topic sentence or thesis statement?

EXERCISE 8-23 . . . WRITING A WORKS CITED/REFERENCES LIST

Using either MLA style or APA style, add in-text citations and write a Works Cited/ References list for your essay that you revised in Exercise 8-22. Be sure to include entries for all your sources.

SELF-TEST SUMMARY

To test yourself, cover the right column with a sheet of paper and answer the question in the left column. Evaluate each of your answers by sliding the paper down and comparing it with what is printed in the right column.

	QUESTION	ANSWER
1	**How are essays structured?**	An **essay** is a group of paragraphs about one subject. It contains three parts—an introductory paragraph that includes the thesis statement, supporting paragraphs (body), and the conclusion.
2	**How do you prepare to write an essay?**	Prepare to write an essay by **prewriting**, which involves choosing your topic and generating ideas; narrowing your topic; grouping ideas to discover a thesis; writing a preliminary thesis statement; considering purpose, audience, point of view, and tone; organizing ideas; and choosing a method of development.
3	**What is involved in drafting?**	**Drafting** involves writing and rewriting your essay. It includes drafting body paragraphs; evaluating and revising your thesis statement; supporting your thesis with substantial evidence; using transitions to connect your ideas; and writing an introduction, conclusion, and title.
4	**How do you revise an essay?**	**Revision** involves examining your ideas and how effectively you have expressed them. Use revision maps to evaluate your essay's content and structure, paragraphs, sentences, and words.
5	**How do you edit and proofread?**	**Editing and proofreading** involve making certain your essay is clear, error free, and presented in acceptable manuscript form. Correct errors in spelling, punctuation, and grammar, as well as typographical errors.
6	**What is involved when you write essays using sources?**	Writing a paper **using sources** involves finding appropriate sources, recording information from them, and organizing and synthesizing the information to support your thesis.
7	**How do you find appropriate sources?**	To **find sources**, consult a reference librarian; use a systematic approach, starting with general sources; use current and reliable sources; sample different viewpoints; preview by reading abstracts or summaries; read selectively; and follow leads to additional sources.
	What is plagiarism and how do you record sources to avoid plagiarism?	**Plagiarism** is using an author's words or ideas without acknowledging you have done so. Use note cards or a small notebook to record critical source information, photocopy print sources, and download and/or print and bookmark online sources.

QUESTION	ANSWER
8 *How do you use sources to support a thesis and develop an essay?*	**Use sources** to find facts, statistics, and other evidence that support your thesis. Write a first draft, analyze where you need support, revise your thesis if necessary based on new information, research sources to find relevant facts, opinions, and other evidence, and record the sources you use.
9 *What does it mean to synthesize sources?*	**Synthesis** is a process of using information from two or more sources in order to develop new ideas about a topic or to draw conclusions about it. Comparing sources is part of synthesizing; it involves placing sources side by side and examining how they are the same and how they are different.
10 *How do you integrate quotations into essays?*	When you **integrate quotations** into your writing, introduce them with a signal phrase, provide an in-text citation, and use correct punctuation. Short quotations can be built into your sentences, but longer ones are indented as block quotations.
11 *Why is it important to document your sources?*	When you quote, paraphrase, or summarize a source, you must **credit the author in order to avoid plagiarism**. Two common methods for citing and documenting sources are the MLA and APA styles.
What is MLA style, and when is it used?	**The Modern Language Association (MLA) style** is typically used for documenting sources in English and the humanities and consists of in-text citations that refer readers to a Works Cited list of all sources used, organized alphabetically by authors' last names.
What is APA style, and when is it used?	**The American Psychological Association (APA) style** is used for documenting sources in psychology and other social sciences and consists of in-text citations that refer readers to a References list of all sources used, organized alphabetically by authors' last names.

9 Critical Thinking: Reading and Writing

LEARNING OBJECTIVES

1 Make inferences and draw conclusions
2 Assess sources and author qualifications
3 Understand fake news
4 Distinguish fact from opinion
5 Identify the author's purpose
6 Evaluate tone
7 Interpret figurative language
8 Identify bias
9 Evaluate data and evidence
10 Interpret and use visuals

9a   MAKING ACCURATE INFERENCES AND DRAWING CONCLUSIONS

LEARNING OBJECTIVE 1
Make inferences and draw conclusions

Look at the photograph below, which appeared in a psychology textbook. What do you think is happening here? What are the feelings of the participants?

Ronald Sumners/Shutterstock

To answer these questions, you had to use information you could get from the photo and make decisions based on it. The facial expressions, body language, clothing, and musical instruments presented in this photo provide clues. This reasoning process is called **making an inference**. You also had to use your prior knowledge about concerts, performers, musicians, and so forth. When you use both your prior knowledge and information from a text or image, you **draw a conclusion**.

Inferences and **conclusions** are reasoned guesses about what you don't know made on the basis of what you do know. They are common in our everyday lives. When you get on a highway and see a long, slow-moving line of traffic, you might predict that there is an accident or roadwork ahead. When you see a puddle of water under the kitchen sink, you can infer that you have a plumbing problem. The inferences you make may not always be correct, even though you base them on the available information. The water under the sink might have been the result of a spill. The traffic you encountered on the highway might be normal for that time of day, but you didn't know it because you aren't normally on the road at that time. An inference is only the best guess you can make in a situation, given the information you have.

How to Make Accurate Inferences and Conclusions

When you read the material associated with your college courses, you need to make inferences and draw conclusions frequently. Writers do not always present their ideas directly. Instead, they often leave it to you—the reader—to add up and think beyond the facts they present, and to use your prior knowledge about the topic. You are expected to reason out the meaning an author intended (but did not say) on the basis of what he or she did say.

Each inference and conclusion you make depends on the situation, the facts provided, and your own knowledge and experience. Here are a few guidelines to help you see beyond the factual level and make accurate inferences from your reading materials.

Understand the Literal Meaning

You must understand the stated ideas and facts before you can move to higher levels of thinking, which include inference making and drawing conclusions. You should recognize the topic, main idea, key details, and organizational pattern of each paragraph you have read.

Notice Details

As you are reading, pay particular attention to details that are unusual or stand out. Often, such details will offer you clues to help you make inferences. Ask yourself:

- What is unusual or striking about this piece of information?
- Why is it included here?

Read the following excerpt, which is taken from an essay about a young Polish immigrant to the United Kingdom, and mark any details that seem unusual or striking.

Issue: Immigration

An Immigration Plan Gone Awry

Due to her own hardship, Katja was not thrilled when her younger brother called her from Warsaw and said that he was going to join her in the United Kingdom (U.K.). Katja warned him that opportunities were scarce in London for a Polish immigrant. "Don't worry," he said in an effort to soothe her anxiety. "I already have a job in a factory." An advertisement in a Warsaw paper had promised good pay for Polish workers in Birmingham. A broker's fee of $500 and airfare were required, so her brother borrowed the money from their mother. He made the trip with a dozen other young Polish men.

The "broker" picked the young men up at Heathrow [airport] and piled them in a van. They drove directly to Birmingham, and at nightfall the broker dropped the whole crew off at a ramshackle house inside the city. He ordered them to be ready to be picked up in the morning for their first day of work. A bit dazed by the pace, they stretched out on the floor to sleep.

Their rest was brief. In the wee hours of the night, the broker returned with a gang of 10 or so thugs armed with cricket [similar to baseball] bats. They beat the young Polish boys to a pulp and robbed them of all their valuables. Katja's brother took some heavy kicks to the ribs and head, then stumbled out of the house. Once outside, he saw two police cars parked across the street. The officers in the cars obviously chose to ignore the mayhem playing out in front of their eyes. Katja's brother knew better than try to convince them otherwise; the police in Poland would act no differently. Who knows, maybe they were part of the broker's scam. Or maybe they just didn't care about a bunch of poor Polish immigrants "invading" their town.

—Batstone, "Katja's Story," from *Sojourner's*

Did you mark details such as the $500 broker's fee, the promise of a well-paying job despite scarce job opportunities for Polish immigrants, and the terrible sleeping conditions?

Add Up the Facts

Consider all of the facts taken together. To do this, ask yourself the following questions:

- What is the writer trying to suggest with this set of facts?
- What do all these facts and ideas seem to point toward or add up to?
- Why did the author include these facts and details?

Making an inference is somewhat like assembling a complicated jigsaw puzzle; you try to make all the pieces fit together to form a recognizable picture. Answering these questions requires you to add together all the individual pieces of information, which will help you arrive at an inference.

When you add up the facts in the article "An Immigration Plan Gone Awry," you realize that Katja's brother is the victim of a scam.

Be Alert to Clues

Writers often provide you with numerous hints that can point you toward accurate inferences. An awareness of word choices, details included (and omitted), ideas emphasized, and direct commentary can help you determine a writer's attitude toward the topic at hand. In "An Immigration Plan Gone Awry," the "ramshackle" house, the men "piled" into a van, and the immigrants sleeping on the floor are all clues that something is amiss.

Consider the Author's Purpose

Also study the author's purpose for writing. What does he or she hope to accomplish? In "An Immigration Plan Gone Awry," the writer is critical of immigrant brokers and of the police.

Verify Your Inference

Once you have made an inference, check to make sure that it is accurate. Look back at the stated facts to be sure you have sufficient evidence to support the inference. Also be certain you have not overlooked other equally plausible or more plausible inferences that could be drawn from the same set of facts.

EXERCISE 9-1 . . . MAKING INFERENCES AND DRAWING CONCLUSIONS

Study the photograph below and place a check mark in front of each statement that is a reasonable inference or conclusion that can be made from the photograph.

Piotr Wawrzyniuk/Shutterstock

_____ 1. It is likely that the photograph takes place at a march or walk-out.

_____ 2. The participants holding the signs are probably advocates of voter reform.

_____ 3. The participants likely do not believe in climate change.

_____ 4. "There Is No Planet B" means that there is no second chance to save our planet.

_____ 5. "Change the Politics" refers to changing governmental policies or legislation.

EXERCISE 9-2 . . . MAKING INFERENCES AND DRAWING CONCLUSIONS

Read each of the following statements. Place a check mark in front of each sentence that follows that is a reasonable inference or conclusion that can be made from the statement.

1. Many job applicants have found that their postings on Facebook or their tweets on Twitter have had negative effects on their job interviews.

_____ a. Job recruiters look up candidates' online histories.

_____ b. Young people should be careful about what they post online.

_____ c. The majority of people over age 23 now have Facebook accounts.

_____ d. Tweeting has become an accepted method of staying in touch with friends.

2. Reality TV may look spontaneous and unscripted, but reality TV shows are carefully edited before they are televised.

_____ a. In truth, reality TV is not particularly realistic.

_____ b. The directors and producers of reality TV may distort facts and events.

_____ c. Reality TV shows are cheaper to produce because there is no need for writers to write the dialogue.

_____ d. Most people now prefer to watch reality TV rather than sitcoms or dramas.

3. The goal of health care reform in the United States is to ensure that as many people as possible have medical insurance and decent medical care, as in Canada and Europe.

_____ a. The cost of medical care is likely to decrease.

_____ b. Under the old medical care system, many people in the United States had no access to medical care.

_____ c. As a result of health care reform, there is likely to be a shortage of doctors.

_____ d. Canada and Europe currently do a better job of providing health care to their citizens than the United States does.

EXERCISE 9-3 . . . MAKING INFERENCES AND DRAWING CONCLUSIONS

Read each of the following passages. Determine whether the statements following each passage are true or false. Place a T next to each true statement and an F next to each false statement.

A. Issue: Literacy

On the surface, development statistics show impressive gains in education among developing countries. By the early twenty-first century, more than 80 percent of children were enrolled in primary school, and five out of six of the world's adults were literate, according to the United Nations Development Report in 2008. Yet the same report notes that only slightly over one-half of children attend school in sub-Saharan Africa and in many developing countries few children even graduate from primary school. Illiteracy rates in most middle-income nations are much lower, typically less than 20 percent. However, millions of rural and urban children receive no education whatsoever.

—adapted from Thompson and Hickey, *Society in Focus*, p. 239

_____ 1. In middle-income nations, urban children are more likely to be denied an education than rural children.

_____ 2. Today, the great majority of the world's population is literate.

_____ 3. Literacy rates are generally higher in middle-income nations than they are in developing nations.

_____ 4. More than half the children in sub-Saharan Africa will graduate from primary school.

_____ 5. The United Nations Development Report describes social trends in developing (poor) nations.

B. Issue: Family and Family Trends

Many of you have probably grown up on tales of men running from marriage, going to great lengths to avoid being "trapped." This folklore actually runs counter to the reality of women's and men's lives. In reality, men seem to prefer marriage to being single. For example, when asked if they would marry the same person again, they respond in the affirmative twice as often as their wives. In addition, most divorced and widowed men remarry, and the rate of marriage for these men at every age level is higher than the rate for single men. Furthermore, when compared with single men, married men live longer, have better mental and physical health, are less depressed, have a lower rate of suicide, are less likely to be incarcerated for a crime, earn higher incomes, and are more likely to define themselves as happy.

—Schwartz and Scott, *Marriages and Families*, p. 255

_____ 6. Marriage has a number of beneficial effects on men.

_____ 7. Marriage is more beneficial to men than to women.

_____ 8. Married men are less likely to be in jail than married women are.

_____ 9. More men than women are happy in their current marriage.

_____ 10. A man who has been married is not likely to marry again.

EXERCISE 9-4 . . . MAKING INFERENCES AND DRAWING CONCLUSIONS

Read the following passage and the statements that follow. Place a check mark next to the statements that are reasonable inferences or conclusions.

Issue: Police Techniques

August Vollmer was the chief of police of Berkeley, California, from 1905 to 1932. Vollmer's vision of policing was quite different from most of his contemporaries. He believed the police should be a "dedicated body of educated persons comprising a distinctive corporate entity with a prescribed code of behavior." He was critical of his contemporaries and they of him. San Francisco police administrator Charley Dullea, who later became president of the International Association of Chiefs of Police, refused to drive through Berkeley in protest against Vollmer. Fellow California police chiefs may have felt their opposition to Vollmer was justified, given his vocal and strong criticism of other California police departments. For example, Vollmer publicly referred to San Francisco cops as "morons," and in an interview with a newspaper reporter, he called Los Angeles cops "low grade mental defectives."

Because of his emphasis on education, professionalism, and administrative reform, Vollmer often is seen as the counterpart of London's Sir Robert Peel and is sometimes called the "father of modern American policing." Vollmer was decades ahead of his contemporaries, but he was not able to implement significant change in policing during his lifetime. It remained for Vollmer's students to implement change. For example, O.W. Wilson, who became chief of police of Chicago, promoted college education for police officers and wrote a book on police administration that reflected many of Vollmer's philosophies. It was adopted widely by police executives and used as a college textbook well into the 1960s.

Vollmer is credited with a number of innovations. He was an early adopter of the automobile for patrol and the use of radios in police cars. He recruited college-educated police officers. He developed and implemented a 3-year training curriculum for police officers, including classes in physics, chemistry, biology, physiology, anatomy, psychology, psychiatry, anthropology, and criminology. He developed a system of signal boxes for hailing police officers. He adopted the use of typewriters to fill out police reports and records, and officers received training in typing. He surveyed other police departments to gather information about their practices. Many of his initiatives have become common practice within contemporary police departments.

—Fagin, *Criminal Justice*, pp. 245–246

_____ 1. Vollmer did not have a college degree.

_____ 2. Most police officers of Vollmer's time had a limited education.

_____ 3. Vollmer believed police should be held accountable for their actions.

_____ 4. Sir Robert Peel dramatically changed policing procedures in England.

_____ 5. Vollmer received support from most police officers on the street.

_____ 6. Vollmer would support recent technological advances in policing.

_____ 7. Police departments of Vollmer's time were run with a careful eye toward accuracy and fairness.

_____ 8. Vollmer outlawed billy clubs.

Thinking Critically About Inferences as You Write

If you want to be completely sure that your readers understand your message, state it directly. If you only imply an idea and do not directly state it, there is a chance your reader may miss your point. Worse yet, there is a possibility that less than careful readers may infer an idea you had not intended, creating a misunderstanding or miscommunication.

There are occasions in which you may deliberately leave an idea unstated. You may want to lead your readers to an idea, but let them figure it out for themselves, thinking it was their idea. Especially in argument, you may want to lead your readers to take action or accept a particular viewpoint, but you may prefer not to make a direct plea. When following this strategy, be sure to supply enough detail and evidence so your readers make the desired inference.

9b   ASSESSING SOURCES AND AUTHOR QUALIFICATIONS

LEARNING OBJECTIVE 2
Assess sources and author qualifications

Two very important considerations in evaluating any written material are the source in which it was printed and the authority, or qualifications, of the author.

Considering the Source

Your reaction to and evaluation of printed or online material should take into account its source. Often the source of a piece of writing can indicate how accurate, detailed, and well documented an article is. Consider this example: Suppose you are in the library trying to find information on sleepwalking for a term paper. You locate the following sources, each of which contains an article on sleepwalking. Which would you expect to be the most factual, detailed, and scientific?

- an encyclopedia entry on sleepwalking
- an article titled "Strange Things Happen While You Are Sleeping" in *Woman's Day*
- an article titled "An Examination of Research on Sleepwalking" in *Psychological Review*

You would expect the encyclopedia entry to provide only a general overview of the topic. You might expect the article in *Woman's Day* to discuss various abnormalities that occur during sleep, as well as to relate several unusual or extreme cases of sleepwalking, rather than to present a factual analysis of the topic. The article in *Psychological Review*, a journal that reports research in psychology, is the one that would contain a factual, authoritative discussion of sleepwalking. You can see from this example that from the source alone you can make predictions about the content and approach used.

Ask the questions in the following box to evaluate a source:

HOW TO EVALUATE A SOURCE
1. What reputation does the source have?
2. Who is the audience for whom the source is intended?
3. Are references or documentation provided?

Considering the Author's Credentials

To evaluate printed material, you must also consider the competency of the author. Use the following guidelines to assess a writer's expertise.

Checking and Evaluating Author Credentials in . . .

- **Textbooks.** In textbooks, the author's college or university affiliation, and possibly his or her title, may appear on the title page beneath the author's name, in the preface, or on the back cover. Based on his or her education and teaching experience, you can infer whether the author is knowledgeable about the topic.
- **Nonfiction books and general market paperbacks.** A synopsis of the author's credentials and experiences may be included on the book jacket or the back cover. There is also often additional material available on the publisher's and/or author's Web site.
- **Newspapers, magazines, and reference books.** In these sources, you are given little or no information about the writer. You can rely on the judgment of the editors or publishers to assess an author's authority and/or check the Web site for publication, where you may find more biographical information about columnists and reporters. You could also Google a writer to find out more about his or her background and experience.

EXERCISE 9-5 . . . EVALUATING SOURCES

Working with a classmate, predict and discuss how useful and appropriate each of the following sources would be for the situation described.

1. Using an article from *Working Women* on family aggression for a term paper for your sociology class

   _____

   _____

2. Quoting an article in *The New York Times* on recent events in China for a speech titled "Innovation and Change in China"

   _____

3. Reading an article titled "Bilingual Education in the Twenty-First Century" printed in the *Educational Research Quarterly* for a paper arguing for increased federal aid for bilingual education

   _____

   _____

4. Using an article in *TV Guide* on television's coverage of crime and violence for a term paper on the effects of television on society

   _____

   _____

5. Using information from a book written by former First Lady Laura Bush in a class discussion on use and abuse of presidential power

   _____

   _____

Evaluating Internet Sources

Although the Internet contains a great deal of valuable information and resources, it also contains rumor, gossip, hoaxes, and misinformation. In other words, not all Internet sources are trustworthy. You must evaluate a source before accepting it. Here are some guidelines to follow when evaluating Internet sources.

Evaluating the Content of a Web Site

When evaluating the content of a Web site, evaluate its appropriateness, its source, its level of technical detail, its presentation, its completeness, and its links.

- **Evaluate appropriateness.** To be worthwhile, a Web site should contain the information you need. If it does not address your questions in sufficient detail, check the links on the site to see if they lead you to more detailed information, or search for a more useful site.

- **Evaluate the source.** Ask yourself "Who is the sponsor?" and "Why was this site put up on the Web?" The sponsor is the person or organization who paid for the creation and placement of the site on the Web; who they are will often suggest the purpose of a site. For example, a site sponsored by Nike has a commercial purpose, while a site sponsored by a university library is educational or informational. If you are uncertain who sponsors a Web site, check its URL, its copyright, and the links it offers, or try to locate the site's home page.

- **Evaluate the level of technical detail.** A site's level of technical detail should be suited to your purpose. Some sites may provide information that is too sketchy for your search purposes; others assume a level of background knowledge or technical sophistication that you lack.

- **Evaluate the presentation.** Information should be well written and presented. If it is not, you should be suspicious. An author who did not take time to present ideas clearly and correctly may not have taken time to collect accurate information either.

- **Evaluate completeness.** Does the site address all aspects of the topic that you feel it should? If you discover that a site is incomplete, search for sites that provide a more thorough treatment of the topic.

- **Evaluate the links.** Many reputable sites supply links to other related sites. Make sure that the links are current and the sites they link to are reliable sources of information. If the links do not work or the sources appear unreliable, you should question the reliability of the site itself. Also determine whether the links provided are comprehensive or only present a representative sample. Either is acceptable, but the site should make clear the nature of the links it is providing.

EXERCISE 9-6 . . . EVALUATING CONTENT

Evaluate the content of two of the following sites. Explain why you would either trust or distrust each site as a source of reliable content.

1. http://www.innercircleofpoets.com

2. http://www.earlham.edu/~peters/knotlink.htm

3. http://www.age-of-the-sage.org/psychology/

Evaluating the Accuracy and Timeliness of a Web Site

When using information on a Web site for an academic paper, it is important to be sure that you have found accurate and up-to-date information. One way to determine the accuracy of a Web site is to compare it with print sources (periodicals and books) on the same topic. If you find a wide discrepancy between the Web site and the printed sources, do not trust the Web site. Another way to determine a site's accuracy is to compare it with other Web sites that address the same topic. If discrepancies exist, further research is needed to determine which site is more accurate.

Tips for Evaluating Accuracy

The site itself will also provide clues about the accuracy of its information. Ask yourself the following questions:

- **Are the author's name and credentials provided?** A well-known writer with established credentials is likely to author reliable, accurate information. If no author name is given, you should question whether the information is accurate.
- **Is contact information for the author included on the site?** Sites often provide an e-mail address where the author may be contacted.
- **Is the information complete or in summary form?** If it is a summary, use the site to find the original source. Original information has less chance of error and is usually preferred in academic papers.
- **If opinions are offered, are they presented clearly as opinions?** Authors who disguise their opinions as facts are not trustworthy.
- **Does the writer make unsubstantiated assumptions or base his or her ideas on misconceptions?** If so, the information presented may not be accurate.
- **Does the site provide a list of works cited?** As with any form of research, sources used to put information up on a Web site must be documented. If sources are not credited, you should question the accuracy of the Web site.

Although the Web is well known for providing up-to-the-minute information, not all Web sites are current.

Tips for Evaluating Timeliness

Evaluate a site's timeliness by checking the following dates:

- the date on which the Web site was published (put up on the Web)
- the date when the document you are using was added
- the date when the site was last revised
- the date when the links were last checked

This information is usually provided at the end of the site's home page or at the end of the document you are using.

EXERCISE 9-7 . . . EVALUATING ACCURACY AND TIMELINESS

Evaluate the accuracy and timeliness of two of the sites you evaluated for Exercise 9-6.

Thinking Critically About Source and Authority as You Write

As critical thinkers, your readers will assess your qualifications and knowledge of the subject you are writing about. Many factors can create an image of you as a serious, competent writer, qualified to write on your topic. These include the following:

- **A correct, error-free essay that is neatly presented.** Readers may assume that if you have not taken the time to present your paper carefully, you may not have taken the time to research or think through your ideas, either.

- **A well-documented paper.** If you use sources, be sure to give your sources credit using in-text citations and a Works Cited or References list. (See Chapter 8 for more detailed information on how to do this.) Failure to credit sources is dishonest, and your readers may realize you have not done so.

- **An honest approach to the topic.** If you are not an expert on your topic, do not present yourself as one. If you do have expertise on your topic, you might build mention of your expertise into the essay for the purpose of establishing your credibility. For example, if you are a first responder for your community volunteer fire company and are writing about accidents that occur when drivers are texting, you might acknowledge your experience responding to accidents.

9c   UNDERSTANDING FAKE NEWS

LEARNING OBJECTIVE 3
Understand fake news

Fake news is a current topic of discussion and debate in many academic communities. As such, it demands our attention and requires our scrutiny. Fake news may include gossip Web sites that have no basis in reality, blogs that offer opinions that are based on scanty or nonexistent evidence, and news sites that exaggerate or falsely report current events.

What Is Fake News?

Fake news is false information that is deliberately and intentionally presented to mislead readers or listeners. It is often damaging to a person, entity, or agency. It pretends to be from a legitimate, trustworthy source. Most often, it is spread through the Internet, either through Web sites or social media. Fake news is intended to attract attention, and it may generate advertising revenue for high traffic sites.

Here is an example of the phenomenon. False stories and hoaxes often follow horrific events, according to *USA Today*, which reports that following the mass shooting in a Parkland, Florida, high school, a reporter's tweets were doctored, and fake tweets were published. In one false tweet, published before the shooter had even been apprehended, the reporter supposedly asked survivors whether they had photos or videos of dead bodies or whether the shooter was white.[1]

Fake news uses numerous deceptive techniques, including the following:

- Fake news may use misleading headlines, visuals, or graphics.
- Fake news may "doctor" or revise legitimate sources or images to suit their own purposes.
- Fake news may impersonate real, legitimate people or sources.
- Fake news may use truthful content but repurpose it or present it in an unfair context.

How to Identify Fake News

Fake news is often written to appear as legitimate, credible journalism. In fact, some fake news Web sites design their site to very closely resemble the authentic site they are trying to imitate. In addition to the tips provided in the previous section for evaluating a web site's accuracy, consider the following telltale signs of fake news:

1. **It is published in only one source.** If one source announces an "exclusive story that you won't find anywhere else," proceed with caution, especially if the source does not have verified journalistic credentials. It is also possible that multiple sites publish a story, but all of them are obtaining their information from one unverified source.

2. **The source is untrustworthy.** For example, *The National Enquirer* has been spreading celebrity gossip for decades. *The Globe* is another well-known tabloid. Tabloids such as these report absurd stories such as a mini-mermaid found in a tuna sandwich or five U.S. senators being space aliens.

3. **The domain name resembles a reputable journalistic source.** A fake news source may create a domain name that is only a slight variation from a mainstream news source.

4. **Attention-grabbing headlines create an emotional response.** Reliable news sources seek to grab readers' attention with statements that are supported with evidence in the article. Many fake news outlets rely on readers' unwillingness to read the entire article.

---

[1]https://www.usatoday.com/story/tech/news/2018/02/15/florida-school-shooting-doctored-tweets-russian-bots-and-hoaxes-spread-false-news/340349002/

5. **There is no "About Us" page on the site.** Most reputable sources have an "About Us" page or link that states the site's mission, explains who runs it, and provides contact information.

6. **Vague polls and unnamed sources are used.** A source may cite a poll "proving" that most people have a fear of heights or a survey "suggesting" that everyone in America prefers tall, male politicians. Credible sources identify the polling organization, how many people were surveyed, and where. Unnamed sources—often quoted in *The National Enquirer* and gossip Web sites—may very well be fraudulent.

Several Web sites have been created to evaluate news stories and rumors to determine their level of truthfulness. These include FactCheck.org, PolitiFact, and Snopes.org.

How the Term "Fake News" Is Misused

The term "fake news" has been misused to refer to any source or piece of information that does not agree with one's own views and opinions. For example, a research report on the health risks of consuming too many soft drinks could be labeled fake news by members of the soft drink industry because the report conflicts with the industry's position that its drinks are safe and healthy food sources.

EXERCISE 9-8 . . . USING A FACT-CHECKING SITE

Visit the fact-checking site Snopes.com or another recommended by your instructor. Preview the site to discover how it is organized and what it offers. If using Snopes.com, be sure to visit the Fact Check page and look at 5–10 items. For the site you visited, write a one-paragraph summary of what you learned about fake news and how it is used. Include several examples.

9d DISTINGUISHING BETWEEN FACT AND OPINION

LEARNING OBJECTIVE 4
Distinguish fact from opinion

When working with any source, readers and writers should try to determine whether the material is factual or an expression of opinion. **Facts** are statements that are true and can be verified. **Opinions** are statements that express feelings, attitudes, or beliefs and are neither true nor false. Following are examples of each:

Facts

1. Canada, the United States, and Mexico are all members of the North American Free Trade Agreement.
2. Facebook has become the world's most popular social networking site.

Opinions

1. Employers should be banned from spying on employees and reading their e-mail.
2. All immigration into the United States must be halted for a ten-year period.

Facts, when verified or taken from a reputable source, can be accepted and regarded as reliable information. Opinions, on the other hand, are not reliable sources of information and should be questioned and carefully evaluated. Look for evidence that supports the opinion and indicates that it is reasonable. For example, opinion 2 is written to sound like a fact, but look closely. Would everyone agree with this statement? Can it be disputed?

Identifying Facts and Opinions

Some writers signal the reader when they are presenting an opinion. Watch for the following words and phrases as you read.

according to	it is believed that	presumably
apparently	it is likely that	seemingly
in my opinion	one explanation is	this suggests
in my view	possibly	

In the following excerpt from a business textbook, notice how the author uses qualifying words and phrases (underlined), as well as direct quotations from social critics, to indicate opinions on the topic "Are advertising and marketing necessary?"

Issue: Advertising and Ethics

Are Advertising and Marketing Necessary?

More than 50 years ago, the social critic Vance Packard wrote, "Large-scale efforts are being made, often with impressive success, to channel our unthinking habits, our purchasing decisions, and our thought processes by the use of insights gleaned from psychiatry and the social sciences." The economist John Kenneth Galbraith charged that radio and television are important tools to accomplish this manipulation of the masses. Because consumers don't need to be literate to use these media, repetitive and compelling communications can reach almost everyone. This criticism may be even more relevant to online communications, where a simple click delivers a world of information to us.

Many feel that marketers arbitrarily link products to desirable social attributes, fostering a materialistic society in which we are measured by what we own. One influential critic even argued that the problem is that we are not materialistic enough—that is, we do not sufficiently value goods for the utilitarian functions they deliver but instead focus on the irrational value of goods for what they symbolize. According to this view, for example, "Beer would be enough for us, without the additional promise that in drinking it we show ourselves to be manly, young at heart, or neighborly. A washing machine would be a useful machine to wash clothes rather than an indication that we are forward-looking or an object of envy to our neighbors."

—Solomon, *Consumer Behavior*, p. 23

Other authors do just the opposite; they try to make opinions sound like facts, or they mix fact and opinion without making clear distinctions. This is particularly true in the case of **expert opinion**, which is the opinion of a recognized authority on a topic. Political commentators on Sunday news programs (sometimes called "pundits") represent expert opinion on politics, for example. Textbook authors, too, often offer expert opinion, as in the following statement from an American government text.

Ours is a complex system of justice. Sitting at the pinnacle of the judicial system is the Supreme Court, but its importance is often exaggerated.

—Lineberry et al., *Government in America*, p. 540

The authors of this statement have reviewed the available evidence and are providing their expert opinion regarding what the evidence indicates about the Supreme Court. The reader is free to disagree and offer evidence to support an opposing view.

EXERCISE 9-9 . . . DISTINGUISHING FACT AND OPINION

Read each of the following statements and identify whether it is fact (F), opinion (O), or expert opinion (EO).

F/O_ 1. Toyota is the world's largest automaker.

O_ 2. Apple Computer, already one of the world's most successful companies, will continue to be successful because of its history of innovation and product design.

F_ 3. Americans spend approximately $40 billion per year on diet aids, diet books, and diet foods.

O_ 4. The best way to read a book is on the Kindle Fire.

EO_ 5. A capital good, as defined by economists, is a good bought by businesses to increase their productive resources.

F   6. The U.S. government is comprised of three branches: executive, legislative, and judicial.

EO   7. Anthropologists believe that some native communities in the Americas practiced human sacrifice.

EO   8. According to Dr. Elaine Feldman, a psychologist who specializes in anxiety management, deep breathing can greatly help people reduce their stress levels.

O   9. The finest novels in English history were written by Jane Austen.

O   10. Corn-based fuel (biodiesel) is better than gasoline.

EXERCISE 9-10 . . . DISTINGUISHING FACT AND OPINION

Each of the following paragraphs contains both facts and opinions. Read each paragraph and label each sentence as fact (F), opinion (O), or expert opinion (EO).

A. Issue: Slavery and Freedom

[1]Harriet Tubman was born a slave in Maryland in 1820 and escaped to Philadelphia in 1849. [2]Her own escape presumably required tremendous courage, but that was just the beginning. [3]Through her work on the Underground Railroad, Harriet Tubman led more than 300 slaves to freedom. [4]During the Civil War, Tubman continued her efforts toward the abolition of slavery by working as a nurse and a spy for the Union forces. [5]Today, Americans of all races consider Harriet Tubman one of the most heroic figures in our country's history.

Sentences: 1. _____ 2. _____ 3. _____ 4. _____ 5. _____

B. Issue: Drugs and Addiction

[1]Those big stogies that we see celebrities and government figures smoking are nothing more than tobacco fillers wrapped in more tobacco. [2]Since 1993, cigar sales in the United States have increased dramatically, up nearly 124 percent between 1993 and 2007. [3]The fad, especially popular among young men and women, is fueled in part by the willingness of celebrities to be photographed puffing on a cigar. [4]It's also fueled by the fact that cigars cost much less than cigarettes in most states. [5]Also, among some women, cigar smoking symbolizes being slightly outrageous and liberated. [6]According to a recent national survey, about 11 percent of Americans aged 18 to 25 had smoked a cigar in the past month.

—Donatelle, *Access to Health*, p. 386

Sentences: 1. _____ 2. _____ 3. _____ 4. _____ 5. _____ 6. _____

C. Issue: Cultural Similarities and Differences

[1]Some sociologists believe that if any nation deserves the "pro-family" label, it is Sweden. [2]In the past century, the Swedish state, in cooperation with labor, industry, and the feminist and other social movements, has provided money and services to support family life and the employment of women. [3]And, to a lesser degree, it has sought to eliminate gender inequality and laws and customs that reinforce women's secondary place in society. [4]As a result, wrote sociologist Joan Acker, "Swedish women enjoy public programs and economic guarantees that have made Sweden a model for women in other countries."

—adapted from Thompson and Hickey, *Society in Focus*, p. 383

Sentences: 1. _____ 2. _____ 3. _____ 4. _____

Thinking Critically About the Facts and Opinions You Use

Facts are the building blocks of many paragraphs and are essential to good writing. Opinions, however, may or may not be appropriate, depending on your purpose and the nature of the writing task or assignment. If you are writing a summary, for instance, your opinion of the material does not belong in it, unless you have been asked to analyze or comment on the source text. If you are writing a research paper, your personal opinions are not useful or appropriate.

In some other types of assignments, the use of personal opinion may be appropriate, as long as you substantiate or provide evidence to support it. In writing a response to a poem for a literature class, for example, it is certainly appropriate to express your reactions and feelings about it, as long as you support your opinions with references to the poem. Or in writing an essay about Super Bowl advertising, you may express a viewpoint that the commercials are the best part of the show or that they are extravagant wastes of money. Again, you should give reasons, examples, and so forth to support your viewpoint. Never just offer opinions without explanation and justification.

9e   IDENTIFYING THE AUTHOR'S PURPOSE

LEARNING OBJECTIVE 5
Identify the author's purpose

Writers have many different reasons or purposes for writing. Read the following statements and try to decide why each was written:

1. In 2011, about 17.5 million people traveled through the Chunnel, the tunnel that connects France and England. This averages to about 48,000 people per day.

2. *New Vegetable Sticks in Sensible Portions.* Finally, a snack made from real vegetables with no added sugar or fats. We lightly sauté the vegetables so that they're crispy and crunchy, and then we package them in 100-calorie packets. Buy a box this week.
3. I don't like when people repeat themselves. I also do not like when they are redundant or repetitive, or when they repeat themselves.
4. To prevent yourself from being attacked by mosquitoes or ticks on a hike, be sure to use an insect repellent made with Deet.

Statement 1 was written to give information, 2 to persuade you to buy vegetable sticks, 3 to amuse you and make a comment on human behavior, 4 to give advice.

Determining an Author's Purpose

Often, a writer's purpose is fairly clear, as it is in most textbooks (to present information), newspaper articles (to communicate local, national, or world events), and reference books (to compile facts). However, in many other types of writing—especially materials concerning controversial contemporary issues—writers have varied, sometimes less obvious, purposes. In these cases, the writer's purpose must be inferred.

Often a writer's purpose is to express an opinion directly or indirectly. The writer may also want to encourage the reader to think about a particular issue or problem. Writers achieve their purposes by manipulating and controlling what they say and how they say it.

EXERCISE 9-11 . . . IDENTIFYING THE AUTHOR'S PURPOSE

Read each of the following statements. Then find the author's purpose for each statement in the box below and write it in the space provided.

to persuade	to entertain	to inform
to advise	to criticize	

_____ 1. When choosing your courses for next year, try to find a balance between required courses and electives that you will enjoy.

_____ 2. I don't want to belong to any club that will accept me as a member. (Groucho Marx)

_____ 3. Travelers to Saudi Arabia should be aware that non-Muslims are not permitted in the cities of Mecca and Medina.

_____   4. Now is the time to support gun-control legislation, before more innocent lives are lost to illegal firearms.

_____   5. The mayor's plan to limit the sizes of sugary soft drinks to a maximum of 16 ounces is simply ridiculous. It is an example of intrusive government at its worst.

Determining Your Purpose for Writing

Every piece of writing should be written with a specific purpose in mind. Your purpose is what you want your essay to accomplish. In general, there are three main purposes:

1. **To express or share ideas or feelings.** You might write an essay expressing outrage at the rudeness of people in a movie theater, or you might write a letter to the editor of your campus newspaper sharing your feelings about a campus issue.

2. **To inform your readers.** You might write an essay presenting information about recent internet scams and offering advice on how your readers can protect themselves, for instance.

3. **To persuade your readers.** You might write an essay persuading your readers that they should become organ donors, for example, or should adopt pets from shelters rather than purchase them from breeders.

It is possible for an essay to have more than one purpose. An essay written to explain a vegan diet may also encourage readers to gradually move to a meatless diet.

9f   EVALUATING TONE

LEARNING OBJECTIVE 6
Evaluate tone

The tone of a speaker's voice helps you interpret what he or she is saying. If the following sentence were spoken, the speaker's voice would tell you how to interpret it: "Would you mind closing the door?" In print you cannot tell whether the speaker is polite, insistent, or angry.

Assessing an Author's Tone

Tone refers to the attitude or feeling a writer expresses about his or her subject. Just as a speaker's tone of voice tells how the speaker feels, a writer conveys a tone, or feeling, through his or her writing. The tone of the article "Consequences of Social Class" (p. 8) is informative. The author presents facts, research, and other evidence to support his thesis.

A writer may adopt a sentimental tone, an angry tone, a humorous tone, a sympathetic tone, an instructive tone, a persuasive tone, and so forth. Here are some examples of different tones. How does each make you feel?

- **Instructive**

When purchasing a used car, let the buyer beware. Get a CarFax report that shows the vehicle's history, and ask the seller for a copy of the maintenance records, which will tell you how closely the owner has followed the recommended maintenance schedule.

- **Sympathetic**

Each year, millions of women have miscarriages. My heart goes out to these strong women, who often suffer in silence.

- **Persuasive**

For just 40 cents a day, you can sponsor a poor child in a developing country. Yes, you can make a difference in a child's life for only $12 per month. The question is: How can you afford *not* to contribute?

- **Humorous**

There are two kinds of people in the world: Italians, and those who wish they were Italian.

- **Nostalgic**

Oh, how I long for the simplicity of the 1980s: before everyone was glued to their computers or cell phones every minute of the day; before cable television offered hundreds of channels I cannot possibly watch; before everyone decided to become a singer, celebrity, or reality TV star.

In the first example, the writer offers advice in a straightforward, informative style. In the second, the writer wants you to feel sympathy for women who have miscarried; she encourages this sympathy by describing that these women "often suffer in silence." In the third example, the writer tries to persuade the reader to donate to a worthy cause. In the fourth example, the writer charms with a witty observation, and in the fifth example, the writer fondly reminisces about a simpler time before technology played such a prominent role in society.

To identify an author's tone, pay particular attention to descriptive language and connotations (see Section 3d, p. 90). Ask yourself: "How does the author feel about the subject, and how are these feelings revealed?" It is sometimes difficult to find the right word to describe the author's tone. Table 9-1 lists words that are often used to describe tone. Use this list to help you identify tone. If any of these words are unfamiliar, check their meanings in a dictionary.

TABLE 9-1 WORDS FREQUENTLY USED TO DESCRIBE TONE

amused	condemning	formal	loving	playful
angry	condescending	frustrated	malicious	reverent
arrogant	cynical	hateful	mocking	righteous
assertive	depressing	impassioned	nostalgic	sarcastic
bitter	detached	indignant	objective	serious
caustic	disapproving	indirect	optimistic	sympathetic
celebratory	distressed	informative	outraged	vindictive
cheerful	excited	intimate	pathetic	worried
comic	flippant	irreverent	persuasive	
compassionate	forgiving	joyful	pessimistic	

EXERCISE 9-12 . . . RECOGNIZING TONE

Read each of the following statements. Then choose a word from the box that describes the statement's tone and write it in the space provided. Only some of the tone words are used.

optimistic	angry	admiring	cynical/bitter
excited	humorous	nostalgic	disapproving
formal	informative	sarcastic	

disapproving   1. Cecelia lets her young children stay awake until all hours of the night. Doesn't she realize that growing children need sleep and a predictable schedule?

informative   2. The ostrich is the world's largest bird, the capybara is the world's largest rodent, and the tarantula is the world's largest spider.

admiring   3. Sir Walter Scott was not only a gifted novelist; he was also a kind, generous man who was widely respected and loved.

nostalgic   4. Every time I see figs, I think about the fig tree in my grandfather's garden.

humorous   5. I avoid clichés like the plague, and I eschew obfuscation.

sarcastic   6. What selfless civil servants politicians are! While everyone else struggles in a difficult economy, they vote themselves large pay raises and extended vacations.

optimistic   7. The success of a newly launched news magazine, *The Week*, is proof that print magazines can survive and flourish in the Internet era.

bitter   8. Every time a woman asks me what I do for a living, I wonder if she is trying to figure out how much money I make.

Excited   9. Finally, after years of waiting, I am taking a cruise to Alaska!

formal   10. Mr. and Mrs. Dane LeFever request the honor of your presence at the wedding celebration of their daughter, Sandra Anne, on Wednesday, December 5. Kindly RSVP at your earliest convenience.

EXERCISE 9-13 . . . RECOGNIZING TONE

Read each of the following statements, paying particular attention to the tone. Then write a sentence that describes the tone. Prove your point by listing some of the words that reveal the author's feelings.

1. No one says that wind power is risk free. There are dangers involved in all methods of producing energy. It is true that wind turbines can harm or kill birds. But science and experience have shown us that wind power can be generated cleanly and efficiently. Wind power is at least as safe as, or safer than, many other means of generating power.

    _____

    _____

    _____

2. The state of our schools is shocking. Their hallways are littered with paper and other garbage. Their restrooms are dirty and unsafe for children. The playgrounds are frequented by drug dealers and other unsavory people. Don't we pay school taxes to give our children a safe place to learn and grow?

    _____

    _____

3. I am a tired homeowner. I am tired of mowing the lawn. I'm sick of raking leaves. I'm thoroughly worn out by cleaning and dusting. I am exhausted by leaky faucets, unpainted rooms, and messy basements.

    _____

    _____

4. Cross-country skis have heel plates of different shapes and materials. They may be made of metal, plastic, or rubber. Be sure that they are tacked on the ski right where the heel of your boot will fall. They will keep snow from collecting under your foot and offer some stability.

_____

_____

Thinking Critically About Your Tone

The tone you use contributes to or detracts from your meaning. Be sure to use a tone that is appropriate for your readers. Consider the following factors about your readers.

- **Knowledge of the topic.** If your readers are not knowledgeable about the topic, you might use a supportive, helpful tone. If they are familiar with the topic, the same helpful, supportive tone may be insulting.

- **Background and experience of your readers.** Consider the education level, training, professional position, and factors such as the age and gender of your audience when adopting a tone. A letter written to a panel of community leaders might use a deferential tone because they expect to be treated with respect, while a letter to the editor might use a less formal, but informative tone.

- **Attitudes and beliefs of your readers.** If your readers are likely to agree with your ideas, using a strongly emotional tone may seem inappropriate and unnecessary. If your readers are likely to disagree with your ideas, an energetic, positive, convincing tone may help sway your readers.

9g   INTERPRETING FIGURATIVE LANGUAGE

LEARNING OBJECTIVE 7
Interpret figurative language

Figurative language is a way of describing something that makes sense on an imaginative level but not on a literal or factual level. Many common expressions are figurative:

> It was raining cats and dogs.
> His head is as hard as a rock.
> I was so nervous, I was sweating like a pig.

In each of these expressions, two unlike objects are compared on the basis of some quality they have in common. This is similar, for example, to Hamlet's statement "I will speak daggers to her, but use none." Here the poet (William

Shakespeare) is comparing the features of daggers (sharp, pointed, dangerous, harmful) with something that can be used like daggers—words.

Figurative language is striking, often surprising, sometimes shocking. These reactions are created by the dissimilarity of the two objects being compared. To find the similarity and understand the figurative expression, focus on connotative (the feelings and emotions that a word suggests) rather than literal meanings. For example, read the lines below from Shakespeare's play *Macbeth*.

> "Life's but a walking shadow, a poor player
> That struts and frets his hour upon the stage
> And then is heard no more."
>
> —Shakespeare, *Macbeth*, Act V, Scene V

Here the playwright is comparing an entire life to an actor's brief appearance in a play, implying that life is very short and for all an individual's sense of importance he or she dies leaving no trace.

Analyzing Figurative Language

Figurative expressions, sometimes called **figures of speech**, communicate and emphasize relationships that cannot be communicated through literal meaning. For example, Jonathan Swift's statement "She wears her clothes as if they were thrown on by a pitchfork" creates a stronger image and conveys a more meaningful description than the statement "She dresses sloppily."

The three most common types of figurative expressions are similes, metaphors, and personification. **Similes** make a comparison explicit by using the word *like* or *as*. **Metaphors** directly equate two objects without using the word *like* or *as*. **Personification** is a technique in which human characteristics are given to objects or ideas. For instance, to say "My old computer moans and groans each morning when I turn it on" gives the computer human characteristics of moaning and groaning.

- **Similes**

She dressed like a rag doll.
Sam was as happy as a clam.

- **Metaphors**

Jane wears her heart on her sleeve.
My life is a junkyard of broken dreams.

- **Personification**

The earthquake has swallowed all my future plans.
Nature abhors a peaceful man.

EXERCISE 9-14 . . . USING FIGURATIVE LANGUAGE

Study the figurative expression in each of the following statements. Then, in the space provided, explain the meaning of each.

1. Hope is like a feather, ready to blow away.

   _____

   _____

2. Once Alma realized she had made an embarrassing error, the blush spread across her face like spilled paint.

   _____

   _____

   _____

3. A powerboat, or any other sports vehicle, devours money.

   _____

4. Sally's skin was like a smooth, highly polished apple.

   _____

5. Upon hearing the news, I took shears and shredded my dreams.

   _____

   _____

Using Figurative Language Effectively

Figurative language can make your writing lively, interesting, and engaging. It is also a creative way to describe and explain. To use it effectively, use the following suggestions:

- **Use fresh, interesting figures of speech.** Avoid using tired, overused expressions that have become clichés.

- **Make clear comparisons.** Because figurative language makes a comparison between two unlike things, be sure that you create figurative expressions that compare items for which a likeness is obvious and that do not suggest similarities you do not intend. For example, if you say, "Michael eats like a horse," it is clear that you are comparing only eating qualities and not suggesting that Michael is horselike in other respects. However, if you say, "Michael is a horse, and everyone in the restaurant recognized it," it is unclear what characteristics Michael and the horse share.

- **Avoid figurative expressions when you want to be precise, exact, and direct.** Figurative expressions leave room for interpretation and can lead to misinterpretation.

9h   IDENTIFYING BIAS

LEARNING OBJECTIVE 8
Identify bias

Bias refers to an author's partiality, inclination toward a particular viewpoint, or prejudice. A writer is *biased* if he or she takes one side of a controversial issue and does not recognize opposing viewpoints. Perhaps the best example of bias can be found in advertising. A magazine advertisement for a new car, for instance, describes only positive, marketable features—the ad does not recognize the car's limitations or faults.

Spotting Bias

Sometimes writers are direct and forthright in expressing their bias; other times a writer's bias might be hidden and discovered only through careful analysis. Read the following comparison of organic farming and conventional farming. The authors express a favorable attitude toward organic farming and a negative one toward conventional farming, while also recognizing the reality that a sudden change to the type of farming they support would have serious consequences. Notice, in particular, the underlined words and phrases.

Issue: Environmental Issues

Organic Farming vs. Conventional Farming

Organic farming is carried out without the use of <u>synthetic</u> fertilizers or pesticides. Organic farmers (and gardeners) use manure from farm animals for fertilizer, and they rotate other crops with legumes to <u>restore</u> nitrogen to the soil. They control insects by planting a variety of crops, alternating the use of fields. (A corn pest has a hard time surviving during the year that its home field is planted in soybeans.) Organic farming is also <u>less energy intensive</u>. According to a study by the Center for the Biology of Natural Systems at Washington University, <u>comparable conventional farms used 2.3 times as much energy</u> as organic farms. Production on organic farms was 10% lower, but <u>costs were comparably</u> lower. Organic farms require 12% more labor than conventional ones. Human labor is a <u>renewable resource</u>, though, whereas petroleum is not. Compared with conventional methods, organic farming uses <u>less energy</u> and leads to <u>healthier soils</u>.

In addition to organic practices, sustainable agriculture involves buying <u>local products</u> and using local services when possible, thus avoiding the cost of transportation while getting fresher goods and strengthening the economy of the local community.

Sustainable agriculture promotes independent farmers and ranchers producing good food and making a good living while protecting the environment.

Conventional agriculture can result in severe soil erosion and is the source of considerable water pollution. No doubt we should practice organic farming to the limits of our ability to do so. But we should not delude ourselves. Abrupt banning of synthetic fertilizers and pesticides would likely lead to a drastic drop in food production.

—Hill, McCreary, and Kolb, *Chemistry for Changing Times*, p. 634

Ways to Identify Bias

To identify bias, use the following suggestions:

1. **Analyze connotative meanings.** Do you encounter a large number of positive or negative terms in the reading selection?
2. **Notice descriptive language.** What impression is created?
3. **Analyze the tone.** The author's tone often provides important clues.
4. **Look for opposing viewpoints.**

EXERCISE 9-15 ... DETECTING BIAS

Read each of the following statements and place a check mark in front of each one that reveals bias.

_____ 1. Killing innocent animals so that wealthy women can wear fur coats is a crime against life.

_____ 2. Organic chemistry studies substances that contain carbon, the element essential to life.

_____ 3. While most Americans identify themselves as either Republicans or Democrats, an increasing number of U.S. citizens are defining themselves as Independent.

_____ 4. There's no better way to teach responsibility to children than giving them daily chores to complete.

_____ 5. Without a doubt, the islands of the Caribbean are the most beautiful in the world.

EXERCISE 9-16 ... DETECTING BIAS

Read the following passages and then write a sentence describing the authors' bias.

Issue: Advertising and Ethics

The only essential ingredient in shampoo is a detergent of some sort. What, then, is all the advertising about? You can buy shampoos that are fruit or herb scented, protein enriched, and pH balanced or made especially for oily or dry hair. Shampoos for oily, normal, and dry hair seem to differ primarily in the concentration of the detergent. Shampoo for oily hair is more concentrated; shampoo for dry hair is more dilute.

—Hill, McCreary, and Kolb, *Chemistry for Changing Times*, p. 671

Issue: Classical Music

In the United States, classical music is treated as an elitist activity. Performances are very formal: members of the audience sit listening very quietly until the end of each piece. Most of the music that is performed in classical music concerts was composed in past centuries. The society treats the music of the past with great reverence. There is a written musical tradition stretching back over a thousand years, although most of the music that is performed is between 100 and 250 years old. Concerts often feature the same pieces by a relatively small roster of composers, from one concert to another and from one year to the next.

—Yudkin, *Understanding Music*, p. 4

Handling Bias Openly When You Write

Readers appreciate the open and straightforward expression of ideas and mistrust writers who pretend to be objective while actually presenting a one-sided viewpoint. There are writing situations in which you will want to express your opinions and reveal your bias. When these occur, be sure to do so openly. One way to make it clear that you are expressing a bias is to include phrases such as "in my opinion," "one viewpoint is," or "one way of looking at." It is also helpful to mention opposing viewpoints by referring to or summarizing them, and by refuting them, if you choose.

9i   EVALUATING THE RELIABILITY OF DATA AND EVIDENCE

LEARNING OBJECTIVE 9
Evaluate data and evidence

Many writers who express opinions or state viewpoints provide readers with data or evidence to support their ideas. Your task as a critical reader and writer is to weigh and evaluate the quality of this evidence. You must examine the evidence and assess its adequacy. You should be concerned with two factors: (1) the type of evidence being presented, and (2) the relevance of that evidence.

There are various types of evidence an author can use:

- personal experience or observation
- expert opinion
- research citation
- statistical data
- examples, descriptions of particular events, or illustrative situations
- analogies (comparisons with similar situations)
- historical documentation
- quotations
- description

EXERCISE 9-17 ... EVALUATING TYPES OF EVIDENCE

Refer to the article "Consequences of Social Class," on pages 8–10. For each of the following paragraphs, identify the type(s) of evidence the author provides.

1. Paragraph 2 _____

2. Paragraph 7 _____

3. Paragraph 11 _____

4. Paragraph 13 _____

EXERCISE 9-18 ... IDENTIFYING TYPES OF EVIDENCE

For each of the following statements, discuss the type or types of evidence that you would need in order to support and evaluate the statement.

1. Individuals must accept primary responsibility for the health and safety of their babies.

2. Apologizing is often seen as a sign of weakness, especially among men.

3. There has been a steady increase in illegal immigration over the past 50 years.

4. More college women than college men agree that marijuana should be legalized.

5. Car advertisements sell fantasy experiences, not the means of transportation.

Evaluating Data and Evidence

Each type of evidence a writer uses must be weighed in relation to the statement it supports. Acceptable evidence should directly, clearly, and indisputably support the case or issue in question. Three overall factors point to reliable, trustworthy writing:

- Quantity of information
- Relevance of information
- Timeliness of information

Evaluating the Quantity of Information

As a general rule, the more evidence writers provide to support the thesis statement and main ideas of the selection, the more convincing their writing is likely to be. Suppose an article includes the following thesis statement:

Married people lead healthier, happier lives than unmarried people.

Now suppose the writer includes just one fact to support this statement: "Research shows that most married people report higher levels of happiness than unmarried people do." Does this one piece of evidence provide full support for the thesis statement? Most likely, you would argue that it does not. You may know plenty of single people who are very happy and some married people who are miserable.

Now consider an article that supports the thesis statement with the following evidence:

- Married people have a larger support network that helps them stay healthy.
- Both married women and married men earn more money than their single co-workers.
- Research has shown that married people live longer.
- Married people report lower levels of stress and depression than single people do.

Each of these supporting pieces of evidence on its own may not be enough to help the writer prove his or her thesis statement, but as a whole they greatly strengthen the argument.

Evaluating the Relevance of Information

Supporting evidence must be relevant to be convincing. That is, it must be closely connected to the thesis statement and to the subject under discussion. It is easy to be distracted by interesting pieces of information that are not relevant to the writer's thesis statement.

Consider the discussion of marriage and happiness above. For example, it is interesting that 48% of Americans are married, but this fact is not relevant to the thesis statement "Married people live healthier, happier lives than those who are single." When you encounter irrelevant information, ask yourself: "Why has the writer included this? Is it intended to steer my thinking in a specific direction, away from the topic at hand?"

Evaluating the Timeliness of Information

When evaluating the information provided by the writer, check how recent the examples, statistics, data, and research are. In general, more current facts, figures, and research are better and more reliable. In the computer age, new information and knowledge are being generated at an astonishing rate, so articles published as recently as two years ago may be out of date, and the information they contain may be obsolete. For tips on evaluating the timeliness of a Web site, see page 274.

Keep in mind, though, that some things do not change. The components of the human body are the same today as they were 200 years ago. The principles of mathematics have not changed and are not likely to change. The U.S. Constitution, great works of literature, and other important documents remain the same today as when they were written.

EXERCISE 9-19 . . . EVALUATING QUALITY AND RELEVANCE OF INFORMATION

A magazine article has the following thesis statement: "It has been proven that animal companions, sometimes known as pets, have many benefits for their owners." A list of possible statements to support this thesis sentence follows. Place a check mark next to each statement that is relevant to the thesis statement.

_____ 1. The U.S. Centers for Disease Control, an important source of medical information in the United States, has stated that owning a pet can decrease your blood pressure and cholesterol levels.

_____ 2. Men tend to prefer having dogs as pets, while women seem to prefer owning cats.

_____ 3. Sadly, many animal shelters in the United States are underfunded and desperately in need of donations.

_____ 4. The National Institute of Health has reported widespread benefits of pet ownership for older people.

_____ 5. More than half of all U.S. households have a companion animal.

_____ 6. A growing number of studies have suggested that children who grow up in a home with a "furred animal" are less likely to develop allergies or asthma.

_____ 7. On the dating scene, many singles have reported that their pets have helped them strike up conversations with the opposite sex.

_____ 8. In general, people who own pets report less depression than people who do not own pets.

_____ 9. There are more than 51 million dogs, 56 million cats, and 45 million birds in U.S. households.

_____ 10. One study showed that stockbrokers with high blood pressure who adopted a cat or dog had lower blood pressure readings in stressful situations than people without pets.

EXERCISE 9-20 . . . EVALUATING TIMELINESS OF INFORMATION

Several types of information are provided below. Place a check mark next to each type of information that is not likely to change (that is, cases in which it is acceptable to use an older source of information).

_____ 1. A mathematics textbook teaching students how to add and subtract

_____ 2. A manual teaching you how to use a computer

_____ 3. A diagram of the parts of the human brain

_____ 4. A history textbook explaining the pilgrims' reasons for leaving England

_____ 5. A medical book that suggests the use of leeches to reduce a fever

Thinking Critically About the Evidence You Use

As you draft essays, one of your main tasks is to provide adequate, reliable, and appropriate data and evidence to support your thesis statement. (For more on using evidence to support your thesis, see Chapter 8, p. 244.) Good writers try to vary the data they choose to suit their audience and their purpose. Examples may be appropriate for one audience, but facts and statistics may be more appealing to another. To achieve your purpose, select your evidence carefully. If your purpose is to persuade your readers to take action, such as to vote for a particular political candidate, reasons are needed. But you may also want to include descriptions of the candidate's achievements or draw comparisons to other successful political figures.

Be sure not to omit details that are relevant and important to the topic. Doing so will make your readers distrust you and question your ideas.

9j   INTERPRETING AND USING VISUALS

LEARNING OBJECTIVE 10
Interpret and use visuals

Many textbooks and other reading materials include graphics and photographs. All **visual aids** share one goal: to illustrate concepts and help you understand them better. As a reader, your key goal is to extract important information from them. Visual aids work best when you read them *in addition to* the text, not *instead of* the text. As a writer, you need to be able to use, interpret, and condense information from visual aids as you make text-to-text and text-to-world connections.

Keep in mind that the author chose the visual aid for a specific purpose. To fully understand it, be sure you can explain its purpose.

A General Approach to Reading Graphics

You will encounter many types of **graphics** in your reading materials. These include

- maps
- charts
- graphs
- diagrams

Here is a step-by-step approach to reading any type of graphic effectively. As you read, apply each step to Figure 9-1.

FIGURE 9-1 THE GENDER PAY GAP, BY EDUCATION[1]

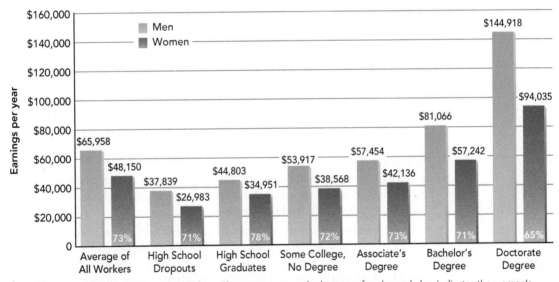

[1]Mean earnings of full-time year-round workers. The percentage at the bottom of each purple bar indicates the women's percentage of the men's income.

Source: By the author. Based on U.S. Census Bureau, *Current Population Survey*, Annual Social and Economic (ASEC) Supplement, 2014: Table PINC-04.

—Henslin, *Sociology: A Down-to-Earth Approach*, 13e, p. 318. By the author. Based on U.S. Census Bureau, *Current Population Survey*, Annual Social and Economic (ASEC) Supplement, 2014: Table PINC-04.

1. **Make connections between written text and graphics.** Look for the reference in the text. The author will usually refer you to each specific graphic. When you see the reference, finish reading the sentence, then look at the

graphic. In some cases, you will need to go back and forth between the text and the graphic, making text-to-text connections, especially if the graphic has multiple parts. Here is the original reference to Figure 9-1: "I'm going to reveal how you can make an extra $1,435 a month between the ages of 25 and 65. You might be wondering if this is hard to do. Actually, it is simple for some and impossible for others. As Figure 9-1 shows, all you have to do is be born a male."

2. **Read the title and caption.** The title will identify the subject, and the caption will provide important information. In some cases, the caption will specify the graphic's key takeaway point. The title of Figure 9-1 makes the graph's subject clear: the differences between men's salaries and women's salaries.

3. **Examine how the graphic is organized and labeled.** Read all headings, labels, and notes. Labels tell you what topics or categories are being discussed. Sometimes a label is turned sideways, like the words "Earnings per year" in Figure 9-1. Note that the title has a note (found at the bottom of the graphic) that provides information on how to read the graphic.

4. **Look at the legend.** The **legend** is the guide to the graphic's colors, terms, and other important information. In Figure 9-1, the legend appears toward the upper left and shows orange for men and purple for women.

5. **Analyze the graphic.** Based on what you see, determine the graphic's key purpose. For example, is its purpose to show change over time, describe a process, present statistics? The purpose of Figure 9-1 is clear: It compares men's and women's salaries for a number of categories based on education level.

6. **Study the data to identify trends or patterns.** If the graphic includes numbers, look for unusual statistics or unexplained variations. What conclusions can you draw from the data?

7. **Write a brief annotation (note to yourself).** In the margin, jot a brief note summarizing the graphic's trend, pattern, or key point. Writing will help cement the idea in your mind. A summary note of Figure 9-1 might read, "Both male and female college graduates earn higher salaries than anyone else, but regardless of education level, men always earn more than women."

Analyzing Photographs

An old saying goes, "A picture is worth a thousand words." Photographs can help writers achieve many different goals. For example, writers can use photos to spark interest, provide perspective, or offer examples. Let's look at the photo in Figure 9-2 and use a step-by-step process to analyze it.

FIGURE 9-2 THE BULLFIGHT: CULTURAL EXPERIENCE OR ANIMAL CRUELTY?

Fresnel6/Fotolia

Many Americans perceive bullfighting as a cruel activity that should be illegal every-where. To most Spaniards, bullfighting is a sport that pits matador and bull in a unifying image of power, courage, and glory. Cultural relativism requires that we suspend our own perspectives in order to grasp the perspectives of others, something easier said than done.

—Henslin, *Sociology*, p. 39

1. **First read the text that refers to the photo.** Photos are not a substitute for the reading. They should be examined *along with* the text. For this reason, many readings include specific references to each photo, usually directly after a key point. For example, in the following paragraph, notice that the reference to a figure immediately follows the author's main point about bullfighting.

Issue: Cultural Relativism

To counter our own tendency to use our own culture as the standard by which we judge other cultures, we can practice cultural relativism; that is, we can try to understand a culture on its own terms. With our own culture so deeply embedded within us, however, practicing cultural relativism can challenge our orientations to life. For example, most U.S. citizens appear to have strong feelings against raising bulls for the purpose of stabbing them to death in front of crowds that shout "Olé!" According to cultural relativism, however, bullfighting must be viewed from the perspective of the culture in which it takes place—*its* history, *its* folklore, *its* ideas of bravery, and *its* ideas of sex roles (Figure 9-2).

—Henslin, *Sociology*, p. 39

Look at the photo as soon as you see the reference. The photo will help you visualize the concept under discussion, making it easier to remember.

2. **Read the photo's title and/or caption.** The caption is usually placed above, below, or to the side of the photo and explains how the photo fits into the discussion.

3. **Ask: What is my first overall impression? Why has the author included this photo?** Because photos can be so powerful, they are often chosen to elicit a strong reaction. Analyze your response to the photo. For example, Figure 9-2 is quite violent; note the blood on the bull's shoulders. What purpose is the author trying to achieve by including this photo?

4. **Examine the details.** Look closely at the picture, examining both the foreground and the background. Details can provide clues regarding the date and location of the photograph. For example, people's hairstyles and clothing often give hints to the year or decade. Landmarks and buildings help point to location. In Figure 9-2, you can see that bullfighting takes place in front of an audience. What point is the author making about the audience's cultural experiences and beliefs regarding bullfighting?

5. **Look for connections to society or your life.** Ask yourself how the photo relates to what you are reading or to your own experiences. For example, what are your own thoughts about bullfighting? Do you know anyone who feels differently? What are the sources of your disagreement?

EXERCISE 9-21 . . . ANALYZING A PHOTOGRAPH

Flip through one of your textbooks and choose a photo of interest to you. Analyze it according to the five-step process outlined on this and the previous page.

Thinking Critically About Incorporating Visuals into Your Writing

Visuals are another way of communicating. They are not a substitute for text, nor are they necessarily the main focus of the text, but a well-chosen visual can serve the following functions:

- Spark interest
- Elicit a reaction
- Provide perspective
- Offer an example
- Help the reader understand a difficult concept

As a writer, you will be the one to choose the visual aids to accompany your text, so be sure you know exactly what you want to accomplish by including them. Placement is also important. If you want to capture the reader's attention, then place the visual in a prominent place, such as at the beginning of an essay or chapter. If you want to support a point you have already made, then insert the visual close to where the point is stated.

There are several ways you can find visuals to include in your writing. Although the Internet contains a large assortment of visual collections, you must use caution when sourcing from the Web.

Guidelines for Finding Visuals

Use the following guidelines for finding appropriate, effective visuals to support your writing:

- **Make sure that you have, at least, a general idea of the type of visual you want to use.** Otherwise, you could waste many hours surfing the Web and never find what you need.

- **Be sure to read the fair use information associated with the particular site that contains the visual you want to use.** Not everything on the Internet is public domain. You may need to seek permission to use a visual, and in some cases, you may even have to pay. For most academic assignments, students may use copyrighted material without permission, but it is always wise to err on the side of caution and check to make sure you can legally use it.

- **Be sure to document the source of the visual in your writing.** See Chapter 8 for documentation sources to consult.

If you cannot find exactly what you want on the Internet, you can always create your own visual. Using computer applications, you can design charts, graphs, or diagrams, and you can even draw your own original creation that perfectly enhances the message of your writing.

SELF-TEST SUMMARY

To test yourself, cover the right column with a sheet of paper and answer the question in the left column. Evaluate each of your answers by sliding the paper down and comparing it with what is printed in the right column.

QUESTION	ANSWER
1 **How can you make accurate inferences and draw conclusions?**	An **inference** is a reasoned guess about what you don't know based on what you do know from the facts and information presented in a text or image. *Combining inference and prior knowledge allows you to draw conclusions.* To make accurate inferences and conclusions, understand the literal meaning of the reading selection, pay attention to details, add up the facts, be alert to clues, and consider the writer's purpose. Once you have made an inference, verify that it is accurate.
2 **How do you evaluate the source of material and the qualifications of the author?**	To **evaluate a source**, consider the source's reputation, the audience for whom the source is intended, and whether documentation or references are provided. Look for a textbook author's credentials on the title page; for nonfiction books and general market paperbacks, look on the book jacket or back cover.
What factors should be considered when evaluating Internet sources?	**Evaluate Internet sources** by considering appropriateness, source, level of technical detail, and presentation. Also evaluate the completeness, accuracy, and timeliness of the site.
3 **How do you identify fake news?**	**Fake news** is false information, pretending to be from a legitimate source, that is intended to mislead its audience. To identify fake news, look out for "exclusive" stories, untrustworthy tabloid sources, domain names tweaked to closely mimic mainstream sources, attention-grabbing headlines, the lack of an "About Us" page, and the use of vague polls and unnamed sources.
4 **How do you distinguish facts from opinions?**	A **fact** is a statement that can be verified (proven to be true or false). An **opinion** expresses feelings, attitudes, and beliefs, and it is neither true nor false. Look for evidence that supports an opinion and indicates that it is reasonable. By distinguishing statements of fact from opinions, you will know which ideas to accept and which to verify or question.
5 **Why should you identify an author's purpose?**	Writers have **different purposes for writing** (for example, to inform, to persuade, to entertain, or to provide an opinion). Recognizing a writer's purpose will help you grasp meaning more quickly and evaluate his or her work.

QUESTION	ANSWER
6 *How do you determine tone?*	**Tone** refers to the attitude or feeling a writer expresses about his or subject. *To determine tone*, pay particular attention to descriptive language and connotations (see Table 9-1, page 285, for a summary of tone words). Recognizing tone will help you evaluate what a writer is attempting to accomplish through his or her writing.
7 *What is figurative language?*	**Figurative language** is a way of describing something that makes sense on an imaginative level but not a literal or factual level. Recognizing and understanding figurative language helps you better understand how a writer views his or her subject. **Similes** make comparisons by using the words *like* or *as*. **Metaphors** make a comparison without using the words *like* or *as*. **Personification** attributes human characteristics to ideas and objects.
8 *How do you identify bias?*	**Bias** refers to a writer's partiality, inclination toward or against a particular viewpoint, or prejudice. A writer is biased when he or she takes one side of a controversial issue and does not recognize opposing viewpoints. To identify bias, examine connotative and descriptive language, analyze tone, and look for opposing viewpoints.
9 *How do you evaluate data and evidence?*	**Types of evidence** include personal experience or observation, expert opinion, research citations, statistical data, examples, analogies, historical documentation, quotations, and descriptions. *Acceptable evidence* should directly, clearly, and indisputably support the issue in question. By evaluating the quantity, relevance, and timeliness of information, you can determine how reliable a source is.
10 *How do you read and use visuals effectively?*	To **read visuals effectively**, make connections between the text and the accompanying visual; examine the title, caption, and legend; study the visual's organization and purpose; identify trends and patterns; and write annotations. To **use visuals** in your writing, determine the purpose of the visual, the message that you want the visual to convey, and the location of the visual within the text. As you source the visual, follow fair use requirements and cite the source.

10 Analyzing Issues and Arguments

LEARNING OBJECTIVES

1 Understand the connection between contemporary issues and arguments
2 Define what constitutes an argument
3 Explain the parts of an argument
4 Use strategies to read arguments
5 Evaluate the validity of arguments
6 Recognize errors in logic
7 Write sound, convincing argument essays

Throughout your college studies you will read many source materials that take a stand on a specific question, such as "What is the best method of decreasing unemployment?" or "How does society go about lowering the crime rate and making the streets safer?" You will discuss these and many other issues in many of your academic courses. Even heavily scientific courses, such as biology, must deal with controversial problems, such as "Is it ethical to perform medical research on human beings?" and "What are the pros and cons of organ donation?"

The best discussions of these issues are based on specific arguments, opinions, and supporting evidence. In this chapter, you will learn the parts of an argument, strategies for reading and evaluating arguments, and how to recognize logical errors. You will also learn to write effective argument paragraphs and essays.

10a CONTEMPORARY ISSUES AND ARGUMENTS

LEARNING OBJECTIVE 1
Understand the connection between contemporary issues and arguments

A **contemporary issue** is a current topic that is relevant to individuals, groups, and society today. Throughout this handbook and Part Two of this text, you will read selections about some of the most talked-about and controversial contemporary issues facing U.S. society today: gun control, drugs and addiction, crime, animal rights, and cultural similarities and differences. This list of contemporary issues could go on for pages.

Most contemporary issues can be phrased in the form of a question, such as the following:

- "Should cosmetics companies be allowed to use animals as test subjects?"
- "What exactly is sexual harassment, and how do we recognize it when we see it?"
- "Do racism and prejudice still exist in U.S. society?"
- "Should single people be allowed to adopt children?"

To answer these questions, writers conduct research, interview people, and read various source materials that help them formulate an opinion. Once their opinion has been formed, they can then write something (an article, a book, a blog, a contribution to a Web site) in which they state their opinion (often as a thesis sentence) and then provide support for their opinion.

10b WHAT IS AN ARGUMENT?

LEARNING OBJECTIVE 2
Define what constitutes an argument

Much of academic writing is based on **arguments**, which are civilized discussions in which people express different points of view about a topic. For example, in a government course you might read arguments for or against the freedom to burn the American flag; in a criminal justice course you might read arguments for or against parole for convicted criminals.

Note that the term *argument*, as used in academic reading and writing, does not have a negative connotation. In common language, an argument is often a heated, emotional, and unpleasant disagreement between two people. In college-level reading (and beyond), an argument is simply a well-thought-out, well-researched piece of writing that offers good reasons to support a particular viewpoint.

A single issue may have many questions and arguments associated with it, as in the following example:

Issue: Terrorism

Question: How do we stop terrorism and prevent terrorist attacks?

- **Argument #1:** The United States must strongly secure the entire length of its borders with Canada and Mexico.
- **Argument #2:** While we must ensure air safety, conducting invasive body searches in airports is not the way to do it. These searches invade the American right to privacy.
- **Argument #3:** The United States must send more financial and military aid to countries that harbor terrorist groups as a way of helping those countries establish pro-democratic, pro-U.S. governments.
- **Argument #4:** The U.S. government should deport any immigrant who comes from a nation that is openly hostile to the United States.

Note that each argument is both an opinion and a thesis statement. Such arguments are likely to be found early in a reading selection, with the remainder of the reading offering various types of support and evidence. In the case of Argument #1, for example, a writer might prepare an essay arguing in favor of increased security at U.S. borders, pointing to the need to keep enemies off U.S. land and providing data showing that increased border controls would not only improve homeland security but also result in more jobs for Americans.

But another writer might disagree with Argument #1. That writer, who does not agree with the idea of spending large sums of money securing the borders, might argue that most terrorists have entered the United States through air travel rather than by crossing the Mexican or Canadian border. The writer might also argue that the money spent on patrolling the borders could be much better used to train bomb-sniffing dogs, develop sophisticated computer software to help identify terrorists, and increase security at major airports.

10c   THE PARTS OF AN ARGUMENT

LEARNING OBJECTIVE 3
Explain the parts of an argument

A good **argument** has three—sometimes four—parts: an issue, a claim about that issue, support for that claim, and, sometimes, a refutation of opposing arguments. Figure 10-1 illustrates the structure of an argument.

FIGURE 10-1 THE STRUCTURE OF AN ARGUMENT

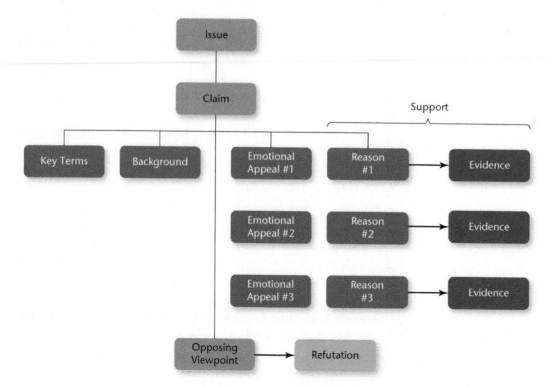

Before we discuss the parts of an argument in more detail, read the following brief argument:

Issue: Ageism and Discrimination

Ageism: Creeping to the Forefront

We all know a little something about the "isms" in society: capitalism, communism, atheism, and so on. "Isms" represent systems of belief and usually encompass stereotypes as well. The time has come to discuss the next big "ism" creeping to the forefront of social stereotypes: ageism. Ageism—prejudice against and discrimination based solely on age—is likely to become more prevalent due in part to the growing population of older individuals in the United States.

Considering society's infatuation with the young and the beautiful, the media—especially TV—has a huge impact on the spread of ageism. In recent years, reality TV shows have flooded the market due to the fact that they are cheaper to produce than scripted shows. Offhand, you'd probably be able to list at least 10 different programs, but ask yourself this: How many participants over the age of 50 can you name? The cast of most shows is young. When the older generation is included in other TV shows, they're often depicted as hunched-over and wrinkled, with gray hair and liver spots. Such depictions reinforce stereotypes that lead to ageism and distort our perceptions of growing older. Recently I took my elderly father to the doctor. I noticed a distinct difference in the way in which we were treated. Often, nurses and the doctor would ask me questions about his health, rather than him. Since he has no impairment, I found this odd. But this subtle type of ageism is widely used when we assume the elderly to be senile, sick, or unable to function. In fact, sociologist Erdman Palmore suggests that medical professionals frequently engage in subtle ageism when they view the symptoms as simply a matter of being old.

—adapted from Carl, *THINK Social Problems*, pp. 71–72

1. **An argument must address an issue—a problem or controversy about which people disagree.** The above brief argument addresses the issue of ageism.

2. **An argument must take a position on an issue.** This position is called a claim. You might think of the claim as a writer's specific viewpoint. The above argument claims that ageism is an unfair practice of discrimination against elderly people. There are three common types of claims:

   - A **claim of fact** is a statement that can be proven or verified by observation or research.

   > Within our children's lifetimes, the average temperature of the planet will increase 2.5 to 10 degrees Fahrenheit.

- A **claim of value** states that one thing or idea is better or more desirable than another. Issues of right versus wrong, or acceptable versus unacceptable, lead to claims of value. In "Ageism: Creeping to the Forefront," the claim of value is that in the United States elderly people are discriminated against and treated unfairly solely based on their age.

- A **claim of policy** suggests what should or ought to be done to solve a problem. The following claim of policy states one writer's position on cyberbullying.

> To control bullying, schools should practice a zero-tolerance policy for any form of bullying, whether on the playground, in the classroom, or over the Internet or smartphones.

3. **The argument must offer support for the claim.** Support consists of reasons and evidence that the claim is reasonable and should be accepted. There are three common types of support:

- A **reason** is a general statement that supports a claim. It explains why the writer's viewpoint is reasonable and should be accepted. In "Ageism: Creeping to the Forefront," the writer offers a good reason why we should be concerned about ageism: the population of older individuals in the United States is growing.

- **Evidence** consists of facts, statistics, experiences, comparisons, and examples that demonstrate why the claim is valid. The author of "Ageism: Creeping to the Forefront" offers a convincing example of the media's influence on society's perception of older people (reality TV).

- **Emotional appeals** are ideas that are targeted toward needs or values that readers are likely to care about. Needs include physiological needs (food, drink, shelter) and psychological needs (sense of belonging, sense of accomplishment, sense of self-worth, sense of competency). In "Ageism: Creeping to the Forefront," the author tells a story about his own elderly father in order to gain the reader's sympathy and agreement. Emotional appeals are often not fair or logical; for information on identifying and evaluating emotional appeals, see Section 10e (p. 319).

4. **Some arguments offer a refutation that considers opposing viewpoints and may attempt to disprove or discredit them.** Not all arguments include refutations, however. In "Ageism: Creeping to the Forefront," the author has not provided any refutation. However, the case might be made that reality TV is far from realistic and that we cannot measure society's approach to an entire group of people through TV shows like *Real Housewives* or *Jersey Shore*.

EXERCISE 10-1 . . . IDENTIFYING CLAIMS

Identify whether each of the following is a claim of fact (F), a claim of value (V), or claim of policy (P).

_____ 1. Convicted criminals who cannot read and write should be required to enroll in literacy programs while serving their time in prison.

_____ 2. Many political scientists believe low voter turnout in elections is the result of voter cynicism and disgust with politics and politicians.

_____ 3. Texting while driving has become a problem of epidemic proportions.

_____ 4. All food-service workers should be required to wear hairnets and plastic gloves.

_____ 5. Testing cosmetics on rabbits and other innocent creatures is wrong.

EXERCISE 10-2 . . . WRITING CLAIMS

For two of the following contemporary issues, write two claims about the issue. For each issue, try to write two different types of claims.

1. selling property in the United States to non-U.S. citizens

2. outsourcing of U.S. jobs abroad (to India, China, and elsewhere)

3. air travel safety

4. employers' electronic monitoring of employees

10d   STRATEGIES FOR READING AN ARGUMENT

LEARNING OBJECTIVE 4
Use strategies to read arguments

Arguments need to be read slowly and carefully. Plan to read an argument more than once. The first time you read it, try to get an overview of its three essential elements: *issue, claim,* and *support.* Then reread it more carefully to closely follow the author's line of reasoning and to identify and evaluate the evidence provided. In this section, the article "Who Are the Animals in Animal Experiments?" (p. 311) will be used as an example and for practice.

Thinking Before You Read

As you prepare to read an argument, ask yourself the following questions:

1. **What does the title suggest?** Before you read, preview following the guidelines in Section 1c on page 6 and ask yourself what the title suggests about the issue, claim, and/or support.

2. **Who is the author, and what are his or her qualifications?** Check to see if you recognize the author or if any information about the author is included in a headnote (or at the end of the book or article). Evaluate whether the author is qualified to write about the issue. The author's specific qualifications signal the credibility of the evidence provided.

3. **What is the date of publication?** Checking the date will prompt you to consider whether new, even possibly contradictory, evidence has recently developed.

4. **What do I already know about the issue or question being discussed?** Try brainstorming using a two-column pro/con list. By thinking about the issue on your own, before you read, you are less likely to be swayed by the writer's appeals and more likely to think about and evaluate the reasons and evidence objectively.

EXERCISE 10-3 . . . PREVIEWING AN ARGUMENT

Preview but do not read "Who Are the Animals in Animal Experiments?" (For previewing guidelines, see Section 1c, p. 6.) After you have previewed the reading, answer the following questions:

1. What does the title suggest about the issue, claim, or evidence?

   _____

2. Is the source current and reliable?

   _____

3. What do you already know about the issue? Brainstorm a two-column "pro/con" list.

   _____

The following article, "Who Are the Animals in Animal Experiments?" appeared in 2014 in *The Huffington Post*. The author, Aysha Akhtar, M.D., M.P.H., is a double Board-certified neurologist and public health specialist. She works for the Office of Counterterrorism and Emerging Threats of the Food and Drug Administration (FDA), serves as Lieutenant Commander in the U.S. Public Health Service, and is a Fellow of the Oxford Centre for Animal Ethics. She also serves on the Leadership Council of the Classy Awards.

Dr. Akhtar is the author of the book *Animals and Public Health: Why Treating Animals Better Is Critical to Human Welfare*. You can learn more about her and the book at her Web site: http://www.ayshaakhtar.com/.

Who Are the Animals in Animal Experiments?

Aysha Akhtar, MD, MPH

1   I once attended a neuroscience conference featuring a talk about spinal cord injury. The presenter showed a brief video clip that haunts me still to this day. The presenter showed a clip of his experiment in which he had crushed a cat's spinal cord and was recording the cat's movement on a treadmill. He had forcibly implanted electrodes into the cat's brain, and she was struggling to keep upright, dragging her paralyzed legs on the treadmill. She repeatedly fell off the machine. At one point, the experimenter lifted her up to reposition her on the treadmill, and the cat did something that was utterly unexpected. *She rubbed her head against the experimenter's hand.*

2   It's difficult for us to imagine what the lives are like for these animals. This is because these secretive experiments are hidden from public view and have been retreated to windowless basement laboratories. We want to believe that those in the white coats are act-

ing responsibly and that the animals are treated humanely; well, I have visited numerous laboratories and witnessed countless experiments on animals, and I can tell you from personal experience that *nothing* is further from the truth.

3   As soon as you walk into a laboratory, you can't help but notice the rows and rows of barren cages holding sad animals living under the glare of fluorescent bulbs. Their bodies

Vit Kovalcik/Fotolia

Vaccine test on laboratory mouse

are burned, mutilated, and scarred. Animals who have had their heads crushed grip their faces and convulse as blood pours out of their noses. You can smell and taste the stench of blood, feces, and fear.

4   Animal protection guidelines and laws serve as smoke and mirrors. They give the impression that animals are protected from suffering when in fact, the guidelines actually serve as a cover for the protection of the experiments. Due to the lobbying efforts of the taxpayer-funded animal experimentation industry, the Animal Welfare Act (AWA) does not include upwards of 95 percent of all animals used in experiments: rats and mice. It also does not cover birds, reptiles, amphibians, and animals used in agricultural experiments. Under the AWA, these animals are not considered animals. Even for the animals covered, the AWA provides minimal protection and leaves enforcement up to the notoriously incompetent U.S. Department of Agriculture (USDA). As explained by Mariann Sullivan, former Deputy Chief Court Attorney at the New York State Supreme Court:

> The standards set forth . . . require little more than that animals be fed, watered, vetted, and kept in reasonably clean and safe enclosures that allow them to make species-appropriate postural adjustments. In other words, the AWA basically stipulates that animals be fed and be allowed to move about, if only a little, in their cages (1).

5   The AWA also requires that experimentation facilities set up so-called "Animal Care and Use Committees" to "consider alternatives" and "minimize discomfort, distress, and pain to the animals." However, the AWA provides loopholes for even these standards, and animal experimenters and their friends dominate the committees. Bottom line: any experiment, no matter how painful or how much suffering it causes, can be justified under the guise of "science."

6   Even when animal welfare violations are found, the fines charged rarely serve as a deterrent for future violations. In December, the USDA fined Harvard Medical School for repeated violations. Two monkeys died because they were not given access to water. One died from strangulation from a toy. The fine? $24,000. For an institution that receives hundreds of millions of our tax dollars to fund its experiments, the fine was a slap on the wrist. If these egregious violations can happen at Harvard, what do you think goes on in laboratories with far less visibility?

7   Surely we can do better than this. The animals used in experiments are much more than furry test tubes left over after years of living in fear. These animals, when given the opportunity, can experience joy, empathy, and affection. Watch a rat laugh as his belly is tickled or he takes a bath, and you can see how much joy they are capable of experiencing.

8   I often find myself thinking back to that cat I watched at the neuroscience conference. I said a quiet prayer that her spinal cord injury wiped out her ability to feel pain in her legs, and I can't help but wonder if anyone else in the audience noticed what I did. Even at the peak of her suffering, the cat was seeking comfort from the very hand that caused it. Ten days later, she was killed and her brain dissected.

9   What does this say about us? Are we going to continue to turn a blind eye to the suffering we cause? Have we, to borrow a phrase from Pink Floyd, become comfortably numb? As Matthew Scully, a special advisor to President George W. Bush, wrote it in his book *Dominion*,

> When scientists abandon moral scruple in the treatment of animals, growing numb to the disfigurement and suffering before their eyes, regarding life itself as a mere instrument to be used and discarded, used and discarded, the habit is hard to shake (382).

10   Isn't it time we shake this habit, take a stand against this senseless suffering, and pursue science that represents us at our best? We don't have to choose between helping animals or humans, and we never did. And I say this as a medical doctor, neurologist, and public health specialist: by ending the abuse of animals in experiments, not only do we save them, but we will also discover the most effective research methods that will save us.

11   Animal experiments don't represent the pinnacle of scientific achievement, but the basement. Unlike the naysayers, I believe that we are capable of so much more. All we need is the courage, vision, and resourcefulness to make it happen. Let's make that our collective resolution.

Reading Actively

Use the following specific strategies as you begin reading an argument.

1. **Read once for an initial impression and the "big picture."** Identify the specific claim the writer is making, and identify the reasons and evidence that support it.

2. **Reread the argument.** Read the argument again to examine whether the writer acknowledges or refutes opposing viewpoints. Evaluate the strength of the evidence and arguments as you read.

3. **Annotate while you read.** Record your thoughts; note ideas you agree with, those you disagree with, questions that come to mind, additional reasons or evidence overlooked by the author, and the counterarguments not addressed by the author. (For more information on annotation, see Section 1g, p. 21.)

4. **Highlight key terms and definitions.** Often, an argument depends on how certain terms are defined. In an argument on the destruction of Amazon rain forests, for example, what does "destruction" mean? Does it mean building homes within a forest, or does it refer to clearing the land for timber or to create fields for growing food crops like corn or wheat?

5. **Use a map or diagram to analyze structure.** Because many arguments are complex, you may find it helpful to map or diagram them (see Sections 1j and 1k, starting on p. 26), which may help you discover bias, claims for which evidence is not provided, or an imbalance between reasons and emotional appeals. You can use the format shown in Figure 10-1 (p. 306) to help you analyze the structure of an argument.

EXERCISE 10-4 . . . READING AN ARGUMENT

Read, reread, and annotate the article "Who Are the Animals in Animal Experiments?" Then answer the questions that follow.

1. What was your initial impression of the article? What additional insights and impressions did you learn upon rereading? _____

_____

2. What is the writer's specific claim?

_____

_____

3. What type of claim does the author make (fact, value, or policy)?

_____

4. Draw a map of the reading and use it to evaluate whether there is a balance or imbalance between reasons and emotional appeals. Write a sentence summarizing what you learned. _____

_____

_____

Recognizing Types of Supporting Evidence

A writer supports a claim by offering reasons and evidence that the claim should be accepted. A **reason** is a general statement that backs up a claim. Here are several reasons that support an argument that more humane treatment of animals used in experiments is needed:

- Animals are kept in inhumane conditions.
- Animals suffer terribly when they are used in laboratory experiments.
- Humans do not act responsibly when conducting research using animals.

However, for any of these reasons to be believable and convincing, they need to be supported with evidence. **Evidence** consists of the following types of information that can be used to demonstrate why a claim is valid:

- **Facts.** Statements that can be verified to be true, facts are commonly used to support an argument and support the accuracy of a claim.
- **Statistics.** Writers commonly use statistics—figures, percentages, averages, and so forth—to support or refute arguments.
- **Quotations and citations.** Writers often substantiate or confirm their ideas by including quotations or citations from experts or authorities on the subject.
- **Examples.** Examples are descriptions of particular situations that are used to illustrate or explain a principle, concept, or idea. Examples should not be used by themselves to prove the concept or idea they

illustrate. The examples given may be atypical, or not representative, of what is common.

- **Personal experience.** A writer may use his or her own personal account or observation of a situation to support an argument. Although a writer's personal experience may provide an interesting perspective on an issue, personal experience should not be accepted as proof.
- **Comparisons and analogies.** Comparisons or analogies (extended comparisons) serve as illustrations. Their reliability depends on how closely the comparison corresponds or how similar it is to the situation to which it is being compared.

10e STRATEGIES FOR EVALUATING AN ARGUMENT

LEARNING OBJECTIVE 5
Evaluate the validity of arguments

Once you have understood an argument by identifying what is asserted and how it is asserted, you are ready to evaluate its soundness, correctness, and validity. The factors you need to consider in evaluating an argument are the accuracy of the evidence and premises, the relevancy and sufficiency of evidence, whether terms are clearly defined, whether relationships claimed to be cause and effect really are, the presence of a stated or implied value system, whether opposing viewpoints are recognized and/or refuted, and the presence of unfair emotional appeals.

Assessing the Accuracy of Evidence and Premises

Evaluating an argument involves assessing the accuracy and correctness of the statements on which the argument is based. As a critical reader, your task is to assess whether the evidence or premises are sufficient to support the claim. Here are some questions to consider when evaluating evidence and premises:

Questions to Ask When Evaluating Evidence and Premises

1. **Is the observer biased?** Did he or she exaggerate or incorrectly perceive a situation?
2. **Are the examples typical and representative?** That is, do the examples fairly represent the situation? Or has the writer used uncommon or rare examples, which weaken the argument?
3. **Are statistics used fairly and clearly?** Many people are impressed by statistics—the reporting of figures, percentages, averages, and so forth—and assume they are irrefutable. Actually, statistics can be misused, misinterpreted, or used selectively to provide a biased or inaccurate view of the situation. Approach statistical evidence with a critical, questioning attitude.
4. **Are comparisons realistic and true?** The reliability of comparisons depends on how closely the comparison corresponds or how similar it is to the situation to which it is being compared. For example, Martin Luther King Jr., in his famous letter from the Birmingham jail, compared nonviolent protesters to a robbed man. To evaluate this comparison, you need to consider how the two are similar and how they are different.

Assessing the Relevancy of Evidence

Evidence that is offered in support of a claim must directly relate to that claim. For example, a friend may offer as a reason for being late for meeting with you that he had a flat tire, but this fact is not relevant if he would have had to walk only one block to see you. Writers may intentionally or unintentionally include information that may seem convincing but when analyzed more closely does not directly apply to the issue.

In the professional essay, "Who Are the Animals in Animal Experiments?" on page 311, if the author had included information about the enrollment or endowment of the medical school while describing the mistreatment of animals at Harvard Medical School in paragraph 6, that information would have been irrelevant because it does not support the main point of the paragraph. To decide whether a statement is relevant, reread the claim and then immediately afterward reread the statement in question. Ask yourself, "Are the two logically connected?"

Assessing the Sufficiency of Evidence

There must be a sufficient number of reasons or pieces of evidence to support a claim. The amount and degree of detail of supporting evidence will vary with the issue, its complexity, and its importance. For any serious issue, it is not usually sufficient to offer a single reason or piece of evidence. For example, to say that our oceans are dying due to coastal development is not convincing because only a portion of the world's oceans are affected by coastal development. Other evidence to support this claim could include industrial waste dumping, oil drilling, ecosystem imbalance, and rising water temperatures.

The evidence a writer offers must also be sufficiently detailed to be convincing and believable. In paragraph 4 of "Who Are the Animals in Animal Experiments?," if the author had omitted information about the percentage of animals that are *not* covered under the Animal Welfare Act or those animals (birds, reptiles, amphibians, and animals used in agricultural experiments) not considered animals, the paragraph would have been unconvincing.

Assessing the Definitions of Terms

A clear and effective argument carefully defines key terms and uses them consistently. The following two paragraphs discuss the topic of illegal immigrants, sometimes called undocumented workers. In the first paragraph, the author defines the terms *underground economy* and *undocumented workers*, explaining how the two terms are related. In the second paragraph, the term *undocumented workers* is used, but the focus is on the controversies involved in preventing illegal immigration from Mexico. The terms *illegal migrant* and *undocumented worker* are not defined. Thus, someone reading the second paragraph might well ask, "But what exactly does *undocumented worker* mean?" Also note the differences in tone and purpose between the two paragraphs.

Issue: Immigration

Paragraph 1: Specific Definitions

The number of illegal immigrants in the United States is on the decline, yet the millions who remain are part of the *underground economy*, an economy of transactions or trades that are not reported to the government. The immigrants who work without authorization are often called *undocumented workers* (called *los sin documentos* in Mexico), and they work for employers who either pay them in cash without reporting their employment to government or look the other way when they provide false documents. There is a big black market for fake green cards. (A green card, also called a Permanent Resident Card, gives an immigrant the right to live and work in the U.S.)

Paragraph 2: Discussion Without Definitions

In 2005, the House of Representatives initiated legislation to reform U.S. immigration policy, particularly to stem a flow of undocumented workers now thought to have brought in 10 million people, more than half from Mexico. Opinions clashed, often along party lines, on proposals for amnesty programs, "guest worker" provisions, and the sanctioning and deportation of illegal migrants.

—adapted from Faragher et al., *Out of Many*, p. 928

In the reading "Who Are the Animals in Animal Experiments?" the author discusses in some detail what the Animal Welfare Act (AWA)—ostensibly designed to protect animals—actually does, using statistics, examples, and a quote from Mariann Sullivan, a former Deputy Chief Attorney, to provide a more accurate definition.

Assessing Cause and Effect Relationships

Arguments are often built around the assumption of a cause and effect relationship. For example, an argument supporting gun-control legislation may claim that ready availability of guns contributes to an increased number of shootings. This argument implies that the easy availability of guns causes increased use of guns. If the writer provides no evidence that this cause and effect relationship exists, you should question the validity of the argument. (For more on cause and effect, see Section 7e, p. 187.)

Assessing Implied or Stated Value Systems

An argument often implies or rests on a **value system** (a consistent set of ethical values regarding what is right, wrong, worthwhile, and important). Although our culture promotes many major common values (murder is wrong, human life is worthwhile, and so forth), there is ample room for disagreement. In addition, everyone possesses a personal value system that may sometimes clash with the larger social value system. For example, one person may think telling lies is always wrong; another person may say that the morality of lying depends on the circumstances. Some people have a value system based on religious beliefs; others may not share those same religious beliefs.

In evaluating an argument, look for value judgments and then decide whether the judgments are consistent with and acceptable to your personal value system. Here are a few examples of value judgments:

- The inhumane treatment that animals receive in some scientific research experiments is morally wrong.
- Marriage should be defined as the union between one man and one woman.
- People with disabilities should have access to the same opportunities and public locations that people without disabilities enjoy.

Recognizing and Refuting Opposing Viewpoints

Many, but not all, arguments recognize opposing viewpoints. For example, an author may argue that gay people should be allowed to marry. However, the author may recognize or admit that opponents believe marriage should only be allowed between a man and a woman.

Many arguments also attempt to refute the opposing viewpoint (explain why it is wrong, flawed, or unacceptable). For example, a writer may refute the notion that gay people should not be allowed to marry by stating that forbidding marriage denies the fundamental freedom of choice of a life partner. Basically, then, refutation is a process of finding weaknesses in an opponent's argument.

When reading arguments that address opposing viewpoints, ask yourself the following questions.

- Does the author address opposing viewpoints clearly and fairly?
- Does the author refute the opposing viewpoint with logic and relevant evidence?

The author of "Who Are the Animals in Animal Experiments?" refutes the idea that the Animal Welfare Act protects animals used in experiments by using statistics, personal observations, and a quotation from an expert authority. She does not directly acknowledge the opposing argument that it is better that animals suffer than that people suffer or die from diseases. Although she does say, "We don't have to choose between helping animals or humans and we never did," she does not explain why we are not forced to choose between animals and people, which could have served as a strong refutation of this counterargument.

EXERCISE 10-5 . . . ANALYZING EVIDENCE

Reread the argument "Who Are the Animals in Animal Experiments?" on page 311, paying particular attention to the type(s) of evidence used. Then answer the questions that follow.

1. What type(s) of evidence is/are used?

   _____

2. Is the evidence convincing? _____

3. Is there sufficient evidence? _____

4. What other types of evidence could have been used to strengthen the argument?

   _____

   _____

5. Which cause and effect relationships does the writer discuss?

   _____

   _____

6. What implied value system is found in the argument?

   _____

7. Does the writer recognize and/or refute opposing viewpoints?

   _____

Recognizing Unfair Emotional Appeals

Emotional appeals attempt to involve or excite readers by appealing to their emotions, thereby shaping their attitude toward a subject. An argument on gun control, for example, may appeal to a reader's need for safety, while an argument favoring restrictions on banks sharing personal or financial information may appeal to a reader's need for privacy and financial security. Several types of emotional appeals are described below.

1. **Emotionally charged or biased language.** By using words that create an emotional response, writers establish positive or negative feelings. For example, an advertisement for a new line of fragrances promises to "indulge," "refresh," "nourish," and "pamper" the user, all positive terms that invite the reader to buy the product. In contrast, in paragraph 3 of "Who Are the Animals in Animal Experiments," the author's description of the plight of research animals is designed to evoke an emotional reaction

of horror: "Animals who have had their heads crushed grip their faces and convulse as blood pours out of their noses. You can smell and taste the stench of blood, feces, and fear."

2. **False authority.** False authority involves using the opinion or action of a well-known or famous person. We have all seen athletes endorsing underwear or movie stars selling shampoo. This type of appeal works on the notion that people admire celebrities and strive to be like them, respect their opinion, and are willing to accept their viewpoint.

3. **Association.** An emotional appeal also is made by associating a product, idea, or position with other things that are already accepted or highly regarded. Patriotism is already valued, so to call a product All-American in an advertisement is an appeal to the emotions. A car being named a Cougar to remind you of a fast, sleek animal, a cigarette ad picturing a scenic waterfall, or a speaker standing in front of an American flag are other examples.

4. **Appeal to "common folk."** Some people distrust those who are well educated, wealthy, highly artistic, or in other ways distinctly different from the average person. An emotional appeal to this group is made by indicating that a product or idea originated from, is held by, or is bought by ordinary citizens. A commercial may advertise a product by showing its use in an average household. A politician may describe her background and education to suggest that she is like everyone else; a salesperson may dress in styles similar to his clients.

5. **Ad hominem.** An argument that attacks the holder of an opposing viewpoint rather than his or her viewpoint is known as *ad hominem*, or an attack on the man. For example, the statement, "How could a woman who does not even hold a college degree criticize a judicial decision?" attacks the woman's level of education, not her viewpoint.

6. **"Join the crowd" appeal.** The appeal to do, believe, or buy what everyone else is doing, believing, or buying is known as *crowd appeal* or the *bandwagon appeal*. Commercials that proclaim their product the "#1 best-selling car in America" are appealing to this motive. Essays in support of a position that cite opinion polls on a controversial issue—"68 percent of Americans favor capital punishment"—are also using this appeal.

EXERCISE 10-6 . . . ANALYZING EMOTIONAL APPEALS

All of the following statements make use of an emotional appeal. Specify which emotional appeal on the line provided.

_____ 1. Now you, too, can have hair as beautiful as Jennifer Aniston's.

_____ 2. Give your family the best by using Tide, America's best-selling laundry detergent.

                  3. Does anyone really agree with fat, unattractive Rush Limbaugh's opinions on immigration?

                  4. Vote for Jane Rodriguez. She knows what it's like to struggle to raise a family and pay the bills.

                  5. Tolerance of polygamy can only lead to the death of the American family and the complete destruction of American morality.

10f   ERRORS IN LOGIC

LEARNING OBJECTIVE 6
Recognize errors in logic

Errors in reasoning, often called **logical fallacies**, invalidate arguments or render them flawed. Sometimes authors genuinely make a mistake when providing support for an argument; other times they are deliberately misleading. Your job as a critical thinker is to read arguments carefully to see if the author has committed any of the following common errors in logic, evaluate how or why they included erroneous reasoning, and determine whether the argument still stands if any of the support is incorrect or deceptive.

Circular Reasoning

Also known as *begging the question*, **circular reasoning** involves using part of the conclusion as evidence to support that conclusion. Here are two examples.

- Female firefighters should not be sent to fight blazing fires because firefighting is a man's job.
- Cruel bullying of children is inhumane.

    In an argument that uses circular reasoning, there is no reason to accept the conclusion because no evidence is given to support the claim.

False Analogy

An analogy is an extended comparison between two otherwise unlike things. A sound analogy addresses aspects of the two things that are alike. A **false analogy** compares two things that do not share a likeness. A writer arguing against gun control may say,

"Guns are not a major problem in this country. Fatal accidents on the road, in the workplace, and at home kill many more people than guns do."

    Here the writer is suggesting that death by guns is similar to fatal accidents in the car, on the job, or at home. Yet, accidents and murder are not similar.

Hasty Generalization

Hasty generalization occurs when a conclusion is derived from insufficient evidence. Here are two examples:

- A person listens to one piece of classical music and does not like it, so she concludes that she does not like classical music.
- By observing one performance of a musical group, a person concludes the group is unfit to perform.

Non Sequitur ("It Does Not Follow")

The false establishment of cause and effect is a **non sequitur** (from Latin for "it does not follow"). For example, "Because my doctor is young, I'm sure she'll be a good doctor" is a non sequitur because youth does not ensure good medical practices. Here is another example of a non sequitur: "Arturo Alvarez is the best choice for state senator because he is well-known for his community service." Being a community service volunteer will not necessarily make someone an effective senator.

False Cause

The **false cause** fallacy is the incorrect assumption that two events that happen in sequence are causally related. In other words, false cause implies that an event that happened later had to be caused by an event that happened earlier. Suppose you open an umbrella and then trip on an uneven sidewalk. If you said you tripped because you opened the umbrella, you would be committing the error of false cause. Or suppose you walk out of your house and it starts to rain. You would be committing the false cause error if you suggest that it started to rain because you walked out of your house.

Either–Or Fallacy

The **either–or fallacy** assumes that an issue has only two sides, or that there are only two choices or alternatives for a particular situation. In other words, there is no middle ground. Consider the issue of censoring TV violence. An either-or fallacy would assume that TV violence must be either permitted or banned. This fallacy does not recognize other alternatives such as limiting access through viewing hours, restricting certain types of violence, and so on.

Abstract Concepts as Reality

Writers occasionally treat abstract concepts as absolute truths with a single acceptable position or outcome. For example, a writer may say, "Research proves that divorce is harmful to children." Actually, there are hundreds of pieces of research on the effects of divorce, and they offer diverse findings and conclusions. Some but not all research reports harmful effects. Here is another example: "Criminology shows us that prisons are seldom effective in controlling crime." Writers tend to use this device to make it seem as if all authorities are in agreement with their position. This device also allows writers to ignore contrary or contradictory evidence or opinions.

Red Herring

A **red herring** is something added to an argument to divert attention from the issue at hand. It is introduced into an argument to throw readers off track. Think of a red herring as an argumentative tactic rather than an error in reasoning. Suppose you are reading an essay that argues against the death penalty. If the author suddenly starts reporting the horrific living conditions in death-row prisons and the unjust treatment of prisoners, the writer is introducing a red herring. The living conditions and treatment of prisoners on death row are valid issues, but they are not relevant to an argument that the death penalty is unjust.

EXERCISE 10-7 . . . IDENTIFYING ERRORS IN LOGIC

Identify the logical fallacy in each of the following statements.

_____   1. All Asian American students in my economics class earned A grades, so Asian Americans must excel in studying economics.

_____   2. If you don't believe in global warming, then you clearly don't care about the earth.

_____   3. My sister cannot do mathematical computations or balance her checkbook because she suffers from depression.

_____   4. A well-known governor, noting a decline in the crime rate in the four largest cities in his state, quickly announced that his new "get tough on criminals" policy was successful and took credit for the decline.

_____   5. The instructor's apartment was robbed because she left her apartment without her cell phone.

EXERCISE 10-8 . . . EVALUATING AN ARGUMENT

Reread the essay "Who Are the Animals in Animal Experiments?" on page 311, and then complete the following.

1. Summarize the author's argument. Include the issue, the author's claim about it, and the main supporting points.

2. Indicate what type of evidence the author uses.

3. Determine whether the evidence is adequate and sufficient to support the author's point.

4. What other types of evidence could have been used?

5. How does the author attempt to win readers over to her viewpoint?

6. Evaluate the overall effectiveness of the argument. Was it convincing? Why or why not?

10g   WRITING ARGUMENT ESSAYS

LEARNING OBJECTIVE 7
Write sound, convincing argument essays

Now that you are familiar with the components of an argument essay, it is time to write one.

Chapter 9 provides detailed coverage of essay writing techniques. Using those strategies and the guidelines that follow will help you to write a well-reasoned argument. Throughout this section, the student essay below will be used as a model.

EXAMINING STUDENT ARGUMENTATIVE WRITING

The following essay was written by Sarah Frey, a student at The University of North Carolina at Chapel Hill. Read the essay carefully, paying special attention to the annotations that show the main elements of an argument essay.

Sarah Frey

Frey 1

Sarah Frey

Dr. Thomas

Psychology 356

26 January 2015

Title

→ Standardized Testing: An Argument for Abolishment

Introduction: Sarah provides background on the issue

1   SATs and ACTs often bring unnecessary stress into the lives of high school

→ students as they begin to think about and prepare for college. But

Frey 2

standardized testing does not stop with admittance into college; in order to apply for graduate school, college students are required to take the Graduate Record Examinations (GRE) or the Graduate Management Admission Test (GMAT). Often standardized testing is coupled with a student's GPA and extracurricular activities as a way to judge whether he or she will fit into the specific college or graduate school to which he or she is applying. Taking these tests causes stress in the lives of the high school and college students, and there is no guarantee that these tests will even get them into school. The argument for the abolishment of standardized testing as a gateway into higher education is a strong one, and parents and students across the country would support a law that would take this action.

Thesis statement identifies the issue and states the author's claim about it

2   The lack of non-academic or creative subjects in standardized testing makes them extremely difficult for some students. Students who are not strong in math and verbal skills tend to struggle with these tests because their gifts lie in other areas. Students may have real talent for the dramatic arts, art media, music, design, or any other non-traditional academic areas, and it is these students who are not even given an opportunity to showcase their talent (Webb). The field of psychology has adopted Gardner's Theory of Multiple Intelligences, in which Gardner proposes that human beings do not just possess a single intelligence, but rather humans can be better described as having a set of intelligences. Gardner's theory proposes nine discrete intelligences: musical, visual, verbal, logical, bodily, interpersonal, intrapersonal, naturalist, and existential. However, the standardized testing that students are forced to take to gain admittance to college or graduate school focuses on only two or, at best, three of these intelligences.

Reason 1

Evidence: Citation from authority

Frey 3

3   In addition to the close-minded approach to the subject of the tests, there

Reason 2

is a socio-economic bias affiliated with the tests themselves. Not only are

students required to pay to take the exam itself, but they are also required to

pay to have their scores sent to their school of choice. In addition to these

fees, students are often encouraged by their high schools to seek out an SAT

or ACT prep course in order to ready them for the exam; these courses also

cost money. All of these fees discourage low-income students from taking the

exam, and if they do choose to take it, their scores tend to be lower than

those of their wealthier peers. According to the *New York Times*, there is a

strong positive correlation between parental income and SAT test scores

(Rampell). Additionally, in every test section, moving up an income category

Statistical evidence

also meant a score boost of over 12 points (Rampell). These boosts may be

attributed to better preparation for the student or better resources that they

were provided.

4   Students tend to have to take these standardized tests on top of all of

Reason 3

their other school work, especially college students taking the GRE or GMAT,

the Medical College Admissions Test (MCAT), or even the Law School

Admissions Test (LSAT). There comes a point for all college students when

they must decide what comes next, and with the direction the world is going

right now, many of them are choosing graduate school. But when they make

that decision, they are also choosing to take on another beast: the graduate

test associated with their chosen path. On top of their already full plates,

Facts as evidence

these students are delegating time and resources to study for yet another

test, in hope of continuing their education (Blackman). Most of the time,

Frey 4

adding a prep course for the graduate test also adds homework and study time to an already busy schedule. And although data suggest that the scores are higher when the test is taken in college rather than post-college, the scores are only good for three to five years. What this means is that the window to apply with a score from a test taken in college may close before students attain the three to five years of work experience required by most schools (Burnsed).

5   There are those who think that standardized testing is the most fair and

Recognition and refutation of opposing viewpoint → unbiased way to evaluate college and graduate school acceptance. According to CollegeBoard, the SAT has questions that are heavily researched in order to make sure that students from all backgrounds have an equal chance of doing well. Additionally, CollegeBoard claims that there are no tricks specifically to trip up students, as the test is designed so that students who do well in the classroom should also do well on the SAT (CollegeBoard). Unfortunately, the scores on the test say otherwise. According to the *Journal of Blacks in Higher Education*, in 2005 there was a seventeen percent difference in the scores of

Statistical evidence → white and black students ("Widening Racial Scoring Gap"). In addition, *USA Today* reports that the highest average scores on the SAT come from students who said their families earned more than $200,000 a year, whereas students who reported family incomes of less than $20,000 a year averaged a 22% deficit (Marklein).

6   If colleges agreed that the test was a fair and just one for students of

Refutation continues → all backgrounds, ethnic or socioeconomic, there would not be a movement away from standardized testing by some schools in favor of just using students' high school records, resumes, and/or portfolios as

Frey 5

acceptance criteria (Peligri). These schools are called "test-optional" schools, and they do not require applicants to take standardized tests but also do not completely disregard them if students submit their test scores. The decision to eliminate standardized testing is meant to alleviate the pressure on many high school seniors to tally high scores on the SAT or ACT exams (Peligri). Graduate schools are still, for the most part, requiring applicants to take the relevant standardized test, but perhaps the idea that a person's intelligence should not be based on a number will reach them soon.

> Conclusion: Sarah recaps her reasons and makes a final statement

7   The abolishment of standardized testing as a gateway into college and graduate school would help students across the country. It would alleviate stress levels when it comes to preparing for such tests, and students could harness that energy for other things. The idea that students only need skills in math and reading and writing is an outdated one, and the world of education seems to be moving away from it with the introduction of test-optional applications and even schools that completely reject the idea of using these scores. Not to mention, it would allow students from less privileged and advantaged communities to be evaluated as people, not just as numbers. The idea of standardized testing is outdated, and it is time for a change. Standardized testing should not be a factor in colleges and graduate programs' decisions to admit or reject potential students.

Frey 6

Works Cited

Blackman, Stacy. "Decide Between GMAT, GRE." *U.S. News & World Report*, 29 July

    2011, www.usnews.com/education/blogs/mba-admissions-strictly-business

    /2011/07/29/decide-between-gmat-gre.

Burnsed, Brian. "Pros and Cons of Taking the GMAT in College." *U.S. News & World*

    Report, 22 June 2011,

    www.usnews.com/education/best-graduate-schools/top-business-schools

    /articles/2011/06/22/pros-and-cons-of-taking-the-gmat-in-college.

CollegeBoard. "Why Take the SAT." 2014. Accessed 9 Nov. 2014.

Gardner, Howard. *Frames of Mind: The Theory of Multiple Intelligences*. Basic Books,

    1993.

Marklein, Mary Best. "SAT Scores Show Disparities by Race, Gender, Family

    Income." *USA Today*, 26 Aug. 2009, usatoday30.usatoday.com/news

    /education/2009-08-25-SAT-scores_N.htm.

Peligri, Justin. "No, the SAT Is Not Required. More Colleges Join Test-optional

    Train." *USA Today*, 7 July 2014, college.usatoday.com/2014/07/07

    /no-the-sat-is-not-required-more-colleges-join-test-optional-train/.

Rampell, Catherine. "SAT Scores and Family Income." *The New York Times*, 27 Aug.

    2009,

    economix.blogs.nytimes.com/2009/08/27/sat-scores-and-family-

    income/?_r=0.

Webb, Candace. "Pro & Cons of the SAT Test." *Synonym*, classroom.synonym.com

    /pro-cons-sat-test-5423.html. Accessed 9 Nov. 2014.

"The Widening Racial Scoring Gap on the SAT College Admissions Test." *The Journal*

    of Blacks in Higher Education, vol. 49, Autumn 2005, www.jbhe.com/features

    /49_25-SAT-scores_N.htm. Accessed 16 Nov. 2014.

Writing an Argumentative Thesis Statement

Your thesis statement should identify the issue and state your claim about it. It may also suggest the primary reasons for accepting the claim. Place your thesis statement where it will be most effective. There are three common placements:

1. Thesis statement in the introduction
2. Thesis statement after responding to objections
3. Thesis statement at the end of the essay

In general, placing the thesis in the introduction is best when addressing an audience in agreement with your claim or one that is neutral about the topic under discussion. For an audience that does not agree with your argument, a later placement gives you the opportunity to respond to the audience's objections before you present your thesis.

In Sarah's essay, the topic was standardized testing and the issue was the requirement of standardized test scores for admission into higher education. Sarah chose to use her introductory paragraph to provide background on the issue, and she placed her thesis statement at the end of the paragraph.

Analyzing Your Audience

Analyzing your audience is a crucial step in planning a convincing argument. There are three types of audiences:

- **Audiences who agree with your claim.** Audiences in agreement with you are likely to be easier to write for because they think the same way you do about the issue. For this audience, state your claim and explain why you think it is correct.

- **Neutral audiences.** These readers have not made up their minds or have not given much thought to the issue. They may have questions, they may misunderstand the issue, or they may have heard arguments supporting the opposing viewpoint. An essay written for a neutral audience should be direct and straightforward, like those written for an audience in agreement with your point of view. However, a fuller explanation of the issue is necessary to answer questions, clear up misunderstandings, and respond to opposing arguments.

- **Audiences who disagree with your claim.** These are the most difficult to address. Some members will have thought about the issue and taken a position that opposes yours. Others who disagree may not have examined the issue at all and may be making superficial judgments or may be relying on misinformation. Both types think their position is correct, so they will not be eager to change their minds. They may also distrust you because you think differently from them. For such an audience, your biggest challenge is to build trust and confidence. Before writing, carefully analyze this audience and try to answer these questions:

- Why does your audience disagree with your claim?
- Is their position based on real facts and sound evidence, or on personal opinion? If it is based on evidence, what type?
- What type of arguments or reasons are most likely to appeal to your audience? For example, will they be convinced by facts and statistics or by statements made by authorities? Would personal anecdotes and examples work well?

Once you understand how your audience thinks, you can plan your essay more effectively. Although Sarah's audience was her psychology professor, her "real life" audience could be students and others in the field of education. Some members of her audience would support her position while others would reject it.

Providing Adequate Supporting Evidence

Here are five types of supporting evidence you can use to develop your thesis.

Facts and Statistics

As in writing any other type of paragraph or essay, you must choose facts that directly support the position you express in your topic sentence. It is usually more effective to present more than one statistic. Suppose you are writing to convince taxpayers that state lotteries have become profitable businesses. You might state that more than 60 percent of the adult population now buy lottery tickets regularly. This statistic would have little meaning by itself. However, if you were to state that 60 percent of adults now purchase lottery tickets, whereas five years ago only 30 percent purchased them, the first statistic would become more meaningful.

In paragraph 5 of Sarah's essay (p. 327), she uses both facts and statistics to refute the argument that standardized testing is fair and unbiased.

According to the *Journal of Blacks in Higher Education*, in 2005 there was a seventeen percent difference in the scores of white and black students ("Widening Racial Scoring Gap"). In addition, *USA Today* reports that the highest average scores on the SAT come from students who said their families earned more than $200,000 a year, whereas students who reported family incomes of less than $20,000 a year averaged a 22% deficit (Marklein).

In selecting statistics to support your position, be sure to consider the following:

1. **Obtain statistics from reliable print or online sources.** These include almanacs, encyclopedias, articles in reputable journals and magazines, or other trustworthy reference materials from your library. Online sources include databases, online journals, and scholarly Web sites.

2. **Use up-to-date information, preferably from the past year or two.** Dated statistics may be incorrect or misleading.

3. **Make sure you define terms and units of measurement.** For example, if you say that 60 percent of adults regularly play the lottery, you should define what "regularly" means. Does it mean daily, weekly, or monthly?

4. **Verify that the statistics you obtain from more than one source are comparable.** For example, if you compare the crime rates in New York City and Los Angeles, be sure that each crime rate was computed the same way, that each represents the same types of crimes, and that report sources were similar.

Quotations or Citations from Authorities

You can also support your claim by using expert or authoritative statements of opinion or conclusions. **Experts** or **authorities** are those who have studied a subject extensively, conducted research on it, or written widely about it. For example, if you are writing an essay calling for stricter preschool-monitoring requirements to prevent child abuse, the opinion of a psychiatrist who works extensively with abused children would provide convincing support.

In the example below, Sarah cited the work of Howard Gardner, a noted authority in the field of psychology.

> The field of psychology has adopted Gardner's Theory of Multiple Intelligences, in which Gardner proposes that human beings do not just possess a single intelligence, but rather humans can be better described as having a set of intelligences.

Examples

Refer to Chapter 5 for a review of how to use examples as supporting details. In an argument essay, your examples must represent your claim and should illustrate as many aspects of your claim as possible. Suppose your claim is that a particular movie should have been rated NC-17 because it contains excessive violence. The evidence you choose to support this claim should be clear, vivid examples of violent scenes.

The examples you choose should also, if possible, relate to your audience's experience. Familiar examples are more appealing, convincing, and understandable. Suppose you are taking a position on abortion. Your audience consists of career women between 30 and 40 years old. It would be most effective to use as examples women of the same age and occupational status.

Sarah used examples throughout her essay. This sentence from paragraph 7 provides examples to support her claim that abolishing standardized testing would help students across the country:

> It would alleviate stress levels when it comes to preparing for such tests, and students could harness that energy for other things.

Personal Experience

If you are knowledgeable about a subject, your personal experiences can be convincing evidence. For example, if you were writing an essay supporting the position that physical separation from parents encourages a teenager or young adult to mature, you could discuss your own experiences with leaving home and assuming new responsibilities.

Although Sarah did not include any personal experience as support, she certainly could have. She could have written of her own experience of working with a tutor before she took the SAT, being stressed about scoring high enough to get into the college of her choice, and struggling with the decision to study for the GRE while taking a full load of courses in college.

Comparisons and Analogies

Comparison and analogies (extended comparisons) are useful, especially when writing for an audience that lacks background and experience with your subject. By comparing something unknown to something that is known and familiar, you can make your readers comfortable and non-threatened. For example, you could explain a new dance step by likening it to dance steps that are traditional and familiar to most readers. Be sure to make it clear which characteristics or features are similar and which are not.

EXERCISE 10-9 . . . SUPPORTING A TOPIC SENTENCE

Select a topic from the list below, generate ideas, and write a thesis statement. Then generate reasons and evidence to support your thesis.

1. advantages of nanotechnology
2. the right of insurance companies to deny medical coverage to certain individuals
3. preventing teenage pregnancy
4. disposing of toxic waste
5. why people should be vegetarians
6. buying American-made products
7. wetland preservation
8. prosecuting people who illegally download music
9. why people should vote

Researching Your Topic

An argument essay must provide specific and convincing evidence that supports the thesis statement. Often it is necessary to go beyond your own knowledge and experience. You may need to research your topic. For example, if you were writing to urge the creation of an environmentally protected wetland area, you would need to find out what types of wildlife live there, which are endangered, and how successful other protected wetland sites have been in protecting wildlife.

At other times, you may need to interview people who are experts on your topic or directly involved with it. Suppose you are writing a memo urging other employees in your department to participate in a walk-a-thon. It is being held to benefit a local shelter for homeless men and women. The director of the shelter or one of her employees could offer useful statistics, share personal experiences, and provide specific details about the clientele the shelter serves that would help you make a convincing case.

As you examine Sarah's Works Cited page, you will see that she used a variety of sources for her essay. The facts, statistics, and citations from authorities provide specific and convincing evidence that support her thesis statement. Although she chose not to, she could have interviewed her peers and included their personal experiences as further support.

EXERCISE 10-10 . . . EVALUATING EVIDENCE

Evaluate the evidence you collected in Exercise 10-9, and research your topic further if needed. Write the first draft of the essay. Exchange essays with a classmate and critique each other's essays. Revise using your classmate's suggestions.

Responding to Opposing Ideas

It is helpful to respond to opposing ideas that do not support your claim. Your readers will regard you as fair and honest if you admit that there are ideas, opinions, and evidence that express opposite or differing viewpoints about your topic. There are three ways you can accomplish this.

1. **You can acknowledge the opposing viewpoint.** This means you admit that other viewpoints exist and that you have considered them. For example, if you are writing that voluntary community service should be a mandatory part of a college degree program, you can admit that college students are already stressed from studying and working.

2. **You can accommodate the opposing viewpoint by using part of it in your own argument.** For the argument about mandatory community service, you could write that although college students are already busy and stressed, community service would help relieve that pressure and stress by providing a hands-on, uplifting experience.

3. **You can refute the opposing viewpoint by explaining why it is wrong.**
For the community service argument, you could refute the opposing idea that college students cannot waste time with community service by arguing that it will give students new viewpoints and experiences that will help them in securing work after they graduate.

In paragraphs 5 and 6 of her essay (pp. 327–328), Sarah outlines, and supports, several reasons why she believes that standardized testing is unfair: the statistical differences in scores between black and white students, the correlation between high students scores and high parent incomes, and the growing movement amongst some colleges towards a test-optional admission standard.

EXERCISE 10-11 . . . EXAMINING WRITING

Analyze the student essay starting on page 324 and answer the following questions.

1. For what type of audience does Sarah seem to be writing—neutral, in agreement, or not in agreement?

2. Did you find her argument convincing? Why or why not?

3. What other reasons could Sarah have included?

4. Does Sarah rely too heavily on citations from authorities? Why or why not? What other types of evidence could she have included?

SELF-TEST SUMMARY

To test yourself, cover the right column with a sheet of paper and answer the question in the left column. Evaluate each of your answers by sliding the paper down and comparing it with what is printed in the right column.

QUESTION	ANSWER
1 **How are contemporary issues and arguments connected?**	A contemporary issue is a topic that is relevant to individuals, groups, and societies today. Writers often ask questions about aspects of these issues and then write an article, a book, or a blog post in which they state their opinion (often as a thesis sentence) and provide support for their opinion.
2 **What is an argument?**	An argument is a discussion in which a person expresses his or her point of view about a topic. A single issue may have many questions and arguments associated with it.
3 **What are the elements of an argument?**	A good argument has three (sometimes four) parts. *First*, it addresses an issue, problem, or controversy about which people disagree. *Second*, it takes a position (called a claim) on the issue. *Third*, the argument offers support for the claim, usually in the form of reasons, evidence, and sometimes emotional appeals. *Fourth*, some arguments consider opposing viewpoints.
4 **How do you read an argument effectively?**	To read an argument, think before you read. Ask yourself: What does the title suggest? Who is the author, and what are his or her qualifications? What is the date of publication? What do I already know about the topic? Then read actively, once for an initial impression, then for specific information. Annotate and highlight key terms. Draw a diagram or map to analyze the argument's structure.
5 **How do you evaluate an argument?**	To evaluate an argument, consider the accuracy of the evidence and premises. Next, examine the relevancy and sufficiency of evidence and whether terms have been clearly and fully defined. Finally, look for unfair emotional appeals (such as *emotionally charged language, false authority, association, appeal to common folk, ad hominem,* and *join the crowd appeal*) and evaluate the author's use of them.
6 **What are errors in logic and how do you recognize them?**	Errors in logic, or *logical fallacies*, invalidate an argument or render it flawed. Be on the lookout for *circular reasoning, false analogies, hasty generalizations, non sequiturs, false causes, the either–or fallacy, abstract concepts presented as reality,* and *red herrings.*
7 **How do you structure an argument essay?**	To write an argument essay, create a thesis statement that identifies the issue and states your claim. Determine what type of audience you have and provide adequate support for your claim, using reasons, examples, facts, statistics, expert opinion, personal experience, and comparisons and analogies. Consider and refute opposing arguments.

Reading and Writing About Contemporary Issues

Monkey Business Images/Shutterstock

Defining Ourselves: Our Multiple Identities

11

Who are you?

Some people might answer that question by stating their name. But many people would pause because they can't give a simple answer. Consider Pang Xu, a student at San Francisco City College. Thinking about the many roles she plays, Pang might see herself in many ways. She might say:

- I am a woman.
- I am a daughter.
- I am the mother of a two-year-old boy.
- I am a wife.
- I am an immigrant.
- I am Chinese American.
- I am a student.
- I am an employee at Target.
- I am a lover of animals.

And the list could go on and on.

The readings in this chapter focus on *identity*: How we define ourselves, not only in our own heads but also in relationship to other people, groups, and society. Each reading in this chapter focuses on at least one type of identity, but sometimes multiple identities.

WHY IS IDENTITY SUCH AN IMPORTANT CONTEMPORARY ISSUE?

Much of what you read in the contemporary press revolves around identity politics—groups' definitions of themselves and how others perceive them. These perceptions color individuals' experiences, expectations, and even the set of choices they face or the challenges they encounter. For example, government policies may offer assistance to people belonging to certain groups (e.g., people with disabilities, elderly people, sick people). But to offer help, the government must clearly define these terms. What exactly does *disabled* mean? At what age does a person become *elderly*? Should people with the flu be considered as sick as those with cancer?

How Does the Concept of Identity Tie in to My College Courses?

Identity is a core theme running through most humanities and social science courses. In a sociology course, for example, you might study ethnic groups in the United States and how some of them came to be considered ethnic minorities. Literature often focuses on self-expression and the quest for identity. In history and government courses, you will learn about the U.S. Census, which in recent years has struggled with defining racial and ethnic groups due to the huge diversity of the U.S. population. Abraham Maslow, a famous psychologist, defined a strong sense of self-identity as the ultimate achievement for any human being.

TIPS FOR READING ABOUT IDENTITY	Here are some tips for reading not only the selections in this chapter, but any reading about identity.

- **Consider the author's background.** Check the first section before each reading to learn more about the author. Doing so may give you perspective on his or her viewpoints. (Outside this text, check for any biographical information provided about the author.)

- **Keep an open mind.** Some of these readings may challenge your ideas or preconceptions about a topic. You may have an emotional response because some of the readings discuss difficult topics like obesity. Once you have experienced the emotion, reread the article more objectively, with a more critical eye, to better analyze and evaluate the author's thesis.

- **Look for similarities to your own life.** As you read, ask yourself whether the author's perceptions match yours. Have you had personal experiences with the topic? If so, do your opinions match the author's? Why or why not?

Study the Annotations

Each of the three readings in this chapter has been annotated to demonstrate the kinds of thinking and questioning that should occur as you read.

Reading is complex, and readers need to do many kinds of thinking at the same time. However, to demonstrate various levels and types of thinking, the annotations for each reading are limited to one level of thinking. The annotations for Selection 1: "Enhancing Your Body Image" show you how to grasp, connect, and organize the author's ideas. In Selection 2: "'Hurtful and Beautiful': Life with Multiple Sclerosis", the annotations examine the strategies the author uses to express her ideas. The annotations for Selection 3: "All Guts, No Glory" model how to assess and evaluate the worth and value of the author's ideas.

The remaining readings in this book are not annotated. Instead, you are encouraged to annotate your own thoughts and questions as your read. Refer back to these three sets of annotations for ideas, if you need help.

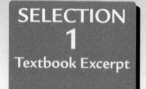

Enhancing Your Body Image

Rebecca J. Donatelle

(WITH CONTEXTUALIZED ANNOTATIONS: STRENGTHENING COMPREHENSION SKILLS)

The following reading was taken from the textbook *Access to Health*, by Rebecca J. Donatelle. Professor Donatelle teaches at Oregon State University in the College of Public Health and Human Sciences. In the introduction to her textbook, the author says her goal is "to empower students to identify their health risks, create plans for change, and make healthy lifestyle changes part of their daily routines." She also states that her book is based on scientifically valid information in order to help students "be smarter in their health decision making, more involved in their personal health, and more active as [advocates] for healthy changes in their community."

GETTING READY TO READ

PREVIEW IT

Preview the reading using the guidelines on page 6. When you have finished, complete the following items:

1. The topic of the reading is _____.

2. List three factors that influence body image.

   a. _____

   b. _____

   c. _____

LOOK IT UP

Rebecca J. Donatelle says she strives to help students "be smarter in their health decision making." In this reading, she focuses specifically on body image. Before you read this selection, spend some time researching the issue on the Internet. Look up positive and negative body images, the factors that influence body image, and the various ways people try to control their body image.

DISCUSS IT

In a group with three or four of your classmates, discuss the findings of your research on body image. Broaden your discussion to include the difference in men and women's perceptions of their body and people you may know about who have taken extreme measures to enhance their body image.

WRITE ABOUT IT

Connect the reading to your own experience by writing a paragraph about how TV shows, movies, and advertisements portray the "ideal" body type for a woman and how that differs for a man. Also, consider the following questions as you write: How much control does a person have over his or her physical appearance? Is there an ideal balance between being healthy and being overly concerned with physical appearance?

STUDY THE MARGINAL ANNOTATIONS: STRENGTHENING COMPREHENSION SKILLS

The marginal annotations and highlighting in this reading are included to help you build your comprehension skills by showing you the kinds of things to look for, notice, and remember.

READING IT

Take a look at the questions that follow the reading before beginning to read so that you can understand the level of recall that is expected. Also, be sure to focus on the author's main points.

Topic sentences are highlighted in yellow.
Transitional words and phrases are highlighted in pink.

The annotations point out features of the text that will help you understand the author's message.

Enhancing Your Body Image

Rebecca J. Donatelle

While this opening story builds interest, there is no need to remember its details.

1   As he began his arm curls, Ali checked his form in the full-length mirror on the weight-room wall. His biceps were bulking up, but after six months of regular weight training, he expected more. His pecs, too, still lacked definition, and his abdomen wasn't the washboard he envisioned. So after a 45-minute upper-body workout, he added 200 sit-ups. Then he left the gym to shower back at his apartment: No way was he going to risk any of the gym regulars seeing his flabby torso unclothed. But by the time Ali got home and looked in the mirror, frustration had turned to anger. He was just too fat! To punish himself for his slow progress, instead of taking a shower, he put on his Nikes and went for a four-mile run.

The phrase "For instance" tells you that an example is coming that illustrates the thesis.

2   When you look in the mirror, do you like what you see? If you feel disappointed, frustrated, or even angry like Ali, you're not alone. A spate of recent studies is revealing that a majority of adults are dissatisfied with their bodies. For instance, a study of men in the United States, Austria, and France found that the ideal bodies they envisioned for themselves were an average of 28 pounds more muscular than their actual bodies. Most adult women—80 percent in one study—are also dissatisfied with their appearance, but for a different reason: most want to lose weight. Tragically, negative feelings about one's body can contribute to disordered eating, excessive exercise, and other behaviors that can threaten

Dissatisfaction with one's appearance and shape is an all-too-common feeling in today's society that can foster unhealthy attitudes and thought patterns, as well as disordered eating and exercising patterns.

your health—and your life. Having a healthy body image is a key indicator of self-esteem and can contribute to reduced stress, an increased sense of personal empowerment, and more joyful living.

What Is Body Image?

Headings tell you what you need to learn and remember in the sections that follow

3

Body image is fundamental to our sense of who we are. Consider the fact that mirrors made from polished stone have been found at archaeological sites dating from before 6000 BCE; humans have been viewing themselves for millennia. But the term *body image* refers to more than just what you see when you look in a mirror. The National Eating Disorders Association (NEDA) identifies several additional components of body image:

Don't miss this part of the definition, even though it is not part of the bulleted list below.

- How you see yourself in your mind
- What you believe about your own appearance (including your memories, assumptions, and generalizations)
- How you feel about your body, including your height, shape, and weight
- How you sense and control your body as you move

Don't miss this two-part definition. Notice the circled words that tie the definition together.

4

NEDA identifies a *negative body image* as (either) a distorted perception of your shape, or feelings of discomfort, shame, (or) anxiety about your body. You may be convinced that only other people are attractive, whereas your own body is a sign of personal failure. Does this attitude remind you of Ali? It should, because he clearly exhibits signs of a negative body image. In contrast, NEDA describes a *positive body image* as a true perception of your appearance: you see yourself as you really are. You understand that everyone is different, and you celebrate your uniqueness—including your "flaws," which you know have nothing to do with your value as a person.

To make the concept understandable, the author uses a comparison to something everyday.

5

Is your body image negative or positive—or is it somewhere in between? Researchers at the University of Arizona have developed a body image continuum that may help you decide (see Figure 1, p. 344). Like a spectrum of light, a continuum represents a series of stages that aren't entirely distinct. Notice that the continuum identifies behaviors associated with particular states, from total dissociation with one's body to body acceptance and body ownership.

Many Factors Influence Body Image

This is an announcement of what is coming next in the reading.

6   You're not born with a body image, but you do begin to develop one at an early age as you compare yourself against images you see in the world around you and interpret the responses of family members and peers to your appearance. Let's look more closely at the factors that probably played a role in the development of your body image.

The Media and Popular Culture

7   Today images of six-pack loaded actors such as Taylor Lautner send young women to the movies in hoards and snapshots of emaciated celebrities such as Lindsay Lohan and Paris Hilton dominate the tabloids and sell magazines. The images and celebrities in the media set the standard for what we find attractive, leading some people to go to dangerous extremes to have the biggest biceps or fit into size 2 jeans. **Most of us think of this obsession with appearance as a recent phenomenon. The truth is, it has long been part of American culture.** During the early twentieth century, while men idolized the hearty outdoorsman President Teddy Roosevelt, women pulled their corsets ever tighter to achieve unrealistically tiny waists. In the 1920s and 1930s, men emulated the burly cops and robbers in gangster films, while women dieted and bound their breasts to achieve the boyish "flapper" look. After World War II, both men and women strove for a healthy, wholesome appearance, but by the 1960s, tough guys like Clint Eastwood and Marlon Brando were the male ideal, whereas rail-thin supermodel Twiggy embodied the nation's standard of female beauty.

Two sentences together express the main point.

8   Today, more than 66 percent of Americans are overweight or obese; thus, a significant disconnect exists between the media's idealized images of male and female bodies and the typical American body. At the same time, the media—in the form of television, the Internet, movies, and print publications—is a more powerful and pervasive presence than ever before. In fact, one study of more than 4,000 television commercials revealed that approximately one out of every four sends some sort of "attractiveness message." Thus, Americans are bombarded daily with messages telling us that we just don't measure up.

These details lead up to the topic sentence, stated at the end of the paragraph.

The word "Thus" provides a clue that the author is stating a conclusion.

Family, Community, and Cultural Groups

9   The members of society with whom we most often interact—our family members, friends, and others—strongly influence the way we see ourselves. **Parents are especially influential in body image development.** For instance, it's common and natural for fathers of adolescent girls to experience feelings of discomfort related to their daughters' changing bodies. If they are able to navigate these feelings successfully and validate the acceptability of their daughters' appearance throughout puberty, it's likely that they'll help their daughters maintain a positive body image. In contrast, if they verbalize or indicate even subtle judgments about their daughters' changing bodies, girls may begin to question how members of the opposite sex view their bodies in general. In addition, mothers who model body acceptance or body ownership may be more likely to foster a similar positive body image in their daughters, whereas mothers who are frustrated with or ashamed of their bodies may have a greater chance of fostering these attitudes in their daughters.

The first sentence looks like the topic until you read the second sentence. The paragraph is limited to talking about parents and children.

An opposite idea is to follow.

10   Interactions with siblings and other relatives, peers, teachers, coworkers, and other community members can also influence body image development. For instance, peer harassment (teasing and bullying) is widely acknowledged to contribute to a negative body image. Moreover, associations within one's cultural group appear to influence body

This example supports the topic sentence.

FIGURE 1   BODY IMAGE CONTINUUM

This is part of a two-part continuum. Individuals whose responses fall to the far left side of the continuum have a highly negative body image, whereas responses to the right indicate a positive body image.

	BODY HATE/ DISSOCIATION	DISTORTED BODY IMAGE	BODY PREOCCUPIED/ OBSESSED	BODY ACCEPTANCE	BODY OWNERSHIP
Important stages →	I often feel separated and distant from my body—as if it belongs to someone else.	I spend a significant amount of time exercising and dieting to change my body.	I spend a significant amount of time viewing my body in the mirror.	I base my body image equally on social norms and my own self-concept.	My body is beautiful to me.
Use these items to help you understand the stages. However, you do not need to learn each one. →	I don't see anything positive or even neutral about my body shape and size. I don't believe others when they tell me I look ok. I hate the way I look in the mirror and often isolate myself from others.	My body shape and size keep me from dating or finding someone who will treat me the way I want to be treated. I have considered changing or have changed my body shape and size through surgical means so I can accept myself.	I spend a significant amount of time comparing my body to others. I have days when I feel fat. I am preoccupied with my body. I accept society's ideal body shape and size as the best body shape and size.	I pay attention to my body and my appearance because it is important to me, but it only occupies a small part of my day. I nourish my body so it has strength and energy to achieve my physical goals.	My feelings about my body are not influenced by society's concept of an ideal body shape. I know that the significant others in my life will always find me attractive.

Source: Based on Smiley, King, and Avey, "Eating Issues and Body Image Continuum."

image. For example, studies have found that European American females experience the highest rates of body dissatisfaction, and as a minority group becomes more acculturated into the mainstream, the body dissatisfaction levels of women in that group increase.

11   Body image also reflects the larger culture in which you live. In parts of Africa, for example, obesity has been associated with abundance, erotic desirability, and fertility. Girls in Mauritania traditionally were force-fed to increase their body size in order to signal a family's wealth, although the practice has become much less common in recent years.

> This example supports the topic sentence.

Physiological and Psychological Factors

12   Recent neurological research has suggested that people who have been diagnosed with a body image disorder show differences in the brain's ability to regulate chemicals called *neurotransmitters*, which are linked to mood. Poor regulation of neurotransmitters is also involved in depression and in anxiety disorders, including obsessive-compulsive disorder. One study linked distortions in body image to a malfunctioning in the brain's visual processing region that was revealed by MRI scanning.

How Can I Build a More Positive Body Image?

> These sentences announce the purpose of the next four paragraphs.

13   If you want to develop a more positive body image, your first step might be to bust some toxic myths and challenge some commonly held attitudes in contemporary society. Have you been accepting these four myths? How would you answer the questions that accompany them?

14   **Myth 1: How you look is more important than who you are.** Do you think your weight is important in defining who you are? How much does your weight matter to your success? How much does it matter to you to have friends who are thin and attractive? How important do you think being thin is in trying to attract your ideal partner?

IS THE MEDIA'S OBSESSION WITH APPEARANCE A NEW PHENOMENON?

CBS Photo Archive/Getty Images

Paul Popper/Popperfoto/Getty Images

Although the exact nature of the "in" look may change from generation to generation, unrealistic images of both male and female celebrities are nothing new. For example, in the 1960s, images of brawny film stars such as Clint Eastwood and ultrathin models such as Twiggy dominated the media.

15   **Myth 2: Anyone can be slender and attractive if they work at it.** When you see someone who is extremely thin, what assumptions do you make about that person? When you see someone who is overweight or obese, what assumptions do you make? Have you ever berated yourself for not having the "willpower" to change some aspect of your body?

This article lacks a conclusion because it is taken from a textbook chapter which continues discussing aspects of the topic.

16   **Myth 3: Extreme dieting is an effective weight-loss strategy.** Do you believe in trying fad diets or "quick-weight-loss" products? How far would you be willing to go to attain the "perfect" body?

17   **Myth 4: Appearance is more important than health.** How do you evaluate whether a person is healthy? Do you believe it's possible for overweight people to be healthy? Is your desire to change some aspect of your body motivated by health reasons or by concerns about appearance?

UNDERSTANDING AND ANALYZING THE READING

A. BUILDING VOCABULARY

Context

Using context and a dictionary, if necessary, determine the meaning of each word as it is used in the selection.

_____ 1. spate (paragraph 2)
    a. large number in quick succession
    b. type of malice
    c. unscientific research study
    d. set of possible answers

_____ 2. continuum (paragraph 5)
    a. ongoing process
    b. sequence
    c. natural light
    d. questionnaire

_____ 3. peers (paragraphs 6 and 10)
    a. close relatives
    b. ancestors
    c. people of the same age
    d. English royalty

_____ 4. emaciated (paragraph 7)
    a. attacked
    b. world-famous
    c. overpaid
    d. extremely thin

_____ 5. obese (paragraph 8)
    a. slightly overweight
    b. disproportionate
    c. very heavy
    d. unhealthy

_____ 6. toxic (paragraph 13)
    a. poisonous
    b. common
    c. unrealistic
    d. silly

Word Parts

> ## A REVIEW OF PREFIXES AND ROOTS
>
> **DIS-**   means *apart, away,* or *not.*
>
> **NEURO**   means *nerve.*

Use your knowledge of word parts and the review above to fill in the blanks in the following sentences.

1. A person who is *dissatisfied* (paragraph 2) with his or her body is _____ satisfied with his or her appearance.

2. *Neurotransmitters* (paragraph 12) transmit electrical impulses between _____, while *neurology* is the study of _____ and _____.

B. UNDERSTANDING THE THESIS AND MAIN IDEAS

Select the best answer.

_____ 1. Which of the following is the best statement of the selection's thesis or central thought?

    a. Understanding four common myths regarding weight loss can help people set more realistic goals when they begin a diet.

    b. Many people suffer from a negative body image that is reinforced by Hollywood celebrities, media, and companies that are trying to sell products.

    c. Body image is important to emotional well-being, and people vary greatly in their body acceptance, often subscribing to commonly held myths about physical appearance.

    d. Ideal body images change over time; women used to want voluptuous bodies but now want to be thin, while men used to prefer thinness but now want to be muscular.

_____ 2. The topic of paragraph 11 is

    a. the connection between body image and culture.

    b. body image in African countries.

    c. the connection between body image and fertility.

    d. the relationship between being wealthy and being overweight.

C. INTERPRETING SUPPORTING DETAILS

Select the best answer.

_____ 1. The author uses a series of questions in paragraphs 14–17 in order to
   a. allow readers to determine the category of the body image continuum into which they fit.
   b. help students prepare for likely exam questions about this reading.
   c. aid readers in distinguishing weight problems caused by physiological issues from weight problems caused by psychological issues.
   d. get readers to examine their own ideas and assumptions about body image and physical appearance.

_____ 2. To support her thesis, the author uses all of the following except
   a. her own personal experience.
   b. historical examples.
   c. statistics.
   d. research studies conducted by academic groups.

_____ 3. Which of the following is *not* a result of having a healthy body image?
   a. an increased sense of personal empowerment
   b. increased self-esteem
   c. a lower level of stress
   d. a higher income level

_____ 4. Which of the following is *not* a component of your body image, as defined by the National Eating Disorders Association (NEDA)?
   a. how you feel about the shape and weight of your body
   b. how others perceive your physical appearance
   c. what you believe about your own appearance
   d. how you control your body as you move

D. RECOGNIZING METHODS OF ORGANIZATION AND TRANSITIONS

Select the best answer. See Chapter 7 for information on patterns of organization.

_____ 1. The pattern of organization used in paragraph 3 is
   a. classification.
   b. definition.
   c. cause and effect.
   d. process.

_____ 2. Which transitional word or phrase signals the organizational pattern of paragraph 3?

    a. *fundamental to*

    b. *consider the fact that*

    c. *refers to*

    d. *what you believe*

_____ 3. The overall pattern of organization used for paragraphs 6–12 (under the heading "Many Factors Influence Body Image") is

    a. classification.

    b. order of importance.

    c. chronological order.

    d. definition.

E. FIGURING OUT IMPLIED MEANINGS

Indicate whether each statement is true (T) or false (F).

_____ 1. Force-feeding girls to signify their families' wealth is common in Mauritania today.

_____ 2. An older woman who thinks "My body is beautiful to me" has a sense of body ownership.

_____ 3. Emphasis on body image in America is mostly a twenty-first-century phenomenon.

_____ 4. A person who is bullied is more likely to develop a negative body image than one who is not bullied.

_____ 5. Almost all people fit perfectly into one of the five categories of the body image continuum.

F. THINKING CRITICALLY ABOUT THE READING

Select the best answer. See Chapter 9 for information on thinking critically about a reading.

_____ 1. The author begins the selection with Ali's story in order to

    a. criticize people who are obsessed with their bodies.

    b. imply that Ali needs to change his diet to achieve his fitness goals.

    c. provide a common example of a person with a negative body image.

    d. offer a role model for those who are trying to "bulk up."

_____ 2. The author's primary purpose in "Enhancing Your Body Image" is to

    a. motivate overweight readers to begin a stricter exercise regimen and a healthier diet.

    b. challenge the "perfect body" stereotypes that are perpetuated by advertising agencies and the media.

    c. make readers aware of the importance of a healthy body image and the factors that affect it.

    d. emphasize the role of body chemistry and personal physiology in determining a person's weight and overall health.

_____ 3. Mariah looks in a mirror and thinks, "No matter how hard I exercise, my hips are too wide and I have too much belly flab. If I'm ever going to find anyone who's interested in dating me or marrying me, I'll need to have plastic surgery first." In which category of the body image continuum does Mariah fall?

    a. body preoccupied/obsessed

    b. body hate/dissociation

    c. distorted body image

    d. body acceptance

_____ 4. The author's tone is best described as

    a. informative.

    b. irreverent.

    c. self-righteous.

    d. abstract.

_____ 5. Three of the following sentences from the reading are facts. One is an opinion. Which one is the opinion?

    a. "A spate of recent studies is revealing that a majority of adults are dissatisfied with their bodies." (paragraph 2)

    b. "Consider the fact that mirrors made from polished stone have been found at archaeological sites dating from before 6000 BCE; humans have been viewing themselves for millennia." (paragraph 3)

    c. "The images and celebrities in the media set the standard for what we find attractive, leading some people to go to dangerous extremes to have the biggest biceps or fit into size 2 jeans." (paragraph 7)

    d. "Today, more than 66 percent of Americans are overweight or obese." (paragraph 8)

_____ 6. In which paragraph can you find the author's key assumption about the benefits of a healthy body image?

     a. paragraph 1

     b. paragraph 2

     c. paragraph 5

     d. paragraph 6

Answer the following open-ended questions in complete sentence format.

7. What does the phrase "attractiveness message" mean in paragraph 8?

8. Evaluate the reading using the following criteria:

     a. Is the reading timely?

     b. Has the author provided sufficient evidence to support her main idea? What other types of evidence might she provide to further support her main idea?

     c. Does the source from which the reading is taken help you determine the credibility of the information presented? Please explain your answer. What is the author's background? Is she qualified to write about the topic? Why or why not?

9. Do you find any bias in the selection? Explain your answer.

10. In paragraph 4, the author speaks of "celebrat[ing] your uniqueness." What does this phrase mean?

WRITING IN RESPONSE TO THE READING ▄▄▄▄▄▄▄▄▄▄▄▄▄▄

G. REVIEWING AND ORGANIZING IDEAS WITH A SUMMARY

Write a clear and concise summary of the section of the reading titled "What Is Body Image?" (paragraphs 3–5). See page 31 for information about writing a summary.

H. ANALYZING THE ISSUE

Discuss in class or write in your journal a response to the following questions.

1. Identify at least three contemporary issues discussed in this reading. Then phrase each as a question that the author raises or answers.

Example

Issue	Question
Obesity in America	Why are 66 percent of Americans overweight or obese?

2. Write a statement that briefly summarizes the author's stance on enhancing one's body image.

3. The theme of this chapter is "defining ourselves: our multiple identities." Analyze the reading by addressing the following questions:
    a. What type of identity does the author focus on?
    b. How is this identity formed?
    c. What factors influence the development of this identity?
    d. How do men and women view this identity differently?
    e. How can this identity either negatively or positively define a person?

4. React to this statement: "The images and celebrities in the media set the standard for what we find attractive." (paragraph 7)

5. The author suggests four myths that need to be busted in order for a person to develop a more positive body image (paragraphs 14–17). What other myths can you add to the list? Try to think of at least two additional myths.

I. WRITING PARAGRAPHS AND ESSAYS

Write a paragraph or essay in response to the following writing prompts.

1. The author discusses body image in detail and talks about how to develop a positive body image as a way of living a "more joyful" life. Write a paragraph in which you explain some other factors that will help you lead a happy, healthy life.

2. The author mentions celebrities who demonstrate the current "body ideal" for women and men, but can you think of any popular figures who do not match this ideal? Write a paragraph describing one such figure, explaining how he or she does not match the image that the media portray as the ideal.

3. On page 345 the author provides photos of two celebrities of a previous generation: Clint Eastwood and Twiggy. Which celebrities would you suggest to the author as the embodiment of what is considered the "ideal" body type for men and women today? Write a paragraph outlining your recommendations to the author.

4. The author talks about obesity, but she doesn't explore the reasons why so many Americans are overweight. Write an essay in which you explore the reasons for Americans' obesity and outline some solutions to the problem.

5. Write an essay about someone you know (you do not have to provide his or her real name). Where do you think he or she falls on the body image continuum? Based on this reading, what recommendations would you give this person?

6. The author claims that the media send strong signals regarding what is attractive in our society. These signals are reinforced by advertisements. Write an essay exploring some ways you can affect or help change the practices of the media and advertisers who contribute to the high levels of negative body image in U.S. society.

"Hurtful and Beautiful": Life With Multiple Sclerosis

Alice G. Walton

(WITH CONTEXTUALIZED ANNOTATIONS: ANALYZING THE AUTHOR'S TECHNIQUES)

In the following reading from *The Atlantic* magazine, poet and teacher Laurie Lambeth tells the author about the challenges and rewards of living with multiple sclerosis. Read the selection to learn about Lambeth's perspective on her disease as she adapts to each "new normal" in her life.

GETTING READY TO READ

PREVIEW IT

Preview the reading using the guidelines on page 6. When you have finished, indicate whether the following statements are true (T) or false (F).

_____ a. Laurie Lambeth was just recently diagnosed with multiple sclerosis.

_____ b. Lambeth continues to teach and write, despite her disease.

LOOK IT UP

Laurie Lambeth suffers from multiple sclerosis (MS). Before you read the essay, spend some time on the Internet researching this disease and the effects it has on those who live with it. Take notes on your findings so that you can share with your discussion group.

DISCUSS IT

In a group with three or four of your classmates, discuss the findings of your research on multiple sclerosis. Broaden your discussion by considering the impact this disease would have on your ability to function in your day to day life, the barriers that exist, and also the accomodations that you would need to function as close to normal as possible. If you have a friend or family member who has MS, share this person's experiences with your group. Be prepared to share the highlights of your discussion with the class.

WRITE ABOUT IT

Connect the reading to your own experience by writing a paragraph about someone you know who has experienced physical or mental challenges because of a disease that has attacked his or her body or mind. How has this person responded to the challenges brought on by the disease? How do you feel when you are with this person? How has the person's family responded to his or her physical or mental challenges? Put yourself in this person's shoes and imagine how you would respond if you had the same disease.

STUDY THE MARGINAL ANNOTATIONS AS YOU READ: ANALYZING THE AUTHOR'S TECHNIQUES

The marginal annotations in this reading focus on *what* the author means and *how* she expresses her ideas. You might read the selection once to understand the author's ideas, and then go back and study the annotations as you begin to think critically about the reading.

READT IT

Because this reading deals with a medical issue, it uses some medical vocabulary. Use word parts to determine the meanings of unfamiliar words, such as "neurological" and "anticonvulsive." When in doubt, consult a dictionary.

Take a look at the questions that follow before you begin reading so that you can understand the level of recall that is expected.

"Hurtful and Beautiful": Life With Multiple Sclerosis

Alice G. Walton

Title presents contrasting ideas that are further developed in the reading.

The author offers background to build interest in Lambeth and help readers understand the disease.

1   The fact that Laurie Lambeth's diagnosis of multiple sclerosis (MS) came after only one month—and after only one "event"—made it a relatively uncommon one. Most people have at least a couple separate events (symptoms or flare-ups) before they're diagnosed. Lambeth's first symptom, at age 17, was numbness that spread up her left arm and down her body. She had been snapping her fingers to music one day, and the next her hand went numb, a sensation, or absence thereof, which diffused across her left side. As the result of this early onset, Lambeth—who is now 43, a PhD, and a prize-winning poet—has lived

This sentence defines Walton's purpose for writing the essay.

with the degenerative neurological disease for all of her adult life. How the disease informs her life, poetry, and concept of "normal" is itself a work in progress.

Ian Lambeth

2   Despite Lambeth's young age at the time, the diagnosis itself was not particularly distressing. Her neurologist's nonchalant attitude about MS made for a diagnosis that was pretty low-key. "My neurologist said to me, 'Think of it as minor inconvenience. Avoid hot tubs. Have a nice life.' That was it. There was no hysteria about it for me because he minimized it so."

Throughout the essay, Walton makes a statement and then substantiates it with quotations from Lambeth.

3   That was in her senior year of high school. As the realization set in more, however, Lambeth began pouring more of herself into academics, which had not previously been her driving force (training horses and her involvement in the visual arts had played center stage). "I tried a lot harder in high school after my diagnosis, and then threw myself into college," says Lambeth. "I thought that if I could no longer count on my body, I could at least rely on my mind. I didn't know that my cognitive abilities would change, that following and synthesizing a number of strands of discussion would come less easily, or that remembering simple words would be much harder for me than for others my age."

Although Walton presents factual information about Lambeth, it is easy to sense her admiration.

4   Despite the physical and cognitive challenges of MS, Lambeth went on to get her BA at Loyola Marymount College and then her MFA and PhD in creative writing at the University of Houston, where she teaches now.

5   In many ways MS informs Lambeth's work just as its presence throughout her adult life has informed her relationship with her own body and with the world around her. "Since I couldn't feel the difference between fabric and a hand on my leg, I began to see the world more abstractly," she says. So Lambeth began creating metaphors—privately, at first, as an outgrowth of her personal experience, and then on paper, to express it to others.

Mention of Lambeth's publications gives her credibility and respect.

6   Lambeth's work has appeared in the *Paris Review*, *Crazyhorse*, and the *Mid-American Review*. She has also published a book of poems and "fragmented" prose, *Veil and Burn*, which won a National Poetry Series award in 2006, and is working on a second. Much of her writing explores the relationship between the self and the other, and even how we may experience sensation through another. Some of her poems articulate the physical sensations of MS, even the numbness, which she describes as a presence, an entity in its own right. Pain, she says, on the other hand, is virtually impossible to convert into words effectively. She also doesn't particularly want to invoke pity in her reader.

7   Finding a new normal has been an ongoing theme in Lambeth's life and work. "I have to say that for the majority of the time I have had MS, I was under the impression that relapsing-remitting meant that my MS would never progress. I was wrong, clearly. It gets harder and harder to recover from a flare-up and get back to normal. Normal itself keeps shifting, and the area I can walk has shrunk." Exacerbations, or flare-ups, may occur during times of stress, or randomly, and the recovery may not be so complete as it once was, making "normal" an ever-changing concept.

8   "My early impression that relapsing-remitting MS would remain so," adds Lambeth, "on an even course of ups and downs and miraculous recoveries, has since been trumped by the degenerative nature of the disease, something I never thought would happen to me. What that disillusionment did to me was simply to make me value uncertainty over full-blown positivity, and to acknowledge that nothing in life is ever certain, explainable, or permanently and easily defined."

The author generalizes about Lambeth's experience and then substantiates it with Lambeth's quotation.

Walton includes this quotation to reveal Lambeth's sense of humor.

9   One thing Lambeth doesn't do is sugarcoat her experience. Living with MS for the majority of her life has in some ways led to certain benefits—psychological depth and, perhaps, professional accomplishments—but she isn't universally thankful for her condition. "The grief I feel occurs when I develop new symptoms or when an exacerbation sticks around for many months. Ideas of permanence within the flux of my MS haunt me at odd times. 'Okay, you can stop it now, I get it,' I want to say to my body. 'That's enough.'" On the other hand, she is grateful to MS for some things. "I do feel, as I felt fairly early on (I at least felt special), that I have been blessed in a way by having MS and having some perceptual walls broken down that helped me become more aware of the body's variability and oddness. In other words, instead of doing drugs in college, I had MS, which is quite a trip in and of itself."

10   Lambeth brings up a dichotomy that she's been interested in for many years: "I learned from the poet Gregory Orr that the French word *blesser* means to wound rather than to bless, and in Old English, it meant to sprinkle with blood. I like the idea that the wound is the blessing that leads you to create. It's hurtful and beautiful at the same time." So too has been her treatment, although in this case, the hurtful portion has mostly trumped the healing. Lambeth has been on just about every MS drug there is: Copaxone, each of the interferons, Tysabri, even an anticonvulsive. Since there is no cure, MS treatments are aimed at slowing the progression of the disease. But the side effects of each she tried were ultimately too severe, with one of the drugs regularly triggering anaphylaxis, and another bringing on persistent flulike symptoms. "The thing that helps you is so often the thing that hurts you," says Lambeth, who continues the once-a-month Tysabri infusion and takes an anticonvulsive, mainly to mask symptoms.

Lambeth uses an electrical cord as a metaphor to explain to her students what MS is doing to her body

Horiyan/Shutterstock

> Walton is drawing a connection with the dichotomy (two contradictory ideas) mentioned in the title.

> Lambeth uses this contrast to explain treatment difficulties.

11   One of the undergraduate classes Lambeth teaches is called Literature and Medicine. She tells her class about her condition on the first day, by making an analogy between a neuron and an electrical cord. "Susan Sontag says we shouldn't use metaphors," laughs Lambeth. "But on the first day of class, I hold up an electrical cord and ask my students if they know what the outer coating does and what would happen to the function of the cord if it were gone. Most guess correctly that if the insulation were gone, the cord wouldn't be able to carry the charge very well or at all. And I tell them that this is what's happening inside my body." Like first-year medical students, a few of her students inevitably confide in her the tinglings or aches they've experienced in their bodies and ask her if she thinks it's anything to worry about. She tries to reassure them (without letting on an inward chuckle) that they're probably OK, but if they're really concerned, to go see a doctor. The students who do have chronic medical conditions seem to find comfort in having a teacher who shares similar struggles.

> This paragraph presents Lambeth as likable and friendly.

> Walton offers her opinion about the situation.

12   Whether MS has enhanced her career or held her back professionally is a question with which Lambeth has grappled for a while. "Strange: I don't usually blame my MS for anything, but instead I blame stigma or poor interview performance or the barriers themselves for most of the professional obstacles I have faced. The thing is, I know I'm a good teacher, but the market is tough right now, and I can't teach a large number of classes at the same time, and that does have something to do with MS. I often tell people I am a part-time professor and a full-time patient with 'years of experience.' And of course, my writing, which receives so little of my time but means so much to me, is my true vocation."

> In this ironic situation, the opposite of what is expected occurs and demonstrates Lambeth's resilience.

13   About ten years ago, Lambeth started experiencing significant vision loss—optic neuritis, a common symptom of MS and the one Lambeth dreaded most, given her profession. "I always thought, 'I'll be ok as long as I don't go blind.' And then I essentially started going blind." After a year of significant vision loss and difficulty working, her vision did return for the most part. For the vision symptoms she still experiences, she's made some adjustments to help her do her work. It's just another reality of an evolving norm, a reminder for her or for any one of us that "Physical ability is tenuous at best."

Conclusion: the author moves readers away from Lambeth's experience and interprets it within the context of life in general.

14   Lambeth continues to adjust and readjust to new normals, teaching, writing, and enjoying life with her husband of 12 years. She underlines that for any person, the struggle is always to adapt, whether adverse conditions should arise from inside or outside the body; the task may just be a bit more pronounced for someone with MS or any health condition. Old symptoms may haunt Lambeth, and new ones will inevitably arise. "Specters of old flare-ups keep returning at odd moments, and that is part of my new normal. But developing new normals is a huge part of being human—being alive—isn't it?"

UNDERSTANDING AND ANALYZING THE READING

A. BUILDING VOCABULARY

Context

Using context and a dictionary, if necessary, determine the meaning of each word as it is used in the selection.

_____ 1. diffused (paragraph 1)
   a. attempted
 * b. spread
   c. observed
   d. offered

_____ 2. nonchalant (paragraph 2)
 * a. casual
   b. useful
   c. uncaring
   d. hostile

_____ 3. synthesizing (paragraph 3)
   a. copying
   b. removing
 * c. combining
   d. agreeing

_____ 4. articulate (paragraph 6)
   a. replace
   b. pretend to know
   c. take away from
 * d. describe or put into words

_____ 5. flux (paragraph 9)
   a. routine
 * b. instability or change
   c. direction
   d. arrival

_____ 6. tenuous (paragraph 13)
   a. unusual
   b. poor
   c. questionable
   d. dangerous

Word Parts

A REVIEW OF ROOTS AND SUFFIXES

COG means *to learn.*   **-IVE** means *performing action.*

VOC means *call.*   **-ATION** means *action* or *process.*

Use your knowledge of word parts and the review above to fill in the blanks in the following sentences.

1. A person's *cognitive* (paragraph 3) abilities include mental activities such as _____, thinking, and remembering.

2. Although Laurie Lambeth works as a teacher, she considers writing to be her *vocation* (paragraph 12) or what she is _____ to do.

B. UNDERSTANDING THE THESIS AND MAIN IDEAS

Select the best answer.

_____ 1. Which of the following best states the thesis or central thought of "'Hurtful and Beautiful'"?

   a. Multiple sclerosis is a degenerative neurological disease that severely limits a person's ability to work.

   b. By adopting a calm attitude, physicians can help make a diagnosis of serious disease less upsetting for the patient.

   c. Learning to live with a degenerative disease presents certain challenges and rewards, but adapting to changing conditions is an important part of being human.

   d. Because there is no cure for MS, the treatments are primarily aimed at slowing the progression of the disease.

_____ 2. The topic of paragraph 6 is

   a. the symptoms of MS.

   b. Lambeth's work.

   c. poetry.

   d. the *Paris Review*.

_____ 3. The main idea of paragraph 7 is found in the

   a. first sentence.

   b. second sentence.

   c. third sentence.

   d. last sentence.

C. INTERPRETING SUPPORTING DETAILS

Select the best answer.

_____ 1. Lambeth uses the phrase "hurtful and beautiful" to refer to

   a. the side effects of her MS treatment.

   b. the title of her latest book of poems and prose.

    c. her students' responses to her diagnosis.

    d. the creativity that can result from pain.

_____ 2. The key type of evidence the author uses to support her main ideas and her thesis is

    a. hospital and research studies.

    b. quotations from neurologists who treat MS.

    c. the personal experience of her subject.

    d. case studies of people with chronic medical conditions.

_____ 3. In paragraph 8, Lambeth's "disillusionment" about the nature of MS caused her to

    a. believe that she would have a miraculous recovery.

    b. acknowledge and embrace the uncertainty of life.

    c. become completely grateful for her condition.

    d. decide to try experimental treatments.

_____ 4. In paragraph 12, Lambeth implies that her job as a part-time professor is

    a. an arrangement she requested so that she could devote more time to her writing.

    b. physically challenging to her.

    c. a position that she had to fight to keep.

    d. a position that she had to settle for.

D. RECOGNIZING METHODS OF ORGANIZATION AND TRANSITIONS

Select the best answer. See Chapter 7 for information on patterns of organization.

_____ 1. The overall organizational pattern of the reading is

    a. definition.

    b. cause and effect.

    c. process.

    d. order of importance.

_____ 2. A transitional word or phrase used in paragraph 5 to signal a cause and effect pattern of organization is

    a. *in many ways.*

    b. *since.*

    c. *at first.*

    d. *then.*

_____ 3. What is the dominant pattern of organization in paragraph 10?

    a. listing

    b. classification

    c. comparison and contrast

    d. chronological order

E. FIGURING OUT IMPLIED MEANINGS

Indicate whether each statement is true (T) or false (F).

_____ 1. The neurologist's attitude toward MS made the diagnosis worse for Lambeth.

_____ 2. Lambeth did not let the challenges of MS prevent her from excelling academically.

_____ 3. Lambeth did not initially realize how her disease would affect her life and her work.

_____ 4. Lambeth blames her disease for all of the obstacles she has faced in her professional life.

_____ 5. Lambeth is still able to write and teach despite having some vision loss.

F. THINKING CRITICALLY ABOUT THE READING

Select the best answer. See Chapter 9 for information on thinking critically about a reading.

_____ 1. The author's overall purpose in "'Hurtful and Beautiful'" is to

    a. describe MS and explore the research surrounding the causes and effects of this disease.

    b. explain how one woman has successfully responded and adapted to the challenges brought on by living with MS.

    c. make the case that side effects of medication and treatment may cause more harm to a patient than the disease itself.

    d. compare and contrast what "normal" means for healthy people and for people living with chronic medical conditions.

_____ 2. The overall tone of the reading selection is best described as

    a. informative and sympathetic.

    b. emotional and angry.

    c. serious and pessimistic.

    d. light and insubstantial.

_____ 3. In paragraph 9, the author states that Lambeth "doesn't . . . sugarcoat her experience," meaning that she

    a. sees only the negative aspects of her disease.

    b. does not like to talk about her experience.

    c. is honest about the positive and negative effects of MS on her life.

    d. wants people to know how difficult the treatment is for MS.

_____ 4. Laurie Lambeth can best be described as

    a. self-centered.

    b. disillusioned.

    c. determined.

    d. inventive.

_____ 5. Three of the following sentences from the reading are facts. One is an opinion. Which one is the opinion?

    a. "I do feel, as I felt fairly early on (I at least felt special), that I have been blessed in a way by having MS and having some perceptual walls broken down that helped me become more aware of the body's variability and oddness." (paragraph 9)

    b. "I learned from the poet Gregory Orr that the French word _blesser_ means to wound rather than to bless, and in Old English, it meant to sprinkle with blood." (paragraph 10)

    c. "Like first-year medical students, a few of her students inevitably confide in her the tinglings or aches they've experienced in their bodies and ask her if she thinks it's anything to worry about." (paragraph 11)

    d. "After a year of significant vision loss and difficulty working, her vision did return for the most part." (paragraph 13)

_____ 6. Why might the author have included the photo on page 356?

    a. to illustrate the interconnectedness that we all have in our suffering

    b. to imply that just as electricity often seems mysterious to us, so does MS

    c. to emphasize the pain and discomfort that accompany this neurological disease

    d. to explain MS in a way that everyone can understand

Answer the following open-ended questions in complete sentence format.

7. Identify two or three issues presented in this reading. Then phrase each issue as a question that the author raises, discusses, or answers.

8. Has the author provided sufficient evidence to support her thesis? What other types of evidence might she provide to strengthen the reading?

9. Do you find any evidence of bias in the reading? Explain your answer.

10. How did the doctor's statement in paragraph 2 make you feel? Why do you think the doctor was so non chalant in pronouncing the diagnosis?

WRITING IN RESPONSE TO THE READING ▆▆▆▆▆▆▆▆▆

G. REVIEWING AND ORGANIZING IDEAS WITH A PARAPHRASE

Complete the following paraphrase of paragraph 1.

Most people are diagnosed with multiple sclerosis after having a few different episodes, so it was unusual that Laurie Lambeth was diagnosed with MS after just

_____

_____

_____

_____

_____

_____

For paragraph 2 of the reading, write your own two-sentence paraphrase.

_____

_____

_____

_____

H. ANALYZING THE ISSUE

Discuss in class or write in your journal a response to the following questions.

1. How does the author help you understand what MS is? Explain in your own words what you have learned about the disease from this article. What questions do you have that were not addressed in the article?

2. In your opinion, how does the author's frequent use of Lambeth's own words add to or detract from the story? What other types of supporting details could the author have included?

3. The theme of this chapter is "Defining Ourselves: Our Multiple Identities." Analyze the reading by addressing the following questions:

   a. How do you think Laurie Lambeth would define herself, based on what you read about her in the article?

b. How do you think Lambeth's friends, students, and colleagues would define her?

c. How do you think those who did not know Lambeth would define her?

d. In our society, what does it mean to be normal?

e. What are some misconceptions about those in our society who are physically challenged?

4. How does Lambeth's analogy in paragraph 11 help you understand the effects of the disease? Discuss her explanation and her subsequent interaction with her students. What do these details reveal about who she is and how she approaches her disease?

5. To what audience is the author appealing? Explain your answer.

I. WRITING PARAGRAPHS AND ESSAYS

Write a paragraph or essay in response to the following writing prompts.

1. Laurie Lambeth describes feeling both grief and gratitude toward her disease. Write a paragraph in which you summarize these two aspects of her feelings about living with MS.

2. In paragraph 8, Lambeth says that the degenerative nature of MS has led her to "value uncertainty over full-blown positivity." What does she mean by this? Do you, like Lambeth, value uncertainty over positivity? Write a paragraph in which you explain why or why not.

3. Consider the concept of "hurtful and beautiful," or the idea that "the wound is the blessing that leads you to create." Write a paragraph explaining this idea in your own words, using examples from your own experience, if possible.

4. Lambeth works as a teacher but considers writing her true vocation. What do you see as your true vocation at this point in your life? If you work, is your job the same as your true vocation? Why or why not? Write an essay in which you describe your true vocation and answer these questions.

5. In the last line of the selection, Lambeth asks the question, "But developing new normals is a huge part of being human—being alive—isn't it?" Do you agree? Write an essay in which you explore the ways that you have developed "new normals" in your own life and the ways that you have adapted to adverse (or simply changing) conditions arising from inside or outside your body.

All Guts, No Glory

Molly M. Ginty

(WITH CONTEXTUALIZED ANNOTATIONS:
EVALUATING THE AUTHOR'S IDEAS)

A longer version of this article originally appeared in *Ms.* Magazine, a women's-rights magazine founded in 1971. According to its Web site, *Ms.* was the first U.S. magazine to explain and advocate for the ERA (equal rights amendment), rate presidential candidates on women's issues, put domestic violence and sexual harassment on the cover of a women's magazine, and blow the whistle on the influence of advertising on journalism. The author, Molly M. Ginty, has written not only for *Ms.*, but also for *On the Issues Magazine, Women's eNews,* and PBS.org.

GETTING READY TO READ

PREVIEW IT

Preview the reading using the guidelines on page 6. When you have finished, complete the following items:

The topic of this reading is _____.

Indicate whether each statement is true (T) or false (F).

_____ a. The article will probably contain examples of specific women's experiences.

_____ b. Women in the military often risk their lives and suffer serious injuries.

LOOK IT UP

Molly Ginty addresses the issue of women in the armed forces serving in "combat operations." Before you read her story, spend some time researching this issue on the Internet. Try to find information on both sides of the issue—for and against women serving in combat operations. Take notes on your findings so that you can share with your discussion group.

DISCUSS IT

In a group with three or four of your classmates, discuss the findings of your research on the issue of women serving in "combat operations." Be sure to balance your discussion by examining both the pros and cons of the issue. Be prepared to share the highlights of your discussion with the class.

WRITE ABOUT IT

Connect the reading to your own experience by writing about the issue of women in the military. Have you ever served in the military, or do you know someone who has? If so, what roles have women played in the armed services? Do you know any women who have served in the military? Have you ever discussed their experiences with them? How is it possible to be injured in wartime without serving on the battlefield? Should women fight alongside men in armed combat?

STUDY THE MARGINAL ANNOTATIONS: EVALUATING THE AUTHOR'S IDEAS

The marginal annotations in this reading are included to model the types of thinking that will enable you to interpret and evaluate the author's ideas and assess their accuracy, value, and worth. You might read the selection once to understand the author's message and then return to the reading to study the annotations as you begin thinking critically about the reading.

READID

Take a look at the questions that follow the reading before you begin reading so that you can understand the level of recall that is expected. Also, keep track of the types of evidence the author uses to support her thesis and argument.

All Guts, No Glory

Molly M. Ginty

The connotative meaning of the circled words reveals the author's attitude toward each event.

1   Captain Dawn Halfaker saw a flash of light and heard an explosion—then suffered shrapnel wounds, a 12-day coma, and the amputation of her right arm.

2   Sergeant Rebekah Havrilla collected the remains of a suicide bomber and his victims from a room where blood ran down the walls—then endured years of nightmares.

By beginning with these 3 examples, the author suggests her bias about women in combat.

3   Private First Class Lori Piestewa was ambushed by insurgents, who killed three of the passengers in her Humvee—then was taken captive and died of her head wounds.

4   If you ask the U.S. military, none of these women officially served in battle. That's because females in the armed forces don't technically fight in ground combat. But the Department of Defense (DOD) policy belies the reality of the conflicts in Iraq and Afghanistan, and its willful avoidance of the truth denies military women safety training, health care, and career advancement.

Foote's position is stated, but her supporting reasons are not offered. Would they be helpful?

5   "It's time to give servicewomen the recognition they deserve," says Brigadier General Evelyn Foote, president emerita of the Alliance for National Defense in Alexandria, Virginia. "Let's join the 21st century and shed this exclusionary policy."

6   Military women today constitute almost one-sixth of the armed forces, but for most of its history, the U.S. military kept women out of battle, relegating them to support positions such as nursing. Although more than 80 percent of military jobs are now open to women, the DOD moved in 1994 to ban women from serving in "combat operations" such as the short-range field artillery, Special Forces, and infantry.

Prestigious organizations are mentioned here to give the author's position credibility.

7   Is there a good reason for these bans? Not according to a 1997 report conducted by the Rand Corporation, which found that full gender integration in the armed services would have little effect on "readiness, cohesion, and morale." And both the Military Leadership Diversity Commission and the Defense Advisory Committee on Women in the Services have urged the DOD to lift the combat ban.

More examples might be useful to explain the conflicts.

8   Modern military conflicts put every soldier, male or female, directly in the line of fire. For instance, according to Patricia Hayes, national director of women's health for the Veterans Health Administration, one of the most dangerous jobs in the military today is driving a truck—a position that many women hold.

Are these credentials dated?

9   "The issue of women in battle is coming to a head now because there's no demarcation between combat and non-combat in the Middle East," says former U.S. Representative Pat Schroeder (D-Colo.), who served on the U.S. House Armed Services Committee from 1973 to 1996. "As it stands, there no longer is an official front line."

More details are needed to clearly understand why everyone is exposed to combat.

10   Today, women represent 15 percent of the active military, 18 percent of the reserve, and 20 percent of all new recruits. With so many women in service (and with submarine assignments just opened to women in 2010), the DOD may no longer be able to keep arguing that it can legally bar women from certain jobs. "Everyone in uniform is in combat," says Representative Susan Davis (D-Calif.), ranking member of the House Subcommittee on Military Personnel. "Yet women in uniform are not afforded the proper training for combat since they are technically barred from engaging the enemy this way."

11   If they were officially allowed to serve in battle, military women could better protect themselves from injury and could get better care if they were hurt. Consider the bind of the military's "lioness" and "female engagement" teams of women soldiers who gather information from conservative Muslim women whose beliefs prevent them from talking directly to men.

12   "These female intelligence service members are 'attached' to units and not directly assigned to them," explains Greg Jacob, policy director for the New York City–based Servicewomen's Action Network. "And when their work is not documented by their parent command, their record doesn't always reflect their combat-related injuries."

Is this perspective dated?

13   Captain Barbara Wilson, creator of the website American Women in Uniform, says that when she served in the Air Force back in the 1950s, the men in her unit treated women recruits as "nothing more than secretaries in uniform." Even though Wilson could best them all at firing practice, the men claimed women couldn't operate machinery. "There was only one way to respond to this discrimination," says Wilson. "I tuned it out and just focused on my work."

14   When Wilson entered the service, critics also said women were too delicate to fight, or to pull fallen male soldiers to safety. They said the distraction of women batting their eyelashes would destroy military units' camaraderie. They predicted that if women and men served in battle together, they would be too busy flirting, or feuding, to effectively ward off the enemy. "None of these ridiculous prophecies came true," says Pat Schroeder.

615 Collection/Alamy Stock Photo

Military women today constitute almost one-sixth of the armed forces, yet their efforts are seldom recognized.

15   "From the push-ups and drills of basic training onward, I busted my ass to keep up with the men so they had no reason to give me grief over my gender," says Sergeant Rebekah Havrilla, who spent a year in Afghanistan defusing bombs. "But I was the only female on my team and had to fend off sexual, emotional, and verbal abuse every day." — Cons

16   When it comes to rape, which Havrilla suffered in 2007 at the hands of a male colleague, the military's misogyny shows itself at its worst. Military women are twice as likely as civilian women to be assaulted, often by the very men who are supposedly their comrades. One in three female vets reports rape or attempted rape. And if a soldier becomes pregnant as a result of sexual assault, military health benefits won't cover an abortion.

17   Women in the military say they are afraid to visit latrines at night because they could be assaulted. During recent congressional hearings (which keep racking up in number but do little to stem rampant rapes), one woman said she was reluctant to report being attacked because she feared she would be demoted for failing to carry a weapon when it happened.

Does the paragraph provide sufficient evidence?

18   "Opening more military jobs to women could help address the rampant problem of sexual assault," says Nancy Duff Campbell, copresident of the Washington-based National Women's Law Center. "We know from experience in other nontraditional employment environments—for example, with women police and firefighters—that when their members hit critical mass, incidents of sexual harassment declined." → PPO

The comparison of U.S. policy with that of other countries strengthens the author's case.

19   While the U.S. government says women are not fit to serve in combat, the rest of the world doesn't agree—at least not Belgium, Canada, Denmark, France, Germany, Hungary, India, Israel, the Netherlands, New Zealand, Norway, Portugal, South Africa, South Korea, and Sweden.)Pro

20   In late September, Australia, which contributes the largest contingent of non-NATO soldiers to Afghanistan, was added to that list. "In the future," announced Australia's Defense Minister Stephen Smith, "your role in the defense force will be determined on your ability, not on the basis of your sex."

Are the details of the lives of these two women after combat relevant? Why or why not?

21   There's also no denying that U.S. women are already serving with valor in battle in Iraq and Afghanistan right now.

22   Consider Nashville's Sergeant Leigh Ann Hester, who was awarded the Silver Star for saving members of her convoy when it was ambushed by 34 enemy soldiers. Or consider Lieutenant Tammy Duckworth, who lost both her legs and shattered her right arm when her helicopter was shot down in Iraq. Duckworth went on to serve as a high-ranking Veterans Affairs administrator, to race two Chicago Marathons on a hand-cranked bicycle, and to recently launch a vigorous campaign for Congress in Illinois. Oh yes, and she's still a member of the Illinois Army National Guard.[1]

Description of loss of life presents both a rational and emotional appeal.

23   According to the iCasualties website, 126 servicewomen have died in Iraq and Afghanistan since 2001, and by the DOD's own admission, 60 percent of these deaths have stemmed from "hostile attacks." "The loss of life in battle can be the ultimate act of bravery," says retired Air Force pilot Brigadier General Wilma Vaught, president of the Women in Military Service for America Memorial Foundation in Arlington, Virginia. "There's nothing more frustrating than hearing it said that this sacrifice isn't happening, that somehow the loss of a servicewoman's life in battle isn't as noble or heroic or as meaningful."

Molly M. Ginty is an award-winning reporter who has written for Ms.,
On the Issues Magazine, Women's eNews, *PBS, Planned Parenthood,*
and RH Reality Check.

---

[1]Update: Duckworth retired from the Army in 2014. After two terms in the House of Representatives, she is currently serving as junior U.S. Senator for Illinois.

UNDERSTANDING AND ANALYZING THE READING

A. BUILDING VOCABULARY

Context

Using context and a dictionary, if necessary, determine the meaning of each word as it is used in the selection.

_____ 1. exclusionary (paragraph 5)
   a. leaving people out
   b. old-fashioned
   c. based on social class
   d. belonging to the special-forces unit

_____ 2. cohesion (paragraph 7)
   a. readiness for battle
   b. unity
   c. power
   d. preparation

_____ 3. demarcation (paragraph 9)
   a. relationship
   b. connection
   c. prejudice
   d. distinction

_____ 4. camaraderie (paragraph 14)
   a. friendship
   b. jealousy
   c. dislike
   d. anger

_____ 5. latrine (paragraph 17)
   a. cafeteria
   b. toilet
   c. shower
   d. recreational center

_____ 6. rampant (paragraph 18)
   a. widespread
   b. unacknowledged
   c. serious
   d. secretive

Word Parts

A REVIEW OF PREFIXES AND ROOTS

SUB-	means *under or below.*
GYN	means *woman.*

Use your knowledge of word parts and the review above to fill in the blanks in the following sentences.

1. A *submarine* (paragraph 10) is a ship that sails _____ the water.

2. *Misogyny* (paragraph 16) means the dislike or hatred of _____.

B. UNDERSTANDING THE THESIS AND MAIN IDEAS

Select the best answer.

_____ 1. Which of the following is the best statement of the selection's thesis or central thought?

    a. The many women who have been injured or died in the wars in Iraq and Afghanistan have not received proper health care or an honorable burial by the military.

    b. In most of the world's countries, men and women play equal roles in the military.

    c. Women represent 20 percent of new recruits to the military and should therefore have special rights and living accommodations when they report for active duty.

    d. Because women in the U.S. military perform essential roles in which they may be injured or killed, the U.S. military should classify them as having served in battle.

_____ 2. The main idea of paragraph 10 can be found in the

    a. first sentence.

    b. second sentence.

    c. third sentence.

    d. fourth sentence.

_____ 3. What is the implied main idea of paragraph 14?

    a. Women lack the physical strength that men have.

    b. Early predictions about women's ability to serve in the military have proven false.

    c. On the battlefield, there is a real concern that men will find women a distraction from combat.

    d. Most male-female relationships are based on either flirting or fighting.

_____ 4. What is the topic of paragraph 16?

    a. female veterans

    b. pregnancy

    c. sexual assault in the military

    d. health benefits

C. INTERPRETING SUPPORTING DETAILS

Select the best answer.

_____ 1. The author begins her article with three women's stories in order to

    a. imply that women play a larger role in the military than men do.

    b. emphasize that U.S. military women suffer serious physical and emotional damage on the job.

    c. contrast the experience of women who serve as officers in the U.S. military with the experiences of women who fight on the front lines.

    d. call attention to a few isolated cases to prove her larger point that military women rarely experience injuries.

_____ 2. What is the role of the military's "lioness" and "female engagement teams"?

    a. to advocate for women's rights in the military

    b. to ensure that the families of women in the military receive proper care when a woman is deployed on a mission

    c. to gather information from Muslim women who will not talk to men

    d. to investigate alleged sexual assaults that have taken place on or off base

_____ 3. When Brigadier General Evelyn Foote says, "Let's join the 21st century" (paragraph 5), she means

    a. the leaders of the U.S. military should change policies that are based on outdated, disproven assumptions.

    b. the United States should adopt the sophisticated, satellite-based methods of warfare used by other countries.

    c. all of the world's nations should band together to put an end to warfare once and for all.

    d. the time has come to make men more aware of what constitutes sexual harassment and sexual assault and that such practices must cease immediately.

_____ 4. To support her thesis, the author uses all of the following *except*

    a. her own personal experience.

    b. quotations from experts.

    c. statistics.

    d. historical examples.

D. RECOGNIZING METHODS OF ORGANIZATION AND TRANSITIONS

Select the best answer. See Chapter 7 for information on patterns of organization.

_____ 1. The pattern of organization used in paragraphs 11 and 12 is
   a. cause and effect.
   b. classification.
   c. definition.
   d. order of importance.

_____ 2. The pattern of organization used in paragraph 19 is
   a. chronology.
   b. process.
   c. contrast.
   d. definition.

_____ 3. Which word or phrase used in paragraph 21 signals the addition pattern?
   a. *also*
   b. *valor*
   c. *already*
   d. *right now*

E. FIGURING OUT IMPLIED MEANINGS

Indicate whether each statement is true (T) or false (F).

_____ 1. Canada is the most recent country to allow women to serve in combat.

_____ 2. For most of U.S. history, women in the military served as nurses, secretaries, or in other noncombat roles.

_____ 3. Early opponents of women serving in combat argued that women were too weak to perform battlefield duties.

_____ 4. Both Israel and South Korea have a more progressive approach to women in the military than the United States does.

_____ 5. Women constitute one quarter of the U.S. armed forces.

F. THINKING CRITICALLY ABOUT THE READING

Select the best answer. See Chapter 9 for information on thinking critically about a reading.

_____ 1. The author's primary purpose in "All Guts, No Glory" is to

    a. provide inspirational stories regarding women in combat.

    b. emphasize the bloody nature of warfare and the general population's ignorance of what happens on the battlefield.

    c. call attention to the problems of sexual harassment in military organizations around the globe.

    d. argue that U.S. servicewomen should receive the recognition and benefits they deserve.

_____ 2. The author's tone in paragraph 22 could best be described as

    a. worried.

    b. cynical.

    c. admiring.

    d. nostalgic.

_____ 3. The photograph on page 366 was most likely included to

    a. emphasize that women in the military play different roles than men.

    b. create an emotional response to the issue.

    c. illustrate that women face risks and dangers in the military.

    d. suggest that women are treated unfairly in the military.

_____ 4. Which of the following statements is an expression of an opinion?

    a. "Captain Dawn Halfaker saw a flash of light and heard an explosion . . ." (paragraph 1)

    b. "These female intelligence service members are 'attached' to units and not directly assigned to them . . ." (paragraph 12)

    c. ". . . the distraction of women batting their eyelashes would destroy military units' camaraderie." (paragraph 14)

    d. "Women in the military say they are afraid to visit latrines at night . . ." (paragraph 17)

_____ 5. Which paragraph outlines the assumptions made about female military personnel in the 1950s?

    a. paragraph 10

    b. paragraph 14

    c. paragraph 16

    d. paragraph 19

_____ 6. Which of the following is not a key component of the author's overall thesis and argument?

  a. Most women enter the U.S. military specifically because they want to take part in combat.

  b. The U.S. military's approach to women is outdated and unfair.

  c. Reclassifying women as combatants will help them receive better medical care and benefits.

  d. Recognizing that women have served or died in battle is an acknowledgment of their bravery and heroism.

Answer the following open-ended questions in complete sentence format.

7. In paragraph 11, the author writes, "If they were officially allowed to serve in battle, military women could better protect themselves from injury and get better care if they were hurt." The author uses an example about Muslim women to back up this assertion. Explain this example in your own words. Does the author's reasoning seem logical to you or not? Explain your answer.

8. In one sentence, summarize the author's position on the issue.

9. What does the phrase "the military's lioness" mean in paragraph 11?

10. How would you best describe the author's tone in paragraph 14?

WRITING IN RESPONSE TO THE READING

G. REVIEWING AND ORGANIZING IDEAS WITH A MAP OR OUTLINE

Create a contextual map or write an outline of the reading selection. See page 28 for information on mapping and page 26 for outlining.

H. ANALYZING THE ISSUE AND THE ARGUMENT

Discuss in class or write in your journal a response to the following questions.

1. The theme of this chapter is "defining ourselves: our multiple identities." Analyze the reading by addressing the following questions:

  a. How do women in the military perceive themselves?

  b. How do men in the military perceive women in the military?

  c. How does society perceive women and men in the military, and what does society expect from each of the groups?

  d. How does the Department of Defense (DOD) perceive female military personnel? What evidence from the reading supports your answer to this question?

2. What techniques does the author use to make her arguments? For example, does she speak about her own military service record, or does she allow experts to help her make those arguments?

3. Identify at least one claim of fact, one claim of value, and one claim of policy in the reading.

4. What is the author's background, and is she qualified is to write about the topic? Why or why not? Do you find any bias in the selection?

5. Evaluate the argument on the following criteria:

   a. Is the argument timely?

   b. Are the statistics used fairly and clearly?

   c. Has the author provided sufficient evidence to support her argument?

   d. Does the author offer any opposing viewpoints?

   e. Does the author quote only women, or does she also quote men?

   f. Does the article offer any emotional appeals? If so, identify them and evaluate their fairness.

I. WRITING PARAGRAPHS AND ESSAYS

Write a paragraph or essay in response to the following writing prompts.

1. You might think of the question "Should women be allowed to participate in combat?" as an issue that can be considered in pro and con terms. "All Guts, No Glory" falls into the pro category. Write a paragraph in which you outline some of the cons.

2. How are the arguments from the 1950s against women serving in combat (discussed in paragraphs 13 and 14) similar to the arguments against gay people serving in the military? How are they different? Write a paragraph in which you discuss the similarities and differences.

3. Write a paragraph in which you describe your reaction to the photograph on page 366. You looked at the photo during your preview of the selection. Do you feel differently about the photo *after* reading the selection?

4. Do you think certain professions are better suited to men, while other professions are better suited to women? If so, which ones? If not, why not? Write an essay in which you explore this topic.

5. Gender issues have come to the forefront not only in the military, but also in other careers. For example, recent controversies have arisen over women as firefighters. Research this topic and write an essay in which you explain both sides of the argument—pro and con—for allowing women to serve as firefighters. Explain which side of the argument you agree with, and why. (You may also choose to examine a career other than firefighter, if you wish.)

6. If you have served in the military, write an essay about your experiences of working with the opposite sex. If you have not served, write about your experiences and opinions regarding your interactions with the opposite sex in another work-related situation. Do your experiences strengthen or weaken the argument in "All Guts, No Glory"?

ACTIVITIES: EXPLORING IDENTITY

On your own or with a group of classmates, complete two of the following four activities.

1. List at least five aspects of your identity. Are any of these aspects in conflict with each other? If so, how do you negotiate the space in between?

   _____

   _____

   _____

2. Collect at least five advertisements (from newspapers, magazines, Web sites, or any other source) that signal the "ideal" body type for men and women in the United States. What features do the women share? What features do the men share? How closely do these images reflect the faces and body types you see in your classroom?

   _____

   _____

   _____

3. Visit a U.S. military Web site (for example, the U.S. Army or the U.S. Navy). What are the expectations for recruits (people who wish to join that branch of the military)? Would you make a good military officer? Why or why not? If you had to join a specific military branch, which one would you join and why?

   _____

   _____

   _____

4. The topic of identity is so broad that entire encyclopedias have been written about it. This chapter discussed just a few aspects of the topic. Other types of identity include (but are not limited to):

   - **family identity** (for example, being a mother, father, brother, sister, child, or grandchild)
   - **sexual and gender identity** (for example, being male, female, straight, gay, or transgender)
   - **participation in a subculture** (for example, bikers, hip-hop, Goth, tattoo culture)
   - **religious identity** (for example, affiliation with a particular religion or style of worship)

   Write an essay or prepare a class presentation about an aspect of one these identities and how it affects other parts of a person's identity. You may, of course, draw on personal experience. For instance, you might think about the grandmother's role in Latino families. How does a woman's life change when she goes from being a mother to being both a mother and a grandmother? What social expectations does she face in her new role?

   This is a very broad assignment, so you should feel free to make it your own and write or present on any aspect of the topic that you find interesting.

MAKING CONNECTIONS: THINKING WITHIN THE ISSUES

This section requires you to draw connections between the readings on the issue explored within the chapter. The activities and assignments below will give you practice synthesizing information and thinking critically about the relationship of the chapter readings.

1. "'Hurtful and Beautiful': Life with Multiple Sclerosis" (Selection 2, p. 353) is one woman's reflections on the rewards and challenges of living with a progressive disease, and "All Guts, No Glory" (Selection 3, p. 364) focuses on women in military service and combat. Yet these descriptions over-simplify the concept of identity: female soldiers are more than just members of the military, and Laurie Lambeth is more than just a woman with multiple sclerosis. What other aspects of their identities might the subjects of these readings identify? List three components of identity that are not directly considered in the readings. For example, the female soldiers in "All Guts, No Glory" may also be mothers.

2. In "Enhancing Your Body Image" (Selection 1, p. 340), Rebecca Donatelle presents the following self-evaluative questions about body image:

   - What do you see when you look in the mirror?
   - How do you see yourself in your mind?
   - What do you believe about your own appearance?
   - How do you feel about your height, weight, and shape?
   - How do you sense and control your body as you move?

   How do you think Laurie Lambeth, the woman in "'Hurtful and Beautiful'" (Selection 2, p. 353) with multiple sclerosis, would answer the questions? How do you think a woman in the military, like those described in "All Guts, No Glory" (Selection 3, p. 364) would answer the five questions? Also, do your answers about these two women reveal any bias on your part? Create a chart to show the comparison between the answers you provided about the body image of the two women.

Our Environment: Problems and Solutions

12

What is the environment?

You often hear people talking about "the environment." But what exactly is the environment, and why are so many people talking and writing about it? In general, the *environment* refers to nature and to the surroundings or conditions in which people, animals, and plants live. But you can think about the term in many different ways:

- You can think about your local environment as the conditions on your street, in your neighborhood, or in your city.
- You can think of the environments of larger regions (such as states) or entire parts of the country (such as the West Coast or the Midwest).
- You can think of the environmental issues facing entire countries or continents, such as Asia or South America. (For example, China has become one of the most polluted places on Earth.)
- You can think about the environment as encompassing the entire Earth, including all its individual components, such as the land and the oceans.

The environment starts inside the Earth and continues up into the atmosphere. So, for example, oil companies drilling for oil deep inside the Earth can affect the environment on a local, regional, and even global scale. Factories that release pollution into the air or water can affect people half a world away. When a volcano explodes in Europe, weather in North America may reflect the effects.

All the readings in this chapter focus on *the environment*: how humans affect it, how it affects humans, debates about the effects of technology, and how humans can make small changes that will have a great impact.

WHY IS THE ENVIRONMENT SUCH AN IMPORTANT CONTEMPORARY ISSUE?

In recent decades, many scientists have sent up an alarm: human beings, they argue, are burning too many fossil fuels (coal, oil, and gasoline), which is producing carbon dioxide and leading to global warming. Those who believe in global warming argue that the Earth cannot process all this pollution. Those who are more skeptical argue that Earth goes through many warming and cooling cycles over hundreds or thousands of years, and that we are simply now in a warmer period.

It is important to understand these debates because government policies (and even campus policies) are increasingly focused on human beings' roles as caretakers of the natural environment. You probably heard about these issues long before you started this chapter, but the readings here will help you understand some of these issues in greater detail.

How Does the Concept of Environment Tie in to My College Courses?

Much of what you read, particularly in college science courses and even in general-interest newspapers and magazines, will discuss environmental issues. Courses in environmental science, geology, and ecology are concerned primarily with the environment. Because pollution often affects the poor more than the rich, you'll learn about the environment in sociology and political science courses as well. Business courses frequently examine companies and the roles they play in polluting the environment, as well as the steps they have taken and can take toward greater social responsibility.

TIPS FOR READING ABOUT THE ENVIRONMENT

Here are some tips for reading not only the selections in this chapter, but any reading about the environment.

- **Look for scientific reasoning and data.** Scientists collect data and perform numerous experiments to learn how people and the environment interact. You may need to decrease your reading speed so that you can fully understand scientific concepts with which you are not familiar.

- **Think about your life, how you affect the environment, and how the environment affects you.** For example, how does the car you drive (and the gas mileage it gets) affect you and your community? Do you take part in any recycling programs? Do you feel you have any control over environmental issues? Do you use BPA-free products?

- **Familiarize yourself with some key concepts in environmental studies.** You will often encounter the following terms when reading about the environment. Make sure you understand these concepts before you undertake any of the readings in this chapter.

  - *Green* is a word used to describe a movement that is intended to decrease humans' impact on the environment.

  - *Toxins* is a term that refers to poisonous substances that can cause disease and damage when introduced into body tissues.

  - *Global warming* and *global climate change* are terms some people use to refer to the slow and steady increase in temperatures around the world. Some people also see global warming as the cause of the increased number of natural disasters, such as hurricanes and extreme winters, in recent years.

- *Greenhouse gases* (water vapor, methane, nitrous oxide, carbon dioxide, and fluorinated gases) act to slow or prevent heat from leaving the atmosphere. Many scientists believe these gases, particularly carbon dioxide, are responsible for the warming of Earth's climate.
- *Biodegradable* refers to a product that will break down over time into natural (organic) components through the action of living organisms.

SELECTION 4
Magazine Article
MySkillsLab

'Katrina Brain': The Invisible Long-term Toll of Megastorms

Christine Vestal

In the following article, which appeared in *The Agenda* section of Politico.com in October 2017, the author writes about the mental health effects of extreme weather events.

GETTING READY TO READY

PREVIEW IT

Preview the reading using the guidelines on page 6. When you have finished, complete the following items:

1. The topic of the selection is _____.

_____ 2. You can reasonably expect the reading to include all of the following except

   a. stories of survivors.

   b. descriptive details.

   c. quotations from experts.

   d. links to websites.

LOOK IT UP

In the reading, the author explores the mental health effects of megastorms by focusing on one storm in particular, Hurricane Katrina. Before you begin reading the article, spend some time on the Internet researching Hurricane Katrina and the devastating blow it dealt to the city and the people of New Orleans. Take notes on your findings so that you can share with your discussion group.

DISCUSS IT

In a group with three or four of your classmates, discuss the findings of your research on the devastating effects of Hurricane Katrina to the city and the people of New Orleans. Be prepared to share the highlights of your discussion with the class.

WRITE ABOUT IT

Connect the reading to your own experience by writing a paragraph about a catastrophic weather event that you have seen reported on television. Perhaps it was a wildfire, a flood, a tornado, a hurricane, or an earthquake. Consider these questions as you write: What were the effects of the event on the survivors who were shown in the newscast? How did the experience of seeing the devastation and hearing the survivors speaking affect you? Were you able to put the news behind you and move on, or were you "glued" to the television coverage of the event? Did it remind you of an anxiety-producing storm you might have experienced?

READ IT

As you read, keep track of the types of evidence the author uses to support her thesis.

Also, be sure to highlight and annotate the text so that you can answer the detailed questions that follow the reading. Take a look at the questions before reading so that you can understand the level of recall that is expected.

'Katrina Brain': The Invisible Long-term Toll of Megastorms

Christine Vestal

Long after a big hurricane blows through, its effects hammer the mental health system.

1   Brandi Wagner thought she had survived Hurricane Katrina. She hung tough while the storm's 125-mph winds pummeled her home, and she powered through two months of sleeping in a sweltering camper outside the city with her boyfriend's mother. It was later, after the storm waters had receded and Wagner went back to New Orleans to rebuild her home and her life, that she fell apart. "I didn't think it was the storm at first. I didn't really know what was happening to me," Wagner, now 48, recalls. "We could see the waterline on houses, and rooftop signs with 'please help us,' and that big X where dead bodies were found. I started sobbing and couldn't stop. I was crying all the time, just really losing it."

2   Twelve years later, Wagner is disabled and unable to work because of the depression and anxiety she developed in the wake of the 2005 storm. She's also in treatment for an opioid addiction that developed after she started popping prescription painkillers and drinking heavily to blunt the day-to-day reality of recovering from Katrina.

3   More than 1,800 people died in Katrina from drowning and other immediate injuries. But public health officials say that, in the aftermath of an extreme weather event like a hurricane, the toll of long-term psychological injuries builds in the months and years that follow, outpacing more immediate injuries and swamping the health care system long after emergency workers go home and shelters shut down. That's the rough reality that will soon confront regions affected by this year's string of destructive hurricanes. As flood waters recede from Hurricane Harvey, Irma, Maria, and Nate, and survivors work to rebuild communities in Texas, Florida, and the Caribbean, mental health experts warn that the hidden psychological toll will mount over time, expressed in heightened rates of depression, anxiety, post-traumatic stress disorder, substance abuse, domestic violence, divorce, murder, and suicide.

4   Renee Funk, who manages hurricane response teams for the Centers for Disease Control and Prevention, says it has become clear since Katrina that mental illness and substance abuse aren't just secondary problems—they are the primary long-term effect of natural disasters. "People have trouble coping with the new normal after a storm," Funk said. "Many have lost everything, including their jobs. Some may have lost loved ones, and now they have to rebuild their lives. They're faced with a lot of barriers, including mental illness itself," she said.

5   In New Orleans, doctors are still treating the psychological devastation of Katrina. More than 8,000 patients receive care for mental illness and addictive disorders just from Jefferson Parish Human Services Authority, which runs two health centers in the New Orleans metropolitan area. At least 90 percent of the patients lived through Katrina, and many still suffer from storm-related disorders, according to medical director and chief psychiatrist Thomas Hauth, who adds that he and most of his fellow clinicians also suffer from some level of long-term anxiety from the storm. "Every year about this time, I start checking the National Weather Service at least three times a day," he said.

6   These long-term mental health effects of extreme weather are a hidden public health epidemic, one that is expected to strain the U.S. health care system as the intensity and frequency of hurricanes, tornadoes, floods, wildfires, earthquakes, and other natural disasters increase in coming decades because of global warming and other planetary shifts. With climatologists promising more extreme weather across the country, mental and behavioral health systems need to start preparing and expanding dramatically, or demand for treatment of the long-term psychological effects of future natural disasters will vastly outstrip the supply of practitioners, said Georges Benjamin, director of the American Public Health Association. "On a blue sky day, our mental health resources are stretched," said Carol North, researcher and professor of psychiatry at University of Texas Southwestern in Dallas. "There's a lot we don't know yet, but common sense tells us that more disasters and worse disasters will lead to worse psychological effects."

"Katrina brain"

7   For climate change believers, this year's string of record-breaking Atlantic hurricanes was just a warm-up for what scientists predict will be more frequent extreme weather events in the future. When an entire city experiences a significant trauma at the same time, as New Orleans did during Katrina and Houston did during Harvey, it can push a lot of people over the edge, said Eric Kramer, another doctor who worked in the Jefferson Parish clinic: "Some people can rely on their inner strength and resilience to get through it, but others can't."

8   In the aftermath of Katrina, many survivors struggled with short-term memory loss and cognitive impairment, a syndrome dubbed "Katrina brain," according to a report by Ken Sakauye, a University of Tennessee professor of psychiatry who was at Louisiana State University at the time. Even though more than half the population of New Orleans had evacuated, psychiatric helpline calls increased 61 percent in the months after Katrina, compared with the same period before the storm, death notices increased 25 percent, and the city's murder rate rose 37 percent, Sakauye wrote.

9   A year after Katrina, psychiatrist James Barbee reported that many of his patients in New Orleans had deteriorated from post-Katrina anxiety to more serious cases of depression and anxiety. "People are just wearing down," Barbee said. "There was an initial spirit about bouncing back and recovering, but it's diminished over time, as weeks have become

months." In a longitudinal study comparing the mental health of low-income single moms in New Orleans before and after Katrina, one in five participants reported elevated anxiety and depression that had not returned to pre-storm levels four years later, said Jean Rhodes, study co-author and professor of psychiatry at University of Massachusetts Boston. For a smaller percentage of people in the study, particularly people with no access to treatment, symptoms of anxiety developed into more serious, chronic conditions such as post-traumatic stress disorder, the researchers found.

10   These aren't cheap conditions to treat. One study cited by the CDC estimated the cost of treating even the short-term effects of anxiety disorders at more than $42 billion annually; double-digit regional leaps in rates of anxiety could cause serious financial strain to patients, employers, insurers and the government.

Vicarious Reactions

11   Some damage can take place outside the storm-hit region. Even for people who have never experienced the raging winds, floods, and prolonged power outages of a hurricane, this season's repeated images of people struggling against the storms on television and other news and social media created unprecedented levels of anxiety and depression nationwide, said Washington, D.C., psychiatrist and environmental activist Lise Van Susteren. "There is a vicarious reaction. When we see people flooded out of their homes, pets lost, belongings rotting in the streets, and people scared out of their wits, we experience an empathic identification with the victims," she said.

12   "People come in saying they can't sleep, they're drinking too much, they're having trouble with their kids, their jobs or their marriages are falling apart. They may not know where the anxiety is coming from, but everyone is affected by the stress of climate change."

13   The same kind of vicarious reactions were documented after the September 11, 2001, terrorist attacks in New York and Washington and after Hurricane Katrina, particularly in children, said Columbia University pediatrician and disaster preparedness expert Irwin Redlener. "The mental health effects of natural disasters are really important and vastly overlooked, not only acutely but over the long term," he said.

14   Everyone who lives through a major storm experiences some level of anxiety and depression. But for low-income people and those without strong social supports, the symptoms are much worse, said Ronald Kessler, an epidemiologist and disaster policy expert at Harvard Medical School. The same is true for people who already suffered from mental illness or drug or alcohol addiction before the disaster occurred.

15   Repeated exposure to weather disasters is another risk factor for mental and behavioral disorders. Hurricane Katrina decimated New Orleans on August 29, 2005, followed by Hurricane Rita less than a month later. Three years after that, Hurricane Gustave hit the Louisiana coast, followed by Hurricane

123rf.com

A home completely destroyed by Hurricane Katrina in the Ninth Ward of New Orleans, Louisiana.

Ike two weeks later. In September, many who had fled Hurricane Katrina and resettled in Houston had to relive the same horrors all over again, putting them at higher risk for long-term mental health problems.

16   But perhaps the greatest risk of adverse mental health reactions to storms occurs when an entire community like New Orleans's Lower Ninth Ward is so completely destroyed that people can't return to normal for months or years, if ever. For those who left and went to live in Houston, Atlanta, and other far-flung cities, the dislocation and loss of community was equally harmful, researchers say. People are only physically and mentally resilient to a point, and then they are either irretrievably injured or they die," Kessler said. If storms intensify in the future, the kind of devastation parts of New Orleans experienced could become more common, he said.

Psychiatric First Aid

17   In the past decade, first responders and public health workers began training in a type of mental health first aid that research has shown to be effective in lowering anxiety and reducing the risk that the traumas experienced during a storm will lead to serious mental illness. Using evidence-based techniques, rescue workers reassure storm survivors that feelings of sadness, anger, and fear are normal and that they are likely to go away quickly. But when survivors complain that they've been crying nonstop, haven't slept for days, or are having suicidal thoughts, rescue workers are trained to make sure they get more intensive mental health care immediately.

18   In Houston, for example, teams of doctors, nurses, mental health counselors, and other health care professionals offered both physical and mental health services at clinics set up in every storm shelter. The city's emergency medical director, David Persse, said the clinics were so successful that local hospital emergency departments reported no surges in patients with psychiatric distress or minor injuries.

19   Another important factor in reducing the psychological impacts of a storm is avoiding secondary traumas like being stranded for weeks in the convention center in New Orleans, said Sarah Lowe, a co-author of the Katrina study who teaches psychology at Montclair State University in New Jersey. "Repeated traumas can pile up almost the way concussions do. What I'm seeing in Harvey and Irma is there's more mitigation of secondary trauma," Lowe said. People were allowed to take their pets to the shelters with them, for example. In Katrina, survivors either had to leave their pets behind or stay in their homes and be more exposed to physical and mental dangers.

Evacuation and Relocation

20   Some public health experts say that we need to start thinking of longer-term solutions to the longer-term problem of severe weather; instead of trying to treat post-storm psychological damage, we should avoid it in the first place by persuading residents to move out of storm-prone areas.

21   "We do a great job with preparedness and response to hurricanes in this country. It's an amazing accomplishment," said Mark Keim, an Atlanta-based consultant who works with the CDC and the National Center for Disaster Medicine and Health. "But as climate change progresses over the next one hundred years, what are we going to do—respond, respond, respond? We can't afford that anymore." According to Keim, much of the rest of the world is already taking that approach: "Hurricanes can't be prevented, but by refusing to rebuild

in flood plains and developing the infrastructure needed to reduce inland flooding and coastal surges, we can avoid much of the human exposure to the coming storms. That's where the world is right now in disaster management. Preparedness and response are older approaches."

22   Climate change experts agree. To avoid increasing loss of lives from the megastorms expected in the decades ahead, large coastal populations should relocate, researchers say. Matthew Hauer, a demographer at the University of Georgia, recently found that a predicted six-foot rise in sea levels by 2100 would put 13 million people in more than 300 U.S. coastal counties at risk of major flooding. But relocating large populations has its own risks. For the hundreds of thousands of New Orleans residents who rebuilt their lives far from home after Katrina, the loss of social ties and the stress of adapting to new surroundings also took a heavy psychological toll, according to recent research at the University of California. There's another problem with relocating people from coastal regions. It's not just hurricanes that are expected to plague the planet as the climate shifts. Wildfires, droughts, inland flooding, tornadoes, earthquakes, and other natural disasters are also expected to increase in frequency and intensity, making it hard to find a safe place to put down new roots.

23   "Whether people decide to stay or decide to move, which means giving up a way of life, the long-term psychological costs of climate change appear to be inevitable," Harvard's Kessler said. "We can expect a growing number of people to have to face that dilemma. They'll be affected by extreme weather one way or another, and they will need psychological help that already is in short supply."

UNDERSTANDING AND ANALYZING THE READING

A. BUILDING VOCABULARY

Context

Using context and a dictionary, if necessary, determine the meaning of each word as it is used in the selection.

_____ 1. pummeled (paragraph 1)
   a. shook
   b. beat
   c. threatened
   d. collapsed

_____ 2. blunt (paragraph 2)
   a. enhance
   b. compound
   c. hide
   d. weaken

_____ 3. resilience (paragraph 7)
   a. faith
   b. positivity
   c. toughness
   d. stamina

_____ 4. vicarious (paragraph 11)
   a. secondhand
   b. imagined
   c. unexpected
   d. experiential

_____ 5. empathic (paragraph 11)

    a. comprehending the seriousness of an event

    b. understanding the cause of a problem

    c. responding appropriately

    d. understanding others' feelings

_____ 6. mitigation (paragraph 19)

    a. understanding

    b. moderation

    c. incidence

    d. inclusion

Word Parts

A REVIEW OF PREFIXES AND SUFFIXES

RE-	means *back* or *again*.
POST-	means *after*.
-ATION	means *the act of.*

Use your knowledge of word parts and the review above to fill in the blanks in the following sentences.

1. Many survivors of Katrina who had to *rebuild* (paragraph 4) their lives had to build them _____.

2. *Post-traumatic stress* (paragraph 9) is stress that occurs _____ a traumatic event.

3. *Identification* with the Katrina survivors (paragraph 11) is the _____ identifying with them.

B. UNDERSTANDING THE THESIS AND MAIN IDEAS

Select the best answer.

_____ 1. Which of the following best states the thesis or central thought of the reading?

    a. The segment of the population most affected by an extreme weather event is the poor who lack the resources to get the mental health assistance they need.

    b. The long-term psychological issues associated with extreme weather events affect both survivors and the already strained mental health systems that struggle to treat them.

    c. The efforts of climatologists to predict extreme weather and the preparedness of response teams are key to managing the psychological toll of mega-storms.

    d. Psychological issues associated with extreme weather affect all people in one way or another.

_____ 2. The topic of paragraph 3 is
   a. the death toll from Hurricane Katrina.
   b. the struggle that mental health providers have in treating weather-related issues.
   c. the hidden psychological effects of catastrophic weather events.
   d. the increased risk of suicide after catastrophic weather events.

_____ 3. The topic of paragraph 9 is
   a. the progression of anxiety for some survivors of Hurricane Katrina.
   b. the absence of treatment during the years after Hurricane Katrina.
   c. the lack of resilience in people with no access to treatment.
   d. the length of time needed to successfully recover from a catastrophic weather event like Hurricane Katrina.

_____ 4. Of the following statements, which one best expresses the implied main idea of paragraph 22?
   a. Nothing could have helped the survivors of Katrina avoid serious psychological trauma.
   b. Climate change experts are able to accurately identify communities that need to relocate.
   c. Relocating coastal populations is not the only solution to surviving extreme weather events and remaining psychologically sound, but it is one way to help alleviate some of the problems.
   d. The difficulty of finding a truly safe place to live rules out relocation as a viable option for protecting people from extreme weather events.

C. INTERPRETING SUPPORTING DETAILS

Select the best answer.

_____ 1. One reason that lower income people struggle with long-term anxiety and depression issues after an extreme weather event is because
   a. they do not have the funds to rebuild their homes and start their lives over.
   b. many are single moms who cannot find help for their children.
   c. they cannot afford mental health assistance.
   d. they lack resilience.

_____ 2. Evidence-based techniques used by first responders and public health workers depend upon the survivors to be able to

    a. describe their symptoms accurately.

    b. seek mental health care quickly.

    c. find help outside of local emergency rooms.

    d. admit that they have a problem.

_____ 3. What was it that finally put Brandi Wagner "over the edge"?

    a. the visible reality of the storm's damage

    b. the relocation to a sweltering trailer

    c. the loss of her family

    d. the winds that relentlessly pounded her house

_____ 4. In paragraph 19, Sarah Lowe, a psychologist, compares repeated traumas to concussions. What point is she trying to make?

    a. Just as with concussions, repeated trauma victims must rest and give their brains time to heal.

    b. The more physical damage one sustains, the harder the recovery will be.

    c. Concussions and traumas are likely to cause damage to the brain.

    d. The more trauma one endures, the more serious the impact.

D. RECOGNIZING METHODS OF ORGANIZATION AND TRANSITIONS

Select the best answer. See Chapter 7 for information on patterns of organization.

_____ 1. The overall pattern of organization in this reading is

    a. comparison and contrast.

    b. classification.

    c. cause and effect.

    d. definition.

_____ 2. The dominant organizational pattern in paragraph 18 is

    a. classification.

    b. illustration.

    c. cause and effect.

    d. process.

_____ 3. Which transitional word or phrase is a clue to the dominant organizational pattern of paragraph 19?

    a. *for weeks*

    b. *another important factor*

    c. *in Harvey and Irma*

    d. *in the convention center*

E. FIGURING OUT IMPLIED MEANINGS

Indicate whether each statement is true (T) or false (F).

_____ 1. The author understands that not everyone believes in climate change and global warning.

_____ 2. The author believes that the mental health system in New Orleans was doing all it could do to help Katrina survivors.

_____ 3. The author is critical of the National Weather Service and its ability to accurately predict extreme weather events.

_____ 4. The author believes that the CDC grossly over-estimated the annual cost of treating anxiety disorders.

_____ 5. The author believes that with the right services in place, survivors of extreme weather events can avoid psychological damage altogether.

F. THINKING CRITICALLY ABOUT THE READING

Select the best answer. See Chapter 9 for information on thinking critically about a reading.

_____ 1. The author's overall purpose in "'Katrina Brain': The Invisible Long-term Toll of Megastorms" is

    a. to encourage people who are still suffering the effects of a megastorm and assure them that their issues are common to those who have survived a traumatic event.

    b. to compare the severity of the effects of an extreme weather event and the access to help between the impoverished and the wealthy in society.

    c. to inform readers of the lasting effects on survivors of a megastorm, to highlight the challenges associated with treatment of these individuals, and to propose possible longer-term solutions to these problems.

    d. to help readers understand the devastation that hurricanes can deliver and to educate them on the various kinds of agencies that exist to help survivors of such an event.

_____ 2. The overall tone of the reading selection is best described as

    a. critical and skeptical.

    b. objective and informative.

    c. bitter and disapproving.

    d. condescending and indifferent.

_____ 3. The author uses all of the following types of evidence to support her main ideas *except*

    a. examples and quotations from experts.

    b. personal experience and Wikipedia citations.

    c. information from government agencies.

    d. research studies conducted by academics.

_____ 4. Which of the following statements from the reading is an opinion, not a fact?

    a. "People have trouble coping with the new normal after a storm." (paragraph 4)

    b. "More than 8,000 patients receive care for mental illness and addictive disorders just from Jefferson Parish Human Services Authority. . . ." (paragraph 5)

    c. "For climate change believers, this year's string of record-breaking Atlantic hurricanes was just a warm-up for what scientists predict will be more frequent extreme weather events in the future." (paragraph 7)

    d. "Another important factor in reducing the psychological impacts of a storm is avoiding secondary traumas. . . ." (paragraph 19)

_____ 5. According to mental health experts, the one factor that causes post-storm anxiety to deteriorate into full-blown depression is

    a. the length of time that the effects of the storm linger.

    b. the type of extreme weather event.

    c. the quality of available mental health assistance.

    d. the availability of financial resources.

_____ 6. Which group does the author **NOT** mention as being affected by an extreme weather event?

    a. children

    b. students

    c. mental health patients

    d. mental health professionals

Answer the following questions in complete sentence format.

7. What does the photograph that accompanies this reading communicate to readers?

8. In two or three sentences, explain how television coverage of extreme weather events affects viewers.

9. In paragraph 4, Renee Funk of the Centers for Disease Control and Prevention, says, "They're [survivors] faced with a lot of barriers, including mental illness itself." What is she implying about society's assumptions regarding mental illness? Why would mental illness be considered a barrier?

10. In paragraph 8, a professor from Louisiana State University at the time of Hurricane Katrina stated that the murder rate in New Orleans rose 37% in the months following the storm. Why do you think this occurred? Explain your answer in two to three sentences.

WRITING IN RESPONSE TO THE READING

G. REVIEWING AND ORGANIZING IDEAS WITH A PARAPHRASE

Complete the following paraphrase of paragraph 22. Begin your paraphrase with the following sentence.

Researchers and scientists agree that the way to protect people living near the coast from future major storms is to convince entire communities to move inland.

_____

_____

_____

_____

_____

_____

_____

_____

_____

_____

For paragraph 1, write your own two- or three-sentence paraphrase.

_____

_____

_____

_____

_____

_____

_____

H. ANALYZING THE ISSUE

1. The theme of this chapter is "our environment: problems and solutions." Answer the following questions as they relate to this theme:

   a. Identify at least three problems and three solutions discussed in this reading.

   b. What short-term solutions actually became problems during and after Hurricane Katrina?

   c. What barriers to solving the problems existed during and after Hurricane Katrina?

2. Is the first paragraph an effective introduction to the reading? Why or why not?

3. What are some common misconceptions about mental illness?

4. Suppose you are going to give a PowerPoint presentation that summarizes the reading. You will have five slides, and you will put one key point on each slide. What would your five key points be?

5. Would you consider the author biased? That is, does she tell only one side of the story, or does she explore alternate viewpoints? Explain.

I. WRITING PARAGRAPHS AND ESSAYS

Write a paragraph or essay in response to the following writing prompts.

1. In a paragraph, react to this statement: homelessness is more than not having a house. Relate this statement to the people who have been rendered homeless by a recent extreme weather event. What have they lost in addition to their homes?

2. To fully understand this reading, you must understand a little bit about climate change and how it contributes to the intensity and frequency of extreme weather events. You may first need to research this topic. After researching the topic, write a paragraph summarizing your findings.

3. Does someone you know have an extreme fear of storms or other weather events? How does word of an impending storm affect that person? When did this fear develop? Why do you think he or she is so afraid of this event? Write a paragraph or an essay that both describes and explains the fear.

4. Ronald Kessler, an epidemiologist and disaster policy expert at Harvard Medical School, says, "People are only physically and mentally resilient to a point, and then they are either irretrievably injured or they die." Think of a trauma that either you or someone you know has experienced. In an essay, show how another person or you have persevered over time and then "crashed and burned."

5. In paragraph 19, Sarah Lowe, a psychology instructor, talks about the comfort that people experienced when they were allowed to take their pets to a storm shelter. If you had to evacuate to a storm shelter, what three things would you take to comfort you? Write an essay in which you describe these three items and also explain how/why they bring comfort to you.

SELECTION 5
Web Article
MySkillsLab

Our E-Waste Problem Is Ridiculous, and Gadget Makers Aren't Helping

Christina Bonnington

This article originally appeared in *Wired.com*, an online magazine. Available in both print and online, *Wired* provides "in-depth coverage of current and future trends in technology, and how they are shaping business, entertainment, communications, science, politics, and culture." The author, Christina Bonnington, is a technology journalist who works as a staff writer for *Wired*. She has contributed numerous articles on a variety of technology-related topics, and she also appeared on *Wired's* video podcast, Gadget Lab.

GETTING READY TO READ

PREVIEW IT

Preview the reading using the guidelines on page 6. When you have finished, complete the following items:

1. This reading is about the problems associated with the _____
   _____

2. List three topics you expect the author to discuss in the reading.

   a. _____

   b. _____

   c. _____

LOOK IT UP

The number of technological gadgets that are in the hands of consumers has created a serious e-waste problem. Where do our throwaway gadgets go when we are tired of them? Before you read this selection, spend some time on the Internet researching the issue of e-waste in the United States. Take notes on your findings so that you can share with your discussion group.

DISCUSS IT

In a group with three or four of your classmates, discuss the findings of your research on the issue of e-waste. Broaden your discussion to include other related issues, such as consumer irresponsibility, corporate lack of cooperation, design limitations, and suggestions for improvement. Be prepared to share the highlights of your discussion with the class.

WRITE ABOUT IT

Connect the reading to your own experience by writing a paragraph about your own electronic gadgets. What do you do with your devices when you upgrade to a newer model? Have you ever thought about what happens to your discarded devices once you dispose of them? Have you ever just thrown a small gadget into the garbage? Do you know where it goes and what happens to it once it leaves your trash receptacle?

READ IT

This reading offers ample opportunity for critical thinking. As you read, take note of the various causes and effects presented by the author, and consider the proposed solutions. Also, be sure to highlight and annotate the text so that you can answer the detailed questions that follow the reading. Look at the questions before reading so that you can understand the level of recall that is expected.

Our E-Waste Problem Is Ridiculous, and Gadget Makers Aren't Helping

Christina Bonnington

1   Chances are high that you'll be getting or giving new electronics this year: an iPhone upgrade for mom perhaps, or maybe a new Windows 8 ultrabook. Device upgrades have become increasingly frequent for many of us. Unfortunately, too many people give virtually no thought to what becomes of all these **discarded** gadgets. And neither do most device manufacturers. Some 41.5 million tons of electronic waste was generated in 2011, and that number is expected to rise to 93.5 million by 2016, according to the research firm MarketsandMarkets. Right now, 70 to 80 percent of all that old gadgetry goes straight to landfills.

Junked motherboards

discarded
thrown away

stats

2   Oh sure, many companies have green initiatives. Apple in particular has made notable, documented efforts to reduce its carbon footprint, powering a majority of its retail stores and data centers with renewable energy, developing more efficient packaging design, and designing products that use less power than their predecessors. But if your products are going to be tossed out in a year, none of that is particularly brag-worthy. That's a tremendous amount of wasted resources.

recycling problem

3   In the past, computers were designed to be relatively easy to disassemble, like HP's towers and older versions of the Mac Mini. You could swap out dead parts and batteries, add more memory if it got sluggish, even replace a motherboard. But in the mid-2000s, things started to change. Apple introduced the ultra-thin, ultra-light MacBook Air and the industry enthusiastically followed with heaping helpings of devices that, while slim, were very difficult to repair due to the construction compromises required to achieve that svelte profile. Smartphones and tablets followed with an even faster purchasing and chucking cycle.

4   As mobile gadgets exploded, we became a culture that abandoned its gear regularly, on a massive scale. It's an epic environmental and economic problem not simply because people aren't properly recycling their old devices, but because many devices are all but impossible to recycle efficiently.

5   Electronics include a host of environmentally deleterious chemicals like mercury, cadmium, lead, phosphors, arsenic, and beryllium. When they end up in a landfill, these chemicals eventually seep into the ground and into our water supply. Thus, properly disposing of them through programs offered by device manufacturers like Asus, Samsung, or Apple, or retailers like Best Buy or Staples, is paramount. But that's only part of the equation. Manufacturers also play a vital role in the success (or failure) of this endeavor.

The Recycling Process

6   When you turn your device in to get recycled, a few things happen. First, it's assessed. Does it have dents or scratches? A broken screen? Does it turn on? If it's in good shape, the product is wiped of any remaining data and repackaged to be resold. This is generally done by hand. "You can mechanize the cleaning, but the assessment, fixing, re-testing, and repackaging is still a very human and touch-related business," said John Shegerian, the CEO of ERI. The company is among the world's largest e-waste recyclers, with more than one billion pounds of material recycled since 2005.

7   If a product's not fit to resell or the manufacturer isn't interested in selling refurbished gadgets, it is disassembled and shredded so things like steel, copper, and aluminum can be recycled. Glass is also melted down and recycled. When you send your device to a recycling outfit like ERI, nothing ends up in the landfill. But for such an effort to be worthwhile, two things must be considered: what's the value of the raw materials that can be recovered from the device, and how much effort does it take to get them? If retrieving all that material costs more than it's worth, it simply isn't worth the effort because the recycler is operating at a loss. Therefore, the easier it is to disassemble something, the more likely it is to be worth someone's time to recycle it. And that's where issues arise.

Recycling Challenges

8   "The big problem the electronics industry is facing as a whole is products are getting lighter and lighter," iFixit's Kyle Wiens said. "This is great for consumers but a nightmare for recyclers." Smaller, lighter products can be tricky to take apart, and yield a lower volume of raw materials.

9   Safety is a big concern for the workers tasked with dismantling discarded gadgetry. iFixit, which tears down electronic devices and posts online repair manuals, often works with recyclers to ensure everything is safely and efficiently disassembled. Device manufacturers usually don't do that.

10   Glue and adhesives are a common hurdle. Products like the iPad and Microsoft Surface achieve a slim form factor by using "a metric duckload of adhesive," as Wiens once put it, particularly to keep the battery in place. All that glue must be removed before any recyclable material can be melted down. And battery recycling is a risky endeavor in the best of circumstances—under the right conditions, a damaged battery can cause a fiery explosion. Tack onto that the need to painstakingly pry a battery from its glue-smeared lodging and you've got a delicate task indeed. For items with a lot of glue, like a tablet display, Sims Recycling Solutions heats the glue, then uses suction cups to apply pressure across the glass so it can be removed without cracking.

11   Other things that can make a product more challenging to recycle include the number of screws (particularly non-standard screws), the inclusion of hazardous materials like mercury (which is declining, due to the rising popularity of LEDs instead of bulbs), large amounts of glass, and plastics. Waterproof and tightly sealed products also are more arduous to deal with.

Designing Recyclable Products

12   While no one we spoke with would say so **outright**, Apple products are among the most difficult to recycle. (Apple did not respond to repeated requests for comment.) The very things that make them the most marketable—multiple colors, thin profile, big glass displays, seamless cases—also make them difficult to disassemble. However, Sims, the company Apple officially contracts with for recycling, suggested that Apple works with them to develop and provide tools workers can use, and is very engaged in helping them figure out the best way to recycle products at the end of their useful lives.

13   Not all device makers, and not all recycling facilities, get this same level of help though. Sometimes, between the time it takes to dismantle products and the injuries workers get in the process, lucrative contracts with specific manufacturers are barely worth the trouble.

14   As we rush headlong into a world in which we're disposing of more and more gadgets each year, making them easily recyclable should be a growing priority of device makers. Just as display size, processor speed, and energy efficiency are marketing points, so too should recyclability.

15   David Thompson, Panasonic's head of environmental affairs, says the standardization of screws and plastic resin materials, not **thermally** setting screws in plastic, and minimizing the use of glue will boost recycling efforts, as will designing products for easier disassembly. Would consumers really decry, or even notice, these changes? Probably not. But such changes could require concessions to slim dimensions and light weight. And for manufacturers, increased standardization may mean fewer distinctions between competing products. Take a plastic smartphone housing: Currently there are hundreds of variations (soft touch, textures, and metallic colors, to name a few). Standardization could limit that very marketable variety.

16   Even so, some products are embracing such ideals. Dell won The Institute for Scrap Recycling Industries 2014 Design for Recycling award for the Latitude 10 and XPS 10 tablets and Latitude E7240 notebook. Aside from making its products cheap and easy to recycle, Dell has used nearly 8 million pounds of recycled plastic in its desktop and display production. And it is not alone. "Companies are getting better at making greener, more recyclable products. They're asking to visit our facilities and learn from our pain points," Shegerian said.

17   More manufacturers need to start doing this. An old smartphone or laptop can only be reused ("The truest form of recycling," says Sims sales and marketing vice president Sean Magann) so many times. The pattern of gadget manufacturing, use, and disposal needs to become circular to ensure our environment doesn't turn into a *Wall-E*-esque landscape of toxic landfills, and to ensure the continued availability of the stuff that's needed to keep making all these gadgets. We aren't going to stop buying things any time soon. ✳

UNDERSTANDING AND ANALYZING THE READING

A. BUILDING VOCABULARY

Context

Using context and a dictionary, if necessary, determine the meaning of each word as it is used in the selection.

_____ 1. predecessors (paragraph 2)
    a. competition from other sources
    b. prototypes
    c. things that came before
    d. things that occurred afterward

_____ 2. svelte (paragraph 3)
    a. attractive
    b. compact
    c. desirable
    d. slender

_____ 3. deleterious (paragraph 5)
    a. harmful
    b. metallic
    c. distasteful
    d. beneficial

_____ 4. arduous (paragraph 11)
    a. dangerous
    b. difficult
    c. sensitive
    d. subtle

_____ 5. lucrative (paragraph 13)
    a. minimal
    b. favorable
    c. expensive
    d. profitable

_____ 6. decry (paragraph 15)
    a. support
    b. refuse
    c. denounce
    d. recommend

Word Parts

A REVIEW OF PREFIXES AND SUFFIXES

-ABLE	means *capable of.*	**RE-**	means *back* or *again.*
DIS-	means *apart, away,* or *not.*	**-TION**	means *a process.*
-IZE	means *to make.*		

Use your knowledge of word parts and the review above to fill in the blanks in the following sentences.

1. A resource that is *renewable* (paragraph 2) is _____ being made new _____.

2. To *disassemble* (paragraph 3) something is to take it _____.

3. *Standardization* (paragraph 15) is the process of making something _____.

B. UNDERSTANDING THE THESIS AND MAIN IDEAS

Select the best answer.

_____ 1. The thesis or central thought of the selection can be found in
   a. paragraph 1.
   b. paragraph 4.
   c. paragraph 8.
   d. paragraph 17.

_____ 2. The topic of paragraphs 6 and 7 is
   a. the recycling process.
   b. reclaimed metals.
   c. John Shegerian.
   d. the role of profit.

_____ 3. The main idea of paragraph 10 is found in the
   a. first sentence.
   b. second sentence.
   c. fifth sentence.
   d. last sentence.

C. INTERPRETING SUPPORTING DETAILS

Select the best answer.

_____ 1. According to David Thompson, all of the following will boost recycling of electronic products *except*
   a. designing products for easier disassembly.
   b. minimizing the use of glue.
   c. standardizing screws and plastic resin materials.
   d. new laws that require people to recycle old electronics.

_____ 2. The author uses all of the following to support her main ideas *except*

a. quotations from experts.

b. statistics.

c. examples.

d. personal experience.

_____ 3. At which company does the author direct subtle and not-so-subtle criticisms?

a. Apple

b. Dell

c. Panasonic

d. Samsung

_____ 4. In paragraph 2, the author includes details to support her opinion that

a. big corporations have greater green initiatives than small companies.

b. green initiatives are not a big deal if companies continue to make products that are essentially disposable after a short period of time.

c. Apple is the only big corporation to take seriously the problem of e-waste.

d. the e-waste problem could be simply solved if manufacturers would make longer lasting products.

D. RECOGNIZING METHODS OF ORGANIZATION AND TRANSITIONS

Select the best answer. See Chapter 7 for information on patterns of organization.

_____ 1. The primary organizational pattern used in paragraph 3 is _____ combined with chronological order.

a. definition

b. comparison and contrast

c. classification

d. illustration

_____ 2. Which organizational pattern is used in paragraph 11?

a. process analysis

b. cause and effect

c. illustration

d. definition

___ 3. Which transitional word or phrase signals the use of process in paragraphs 6 and 7?

a. *a few things happen*

b. *first*

c. *among the world's largest*

d. *therefore*

E. FIGURING OUT IMPLIED MEANINGS

Indicate whether each statement is true (T) or false (F).

___ 1. The author refuses to accept the fact that many people are always going to want the latest technology.

___ 2. The author believes that earlier generations of computers were much preferable to today's computers.

___ 3. The author is supportive of the recycling programs sponsored by retail stores like Best Buy and Staples.

___ 4. The author understands that electronics-recycling businesses need to make a profit to remain in business.

___ 5. The author supports Dell's efforts with regard to computer design and recycling.

F. THINKING CRITICALLY ABOUT THE READING

Select the best answer. See Chapter 9 for information on critical thinking about a reading.

___ 1. The author's purpose for writing "Our E-Waste Problem Is Ridiculous" is to

a. provide an in-depth look at how consumer electronics are discarded and recycled.

b. provide basic facts about e-waste and recycling, and to argue for increased efforts to recycle discarded electronics.

c. criticize the technology-recycling industry for its unwillingness to do more to help the environment.

d. explain why adhesives make the recycling of technology next to impossible and why these adhesives should be prohibited.

___ 2. The tone of the reading is best described as

e. furious.

f. nostalgic.

g. apathetic.

h. concerned.

_____ 3. The photograph on p. 395 was most likely included with the reading to

a. urge individuals to recycle more electronic waste.

b. emphasize the environmental threat of electronic waste.

c. illustrate the large amount of electronic waste that has been created.

d. encourage manufacturers to develop devices that are less harmful to the environment.

_____ 4. Which of the following statements from the reading is an opinion, not a fact?

a. "Some 41.5 million tons of electronic waste was generated in 2011." (paragraph 1)

b. "If it's in good shape, the product is wiped of any remaining data and repackaged to be resold." (paragraph 6)

c. "Safety is a big concern for the workers tasked with dismantling discarded gadgetry." (paragraph 9)

d. "Just as display size, processor speed, and energy efficiency are marketing points, so too should recyclability." (paragraph 14)

_____ 5. In paragraph 8, iFixit's Kyle Wiens says that the lighter and smaller electronic devices are "great for consumers but a nightmare for recyclers." What figurative language appears in the quoted material?

a. a simile

b. a metaphor

c. personification

d. hyperbole

_____ 6. In paragraph 10, iFixit's Kyle Wiens uses the expression, "a metric duckload of adhesive." From the context of the sentence, what do you think the meaning of duckload is?

a. an amount measured by its weight in water

b. a measurement of water content

c. a metric measurement

d. a very large amount

Answer the following open-ended questions in complete sentence format.

7. In paragraph 3, what does the author mean when she writes of the "purchase and chucking cycle"?

8. Identify at least three issues presented in this reading. Then phrase each issue as a question that the author raises, discusses, or answers.

9. Explain what Sean Magann (paragraph 17) considers to be the truest form of recycling. How is this form of recycling different from the more widely accepted definition of recycling?

10. What one word best describes the author's tone in paragraph 2?

WRITING IN RESPONSE TO THE READING ▆▆▆▆▆▆

G. REVIEWING AND ORGANIZING IDEAS WITH A MAP OR OUTLINE

Create a conceptual map or write an outline of the reading selection. See page 28 for information about mapping and page 26 for outlining.

H. ANALYZING THE ISSUE

1. The theme of this chapter is "our environment: problems and solutions." Analyze the reading by addressing the following questions:

   a. Does the author clearly present the problem? What is the overriding problem? What other problems does the author present?

   b. What solutions does the author propose? Are the proposed solutions reasonable and realistic? Are there other solutions that the author fails to mention? If so, what are they?

   c. Do you need to understand the inner workings of computers and technology in order to understand the selection and the issue? Why or why not?

   d. How do you think the general public would react to this reading selection? Explain your answer.

   e. What is your reaction to this selection?

   f. Other than e-waste, are there other ways that technology negatively impacts our environment? Explain your answer.

2. Evaluate the author's use of evidence. Does she provide ample, varied evidence to support her argument? What other types of evidence could she have used to strengthen her argument?

3. What is the assumption or generalization on which the entire argument is based?

4. Evaluate the author's level of bias. Is she highly biased, moderately biased, or unbiased? Explain your answer.

5. Examine the author's use of language, which is sometimes informal—for example, "none of that is particularly brag-worthy" (paragraph 2). How does the author's informal language aid (or detract from) her argument?

I. WRITING PARAGRAPHS AND ESSAYS

Write a paragraph or essay in response to the following writing prompts.

1. The title of the selection includes the word *gadget*. Write a paragraph in which you define *gadget*. What connotations does the word have? Which technologies would you consider gadgets, and which are important tools for school and/or workplace productivity?

2. You most likely have more than one piece of technology. If you had to give up one, which one would you choose? Write a paragraph explaining your answer.

3. How does the recycling of electronic waste differ from the recycling of other materials, such as paper, glass, and plastic? Write a paragraph explaining your answer.

4. You most likely have seen (or used) products made by Apple, which is one of the most successful companies in the world. Write an essay in which you explain what makes Apple's products so desirable and successful.

5. Does your campus or community sponsor an e-waste recycling program? If so, write an essay explaining the program and how effective it has been (you may need to do a bit of research). If not, write an essay explaining how you would set up and run a campus recycling program. What would you do to advertise the program? How would you get the word out?

SELECTION
6
Textbook Excerpt
MySkillsLab

Poison in the Bottle: How Safe Is Bisphenol A?

Jay Withgott and Matthew Laposata

This reading is taken from an environmental science textbook, *Environment: The Science Behind the Stories*. Environmental science is *multidisciplinary*, meaning it draws from many disciplines, including biology, economics, geography, chemistry, and earth science. In their preface, the authors write, "Environmental science helps show us how Earth's systems function and how we influence these systems. It gives us a big-picture understanding of the world and our place in it. Studying environmental science helps us comprehend the problems we create, and it can reveal ways to fix those problems. Environmental science is not just some subject you learn in college; it's something that relates to everything around you for your entire life!"

GETTING READY TO READ

PREVIEW IT

Preview the reading using the guidelines on page 6. When you have finished, complete the following items:

1. This reading is about the safety of a synthetic _____ called _____ found in many products that we use every day.

2. Give a few examples of problems and risks this chemical can cause.

LOOK IT UP

Before you read this article about BPA and its effects on human health, spend some time on the Internet researching the issue of its use. Take notes on your findings so that you can share with your discussion group.

DISCUSS IT

In a group with three or four of your classmates, discuss the findings of your research on the issue of BPA and its effects on human health. Broaden your discussion to include the pros and cons of BPA use and your own personal opinion on this issue. Be prepared to share the highlights of your discussion with the class.

Connect the reading to your own experience by writing a paragraph about BPA as an environmental health hazard. Consider the following questions as you write: Before researching the issue, had you ever heard of BPA? If you had, did it concern you? Why or why not? Do you ever consider what might be in products that you use or eat? Are there things that you typically avoid consuming? If so, why do you avoid them? When you hear about a research study on potential risk to human health, do you take it seriously? Why or why not?

READ IT

This scientific reading makes use of many vocabulary terms used in environmental science courses. As you encounter unfamiliar words, try to figure out the definitions of the words before looking them up in a dictionary. Often, the examples and context that follow will provide clues to the definitions.

As you read the selection, highlight and annotate the text so that you can answer the detailed questions that follow. Take a look at the questions before reading so that you can understand the level of recall that is expected.

Poison in the Bottle: How Safe Is Bisphenol A?

Jay Withgott and Matthew Laposata

"This chemical is harming snails, insects, lobsters, fish, frogs, reptiles, birds, and rats, and the chemical industry is telling people that because you're human, unless there's human data, you can feel completely safe."

—Dr. Frederick vom Saal, BPA researcher

"There is no basis for human health concerns from exposure to BPA."

—The American Chemistry Council

1   How is it that a chemical found to alter reproductive development in animals gets used in baby bottles? How can it be that a substance linked to breast cancer, prostate cancer, and heart disease is routinely used in food and drink containers? The chemical bisphenol A (BPA for short) has been associated with everything from neurological effects to miscarriages. Yet it's in hundreds of products we use every day, and there's a better than nine in 10 chance that it is coursing through your body right now.

2   To understand how chemicals that may pose health risks come to be widespread in our society, we need to explore how scientists and policymakers study toxic substances and other environmental health risks—and the vexing challenges these pursuits entail.

3   Chemists first synthesized BPA, an organic compound with the chemical formula $C_{15}H_{16}O_2$, in 1891. As they began producing plastics in the 1950s, chemists found BPA to be useful in creating epoxy resins used in lacquers and coatings. Epoxy resins containing BPA were soon being used to line the insides of metal food and drink cans and the insides of pipes for our water supply, as well as in enamels, varnishes, adhesives, and even dental sealants for our teeth.

4   Chemists also found that linking BPA molecules into polymers helped create polycarbonate plastic, a hard, clear type of plastic that soon found use in water bottles, food containers, eating utensils, eyeglass lenses, CDs and DVDs, laptops and other electronics, auto parts, sports equipment, baby bottles, and children's toys. With so many uses, BPA has become one of the world's most-produced chemicals; each year we make about half a kilogram (1 lb) of BPA for each person on the planet, and 9 kg (20 lb) per person in the United States!

5   Unfortunately, BPA leaches out of its many products and into our food, water, air, and bodies. Fully 93% of Americans carry detectable concentrations in their urine, according to the latest National Health and Nutrition Examination Survey conducted by the Centers for Disease Control and Prevention (CDC). Because most BPA passes through the body within hours, these data suggest that we are receiving almost continuous exposure. Babies and children have higher relative exposure to BPA because they eat more for their body weight and metabolize the chemical less effectively.

6   What, if anything, is BPA doing to us? To address such questions, scientists run experiments on laboratory animals, administering known doses of the substance and measuring the health impacts that result. Hundreds of studies with rats, mice, and other animals have shown many apparent effects of BPA, including a wide range of reproductive abnormalities. Recent studies suggest humans suffer health impacts from BPA as well.

7   Many of these effects occur when BPA is present at extremely low doses—much lower than the exposure levels set so far by regulatory agencies for human safety. Scientists say this is because BPA mimics the female sex hormone estrogen; that is, it is structurally similar to estrogen and can induce some of its effects in animals. Hormones such as estrogen function at minute concentrations, so when a synthetic chemical similar to estrogen reaches the body in a similarly low concentration, it can fool the body into responding.

8   In reaction to research involving animals, a growing number of researchers, doctors, and consumer advocates are calling on governments to regulate BPA and for manufacturers to stop using it. The chemical industry insists that BPA is safe, pointing to industry-sponsored research that find no health impacts.

9   To sort through the debate, several expert panels have convened to assess the fast-growing body of scientific studies. Some panels have found typical BPA exposure to be a cause for concern, whereas others have concluded such exposure is not a meaningful health risk. Regardless of their conclusion, however, most of these panels have indicated a need for the development of federally approved testing protocols for studies of hormone-mimicking substances. Such guidelines would make more studies available for consideration by expert panels, who can evaluate only studies that meet established federal guidelines for toxicological research. As existing guidelines are designed for substances that have "traditional" toxicity profiles, such as increasing adverse effects with increasing exposure to the toxin, new guidelines need to be developed for hormone-mimicking substances that have unconventional toxicity profiles and exert effects at very low doses. Indeed, dealing with substances like BPA is forcing us toward a challenging paradigm shift in the way we assess environmental health risks.

10   As governments continue to consider differing regulatory approaches for products containing BPA, studies suggesting human health impacts of the chemical are now emerging. A 2013 review found 91 studies that examined the relationship between the level of BPA in research participants' urine or blood and a variety of health problems (see Figure A). Although these studies are correlative, they collectively suggest that exposure to elevated BPA levels may be harmful to humans.

FIGURE A

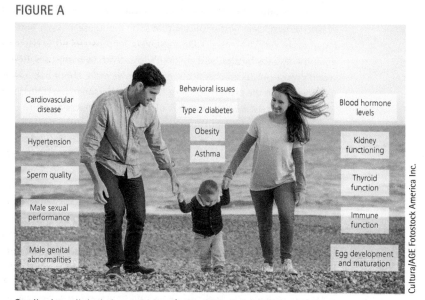

Cultura/AGE Fotostock America Inc.

Studies have linked elevated blood/urine BPA concentrations to numerous health impacts in humans. Although these correlative studies do not conclusively prove that BPA causes each observed ailment, they indicate topics for further research.

11   In light of a growing body of research, some governments have taken steps to regulate the use of BPA in consumer products. Canada, for example, has banned BPA completely. In many other nations, including the United States, its use in products for babies and small children has been restricted. Accordingly, concerned parents can now more easily find BPA-free items for their infants and children, but the rest of us remain exposed through most food cans, many drink containers, and thousands of other products.

12   In the face of mounting public concern about the safety of BPA, many companies are voluntarily choosing to remove it from their products, even in the absence of regulation by the U.S. government. WalMart and Toys "R" Us, for example, decided to stop carrying children's products with BPA several years before the U.S. Food and Drug Administration (FDA) banned BPA use in baby bottles in 2012. (In March of 2018, Toys "R" Us announced the closing of all of its stores in the U.S.) Campbell's has announced that it is transitioning away from the use of BPA in its soup can liners, and food giants ConAgra, Nestle, and Heinz have also pledged to remove BPA from their food packaging. There is precedent for such efforts, because BPA was voluntarily phased out of can liners in Japan starting in the late 1990s.

13   Although we don't yet know everything there is to know about BPA, it isn't likely to be among our greatest environmental health threats. However, it provides a timely example of how we as a society assess health risks and decide how to manage them. As scientists and government regulators assess BPA's potential risks, their efforts give us a window on how hormone-disrupting chemicals are challenging the way we appraise and control the environmental health risks we face.

14   International agreements such as REACH and the Stockholm Convention indicate that governments may act to protect the world's people, wildlife, and ecosystems from toxic

substances and other environmental hazards such as BPA. At the same time, solutions often come more easily when they do not arise from government regulation alone. Consumer choice exercised through the market can often be an effective way to influence industry's decision making, but this requires consumers to have full information from scientific research regarding the risks involved. Once scientific results are in, a society's philosophical approach to risk management will determine what policy decisions are made.

15   All of these factors have come into play regarding regulation of BPA in consumer products. Although some nations have banned the chemical, many others have only restricted its use in children's products or chosen not to restrict BPA at all. But growing consumer concern over the presence of BPA, brought about by media attention, has spurred some companies to remove BPA from their products, even in the absence of governmental regulation in the United States.

16   It is important to remember, however, that synthetic chemicals, while exposing people to some risk, have brought us innumerable modern conveniences, a larger food supply, and medical advances that save and extend human lives. The lining of cans that contain BPA, for example, can affect human health by leaching BPA into foods but also serves a beneficial function by preventing corrosion and contamination of canned goods. A safer and happier future, one that safeguards the well-being of both people and the environment, therefore depends on knowing the risks that some hazards pose, assessing these risks, and having means in place to phase out harmful substances and replace them with safer ones whenever possible.

UNDERSTANDING AND ANALYZING THE READING

A. BUILDING VOCABULARY

Context

Using context and a dictionary, if necessary, determine the meaning of each word as it is used in the selection.

_____ 1. coursing (paragraph 1)
   a. growing
   b. draining
   c. existing
   d. moving

_____ 2. vexing (paragraph 2)
   a. numerous
   b. bothersome
   c. anticipated
   d. usual

_____ 3. leaches (paragraph 5)
   a. passes
   b. runs
   c. reaches
   d. transitions

_____ 4. minute (paragraph 7)
   a. small
   b. expected
   c. saturated
   d. detectable

_____ 5. toxin (paragraph 9)

     a. chemical

     b. hormone

     c. poison

     d. risk

_____ 6. precedent (paragraph 12)

     a. support

     b. praise

     c. a reason

     d. a model

Word Parts

A REVIEW OF PREFIXES AND ROOTS

IN- means *not*.	**NEURO** means *nerve*.	
RE- means *back* or *again*.	**BENE** means *good* or *well*.	

Use your knowledge of word parts and the review above to fill in the blanks in the following sentences.

1. A *neurological* effect associated with BPA (paragraph 1) is one that affects the body's _____.

2. A *beneficial* function of BPA (paragraph 16) is one that has a _____ use.

3. The field of *reproductive* biology (paragraph 1) studies how animals _____ by natural process.

4. The *innumerable* (paragraph 16) conveniences that BPA affords us can _____ be numbered.

B. UNDERSTANDING THE THESIS AND MAIN IDEAS

Select the best answer.

_____ 1. Which of the following is the best statement of the selection's thesis or main idea?

     a. Consumer concern and choice exercised in the marketplace have forced industries to more closely assess and manage the health risks associated with BPA.

     b. Synthetic chemicals have made possible medical advances that save lives while, at the same time, posing a threat to human health.

     c. There is no industry-wide consensus that BPA exposure poses a meaningful health risk.

     d. Substances like BPA are forcing scientists and regulators to change the way in which they assess environmental health threats.

_____ 2. The topic of paragraph 11 is

    a. the ban of BPA in Canada.

    b. government regulation of BPA.

    c. BPA-free items for babies.

    d. the many products that still contain BPA.

_____ 3. Which statement best restates the topic of paragraph 9?

    a. Expert panels believe that the federal government needs to develop testing standards for substances like BPA.

    b. Currently, expert panels can only evaluate those studies that meet federal guidelines for traditional toxicity research.

    c. Expert panels are currently assessing the scientific studies associated with BPA.

    d. Expert panels do not agree on the health risks of BPA.

_____ 4. The topic of paragraph 12 is

    a. the voluntary removal of BPA-containing products by some companies.

    b. the FDA's ban of BPA's use in baby bottles.

    c. companies who have removed BPA from food packaging.

    d. Japan's lead in removing BPA from can liners.

C. INTERPRETING SUPPORTING DETAILS

Select the best answer.

_____ 1. What do the authors mean by the term "paradigm shift" used in paragraph 9?

    a. a movement away from the traditional model of assessing environmental health risks

    b. a shift in the level of responsibility of those who assess environmental health risks

    c. a change to a pared down process of assessing environmental health risks

    d. a shift to a more conventional process of assessing environmental health risks

_____ 2. To support their thesis, the authors use all of the following *except*

    a. quotations from experts.

    b. facts and statistics.

    c. personal experience.

    d. examples.

_____ 3. To what group do the authors give credit for the growing consumer concern about the health risks of BPA?

    a. the medical profession

    b. the Center for Disease Control and Prevention

    c. consumer advocates

    d. the media

_____ 4. According to the article, BPA may cause all of the following medical problems *except*

    a. miscarriages.

    b. neurological disorders.

    c. reproductive abnormalities.

    d. physical deformities.

D. RECOGNIZING METHODS OF ORGANIZATION AND TRANSITIONS

Select the best answer. See Chapter 7 for information on patterns of organization.

_____ 1. The author explains the dangers of BPA primarily by

    a. ranking ideas in order of importance.

    b. explaining a process.

    c. making comparisons.

    d. giving examples.

_____ 2. The organizational pattern used in paragraph 5 is

    a. cause and effect.

    b. definition.

    c. classification.

    d. order of importance.

_____ 3. The organizational pattern used in paragraphs 3 and 4 is

    a. cause and effect.

    b. process.

    c. definition.

    d. enumeration.

_____ 4. Which word or phrase used in paragraph 12 signals the addition pattern?

  a. *because*

  b. *for example*

  c. *In the face of*

  d. *also*

E. FIGURING OUT IMPLIED MEANINGS

Indicate whether each statement is true (T) or false (F).

_____ 1. The authors believe that BPA poses a more significant risk to the safety and health of animals than it does to humans, mostly because of their low body weight.

_____ 2. The authors believe that consumers can force industry-wide change by voting with their money in the marketplace.

_____ 3. The authors believe that consumers have the right to be fully informed about the potential environmental health risks.

_____ 4. The authors believe that the United States government should extend its ban of BPA to all consumer products.

_____ 5. The authors believe that the chemical industry is misleading the public and jeopardizing their health by insisting on BPA's safety.

F. THINKING CRITICALLY ABOUT THE READING

Select the best answer. See Chapter 9 for information about thinking critically about a reading.

_____ 1. The authors' primary purpose in writing "Poison in the Bottle: How Safe Is Bisphenol A?" is to

  a. provide a definition of BPA and underscore the necessity of changing the way environmental health risks are assessed and controlled.

  b. educate readers about the effects of exposure to Bisphenol A.

  c. point the finger of shame at the chemical industry and manufacturers who use BPA in their products.

  d. argue that BPA should be banned from all products manufactured in the United States.

_____ 2. The overall tone of the reading is

    a. informative.

    b. unbiased.

    c. disapproving.

    d. neutral.

_____ 3. The authors begin the reading with two questions in order to

    a. indicate the target audience of the reading.

    b. imply that BPA is dangerous to babies and those with compromised immune systems.

    c. involve readers by appealing to their emotions.

    d. criticize people who continue to use products that contain BPA when they know of the associated risks involved.

_____ 4. In paragraph 13, the authors state, "Although we don't yet know everything there is to know about BPA, it isn't likely to be among our greatest environmental health threats." By this statement, they mean

    a. we can learn from how scientists and governmental regulators have handled the BPA issue and apply that learning to other more serious environmental health threats.

    b. people should not get so upset about BPA; there are much more serious environmental health risks that we unknowingly encounter every day.

    c. BPA is simply the environmental health threat that is getting press at the moment.

    d. chemical companies have been successful, thus far, in hiding or minimizing some very serious environmental health threats.

_____ 5. How do the authors lead you to be worried and concerned about the dangers of BPA?

    a. by explaining the issues with current research studies

    b. by including the visual

    c. by citing information from chemical companies

    d. by comparing the regulatory practices of the United States with those of Japan

_____ 6. Which one of the following agencies/corporations represents the minority opinion presented in the reading?

    a. the U.S. Food and Drug Administration

    b. the Canadian government

    c. the chemical industry

    d. Campbell's and Heinz

Answer the following open-ended questions in complete sentence format.

7. Why do you think the authors chose to use the infographic (Figure A)? How does it support the thesis? What message does it send to the reader?

8. What other type of graphic could the authors have used to support their thesis?

9. The reading opens with two quotations—one from a researcher and one from the American Chemistry Council. What is missing is a quote from you—a consumer. In one sentence, write a statement that expresses your opinion on BPA exposure. Use the contents of the reading as the basis for your opinion.

WRITING IN RESPONSE TO THE READING

G. REVIEWING AND ORGANIZING IDEAS WITH A SUMMARY

Write a clear and concise summary of paragraphs 5–12. See page 31 for information on writing a summary.

H. ANALYZING THE ISSUE

1. Identify at least three contemporary issues presented in this reading. Then phrase each as a question that the authors raise, discuss, or answer.

2. Have the authors provided sufficient evidence to support their thesis? What other types of evidence could they have included? Why would these types of evidence be helpful?

3. Does the source from which this reading is taken help you determine the authors' credibility? Do you find any bias in the selection?

4. The theme of this chapter is "our environment: problems and solutions." As you focus on the solutions presented in this reading, explain which of the solutions is the most viable one and why. What other solutions, other than those mentioned in the reading, might work?

5. Does the article offer any emotional appeals? If so, identify them and evaluate their fairness.

I. WRITING PARAGRAPHS AND ESSAYS

Write a paragraph or essay in response to the following writing prompts.

1. What is your initial reaction to the reading? How concerned are you about the presence of BPA in products you use? Write a paragraph response to these two questions.

2. Take a close look at the BPA-containing products you use or consume in your daily life (see paragraphs 3, 4, and 5 for some ideas) and then write an

essay outlining the ways you could limit your exposure to BPA. What would you need to avoid using? Are there products you could use in place of BPA-containing products? Are there places you would shop (or not shop)?

3. The involvement of the government in the business of corporations is often a point of contention. Do you think the government should force companies to remove BPA from their products, or do you think that companies should have a choice about removing it? Write an essay in which you present your opinion on this issue. Be sure to support your opinion with convincing evidence.

4. Write a letter to one of the following people:

    * the president of a chemical company that manufactures BPA

        OR

    * the CEO of WalMart

    In the letter, express your thoughts about the presence of BPA in the hundreds of products we use every day and share your opinion about the action this person's company has taken in regards to BPA.

ACTIVITIES: EXPLORING ENVIRONMENTAL ISSUES

On your own or with a group of classmates, complete two of the following four activities.

1. List at least five ways you can have a positive effect on the environment. These can be local/personal activities (for example, not using Styrofoam cups, which clog up landfills and do not break down into natural components) or community-based, national, or international activities (for example, volunteering for a committee that cleans up local parks).

   _____

   _____

   _____

   _____

   _____

2. Conduct a Web search for an organization that is devoted to preserving the environment, such as the World Wildlife Federation, Greenpeace, or the Sierra Club. What is the organization's mission? Read a couple of the articles on the organization's home page and summarize them. Would you consider joining one of these organizations? Why or why not?

3. As we mentioned at the start of this chapter, the environment is a very broad topic. This chapter discussed just a few aspects of the topic. Other environmental issues include the following:

   - The development of alternative energy sources, such as biofuels
   - The effects of "fracking" (drilling for natural gas) on the land
   - *Environmental racism*, which refers to the fact that poor people are much more likely to live close to heavily polluted areas
   - *Carbon footprints* and how companies are trying to reduce their impact on the environment in an effort to be more socially conscious
   - *Deforestation* and resultant loss of biodiversity.

   Write an essay or prepare a class presentation about any of these topics, or any other environmental topic you are interested in.

4. Perform an "energy audit" of your home or a part of your campus. Where do you see natural resources and utilities (such as gas, electricity, and lighting) being used in an environmentally friendly way? Where do you see waste? For the areas of waste, suggest improvements that might be made.

MAKING CONNECTIONS: THINKING WITHIN THE ISSUES

This section requires you to draw connections between the readings on this issue explored within the chapter. The activities and assignments below will give you practice in synthesizing information and thinking critically about the relationship of the chapter readings.

1. In "Poison in the Bottle: How Safe Is Bisphenol A?" (Selection 6, p. 406), Jay Withgott and Matthew Lapasata write, "A safer and happier future, one that safeguards the well-being of both people and the environment, therefore depends on knowing the risks that some hazards pose, assessing these risks, and having means in place to phase out harmful substances and replace them with safer ones wherever possible."

   Imagine that you must convince your college administration to institute a new program that will enhance the environment and make it safer for people. The two programs they are considering are identifying the BPA-containing products they use in their food services division and substituting safer products in place of them and e-waste recycling. Using "Poison in the Bottle: How Safe Is Bisphenol A?" (Selection 6, p. 406) and "Our E-Waste Problem Is Ridiculous and Gadget Makers Aren't Helping" (Selection 5, p. 395) as resources, write an essay in which you compare and contrast the two initiatives on the basis of their impact on the environment and on humans and their ease of implementation. Be sure to address the obstacles that might interfere with implementation and ways to overcome these obstacles. In your conclusion, you will make a recommendation to the college administration as to which initiative they should begin.

2. In "'Katrina Brain': The Invisible Long-term Toll of Megastorms" (Selection 4, p. 381) and "Poison in the Bottle: How Safe Is Bisphenol A?" (Selection 6, p. 406), the authors discuss the power of the media. In "Katrina Brain," the author focuses on a more negative influence of the media on the public, while in "Poison in the Bottle," the focus is on positive influence of the media. In both instances, the purpose of the media's coverage of the issues was to inform the public. In an essay, discuss the power of the media presented in these two readings, and then discuss one or two more environmental issues that have been addressed by the media. Be sure to discuss how the media presented these issues, and the outcome of the media coverage.

Relationships: Our Friends, Families, and Communities

How many people do you interact with daily?

If you're like most people, you don't keep track of the dozens, even hundreds, of people you see each day. Sociologists and psychologists often call humans "the social animal" because the vast majority of human beings seek the company of others. John Donne, the English poet, wrote a famous poem titled "No Man Is an Island," which begins:

> No man is an island,
> Entire of itself.
> Each is a piece of the continent,
> A part of the main.

But human relationships aren't necessarily easy. In fact, they often require a good deal of work, and they are at the center of many contemporary issues. Consider the following questions, which are often debated:

- Is marriage a religious institution, or is it secular (nonreligious)?
- Is marriage the ideal situation for most people, or should society embrace looser definitions of what constitutes a "couple"?
- When should a relationship end? How do divorces and breakups affect not only the couple breaking up, but also their friends, family, and children?

The readings in this chapter look at just a few of the many issues surrounding interpersonal relationships today. Should two people have sex before they get married, or even on the first date? How does mobile phone usage negatively affect your relationships with others? Is it possible to fall in love successfully online?

WHY ARE RELATIONSHIPS SUCH AN IMPORTANT CONTEMPORARY ISSUE?

Human beings are constantly redefining their relationships with other people, starting new relationships and sometimes ending other ones. Society's views of relationships affect people at the core of their being and influence their decisions. For example, it is often suggested that gay people tend to gather in liberal cities as a particular area's acceptance can have major effects on spouses, ex-spouses, in-laws, and children.

How Do Relationships Tie in to My College Experience?

The phrase "college experience" connotes much more than simply taking courses and studying for exams. Rather, it refers to an entire constellation of experiences you will encounter in college—from having a roommate, to developing relationships with your instructors, to managing your life, to planning your career. Relationships are involved in almost every aspect of the college experience and in many college courses. For example, business courses often require teamwork, which requires getting along with others in a group setting. In science labs, you will often have a lab partner with whom you share the work, and entire disciplines (such as sociology and communications) focus on human interactions and relationships.

TIPS FOR READING ABOUT RELATIONSHIPS	Here are some tips for reading not only the selections in this chapter, but any reading about relationships.

- **Apply the reading to your own experiences and life.** Students often find readings about relationships to be fairly "easy" and immediately applicable to their lives. As you read, think about how the selection applies to you or to other people you know. This is an excellent way to learn the concepts and ideas discussed in the reading.

- **Distinguish between the writer's opinions and research presented as evidence to support a thesis or main idea.** Much of what you read about relationships will be based on the writer's personal experiences. Such readings can be illuminating, but they may not be representative of the way most people feel. They are therefore mostly opinion pieces. In contrast, scientific research presented in a reading is more fact based. Most writers give credit to the person who conducted the research, either directly (by giving the person's name and affiliation) or indirectly, by using a parenthetical research citation. For example, (Smith, 2009) refers to a research study conducted by someone named Smith, who published his or her results in 2009. Complete sources for parenthetical citations are usually found in footnotes or endnotes.

- **Keep an open mind.** Some readings about relationships may make you uncomfortable if they challenge your beliefs or expectations. Read carefully, keeping an open mind, and engage in critical thinking. Annotate the reading to record your reactions, and then analyze your reactions, asking yourself why you reacted the way you did.

SELECTION 7
Textbook Selection

Hooking Up

Jenifer Kunz

The following reading was taken from an introductory textbook, *Think Marriages and Families*, by Jenifer Kunz. This selection comes from a chapter titled "Friendship, Affection, Love, and Intimacy." The author is a professor of sociology at West Texas A&M University. According to her biography, Dr. Kunz's interest in studying the family grew out of her experiences of growing up in her own family. "We worked hard, played hard, and had fun together," she says. "I came to learn and understand that the family is the most important and most influential social institution in the world." In "Hooking Up," Dr. Kunz takes a look at recent trends in the sexual behaviors of college students.

GETTING READY TO READ

PREVIEW IT

Preview the reading using the guidelines on page 6. When you have finished, indicate whether the following statements are true (T) or false (F).

_____ a. The reading will offer criticisms of hooking up, explaining why it has negative effects on those who hook up.

_____ b. The sexual double standard allows modern young men and women to enjoy healthy, active sex lives without guilt or negative effects on self-esteem.

LOOK IT UP

"Hooking Up" is a research-based look at the sexual behavior of college students. Before you begin reading this selection, spend some time on the Internet doing some research of your own on this issue. Look for studies that focus on the causes and the effects of "hooking up." Take notes on your findings so that you can share with your discussion group.

DISCUSS IT

In a group with three or four of your classmates, discuss the findings of your research on the issue of "hooking up." Broaden your discussion to include the pros and cons of this type of relationship. Be prepared to share the highlights of your discussion with the class.

WRITE ABOUT IT

Connect the reading to your own experience by writing a paragraph about "hooking up." What does the term mean to you? Who does it, and why? Are there other "adultlike" behaviors that students experiment with when they enter college?

READ IT

Readings about some contemporary issues may make you slightly uncomfortable, especially when they discuss sensitive topics like sex. As you read "Hooking Up," focus on the definitions and on the research that attempts to shed light on the sexual behavior of college students. Pay close attention to the author's tone, purpose, and audience, and look for evidence of bias in the reading.

As you read the selection, highlight and annotate the text so that you can answer the detailed questions that follow. Take a look at the questions before you begin reading so that you can understand the level of recall that is expected.

Hooking Up

Jenifer Kunz

1   One day, dating might be considered an old-fashioned quirk of almost Victorian taste and prudery, as quaint as a woman dropping an embroidered handkerchief to encourage a man to approach her. On that day, "hooking up" will be the **norm**. This postmodern view of romance may just be one of the latest fashions of the sometimes alarmist media. Before losing all hope, we should ask ourselves, "What does 'hooking up' really mean?"

norm normal, expected behavior

2   "Hooking up" is a term used to describe casual sexual activity with no strings attached between heterosexual college students who are strangers or brief acquaintances. When did people start to hook up? Although the term became common in the 1990s, its use with its modern meaning has been documented as early as the mid-1980s. Studies from the early 2000s show that hooking up was already a fairly common practice on U.S. campuses, practiced by as much as 40 percent of female college students. More recent studies have shed some light on the demographic and

>>> A 2003 study of the phenomenon of "hooking up" among college students revealed that people thought their peers were more comfortable with hookups than they were. **Based on these results, how do you think peer pressure affects sexual behavior in teenagers and young adults?**

Sam Edwards/OJO Images/Getty Images

correlatives
two or more
factors
working
together

extroversion
outgoing
personality
type; the
opposite is
introversion,
which refers
to people
who are more
solitary

psychological **correlatives** of hooking up. In a 2007 study involving 832 college students, it emerged that hooking up is practiced less by African-American than Caucasian students. Hooking up is also associated with the use of alcohol and, interestingly, with higher parental income. Increased financial resources may give teens and young adults more opportunities to socialize and hook up. As far as personality traits, hookups seem to be more common for people displaying **extroversion**, although it is also common in neuroticism. Neuroticism is a personality trait characterized by negative emotions such as depression, anxiety, anger, embarrassment, vulnerability, and impulsiveness combined with emotional instability that may lead neurotics to hook up as a way to cope with fears and anxieties. The emotions stirred by hookups are varied, and women seem to be more likely than men to experience regret after a hookup, especially when sexual intercourse is involved.

3   Not surprisingly, hooking up has received much criticism. Psychologists blame the hookup culture for young people's fear of commitment, saying that focusing only on sex does not teach people to respond to the emotional and romantic needs of the partner. In this sense, hookups are described as the worst possible preparation for long-term relationships and marriage. Other critics argue that the hookup culture has its risks, too, especially when it's strongly characterized by alcohol consumption. A 2007 study of 178 college students concluded that 23 percent of women and 7 percent of men had experienced unwanted sexual intercourse, including regretful or harmful sexual behavior such as assault and rape (although assault and rape were reported only by a small minority of interviewees). More significantly, 78 percent of unwanted sexual intercourse experienced by the interviewees took place during a hookup. Of course, unwanted sexual intercourse is not characteristic of hookups only, and dating is not exempt from it.

Hookups and Dating

4   How does "hooking up" differ from dating? According to author Kathleen A. Bogle, the most significant difference lies in the timing of sex, where the term "sex" refers to any sexual activity from kissing to sexual intercourse. In dating, sex usually is postponed until the couple has gone on a few dates, whereas in a hookup, sex frequently happens on the first encounter. Second, when dating, two people get to know each other and possibly start a romantic relationship, which is not required in hooking up. Alcohol consumed in large quantities is also more characteristic of hookups than dating, since casual sex is more likely when **inhibitions** are lowered. Hooking up also differs from dating in terms of privacy: dates tend to have a public nature (they take place in restaurants, movie theaters, etc.), whereas hookups are more spontaneous and often private. The private nature of the hookup culture has been facilitated by technology advancements in the last decades, such as mobile phones and the Internet. This new technology makes it much easier to get in touch with acquaintances through private channels.

inhibition
mental block
imposing
restraint or
restriction

5   In a time of economic crisis, it might be tempting to hook up just to save money. Unlike dates, hookups do not require spending any money on nice dinners and flowers. It is also important to realize that hooking up is most common among college students, and that it is not necessarily representative of the entire single population. College years are often viewed as the last chance to have fun before settling down, so hookups may represent a chance to experiment sexually—something that dating does not provide.

initiation
action that
makes
something start

6   Hookups also show more gender equality in the **initiation** of the script, or sequence of automatic behaviors, although research shows that men still maintain more power in deciding whether the hookup will be a one night stand or lead to something more. In this

regard, sexual exploitation is still very common both in the hookup and dating culture, meaning that men are often capable of keeping a partner just for sexual enjoyment regardless of the woman's true desires. This seems to stem from the fear that women have of being rejected if they don't perform to a man's standard. There is still a stigma attached to women with a more intense sexual life or those who have had many sexual partners. As liberating as the hookup script might seem, the sexual double standard that condemns women and praises men for the same level of sexual experience is still present today.

Case Study: Hooking Up Versus Commitment

7   Kara is a sophomore in college. She hooked up a lot during her first year of school but is now ready for a deeper relationship.

8   "When I first got to college, I was ready to have fun. Leaving home for the first time gave me a sense of adventure that carried over into my idea of relationships. I didn't want anything serious, but I wanted to see what was out there. During the first months of school, I hooked up with a lot of guys, mostly people I met at parties. I loved not having the pressure of a relationship on top of school.

9   "Then I hooked up with Bill, a guy from my biology class. Since he wasn't a stranger, this encounter was slightly more intimate than what I'd been used to. I'd never thought about Bill romantically, but after we made out, I started to think that way.

10   "Bill and I didn't become a couple, but our relationship made me realize that hooking up can be fun for a while, but ultimately I'd like to have someone to get close to. I want a guy who doesn't leave first thing in the morning and who calls me for something other than one passionate night."

UNDERSTANDING AND ANALYZING THE READING

A. BUILDING VOCABULARY

Context

Using context and a dictionary, if necessary, determine the meaning of each word as it is used in the selection.

_____ 1. quirk (paragraph 1)
    a. tradition
    b. habit
    c. law
    d. oddity

_____ 2. alarmist (paragraph 1)
    a. biased and untrustworthy
    b. loud and crass
    c. exaggerating dangers
    d. reporting on a specific topic

_____ 3. demographic (paragraph 2)
    a. having psychological issues
    b. enrolled in college
    c. specific part of the population
    d. inclined to bragging

_____ 4. spontaneous (paragraph 4)
    a. unplanned
    b. frequent
    c. lighthearted
    d. enjoyable

_____ 5. facilitated (paragraph 4)

    a. exposed

    b. helped

    c. stopped

    d. affected

_____ 6. stigma (paragraph 6)

    a. mark of disgrace

    b. role of women

    c. signal of trust

    d. problem

Word Parts

> **A REVIEW OF PREFIXES AND SUFFIXES**
>
> **HETERO-**   means *different* or *other*.
>
> **-FUL**   refers to the *state*, *condition*, or *quality*; in this case, "full of."

Use your knowledge of word parts and the review above to fill in the blanks in the following sentences.

1. A *heterosexual* (paragraph 2) couple is composed of people of two _____ sexes: male and female.

2. Someone who is *regretful* (paragraph 3) about a particular situation is full of _____ about what happened.

B. UNDERSTANDING THE THESIS AND MAIN IDEAS

Select the best answer.

_____ 1. The thesis or central thought of "Hooking Up" is best stated as

    a. In the modern world, hooking up is simply a rite of passage between adolescence and adulthood.

    b. Hooking up, a term used to refer to casual sexual activity between straight college students, is associated with specific demographic and psychological factors; it is fairly common but appears to have more drawbacks than benefits.

    c. Society has come a long way since Victorian days, when sexual prudery was the norm; now, casual sex is commonplace, and it no longer carries any negative connotations for college-aged men and women.

    d. Research studies regarding the hooking-up phenomenon have been inconsistent in their findings, but for the most part they reveal that young, black, straight people hook up much more frequently than older, white, gay people.

_____ 2. The topic of paragraph 3 is
   a. relationships and marriage.
   b. criticisms of hooking up.
   c. unwanted sexual intercourse.
   d. women's emotional needs.

_____ 3. The main idea of paragraph 6 is found in the
   a. first sentence.
   b. second sentence.
   c. third sentence.
   d. last sentence.

C. INTERPRETING SUPPORTING DETAILS

Select the best answer.

_____ 1. The author's purpose for including Kara's story in the box titled "Hooking Up Versus Commitment" (paragraphs 7–10, p. 424) is to
   a. show that young college women are more likely to hook up than older women.
   b. indicate that hooking up is more common among freshmen and sophomores than among juniors and seniors.
   c. imply that romance and dating are more emotionally fulfilling than hooking up.
   d. provide a case study of one college student who holds very conservative views about dating and sex.

_____ 2. According to Kathleen A. Bogle, what is the key difference between dating and hooking up?
   a. Two people who hook up tend to know each other longer than two people who go out on their first date.
   b. Two people who hook up tend to come from lower-income families than two people who go out on a first date.
   c. In a hookup, two people have sex on the first date; in dating, sex is usually postponed until the couple has gone out on a few dates.
   d. In a hookup, the two people usually have roommates; in dating, the two people usually have their own apartments or live independently.

_____ 3. Which of the following is not a trait of neuroticism?

    a. shyness

    b. impulsiveness

    c. anxiety

    d. anger

_____ 4. The key type of evidence the author uses to support her main ideas and her thesis is

    a. personal experience.

    b. research studies.

    c. historical information.

    d. reports from government-funded agencies.

D. RECOGNIZING METHODS OF ORGANIZATION AND TRANSITIONS

Select the best answer. See Chapter 7 for information on patterns of organization.

_____ 1. What is the overall organizational pattern of the reading?

    a. definition

    b. classification

    c. process

    d. cause and effect

_____ 2. Paragraph 3 focuses on

    a. reasons why hooking up has received criticism.

    b. the characteristics of hooking up.

    c. differences between hooking up and marriage.

    d. the importance of defining risks.

_____ 3. The primary pattern of organization used in paragraph 4 is

    a. spatial order.

    b. cause and effect.

    c. comparison and contrast.

    d. process.

_____ 4. A transitional word or phrase used in paragraph 4 to signal its pattern of organization is

    a. *how.*

    b. *whereas.*

    c. *refers to.*

    d. *such as.*

E. FIGURING OUT IMPLIED MEANINGS

Indicate whether each statement is true (T) or false (F).

_____ 1. White students hook up more often than black students.

_____ 2. Poor people have more time on their hands and thus are more likely than rich people to hook up.

_____ 3. The author sees a connection between the rise of the Internet and the increase in hooking up.

_____ 4. In this reading, the term "hooking up" does not apply to college graduates or gay people.

_____ 5. Extroverts are more likely to hook up than introverts.

F. THINKING CRITICALLY ABOUT THE READING

Select the best answer. See Chapter 9 for information about thinking critically about a reading.

_____ 1. The author's overall purpose in "Hooking Up" is to

    a. define the term "hooking up" and explore the research surrounding the causes and effects of this common behavior.

    b. encourage young people to experiment with a variety of different lifestyles before choosing to settle down with one mate.

    c. make the case that young men, who have more power in romantic and sexual relationships, should engage in more responsible sexual behaviors.

    d. compare and contrast neurotic behaviors with other common behaviors that do not have psychological underpinnings.

_____ 2. The overall tone of the reading selection is best described as

    a. emotional and angry.

    b. concerned and somewhat biased.

    c. neutral and inoffensive.

    d. light and insubstantial.

_____ 3. With which of the following statements would the author of "Hooking Up" *not* agree?

    a. Hooking up may be a way for college students to have fun before they settle down with a lifetime partner.

    b. It usually costs more money to date than to hook up.

    c. Overall, men have more power than women do in deciding whether a hookup will be a one night stand or lead to something more.

    d. The sexual double standard has led to greater equality between women and men.

_____ 4. The author of this reading selection, Jenifer Kunz, can best be described as

    a. old-fashioned.

    b. self-centered.

    c. closed-minded.

    d. feminist.

_____ 5. Which of the following statements best summarizes the "postmodern view of romance" to which the author refers in paragraph 1?

    a. Hooking up is much harder work than dating.

    b. Hooking up is normal, expected behavior.

    c. Hooking up is necessary before a romance can get started.

    d. Hooking up is the next logical step in women's liberation from outmoded ideas.

_____ 6. The author likely included the photo on page 422 in order to

    a. illustrate what typical college students look like.

    b. imply that attractive people are more likely to hook up than unattractive people.

    c. emphasize that homosexuals do not hook up.

    d. provide a visual reminder of the group of people who are most likely to hook up.

Answer the following open-ended questions in complete sentence format.

7. In paragraph 6, the author states that hookups "show more gender equality in the initiation of the script." What does she mean?

8. In paragraph 1, the author writes that "This postmodern view of romance may just be one of the latest fashions of the sometimes alarmist media." What is the meaning of this statement?

9. Why do you think "hooking up" is more common for extroverts than introverts (paragraph 2)?

WRITING IN RESPONSE TO THE READING ▮▮▮▮▮

G. REVIEWING AND ORGANIZING IDEAS WITH A PARAPHRASE

Complete the following paraphrase of paragraph 4. Begin your paraphrase with the following sentence.

Kathleen Bogle has written about the differences between hooking up and dating.

_____

_____

_____

_____

_____

_____

_____

_____

For paragraph 5 of the reading, write your own two-sentence paraphrase.

_____

_____

_____

H. ANALYZING THE ISSUE

Discuss in class or write in your journal a response to the following questions.

1. The theme of this chapter is "relationships: our friends, families, and communities." Analyze the reading by addressing the following questions:
   a. How would you define a relationship? Does hooking up qualify as a relationship according to your definition? Explain your answer.
   b. How do you think Kara (paragraphs 7–10) would define a relationship?
   c. How does the author feel about "hooking up"? What evidence exists to support your answer?
   d. Taking into account friends, family, and community, what impact would a person's hookup experience possibly have on his/her other relationships?

2. Does the author provide adequate background information about the topic of hooking up? If not, what is lacking?

3. How does the photo on page 422 help you learn?

4. Assume this material is to be included on an upcoming exam. Discuss how you would prepare for the exam.

5. How does the information about the source of the reading and the author help you to understand the reading better?

I. WRITING PARAGRAPHS AND ESSAYS

Write a paragraph or essay in response to the following writing prompts.

1. Do you think hooking up is a common occurrence among the students on your campus? Write a paragraph explaining your answer.

2. Do you think men and women would be equally likely to give an honest answer to the following question: "When was the last time you hooked up?" Write a paragraph in which you explain your opinion.

3. The boxed insert within the reading (p. 422) begins "A 2003 study" and closes with the question "Based on these results, how do you think peer pressure affects sexual behavior in teenagers and young adults?" Write an essay in which you answer this question.

4. "Hooking Up" discusses one common type of behavior among college students, suggesting that it is a form of experimentation. What other types of common experimental behaviors do you see among college students? Write an essay in which you explore some of these behaviors and the possible motivations behind them.

5. In paragraph 1, the author refers to the "alarmist media." How would you describe today's media, from newspapers to TV newscasts to Web sites? Write an essay in which you explore the types of stories that receive the most press coverage. How newsworthy are these stories?

SELECTION
8
Magazine Article

Are You 'Phubbing' Right Now?
What It Is and Why Science Says It's Bad For Your Relationships

Emma Seppälä

This reading originally appeared in *Greater Good Magazine: Science-Based Insights for a Meaningful Life*, published by the Greater Good Science Center at the University of California Berkeley. The author, Emma Seppälä, PhD, is the author of a book entitled *The Happiness Track*, published in 2016 by HarperOne. In addition, she is the Science Director of Stanford University's Center for Compassion and Altruism Research and Education and Co-Director of the Yale College Well-being Program at the Yale Center for Emotional Intelligence. She also teaches a course at Yale College entitled "The Psychology of Happiness."

GETTING READY TO READ

PREVIEW IT

Preview the reading using the guidelines on page 6. When you have finished, complete the following items:

1. This reading is about _____
   _____.

2. List two topics you expect the author to discuss in the reading.

   a. _____

   b. _____

LOOK IT UP

Before reading this article, conduct an Internet search for information on phubbing. Be sure to look for articles other than the one you will be reading for class. Pay special attention to any research studies and experts in the field that you may find as you search. Take notes on your findings so that you can share with your discussion group.

DISCUSS IT

In a group with three or four of your classmates, discuss the findings of your research on phubbing. Be prepared to share the highlights of your discussion with the class.

WRITE ABOUT IT

Connect the reading to your own experience by writing a paragraph about phubbing. What does the term mean to you? Are you guilty of phubbing? How frequently do you phub others, and who do you phub? Do others phub you? How does it make you feel? What do you do when it happens to you?

READ IT

Phubbing may seem to be a harmless practice, but it can negatively impact your relationships with others. As you read, pay special attention to the consequences of phubbing presented by the author.

Also, be sure to highlight and annotate the text as you read so that you can answer the detailed questions that follow the reading. Take a look at the questions before reading so that you can understand the level of recall that is expected.

Are You 'Phubbing' Right Now?

What It Is and Why Science Says It's Bad For Your Relationships

Emma Seppälä

1   "Phubbing" is the practice of snubbing others in favor of our mobile phones. We've all been there, as either victim or perpetrator. We may no longer even notice when we've been phubbed (or are phubbing), it has become such a normal part of life. However, research is revealing the profound impact this sort of snubbing can have on our relationships and well-being. There's an irony here. When we're staring at our phones, we're often connecting with someone on social media or through texting. Sometimes, we're flipping through our pictures the way we once turned the pages of photo albums, remembering moments with people we love. Unfortunately, however, this can severely disrupt our actual, present-moment, in-person relationships, which also tend to be our most important ones.

2   In a study poignantly titled, "My life has become a major distraction from my cell phone," Meredith David and James Roberts suggest that overuse of our phones in the presence of others can lead to a decline in one of the most important relationships we can have as an adult: the one with our life partner. According to their

Cell phone distraction can severely disrupt in-person relationships.

Rommel Canlas/Shutterstock

study of 145 adults, phubbing decreases marital satisfaction, in part because it leads to conflict over phone use. A follow-up study by Chinese scientists assessed 243 married adults with similar results: partner phubbing, because it was associated with lower marital satisfaction, contributed to greater likelihood of depression.

3   This behavior also affects our casual friendships. Not surprisingly to anyone who has been phubbed, phone users are generally seen as less polite and attentive. When someone's eyes wander, we intuitively know what brain studies show: the mind is wandering. We feel unheard, disrespected, disregarded. A set of studies actually showed that just having a phone out and present during a conversation (say, on the table between you) interferes with your sense of connection to the other person, the feelings of closeness experienced, and the quality of the conversation. Especially during meaningful conversations, you lose the opportunity for true and authentic connection to another person, the core tenet of any friendship or relationship. These findings hold true regardless of people's age, ethnicity, gender, or mood. We feel more empathy when smart phones are put away. This makes sense. When we are on our phones, we are not looking at other people and not reading their facial expressions. We don't hear the nuances in their tone of voice or notice their body posture.

4   So how do those who are phubbed react to being ignored? According to a study published in March of this year, they themselves start to turn to social media. Presumably, they do so to seek inclusion. They may turn to their cell phone to distract themselves from the very painful feelings of being socially neglected. We know from brain imaging research that being excluded registers as actual physical pain in the brain. People snubbed in favor of technology in turn become more likely to attach themselves to their phones in unhealthy ways, thereby increasing their own feelings of stress and depression. "It is ironic that cell phones, originally designed as a communication tool, may actually hinder rather than foster interpersonal connectedness," write David and Roberts in their study, "Phubbed and Alone." Their results suggest the creation of a vicious circle: a phubbed individual turns to social media, and their compulsive behavior presumably leads them to phub others—perpetuating and normalizing the practice and problem of "phubbing."

5   Why do people get into the phubbing habit in the first place? Not surprisingly, fear of missing out and lack of self-control predict phubbing. However, the most important predictor is addiction—to social media, to the phone, and to the Internet. Internet addiction has similar brain correlates to physiological forms like addiction to heroin and other recreational drugs. The impact of this addiction is particularly worrisome for children whose brain and social skills are still under development.

6   Consider this: the urge to check social media is stronger than the urge for sex, according to research by Chicago University's Wilhelm Hoffman. In some ways, these findings come as no surprise. We are profoundly social people for whom connection and a sense of belonging are crucial for health and happiness. (In fact, the lack thereof is worse for you than smoking, high blood pressure, and obesity.) So, we err sometimes. We look for connection on social media at the cost of face-to-face opportunities for true intimacy.

7   Awareness is the only solution. Know that what drives you and others is to connect and to belong. While you may not be able to control the behavior of others, you yourself have opportunities to model something different. Research by Barbara Fredrickson, beautifully described in her book *Love 2.0*, suggests that intimacy happens in micro-moments: talking over breakfast, the exchange with the UPS guy, the smile of a child. The key is to be present and mindful. A revealing study showed that we are happiest when we are present, no matter what we are doing. Can we be present with the person in front of us right now, no matter who it is?

8   The most essential and intimate form of connection is eye contact. Posture and the most minute facial expressions (the tightening of our lips, the crow's feet of smiling eyes, upturned eyebrows in sympathy or apology) communicate more than our words. Most importantly, they are at the root of empathy—the ability to sense what another person is feeling—which is so critical to authentic human connection. True connection thrives on presence, openness, observation, compassion, and, as Brene Brown has so beautifully shared in her TED talk and her bestselling book *Daring Greatly*, vulnerability. It takes courage to connect to another person authentically, yet it is also the key to fulfillment.

9   What if someone in your presence snubs you for their phone? Patience and compassion are key here. Understand that the person is probably not doing it with malicious intent, but rather is following an impulse (sometimes irresistible) to connect. Just like you or I, their goal is not to exclude. To the contrary, they are looking for a feeling of inclusion. After all, a telling sociological study shows that loneliness is rising at an alarming rate in our society.

10   What's more, age and gender play a role in people's reactions to this behavior. According to studies, older participants and women advocate for more restricted phone use in most social situations. Men differ from women in that they viewed phone calls as more appropriate in virtually all environments including intimate settings. Similarly, in classrooms, male students find phubbing far less disturbing than their female counterparts.

11   Perhaps even worse than disconnecting from others, however, Internet addiction and phubbing disconnect us from ourselves. Plunged into a virtual world, we hunch over a screen, strain our eyes unnecessarily, and tune out completely from our own needs—for sleep, exercise, even food. So, the next time you're with another human and you feel temped to pull out your phone—stop. Put it away. Look them in the eyes, and listen to what they have to say.

UNDERSTANDING AND ANALYZING THE READING

A. BUILDING VOCABULARY

Context

Using context and a dictionary, if necessary, determine the meaning of each word as it is used in the selection.

_____ 1. perpetrator (paragraph 1)
   a. one who is wronged
   b. one who witnesses a crime
   c. one who is taken advantage of
   d. one who carries out a harmful act

_____ 2. tenet (paragraph 3)
   a. meaning
   b. cause
   c. policy
   d. principle

_____ 3. empathy (paragraph 3)

      a. the ability to have meaningful conversations

      b. a feeling of self-satisfaction

      c. the ability to sense others' feelings

      d. a feeling of disrespect

_____ 4. nuance (paragraph 3)

      a. word

      b. concept

      c. subtlety

      d. activity

_____ 5. vulnerability (paragraph 8)

      a. consideration

      b. exposure

      c. refusal

      d. connection

_____ 6. malicious (paragraph 9)

      a. spiteful

      b. spirited

      c. impulsive

      d. intentional

Word Parts

A REVIEW OF PREFIXES, ROOTS, AND SUFFIXES

COM-	means *with*.
PATH/PASS	means *feeling*.
-SHIP	means *pertaining to*.

Use your knowledge of word parts and the review above to fill in the blanks in the following sentences.

1. People who have casual *friendships* (paragraph 3) with others have relationships that pertain to _____.

2. One who responds with *compassion* (paragraph 9) is someone who responds with _____.

B. UNDERSTANDING THE THESIS AND MAIN IDEAS

Select the best answer.

_____ 1. Which of the following best states the thesis or central thought of the reading?

    a. Overuse of cell phones has been found to be the primary cause of marital dissatisfaction.

    b. Overuse of cell phones while in the presence of others can negatively affect your relationship with them and your well-being.

    c. While cell phones can enhance relationships by enabling people to communicate over long distances, they can also hurt relationships by limiting authentic connection.

    d. Phubbing is bad for relationships because it leads to an addiction to social media for the perpetrator and the victim.

_____ 2. The topic of paragraph 3 is

    a. the importance of meaningful connection.

    b. the meaning of true friendship.

    c. the effects of phubbing on relationships with friends.

    d. the role of empathy in casual friendships.

_____ 3. Which of the following is the best statement of the implied main idea of paragraph 10?

    a. Older people and women are generally more conservative in thought and action than younger people and men.

    b. Men are more comfortable with technology than women are.

    c. In general, women tend to be more attuned to the feelings of others than men are.

    d. In classrooms, male students are more adept at multi-tasking than female students are.

C. INTERPRETING SUPPORTING DETAILS

Select the best answer.

_____ 1. Which one of the following statements presented by the author *cannot* be substantiated by brain research?

    a. Lack of direct visual contact indicates a lack of connection between two people.

    b. The physiological addiction to the Internet is similar to drug addiction.

    c. Not being included by others is perceived as pain by the brain.

    d. The brains of children are not developed enough to be able to handle anything other than face-to-face communication.

_____ 2. The reading discusses all of the following effects of phubbing on relationships *except*

   a. lack of presence.

   b. feelings of disrespect.

   c. feelings of hostility.

   d. feelings of neglect.

_____ 3. With which of the following statements would the author of this reading *disagree*?

   a. Even the presence of a cell phone can be a deterrent to a conversation.

   b. People who are victims of phubbing may become phubbers themselves.

   c. With meaningful conversation, true intimacy can occur over the phone.

   d. People who phub others are generally thought of as being rude.

_____ 4. The author uses all of the following to support her main ideas *except*

   a. sociological studies.

   b. direct quotations from university professors.

   c. references to books and videos.

   d. brain-imaging studies.

D. RECOGNIZING METHODS OF ORGANIZATION AND TRANSITIONS

Select the best answer. See Chapter 7 for information on patterns of organization.

_____ 1. The dominant organizational pattern of the reading is

   a. process.

   b. spatial order.

   c. classification.

   d. cause and effect.

_____ 2. Which organizational pattern is used in paragraph 10?

   a. classification

   b. chronological order

   c. comparison and contrast

   d. definition

_____ 3. Which transitional word or phrase points to the use of cause and effect in paragraph 2?

    a. *because*

    b. *according to*

    c. *in part*

    d. *greater likelihood*

E. FIGURING OUT IMPLIED MEANINGS

Indicate whether each statement is true (T) or false (F).

_____ 1. The author believes that overuse of cell phones can have a detrimental effect on a marriage.

_____ 2. The author believes that in order for a true friendship to exist, there must be a mutual understanding of what phubbing is and to what extent it will be tolerated.

_____ 3. The author believes that the intense desire for belonging drives people to social media as a way to connect with others.

_____ 4. The author believes that when a person is phubbed, he or she should retaliate by phubbing the perpetrator in order to demonstrate the rudeness of the behavior.

_____ 5. The author believes that it can be difficult or impossible to forge a genuine connection with another person online.

F. THINKING CRITICALLY ABOUT THE READING

Select the best answer. See Chapter 9 for information about thinking critically about a reading.

_____ 1. The author's purpose in writing "Are You 'Phubbing' Right Now?" is to

    a. use research to convince skeptics of the dangers of cell phone overuse.

    b. explain the causes and effects of cell phone snubbing behavior and encourage people to strive for authentic connection.

    c. outline some key research studies that demonstrate how socially isolated people can use social media to connect with others.

    d. criticize the people who spend too much time online instead of working to establish true face-to-face relationships.

_____ 2. The tone of the reading can best be described as

    a. informative and understanding.

    b. curious and open-minded.

    c. bitter and cutting.

    d. skeptical and questioning.

_____ 3. Which of the following excerpts from the reading is an opinion?

    a. "According to their study of 145 adults, phubbing decreases marital satisfaction, in part because it leads to conflict over phone use." (paragraph 2)

    b. "Internet addiction has similar brain correlates to physiological forms like addiction to heroin and other recreational drugs." (paragraph 5)

    c. "True connection thrives on presence, openness, observation, compassion, and, as Brene Brown has so beautifully shared in her TED talk and her bestselling book *Daring Greatly*, vulnerability." (paragraph 8)

    d. "Internet addiction and phubbing disconnect us from ourselves." (paragraph 11)

_____ 4. What does the author mean when she says that the key to true intimacy is to be present and mindful? (paragraph 7)

    a. In order to connect with a person, you must sit or stand in front of him or her and show that you are thinking about the relationship.

    b. To have a relationship with a person, you must arrange to meet with him or her and share ideas, hopes, and dreams.

    c. To have an authentic connection with someone, you must be with him or her in a face-to-face environment, intently focused on the person, and responding both verbally and with engaging facial expressions.

    d. To have an in-person relationship with someone, you must disconnect from social networks and invest time and energy in the relationship.

_____ 5. What is ironic about the way that victims of phubbing often react? (paragraphs 4 and 5)

    a. After the painful experience of being phubbed, the victims often retreat to pleasurable experiences on their phones.

    b. Those who are phubbed often become the ones who phub others.

    c. Those who feel socially neglected turn to social media for connection.

    d. Being face-to-face with a phubber is a lonely experience.

_____ 6. Based on the evidence in this reading, how do you think the author would respond to someone who snubs her in favor of his or her phone?

    a. "Why don't you put your phone down and talk to me?"

    b. "I hate it when you ignore me. Have I done something to make you mad?"

    c. "I know you like to check your phone often, but I would really like it if you would put it away so that we could talk for a while."

    d. "I understand that you have an addiction, but I feel left out when you choose to interact with your phone rather than with me."

Answer the following open-ended questions in complete sentence format.

7. Has the author provided sufficient evidence to support her main ideas? What other types of evidence might she provide to strengthen the reading?

8. An old Yiddish proverb says, "The eyes are the mirror of the soul." How does this saying relate to the information in paragraph 8?

9. How does the photo included with this reading illustrate the theme? If you had to choose a photo for the reading, what would it look like and what message would it convey?

10. Is the author qualified to write on the topic? Why or why not? Why do you think this topic would be of special interest to her?

WRITING IN RESPONSE TO THE READING

G. REVIEWING AND ORGANIZING IDEAS WITH A MAP

Create a conceptual map of the reading selection. See page 28 for information about mapping.

H. ANALYZING THE ISSUE

Discuss in class or write in your journal a response to the following questions.

1. Identify at least three contemporary issues presented in this reading.

2. The theme of this chapter is "relationships: our friends, families, and communities." In a few sentences, explain how phubbing affects friends, families, and communities.

3. In a sentence or two, describe the author's version of an ideal relationship.

4. For what audience is the author writing? What makes you think this? How do you think her message would be received by this audience? How convincing of her claim do you think she is?

5. List the major points of the author's argument presented in this reading.

I. WRITING PARAGRAPHS AND ESSAYS

Write a paragraph or essay in response to the following writing prompts.

1. Suppose you just spent an hour with a good friend at a coffee shop, and for all but five minutes of the hour, your friend phubbed you by staring at his/her phone as he/she texted and connected with another friend via social media. How did this make you feel? What did this say about the relationship you have with your friend? Write your friend a letter describing exactly what happened at the coffee shop, detailing how the phubbing made you feel, and the effect this could possibly have on the relationship.

2. Consider all of the relationships you have in your present life. What is the best relationship you have and what makes it so satisfying? Write a paragraph in which you discuss these questions.

3. In paragraph 6, the author says, "We look for connection on social media at the cost of face-to-face opportunities for true intimacy." Do you agree with this statement? Does this describe you or someone you know? Write a paragraph or essay about this behavior, the causes of it, and the results of it. Be sure to use support from your own experiences or the experiences of someone you know.

4. Several talks by Emma Seppälä, the author of "Are You 'Phubbing' Right Now?" can be found on TED talks. Search the TED table of contents for one of her talks on relationships and spend some time listening to it and taking notes. In an essay, provide a concise summary of the article, explain how the talk in some way relates to the reading on phubbing, and discuss whether or not you agree with Seppälä's major points.

5. Take an honest look at your cell phone usage. Are you mindful of when and how you use your phone and how your cell phone usage affects others? Do you spend more time connecting with others on social media or through texting than you do in person with others? Would other people consider your cell phone habits to be rude or disrespectful? Write an essay about your cell phone usage habits. What benefits have you experienced by having a cell phone and using it as you do? Have you experienced any negative effects associated with your cell phone usage? Are there some bad habits that you need to change? How will you go about making those changes?

SELECTION 9
Magazine Article

Why It's Really Possible to Fall in Love Online*

Brenna Ehrlich

In the following article, which first appeared as a special to CNN, the author explores the possibility of falling in love with a person without ever having met him or her face-to-face.

GETTING READY TO READ

PREVIEW IT

Preview the reading using the guidelines on page 6. When you have finished, complete the following items:

1. The topic of the selection is _____.

2. How does the author begin the article? _____.

_____ 3. _____

    a. research findings

    b. true stories

    c. links to dating sites

    d. expert opinions

LOOK IT UP

The Internet has many articles on online romantic relationships. Conduct a search and find an article that relates to the topic of this reading. Read and take notes on the article so that you can share the information with your discussion group.

DISCUSS IT

In a group with three or four of your classmates, discuss the major points of the articles that you and your group members read. Broaden your discussion to include the pros and cons of online romantic relationships you might have encountered in the readings. Be prepared to share the highlights of your discussion with the class.

---

*Ehrlich, Brenna. "Why It's Really Possible To Fall In Love Online." From CNN.com, 14 Feb © 2013 Turner Broadcast Systems. All rights reserved. Used by permission and protected by the Copyright Laws of the United States. The printing, copying, redistribution, or retransmission of this Content without express written permission is prohibited.

WRITE ABOUT IT

Connect the reading to your own experience by writing a paragraph about online romances. Consider the following questions as you write: Have you ever had an online romance? If so, how did it turn out? Do you know anyone who met his or her wife or husband online? What details do you know about that experience? Do you think you would ever be able to fall in love with someone you have never seen? Why or why not?

READmIT ▐▬▬▬▬▬▬▬▬▬▬▬▬▬▬▬▬▬▬▬▬▐

Read this article with an open mind, being careful to distinguish between facts and opinions. Also, pay special attention to the findings of the research studies cited by the author.

Highlighting and annotating the text as you read will prepare you to answer the detailed questions that follow the reading. Take a look at the questions before you begin reading so that you can understand the level of recall that is expected.

Why It's Really Possible to Fall in Love Online

Brenna Ehrlich

1   Jon's plane taxied to a gate at Los Angeles International Airport, and although he had been flying for 30 hours on a journey from South Asia to California, his heart pounded at the prospect of wrapping Katie, his fiancée-to-be, in a bear hug. In a week and a half, Jon would put his grandmother's diamond ring on Katie's finger and the ring would be woefully too big. The oversight was not due to thoughtlessness on his part, nor a mishap at the jeweler; Jon had never once held that hand in real life.

2   Katie, 24, is not a modern-day mail-order bride and Jon, 32, is not a moneyed lonely heart. The couple, who work as Christian missionaries and requested their last names not be published for security reasons, met online while she was in San Diego and he was on a mission in South Asia. Two months prior to their October 2011 meeting in Los Angeles, Katie had sent Jon an email, hoping to join his mission group. Jon, curious, had clicked through to her blog, which was replete with references to obscure devotional writers that he also admired. That initial contact led to months of emails and phone calls, costing Katie $600 in phone bills, culminating, at last, in their decision to meet in the flesh. Today the couple are happily married with a baby girl.

3   Their relationship may seem like an outlier at a time when the world is looking askance at online relationships. As we all learned, the Internet enabled Notre Dame football star Manti Te'o to fall for Lennay Kekua, a woman who does not exist. "Catfish," a popular MTV series based on a movie by the same name, captures audiences with tales of online love that quickly devolve into lies. And all over the Web, onlookers have been wondering: Is it possible to fall in love with someone you've never met?

A Fast Connection

4   Despite the current atmosphere of distrust, falling in love sight unseen, often through the written word, has been happening for centuries. The Web has only made it easier. Some experts say communicating online before meeting IRL (that's In Real Life) can actually foster strong relationships by helping those with similar interests come together over great distances. Potential lovers overlook superficial turnoffs, and people open up to each other faster and more deeply. "Online technology, as well as SMS [Short Messaging Service (text message)] enables having a connection that is faster and more direct," said Aaron Ben-Ze'ev, a philosophy professor at the University of Haifa and author of the book *Love Online: Emotions on The Internet*. "It also enables ongoing dialogue as compared to the slow interactions that are typical of letters." Translation: while it may have taken months to a year for couples to communicate and therefore grow closer in the past, today we can have lengthy, deep interactions with a stroke of a key (or touchscreen).

5   Grey Howe counts his relationship with his wife Michelle, both in their late 30s, as one of the earliest examples of online dating. "It was 1994, so there was not really an Internet as you know it today," he said. "We met through IRC." IRC refers to "Internet Relay Chat," a form of computer-based conversation that was developed in the late 1980s. "Internet Relay Chat, at the time, you had to know your stuff," Howe said. "So if you were on IRC, you were pretty much guaranteed to be talking to the smart people. And I lucked out; I talked to a smart woman." Grey talked with Michelle for about six months on the phone and via IRC before climbing on his motorcycle and driving from San Diego to Denver to see her in person for the first time. He never left. Thirteen years later, they got married, ironically enough for the technologically inclined couple, in an 1870s Victorian-themed ceremony.

6   Since Grey and Michelle's 1994 love connection, the prospect of online love has become more and more mainstream. A 2010 study found that nearly one-quarter of heterosexual couples surveyed had met via the Web, making the Internet the second-most-common way to find a partner after meeting through friends.

Someone Like You (Who's Like Me)

7   So what makes these digital relationships successful? According to a 2002 study, "Relationship Formation on the Internet: What's the Big Attraction?" one of the key draws of Internet relationships of all kinds is the ability to find people who like the same stuff that you do. This was the case for Amanda Goldstein Marks, 35, who met her future husband Aaron in 1999 via the Jewish dating site JDate. In the beginning, Amanda signed up for the site without any intention of going on dates; she only wanted to look at her cousin's pictures. But soon after putting up her profile, sans photos, she met Aaron, who was drawn to the mention of Jewish summer camp on her page. Amanda talked with Aaron for months, without seeing any pictures of him, before the couple finally met—like Jon and Katie, at an airport—when he returned from summer vacation to attend college. "I watched him walk off the plane, and I remember thinking, 'This is so weird because it's not weird.' It felt like I was meeting an old friend," she said.

8   A year later, by which point they were officially dating, the two discovered that their grandmothers had attended the same Jewish summer camp in Cleveland, Ohio, a strange coincidence considering Amanda grew up in Alabama and Aaron in New Mexico. "[Jewish summer camp] was important to us, and it was important to us because it was important to our parents, because it was important to our grandparents," said Amanda, who works at an ad agency. "So it kind of felt like my fate was sealed." While Amanda says that the two were not

officially dating during the months preceding their first meeting, and although she had never seen a picture of Aaron, she still says their connection was deep. "All I knew was that he was tall and had brown hair and blue eyes, so every guy I saw who kind of fit that description, I would look at him and I would say, 'If that were Aaron, would I still like him?'" said Amanda, who now lives with Aaron in Decatur, Georgia. "The answer was always yes."

Love Can Be Blind—Literally

9   Amanda's attraction to a man she had never seen before is not uncommon: studies have been done on this phenomenon for decades. One of the most famous is 1973's ominous sounding "Deviance in the Dark," in which interactions between students were observed in both pitch-dark and well-lit rooms. Those who met in the dark room, on the whole, were much more open and intimate with their fellow participants than those who met face-to-face under the fluorescents. In short, when you get rid of all the stress attached to face-to-face meetings, people feel more free to be themselves and get to know each other.

10   That approach worked for Keith A. Masterson, 41, and Gabriel-Thomas Masterson, 37. After meeting via a Facebook group comment chain, the couple spent hours daily chatting on Facebook and the phone before meeting two months later. The couple are now married and living in Colonial Heights, Virginia. "In our situation, (meeting online) gave me the opportunity to ask questions that I probably would not have asked face-to-face at that time," Keith said. Gabriel-Thomas agreed: "One of the reasons we moved so quickly was because we spent so much time on the phone talking."

11   Some research also suggests that chatting online first can have a beneficial effect on face-to-face relationships. In the "Relationship Formation on the Internet" study, the authors tested whether a group of students liked each other more after an online or in-person meeting. They found the online group was much more chummy, in part because of the quality of the digital interaction itself. In short, the Web allowed participants to pare away interpersonal distractions and focus on communicating openly and honestly.

12   Granted, there are some pitfalls with too much online interaction before meeting in person. Dr. Artemio Ramirez, Jr., associate professor of communications at the University of South Florida, has done his own research on the effects of online communications on offline relationships. "If you meet someone face-to-face shortly after you meet them online, it's not necessarily going to lead to someone having a positive relationship, but waiting longer increases the possibility that things are not going to work out," he said. "We tend to develop in our heads these impressions of what we think that person is like, even though the realities of communication do not reflect that."

13   Still, Ramirez says the effect of idealization can be mitigated by expanding a relationship beyond the bounds of the written word. "When people rely on more text-based forms of communication, that's where you really see people idealizing. When people in relationships can talk on the phone or via Skype, it's more of a reality check," he said. "Each new form of communication incrementally gives us more information about that person."

"Catfishing" Goes Mainstream

14   Of course, not all online love affairs pay off as well as those detailed above. Manti Te'o fell for a woman he was told died of cancer, a woman he had to say "goodbye" to twice after he found out she never existed. The Web is full of tricksters. One 2008 study found that 81% of online daters admitted to lying about their weight, height, age or a combination

of the three on their profiles. The Web allows users to present their best selves to the public, and sometimes those selves are exaggerated.

sifotography/123rf.com

Portrait of happy man sending love sms text message on mobile phone with red hearts flying away from screen isolated on grey wall background.

15 However, just because the object of one's online affections isn't real doesn't mean that one's feelings aren't. Nev Schulman, the protagonist in the 2010 documentary "Catfish," knows better than anyone about the heartbreak caused by falling for someone who doesn't exist. The movie details how he fell for a Michigan woman named Megan Faccio, who turned out to be an intricate fabrication created by a lonely wife and mother. The film, and the related TV series, has raised awareness of such hoaxes and even given the public a term with which to categorize them: "catfishing." "Once I kind of came to terms with the reality that this daily soap opera that I was tuning into and the long-distance love affair that I was having got canceled and everything sort of shut down, at first I was incredibly lonely," Schulman said.

16 "It's a double insult," said Dr. Michael Adamse, author of *Affairs of the Net: The Cybershrinks' Guide to Online Relationships*. "Because on one hand it's the loss of a love object. . . . There's also the humiliation attached to it, too, feeling badly about yourself. Not only have I lost somebody that was never really in love with me, but I've also been duped." Despite what happened to Schulman and the unlucky souls on his show who fell in love with mirages, both he and his "Catfish" co-host, Max Joseph, say that it is possible to fall in love successfully online. "Everyone, when they meet one of us, they want to tell us that they know people who have been in online relationships, and half the time the stories are really positive," Joseph said. "They have really happy endings." The trick, they said, is to be smart about your online love affair before getting in too deep.

To Have and to Hold

17 All the couples interviewed for this story have one integral thing in common: Each and every one of them eventually met in real life to solidify their relationship. "If you're really starting to 'fall' for somebody, it's very important to have that IRL to see if the fantasy matches the reality," said Adamse. "Not until you're actually in a situation where you're face-to-face with that person, spending time with that person, will you be able to access really what that reality is."

18 When Jon the missionary got off that plane in Los Angeles, after flying halfway around the world, he was moments away from finding out if his fantasy matched the woman waiting

for him, the one he described as "my heart in the form of a girl." The one he was so sure about that he had procured the (too big) ring and planned to put it on her finger in the presence of family and friends. "Everything struck me about her," he said years later, recalling that day when he stepped off the plane and into Katie's arms. "In all reality, the thing that attracted me the most about Katie all along was her heart, which was and is incredibly beautiful. But when I saw her in person I was able to see her inner beauty radiate through her eyes and her smile. I was a goner pretty quick."

UNDERSTANDING AND ANALYZING THE READING

A. BUILDING VOCABULARY

Context

Using context and a dictionary, if necessary, determine the meaning of each word as it is used in the selection.

_____ 1. askance (paragraph 3)
  a. with an attitude of approval
  b. with an attitude of optimism
  c. with an attitude of curiosity
  d. with an attitude of suspicion

_____ 2. pare (paragraph 11)
  a. send
  b. trim
  c. run
  d. explain

_____ 3. mitigated (paragraph 13)
  a. increased
  b. multiplied
  c. reduced
  d. developed

_____ 4. fabrication (paragraph 15)
  a. imagination
  b. model
  c. invention
  d. dream

_____ 5. mirages (paragraph 16)
  a. affairs
  b. realities
  c. destinies
  d. illusions

_____ 6. procured (paragraph 18)
  a. inherited
  b. borrowed
  c. saved
  d. obtained

Word Parts

A REVIEW OF PREFIXES AND SUFFIXES

DIS-	means *not*.
INTER-	means *between*.
-ION	means *action* or *process*.
-ANT	means *one who*.

Use your knowledge of word parts and the review above to fill in the blanks in the following sentences.

1. An atmosphere of *distrust* (paragraph 4) is one in which there is _____ trust.

2. Compared to the Internet, letters are slow *interactions* (paragraph 4) because they increase the time it takes for action to occur _____ senders and receivers.

3. Online technology makes *connection* (paragraph 4) or the process of _____ with others both faster and more direct.

4. The *participants* (paragraph 9) in the "Deviance in the Dark" study were the ones who _____ in the study by meeting either in a dark or a well-lit room.

B. UNDERSTANDING THE THESIS AND MAIN IDEAS

Select the best answer.

_____ 1. Which of the following best states the thesis or central thought of the reading?
   a. The odds are stacked against a successful online romance because real and lasting trust can only be established in a face-to-face relationship.
   b. People who fall in love successfully online attribute the success of their relationship to looking at the heart rather than the outward appearance of their mate.
   c. Given the right circumstances, it is possible for people to fall in love successfully online.
   d. Despite the success of some online relationships, most people are skeptical about the ability of people to fall in love with someone without ever seeing the person.

_____ 2. The topic of paragraph 14 is
   a. Manti Te'o's online love affair.
   b. how tricksters are attracted to the Web.
   c. the lack of censorship on the Web.
   d. personal misrepresentation on the Web.

_____ 3. The main idea of paragraph 16 is
   a. proceed with caution in an online relationship.
   b. learn from your past online relationship mistakes.
   c. avoid humiliation at all cost.
   d. have an open mind about the possibility of an online relationship.

_____ 4. What is the implied main idea of paragraph 4?

    a. Communication between two people with dissimilar interests is difficult at best.

    b. Communication is a key component of lasting relationships.

    c. Communication is easier when superficial distractions, like physical appearance, are eliminated.

    d. People are more likely to carry on extended conversations online because of the ease and speed of typing rather than talking.

C. INTERPRETING SUPPORTING DETAILS

Select the best answer.

_____ 1. According to the author, there are certain practices that increase the likelihood of two people falling in love successfully online. The author cites all of the following *except*

    a. communicating with more than text-based language.

    b. meeting face-to-face.

    c. shared interests.

    d. technological savvy.

_____ 2. The key type of evidence the author uses to support her main ideas and her thesis are

    a. television shows about online romances.

    b. books and advice columns on how to fall in love online.

    c. personal accounts of successful online love affairs.

    d. historical information on online dating.

_____ 3. According to the reading, all of the following factors contribute to an unrealistic impression of an online lover *except*

    a. refusing to allow the other person to see a picture of oneself.

    b. the tendency of some people to lie while hiding behind a screen.

    c. the tendency of people to create an ideal person in their mind while ignoring the realities that exist online.

    d. communicating with only typed words.

_____ 4. The author likely included the photo on page 424 in order to

    a. stress the importance of being able to pick up on the often-subtle signs that online users are lying.

    b. show the effects of heartbreak that can result from being duped in an online relationship.

c. help the reader understand the prevalence of catfishing.

d. stress the importance of proceeding with caution and wisdom in an online relationship.

D. RECOGNIZING METHODS OF ORGANIZATION AND TRANSITIONS

Select the best answer. See Chapter 7 for information on patterns of organization.

_____ 1. The pattern of organization used in paragraph 12 is

    a. classification.

    b. cause and effect.

    c. comparison and contrast.

    d. process.

_____ 2. The organizational pattern used in paragraphs 1 and 2 is

    a. illustration.

    b. classification

    c. definition.

    d. chronological order.

_____ 3. The transitional word or phrase that provides a clue to the organizational pattern used in paragraph 15 is

    a. *because.*

    b. *however.*

    c. *at first.*

    d. *that I was tuning into.*

E. FIGURING OUT IMPLIED MEANINGS

Indicate whether each statement is true (T) or false (F).

_____ 1. The author believes that true reality can only be assessed when two people meet in a face-to-face environment.

_____ 2. The author believes that most people who lie on the Web are doing so to make themselves look good.

_____ 3. The author implies that only smart people should have online relationships.

_____ 4. According to the author, although finding a partner online is becoming a more acceptable way in the public's eye, the most common way is still meeting someone through friends.

_____ 5. The author thinks that online couples who marry are at a greater risk of divorce than are those who meet and date in person.

F. THINKING CRITICALLY ABOUT THE READING

Select the best answer. See Chapter 9 for information about thinking critically about a reading.

_____ 1. The author's primary purpose in "Why It's Really Possible to Fall in Love Online" is to

    a. discuss the pitfalls of online romances.

    b. educate people about the successes and failures of online relationships.

    c. help people to understand the factors that contribute to a successful online love affair.

    d. expose people to the research surrounding online romances so that they can make a more-informed decision about how to go about finding a partner.

_____ 2. Overall, the author's tone in this selection can best be described as

    a. sarcastic.

    b. sympathetic.

    c. informative.

    d. persuasive.

_____ 3. Which of the following is a fact, not an opinion?

    a. "It was 1994, so there was not really an Internet as you know it today." (paragraph 5)

    b. "And I lucked out; I talked to a smart woman." (paragraph 5)

    c. "It felt like I was meeting an old friend." (paragraph 7)

    d. ". . . the thing that attracted me the most about Katie all along was her heart, which was and is incredibly beautiful." (paragraph 18)

_____ 4. In paragraph 2, the author notes that "Katie, 24, is not a modern-day mail-order bride and Jon, 32, is not a moneyed lonely heart." What does she mean?

    a. Katie was not necessarily looking for a man with money.

    b. Neither Katie or Jon were desperate souls looking for a mate.

    c. Although Jon was a missionary in South Asia, he had a support network that kept him from being lonely.

    d. Neither Katie nor Jon falsely represented themselves in the early days of their online relationship.

_____ 5. Based on what you have read in this article, what do you think a "catfish" is?

    a. a person who is less desirable than most but through deception tries to present himself or herself in a positive light

    b. a person who creates a fake identity and uses social media to lure someone into a romantic relationship

    c. a slippery, sneaky person, who takes the online "bait" that comes his way and gives nothing in return

    d. a "good catch"

_____ 6. In paragraph 15, Nev Schulman directly equates his online love affair with Megan Faccio to a daily soap opera. This comparison is an example of

    a. a rhetorical question.

    b. personification.

    c. a metaphor.

    d. a simile.

Answer the following open-ended questions in complete sentence format.

7. In a sentence or two, explain the irony of the wedding theme of Grey and Michelle. (paragraph 6)

8. How does the saying "love can be blind" relate to the practice of online dating and romance as presented in this reading selection?

9. Has the author provided sufficient evidence to support her main ideas? What other types of evidence might she provide to strengthen the reading?

10. If you had to choose another photo for the reading, what would it look like and what message would it convey?

WRITING IN RESPONSE TO THE READING

G. REVIEWING AND ORGANIZING IDEAS WITH A SUMMARY

Write a clear and concise summary of the section of the reading titled "'Catfishing' goes mainstream" (paragraphs 14–16). See page 31 for information about writing a summary.

H. ANALYZING THE ISSUE

1. What issues does the author bring up in this reading? List at least three.

2. The theme of this chapter is "relationships: our friends, families, and communities." Analyze the reading by addressing the following questions:

    a. What examples of relationships has the author provided?

    b. What did Jon learn about relationships? (paragraphs 1, 2, and 18)

    c. What did Amanda learn about relationships? (paragraphs 7 and 8)

    d. How is the relationship with friends addressed in the reading? How about the relationship with community?

3. Does the author present a balanced discussion of the pros and cons of online relationships? Explain your answer and include what, if any, information she should have included.

4. What are some misconceptions about online dating and online romance?

5. What assumptions about online dating and/or marriage does the author make?

I. WRITING PARAGRAPHS AND ESSAYS

Write a paragraph or an essay in response to the following writing prompts.

1. Write a paragraph detailing the first time you went out on a date with a particular person. How did you meet the person? What did you talk about on the date? Were you stressed out about your first meeting with this person? What were some of the stresses you felt? If you went on a second date, how was it different from the first one?

2. The tv series "Catfish" featured "unlucky souls who fell in love with mirages." Would you find a show like this entertaining? Do you think there is anything ethically wrong with a show like this? Write a paragraph in which you address these questions.

3. In a paragraph or essay, describe your ideal life partner. If you are already in a relationship with your ideal life partner, describe that person and the traits he or she embodies.

4. Write an essay in which you present both the pros and cons of online dating. Do not use any information from "Why It's Really Possible to Fall in Love Online." Instead, conduct an Internet search for articles that contain information that supports your major points. Be sure to properly document your sources.

5. Is love blind? Write an essay in which you either agree or disagree with this saying. Be sure to use examples from real life to support your thesis.

ACTIVITIES: EXPLORING RELATIONSHIPS

On your own or with a group of classmates, complete two of the following four activities.

1. Compile a list of ten people with whom you have a relationship. Then define your relationship. For example, is the relationship a close friendship? A casual romantic relationship? A classmate whom you like but probably won't stay in touch with after the term ends?

2. Take a poll among ten friends, acquaintances, co-workers, or classmates. How many of them have used a dating Web site to meet other people? How many met current or ex- boyfriends or girlfriends through social media like Facebook or Twitter? Write an essay or give a presentation to the class about their experiences. Overall, how do they think online dating compares to old-fashioned dating? Do they prefer one or the other, and why?

3. The three readings in this chapter address only a few of the issues surrounding relationships today. Some other often-discussed questions include the following:

   - Are "friends" on Facebook real friends? How do online friendships differ from offline friendships?

   - Are portable technologies, such as cell phones and smartphones, taking the place of personal relationships? What are the benefits and dangers of conducing relationships in the "virtual" world?

   - How are gender roles changing in the modern world, and how are these changes affecting relationships? (For example, more than ever before, women are acting as the main breadwinners in a relationship, while men stay home and care for the children.)

   - Should romantic relationships be prohibited in the workplace? Why or why not?

   Write an essay or prepare a class presentation about any of these topics, or any other relationship issue in which you are interested.

4. The readings in this chapter focused on different aspects of relationships: hooking up, "phubbing" and its effect on relationships, and falling in love online. One topic not discussed in detail is friendship. How exactly would you define a friend? Are there different types of friends for different situations? Write an essay about friendship, choosing the best organizational pattern to suit your purpose. For example, you might write a definition essay in which you define friendship, or you might write a classification essay in which you describe different types of friends.

MAKING CONNECTIONS: THINKING WITHIN THE ISSUES

In many college courses, instructors will expect you to read and evaluate a wide variety of materials. This activity is designed to provide practice in synthesizing or pulling together ideas from a variety of sources.

1. Both "Are You 'Phubbing' Right Now?" (Selection 8, p. 432) and "Why It's Really Possible to Fall in Love Online" (Selection 9, p. 443) examine human interactions and technology. How has technology positively and negatively impacted our interaction with other people? Do you think people retreat to their phones/computers and prefer virtual communities because they perceive online relationships as somehow "easier" or less stressful than in-person relationships? Consider these questions as you write a one-page reflection on virtual communities and the effects of technology on relationships.

2. The English poet John Donne wrote a famous poem titled "No Man Is an Island." The beginning of the poem appeared at the beginning of this chapter:

   > No man is an island,
   > Entire of itself.
   > Each is a piece of the continent,
   > A part of the main.

   Write an essay in which you explain the meaning of this poem as it relates to each of the reading selections in this chapter: "Hooking Up" (Selection 7, p. 421), "Are You 'Phubbing' Right Now?" (Selection 8, p. 432), and "Why It's Really Possible to Fall in Love Online" (Selection 9, p. 443).

 Medical Ethics: Where Do We Draw the Line?

How many of the things you use in your daily life were available five or ten years ago?

If you want to see progress, just look around you. Science lies at the heart of most medical advances, along with advances in technology, communications, and many other fields. At the heart of science is the *experimental method*, which offers a specific structure to help scientists formulate theories and test them. In the past, research was a long-term process. Today, ultrafast computers help scientists test their theories much more quickly. Science and technology have produced rapid medical developments, some of which are controversial.

In fact, medicine itself is controversial. Consider the following questions, which are often debated:

- Does a doctor have the right to stop seeing a patient who repeatedly fails to comply with the his or her orders?

- Should a person be allowed to buy an organ for transplant (as opposed to waiting an indefinite amount of time on a transplant list) in order to expedite the process?

- What role do a person's religious beliefs play in the type of medical care he or she can receive? For instance, some religions will not allow people to accept a blood transfusion.

These are all complicated questions. Medicine may be able to provide solutions, but it almost always encounters questions of ethics at the same time. *Ethics* are moral principles. They guide people's behavior by telling them what is right and what is wrong. But ethical codes can come into conflict.

The readings in this chapter look at just a few of the many medical/ethical issues facing society today. How do people and societies attempt to reconcile medicine with ethics? For example, how does the fertility industry work, and does it take advantage of desperate couples and underprivileged young women? Does a person with an incurable disease have a right to take his/her own life? Do health care providers have an ethical responsibility to care for their clients' needs even when they conflict with state laws or the needs and wishes of families or employers?

WHY IS MEDICAL ETHICS SUCH AN IMPORTANT CONTEMPORARY ISSUE?

A society tries to establish a basic moral code that most people can agree on. For example, in almost all societies, most people agree that murder is wrong. But on many other issues, there is a wide range of beliefs that are formed by a person's family background, age, religious affiliation, and other factors. Understanding these multiple perspectives helps the larger society agree on what is allowed and what isn't—what is lawful and what is unlawful. All of these decisions are the results of many decades of debate and argument. Ultimately, the question becomes where do we draw the line between what is right and what is wrong?

How Do Medicine and Ethics Tie in to My College Experience?

At one level, the honor code on your campus is an ethical system—it clearly states the rules regarding campus behavior, plagiarism, cheating, individual responsibility, and other aspects of campus life. In individual courses, though, you will learn about the ethics of medical research and examine whether experiments are ethical or unethical. Psychology and sociology courses are filled with examples of famous studies that would be considered unethical today. Business courses discuss the ethical issues that companies face (you may have heard about controversies in the pharmaceutical industry involving severe price hikes on medications). Thinking about ethical issues expands your critical-thinking abilities and gets you considering a wide variety of topics in depth.

TIPS FOR READING ABOUT MEDICINE AND ETHICS

Here are some tips for reading not only the selections in this chapter but any reading about medical science and ethics.

- **Carefully distinguish between facts and opinions.** Ethical codes are often based on personal opinions and experiences. As you read, check to see whether any opinions are stated as facts.

- **Look for bias in the selection.** Many articles concerning medical ethics have an agenda. For example, the written results of a new drug's effectiveness may be very different depending on whether the report was written by the drug company or by a neutral researcher.

- **Weigh the process against the results.** In scientific/medical readings, the assumption is sometimes made that "the ends justify the means." In other words, some people argue that (for example) it would be quite acceptable to perform gruesome experiments on monkeys if those experiments led to a cure for cancer. Ask yourself whether this assumption underlies what you are reading, and whether you agree with it or not.

SELECTION 10
Personal Essay

Eggs for Sale

M. A. Garcia

The following personal essay was written for a college composition course at Moorpark College in California. To protect her privacy, the author has chosen to use a *pseudonym*, or false name. Read "Eggs for Sale" to learn about one young woman's experiences serving as an egg donor for couples who are unable to have children of their own.

GETTING READY TO READ

PREVIEW IT

Preview the reading using the guidelines on page 6. When you have finished, complete the following items:

1. This reading is about a woman who sells her ＿＿＿ and discovers that she has given an infertile couple the best possible gift.

2. The screening process consisted of a psychological examination, a ＿＿＿＿＿＿ ＿＿＿＿＿＿, and a legal consultation.

LOOK IT UP

M. A. Garcia sold her eggs to give an infertile couple a chance to have a child. Before you read her story, spend some time on the Internet researching the issue of egg donation and the pros and cons associated with the issue. Take notes on your findings so that you can share with your discussion group.

DISCUSS IT

In a group with three or four of your classmates, discuss the findings of your research on the issue of egg donation. Broaden your discussion to include the ethical ramifications of egg donation and other infertility treatments you may know about. Be prepared to share the highlights of your discussion with the class.

WRITE ABOUT IT

Connect the reading to your own experience by writing a paragraph about any couples you know who are trying to have children. What other options are available to people who cannot conceive children of their own? You may also reflect on how you would feel if you or one of your family members or friends were the one who had made the decision to donate her eggs.

READIT

As you read the essay, trace the narrator's/author's state of mind. How does she feel at the beginning of the process? How does she feel at the end of the process? How did donating her eggs change her outlook on life?

Also, highlight and annotate the text as you read so that you can answer the detailed questions that follow the reading. Take a look at these questions before reading so that you can understand the level of recall that is expected.

Eggs for Sale

M. A. Garcia

1   Two months later, the long-awaited day was finally here. The night before I had self-administered what fertility doctors call a trigger shot, and I was told to shower and not use any products on my hair or skin. This moment was the reason I had been injected with what seemed like hundreds of needles. I was going to be put under and cut open, and my eggs were going to be aspirated as though they had a little sign that read, "Fertile Eggs for Sale." I clearly remember the last ten minutes before I underwent the procedure. I lay in a cold operating room, staring at the brightly lit ceiling. I had goose bumps all over my body, and I wasn't sure if it was because of how cold I was or simply because reality was in full effect. My emotions started running all over the place. Immediately I felt a sense of satisfaction and knew that I had made the correct decision in donating my eggs to an infertile couple. In about nine months, if everything went as planned, there would be a start of a child's life. As the anesthesiologist depressed the syringe into my IV, a last thought jumped into my head right before I was knocked out. I was giving this couple something I had never given anyone before: "the gift of life." This day was a turning point in my life because after going through an extensive and thorough screening, a painful stimulating egg production cycle, and the actual egg retrieval procedure, I learned to value life and fertility for everything they are worth. This newfound feeling of giving for a lifetime of happiness was the culmination of my current journey through egg donation.

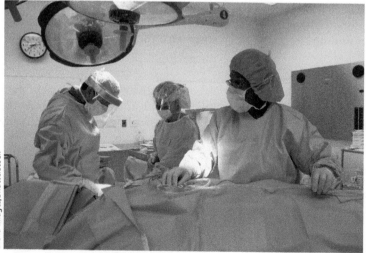

Blend Images/Shutterstock

2   When I first decided to fill out a donor application at Donor Source, I did it in hopes that I would get picked only because of the monetary compensation. After I filled it out, it was

processed and approved within a week. I then created an online profile where infertile couples could select a donor based on their particular needs. Only two weeks had gone by when I received a call from Donor Source. They told me a couple in Phoenix, Arizona, was interested in purchasing my eggs and wanted to immediately start the screening process. I hadn't hung the phone up and I was already thinking of things to do with the money I was getting. Everything happened so quickly; I agreed to becoming a donor as easily as I would have agreed to my sister borrowing my shoes.

3   The screening process consisted of a psychological and medical examination and a legal consultation. During my psychological screening I remember thinking what would happen if the psychologist found out that at this point I was only interested in the money and couldn't care less where my eggs went. In fear of rejection I lied and told her I had always considered egg donation. I definitely didn't tell her I already had a list of things I wanted to buy but had never thought about what it actually meant to donate my eggs. Even after I cleared the psychological screening and moved onto medical screening, my mind was still focused on the materialistic aspect of things. The medical screening was quick. I went in, had blood drawn, and underwent an **ultrasound probe**. The probe was used to look at my ovaries, uterus, and other pelvic organs. Once the doctors determined I was 100% disease-free and healthy, I received a phone call from the agency's lawyer. During this two-hour conversation he went into detail about my legal rights and my responsibilities. In thinking back, this is one of those moments that made this process seem so real and life-changing for me. I felt like at this point nothing was going to be as easy as I thought. I couldn't just hand over my eggs to this couple and pretend they were never a part of me. And I couldn't pretend it never happened because I had just agreed to be contacted in case the child had an illness in which either my organs or blood would help him or her live. I also agreed that if after his or her eighteenth birthday the child wanted to know who I was, he or she was allowed to contact me. This no longer was something I could brush off. I thought about how I would react if years from now a young man or woman knocked on my door. Would he be thankful? Upset? Or tell me he had a crappy life? This made me ask myself if what I was doing was the right thing for all parties, not just myself. I didn't have an answer, and all I did was hope that the intended parents would give their soon-to-be child a life full of love and happiness.

4   After the consultation with the lawyer, I was constantly asking, "What if?" What if the parents are awful? What if the child gets cancer? What if? What if? At this time, I was also put on birth control in order to synchronize my menstrual cycle with the intending mother's. At this point, I knew what I was doing, but I had not come to terms with reality. Reality slowly started seeping in the day I came home from work and saw a large FedEx box sitting right at my door. I stared at the box for a couple minutes. I knew what was inside because the nurses had previously told me, and the mailing address indicated the package had come from a fertility clinic. What I didn't know was how real everything was going to be once I opened it and how my life for the next two months was all put into this single box. This box contained a large number of needles, vials, and what looked like a chunky blue pen. I carefully inspected each and found out the chunky pen was actually a Follistim pen and the vials contained Follistim (follicle stimulating hormone). The vials also held Lupron (used to suppress the pituitary gland and prevent premature ovulation) and HCG (used to induce final maturation of the eggs). It was here that I knew there was no turning back.

5   All of these medications were going to be used to activate my ovaries, to get them to create multiple eggs in a single cycle. The first medication I used was the Follistim. For my

ultrasound probe a medical device that uses sound waves to perform a medical examination

first application I got everything ready, and I thought I was going to do it quickly and be over with it, but I was wrong. I sat in front of the mirror for an hour and realized injecting myself wasn't going to be easy. I watched several videos on YouTube before I got over my fear and finally just did it. After a couple of days, this procedure became routine, but it didn't stop it from being uncomfortable. Little bruises formed around the injection sites, and my stomach would sting if I went near or on top of a previous site. During this time I also paid multiple visits to a monitoring clinic to make sure the Follistim was working. The clinic reviewed my progress by withdrawing what seemed like quarts and quarts of blood. It got to the point where I couldn't go out in public wearing a short-sleeve shirt because I looked like a heroin addict with bruised arms and needle trails everywhere. The pain and discomfort from the blood work are what made me question if this was worth it. At times I hated it and wanted it all to end, and other times I felt good about what I was doing, but I never was 100% sure of what I felt. So I was relieved when the doctor told me the next visit was going to be my last in California. On my last visit to the clinic, the doctor verified everything was going as planned and authorized me to fly to Phoenix.

6   The day I flew into Phoenix I went straight to the fertility clinic at which the retrieval would be performed. The nurse told me step by step what was going to happen that week. I didn't take much into consideration because by this time the Follistim made me feel tired, moody, and hungry. All I wanted was to go to my hotel room and sleep. In Phoenix I was scheduled to get blood work daily. During this time the fertility clinic wanted to make sure it estimated the time correctly to retrieve my eggs at their most fertile state.

7   On the fourth day of going through this routine, I was ordered to take the trigger shot. I had seen the needle before, but I guess I never paid attention to the size because I was in shock when I picked it up. This needle was almost as thick as a toothpick. I found myself feeling the same way I did when I first attempted to inject the Follistim. I did not want to inject myself with this toothpick, so I sat on the hotel bed thinking of 101 ways to avoid it. But there was no avoiding it; this was something I had to do. I didn't come this far along to give up now. This was literally the step before the last, and I felt guilty for even thinking about not doing it. A couple was counting on me, and I couldn't let them down, so I finally summoned enough guts to inject myself. This shot sent a message to my ovaries to begin ovulation, which was needed for the retrieval to be successful.

8   The egg retrieval process took about 25 minutes, if that. The worst pain I felt through this process was when the nurse inserted an IV in my wrist so that the anesthesia could be administered; funny how I had to feel pain in order not to feel pain during surgery. I remember feeling cold, and I started realizing that I was 100% certain that this was all worth it. I was sure of what I was doing, and I couldn't be any happier. It had been weeks and weeks since I had given the monetary compensation thought. I was content and can't remember another time in my life when I felt better about myself. From the eggs they were retrieving, a new life would be born, and that life was going to give an infertile couple a chance that without me they would've never had—to be parents. I thought about how many of us don't value life or even the fact that we are fertile. And before I knew it I was asleep.

9   While I was pain-free and sedated, the doctors performed the ultrasound aspiration. They attached a tube to the ultrasound probe, and using that they guided a suctioning needle to remove mature eggs from each of my ovaries. The actual procedure I do not remember at all. I woke up still sleepy and crampy, and my stomach was beyond bloated. But none of this mattered because I felt like I had experienced a wake-up call. At the beginning of the

process, I did not expect to feel this way, and all I cared about was how I was going to be compensated. But throughout the process I came to understand that my eggs aren't just eggs and that from them a living and breathing being would result, and that is the best compensation of all. Egg donation has made me appreciate and value everything in life, life itself, and fertility more now than I ever have before.

UNDERSTANDING AND ANALYZING THE READING

A. BUILDING VOCABULARY

Context

Using context and a dictionary, if necessary, determine the meaning of each word as it is used in the selection.

_____ 1. extensive (paragraph 1)
  a. painful
  b. medical
  c. comprehensive
  d. inexpensive

_____ 2. culmination (paragraph 1)
  a. climax
  b. beginning
  c. middle
  d. temptation

_____ 3. compensation (paragraph 2)
  a. commitment
  b. answer
  c. payment
  d. option

_____ 4. materialistic (paragraph 3)
  a. related to material
  b. related to acquiring things
  c. related to fabric
  d. related to being a mother

_____ 5. seeping (paragraph 4)
  a. hitting
  b. oozing
  c. breaking
  d. cracking

_____ 6. vials (paragraph 4)
  a. small containers
  b. arguments
  c. syringes
  d. writing implements

Word Parts

A REVIEW OF PREFIXES AND SUFFIXES

IN-	means *not.*
-OR	means *one who.*

Use your knowledge of word parts and the review above to fill in the blanks in the following sentences.

1. A woman who is *infertile* (paragraph 1) is _____ fertile. That is, she is unable to conceive a child.

2. A *donor* (paragraph 2) is one who gives or _____.

B. UNDERSTANDING THE THESIS AND MAIN IDEAS

Select the best answer.

_____ 1. The best statement of the thesis or central thought of "Eggs for Sale" is

    a. Egg donation is only available to women who are in excellent physical and emotional health.

    b. While the author first chose to be an egg donor for the money, she came to see it as the most rewarding experience of her life.

    c. Those who donate eggs need to prepare themselves for all the emotional and physical hardship that the process will put them through.

    d. There are many reasons that women cannot conceive a child, and for these women, receiving a donated egg is the best possible way of coping with that situation.

_____ 2. The topic of paragraph 3 is

    a. the reasons for donating eggs to infertile couples.

    b. the unreasonable demands made on the author by Donor Source.

    c. the psychological, medical, and legal screening process for potential egg donors.

    d. the author's serious concerns about the child who might someday contact her.

_____ 3. The main idea of paragraph 9 can be found in the

    a. first sentence.

    b. second sentence.

    c. sixth sentence.

    d. last sentence.

C. INTERPRETING SUPPORTING DETAILS

Select the best answer.

_____ 1. To support her thesis, the author uses primarily
   a. her personal experiences.
   b. quotations from experts.
   c. references from medical journals.
   d. statistics about fertility.

_____ 2. What is the "trigger shot" to which the author refers?
   a. the shot of hormones that will synchronize the author's menstrual cycle with that of the woman to whom she is donating her eggs
   b. the final hormone shot before she undergoes a medical procedure to remove the eggs from her body
   c. the genetic-defect screening injection that will identify possible birth defects that might result from her eggs
   d. the moment at which she legally signs over her eggs to Donor Source

_____ 3. In paragraph 8, the author says, "funny how I had to feel pain in order not to feel pain during surgery." By "funny how I had to feel pain," the author is referring to
   a. the IV for anesthesia.
   b. emotional pain.
   c. the Follistim injections.
   d. the clinic's uncaring attitude toward her.

_____ 4. In paragraph 2, the author says, "I agreed to becoming a donor as easily as I would have agreed to my sister borrowing my shoes." What is she trying to communicate by using this comparison?
   a. She made the decision hesitantly wondering if she would get anything in return.
   b. She made the decision confidently because it was the right thing to do.
   c. She made the decision easily because she considered it to be insignificant.
   d. She made the decision quickly and easily because she had little time to think about it.

D. RECOGNIZING METHODS OF ORGANIZATION AND TRANSITIONS

Select the best answer. See Chapter 7 for information on patterns of organization.

_____ 1. The *overall* primary pattern of organization used in "Eggs for Sale" is
   a. classification.
   b. process.
   c. order of importance.
   d. comparison and contrast.

_____ 2. A minor pattern of organization in the essay contrasts which two elements?
   a. the author's life and the lives of adopted children
   b. the experiences of infertile men and infertile women
   c. the author's feelings before egg donation and after egg donation
   d. the experience of being on drugs and the experience of being drug free

_____ 3. In paragraph 4, the type of punctuation that is used to indicate the definition of Follistim is
   a. parentheses.
   b. semicolon.
   c. comma.
   d. dash.

_____ 4. The transitional word or phrase in paragraphs 6–8 that provides a clue regarding the reading's overall organizational pattern is
   a. *step by step* (paragraph 6).
   b. *consideration* (paragraph 6).
   c. *counting on me* (paragraph 7).
   d. *I remember* (paragraph 8).

E. FIGURING OUT IMPLIED MEANINGS

Indicate whether each statement is true (T) or false (F).

_____ 1. If the author had not been completely healthy and free of diseases, she would likely have been rejected as an egg donor.

_____ 2. The author sees egg donation as primarily a financial transaction that will help young women support themselves and pay their bills.

_____ 3. Donor Source matches potential eggs donors with infertile couples who wish to purchase eggs.

_____ 4. The author finds the blood work and internal examinations she must undergo to be quite uncomfortable.

F. THINKING CRITICALLY ABOUT THE READING

Select the best answer. See Chapter 9 for information about thinking critically about a reading.

_____ 1. The author's overall purpose in "Eggs for Sale" is to
   a. lobby the government for better legal oversight of the egg donation process and the possible problems that can result.
   b. advertise her willingness to serve as a surrogate mother for childless couples.
   c. describe the effects of fertility drugs on a woman's body and mind.
   d. explain how her feelings about egg donation changed after she became an egg donor.

_____ 2. The overall tone of *most* of the selection can best be described as
   a. angry.
   b. uncertain.
   c. ashamed.
   d. weak.

_____ 3. The tone of paragraph 9 is best described as
   a. greedy.
   b. cynical.
   c. proud.
   d. guilty.

_____ 4. Throughout the emotional journey of making the decision to donate her eggs and then actually donating them, the author feels all of the following *except*
   a. materialistic.
   b. reluctant.
   c. depressed.
   d. appreciative of life.

_____ 5. Which piece of advice do you think the author would be *most* likely to give young women?

a. "Don't donate your eggs. The money is not worth the time, the pain, and the hassle."

b. "Before you donate eggs, make sure you have very carefully investigated the people who will be buying them."

c. "The decision to donate your eggs may seem easy, but it's actually very emotionally complicated and ultimately very rewarding."

d. "The best way to get in touch with yourself, and to determine what kind of mother you will be, is to go through the process of egg donation, which really makes you think about your attitude toward children."

_____ 6. What does the photo of the operating room contribute to the reading?

a. It raises questions about the safety of egg donation.

b. It emphasizes the serious nature of egg donation.

c. It raises the issue of the legality of egg donation.

d. It illustrates the emotional aspects of egg donation.

Answer the following open-ended questions in complete sentence format.

7. If you were asked to provide another visual for this reading, what would it look like? What message would it convey?

8. How does the title relate to the story? Does the title have a positive or negative connotation? Suggest another title that would capture the essence of the story.

9. Identify at least three issues presented in the reading. Then phrase each issue as a question that the author raises, discusses, or answers.

10. Do you find any evidence of bias in the reading? Explain.

WRITING IN RESPONSE TO THE READING

G. REVIEWING AND ORGANIZING IDEAS WITH A PARAPHRASE

Complete the following paraphrase of paragraph 5. Begin your paraphrase with the following sentence.

M. A. Garcia writes about one of the medicines she took during the process of egg donation.

_____

_____

_____

_____

_____

_____

_____

_____

_____

_____

_____

_____

_____

For paragraph 6, write your own two sentence paraphrase.

_____

_____

_____

_____

H. ANALYZING THE ISSUE

Discuss in class or write in your journal a response to the following questions.

1. The theme of this chapter is "medical ethics: where do we draw the line?" Analyze the reading by addressing the following questions:

    a. What is the ethical issue or issues presented in this reading?

    b. How did the ethics of the issue impact the author's decision?

    c. Do you think ethical considerations account for the author's decision to use a pseudonym rather than her real name?

    d. Are there emotional components of this issue that prevent some people from thinking rationally about the issue? If so, what are the emotional components?

    e. For those who consider this issue to be unethical, what is the basis for their belief?

2. What stated or implied value system do you find in the selection?

3. Has the author provided sufficient evidence to support her main ideas? What other types of evidence might she provide to further support her main ideas?

4. Does the source from which the reading is taken help you determine the credibility of the information presented? Please explain your answer. What is the author's background? Is she qualified to write about the topic? Why or why not?

5. What audience do you think the author is addressing? Use evidence from the reading to support your answer.

I. WRITING PARAGRAPHS AND ESSAYS

Write a paragraph or essay in response to the following writing prompts.

1. The title of this essay is provocative. Write an essay in which you examine or dissect the title. Do you think the title reflects the author's state of mind more at the beginning of the process, or more at the end of the process?

2. The author talks about the pain of the injections she had to give herself. Write a paragraph in which you describe the worst physical pain you ever felt. What caused it?

3. "Eggs for Sale" might be considered the "pro" side of the question "Should women donate their eggs to infertile couples?" Write an essay in which you explore the "con" side, offering several reasons why donating eggs might not be a good idea.

4. This reading focuses on one avenue that infertile couples can pursue to bring a child into their lives. Write an essay in which you explore several other options they might pursue, including some of the pros and cons of each.

5. Suppose you are part of an infertile couple. How would you feel about purchasing eggs from a donor? Are you comfortable with the idea? Do you have reservations—and if so, what are they? How does your background influence your thinking on this subject? Write an essay in which you explore your position on the subject.

SELECTION 11
Web Article

Why the Right to Die Movement Needed Brittany Maynard

Keisha Ray

The author of this reading, Keisha Ray, holds a Ph.D. with a specialty in bio-ethics, specifically the ethical and socially just uses of biotechnology. She has written on a variety of topics in the bioethics field for *Bioethics.net*. This partic-ular article appeared as a blog on *Bioethics.net*.

GETTING READY TO READ

PREVIEW IT

Preview the reading using the guidelines on page 6. When you have finished, complete the following items:

1. This reading is about the _____ movement.

2. List three topics you expect the author to discuss in the reading.

   a. _____

   b. _____

   c. _____

LOOK IT UP

Brittany Maynard chose to end her own life and die with dignity before brain cancer robbed her of her life. Before you read this selection, spend some time on the Internet researching Maynard's story, the right to die movement, and those who oppose the movement and their reasons for doing so. Take notes on your findings so that you can share with your discussion group.

DISCUSS IT

In a group with three or four of your classmates, discuss the findings of your research on the issue of a terminally ill person's right to die. Broaden your dis-cussion to include various cases you may have discovered during your research and also the views of those who oppose the right to die movement. Be prepared to share the highlights of your discussion with the class.

WRITE ABOUT IT

Connect the reading to your own experience by writing a paragraph about "death with dignity." What does the phrase mean to you? What are your feelings about euthanasia? Do you know what the laws are in your state concerning assisted suicide? Think about how you would vote on the issue if your state proposed a "death with dignity" law.

READ IT

As you read the selection, highlight the author's main points in support of her argument and notice how she responds to opposing ideas. Also, annotate the text so that you can answer the detailed questions that follow the reading. Take a look at these questions before reading so that you can understand the level of recall that is expected.

Why the Right to Die Movement Needed Brittany Maynard

Keisha Ray

1   Brittany Maynard was diagnosed with brain cancer. At the age of 29, she decided to end her own life and "die with dignity" under Oregon's "Death with Dignity Act." There have been many articles written in support of Maynard's choice and many articles written condemning her choice to die. The right to die movement has many hurdles that it must overcome to draw in more supporters and hopefully influence public policy. Some of those hurdles include misconceptions about the kinds of people that want to end their lives and why people who have been diagnosed with terminal illness want to have the choice to take their own lives. To anyone who was watching and willing to consider her point of view, Maynard gave the right to die movement a significant push by dispelling some strong misconceptions.

Choice

2   In life many choices are not our own, but how we live our life is our choice. Maynard did not choose to have cancer invade her brain, but she did choose how to live her life after her diagnosis. After her diagnosis, Maynard continued to engage in the activities that had always made her life fulfilling—traveling, volunteering, and spending time with family and friends. Maynard made an informed choice to not let brain cancer kill her. She made the decision to choose how her life ends. And that's one of the major aims of the right to die movement—that terminally ill patients ought to be able to choose how long they live with their disease and whether their disease will be the cause of their death. Disease takes away so many choices and puts people at the mercy of doctors and nurses. Most importantly, it puts people at the mercy of their failing body. The right to die movement aims to take some of that power back.

3   Some opponents of the right to die movement believe that no one should choose to die. But for people in situations like Maynard's, the decision to die was made for her—by her disease. Rather than let her disease make the decision for her, she exercised the ultimate act of **autonomy** and made the decision for herself. If Maynard had let the disease kill her, she would have been relinquishing the reins of her life over to her brain cancer.

autonomy freedom to act or function independently

4   Of course, since the right to die movement is concerned with autonomy, one could express one's autonomy by choosing to live and let the disease take one's life. This is not incompatible with the right to die movement as individuals like Nadin Naumann would lead us to believe. In an article that she wrote, Naumann stated, "My mom has the same brain cancer diagnosis as Brittany Maynard; she's fighting to live." In Naumann's condemnation of Maynard's decision to die, she tells the story of her mother who has the same brain cancer as Maynard but is choosing not to **euthanize** herself. After recalling the praise that Maynard received for "dying with dignity," Naumann states, "but what about people like my mom? How about the individual who chooses to fight knowing all the consequences that he or she could face?" What Naumann fails to mention is that the right to die movement does not aim to force all terminally ill people to kill themselves; rather, they believe that the choice to end their life should be a right that all terminally ill people should possess. The point is that the choice should be ours: to live with the disease and fight a noble fight, or to die before the disease kills us and have a noble death.

euthanize put a living being to death humanely

Lack of Caregivers

5   There is also a misconception that people who want to end their lives want to do so because they don't have anyone to care for them while their health declines. The image of a lonely, dying person is one that opponents of the right to die movement frequently call upon. The right to die movement needed Maynard because she showed us that this is not always the case. Maynard was surrounded by family—a husband, parents, brothers, and her husband's parents. We can assume that her family would have been willing to care for her based on their active presence in her life before and after her diagnosis. Giving us an image of a loving, caring family that stands behind their loved one's choice, whatever it may be, was needed to dispel misconceptions about the kinds of people who choose to end their lives.

Fear of Death

6   Individuals who want to end their life have often been accused of fearing death. For example, in regard to Maynard's choice to die, one article states that she feared death, which led her to a mistaken decision: "But taking one's life out of fear of what life might bring is, at the very least, to be regretted. It was an understandable decision, but it was also the wrong decision. A case of cutting off your face to spite your nose."

Brittany Maynard's mother holds a picture of Maynard.

Rich Pedroncelli/AP Images

7   Fear of death is understandable. But what this article and others miss when they accuse terminally ill people of fearing death is the great courage needed to end one's own life. It's hard to imagine a person fearing death yet taking steps that she knows will end with her own death. Choosing to end one's life is not a fear of death but a fear of the life you have left lacking such quality that it's not a life that you recognize or a life that you want, but are being forced to live.

8   People who are terminally ill are forced to face their mortality in ways that those who are not terminally ill are not forced to face it. We all know we are going to die one day, but the terminally ill are given a time frame for when they are going to die. They are told that they have a very limited amount of time before their disease will kill them. I imagine that would scare some people. It would certainly scare me. But making the decision to end one's life has to be one of the greatest acts of facing that fear, and I imagine not many people would be able to overcome this kind of fear.

hypoallergenic having little likelihood of causing an allergic response

9   When I think of a fear of death, I imagine a person living in a **hypoallergenic** bubble, who sits at home afraid of life. I certainly don't imagine someone like Maynard who chose to live out her last days by living life to the fullest, doing those things that she always loved to do. I certainly don't think of someone who chooses to end her life on her own terms, which is an image the right to die movement so desperately needed to dispel misconceptions about why terminally ill people choose to die.

Youth and Beauty

10   In our appearance driven society, movements need youth and beauty to be the face of their cause to get people to pay attention. This is why celebrities are often the face of health and social justice movements (e.g., Angelina Jolie for child hunger and poverty, Emma Watson for feminism, and the list goes on and on). Brittany Maynard was articulate, intelligent, and college educated. But Maynard was also young and beautiful. She was not the first to euthanize herself using right to die laws, but the media was drawn to her and her story. To be clear, I'm not discrediting Maynard's story. But the right to die movement needed a young and beautiful person who wanted to exercise her choice to end her life to show that it is not just the very old who want the right to die.

11   Opponents of the right to die movement often used age and beauty against Maynard, making statements like "But she's so beautiful, why would she want to die?" Although misguided, even people who made these kinds of statements were drawn to Maynard's story, and you can't sway the opinions of people who aren't paying attention. Unfortunately, sometimes this is what a movement needs to gain more momentum, and unfortunately, sometimes people only listen to the story if the person telling the story is aesthetically appealing.

12   The right to die movement needed Brittany Maynard to show others the true goals of the movement—being able to choose how we live and die and embracing our mortality, evidenced by making the choice to die. The right to die movement does not aim to euthanize every terminally ill patient. Its aim is to give people more power over their lives than their disease has.

UNDERSTANDING AND ANALYZING THE READING

A. BUILDING VOCABULARY

Context

Using context and a dictionary, if necessary, determine the meaning of each word as it is used in the selection.

_____ 1. misconceptions (paragraph 1)
    a. misfortunes
    b. misrepresentations
    c. misappropriations
    d. misunderstandings

_____ 4. condemnation (paragraph 4)
    a. firm denial
    b. whole-hearted support
    c. strong disapproval
    d. loyal devotion

_____ 2. relinquishing (paragraph 3)
    a. possessing
    b. granting
    c. surrendering
    d. replacing

_____ 5. misguided (paragraph 11)
    a. confused
    b. mistaken
    c. condemned
    d. unsure

_____ 3. incompatible (paragraph 4)
    a. inconsistent with
    b. unable to be defended
    c. unable to agree upon
    d. unable to commit to

_____ 6. aesthetically (paragraph 11)
    a. pertaining to youthfulness
    b. pertaining to a sense of beauty
    c. pertaining to an illness
    d. pertaining to pleasure

Word Parts

A REVIEW OF PREFIXES, ROOTS, AND SUFFIXES	
DIS-	means *not*.
MORT	means *death*.
CRED	means *believe*.
-ITY	means *state* or *quality*.

Use your knowledge of word parts and the review above to fill in the blanks in the following sentences.

1. Facing our *mortality* (paragraph 8) means accepting the idea that, as living beings, we are subject to _____.

2. A person who is *discrediting* (paragraph 10) a story is indicating that he or she does not _____ it.

B. UNDERSTANDING THE THESIS AND MAIN IDEAS

Select the best answer.

_____ 1. The thesis or central thought of this reading can be found in
   a. paragraph 1.
   b. paragraph 3.
   c. paragraph 5.
   d. paragraph 10.

_____ 2. The topic of paragraphs 2–4 is
   a. choosing to fight a terminal illness.
   b. being diagnosed with a disease.
   c. having the choice to live or die.
   d. dispelling misconceptions about the right to die movement.

_____ 3. Which of the following is the best statement of the implied main
   idea of paragraph 5?
   a. People who want to end their lives don't have anyone to care for
      them while their health declines.
   b. Those who oppose the right to die movement often promote
      the image of a lonely, dying person with no caregivers.
   c. Brittany Maynard's family seemed willing to care for her because
      they were involved in her life before and after her diagnosis.
   d. Brittany Maynard was important to the right to die movement
      because she provided an image of someone whose family
      supported her decision to die.

_____ 4. The topic of paragraph 8 is
   a. choosing to fight a terminal illness.
   b. facing the fear of imminent death.
   c. the inevitability of death.
   d. how the terminally ill are different from healthy people.

C. INTERPRETING SUPPORTING DETAILS

Select the best answer.

_____ 1. Which of the following details from the reading is *not* true?
   a. After Brittany Maynard was diagnosed with brain cancer, she
      traveled and spent time with her family and friends.
   b. Maynard chose to end her life at the age of 29.

    c. The right to die law in Oregon is called the "Death with Dignity Act."

    d. Maynard was the first person to euthanize herself using right to die laws.

_____ 2. The purpose of Nadin Naumann's article was to describe her mother's

    a. choice to fight brain cancer.

    b. strong support of right to die laws.

    c. friendship with Brittany Maynard.

    d. fear of death.

_____ 3. The author mentions Angelina Jolie and Emma Watson because these are celebrities who have

    a. spoken out in favor of the right to die movement.

    b. provided an attractive image for health and social justice movements.

    c. played terminally ill characters in movies.

    d. publicly supported "death with dignity" legislation in California.

_____ 4. Brittany Maynard had all of the following *except*

    a. a living will.

    b. brain cancer.

    c. a supportive family.

    d. youth and beauty.

D. RECOGNIZING METHODS OF ORGANIZATION AND TRANSITIONS

Select the best answer. See Chapter 7 for information on patterns of organization.

_____ 1. The organizational pattern used in paragraph 2 is

    a. chronological order.

    b. spatial order.

    c. process.

    d. definition.

_____ 2. In paragraph 4, Nadin Naumann makes a contrast between

    a. different types of brain cancer diagnoses.

    b. euthanasia and "dying with dignity."

    c. her mother's decision to fight and Maynard's decision to die.

    d. public policy in Oregon and in other states.

_____ 3. In paragraph 10, the phrase *This is why* suggests the author will present a(n)

    a. contrast.

    b. example.

    c. cause.

    d. reason.

E. FIGURING OUT IMPLIED MEANINGS

Indicate whether each statement is true (T) or false (F).

_____ 1. The author believes that Brittany Maynard was helpful in advancing the right to die movement.

_____ 2. The author believes that the right to die movement allows people the choice of living with a disease or dying before the disease kills them.

_____ 3. The author believes most terminally ill people should choose to end their life.

_____ 4. The author believes that it takes great courage to choose to end one's life.

_____ 5. The author disapproves of using youth and beauty to get people to pay attention to social movements.

F. THINKING CRITICALLY ABOUT THE READING

Select the best answer. See Chapter 9 for information about thinking critically about a reading.

_____ 1. The author's purpose in writing "Why the Right to Die Movement Needed Brittany Maynard" is to

    a. criticize opponents of the right to die movement for not understanding the facts about euthanasia.

    b. urge readers to demand the enactment of "death with dignity" legislation in their own states.

    c. explain how Brittany Maynard was able to dispel misunderstandings about the right to die movement.

    d. compare right to die laws in the United States with those in Europe and elsewhere around the world.

_____ 2. The tone of the reading can best be described as

    a. objective.

    b. earnest.

    c. pessimistic.

    d. skeptical.

_____ 3. The author supports her main ideas with all of the following *except*

    a. research studies.

    b. direct quotations.

    c. facts.

    d. opinions.

_____ 4. Which of the following excerpts from the reading is a fact?

    a. "At the age of 29, she decided to end her own life . . . under Oregon's 'Death with Dignity Act.'" (paragraph 1)

    b. "We can assume that her family would have been willing to care for her based on their active presence in her life before and after her diagnosis." (paragraph 5)

    c. "But making the decision to end one's life has to be one of the greatest acts of facing that fear, and I imagine not many people would be able to overcome this kind of fear." (paragraph 8)

    d. "I certainly don't think of someone who chooses to end her life on her own terms, which is an image the right to die movement so desperately needed to dispel misconceptions about why terminally ill people choose to die." (paragraph 9)

_____ 5. When referring to Brittany Maynard's wish to die with dignity, opponents of the right to die movement made statements like "but she's so beautiful, why would she want to die?" (paragraph 11). This question can be characterized as

    a. sensitive.

    b. illogical.

    c. complimentary.

    d. demeaning.

_____ 6. Suppose you were asked to choose an additional visual for this reading that would support the author's thesis. Which of the following visuals would you choose?

    a. an anatomically correct picture of a diseased brain

    b. a group of people demonstrating and holding signs at a right to die rally

    c. a grieving family at a funeral

    d. a beautiful but sickly young woman

Answer the following open ended questions in complete sentence format.

7. What does the author mean when she says, "you can't sway the opinions of people who aren't paying attention" (paragraph 11)?

8. One opponent of the right to die movement referred to taking one's life out of fear of the future as "a case of cutting off your face to spite your nose" (paragraph 6). This is a reversal of a commonly used expression. What do you think the author meant?

9. Is the author qualified to write on the topic? Why or why not? How do her own experiences inform the article?

10. What audience is the author writing for? Do you think she persuaded anyone who disagreed with her claim? Why or why not?

WRITING IN RESPONSE TO THE READING

G. REVIEWING AND ORGANIZING IDEAS WITH A MAP

Create a conceptual map of the reading selection. See page 28 for information about mapping.

H. ANALYZING THE ISSUE AND THE ARGUMENT

Discuss in class or write in your journal a response to the following questions. Evaluate the reading on the following criteria:

1. Identify at least three issues presented in this reading. Then phrase each issue as a question that the author raises, discusses, or answers.

2. The theme of this chapter is "medical ethics: where do we draw the line?" Analyze the reading by addressing the following questions:
   a. What is the basis for the belief of some people that it is ethically and morally right for a terminally ill person to end his/her own life?
   b. What is the basis for the belief of some people that it is ethically and morally wrong for a terminally ill person to end his or her own life?
   c. How do you think the scientific community views euthanasia?
   d. What part did science play in Maynard's decision to end her life?
   e. Ethically, should anyone have the right to criticize Maynard's decision? Explain your answer.

3. Has the author provided sufficient evidence to support her argument? What types of evidence has she provided? What other types of evidence might she provide to strengthen her main ideas?

4. Does the author offer alternative viewpoints on any topics? If so, which topics and which viewpoints does she discuss? Does she present other viewpoints neutrally or fairly, or do you detect any bias? How effectively does she refute other viewpoints?

5. Does the reading offer any emotional appeals? If so, identify them and evaluate their fairness.

I. WRITING PARAGRAPHS AND ESSAYS

Write a paragraph or essay in response to the following writing prompts.

1. Write a paragraph summarizing each of the author's main points regarding Brittany Maynard's effect on the right to die movement.

2. How would you describe the author's feelings toward Brittany Maynard? Write a paragraph explaining how you think the author feels and why. Try to find examples of language from the reading that help reveal the author's feelings.

3. What does the author mean when she says people with disease are "at the mercy of doctors and nurses" (paragraph 2)? How important is it for people to have a sense of power over their own fate, especially when they are ill? Consider a time when you felt you were "at the mercy" of someone else. How did you respond? Write an essay exploring these questions.

4. Consider the author's argument that people should have the choice "to live with the disease and fight a noble fight, or to die before the disease kills us and have a noble death" (paragraph 4). Why does the author use the word "noble" to describe each option? Which choice do you think you would make? Have you known anyone who made either of those choices? Write an essay explaining your answers.

5. Write an essay giving your response to the article. If you agree that Brittany Maynard helped dispel misconceptions in the right to die movement, explain what aspects of the author's argument were most persuasive. If you disagree, write a refutation in which you address each aspect of the author's argument.

Ethical Issues in Medicine

Audrey Berman, Shirlee J. Snyder, and Geralyn Frandsen

This reading was taken from a textbook entitled Kozier & Erb's *Fundamentals of Nursing*. Written for nursing students, this text focuses on the concepts, process, and practice of effective professional nursing.

GETTING READY TO READ

PREVIEW IT

Preview the reading using the guidelines on page 6. When you have finished, complete the following items:

1. This reading is about _____ ethics.

2. The medical profession that is the focus of this reading is _____.

3. List three ethical issues you expect the authors to discuss in the reading.

   a. _____

   b. _____

   c. _____

LOOK IT UP

A real-life scenario appears on the next page (just before the reading selection) describing an ethical dilemma that Alex Wubbels faced as a charge nurse at the University of Utah Hospital. Before you read the selection, take some time to research this dilemma on the Internet. Search for information on William Gray, the patient; Alex Wubbels, the nurse; and the resulting fallout from her decision. Take notes on your findings so that you can share with your discussion group.

DISCUSS IT

In a group with three or four of your classmates, discuss the findings of your research on the medical ethics issue involving the charge nurse at the University of Utah Hospital. If time permits, broaden your discussion to explore other ethical issues that nurses might face while carrying out their professional duties.

WRITE ABOUT IT

Connect the reading to your own experience by writing a paragraph about your understanding of ethics. Consider the following questions: What does the word ethics mean to you? How do you determine what is ethically right or wrong? How do you go about making an ethical decision? What are some ethical decisions you have had to make in your day-to-day living?

READ IT

This textbook selection relates to a specific medical profession, and as such, it may contain some unfamiliar vocabulary. While reading the selection, pay special attention to the bold words, which are often defined within the context of the sentence in which they appear. If there is no definition for an unfamiliar word, try to determine its meaning from context. If you get stuck on a particular word, check the meaning in a dictionary before you continue.

As you read the selection, highlight and annotate the text so that you can answer the detailed questions that follow the reading. Take a look at these questions before reading so that you can understand the level of recall that is expected.

Below is a scenario that will help you tune in to the difficult role medical practitioners face on a daily basis. The reading that follows explores a variety of issues related to medical ethics.

On July 26, 2017, William Gray, a truck driver and part-time Idaho police reserve officer, lay unconscious in the burn unit at the University of Utah Hospital as a result of a vehicle crash. Alex Wubbels was the charge nurse at the hospital that day when a police detective requested that blood be drawn from Gray to determine whether Gray had illicit substances in his blood at the time of the crash. Wubbels explained to the detective that, according to the hospital's policy, the police needed a warrant or consent from the patient or had to put the patient under arrest before she could allow a blood draw. Video footage from police officers' body cameras showed that after Wubbels refused to draw blood based on hospital policy, she was forcibly handcuffed and shoved into a patrol car while she screamed, "Help! Help! Somebody help me! Stop! Stop! I did nothing wrong!"

While Wubbles was not charged, news reports indicated that she was in the patrol car for about 20 minutes. In a statement after the incident, Wubbles said, "The only job I have as a nurse is to keep my patients safe. A blood draw just gets thrown around like it's some simple thing. But blood is your blood, that's your property."

Several months after the incident, Wubbels reached an agreement with Salt Lake City and the University of Utah which resulted in her receiving a settlement of $500,000.

Ethical Issues in Medicine

Audrey Berman, Shirlee J. Snyder, and Geralyn Frandsen

1   Because of their unique position in the health care system, nurses experience conflicts among their loyalties and obligations to clients, families, primary care providers, employing institutions, and licensing bodies. Client needs may conflict with institutional policies, primary care provider preferences, needs of the client's family, or even laws of the state. According to the nursing code of ethics, the nurse's first loyalty is to the client. However, it is not always easy to determine which action best serves the client's needs. For instance, the nurse may be aware that marijuana has been shown to be effective for a condition a client has that has not responded to mainstream therapies. Although legal issues are involved, the nurse must determine if ethically the client should be made aware of a potentially effective alternative. Another example is individual nurses' decisions regarding honoring picket lines during employee strikes. The nurse may experience conflict among feeling the need to support coworkers in their efforts to improve working conditions, feeling the need to ensure clients receive care and are not abandoned, and feeling loyalty to the hospital employer.

Strategies to Enhance Ethical Decisions and Practice

2   Several strategies help nurses overcome possible organizational and social constraints that may hinder the ethical practice of nursing and create moral distress for nurses, such as:

- Become aware of your own values and the ethical aspects of nursing.
- Be familiar with the nursing codes of ethics.
- Seek continuing education opportunities to stay knowledgeable about ethical issues in nursing.
- Respect the values, opinions, and responsibilities of other health care professionals that may be different from your own.
- Participate in or establish ethics rounds. Ethics rounds use hypothetical or real cases that focus on the ethical dimensions of client care rather than the client's clinical diagnosis and treatment.
- Serve on institutional ethics committees.
- Strive for collaborative practice in which nurses function effectively in cooperation with other health care professionals.

Specific Ethical Issues

3   Some of the ethical problems nurses encounter most frequently are issues in the care of clients with HIV/AIDS, abortion, organ or tissue transplantation, end-of-life decisions, cost-containment issues that jeopardize client welfare and access to health care (resource allocation), and breaches of client confidentiality (e.g., computerized information management).

stockbroker/123rf

Acquired Immunodeficiency Syndrome (AIDS)

4   Because of its association with sexual behavior, illicit drug use, and physical decline and death, AIDS bears a social stigma. According to an ANA position statement, the moral obligation to care for a client with HIV infection cannot be set aside unless the risk exceeds the responsibility (ANA, 2006).

5   Other ethical issues center on testing for HIV status and the presence of AIDS in health professionals and clients. Questions arise as to whether testing of all providers and clients should be mandatory or voluntary and whether test results should be released to insurance companies, sexual partners, or caregivers. As with all ethical dilemmas, each possibility has both positive and negative implications for specific individuals.

Abortion

6   Abortion is a highly publicized issue about which many people feel very strongly. Debate continues, pitting the principle of sanctity of life against the principle of autonomy and a woman's right to control her own body. This is an especially volatile issue because no public consensus has yet been reached.

7   Most state laws have provisions known as conscience clauses that permit individual primary care providers and nurses, as well as institutions, to refuse to assist with an abortion if doing so violates their religious or moral principles. However, nurses have no right to impose their values on a client. Nursing codes of ethics support clients' rights to information and counseling in making decisions.

Organ and Tissue Transplantation

8   Organs or tissue for transplantation may come from living donors or from donors who have just died. Many living people choose to become donors by giving consent under the Uniform Anatomical Gift Act. Ethical issues related to organ transplantation include allocation of organs, selling of body parts, involvement of children as potential donors, consent, clear definition of death, and conflicts of interest between potential donors and recipients. In some situations, a person's religious belief may also present conflict. For example, certain religions forbid the mutilation of the body, even for the benefit of another person.

9   Individuals' spiritual beliefs and views on when human life begins have an impact on their opinions about stem cell research. The ANA (2007) supports the ethical use of stem cells for research and therapeutic purposes that impact health. This position is slightly different from a previous position statement regarding cloning (exact duplication of cells or organisms). Stem cell research is the foundation for cell-based therapies in which stem cells are induced to differentiate into the specific cell type required to repair damaged or destroyed cells or tissues. Both embryonic and adult cells are used in this research. Embryonic cells are derived from a five-day preimplantation embryo. Adult cells are undifferentiated cells found in differentiated tissue.

End-of-Life Issues

10   The increase in technologic advances and the growing number of older adults have expanded ethical dilemmas. Providing information and professional assistance, as well as the highest quality of care and caring, is of the utmost importance during the end-of-life

period. Some of the most frequent disturbing ethical problems for nurses involve issues that arise around death and dying. These include euthanasia, assisted suicide, termination of life-sustaining treatment, and withdrawing or withholding of food and fluids.

11   **Advance Directives.** Many moral problems surrounding the end of life can be resolved if clients complete advance directives. Presently, all 50 of the United States have enacted advance directive legislation. Advance directives direct caregivers as to the client's wishes about treatments, providing an ongoing voice for clients when they have lost the capacity to make or communicate their decisions.

12   *Euthanasia,* a Greek word meaning "good death," is popularly known as "mercy killing." **Active euthanasia** involves actions to bring about the client's death directly, with or without client consent. An example of this would be the administration of a lethal medication to end the client's suffering. Regardless of the caregiver's intent, active euthanasia is forbidden by law and can result in criminal charges of murder.

13   **Assisted suicide.** A variation of active euthanasia is **assisted suicide**, or giving clients the means to kill themselves if they request it (e.g., providing lethal doses of pills). Some countries or states have laws permitting assisted suicide for clients who are severely ill, who are near death, and who wish to commit suicide. Although some people may disagree with the concept, assisted suicide is currently legal in the states of Montana, Oregon, Vermont, and Washington and several countries. In any case, the nurse should recall that legality and morality are not the same thing. Determining whether an action is legal is only one aspect of deciding whether it is ethical. The questions of suicide and assisted suicide are still controversial in Western society. The ANA's position statement on assisted suicide and active euthanasia (2013) states that both active euthanasia and assisted suicide are in violation of the *Code of Ethics for Nurses.*

14   **Passive euthanasia,** more commonly referred to now as withdrawing or withholding life-sustaining therapy (WWLST), involves the withdrawal of extraordinary means of life support, such as removing a ventilator or withholding special attempts to revive a client (e.g., giving the client "no code" status) and allowing the client to die of the underlying medical condition. WWLST may be both legally and ethically more acceptable to most people than assisted suicide.

15   **Termination of Life-Sustaining Treatment.** Antibiotics, organ transplants, and technologic advances (e.g., ventilators) help to prolong life, but not necessarily to restore health. Clients may specify that they wish to have life-sustaining measures withdrawn, they may have advance directives on this matter, or they may appoint a surrogate decision maker. However, it is usually more troubling for health care professionals to withdraw a treatment than to decide initially not to begin it. Nurses must understand that a decision to withdraw treatment is not a decision to withdraw care. Nurses must ensure that sensitive care and comfort measures are given as the client's illness progresses. When the client is at home, nurses often provide this type of education and support through hospice services. It is difficult for families to withdraw treatment, which makes it very important that they fully understand the treatment. They often have misunderstandings about which treatments are life sustaining. Keeping clients and families well informed is an ongoing process, allowing them time to ask questions and discuss the situation. It is also essential that they understand that they can reevaluate and change their decision if they wish.

16   **Withdrawing or Withholding Foods and Fluids.** It is generally accepted that providing food and fluids is part of ordinary nursing practice and, therefore, a moral duty. However, when food and fluids are administered by tube to a dying client, or are given over a long period to an unconscious client who is not expected to improve, then some consider it to be an extraordinary, or heroic, measure. A nurse is morally obligated to withhold food and fluids (or any treatment) if it is determined to be more harmful to administer them than to withhold them. The nurse must also honor competent and informed clients' refusal of food and fluids. The ANA *Code of Ethics for Nurses* (2010) supports this position through the nurse's role as a client advocate and through the moral principle of autonomy. However, the debate on ethical, legal, personal, and religious grounds continues—especially as it relates to the care of children who are unable to speak for themselves. In addition, client views on the acceptability of these actions vary according to culture (Preedy, 2011).

Allocation of Scarce Health Resources

17   Allocation of limited supplies of health care goods and services, including organ transplants, artificial joints, and the services of specialists, has become an especially urgent issue as medical costs continue to rise and more stringent cost-containment measures are implemented. The moral principle of autonomy cannot be applied if it is not possible to give each client what he or she chooses. In this situation, health care providers may use the principle of justice—attempting to choose what is most fair to all. Nursing care is also a health resource. Most institutions have been implementing "workplace redesign" to cut costs. Some nurses are concerned that staffing in their institutions is not adequate to give the level of care they value. California is the first state to enact legislation mandating specific nurse-to-client ratios in hospitals and other health care settings. With a nationwide shortage of nurses, an ethical dilemma arises when, in order to provide adequate staffing, facilities must turn away needy clients. Nurses must continue to look for ways to balance economics and caring in the allocation of health resources.

Management of Personal and Health Information

18   In keeping with the principle of autonomy, nurses are obligated to respect clients' privacy and confidentiality. Privacy is both a legal and ethical mandate. The Health Insurance Portability and Accountability Act of 1996 (HIPAA) includes standards protecting the confidentiality, integrity, and availability of data, and standards defining appropriate disclosures of identifiable health information and client rights protection. Clients must be able to trust that nurses will reveal details of their situations only as appropriate and will communicate only the information necessary to provide for their health care. Computerized client records make sensitive data accessible to more people and accent issues of confidentiality. Nurses should help develop and follow security measures and policies to ensure appropriate use of client data.

UNDERSTANDING AND ANALYZING THE READING

A. BUILDING VOCABULARY

Context

Using context and a dictionary, if necessary, determine the meaning of each word as it is used in the selection.

_____ 1. constraints (paragraph 2)
   a. limitations
   b. laws
   c. values
   d. strongholds

_____ 2. collaborative (paragraph 2)
   a. competitive
   b. independent
   c. joint
   d. beneficial

_____ 3. illicit (paragraph 4)
   a. illegal
   b. immoral
   c. unnecessary
   d. unsafe

_____ 4. volatile (paragraph 6)
   a. negotiable
   b. troublesome
   c. explosive
   d. questionable

_____ 5. allocation (paragraphs 8 and 17)
   a. preservation
   b. distribution
   c. donation
   d. evaluation

_____ 6. surrogate (paragraph 15)
   a. substitute
   b. related
   c. legal
   d. possible

Word Parts

A REVIEW OF PREFIXES AND ROOTS
UN-   means *not*.
BENE   means *good* or *well*.
CIDE   means *to kill*.

Use your knowledge of word parts and the review above to fill in the blanks in the following sentences.

1. A practice that exists for the *benefit* of others (paragraph 8) is one that produces a _____ effect for others.

2. *Suicide* (paragraph 10) is the _____ of oneself.

3. An *unconscious* client (paragraph 16) is one who is _____ conscious.

B. UNDERSTANDING THE THESIS AND MAIN IDEAS

Select the best answer.

_____ 1. Which of the following is the best statement of the selection's thesis or central thought?

     a. Medical ethics is the study of the values that doctors and nurses place on the treatment of their patients.

     b. The range of problems that nurses encounter requires that they weigh many competing factors when making ethical decisions about the treatment and welfare of their clients.

     c. Nurses must keep their focus on patient care and put aside all personal feelings in order to make rational decisions about difficult ethical issues involving treatment and standards of care.

     d. Although nurses are on the front line of duty when it comes to patient care, they do not usually act alone when making ethical decisions regarding serious, life-threatening illnesses and end-of-life issues.

_____ 2. What is the implied main idea of paragraph 17?

     a. Institutional policies have contributed to the shortage of nurses in our country.

     b. Nurses would like a voice at the table when staffing cuts are proposed.

     c. Nurses have serious concerns about caring for the needy.

     d. When medical institutions have to cut costs, patient care often suffers.

_____ 3. The topic of paragraph 1 is

     a. the priority of client loyalty.

     b. conflicting loyalties and obligations.

     c. conflicts created by legal issues.

     d. the ethical ramifications of employee strikes.

C. INTERPRETING SUPPORTING DETAILS

Answer each of the following questions.

_____ 1. One characteristic of all ethical dilemmas is

     a. they have legal ramifications for the decision makers.

     b. they require an ethics committee to rule on the decision.

     c. they have positive and negative implications for the individuals involved.

     d. they have data that can be reviewed as part of the decision-making process.

_____ 2. Which of the following is *not* a source of moral distress for nurses?

    a. a conflict that exists between the charge nurse and his or her team of nurses

    b. a conflict between the nurse's personal beliefs and what is best for the patient

    c. a conflict between doing what family members want for their loved one and what is best for the patient

    d. a conflict between doing what is lawful and doing what is in a patient's best interest

_____ 3. All of the following types of ethical issues have a legislative component *except*

    a. advance directives.

    b. organ donation.

    c. withdrawing treatment that sustains life.

    d. active euthanasia.

_____ 4. Of the following types of evidence, which one do the authors *not* use for support in paragraph 13?

    a. examples

    b. academic research

    c. information from experts or authorities

    d. facts

D. RECOGNIZING METHODS OF ORGANIZATION AND TRANSITIONS

Select the best answer. See Chapter 7 for information on patterns of organization.

_____ 1. The organizational pattern of paragraph 2 is

    a. comparison and contrast.

    b. cause and effect.

    c. classification.

    d. process.

_____ 2. The organizational pattern used in paragraphs 10–16 is

    a. cause and effect.

    b. classification.

    c. definition.

    d. illustration.

_____ 3. The transitional word or phrase used to signal the organizational pattern of paragraph 13 is

    a. *a variation of.*

    b. *although.*

    c. *in any case.*

    d. *only one aspect.*

E. FIGURING OUT IMPLIED MEANINGS

Indicate whether each statement is true (T) or false (F).

_____ 1. The ethical questions surrounding medical practices have clear-cut answers.

_____ 2. The authors imply that injustice still exists in the area of access to health care.

_____ 3. When making an ethical decision, input from others adds confusion to the problem and hampers the decision-making process.

_____ 4. Advances in medical treatment have actually created new ethical issues in medicine.

_____ 5. The best training for making ethical decisions in the practice of medicine is on-the-job training.

F. THINKING CRITICALLY ABOUT THE READING

Select the best answer. See Chapter 9 for information about thinking critically about a reading.

_____ 1. The authors' approach to the topic of ethics in medicine can best be described as

    a. skeptical.

    b. impassioned.

    c. uninformed.

    d. objective.

_____ 2. The authors' purpose in writing this selection is to

    a. educate nurses on the conflicts they may encounter when making ethical decisions about patient care and explain specific ethical issues that they may encounter in their line of work.

    b. warn nurses of the religious, cultural, and legal constraints that may create moral distress for them.

   c. build support for justice in the allocation of health resources.

   d. instruct nurses on how to provide quality patient care in an environment in which they encounter new ethical issues almost daily.

_____ 3. Which of the following is *not* a stated or unstated assumption made within the reading?

   a. All patients have the right to voice their wishes about the medical care they desire to receive.

   b. Although making ethical decisions about patient care is a difficult process, there are steps that nurses can take to better equip themselves for the task.

   c. Due to the number of difficult ethical decisions that nurses have to make, it is critical that they have adequate insurance to protect them from suits.

   d. As the lifespan of people increases, so do ethical issues associated with aging.

_____ 4. The principle of autonomy can be applied to all of the following issues *except*

   a. abortion.

   b. advance directives.

   c. withholding nourishment.

   d. allocation of limited resources.

_____ 5. Which of the following actions does a conscience clause permit in the case of abortion?

   a. a refusal by medical personnel to participate in the procedure

   b. an offer of personal advice to the patient

   c. an explanation to the patient of the religious issues surrounding the procedure

   d. an offer of counseling to the patient for before and after the procedure

Answer the following open-ended questions in complete sentence format.

6. What is *moral distress*, and why are nurses susceptible to it?

7. In paragraph 1, the authors mention that "client needs may conflict with institutional policies, primary care provider preferences, needs of the client's family, or even laws of the state." Explain which of these conflicts came into play with Alex Wubbels. What were the immediate needs of the client and to whom was Nurse Wubbels loyal?

8. How does the photo included with this reading illustrate the theme? If you had to choose a photo for the reading, what would it look like and what message would it convey?

WRITING IN RESPONSE TO THE READING

G. REVIEWING AND ORGANIZING IDEAS WITH A SUMMARY

Write a clear and concise summary of the section of the reading titled "End-of-Life Issues" (paragraphs 10–16). See page 31 for information about writing a summary.

H. ANALYZING THE ISSUE

1. The theme of this chapter is "medical ethics: where do we draw the line?" Name three contemporary issues being discussed in this article and explain where you would draw the line for each of the issues.

2. Evaluate the reading using the following criteria:
   a. Is this reading timely? If not, what parts are not?
   b. What audience are the authors writing for? What makes you think this?
   c. Are the terms used in the article carefully defined and explained?
   d. Is ample and relevant evidence provided to support the thesis or central thought? Give examples to support your answer. What other types of evidence could be used to support the selection's main ideas?
   e. Does the source from which the reading is taken help you to determine the credibility of the information presented? Please explain your answer.

I. WRITING PARAGRAPHS AND ESSAYS

Write a paragraph or essay in response to the following writing prompts.

1. In a paragraph, write a description of an ethical dilemma you have faced in your life and explain how you resolved the dilemma.

2. This reading does not have a concluding paragraph. Write a concluding paragraph that effectively sums up the main points and supports the thesis.

3. Put yourself in the place of Alex Wubbels, the charge nurse at the University of Utah Hospital described in the READ IT section that precedes the reading. In a paragraph, record your thoughts about Wubbel's decision. Do you think it was the right or wrong decision for her to make? On what grounds do you base your opinion? Was the police response warranted? Why or why not? What are your thoughts regarding the settlement? What would you have done if you had been put in a similar situation?

4. In paragraph 8, the authors mention the ethical issue of children as potential donors of organs and tissues for transplantation. After researching the topic and thinking through the issue, write an essay in which you take a stand either for or against children as donors. You may use the results of your research as support. Be sure to provide specific details and examples.

5. Write an essay in which you answer this question: what is assisted suicide, and is it ethical? You may research this topic and use the results of your research in your writing. Be sure to provide specific details and examples to support your position.

ACTIVITIES: EXPLORING MEDICINE AND ETHICS

On your own or with a group of classmates, complete two of the following four activities.

1. Many companies and scientists advertise on the radio for volunteers to take part in experiments, often to test new drugs. Participants receive the drug for free, and they are usually paid for their time and participation. In an essay or as part of a group discussion, come up with a list of rules for conducting this type of experiment ethically. What should the researchers do? What should they *not* do?

2. Brittany Maynard's decision to end her life herself rather than letting cancer end it received a lot of publicity and stirred the emotions of many people. There were those who wholeheartedly supported her right to die while others adamantly opposed it. Research both sides of this issue and prepare a debate that highlights the main points of the two arguments.

3. The three readings in this chapter only scratch the surface of the many ethical issues facing doctors and nurses today. Other hotly debated questions include the following:

    - When an organ is donated, who should receive it? There are long waiting lists for all organs, and never enough organs available for transplant.

    - Do doctors "play God" when they help infertile couples become pregnant through the use of scientific technologies?

    - Is it ethical to prolong the life of someone who is brain-dead? Who gets to make the decisions regarding whether a person should continue living or not?

    Write an essay or prepare a class presentation about any of these topics, or any other medical ethics issue in which you are interested.

4. In 1961, a Yale researcher named Stanley Milgram conducted what has become a famous experiment regarding obedience to authority. The results of the study are somewhat disturbing, but also disturbing are the ethical issues raised by the way the study was conducted. Conduct research into the "Milgram experiment," outline its results, and explain the ethical issues involved in it.

MAKING CONNECTIONS: THINKING WITHIN THE ISSUES

In many college courses, instructors will expect you to read and evaluate a wide variety of materials. This activity is designed to provide practice in synthesizing or pulling together ideas from a variety of sources.

1. "Eggs for Sale" (Selection 10, p. 459) and "Why the Right to Die Movement Needed Brittany Maynard" (Selection 11, p. 457) both focus on ethical decisions regarding life and the human body. The reading selections focus on the benefits of donating eggs to an infertile couple and ending one's life before the ravages of cancer destroy it, but arguments can be made against such activities. Thinking critically about the issues, list at least three arguments against transplanting eggs and exercising one's right to die.

2. On the surface, the ethical issues in "Eggs for Sale" (Selection 10, p. 459) seem to be similar to the "Ethical Issues in Medicine" section on "Organ and Tissue Transplantation" (Selection 12, p. 482), but there are differences between the two. Carefully consider the ethical questions surrounding these two issues and write an essay that compares and contrasts the issues and the arguments.

15 Personal Safety and Security: Threats and Protection

Are you safe? Are you sure?

We live in an ever-changing world. One of the biggest changes in the past several decades has been the growing threat to our personal safety and security. The threat takes several forms. Many people no longer feel physically safe in a shopping mall, in a classroom, in an office, or even just walking down the street. Numerous tragic events, including school shootings, have changed the lives of many people. Further, we can no longer feel secure using technology, and in particular, computers. Personal identity theft, security of medical records, genetic profiling, and facial recognition technology are issues that loom large to many. Surveillance, too, threatens personal safety and security, as technology makes it easier for individuals, corporations, and agencies to watch and monitor the activities of private citizens.

The readings in this chapter explore three aspects of personal safety and security: physical safety, surveillance, and technology. Each reading in this chapter focuses on at least one aspect of personal safety and security.

WHY ARE SAFETY AND SECURITY SUCH IMPORTANT CONTEMPORARY ISSUES?

Safety and security are important issues because they affect many aspects of our daily existence. Efforts to curb threats to our security can limit our personal freedoms, present economic consequences, and raise sensitive and controversial moral, political, and ethical questions, including, for example, gun control.

How Does the Concept of Safety and Security Tie in to My College Courses?

Safety and security are underlying themes running through many college courses. In a sociology course, for example, you might study how groups respond to threating situations. Literature often focuses on the perception of self in the face of adversity. In history and government courses, you will study the widespread effects of the 9/11 terrorist attack, seen by many as the beginning of a new era. Criminal justice courses consider means and strategies for keeping citizens safe, given the threat of technological criminal activity.

TIPS FOR READING ABOUT PERSONAL SAFETY AND SECURITY

Here are some tips for reading not only the selections in this chapter, but any reading about personal safety and security.

- **Consider the author's background and experience.** Check the first section before each reading to learn more about the author. Doing so may give you a perspective on his or her viewpoints. (Outside this text, search online for any biographical information provided about the author.)

- **Keep an open mind.** Some of these readings may challenge your ideas or preconceptions about a topic. You may have an emotional response because some of the readings discuss difficult topics like government surveillance or mass shootings. Once you have experienced the emotion, reread the article more objectively, with a more critical eye, to better analyze and evaluate the author's thesis.

- **Compare the author's perception of threats to those you have read about, observed, or experienced.** As you read, ask yourself whether the author's perceptions match yours. Do your opinions match the author's? Why or why not? What evidence does the author offer to support his or her opinions? Is that evidence relevant and sufficient?

SELECTION
13
Magazine Article

How to Protect Yourself During a Mass Shooting

Ed Hinman

The following selection originally appeared in the November 6, 2017 issue of *The Washington Post*. The author of the article is the director of a consulting firm that specializes in international security.

GETTING READY TO READ

PREVIEW IT

Preview the reading using the guidelines on page 6. When you have finished, complete the following items:

1. Based on the title and first paragraph, what do you expect the author's attitude toward learning how to protect yourself during a mass shooting will be? _____

2. List three topics you expect the author to discuss in the reading.

   a. _____

   b. _____

   c. _____

LOOK IT UP

This article focuses on how people can prepare and protect themselves during a mass shooting. Google recent mass shootings in the U.S. and search for interviews and statements from people who survived a mass shooting. Take notes on what actions they took to save their lives and be prepared to share this information with your discussion group.

DISCUSS IT

In a group with three or four of your classmates, discuss the findings of your research on surviving a mass shooting. In addition, broaden your discussion to include the specific details of each mass shooting presented and the common tips for survival that your group found. Be prepared to share the highlights of your discussion with the class.

WRITE ABOUT IT

Connect the reading to your own experience by writing about what you would do if you were in a place where there was an active shooter. Have you ever thought about it before? Do you think about escape routes when you are in certain places? How do you think you would initially respond? Have you had any training at school or work about how to respond in a situation like this?

READ IT

As you read, number each tip for survival that the author presents. Also, underline the specific details about each of the tips. You can later use your underlines and annotations to help you create an outline, map, or summary of the reading. Also, be sure to highlight and annotate the text so that you can answer the detailed questions that follow the reading. Take a look at the questions before reading so that you can understand the level of recall that is expected.

How to Protect Yourself During a Mass Shooting

Ed Hinman

1   After shots were fired at the First Baptist Church in Sutherland Springs, Texas, where 26 people were killed in Sunday's mass shooting, Julius Kepper, who lives nearby, grabbed his gun and ran toward the sound of gunfire, according to the Wall Street Journal, where he saw another neighbor, also armed, confront the suspected killer. Kepper later said, "You just can't conceive of this happening in a small town like this." Carrie Matula, who works nearby, told NBC News "I never thought it would happen here," adding, "This is something that happens in a big city."

2   Not so. Mass shootings occur in rural, suburban and urban settings. In recent years, mass shootings have occurred at gathering places and houses of worship of many different faiths: churches, an Islamic center, a Jewish community center, a Sikh temple. There was Sandy Hook elementary school in 2012, the Pulse nightclub in 2016 and, a few weeks ago, 58 people were killed and hundreds were wounded by a gunman firing on an outdoor country music show in Las Vegas. Mass shootings can happen anywhere, at any time. It's imperative that everyone know how to react.

3   Dave Grossman, author of "On Killing: The Psychological Cost of Learning to Kill in War and Society," speaks regularly on the subject and often begins his lectures with this question: "How many kids in America have died from a school fire in recent years?" His answer: "None." Meanwhile, according to a 2014 FBI study, active shooters killed 117 people in schools between 2000 and 2013. Schools conduct fire drills and adhere to fire codes, but they generally don't do nearly as much, Grossman insists, to train students for a scenario far more likely to kill kids in schools: an active shooter. Most adults lack preventive training, as well.

4   Talking about these attacks can be difficult and heart-wrenching. But we can't avoid preparing ourselves just because the topic is disturbing. As my colleague James Hamilton — who served for years in the FBI and provides training to corporations, government agencies and security personnel for public figures — says, "You must be an active participant in your own survival."

Be an Active Participant in Your Own Survival

5   In the 2007 Virginia Tech massacre, a lone gunman had two handguns and hundreds of rounds of ammunition. He entered the second-floor of Norris Hall and began the final phase of a killing rampage that, in total, left 32 students and faculty members dead. One lesson from that tragedy is that the types of action taken by students and professors inside different classrooms influenced their chances of survival. In Room 206, where students hid beneath

A worker hides under her desk during an Operational Readiness Exercise at the Space and Missile Systems Center at Los Angeles Air Force Base in California. Based on the safety strategies presented in this reading, is hiding under a desk a good defense strategy? Why or why not?

their desks, the gunman killed 10 students and wounded several as he walked up and down the rows of desks. In Room 204, however, where two students were killed, several students jumped out of the second-floor windows, and all of those who managed to escape survived. In Room 205, students barricaded the classroom door with tables and chairs, holding it all in place while lying flat on the ground. Despite the shooter's attempt to breach the barricade, firing two inaccurate rounds into the room, he never entered and everyone inside survived.

6   During an active-shooter event, as the recent attacks in Texas and Las Vegas sadly demonstrate, some things are outside our control. Yet, like the students in Rooms 204 and 205, we can take actions that may improve the chances of survival.

Take Time to Prepare an Emergency Action Plan

7   Recently, in a coffee shop with my wife, I nodded toward the door and asked her, "What would you do if a man holding a gun walked through that door right now?" She answered, "I would throw my hot coffee at his face and distract him long enough to run out that side door." I loved her response. She had a plan.

8   When I asked a security professional and colleague, Nick Perez — who attended the Las Vegas concert with his girlfriend — what he credits most for their survival, he said, "I had a plan." Before attending the show, Perez reviewed the festival's app on his phone. He noted the venue's layout, including the entrances and emergency exit points. He said, "I thought ahead because I'm trained to do so. I always want to know a location's layout in case I need to make a quick exit or find on-site security or medical services. And, to be honest," he said, "I wasn't thinking about a mass shooting but more common occurrences like a medical emergency or a fight."

9   In the world of bodyguards and close protection, we call his actions "advancing" a location — preparing for the arrival of our protectee. We want to know the location of on-site security and paramedics, exit points and, most of all, our planned evacuation routes in case we need to evacuate the area because of an emergency, such as a fire or a shooter.

10   When you're out in public, before settling into your seat or spot, ask yourself: If there's an attack, what will I do? It only takes a moment to answer this question before you sit back, relax and enjoy your outing. Think of it as making regular deposits in a survival bank and then, if an emergency arises, being able to make a potentially lifesaving withdrawal.

Practice Situational Awareness

11   At theaters and concerts, consider choosing seats on the aisle and close to exits. At restaurants, sit with your back to the wall and face the entrance. Before you relax, identify your escape routes and exit points, including turnstiles, doors, scalable fences and accessible windows. If escaping a building isn't a viable option during an attack, consider moving into rooms where you're able to barricade yourself and others from the attacker. If the attacker breaches that room, be ready to use an improvised weapon — fire extinguisher, scissors, pen, etc. — to incapacitate him with speed, surprise and violence of action.

12   Perez told me that he stood with his girlfriend just 30 feet from the stage when gunfire tore through the crowd. "After the second burst of gunfire," he said, "I knew it wasn't firecrackers, I knew we were under attack." How did he know? "I saw a police car racing down Las Vegas Boulevard, toward the hotel." "Right then," he said, "I grabbed my girlfriend's hand and sprinted in the opposite direction to the exit I remembered from the venue's layout on the festival app."

13   When arriving at a new location, such as a restaurant or hotel lobby, in addition to considering your emergency action plan, pause for a moment and allow your senses to absorb all that's "normal" within the new environment — the sights, the sounds, the smells, etc. Once you establish a baseline of normalcy, it's easier to identify all that is not normal, and possibly, dangerous. At the gun range, firearms and gunshots are normal. Nearly everywhere else, they are not. At a concert, yelling is normal. At a restaurant, it is not. Anything that "is not" catches my attention as "not normal" for that environment and is possibly an indication of danger.

14   If I see a man walk through the front entrance of an establishment dressed in a wool trench coat on a hot August day, his winter attire would disrupt my baseline sense of normalcy. As a result, I'd observe his behavior a bit longer. If his actions continue to suggest abnormal behavior and cause me unease, I'll listen to my intuition like any animal bent on survival and respond to the perceived danger. That response might simply be continued observation or something more, like me moving closer to the exit. And if the strange-acting man, whom I'm now intuiting as possibly dangerous, reveals a rifle beneath his wool coat, I don't need to hear the first shot. I'm already executing my evacuation plan before anyone else.

Get out of the Kill Zone

15   When one of the teachers at Columbine High School heard shots fired during that school's 1999 mass shooting, she ran into the library and called 911. At one point, she told students in the library to "get down" and hide under desks and tables. When the gunmen entered the library, it became a kill zone and teenagers, caught sitting statically underneath those tables, began to die.

16   If you're caught by surprise in a kill zone, getting down is beneficial if the shooter is firing from a position level to yours. But whatever you do, don't stay down for long. As soon as

it's possible, "move off the X," as we say in personal security. Hiding under a table or desk offers little protection and provides the shooter a static human target to shoot. In the case of Columbine and Virginia Tech, to shoot at close range. Targets moving through the kill zone, however, are harder to hit. And targets that have evacuated the kill zone altogether are much harder to hit.

17   If you're being shot at and you know the gunman is firing from an elevated position, do not "get down" or stay down. Doing so creates a stationary human target with a larger surface area for his barrage of descending bullets. Instead, flee the kill zone immediately toward your preplanned exit points and eventually find cover, either terrain or structures that can probably stop bullets.

18   If like many of the Las Vegas concertgoers, you don't know the killer's location and you lack nearby cover, you can still attempt to flee the kill zone. It's your best option. And when you evacuate the kill zone, try to take others with you. If more people are running away from the kill zone than remaining paralyzed in it, others will follow.

UNDERSTANDING AND ANALYZING THE READING

A. BUILDING VOCABULARY

Context

Using context and a dictionary, if necessary, determine the meaning of each word as it is used in the selection.

_____ 1. imperative (paragraph 2)
   a. commanded
   b. suggested
   c. required
   d. crucial

_____ 2. adhere (paragraph 3)
   a. fix
   b. ignore
   c. cover
   d. follow

_____ 3. breach (paragraph 5)
   a. uphold
   b. violate
   c. modify
   d. divide

_____ 4. viable (paragraph 11)
   a. workable
   b. preferable
   c. achievable
   d. imaginable

_____ 5. static (paragraph 16)
   a. vital
   b. ready
   c. stationary
   d. close

_____ 6. barrage (paragraph 17)
   a. heavy burst
   b. range
   c. artillery clip
   d. firing device

Word Parts

A REVIEW OF PREFIXES AND ROOTS

VENT-	means *come*.
PRE-	means *before*.
IN-	means *not*

Use your knowledge of word parts and the preceding review to fill in the blanks in the following sentences.

1. Preventive (paragraph 3) training is one that would _____ an actual event.

2. An inaccurate (paragraph 5) shot is one that does _____ hit the intended target.

B. UNDERSTANDING THE THESIS AND OTHER MAIN IDEAS

Select the best answer.

_____ 1. Which statement best summarizes the thesis or central thought of the selection?

    a. The strategies that are designed to help people survive a school shooting are the same strategies that can be used for other places, such as theaters and churches.

    b. The best way to improve one's chances of surviving a mass shooting is to know and practice how to react in the situation.

    c. As a society, we should treat preparedness for surviving a mass shooting in the same way we treat preparedness for surviving a fire.

    d. A person's chances of surviving a mass shooting depends, in large part, on his or her awareness of the surrounding area.

_____ 2. The topic of paragraph 13 is

    a. how to trick an active shooter.

    b. how to escape a building.

    c. how to block a door.

    d. how to plan for an attack in a public place.

_____ 3. The main idea of paragraph 13 can be found in the

    a. first sentence.

    b. second sentence.

    c. fourth sentence.

    d. last sentence.

_____ 4. The topic of paragraph 18 is

    a. how to react in a kill zone.

    b. how to become a static target in order to avoid being shot at close range.

    c. how to apply the lessons learned from the Columbine and Virginia Tech shootings to any active shooter situation.

    d. how to stay silent and undetected while escaping a kill zone.

C. INTERPRETING SUPPORTING DETAILS

Select the best answer.

_____ 1. Which of the following actions was *not* recommended by the author?

    a. In anticipation of encountering the shooter while hiding, find something that you can use as a makeshift weapon.

    b. If confronted by the shooter, let him know that you have a weapon that you are willing to use.

    c. Regard sights, sounds, and behaviors that are out of the ordinary for a certain environment as signs of potential danger.

    d. Look at all locations you visit as possible sites for a mass shooting and be prepared.

_____ 2. The key type of evidence the author uses to support his main ideas and his thesis is

    a. research studies.

    b. personal experience.

    c. examples.

    d. quotations.

_____ 3. According to the author, if you find yourself in a kill zone, you should

    a. get down and stay down.

    b. hide under a table or desk and remain silent.

    c. assess the normalcy of the situation before making a move.

    d. flee the kill zone as soon as possible.

_____ 4. With which statement would the author most likely agree?

    a. All school shootings that occurred in the U.S. from 2000-2013 could have been prevented if students had been trained on how to react to the situation.

    b. When in a kill zone, do not waste valuable time by trying to get others to flee with you.

    c. There are some active-shooter situations for which we can never be prepared.

    d. When responding to perceived danger, a person should ignore his or her intuition.

D. RECOGNIZING METHODS OF ORGANIZATION AND TRANSITIONS

Select the best answer. See Chapter 7 for information on patterns of organization.

_____ 1. The overall organizational pattern of the reading is

    a. definition

    b. classification

    c. cause and effect

    d. process and analysis

_____ 2. The organizational pattern used in paragraph 15 is

    a. comparison and contrast.

    b. cause and effect.

    c. definition.

    d. classification.

_____ 3. The transitional word or phrase that signals a contrasting idea is to follow in paragraph 2 is

    a. *in recent years.*

    b. *at any time.*

    c. *not so.*

    d. *a few weeks ago.*

E. FIGURING OUT IMPLIED MEANINGS

Indicate whether each statement is true (T) or false (F).

_____ 1. The author suggests that the strategies for surviving a mass shooting in public places are not effective in schools.

_____ 2. The author believes that people must change their thinking about being prepared for a mass shooting.

_____ 3. The author implies that, for most of us, our best chance of surviving a mass shooting is to be armed with survival strategies rather than a gun.

_____ 4. The author would agree that even discussing how to survive a mass shooting is a stressful experience.

_____ 5 The author believes that one of our best defenses in an active-shooter situation is a weapon of any type and the courage to use it.

F. THINKING CRITICALLY ABOUT THE READING

Select the best answer. See Chapter 9 for information about thinking critically about a reading.

_____ 1. The author's overall purpose for writing this selection is to

    a. urge people to always be prepared for a mass shooting by rehearsing the strategies for survival and being aware of their surroundings so as to make a quick exit if needed.

    b. address the claim that there is no real way to survive a mass shooting unless those being attacked have weapons with which to retaliate.

    c. encourage readers to evaluate the strategies used in previous mass shootings to determine what helped and what didn't help people to survive.

    d. provide information on the variety of venues and settings where mass shootings have occurred so that people will not develop a false sense of security based on where they live and gather.

_____ 2. The overall tone of the selection is best described as

    a. objective and optimistic.

    b. informative and serious.

    c. uncertain and worried.

    d. discouraged and skeptical.

_____ 3. In paragraph 10, the author directly equates preventive planning to making deposits in a survival bank. This comparison is an example of

    a. a rhetorical question.

    b. an assumption.

    c. figurative language.

    d. a transitional phrase.

_____ 4. This selection is best described as

    a. based on opinion.

    b. highly influenced by data and other statistics.

    c. based on factual information.

    d. based on government-funded studies.

_____ 5. Which of the following excerpts from the reading is an opinion?

    a. "Carrie Matula, who works nearby, told NBC News 'I never thought it would happen here,' adding, 'This is something that happens in a big city.'" (paragraph 1)

    b. "Meanwhile, according to a 2014 FBI study, active shooters killed 117 people in schools between 2000 and 2013." (paragraph 3)

    c. "One lesson from that tragedy is that the types of action taken by students and professors inside different classrooms influenced their chances of survival." (paragraph 5)

    d. "We want to know the location of on-site security and paramedics, exit points and, most of all, our planned evacuation routes in case we need to evacuate the area because of an emergency, such as a fire or a shooter." (paragraph 11)

_____ 6. What technique does the author use in paragraph 1 to add emphasis to the main idea of the paragraph?

    a. questioning

    b. repetition of a word

    c. description of a photo

    d. a quotation

Answer the following open-ended questions in complete sentence format.

7. Suppose you were asked to choose a visual for this reading that would support the author's thesis. What visual would you choose and why would you choose it?

8. What types of sources does the author use to provide information to support his main idea? Evaluate the credibility of the sources. What other sources could the author have included that would have provided even more support for the thesis?

9. In paragraph 16, what does the author mean when he speaks of "moving off the X?" What is the "X"? Why should one move off the "X"? If you were in an active-shooter situation, would you be able to comply with this directive? Why or why not?

WRITING IN RESPONSE TO THE READING

G. REVIEWING AND ORGANIZING IDEAS WITH A PARAPHRASE

Complete the following paraphrase of paragraph 13. Begin your paraphrase with the following sentence

When you go to a new place, think about your emergency action plan and also pay attention to the normal aspects of the new environment.

_____

_____

_____

_____

_____

_____

For paragraph 17 of the reading, write your own two-sentence paraphrase.

_____

_____

_____

H. ANALYZING THE ISSUE

1. The theme of this chapter is "personal safety and security." The relationship of the reading to the theme of personal safety is obvious. How does the reading relate to the theme of security?

2. For what audience does the author seem to be writing? What assumptions does he make about his audience?

3. Is the first paragraph an effective introduction to the reading? Why or why not? What effect does it have on you as a reader?

4. Identify at least three issues presented in this reading. Then phrase each issue as a question that the author raises, discusses, or answers.

5. Suppose you are going to give a PowerPoint presentation that summarizes the reading. You will have five slides, and you will put one key point on each slide. What would your five key points be?

I. WRITING PARAGRAPHS AND ESSAYS

Write a paragraph or essay in response to the following writing prompts.

1. In paragrah 4, James Hamilton says, "You must be an active participant in your own survival." Write a paragraph in which you react to this statement. How does this statement make you feel? Are you ready and prepared to save your own life? What preparations have you made?

2. Do you think that schools should offer a course to their students on how to survive a mass shooting? Write a paragraph-length response to this question.

3. In paragraph 3, the author includes information on the number of active shooter incidents in U.S. schools between the years of 2000 and 2013. Although we do not have current numbers, we can only assume that the incidents of school and other mass shooting venues have increased. Why do you think the United States has so many mass shootings? Write an essay in which you present and discuss a minimum of three reasons that the incidence of mass shootings has increased in our country.

4. One solution to school shootings that many lawmakers favor is arming teachers. Do you agree or disagree that teachers in K–12 schools and colleges should be issued a gun? In an essay, state your position on this issue and your reasons for believing as you do.

5. Do you feel safe on your college campus? Write a letter to the president of your college and share your feelings about campus safety with him or her. Also, include suggestions for how to make your campus safer for students and faculty.

SELECTION
14
Web Article

China's Surveillance State Should Scare Everyone

Anna Mitchell and Larry Diamond

This reading originally appeared online in the global section of *The Atlantic* magazine. Anna Mitchell, co-author of the article, is a student and a researcher at Stanford University. Larry Diamond is a senior fellow at the Hoover Institute, a public policy research center, and the Freeman Spogli Institute at Stanford, a research and teaching organization that focuses on key international issues.

GETTING TO READY TO READ

PREVIEW IT

Preview the reading using the guidelines on page 6. When you have finished, complete the following items:

1. This reading is about the _____ in China.

2. List three questions you expect the author to answer in the reading.

   a. _____

   b. _____

   _____

   c. _____

   _____

LOOK IT UP

Government surveillance is not new; it is just getting increasingly more sophisticated. The Internet has numerous articles, blogs, and videos that address this issue. One source of especially relevant videos is TED Talks. Google this source and search for videos on surveillance. Select and view one that addresses the issue of government surveillance. Take notes on the main points of the video so that you can share what you have learned with your discussion group.

DISCUSS IT

In a group with three or four of your classmates, discuss the main points of the video you watched and the issues about surveillance that were mentioned. Be prepared to share the highlights of the discussion with the class.

WRITE ABOUT IT

Connect the reading to your own experience by writing a paragraph about the prevalence of surveillance in your day-to-day life. What types of surveillance do you encounter? Where do you encounter this surveillance? What type of personal information is being gathered from the surveillance? Are you comfortable with being "watched" or does it bother you?

READ IT

Pay close attention to the emotionally charged vocabulary that the authors use to describe China's surveillance state. Take note of how that language contributes to the authors' argument. As you read the selection, highlight and annotate the text so that you can answer the detailed questions that follow the reading. Take a look at the questions before reading so that you can understand the level of recall that is expected.

China's Surveillance State Should Scare Everyone

Anna Mitchell and Larry Diamond

The country is perfecting a vast network of digital espionage as a means of social control—with implications for democracies worldwide.

Lou-Foto/Alamy Stock Photo

Surveillance cameras monitor a busy street in Hangzhou, Zhejiang province, China.

1   Imagine a society in which you are rated by the government on your trustworthiness. Your "citizen score" follows you wherever you go. A high score allows you access to faster Internet service or a fast-tracked visa to Europe. If you make political posts online without a permit, or question or contradict the government's official narrative on current events, however, your score decreases. To calculate the score, private companies working with your government constantly trawl through vast amounts of your social media and online shopping data.

2   When you step outside your door, your actions in the physical world are also swept into the dragnet: the government gathers an enormous collection of information through the video cameras placed on your street and

all over your city. If you commit a crime—or simply jaywalk—facial recognition algorithms will match video footage of your face to your photo in a national ID database. It won't be long before the police show up at your door.

3   This society may seem dystopian, but it isn't farfetched: it may be China in a few years. The country is racing to become the first to implement a pervasive system of algorithmic surveillance. Harnessing advances in artificial intelligence and data mining and storage to construct detailed profiles on all citizens, China's communist party-state is developing a "citizen score" to incentivize "good" behavior. A vast accompanying network of surveillance cameras will constantly monitor citizens' movements, purportedly to reduce crime and terrorism. While the expanding Orwellian eye may improve "public safety," it poses a chilling new threat to civil liberties in a country that already has one of the most oppressive and controlling governments in the world.

4   China's evolving algorithmic surveillance system will rely on the security organs of the communist party-state to filter, collect, and analyze staggering volumes of data flowing across the Internet. Justifying controls in the name of national security and social stability, China originally planned to develop what it called a "Golden Shield" surveillance system allowing easy access to local, national, and regional records on each citizen. This ambitious project has so far been mostly confined to a content-filtering Great Firewall, which prohibits foreign Internet sites including Google, Facebook, and *The New York Times*. According to Freedom House, China's level of Internet freedom is already the worst on the planet. Now, the Communist Party of China is finally building the extensive, multilevel data-gathering system it has dreamed of for decades.

5   While the Chinese government has long scrutinized individual citizens for evidence of disloyalty to the regime, only now is it beginning to develop comprehensive, constantly updated, and granular records on each citizen's political persuasions, comments, associations, and even consumer habits. The new social credit system under development will consolidate reams of records from private companies and government bureaucracies into a single "citizen score" for each Chinese citizen. In its comprehensive 2014 planning outline, the Communist Party explains a goal of "keep[ing] trust and constraints against breaking trust." While the system is voluntary for now, it will be mandatory by 2020. Already, 100,000 Chinese citizens have posted on social media about high scores on a "Sesame Credit" app operated by Alibaba, in a private-sector precursor to the proposed government system. The massive e-commerce conglomerate claims its app is only tracking users' financial and credit behavior, but promises to offer a "holistic rating of character." It is not hard to imagine many Chinese boasting soon about their official scores.

6   While it isn't yet clear what data will be considered, commentators are already speculating that the scope of the system will be alarmingly wide. The planned "citizen credit" score will likely weigh far more data than the Western FICO score, which helps lenders make fast and reliable decisions on whether to extend financial credit. While the latter simply tracks whether you've paid back your debts and managed your money well, experts on China and Internet privacy have speculated—based on the vast amounts of online shopping data mined by the government without regard for consumer privacy—that your Chinese credit score could be higher if you buy items the regime likes—like diapers—and lower if you buy ones it doesn't, like video games or alcohol. Well beyond the realm of online consumer purchasing, your political involvement could also heavily affect your score: posting political opinions without prior permission or even posting true news that the Chinese government dislikes could decrease your rank.

7   Even more worrying is that the government will be technically capable of considering the behavior of a Chinese citizen's friends and family in determining his or her score. For example, it is possible that your friend's anti-government political post could lower your own score. Thus, the scoring system would isolate dissidents from their friends and the rest of society, rendering them complete pariahs. Your score might even determine your access to certain privileges taken for granted in the U.S., such as a visa to travel abroad or even the right to travel by train or plane within the country. One Internet privacy expert warns, "What China is doing here is selectively breeding its population to select against the trait of critical, independent thinking."

The Specter of a Chinese Mole in America

8   While Westerners and especially civil liberties groups like the ACLU are horrified by such a prospect—one commentator called the possibility "authoritarianism, gamified"—others argue that because lack of trust is a serious problem in China, many Chinese welcome this potential system. However, a state-run, party-inspired, data-driven monitoring system poses profound questions for the West about the role of private companies in government surveillance. Is it ethical for private companies to assist in massive surveillance and turn over their data to the government? Alibaba (China's Amazon) and Tencent (owner of the popular messaging platform WeChat) possess sweeping data on each Chinese citizen that the government would have to mine to calculate scores. Although Chinese companies now are required to assist in government spying while U.S. companies are not, it is possible to imagine Amazon in Alibaba's position, or Facebook in place of Tencent. While private companies like credit scoring bureaus have always used data to measure consumers' creditworthiness, in any decent society there must be a clear distinction between private-sector and public-sector scoring mechanisms that could determine access to citizen rights and privileges, without recourse.

9   This planned data-focused social credit system is only one facet of China's rapidly expanding system of algorithmic surveillance. Another is a sprawling network of technologies, especially surveillance cameras, to monitor people's physical movements. In 2015, China's national police force—the Ministry of Public Safety—called for the creation of an "omnipresent, completely connected, always on and fully controllable" national video surveillance network. MPS and other agencies stated that law enforcement should use facial recognition technology in combination with the video cameras to catch lawbreakers. One IHS Markit estimate puts the number of cameras in China at 176 million today, with a plan to have 450 million installed by 2020. One hundred percent of Beijing is now blanketed by surveillance cameras, according to the Beijing Public Safety Bureau.

10   The stated goal of this system is to capture and deter criminals. However, it also poses obvious and massive risks to privacy and the modicum of freedom Chinese citizens have managed to gain since the Maoist era. The penalties for small crimes seem unreasonable: authorities in Fuzhou are publishing the names of jaywalkers in local media and even sending them to their employers. More ominous, though, are the likely punishments that will be inflicted on people who associate with dissidents or critics, who circulate a petition or hold up a protest sign, or who simply wind up in the wrong place at the wrong time. Thus, the installation of an all-seeing-eye for the government alarms civil liberties

and privacy advocates worldwide. The government already constantly monitors the cell phones and social media of human-rights activists in the name of "stability mainte- nance." A video surveillance system would enable further pervasive and repressive surveil- lance. Making streams publicly available, too, would threaten every citizen's privacy: a busybody neighbor could easily spy on the activities of the family next door as they run errands or go on vacation.

11   China's experiments with digital surveillance pose a grave new threat to freedom of expression on the Internet and other human rights in China. Increasingly, citizens will refrain from any kind of independent or critical expression for fear that their data will be read or their movements recorded—and penalized—by the government. And that is exactly the point of the program. Moreover, what emerges in China will not stay in China. Its repressive technologies have a pattern of diffusing to other authoritarian regimes around the world. For this reason—not to mention concern for the hundreds of millions of people in China whose meager freedom will be further diminished—democracies around the world must monitor and denounce this sinister creep toward an Orwellian world.

UNDERSTANDING AND ANALYZING THE READING

A. BUILDING VOCABULARY

Context

Using context and a dictionary, if necessary, determine the meaning of each word as it is used in the selection.

_____ 1. trawl (paragraph 1)
    a. crawl
    b. wade
    c. search
    d. read

_____ 2. dystopian (paragraph 3)
    a. like an ideal society
    b. like an oppressive imaginary place
    c. like a police state
    d. like a dictatorship

_____ 3. precursor (paragraph 5)
    a. a forerunner
    b. a product
    c. a competitor
    d. an initiative

_____ 4. pariahs (paragraph 7)
    a. criminals
    b. rebels
    c. outcasts
    d. political prisoners

_____ 5. modicum (paragraph 10)
    a. a gift
    b. a privilege
    c. a limited right
    d. a small amount

_____ 6. repressive (paragraph 10)
    a. oppressive
    b. advanced
    c. limited
    d. secret

Word Parts

> ### A REVIEW OF PREFIXES AND ROOTS
>
> | | |
> |---|---|
> | **CONTRA-** | means *against*. |
> | **DIS-** | means *not*. |
> | **DICT** | means *say*. |

Use your knowledge of word parts and the review above to fill in the blanks in the following sentences.

1. If one were to *contradict* (paragraph 1) a government policy, he would be _____ something that goes _____ it.

2. A person who shows *disloyalty* (paragraph 5) is _____ loyal to someone or something.

B. UNDERSTANDING THE THESIS AND OTHER MAIN IDEAS

Select the best answer.

_____ 1. The thesis or central thought of this reading can be found in
   a. paragraph 1.
   b. paragraph 3.
   c. paragraph 4.
   d. paragraph 6.

_____ 2. The topic of paragraph 5 is
   a. the Chinese government's social credit system.
   b. how Alibaba developed their credit system.
   c. why a social credit system is needed in China.
   d. how the Chinese government hopes to expand its social credit system.

_____ 3. The topic of paragraph 8 is
   a. the difference in private companies' relationship to government in China and the West.
   b. the ethical considerations of government surveillance.
   c. the similarities that exist between Alibaba and Amazon and between Tencent and WeChat.
   d. the role of private companies in government surveillance.

_____ 4. Which of the following statements best expresses the implied main idea of paragraph 10?

    a. The Chinese government has the authority to use technology in any way it sees fit in order to deter crime.

    b. Chinese citizens would actually benefit from the national video surveillance system.

    c. The stated goal of the national video surveillance network is, at best, questionable.

    d. Chinese human-rights activists involved in criminal activity would be the target of the national video surveillance system.

C. INTERPRETING SUPPORTING DETAILS

Select the best answer.

_____ 1. According to the reading, the "citizen score" for each Chinese citizen could possibly be based on all of the following criteria *except*

    a. shopping habits.

    b. marital status.

    c. political involvement.

    d. personal associations with family members and friends.

_____ 2. China's system of algorithmic surveillance currently includes all of the following practices *except*

    a. social media monitoring.

    b. cell phone monitoring.

    c. video surveillance for public citizens' use.

    d. surveillance cameras.

_____ 3. According to the authors, the greatest concern about China's extensive surveillance system is its

    a. threat to human health and welfare.

    b. threat to national security.

    c. threat to social stability.

    d. threat to civil liberties and privacy.

D. RECOGNIZING METHODS OF ORGANIZATION AND TRANSITIONS

Select the best answer. See Chapter 7 for information on patterns of organization.

_____ 1. The overall pattern of pattern in this reading is

    a. process.

    b. comparison and contrast.

    c. illustration.

    d. cause and effect.

_____ 2. The transitional word or phrase that points to the use of chronological order in paragraph 2 is

    a. *also.*

    b. *if.*

    c. *when.*

    d. *through.*

_____ 3. The organization pattern used in paragraph 10 is

    a. classification.

    b. cause and effect.

    c. classification.

    d. comparison and contrast.

E. FIGURING OUT IMPLIED MEANINGS

Indicate whether each statement is true (T) or false (F).

_____ 1. The authors believe that the lack of sophisticated technology would greatly limit the spread of pervasive and oppressive surveillance systems to other countries.

_____ 2. The authors would agree that a society like the one described in the reading benefits the government far more than it benefits the citizenry.

_____ 3. The authors imply that it is unethical for private companies to assist the government in surveillance of its citizens.

_____ 4. The authors imply that "stability maintenance" is simply a smokescreen for more invasive and repressive surveillance practices.

_____ 5. The authors admit that their primary concern is for democratic governments, especially the United States, and not for the citizens of China.

F. THINKING CRITICALLY ABOUT THE READING

Select the best answer. See Chapter 9 for information on critical thinking about a reading.

_____ 1. One purpose of "China's Surveillance State Should Scare Everyone" is to

    a. explore the many ways that surveillance and advanced technology can improve civic engagement.

    b. explain the pros and cons of financial credit scores.

    c. warn countries of the dangers and potential spread of repressive technologies like those in China.

    d. promote the usefulness of video surveillance as a deterrent to crime.

_____ 2. Which one of the following statements from the reading is an opinion, not a fact?

    a. "This society may seem dystopian, but it isn't farfetched: it may be China in a few years." (paragraph 3)

    b. "Now, the Communist Party of China is finally building the extensive, multilevel data-gathering system it has dreamed of for decades." (paragraph 4)

    c. "This planned data-focused social credit system is only one facet of China's rapidly expanding system of algorithmic surveillance." (paragraph 9)

    d. "The stated goal of this system is to capture and deter criminals." (paragraph 10)

_____ 3. The authors primarily support their ideas with

    a. research studies.

    b. facts and statistics.

    c. examples from their personal experience.

    d. quotations from technology experts.

_____ 4. The overall tone of the reading selection is best described as

    a. pessimistic and angry.

    b. skeptical and ironic.

    c. suspicious and cautious.

    d. informative and concerned.

_____ 5. What figure of speech do the authors use when they refer to the network of surveillance cameras as "the expanding Orwellian eye" (paragraph 3)?

    a. simile

    b. metaphor

    c. personification

    d. analogy

_____ 6. What is the authors' tone when they describe the spread of China's repressive technologies as "this sinister creep toward an Orwellian world" (paragraph 11)?

    a. frustrated

    b. cynical

    c. distressed

    d. irreverent

Answer the following open-ended questions in complete sentence format.

7. Why do you think the authors included the picture of surveillance cameras at the beginning of the reading? What message does it convey? What other picture might you suggest they include with the reading?

8. The Great Firewall is the name of the content-filtering firewall in China that keeps out foreign Internet sites. What similarities to the Great Wall of China does the Great Firewall have?

9. In paragraph 3, the authors write about the purpose of the citizen score. Why do you think the authors put *good* in quotation marks when describing the desired behavior of the citizens?

10. In this reading, the authors use many words that have a negative connotation. List five words with a negative connotation and explain how the authors' use of these words influences your opinion.

WRITING IN RESPONSE TO THE READING

G. REVIEWING AND ORGANIZING IDEAS WITH A MAP

Create a conceptual map of the reading selection. See page 28 for information about mapping.

H. ANALYZING THE ISSUE AND THE ARGUMENT

Evaluate the reading on the following criteria:

1. The theme of this chapter is "personal safety and security." What examples of personal safety have the authors provided? What examples of security have the authors provided? How would the Chinese government define the two terms—personal safety and security?

2. How timely is the reading? Is it relevant to your own life?

3. Are the authors qualified to write about this subject? How accurate and reliable are their sources for expert opinions?

4. For what audience do the authors seem to be writing? Explain your answer.

5. What other types of evidence could the authors have used to strengthen their main ideas?

6. Identify at least three issues presented in this reading. Then phrase each issue as a question that the authors raise, discusses, or answer.

I. WRITING PARAGRAPHS AND ESSAYS

Write a paragraph or essay in response to the following writing prompts.

1. In a paragraph, discuss what you think it means to be an independent thinker. What are the characteristics of an independent thinker? Why is it important to be an independent thinker?

2. If the United States government were to develop a "citizen score" to encourage good behavior, what criteria do you think it should include? Why do you think it should include the suggested criteria, and what kind of score do you think you would earn? Write a paragraph response to these questions.

3. Write a paragraph response to the following question: is it ethical for private companies to assist in massive surveillance and turn over their data to the government?

4. The title of this reading is "China's Surveillance State Should Scare Everyone." After reading this article, does the surveillance system scare you? Why or why not? What specifically do you find most scary about the surveillance system? Write an essay that addresses these questions.

5. In an essay, compare and contrast the types of surveillance in China to those we have in the United States. Be sure to also discuss the reasons for surveillance in each of the countries.

6. Civil liberties are the basic rights of an individual citizen that are guaranteed in the Bill of Rights. Conduct a Google search to find a list of these civil liberties. Then, in an essay, discuss three civil liberties that are important to you. In your essay, be sure to define each specific civil liberty, give an example of how this freedom is exercised, and explain any threats to this liberty that exist today. Finally, explain why this liberty is important to you.

Technology in the Fight Against Crime

Frank Schmalleger, Ph.D.

Frank Schmalleger is the author of a textbook titled *Criminology Today: An Integrative Introduction*. The selection that follows is an excerpt from a chapter in his book.

GETTING READY TO READ

PREVIEW IT

Preview the reading using the guidelines on page 6. When you have finished, complete the following items:

1. Why does the author say that technology can be considered a double-edged sword?

   _____

2. List three topics that you expect the author to cover.

   a. _____

   b. _____

   c. _____

LOOK IT UP

Conduct an Internet search for information on using technology to fight crime. Narrow your focus to one specific way that law enforcement personnel are using technology to assist in the war against crime. Take notes on your findings so that you can share with your discussion group.

DISCUSS IT

In a group with three or four of your classmates, discuss the findings of your research on types of technology that can be used to fight crime. Make sure each person gets to share. Appoint a note taker and be prepared to share the highlights of your discussion with the class.

WRITE ABOUT IT

Connect the reading to your own experience by thinking and writing about how you unwittingly record information that, if needed, could be useful to law enforcement personnel. For example, what type of information could the police find on your cell phone that might help them solve a crime that you had absolutely no part in? What other pieces of technology do you use on almost a daily basis that might contain valuable information for law enforcement personnel? Do you ever give any thought to the idea that your personal pieces of technology could be seized? And do you ever think about how police might be able to use the information found in these devices? Write a paragraph in which you discuss these questions.

READ IT

This textbook reading contains a large amount of scientific/technical information. Plan to reread sections, if necessary, and adjust your reading rate to ensure you are achieving full comprehension.

As you read the selection, highlight and annotate the text so that you can answer the detailed questions that follow the reading. Take a look at the questions before reading so that you can understand the level of recall that is expected.

Technology in the Fight Against Crime

Frank Schmalleger

1   Technology is a double-edged sword: it arms evildoers with potent new weapons of crime commission, yet it provides police agencies and criminal justice personnel with powerful tools useful in the battle against crime. These tools include advancing new technologies, DNA evidence, and computer-assisted crime fighting tools. Criminally useful or evasive technologies and law enforcement capabilities commonly leapfrog one another. Consider traffic radar, which has gone from early always-on units through trigger-operated radar devices to today's sophisticated laser-based speed-measuring apparatus—each change being an attempt by enforcement agencies to keep a step ahead of increasingly sophisticated radar-detection devices marketed to drivers. Radar-jamming devices and laser jammers are also now used by people apparently intent on breaking speed-limit laws. Not to be outdone, suppliers to law enforcement agencies have created radar-detector detectors, which are used by authorities in states where radar detectors have been outlawed.

2   Other potent technologies in law enforcement today are computer databases of known offenders (including public access to sex-offender databases), machine-based expert systems, cellular communications, video surveillance (often combined with face-recognition technology), electronic eavesdropping, deoxyribonucleic acid (DNA) analysis, and less-lethal weapons. Transponder-based automated vehicle location (AVL) systems now use patrol car–based transmitters in tandem with orbiting global positioning system (GPS) satellites to pinpoint locations of police vehicles to within 50 feet so that dispatchers can better allocate available resources on a given shift and be able to substantially reduce police response times in crisis situations. (Chip-based transponders are also installed in private vehicles to deter thieves and to help trace stolen automobiles).

3   In jurisdictions with computer-aided dispatch (CAD) systems, police dispatchers are prompted by computers for important information that allows them to distinguish a location (such as a particular McDonald's). CAD systems also quickly provide information about how often officers have been called to a given site and can tell responding officers what they might expect to find based on past calls from that location.

4   More innovative crime-fighting technologies are becoming available. The "Spiderman snare," being tested for its usefulness in incapacitating fleeing suspects, is a 16-foot-wide net that is compressed into a small shotgun-like shell. The net has small weights at its circumference and wraps itself around its target after being fired. The snare's impact is harmless, and test subjects report being able to watch with open eyes as the net wraps around them. Another example is a special-frequency disco-like strobe light which quickly disorients human targets by causing intense dizziness, leaving subjects unable to resist cuffing and arrest (operators wear special glasses designed to counter the influence of the light). Because high-speed chases pose a substantial danger to the public, scientists have developed an electromagnetic pulsing device that can be used to temporarily disable a vehicle's electrical system, causing the engine to stall. The prototype is said to be safe enough to use on vehicles driven by those wearing pacemakers.

5   As new technologies are developed, their potential usefulness in law enforcement activities is evaluated by the FBI, the NIJ (National Institute of Justice), and other agencies. The NIJ's Technology Assessment Program (TAP) focused on four areas of advancing technology: protective equipment, such as bulletproof vests and other body armor; forensic sciences, including advances in DNA technology; transportation and weapons, such as electronic stun guns and other less-lethal weapons; and communications and electronics, including computer security and electronic eavesdropping.

6   Recently, the U.S. Department of Justice's National Law Enforcement and Corrections Technology Center (NLECTC) began testing a high-power compact microwave source designed for vehicle immobilization. The microwave beam emitted by the device can interfere with an automobile's computer circuitry, effectively shutting down a car's engine from up to 35 feet away. As the technology is improved, the device will likely become operable over longer distances, and it may soon become a routine tool in police work.

7   Other groups, such as the National Computer Security Association, the American Cryptography Association, and the American Society for Industrial Security, bring more specialized high-tech expertise to the private-security and public law enforcement profession.

8   A person's genetic code is contained in his or her DNA, whose composition is unique to each individual (except in the case of identical twins). DNA samples can be taken from blood, hair, semen, saliva, or even small flakes of skin left at the scene of a crime. After processing, DNA profiles appear like bar codes on film negatives, codes that can exonerate a suspect or provide nearly irrefutable evidence of guilt.

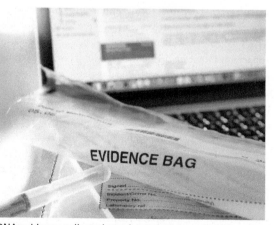

DNA evidence collected at crime scenes can convict a suspect of a crime or exonerate a suspect.

Andrew Brookes/Cultura Creative/Alamy Stock Photo

9   DNA evidence is long lasting—fossilized DNA is now being used to reconstruct genetic maps of long-extinct plant and animal species. Although DNA analysis is theoretically possible using only a single cell, most reputable DNA laboratories require a considerably greater quantity of material to conduct an effective analysis, but that could change. Using a Nobel Prize–winning technique called "polymerase chain-reaction technology," minute strands of DNA can be effectively amplified so that even the identity of a person taking a single puff from a cigarette can be accurately established from the trace DNA left on the cigarette. With costs dropping, these technological advances are expected to soon be available to a range of forensic analysts.

10   The National Research Council has called DNA profiling "a highly reliable forensic tool" but admits that it is not infallible. Obvious differences in scrutinized DNA samples can easily eliminate a suspect, but testing provides less certainty with positive identification, with human error in conducting the tests being perhaps the greatest threat to reliable results. More than 20 states and the federal government generally accept DNA evidence in criminal trials. Other jurisdictions, including California, are less clear in their recognition of DNA testing, and trial judges in those states may offhandedly exclude the use of such evidence when experts disagree as to its validity.

11   One observer, discussing the quality of DNA identification methods, noted, "The challenges today are no longer technical; instead they lie in taking the technology and building a meaningful legal infrastructure around it." As DNA evidence is accepted throughout jurisdictions nationwide and worldwide, digitized forensic DNA databases (similar to widely used fingerprint archives) are useful at the state and national levels, and most of the states and the federal government (through the FBI laboratory) already have them. In 1998 the FBI announced that its National DNA Index System (NDIS)—which enables U.S. forensic laboratories to exchange and compare DNA profiles electronically, thereby linking unsolved serial violent crimes to each other and to known offenders—had begun operation. Shortly thereafter, all 50 states had passed legislation requiring convicted offenders to provide samples for DNA databases, and all states have been invited to participate in NDIS. The federal DNA Identification Act of 1994 authorized the FBI to establish DNA indexes for (1) offenders convicted of crimes, (2) samples recovered from crime scenes, and (3) samples recovered from unidentified human remains. Today, the National DNA Index System is administered under the FBI's Combined DNA Index System (CODIS) and the combined database is known as the CODIS/NDIS. CODIS/NDIS contained more than 11 million offender profiles at the start of 2015.

12   In 1995 the British police, operating under a new nationwide crime bill, became the first national police force in the world to begin routine collection of DNA samples from anyone involved in a "recordable" offense (a serious crime). It appears that genetic profiling will become one of the most significant crime-fighting technologies of the twenty-first century. Genetic profiling—the use of biotechnology to identify the unique characteristics of an individual's DNA—is about to become as prevalent as the Breathalyzer and more important than the fingerprint.

13   Finally, it is important to note that a growing number of jurisdictions are requiring the gathering of DNA information from arrestees, and in 2013 the U.S. Supreme Court held, in the case of *Maryland* v. *King*, that "When officers make an arrest supported by probable cause . . . and bring the suspect to the station to be detained in custody, taking and analyzing a cheek swab of the arrestee's DNA is, like fingerprinting and photographing, a legitimate police booking procedure that is reasonable under the Fourth Amendment."

Computers as Crime-Fighting Tools

14   Computers are used to keep records of every imaginable sort—from point-of-sale contacts to inventory maintenance and production schedules. Computers assist in the design of new technologies and aid in the assignment of resources to problem areas.

15   Computers also connect people. The Internet contains a large number of law-oriented and law enforcement–oriented newsgroups and provides access to the United Nations and worldwide crime data through its link to the United Nations Criminal Justice Information Network. Other computer services provide access to security information and to software useful in law enforcement administration. Innovative computer technologies facilitate the work of enforcement agents. Among them are automated fingerprint identification systems, or AFISs (often with interstate and even international links); computerized crime-scene simulations and reenactments; expert systems; and online clearinghouses containing data on criminal activity and offenders. AFISs allow investigators to complete in a matter of minutes what would otherwise consume weeks or months of work manually matching a suspect's fingerprints against stored records. AFIS computers are able to compare and eliminate from consideration many thousands of fingerprints per second, sometimes leading to the identification of a suspect in a short time. Once crime-related information or profiles of criminal offenders have been generated, they are typically stored in a database and often made accessible to law enforcement agencies at other sites. Other specialized database programs now track inner-city gang activity and gang membership, contain information on known sexual predators, and describe missing children.

Expert systems
A system of computer hardware and software that attempts to duplicate the decision-making processes used by investigators in the analysis of evidence.

16   Forensic expert systems deploy machine-based artificial intelligence to draw conclusions and to make recommendations to investigators and others interested in solving problems related to crime and its commission. **Expert systems**, developed by professional "knowledge engineers" who work with "knowledge bases" and computer software called "inference engines," attempt to duplicate the decision-making processes used by skilled investigators in the analysis of evidence and in the recognition of patterns that such evidence might represent. One such system is currently being perfected by the FBI's National Center for the Analysis of Violent Crime (NCAVC). The NCAVC expert system attempts to profile serial killers by matching clues left at a crime scene with individual personality characteristics.

17   Finally, a number of specialized software programs, such as ImAger, which is produced by Face Software, Inc., and Compu-Sketch, a product of Visatex Corporation, can assist police artists in rendering composite images of suspects and missing victims.

UNDERSTANDING AND ANALYZING THE READING

A. BUILDING VOCABULARY

Context

Using context and a dictionary, if necessary, determine the meaning of each word as it is used in the selection.

_____ 1. tandem (paragraph 2)

    a. existing for one purpose only

    b. operating independently of another

    c. happening at the same time

    d. depending on the position of another

_____ 2. prototype (paragraph 4)

    a. forerunner

    b. model

    c. design

    d. creation

_____ 3. exonerate (paragraph 8)

    a. clear

    b. accuse

    c. implicate

    d. release

_____ 4. reputable (paragraph 9)

    a. experienced

    b. well-known

    c. serious

    d. reliable

_____ 5. infallible (paragraph 10)

    a. unreliable

    b. perfect

    c. valid

    d. faulty

_____ 6. prevalent (paragraph 12)

    a. efficient

    b. important

    c. common

    d. interesting

Word Parts

A REVIEW OF PREFIXES

CIRCUM-	means *the border around something.*
TRANS-	means *across, over.*
IM-	means *not.*

Use your knowledge of word parts and the review above to fill in the blanks in the following sentences.

1. The "Spiderman Snare" has weights at its *circumference* (paragraph 4) and wraps itself _____ the person being chased.

2. Methods of *transportation* (paragraph 5) carry people or things from one place _____ to another.

3. A device designed for vehicle *immobilization* (paragraph 6) is one that makes a vehicle _____ able to move.

B. UNDERSTANDING THE THESIS AND MAIN IDEAS

Select the best answer.

_____ 1. Which of the following best states the thesis or central thought of the reading?

 a. The way that law enforcement personnel used to fight crime is not effective with today's criminals.

 b. In the wrong hands, technology can be dangerous.

 c. Hardened criminals spend most of their time trying to outsmart technology intended to catch them.

 d. Current and future technologies in law enforcement are being used and developed in response to innovative criminal activity.

_____ 2. The implied main idea of paragraph 3 is that

 a. Repeat calls to the same location always mean trouble for police officers.

 b. Not even police officers know all of the trouble spots in a particular area.

 c. Police respond to so many calls that they cannot remember where they have been.

 d. CAD systems provide an extra layer of protection for police officers.

_____ 3. The topic of paragraph 4 is

 a. the "Spiderman snare."

 b. new crime-fighting technologies.

 c. disorienting strobe lights.

 d. vehicle disabling technology.

_____ 4. The main idea of paragraph 15 is found in the

 a. first sentence.

 b. second sentence.

 c. third sentence.

 d. last sentence.

C. INTERPRETING SUPPORTING DETAILS

Select the best answer.

_____ 1. The author mentions all of the following groups of people who have benefitted from innovative crime-fighting technology *except*
   a. public law enforcement personnel.
   b. high-security prison officials.
   c. forensic specialists.
   d. criminal justice personnel.

_____ 2. All of the following statements about DNA are true *except*
   a. Identical twins have the same genetic code contained in their DNA.
   b. DNA evidence can be stored and used long after it has been collected.
   c. When police apprehend a suspect, they have the authority to require the suspect to give a DNA sample.
   d. The law requires convicted criminals to provide DNA samples for inclusion in databases.

_____ 3. The author supports his points with all of the following types of evidence *except*
   a. personal experience.
   b. historical information.
   c. state and federal legislation.
   d. court cases.

_____ 4. The author discusses database programs that do all of the following *except*
   a. help in the search for missing children.
   b. help identify serial killers.
   c. identify people who are likely to commit mass murders.
   d. help identify human remains.

D. RECOGNIZING METHODS OF ORGANIZATION AND TRANSITIONS

Select the best answer. See Chapter 7 for information on patterns of organization.

_____ 1. The pattern of organization used in paragraph 4 is
   a. classification.
   b. illustration/example.
   c. comparison and contrast.
   d. definition.

_____ 2. The transitional phrase that provides a clue to the organizational pattern used in paragraph 4 is

    a. *because.*

    b. *more.*

    c. *is said to be.*

    d. *another example.*

_____ 3. The organizational pattern used in paragraph 9 is

    a. comparison and contrast.

    b. chronological order.

    c. process.

    d. classification.

E. FIGURING OUT IMPLIED MEANINGS

Indicate whether each statement is true (T) or false (F).

_____ 1. The author implies that cigarettes are one of the most reliable sources of DNA evidence.

_____ 2. The author would agree that technology has also helped criminals to be better at committing crimes.

_____ 3. The author believes that the pros and cons of new technology tools must be carefully considered before they are put into widespread practice.

_____ 4. According to the author, genetic profiling will be more useful than the Breathalyzer in deterring criminal activity.

_____ 5. The author disapproves of forensic expert systems that are able to make decisions and recommendations to criminal investigators.

F. THINKING CRITICALLY ABOUT THE READING

Select the best answer. See Chapter 9 for information about thinking critically about a reading.

_____ 1. The author's primary purpose in "Technology in the Fight Against Crime" is to

    a. explain how various technological tools work in the effort to deter crime.

    b. express his concern about the reliability of using DNA technology to convict suspects of violent crimes.

    c. educate his readers about the innovative crime fighting tools that are becoming available to law enforcement personnel.

    d. highlight the federal government's role in approving and implementing new crime-fighting tools.

_____ 2. Overall, the author's tone in this selection can best be described as

    a. critical.

    b. informative.

    c. indifferent.

    d. concerned.

_____ 3. In paragraph 1, the author directly equates technology with a double-edged sword. This comparison is an example of

    a. personification.

    b. a simile.

    c. a metaphor.

    d. a rhetorical question.

_____ 4. What does the author mean when he says, "criminally useful or evasive technologies and law enforcement capabilities commonly leapfrog one another" (paragraph 1)?

    a. Law enforcement personnel employ the help of criminals to help them develop crime-fighting technology.

    b. Criminals are so technologically savvy that they can jump past many of the more rudimentary technological tools and use the more sophisticated ones to commit crimes.

    c. When criminals figure out a way to use technology to break the law, law enforcement personnel have to figure out a way to outsmart the criminal use of technology, and then the cycle repeats itself.

    d. Law enforcement personnel believe that given time, criminals will reveal their secrets, thereby making it easier for law enforcement capabilities to catch up with the technology that criminals use.

_____ 5. In paragraph 12, the author's attitude toward using genetic profiling as a crime-fighting tool seems to be

    a. enthusiastic.

    b. disapproving.

    c. cautiously optimistic.

    d. skeptical.

_____ 6. In paragraph 16, the author writes about artificial intelligence. Within the context of the writing in paragraph 16, which of the following choices describes what a machine with artificial intelligence can do?

    a. mimic human thinking

    b. create knowledge bases

    c. analyze evidence

    d. recognize patterns

Answer the following open-ended questions in complete sentence format.

7. Has the author provided sufficient evidence to support his main ideas? What other types of evidence might he provide to strengthen the reading?

8. If you were to choose a visual to include in this reading, what would you choose and how would it support the main idea of the reading? What caption would you include with the visual?

9. In paragraph 2, the author writes about using patrol car transmitters along with GPS devices as a way to "allocate available resources on a given shift." To what resource is the author referring? How do you know this?

10. In paragraph 4, the author describes an innovative crime-fighting technology tool—a special-frequency disco-like light. He focuses on the positive aspects of this innovative tool but does not mention any negative aspects associated with its use. What negative aspects can you think of, and why do you consider them to be negative?

WRITING IN RESPONSE TO THE READING

G. REVIEWING AND ORGANIZING IDEAS WITH A SUMMARY

Write a clear and concise summary of the section of the reading titled "Computers as Crime-Fighting Tools" (paragraphs 14–17). See page 31 for information about writing a summary.

H. ANALYZING THE ISSUE

1. Identify at least three issues presented in this reading. Then phrase each issue as a question that the author raises, discusses, or answers.

2. The theme of the chapter is "personal safety and security." Analyze the reading by addressing the following questions:

    a. Which technological tool do you think promises the most security to citizens of the United States? Explain your answer.

b. Which technological tool do you think poses the greatest risk to citizens of the United States. Explain your answer.

c. What security issues might arise from using technology to fight crime? Explain your answer.

3. What is the author's background? Is he qualified to write about the topic? Why or why not?

4. Does the source from which this reading is taken help you determine the credibility of the information presented? Do you find any bias in the selection? Please explain both of your answers.

5. Can you find any opinions in this selection, or is the entire piece factually-based? List the opinions that you are able to find in the reading.

I. WRITING PARAGRAPHS AND ESSAYS

Write a paragraph or an essay in response to the following writing prompts.

1. It's your turn to think creatively. Write a paragraph in which you present information on your latest technological crime-fighting invention. Give the invention a name, describe it, and discuss the pros and cons of its use.

2. Using paragraph 5 as a resource, write a paragraph in which you discuss the one innovation discussed in that paragraph that you think has the greatest promise and describe a scenario in which you could envision it being used.

3. In a paragraph or an essay, discuss the pros and cons of collecting and analyzing a DNA sample from an arrestee at the time of his/her booking.

4. The author also mentioned video surveillance, electronic eavesdropping, cellular communications, and facial recognition technology as crime fighting tools. Choose one of these tools and write an essay in which you describe the tool, how it helps to deter crime, and the pros and cons of using the tool. If needed, you may research your chosen topic.

5. In paragraph 1, the author presents the good and the bad about technology. The good is obvious: technology helps law enforcement personnel fight crime. On the other hand, new technology creates new crime, and in the hands of a criminal, technology can become a weapon. Write an essay in which you discuss the downside of technology and crime. Be sure to include at least three different crimes that have arisen as a result of new technology.

ACTIVITIES: EXPLORING PERSONAL SAFETY AND SECURITY ISSUES

On your own or with a group of classmates, complete two of the following four activities.

1. It is likely that you own a smartphone and that you use it to send text messages and/or post to Facebook or some other type of social media. List at least three ways that using a smartphone or a social media site has improved your life. Then list at least three ways in which you see smartphones and/or social media negatively affecting personal safety and security (for example, people who send text messages while driving create extremely dangerous road conditions that can lead to people being killed).

   _____

   _____

   _____

   _____

2. Create a PowerPoint presentation on the top ten ways students can protect their personal safety and security in their everyday life. Do not research this topic. Just focus on practical ways students can protect themselves.

3. Technology can be a double-edged sword when it comes to personal safety and security. This chapter discussed just a few aspects of the topic. Other technological issues include the following:
   - The threat of identity theft through technological means
   - Brain research that suggests the addictive quality of technology
   - Serious privacy concerns as Web browsers track your movements online and then sell that information to companies who want to advertise their products to you
   - The effects of technology on the well-being of young children who spend a lot of time playing on computers
   - Technology's role in the theft of *intellectual property* such as music and books. (If you have ever downloaded a book or a song from a "share" site, you have most likely stolen intellectual property.)

   Write an essay or prepare a class presentation about any of these topics, or any other topic that relates to technology and personal safety and/or security.

4. Cybercrime has become a hot-button issue as technology has become more sophisticated and pervasive. Read about cybercrime (technocrime) on the Internet and narrow your focus to three types of cybercrime that interest you. Take notes on the three types and prepare a five-minute presentation for the class. Be sure to include current and specific examples of the types of cybercrime and explain how they affect one's personal safety and security.

MAKING CONNECTIONS: THINKING WITHIN THE ISSUES

In many college courses, instructors will expect you to read and evaluate a wide variety of materials. This section requires you to draw connections between the readings on this issue explored within the chapter. The activities and assignments below will give you practice in synthesizing information and thinking critically about the relationship of the chapter readings.

1. "China's Surveillance State Should Scare Everyone" (Selection 14, p. 512) and "Technology in the Fight Against Crime" (Selection 15, p. 522) both discuss technology and its use by the government or law enforcement personnel. Choose three technological tools that both countries use and write an essay in which you contrast the ways in which the two countries use similar technologies. For example, both countries use video surveillance, but they use it for very different reasons and in different ways.

2. In your criminal justice class, you have been given the following assignment: Write an essay in which you discuss how technology can be used to reduce the number of mass shootings in the United States. Use both "How to Protect Yourself During a Mass Shooting" (Selection 13, p. 499) and "Technology in the Fight Against Crime" (Selection 15, p. 522) to support your points.

16 Conformity and Nonconformity: Following and Breaking the Rules

Do you follow the rules, or do you break them? Do you do what's expected of you, or do you do your own thing?

Every society is ruled by *norms*, which are spoken or unspoken rules of behavior. We grow up surrounded by these norms, and they become part of us. For example, even as a child, long before you have a driver's license, you learn that a red light means "stop." Many social scientists believe that without norms, society would not be able to function. Those who follow the norms are said to *conform* to social expectations.

Here are some examples of the norms that influence our lives:

- Most children in the United States are required to attend school until they are 16.
- People are expected to behave properly in public and wear clothes that are appropriate for the situation.
- Mothers and fathers are expected to care for their children, and family members are expected to help take care of the elderly and sick.

But not everyone conforms to expected norms. For example, while many people who want to be successful follow the norm of attending college and then looking for a full-time job, others drop out of school and start their own businesses (Bill Gates of Microsoft is a famous example). While many people live a 9-to-5 life of work, family, and home, some people become musicians, living their lives mostly at night and traveling around the country (or the world) for much of the year.

In addition, norms are always undergoing change. In some areas, the "rules" are evolving or have not been defined yet. For instance, what types of etiquette do portable technologies require? Is it acceptable to talk on a cell phone on a crowded bus and in other public places? Should people be allowed to text while driving, or should laws be passed to prevent this?

This chapter offers three readings about conformity and how our personal decisions affect our lives, from the purchases we make, to our behavior and work habits in school, to the lifestyles we choose. Throughout the readings you'll find examples of people who are following society's rules, as well as examples of people who are breaking the rules.

WHY ARE CONFORMITY AND NONCONFORMITY SUCH IMPORTANT CONTEMPORARY ISSUES?

American society has always been individualistic. The image of the tough, rugged American goes back to frontier days, when people built their own houses and farmed the land in order to survive. It's no surprise, then, that so many Americans struggle with the "rules" they feel are imposed on them. For example, feminism was a direct result of women's desire to have more choices in their lives, and the Civil Rights Movement was a direct result of people's desire to see all Americans treated equally and fairly. Many of these struggles are ongoing. To understand the options available to you and others, it is important to understand social expectations. Only then can you think critically about the pros and cons of conformity and decide which decisions are right for you.

How Do Conformity and Nonconformity Tie in to My College Courses?

Understanding the norms of the major social institutions (such as family, education, and religion) is a key goal of most sociology courses. A subfield of psychology, *social psychology*, examines group behavior and expectations, the ways people behave in social settings. Literature courses are filled with tales of people who break the rules and do things their own way, while history and political science courses talk about larger-than-life figures (such as conquerors, generals, and presidents) whose unorthodox or individualistic beliefs and behaviors affected millions of people and changed society. And, of course, business courses teach the "rules" of business, from accounting to management, and talk about the consequences of breaking those rules (from getting fired to ending up in jail).

TIPS FOR READING ABOUT CONFORMITY AND NON-CONFORMITY

Here are some tips for reading not only the selections in this chapter, but any reading about conformity and nonconformity.

- **Consider context.** Different groups of people may be guided by very different sets of norms. For example, as a college student, you are expected to study and attend all your classes. At some colleges, however, student athletes follow a different set of "rules" from most other students. Their main focus may be the sport they play rather than their studies. As you read, ask yourself what specific *part* of society the author is writing about.

- **Pay close attention to the examples.** Readings about conformity and nonconformity often focus on individuals. What exactly are these people doing to follow or break society's rules? What are the consequences of their actions, for themselves and others? What guides their behaviors?

- **Link the reading to your life, experiences, and opinions.** If you are reading a personal essay, put yourself in the author's position. Would you make the same choices or different choices? How would the opinions of others affect (or not affect) your choices?

A Brother Lost

Ashley Womble

In the following article, which first appeared in *Salon* magazine in July 2010, the author writes about Jay, her mentally ill brother who became homeless.

GETTING READY TO READ

PREVIEW IT

Preview the reading using the guidelines on page 6. When you have finished, Complete the following items:

1. The reading is about _____.
2. Write a sentence describing what you learned from previewing the reading.

_____

_____

LOOK IT UP

Ashley Womble's "lost" brother suffers from paranoid schizophrenia. Before you read his story, spend some time searching the Internet on the issue of mental illness and homelessness. Take notes on your findings so that you can share with your discussion group.

DISCUSS IT

In a group with three or four of your classmates, discuss the findings of your research on the issue of mental illness and homelessness. Broaden your discussion to include other segments of the population that belong to the homeless community. Be prepared to share the highlights of your discussion with the class.

WRITE ABOUT IT

Connect the reading to your own experience by writing a paragraph about homelessness. Consider the following questions as you write: What experience have you had with homeless people? How do you feel when you pass by them on the street? Do you ever wonder about their family? Have you ever tried to help someone who did not want your help?

READ IT

We often make assumptions about a certain group of people until we meet a member of that group who challenges us to re-examine our preconceived ideas. Oftentimes, we miss out on opportunities to broaden our circle of friendship because we ignore or shun those folks whose lives do not conform to our societal norms. As you read "A Brother Lost," notice how the author's perception of homelessness changes.

As you read the selection, highlight and annotate the text so that you can answer the detailed questions that follow the reading. Take a look at these questions before reading so that you can understand the level of recall that is expected.

A Brother Lost

Ashley Womble

1   Like any New Yorker, I was no stranger to homeless people. I passed by them on my way to the shiny glass tower where I worked for a glossy women's magazine: the older lady perched atop a milk crate in the subway station, the man curled up in a dirty sleeping bag and clutching a stuffed animal. They were unfortunate ornaments of the city, unlucky in ways I never really considered.

paranoid schizophrenia A chronic mental illness in which a person suffers from delusions and hallucinations

2   Until one hot summer day in 2009 when my little brother Jay left his key on the coffee table and walked out of his house in West Texas to live on the streets. In the days that followed I spent hours on the phone with detectives, social workers, and even the FBI, frantically trying to track him down. A friend designed a "Missing" poster using the most recent picture I had of him; he was wearing a hoodie and a Modest Mouse T-shirt, a can of beer in his hand and a deer-in-headlights expression on his face. I created a Facebook group and contacted old acquaintances still living in our hometown of Lubbock, begging everyone I even remotely knew to help me find him. No luck. If it had been me, a pretty young white woman, chances are my face would have been all over the news—but the sudden disappearance of a 20-year-old guy with **paranoid schizophrenia** didn't exactly warrant an **Amber Alert**.

Amber Alert A public alert system that spreads information about a missing person through broadcast media and electronic billboards on highways

3   In the year and a half that mental illness had ravaged my brother's mind, I'd learned to lower my expectations of what his life would be like.

Arkna/Fotolia

The smart kid who followed politics in elementary school probably wouldn't become a lawyer after all. Instead of going to college after high school, Jay became obsessed with 9/11 conspiracy theories. What began as merely eccentric curdled into something manic and disturbing: he believed the planners of 9/11 were a group of people called "the Cahoots" who had created a 24-hour television network to monitor his actions and control his thoughts. Eventually, his story expanded until the Cahoots became one branch of the New World Order, a government whose purpose was to overturn Christianity, and he had been appointed by God to stop it.

4   This made it hard for him to act normal, even in public. He'd lost his job busing tables after yelling "Stop the filming and hand over the tapes" to everyone dining in the restaurant. Having friends or even a coherent conversation wouldn't be possible unless he took the antipsychotic medication he'd been prescribed while he was in the mental hospital. A legal adult, he was allowed to refuse treatment, and he did. Otherwise the Cahoots would win.

5   I counted each day he'd been missing until they became weeks, until the number was so high I wondered if he was even still alive. That number was about the only thing I continued to keep track of. Dirty clothes and dishes piled up at home, I missed deadlines at work, and I got out of bed only if it was absolutely necessary. I cried often, but especially during thunderstorms, a reminder that wherever my brother was, he was unprotected. Eventually it became clear that I was losing it, too. So I did what my brother wouldn't allow himself to do: I started taking a pill that helped usher away my anxiety and depression.

6   Weeks after Jay disappeared, police in Maryland found him talking to a spider and had him hospitalized. He stayed for 72 hours. Then he went missing again.

7   September 11, 2009, was one of those drizzling mornings when I thought of my brother. There was the usual undertone of reverent sadness in the city, but for me, the date was a reminder of all that had gone wrong inside Jay's mind. And on that day my phone finally rang.

8   "Hello." Jay's Southern drawl was unmistakable. I sat straight up in my desk chair at work wondering what I should do. Record the call? Take notes?

9   "Where are you?" I asked, as images of him sitting in a jail cell or stranded alone in an alley flashed in my head.

10   "Manhattan," he said.

11   My heart filled with hope. Then he asked me if I'd gone to the witchcraft celebration at the World Trade Center, where the Sorcerers had ordered the wind and the rain to destroy the ceremony. Once again, I just felt like a helpless stranger.

12   I asked nervously if I could buy him dinner. To my surprise, he agreed. Twenty minutes later I met him near Penn Station; he was hunched under an awning next to a big blue tarp that covered his backpack and the paisley duffel he'd once borrowed. His pale skin had tanned, and hair covered his face. He was staring at people as they walked by, but he didn't see me until I said his name. Standing face-to-face with him, I could see that he had lost a lot of weight. His cheekbones jutted out from his once-full face. If I had seen his picture I would have gasped. Instead, I just held out my arms.

Zagat a guide to restaurants in a particular city

13   **Zagat** has no recommendations for where to take your homeless brother to dinner. We settled on the Mexican chain Chevys and sat in a booth near the back. He told me about hitchhiking to New York and sleeping in Central Park until the cops kicked him out. He grinned as he talked about sleeping on the steps of a downtown school, his smile still as charming as it had been when he was seven.

14   "Do you consider yourself homeless?" I asked.

15   "Oh, yes!" he answered proudly.

16   I wondered if the constant motion of wandering from town to town helped quiet the voices he heard. If it was his own kind of medication and, if so, could I really tell him that was the wrong way to live?

17   Earlier in the year I'd bribed him with a trip to visit me on the condition that he took his meds. Now he was sitting in front of me, and as much as I wanted to let him stay in my apartment, I knew I couldn't let him (my therapist discouraged it, and my roommate rightly put her foot down). I approached the topic cautiously, my voice shaking as I asked, "Do you know why you can't stay with me?" His voice small and shamed, he answered, "Because I won't take my medication." He had always denied that he had schizophrenia, but his admission gave me hope that maybe some day that would change.

18   I tried to quiet my own inner voice, which told me Jay needed to be in the hospital where a team of psychiatrists could experiment with medications that would fix his mind. I could do some things for my brother: I could give him a little money for cigarettes. I could buy him a new backpack, a sleeping bag, good walking shoes. But the more I pushed him to get help, the more my own sanity escaped me.

19   So I let him go. He went to New Jersey. Florida. Louisiana. To a place where he told me from a pay phone he wouldn't call anymore because he didn't want me to know his whereabouts. I can only imagine what he looks like after a year on the streets: his hair must be long, skin tan and hardened, and his rail-thin body caked in dirt. He probably doesn't look much different from the homeless people I pass by on the streets of New York City. Seeing them makes my heart ache, makes me think about those they may have left behind, people who long to dust them off and put them on the right path but who know, in the end, it's not their choice.

UNDERSTANDING AND ANALYZING THE READING

A. BUILDING VOCABULARY

Context

Using context and a dictionary, if necessary, determine the meaning of each word as it is used in the selection.

_____ 1. warrant (paragraph 2)

    a. cause

    b. justify

    c. offer

    d. document

_____ 2. ravaged (paragraph 3)

    a. starved to death

    b. invaded forcefully

    c. teased mercilessly

    d. caused terrible damage

_____ 3. eccentric (paragraph 3)

    a. inborn

    b. extreme

    c. odd

    d. challenging

_____ 4. curdled (paragraph 3)

    a. molded

    b. floated

    c. turned bad

    d. disappeared

_____ 5. coherent (paragraph 4)

    a. logical

    b. entertaining

    c. serious

    d. illogical

_____ 6. reverent (paragraph 7)

    a. respectful   *church*

    b. uncontrollable

    c. great

    d. approving

Usher = escort

Addmission = confession

Word Parts

A REVIEW OF PREFIXES

ANTI-   means *against.*

DIS-   means *not, apart,* or *away.*

Use your knowledge of word parts and the review above to fill in the blanks in the following sentences.

1. *Antipsychotic* medications (paragraph 4) are medications that work _____ psychosis to improve a person's mental health.

2. The therapist who *discouraged* (paragraph 17) the author did _____ encourage her to let her brother stay with her.

B. UNDERSTANDING THE THESIS AND MAIN IDEAS

Select the best answer.

_____ 1. The best statement of the thesis or central thought of "A Brother Lost" is that

    a. people who suffer from mental illness are lost.

    b. one's preconceived notions about groups of people are oftentimes shattered after one gets to know and understand someone in the group.

    c. love for one's family member cannot be extinguished by the ravages of a mental illness.

    d. it is futile to try to help someone who does not want to be helped.

_____ 2. The topic of paragraph 4 is

    a. the Cahoots.

    b. busing tables.

    c. Jay's abnormal behavior.

    d. the antipsychotic medicine.

_____ 3. What is the implied main idea of paragraph 19?

    a. We cannot help someone who does not want to be helped.

    b. Everyone who is homeless has chosen to be homeless.

    c. Most homeless people have families who love them.

    d. Homeless people are dirty, thin, and sickly.

C. INTERPRETING SUPPORTING DETAILS

Select the best answer.

_____ 1. The purpose of Jay's imagined New World Order was to

    a. control the thoughts of all people.

    b. monitor the actions of all people.

    c. overturn Christianity.

    d. abolish all government.

_____ 2. Jay lost his job because

    a. he couldn't carry on a coherent conversation with customers.

    b. he failed to show up for work regularly.

    c. he yelled out "Stop the filming and hand over the tapes" to customers in the dining room.

    d. he passed out literature and solicited members for the New World Order while at work.

_____ 3. What does Jay believe about 9/11?

    a. It was planned by terrorists who had been appointed by God.

    b. It was planned by the Cahoots.

    c. It was planned and carried out by mentally ill rebels.

    d. It was televised in an attempt to control the minds of Americans.

_____ 4. To support her thesis and main ideas, the author uses all of the following types of evidence _except_

    a. research citations.

    b. personal experience.

    c. examples of bizarre behavior.

    d. description.

D. RECOGNIZING METHODS OF ORGANIZATION AND TRANSITIONS

Select the best answer. See Chapter 7 for information on patterns of organization.

_____ 1. The organizational pattern used in paragraph 2 is
   a. definition
   b. classification.
   c. illustration.
   d. chronological order.

_____ 2. What is the dominant organizational pattern of paragraph 3?
   a. comparison and contrast
   b. illustration
   c. cause and effect
   d. definition

_____ 3. Which transitional word or phrase is a clue to the dominant organizational pattern of paragraph 2?
   a. *in the days that followed*
   b. *created*
   c. *even the FBI*
   d. *still living in our hometown*

E. FIGURING OUT IMPLIED MEANINGS

Indicate whether each statement is true (T) or false (F).

_____ 1. Before the encounter with her brother, the author ignored the homeless people that she passed each day.

_____ 2. The author implies that all homeless people are mentally ill.

_____ 3. According to the author, mentally ill people are not able to hold down a job.

_____ 4. The author implies that the news media are not interested in the plight of the mentally ill.

_____ 5. The author believes that her brother's life would have been different if he had taken his medication.

F. THINKING CRITICALLY ABOUT THE READING

Select the best answer. See Chapter 9 for information about thinking critically about a reading.

_____ 1. The author's main purpose in "A Brother Lost" is to

    a. motivate others to volunteer with organizations that serve the mentally ill and the homeless.

    b. tell the story of her mentally ill and homeless brother in hopes that others will have a greater understanding of this segment of the population.

    c. provide a detailed psychological explanation of what happens to the mentally ill when they do not take their medication.

    d. tell the story of how she lost her brother to mental illness.

_____ 2. The tone of the reading selection can best be described as

    a. serious and introspective.

    b. comic and dismissive.

    c. nostalgic and critical.

    d. admiring and informative.

_____ 3. With which of the following statements would the author of "A Brother Lost" be most likely to *disagree*?

    a. Homeless people are real people.

    b. Love transcends a body caked in dirt and a mind ravaged by mental illness.

    c. Homeless people are unfortunate ornaments of the city.

    d. No matter how difficult it may be, allowing a person to choose his own path is often the right thing to do.

_____ 4. In paragraph 15, the author states that her brother answered *proudly* when asked if he were homeless. Why does the author use this word to describe the manner in which he answered?

    a. She wants the reader to understand that all people have value.

    b. She is implying that her brother is too sick to realize what a dangerous lifestyle he has chosen to live.

    c. She wants to send the reader a message about the pride that comes from choosing one's own path in life.

    d. She wants to encourage others to be proud of their family members no matter what path in life they may choose.

_____ 5. What does the author mean in paragraph 18 when she writes that she "tried to quiet her own inner voice"?

    a. She is hinting that she, too, is a paranoid schizophrenic.

    b. She is implying that her conscience is speaking to her.

    c. She is suggesting that the ideas she has were spoken to her by her psychiatrist.

    d. She means that the voice she hears in her head is so loud that she cannot hear her brother speak.

_____ 6. The author likely chose to include the photo on page 539 to

    a. illustrate the threat that a woman feels when she walks the streets of New York.

    b. illustrate the juxtaposition of good and evil.

    c. illustrate the differences between living in light and living in darkness.

    d. illustrate the indifference people have toward the homeless.

Answer the following open-ended questions in complete sentence format.

7. Is the author qualified to write on the topic? Why or why not? How do her own experiences inform the article?

8. Identify at least three issues presented in this reading. Then phrase each issue as a question that the author raises, discusses, or answers.

9. Evaluate the reading on the following criteria:

    a. Is the reading timely?

    b. Has the author provided sufficient evidence to support her main ideas? What other types of evidence might she provide to strengthen the reading?

    c. Do you find any evidence of bias in the reading? Explain.

WRITING IN RESPONSE TO THE READING

G. REVIEWING AND ORGANIZING IDEAS WITH A PARAPHRASE

Complete the following paraphrase of paragraph 3. Begin your paraphrase with the following sentence.

> The author says that since her brother now struggles with mental illness, she no longer expects much from him.

_____

_____

_____

_____

_____

_____

For paragraph 4, write your own two-sentence paraphrase.

_____

_____

_____

_____

H. ANALYZING THE ISSUE

Discuss in class or write in your journal a response to the following questions.

1. Identify at least three issues presented in this reading. Then phrase each issue as a question that the author raises, discusses, or answers.

2. The theme of this chapter is "conformity and nonconformity: following and breaking the rules." Analyze the reading by addressing the following questions:

   a. What examples of conformity has the author provided?
   b. What examples of nonconformity has the author provided?
   c. What rules does Jay, the nonconformist, break?
   d. How is he treated by those who encounter him?
   e. How does he feel about his nonconformist lifestyle?
   f. What does the author learn from her relationship with her brother, the nonconformist?

3. React to this statement: homelessness is more than not having a house.

4. What are some of the misconceptions about homelessness and the homeless?

5. Is homelessness the fault of society or the individual?

I. WRITING PARAGRAPHS AND ESSAYS

Write a paragraph or essay in response to the following writing prompts.

1. Think of a situation in which you tried to help someone who was unwilling or unable to be helped. Write a paragraph describing that experience.

2. Do you agree with the author that the news media would have been more interested in her disappearance than that of her mentally ill brother? Write a paragraph explaining your answer.

3. Try to put yourself in the author's shoes and imagine what you would have done. Do you think you would have been able to let your loved one go? Write a paragraph explaining your answer.

4. Before her brother became homeless, the author viewed homeless people as "unfortunate ornaments of the city." Her experience shows that each homeless person is someone's brother, sister, daughter, or son. Write an essay explaining how you viewed homeless people before reading this article, and how you view them now, after reading the article.

5. The title of this piece, "A Brother Lost," has multiple meanings. Write an essay discussing at least three of these meanings.

6. In this article, the author must come to terms with letting her brother make his own choice about what is the "right path" for him. Write an essay about freedom of choice. You may focus on a difficult choice you made for yourself, or one that you believe represented the right path for another person. How did the choice work out in the end?

SELECTION 17
Magazine Article

American Schools Are Failing Nonconformist Kids. Here's How. In Defense of the Wild Child

Elizabeth Weil

This reading originally appeared in *The New Republic* magazine, which offers commentary on politics and culture. The author, Elizabeth Weil, has also written a memoir about marriage. In this reading, she describes the failings of the American education system in terms of her own experience as the parent of a nonconformist child.

GETTING READY TO READ

PREVIEW IT

Preview the reading using the guidelines on page 6. When you have finished, complete the following items:

1. This reading is about how _____ try to control nonconformist behavior in students.

2. List three topics you expect the author to discuss in the reading.

   a. _____

   b. _____

   c. _____

LOOK IT UP

In this reading, the author writes about nonconformist kids—those who don't fit the traditional school-kid mold—and how American schools have little tolerance for these independent thinkers. Before you read this selection, spend some time researching the issue of non-traditional kids in traditional schools on the Internet. If your search leads you to some related topics and issues that might be of interest to your classmates, take time to read those articles, as well. Take notes on your findings so that you can share with your discussion group.

DISCUSS IT

In a group with three or four of your classmates, discuss the findings of your research on the issue of schools and nonconformist kids. Broaden your discussion to include other related research that your classmates might have read. Be prepared to share the highlights of your discussion with the class.

WRITE ABOUT IT

Connect the reading to your own experience by writing a paragraph about your own education thus far. If you tend to be a nonconformist, what has your experience been like in school? What challenges have you faced because of your nonconformity? If you tend to be more of a conformist, or one who follows the rules, what has your experience been like? How might your perspective or experience be different as the parent of a nonconformist child?

READ IT

This reading is more difficult than many in this text, but it is typical of many readings you will encounter throughout college. Plan on reading this more than once. Decide how you will handle the difficult vocabulary. You may also encounter some unfamiliar concepts; marginal notes are included to help you understand these concepts. Do an Internet search to obtain needed background information, as needed.

As you read the selection, highlight and annotate the text so that you can answer the detailed questions that follow the reading. Take a look at these questions before reading so that you can understand the level of recall that is expected.

American Schools Are Failing Nonconformist Kids. Here's How. In Defense of the Wild Child

Elizabeth Weil

1   Of the possible child heroes for our times, young people with epic levels of the traits we valorize, the strongest contender has got to be the kid in the marshmallow study. Social scientists are so sick of the story that some threaten suicide if forced to read about him one more time. But to review: The child—or really, nearly one third of the more than 600 children tested in the late 60s at Bing Nursery School on the Stanford University campus—sits in a room with a marshmallow. Having been told that if he abstains for 15 minutes he'll get two marshmallows later, he doesn't eat it. This kid is a paragon of self-restraint, a **savant** of delayed gratification. He'll go on, or so the psychologists say, to show the straight-and-narrow qualities required to secure life's sweeter and more elusive prizes: high SAT scores, money, health.

2   I began to think about the marshmallow kid and how much I wanted my own daughter to be like him one day last fall while I sat in a parent–teacher conference in her second-grade classroom and learned, as many parents do these days, that she needed to work on self-regulation. My daughter is nonconformist by nature, a miniature **Sarah Silverman**. She's wildly, transgressively funny and insists on being original even when it causes her pain. The teacher at her private school, a man so hip and unthreatened that he used to keep a boa constrictor named Elvis in his classroom, had noticed she was not gently going along with the sit-still, raise-your-hand-to-speak-during-circle-time program. "So . . ." he said, in the most caring, best-practices way, "have you thought about occupational therapy?"

savant a person who has unusual or exceptional abilities in a specialized field

Sarah Silverman an American comedian known for her lack of inhibition in addressing controversial topics

3   I did not react well. My husband reacted worse. I could appreciate the role of O.T., as occupational therapy is called, in helping children improve handwriting through better pencil grips. But I found other O.T. practices, and the values wrapped up in them, discomfiting: occupational therapists coaching preschoolers on core-muscle exercises so that they can sit longer; occupational therapists leading social-skills playgroups to boost "behavior management" skills. Fidget toys and wiggle cushions—O.T. staples aimed at helping children vent anxiety and energy—have become commonplace in grammar-school classrooms. Heavy balls and weighted blankets, even bags of rice, are also prescribed on the theory that hefty objects comfort children who feel emotionally out of control. Did our daughter need what sounded like a paperweight for her young body in order to succeed at her job as a second-grader?

Auremar/Fotolia

4   My husband grilled the teacher. How were her reading skills? What about math? Did she have friends? All good, the teacher reassured us. "So what's the problem?" my husband asked. "Is she distracting you?" The teacher stalled, then said yes. "And have you disciplined her?" He had not. This is when I began to realize we'd crossed some weird **Foucaultian** threshold into a world in which authority figures **pathologize** children instead of punishing them. "Self-regulation," "self-discipline," and "emotional regulation" are big buzz words in schools right now. All are aimed at producing "appropriate" behavior, at bringing children's personal styles in line with an implicit emotional **orthodoxy**. That orthodoxy is embodied by a composed, conforming kid who doesn't externalize problems or talk too much or challenge the rules too frequently or move around excessively or complain about the curriculum or have passionate outbursts. He's a master at decoding expectations. He has a keen inner minder to bring rogue impulses into line with them.

5   But at what cost? One mother I spoke to, a doctor in Seattle, has a son who has had trouble sitting cross-legged, as his classroom's protocol demanded. The school sent home a note suggesting she might want to test him for "learning difference." She did—"paid about two thousand dollars for testing," she told me—and started the child in private tutoring. "After the third ride home across the city with him sobbing about how much he hated the sessions, we decided to screw it," she said. She later learned every one of the boys in her son's class had been referred out for testing. Another family, determined to resist such intervention, paid for an outside therapist to provide expert testimony to their son's Oakland school stating that he did not have a mental health disorder. "We wanted them to hear from the therapist directly: he's fine," the mother said. "Being a very strong-willed individual—that's a powerful gift that's going to be unbelievably awesome someday."

Foucaultian related to the philosophy of Michel Foucault, who explored the role played by power in shaping knowledge

pathologize to represent something as a disease

orthodoxy a principle or practice that most people agree with or follow

6   In the meantime, he's part of an education system that has scant tolerance for independence of mind. "We're saying to the kid, 'You're broken. You're defective,'" says Robert Whitaker, author of *Mad in America*. "In some ways, these things become self-fulfilling prophesies."

7   Education is the business of shaping people. It works, however subtly, toward an ideal. At various points, the ideal products of the American school system have been extroverts and right-handed children. (Lefties were believed to show signs of "neurological insult or physical malfunctioning" and had to be broken of their natural tendency.) Individuality has had its moments as well. In the 1930s, for instance, educators made huge efforts to find out what motivated unique students to keep them from dropping out because no jobs existed for them to drop into. Yet here in 2013, even as the United States faces pressure to "win the future," the American education system has swung in the opposite direction, toward the **commodified** data-driven ideas promoted by Frederick Winslow Taylor, who at the turn of the century did time-motion studies of laborers carrying bricks to figure out how people worked most efficiently. Borrowing Taylor's ideas, school was not designed then to foster free thinkers. Nor is it now, thanks to how teacher pay and job security have been tied to student performance on standardized tests. "What we're teaching today is obedience, conformity, following orders," says the education historian Diane Ravitch, author of *The Death and Life of the Great American School System*. "We're certainly not teaching kids to think outside the box."

commodified treated like a product that can be bought or sold

8   As a consumer of education—both as a child and a parent—I'd never thought much about classroom management. The field sounds technical and dull, **inside baseball** for teachers. Scratch two inches below the surface, however, and it becomes fascinating, political philosophy writ small. Is individuality to be contained or nurtured? What relationship to authority do teachers seek to create?

inside baseball a reference to a detail-oriented approach to a subject, appreciated by only a small group of insiders

9   One way to think about classroom management (and discipline in general) is that some tactics are external, and others are internal. External tactics work by inflicting an embarrassing or unpleasant experience on the kid. The classic example is a teacher shaming a child by making him write "I will not ..." whatever on the blackboard 100 times. My own second-grade teacher threw a rubber chicken at a boy who refused to shut up during silent reading. But such means have become "well, *problematic*," says Jonathan Zimmerman, director of the History of Education Program at New York University. In 1975, in *Goss v. Lopez*, the Supreme Court found schoolchildren to have due process rights. "As a result, students can say to teachers with some authority, 'If you do that, my mom is going to sue you.' And that changes the score."

10   In *Goss*'s wake, many educators moved toward what progressive education commentator Alfie Kohn calls the New Disciplines. The philosophy promotes strategies like "shared decision-making," allowing children to decide between, say, following the teacher's rules and staying after school for detention. This sounds great to the contemporary ear. The child is less passive and prone to be a victim, more autonomous and in control of his life. But critics of the technique are harsh. It's "fundamentally dishonest, not to mention manipulative," Kohn has written. "To the injury of punishment is added the insult of a kind of mind game whereby reality is redefined and children are told, in effect, that they wanted something bad to happen to them."

utopian involving idealized but impractical perfection

11   A different, **utopian** approach to classroom management works from the premise that children are natively good and reasonable. If one is misbehaving, he's trying to tell you that

something is wrong. Maybe the curriculum is too easy, too hard, too monotonous. Maybe the child feels disregarded, threatened, or set up to fail. It's a pretty thought, order through authentic, handcrafted curricula. But it's nearly impossible to execute in the schools created through the combination of **No Child Left Behind** and recessionary budget-slashing. And that makes internal discipline very convenient right now.

No Child Left Behind law that requires all schools receiving federal funds to conduct annual, state-wide testing of all students

12   According to the human development theory of Dandelion and Orchid children, certain people are genetically predisposed to grow fairly well in almost any environment while others wilt or blossom spectacularly depending on circumstances and care. Some kids—the dandelions—seem naturally suited to cope with the current system. As Sanford Newmark, head of the Pediatric Integrative Neurodevelopmental Program at the University of California at San Francisco, puts it, "You can feed them three Pop-Tarts for breakfast, they can be in school twelve hours a day, and they can go to kindergarten when they're four, and they would still do OK." But many children crumble.

13   As Stanford Professor James Gross, author of *Handbook of Emotional Regulation*, explains, suppression of feelings is a common regulatory tactic. It's mentally draining. Deliberate acts of regulation also become automatic over time, meaning this habit is likely to interfere with inspiration, which happens when the mind is loose and emotions are running high. Even Paul Tough acknowledges in a short passage in *How Children Succeed* that overly controlled people have a hard time making decisions: they're often "compulsive, anxious, and repressed."

14   Maybe the reason we let ourselves become fixated on children's emotional regulation is that we, the adults, feel our lives are out of control. We've lost faith in our ability to manage our own impulses around food, money, politics, and the distractions of modern life—and we're putting that on our kids. "It's a displacement of parental unease about the future and anxiety about the world in general," says psychologist Wendy Mogel, author of *The Blessing of a Skinned Knee*. "I'm worried our kids are going to file the largest class-action suit in history because we are stealing their childhoods. They're like caged animals or Turkish children forced to sew rugs until they go blind. We're suppressing their natural messy existence."

15   I do worry about my little Sarah Silverman. She's frenetic and disinhibited. My life would be easier if she liked to comply. But we did not send her to O.T. Parents make judgment calls about interventions all the time. What's worth treating: a prominent birthmark? A girl with early puberty? Social and behavioral issues can be especially tricky, as diagnosing comes close to essentializing: *It's not your fault that you're acting this way, honey. It's just who you are.* As one mother told me, "The insidious part is, you can start losing faith in your child. You go down this road . . ." Your child's teacher tells you your child is not showing appropriate emotional regulation. You're directed toward psychological evaluations and therapists. They have a hammer. Your kid becomes the nail. "The saddest, most soul-crushing thing is the negative self-image. We think kids don't understand what's happening, but they do. There's this quiet reinforcement that something is wrong with them. That's the thing that'll kill."

UNDERSTANDING AND ANALYZING THE READING

A. BUILDING VOCABULARY

Context

Using context and a dictionary, if necessary, determine the meaning of each word as it is used in the selection.

_____ 1. valorize (paragraph 1)
   a. overlook
   b. set apart
   c. assign value to
   d. imitate

_____ 2. paragon (paragraph 1)
   a. structure
   b. ideal
   c. opponent
   d. guide

_____ 3. discomfiting (paragraph 3)
   a. disconcerting
   b. allowing
   c. suitable
   d. embarrassing

_____ 4. autonomous (paragraph 10)
   a. necessary
   b. discouraged
   c. independent
   d. artificial

_____ 5. frenetic (paragraph 15)
   a. relaxed
   b. polite
   c. objective
   d. frantic

_____ 6. insidious (paragraph 15)
   a. understandable
   b. treacherous
   c. effective
   d. productive

Word Parts

A REVIEW OF PREFIXES	
TRANS-	means *across, over*.
PRE-	means *before*.
DIS-	means *not*.

Use your knowledge of word parts and the review above to fill in the blanks in the following sentences.

1. A person who is *transgressively* (paragraph 2) funny is someone whose humor goes _____ acceptable boundaries.

2. A child may feel *disregarded* (paragraph 11) if he or she is _____ getting enough attention; a child who is *disinhibited* (paragraph 15) is one who is _____ reserved or inhibited.

3. If you are *predisposed* (paragraph 12) to behave a certain way, you are inclined to that behavior in advance or _____.

B. UNDERSTANDING THE THESIS AND MAIN IDEAS

Select the best answer.

_____ 1. The thesis or central thought of this reading is best expressed as

    a. "Children who conform to school rules go on to achieve higher test scores and greater success in life."

    b. "Occupational therapy can help preschool and grammar-school students develop behavior management skills."

    c. "The trend in American schools is to suppress the free thinking and individuality of students who fail to self-regulate their behavior."

    d. "The most effective classroom management approach combines both external and internal tactics."

_____ 2. The topic of paragraph 2 is

    a. the author's daughter.

    b. parent–teacher conferences.

    c. Sarah Silverman.

    d. private school teachers.

_____ 3. The implied main idea of paragraphs 5 and 6 is that

    a. many young children have trouble sitting still in class.

    b. private tutoring is not the answer for children with learning differences.

    c. therapists can provide expert testimony to help students labeled as nonconformists.

    d. the American school system disregards students who do not conform to school rules and expectations.

_____ 4. The topic of paragraph 7 is

    a. extroverts.

    b. time-motion studies.

    c. the American education system.

    d. standardized tests.

C. INTERPRETING SUPPORTING DETAILS

Select the best answer.

_____ 1. The reading mentions all of the following occupational therapy aids *except*

    a. fidget toys.

    b. wiggle cushions.

     c. weighted blankets.

     d. bags of marshmallows.

_____ 2. The author uses all of the following to support her main ideas *except*

     a. personal experience.

     b. direct quotations from experts in education.

     c. interviews with elementary school principals.

     d. examples from other parents.

_____ 3. The New Disciplines philosophy promotes strategies such as

     a. shaming a child by making him write on the blackboard.

     b. using heavy objects to comfort children who feel out of control.

     c. allowing children to decide between following rules or staying after school.

     d. inflicting an embarrassing or unpleasant experience on a child.

_____ 4. According to the author, all of the following types of students have been fostered by the American school system *except*

     a. free thinkers.

     b. extroverts.

     c. conformists.

     d. right-handed children.

D. RECOGNIZING METHODS OF ORGANIZATION AND TRANSITIONS

Select the best answer. See Chapter 7 for information on patterns of organization.

_____ 1. In paragraphs 2–4, the organizational pattern the author uses to describe a parent–teacher conference is

     a. process.

     b. chronological order.

     c. classification.

     d. definition.

_____ 2. In paragraph 7, the organizational pattern the author uses to describe the various "ideal products" of the American school system is

     a. listing.

     b. cause and effect.

     c. illustration.

     d. definition.

_____ 3. The transitional word or phrase that points to the use of cause and effect in paragraph 14 is

    a. *maybe.*

    b. *because.*

    c. *like.*

    d. *until.*

E. FIGURING OUT IMPLIED MEANINGS

Indicate whether each statement is true (T) or false (F).

_____ 1. The author believes that occupational therapy would help her child in school.

_____ 2. The author and her husband believe the teacher should discipline their daughter when she is distracting in class.

_____ 3. The author believes that teacher pay and job security should be tied to student performance on standardized tests.

_____ 4. The author's own second-grade teacher used external tactics as part of classroom management.

_____ 5. According to the human development theory of Dandelion and Orchid children, orchid children probably have difficulty thriving in the current education system.

F. THINKING CRITICALLY ABOUT THE READING

Select the best answer. See Chapter 9 for information about thinking critically about a reading.

_____ 1. The author's purpose in writing "American Schools Are Failing Nonconformist Kids" is to

    a. persuade parents to resist any kind of emotional regulation of their children in schools.

    b. convince readers that American schools place too much emphasis on emotional regulation at the cost of individuality.

    c. outline key research that promotes a utopian approach to classroom management and discipline.

    d. criticize teachers and schools that are unwilling to tolerate students with different abilities.

_____ 2. The tone of the reading can best be described as

    a. objective and formal.

    b. condescending and indifferent.

    c. concerned and disapproving.

    d. bitter and pessimistic.

_____ 3. The photograph accompanying this selection is included to illustrate children who are
   a. misbehaving in a classroom.
   b. engaged in an occupational therapy exercise.
   c. acting in an impulsive way by eating marshmallows.
   d. taking part in a nontraditional class.

_____ 4. Which of the following excerpts from the reading is a fact?
   a. "She's wildly, transgressively funny and insists on being original even when it causes her pain." (paragraph 2)
   b. "Being a very strong-willed individual—that's a powerful gift that's going to be unbelievably awesome someday." (paragraph 5)
   c. "We're certainly not teaching kids to think outside the box." (paragraph 7)
   d. "In 1975, in *Goss v. Lopez*, the Supreme Court found schoolchildren to have due process rights." (paragraph 9)

_____ 5. The author says she wants her daughter to be like the marshmallow kid because he
   a. went on to earn high SAT scores in high school.
   b. became famous after being in the marshmallow study.
   c. had exceptional reading and math skills.
   d. seemed to be able to control his behavior.

_____ 6. In paragraph 9, Jonathan Zimmerman describes external classroom management tactics as "problematic" because
   a. teachers should never be allowed to embarrass or shame students.
   b. children often become upset when a teacher embarrasses them.
   c. students can threaten to sue teachers who inflict unpleasant experiences on them.
   d. children misbehave when they are trying to tell teachers that something is wrong.

Answer the following open-ended questions in complete sentence format.

7. What does the author mean when she says "They have a hammer. Your kid becomes the nail" (paragraph 15)?

8. In your own words, explain why psychologists referred to in this article say that the kid in the marshmallow study will go on to be a successful adult with money, health, etc. (paragraph 1)

9. In paragraph 2, Elizabeth Weil writes, "'So . . .' he said, in the most caring, best-practices way, 'have you thought about occupational therapy?'" What is the tone of her writing in this sentence? Explain your answer.

10. In light of the theme of this reading selection, what message was the teacher in question 9 trying to convey to the child and her parents?

WRITING IN RESPONSE TO THE READING

G. REVIEWING AND ORGANIZING IDEAS WITH A MAP

Create a conceptual map of the reading selection. See page 29 for information about mapping.

H. ANALYZING THE ISSUE

Discuss in class or write in your journal a response to the following questions.

1. What issues does the author bring up in this reading? List at least two.

2. What makes the author qualified to write on the topic? Do you see any evidence of bias in her writing? If so, how?

3. Does the reading offer any emotional appeals? If so, identify them and evaluate their fairness.

4. What assumptions about parenting and/or education does the author make?

5. The theme of this chapter is "conformity and nonconformity: following and breaking the rules." Analyze the reading by addressing the following questions:
   a. What examples of conformity has the author provided?
   b. What examples of nonconformity has the author provided?
   c. What rules does the little "Sarah Silverman" break?
   d. How is she treated when she breaks the rules?
   e. How do her parents react?
   f. How do you think the child felt? Explain your answer to this question using support from the reading.

I. WRITING PARAGRAPHS AND ESSAYS

Write a paragraph or essay in response to the following writing prompts.

1. Think about your own school experience in second grade (the same age as the author's child). Write a paragraph describing what an ideal school day looked like for you then. What was the "classroom management" like in your second grade? In other words, how did your teacher regulate behavior and get students to accomplish tasks?

2. Do you agree with the author's suggestion that adults are fixated on regulating children's emotions because they feel their own lives are out of control (paragraph 14)? Why or why not? Write a paragraph explaining your answer and addressing the idea that "unease about the future and anxiety about the world in general" is to blame.

3. Write an essay giving your own definition of the word "nonconformist." Illustrate your definition with examples of famous nonconformists or ones you know personally in your own life.

4. Consider the two questions the author asks at the end of paragraph 8: "Is individuality to be contained or nurtured? What relationship to authority do teachers seek to create?" Choose one of these questions and write an essay explaining your answer.

5. In paragraph 7, the author asserts that "Education is the business of shaping people." Do you agree with her statement? Think about other important goals of education. What do you think are the "ideal products" of the American school system? Do you think teaching today consists only of "obedience, conformity, following orders," or are children ever taught to "think outside the box"? Write an essay exploring these questions and supporting your ideas with examples from your own experience.

SELECTION 18
Textbook Selection

Groups and Conformity

Michael R. Solomon

The following reading is taken from a business textbook, *Consumer Behavior: Buying, Having, and Being*. Consumer behavior is often considered a subfield of psychology, and it is the study of how, when, and why people buy (or do not buy) products and services. The author, Michael R. Solomon, is professor of marketing and director of the Center for Consumer Research at Saint Joseph's University.

GETTING READY TO READ

PREVIEW IT

Preview the reading using the guidelines on page 6. When you have finished, complete the following items:

1. This reading is about _____.

2. List three terms you expect to be defined or explained in the reading

    a. _____

    b. _____

    c. _____

LOOK IT UP

This textbook reading is about the psychology of consumer behavior. Before you read this selection, spend some time researching this issue on the Internet. To expand the topic, you can research reference groups, the definition of a reference group, and some examples of reference groups. Take notes on your findings so that you can share with your discussion group.

DISCUSS IT

In a group with three or four of your classmates, discuss the findings of your research on consumer behavior and reference groups. You may broaden your discussion to include personal examples of consumer behavior and also reference groups to which you belong. Be prepared to share the highlights of your discussion with the class.

WRITE ABOUT IT

Connect the reading to your own experience by writing a paragraph about how you go about making decisions regarding what to buy. Does your process differ if you are buying something cheap (for example, gum) versus something more expensive (for example, a car)? If so, how?

READ IT

As you read, pay attention to the italicized terms, which indicate important concepts in the field of consumer behavior. (Note that other textbooks' authors may use boldface instead of italics for emphasis.) Be sure to note how each of these terms relates to your own life and experiences.

Be sure to highlight and annotate the text as you read so that you can answer the detailed questions that follow the reading. Take a look at these questions before reading so that you can understand the level of recall that is expected.

Groups and Conformity

Michael R. Solomon

1   Zachary leads a secret life. During the week, he is a straitlaced stock analyst for a major investment firm. He spends a big chunk of the week worrying about whether he'll have a job, so work is pretty stressful these days. However, his day job only pays his bills to finance his real passion: cruising on his Harley-Davidson Road Glide Custom. His Facebook posts are filled with lunchtime laments about how much he'd rather be out on the road (hopefully his boss won't try to friend him). Actually, Zach feels it's worth the risk: he's participating in Harley's free country social media promotion that encourages riders to post their stories ("freedom statements") on Facebook and Twitter to see if they'll include one of his posts on a Harley banner ad. His girlfriend worries a bit about his getting totaled in an accident, but Zach knows if he stays alert the only way that will probably happen is if he can't kick his habit of texting her while he's driving the bike.

low rider a type of motorcycle in which the rider sits low in the seat, closer to the ground than on a typical motorcycle

crib house or apartment

2   Come Friday evening, it's off with the Brooks Brothers suit and on with the black leather, as he trades his Lexus for his treasured Harley. A dedicated member of the HOG (Harley Owners Group), Zachary belongs to the "RUBs" (rich urban bikers) faction of Harley riders. Everyone in his group wears expensive leather vests with Harley insignias and owns custom **"low riders."** Just this week, Zach finally got his new Harley perforated black leather jacket at the company's Motorclothes Merchandise web page. As one of the Harley web pages observed, "it's one thing to have people buy your products. It's another thing to have them tattoo your name on their bodies." Zach had to restrain himself from buying more Harley stuff; there were vests, eyewear, belts, buckles, scarves, watches, jewelry, even housewares ("home is the road") for sale. He settled for a set of Harley salt-and-pepper shakers that would be perfect for his buddy Dan's new **crib**.

3   Zachary's experiences on social media platforms make him realize the lengths to which some of his fellow enthusiasts go to make sure others know they are hog riders. Two of his riding buddies are in a lively competition to be "mayor" of the local Harley dealership on **Foursquare**, while many others tweet to inform people about a group ride that will occur later in the day—kind of a flashmob on wheels.

Foursquare a social media Web site

Ljupco Smokovski/Shutterstock

4   Zach spends a lot of money to outfit himself to be like the rest of the group, but it's worth it. He feels a real sense of brotherhood with his fellow RUBs. The group rides together in two-column formation to bike rallies that sometimes attract up to 300,000 cycle enthusiasts. What a sense of power he feels when they all cruise together—it's them against the world!

5   Of course, an added benefit is the business networking he's accomplished during his jaunts with his fellow professionals who also wait for the weekend to "ride on the wild side—these days it would be professional suicide to let your contacts get cold, and you can't just count on LinkedIn to stay in the loop" (Schouten and Alexander, 1992).

Reference Groups

6   Humans are social animals. We belong to groups, try to please others, and look to others' behavior for clues about what we should do in public settings. In fact, our desire to "fit in" or to identify with desirable individuals or groups is the primary motivation for many of our consumption behaviors. We may go to great lengths to please the members of a group whose acceptance we covet.

7   Zachary's biker group is an important part of his identity, and this membership influences many of his buying decisions. He has spent many thousands of dollars on parts and accessories since he became a RUB. His fellow riders bond via their consumption choices, so total strangers feel an immediate connection with one another when they meet. The publisher of *American Iron*, an industry magazine, observed, "You don't buy a Harley because it's a superior bike, you buy a Harley to be a part of a family" (Machan, 1997).

8   Zachary doesn't model himself after just *any* biker—only the people with whom he really identifies can exert that kind of influence on him. For example, Zachary's group doesn't have much to do with outlaw clubs whose blue-collar riders sport big Harley tattoos. The members of his group also have only polite contact with "Ma and Pa" bikers, whose rides are the epitome of comfort and feature such niceties as radios, heated handgrips, and floorboards. Essentially, only the RUBs comprise Zachary's *reference group*.

9   A reference group is "an actual or imaginary individual or group conceived of [as] having significant relevance upon an individual's evaluations, aspirations, or behavior" (Park and Lessig, 1977, pp. 102–110). Reference groups influence us in three ways: *informational*, *utilitarian*, and *value-expressive*. Table 16-1 below describes these influences. Other people, whether fellow bikers, coworkers, friends, family, or simply casual acquaintances, influence our purchase decisions. We'll consider how our group memberships shape our preferences because we want others to accept us or even because we mimic the actions of famous people we've never met.

TABLE 16-1 THREE FORMS OF REFERENCE GROUP INFLUENCE

Informational Influence	• The individual seeks information about various brands from an association of professionals or independent group of experts.
	• The individual seeks information from those who work with the product as a profession.
	• The individual seeks brand-related knowledge and experience (such as how Brand A's performance compares to Brand B's) from those friends, neighbors, relatives, or work associates who have reliable information about the brands.
	• The brand the individual selects is influenced by observing a seal of approval of an independent testing agency (such as Good Housekeeping).
	• The individual's observation of what experts do (such as observing the type of car that police drive or the brand of television that repairmen buy) influences his or her choice of a brand.
Utilitarian Influence	• So that he or she satisfies the expectations of fellow work associates, the individual's decision to purchase a particular brand is influenced by their preferences.
	• The individual's decision to purchase a particular brand is influenced by the preferences of people with whom he or she has social interaction.
	• The individual's decision to purchase a particular brand is influenced by the preferences of family members.
	• The desire to satisfy the expectations that others have of him or her has an impact on the individual's brand choice.
Value-Expressive Influence	• The individual feels that the purchase or use of a particular brand will enhance the image others have of him or her.
	• The individual feels that those who purchase or use a particular brand possess the characteristics that he or she would like to have.
	• The individual sometimes feels that it would be nice to be like the type of person that advertisements show using a particular brand.
	• The individual feels that the people who purchase a particular brand are admired or respected by others.
	• The individual feels that the purchase of a particular brand would help show others what he or she is or would like to be (such as an athlete, successful business person, good parent, etc.).

Source: Park, C. Whan and V. Parker Lessig, "Students and Housewives: Differences in Susceptibility to Reference Group Influence," *Journal of Consumer Research* (4 September 1977): 102. By permission of Oxford University Press on behalf of *Journal of Consumer Research*, Inc.

When Are Reference Groups Important?

10   Recent research on smoking cessation programs powerfully illustrates the impact of reference groups. The study found that smokers tend to quit in groups: when one person quits, this creates a ripple effect that motivates others in his or her social network to give up the death sticks also. The researchers followed thousands of smokers and nonsmokers for more than 30 years, and they also tracked their networks of relatives, co-workers, and friends. They discovered that over the years, the smokers tended to cluster together (on average in groups of three). As the overall U.S. smoking rate declined dramatically during this period, the number of clusters in the sample decreased, but the remaining clusters stayed the same size; this indicated that people quit in groups rather than as individuals. Not surprisingly, some social connections were more powerful than others. A spouse who quit had a bigger impact than did a friend, whereas friends had more influence than siblings. Co-workers had an influence only in small firms where everyone knew one another.

11   Reference group influences don't work the same way for all types of products and consumption activities. For example, we're not as likely to take others' preferences into account when we choose products that are not very complex, that are low in perceived risk, or that we can try before we buy. In addition, knowing what others prefer may influence us at a general level (e.g., owning or not owning a computer, eating junk food versus health food), whereas at other times this knowledge guides the specific brands we desire within a product category (e.g., if we wear Levi's jeans versus Diesel jeans, or smoke Marlboro cigarettes rather than Virginia Slims).

Types of Reference Groups

12   Although two or more people normally form a group, we often use the term *reference group* a bit more loosely to describe any external influence that provides social cues. The referent may be a cultural figure who has an impact on many people (e.g., Michelle Obama) or a person or group whose influence operates only in the consumer's immediate environment (e.g., Zachary's biker club). Reference groups that affect consumption can include parents, fellow motorcycle enthusiasts, the Tea Party, or even the Chicago Bears, the Dave Matthews Band, or Spike Lee.

13   Some people influence us simply because we feel similar to them. Have you ever experienced a warm feeling when you pull up at a light next to someone who drives the exact car as yours? One reason that we feel a bond with fellow brand users may be that many of us are a bit narcissistic (not you, of course); we feel an attraction to people and products that remind us of ourselves. That may explain why we feel a connection to others who happen to share our name. Research on the name-letter effect finds that, all things being equal, we like others who share our names or even initials better than those who don't. When researchers look at large databases like Internet phone directories or Social Security records, they find that Johnsons are more likely to wed Johnsons, women named Virginia are more likely to live in (and move to) Virginia, and people whose surname is Lane tend to have addresses that include the word lane, not street. During the 2000 presidential campaign, people whose surnames began with B were more likely to contribute to George Bush, whereas those whose surnames began with G were more likely to contribute to Al Gore.

14   Obviously, some groups and individuals are more powerful than others and affect a broader range of our consumption decisions. For example, our parents may play a pivotal

role as we form our values on many important issues, such as attitudes about marriage or where to go to college. We call this *normative influence*—that is, the reference group helps to set and enforce fundamental standards of conduct. In contrast, a Harley-Davidson club exerts *comparative influence* because it affects members' decisions about specific motorcycle purchases.

Membership Versus Aspirational Reference Groups

15   A *membership reference group* consists of people we actually know, whereas we don't know those in an *aspirational reference group*, but we admire them anyway. These people are likely to be successful businesspeople, athletes, performers, or whoever rocks our world. Not surprisingly, many marketing efforts that specifically adopt a reference group appeal concentrate on highly visible, widely admired figures (such as well-known athletes or performers); they link these people to brands so that the products they use or endorse also take on this aspirational quality. For example, an amateur basketball player who idolizes Miami Heat star Dwayne Wade might drool over a pair of Air Jordan 12 Dwayne Wade PE shoes. One study of business students who aspired to the "executive" role found a strong relationship between products they associated with their *ideal selves* and those they assumed that real executives own. Of course, it's worth noting that as social media usage increases, the line between those we "know" and those we "friend" gets blurrier. Still, whether offline or online, we tend to seek out others who are similar. Indeed, one study even found that people on Twitter tend to follow others who share their mood: people who are happy tend to re-tweet or reply to others who are happy, while those who are sad or lonely tend to do the same with others who also post negative sentiments.

Positive Versus Negative Reference Groups

16   Reference groups impact our buying decisions both positively and negatively. In most cases, we model our behavior to be in line with what we think the group expects us to do. Sometimes, however, we also deliberately do the opposite if we want to distance ourselves from avoidance groups. You may carefully study the dress or mannerisms of a group you dislike (e.g., "nerds," "druggies," or "preppies") and scrupulously avoid buying anything that might identify you with that group. For example, rebellious adolescents do the opposite of what their parents desire to make a statement about their independence. In one study, college freshman reported consuming less alcohol and restaurant patrons selected less fattening food when drinking alcohol and eating junk food were linked to members of avoidance groups.

17   Your motivation to distance yourself from a negative reference group can be as powerful or more powerful than your desire to please a positive group. That's why advertisements occasionally show an undesirable person who uses a competitor's product. This kind of execution subtly makes the point that you can avoid winding up like that kind of person if you just stay away from the products he buys. As a once-popular book reminded us, "Real men don't eat quiche!"

We Like to Do It in Groups

18   We get away with more when we do it in a group. One simple reason: the more people who are together, the less likely it is that any one member will get singled out for attention. That helps to explain why people in larger groups have fewer restraints on their behavior.

For example, we sometimes behave more wildly at costume parties or on Halloween than we do when others can easily identify us. We call this phenomenon *deindividuation*—a process whereby individual identities become submerged within a group.

19   Even shopping behavior changes when people do it in groups. For example, people who shop with at least one other person tend to make more unplanned purchases, buy more, and cover more areas of a store than do those who browse solo. Both normative and informational social influence explains this. A group member may buy something to gain the approval of the others, or the group may simply expose her to more products and stores. Either way, retailers are well advised to encourage group-shopping activities.

20   The famous Tupperware party is a successful example of a home shopping party that capitalizes on group pressures to boost sales. In this format, a company representative makes a sales presentation to a group of people who gather at the home of a friend or acquaintance. The shopping party works due to informational social influence: participants model the behavior of others who provide them with information about how to use certain products, especially because a relatively homogeneous group (e.g., neighborhood homemakers) attends the party. Normative social influence also operates because others can easily observe our actions. Pressures to conform may be particularly intense and may escalate as more and more group members "cave in" (we call this process the *bandwagon effect*).

Conformity

21   The early Bohemians who lived in Paris around 1830 made a point of behaving, well, differently from others. One flamboyant figure of the time earned notoriety because he walked a lobster on a leash through the gardens of the Royal Palace. His friends drank wine from human skulls, cut their beards in strange shapes, and slept in tents on the floors of their **garrets**. Sounds a bit like some frats we've visited.

garret room at the top of a house; attic

22   Although in every age there certainly are those who "march to their own drummers," most people tend to follow society's expectations regarding how they should act and look (with a little improvisation here and there, of course). Conformity is a change in beliefs or actions as a reaction to real or imagined group pressure. In order for a society to function, its members develop norms, or informal rules that govern behavior. Without these rules, we would have chaos. Imagine the confusion if a simple norm such as stopping for a red traffic light did not exist.

23   We conform in many small ways every day, even though we don't always realize it. Unspoken rules govern many aspects of consumption. In addition to norms regarding appropriate use of clothing and other personal items, we conform to rules that include gift-giving (we expect birthday presents from loved ones and get upset if they don't materialize), sex roles (men often pick up the check on a first date), and personal hygiene (our friends expect us to shower regularly). We also observe conformity in the online world; research supports the idea that consumers are more likely to show interest in a product if they see that it is already very popular.

24   One study analyzed how millions of Facebook users adopted apps to personalize their pages. Researchers tracked, on an hourly basis, the rate at which 2,700 apps were installed by 50 million Facebook users. They discovered that once an app had reached a rate of about 55 installations a day, its popularity started to soar. Facebook friends were notified when one of their online buddies adopted a new app, and they could also see a list of the most popular ones. Apparently this popularity feedback was the key driver that determined whether still more users would download the software.

25   Still, we don't mimic others' behaviors all the time, so what makes it more likely that we'll conform? These are some common culprits:

- **Cultural pressures**—Different cultures encourage conformity to a greater or lesser degree. The American slogan "Do your own thing" in the 1960s reflected a movement away from conformity and toward individualism. In contrast, Japanese society emphasizes collective well-being and group loyalty over individuals' needs.
- **Fear of deviance**—The individual may have reason to believe that the group will apply *sanctions* to punish nonconforming behaviors. It's not unusual to observe adolescents shunning a peer who is "different" or a corporation or university passing over a person for promotion because she is not a "team player."
- **Commitment**—The more people are dedicated to a group and value their membership in it, the greater their motivation to conform to the group's wishes. Rock groupies and followers of TV **evangelists** may do anything their idols ask of them, and terrorists willingly die for their cause. According to the *principle of least interest*, the person who is least committed to staying in a relationship has the most power because that party doesn't care as much if the other person rejects him. Remember that on your next date.
- **Group unanimity, size, and expertise**—As groups gain in power, compliance increases. It is often harder to resist the demands of a large number of people than only a few, especially when a "mob mentality" rules.
- **Susceptibility to interpersonal influence**—This trait refers to an individual's need to have others think highly of him or her. Consumers who don't possess this trait are role-relaxed; they tend to be older, affluent, and to have high self-confidence. Subaru created a communications strategy to reach role-relaxed consumers. In one of its commercials, a man proclaims, "I want a car. . . . Don't tell me about wood paneling, about winning the respect of my neighbors. They're my neighbors. They're not my heroes."

evangelists
zealous
advocates of
religious causes

unanimity
total (100
percent)
agreement

UNDERSTANDING AND ANALYZING THE READING

A. BUILDING VOCABULARY

Context

Using context and a dictionary, if necessary, determine the meaning of each word as it is used in the selection.

_____ 1. faction (paragraph 2)

    a. percentage

    b. role model

    c. group within a larger group

    d. extreme enthusiast

_____ 2. covet (paragraph 6)

    a. desire

    b. dislike

    c. need

    d. refuse

_____ 3. narcissistic (paragraph 13)

    a. self-conscious

    b. impatient

    c. self-centered

    d. aging

_____ 4. pivotal (paragraph 14)

    a. central

    b. secondary

    c. unimportant

    d. parental

_____ 5. flamboyant (paragraph 21)

    a. modest

    b. strikingly bold

    c. flammable

    d. floating gently

_____ 6. notoriety (paragraph 21)

    a. significant income

    b. jail time for bad behavior

    c. admiration for bad behavior

    d. being widely and unfavorably well-known

Word Parts

> **A REVIEW OF PREFIXES AND SUFFIXES**
>
> **HOMO-** means *same*.
>
> **-TION** means *the act of*.

Use your knowledge of word parts and the review above to fill in the blanks in the following sentences.

1. In a relatively *homogeneous* (paragraph 20) group, many of the people are _____.

2. *Improvisation* (paragraph 22) is the _____ improvising, or responding without preparation.

B. UNDERSTANDING THE THESIS AND MAIN IDEAS

Select the best answer.

_____ 1. The thesis or central thought of "Groups and Conformity" is best stated as

    a. Conformity is the result of several factors, including cultural pressures, fear of deviance, commitment, group unanimity, and susceptibility to interpersonal influence.

    b. Because human beings are inherently social, they often look to different types of reference groups as they make purchase decisions; and in many of these decisions, the desire to conform to social norms plays an important role.

   c. While most reference groups are based on membership or aspiration, a completely different type of reference group, called an avoidance group, reflects an individual's desire not to be like the members of a group that the individual dislikes or disdains.

   d. While groups are an important determinant of consumer behavior in the United States, the influence of social groups (such as friends and co-workers) is much smaller in other countries, where the dominant culture focuses more on individuality than on group conformity.

_____ 2. The main idea of paragraph 13 is found in the

   a. first sentence.

   b. second sentence.

   c. fifth sentence.

   d. last sentence.

_____ 3. The topic of paragraph 20 is

   a. the bandwagon effect.

   b. group pressures.

   c. Tupperware.

   d. home shopping parties.

For items 4–8, match the term in Column A with its definition in Column B.

Column A: Term	Column B: Definition
_____ 4. aspirational reference	a. a change in actions or beliefs in reaction to imagined or real group pressures
_____ 5. deindividuation	b. the idea that the person who is least committed to being in a relationship holds the most power in that relationship
_____ 6. principle of least interest	c. a process by which individual people, and their identities and personalities, become submerged within a group identity
_____ 7. normative influence	d. a group of people, usually composed of highly visible, widely admired athletes or performers, whose success people wish to associate themselves with (or whose behaviors they seek to emulate)
_____ 8. conformity	e. the process by which a reference group helps establish and enforce basic standards of conduct for its group members

C. INTERPRETING SUPPORTING DETAILS

Select the best answer.

_____ 1. According to the reading, what is the best definition of a "ripple effect" (paragraph 10)?

    a. a pattern that is not easily explained

    b. the likelihood that people will give up smoking in groups instead of individually

    c. the overall decrease in sales of a particular product (such as cigars and cigarettes)

    d. the continuing and spreading results of an event or action

_____ 2. According to the reading, what is the most likely address for a man named Brian Court?

    a. 14 Main Street

    b. 2605 Adriana Road

    c. 173 Phoenix Court

    d. 42689 Palisade Avenue

_____ 3. Suppose you have an aversion to punk rockers. For you, punk ockers are a(n)

    a. aspirational reference group.

    b. utilitarian reference group.

    c. normative group.

    d. avoidance group.

_____ 4. The type of evidence used to support the main ideas in paragraphs 10 and 24 is

    a. the author's personal experience.

    b. quotes from experts.

    c. research studies.

    d. analogies.

D. RECOGNIZING METHODS OF ORGANIZATION AND TRANSITIONS

For items 1–4, match the paragraph in Column A with its organizational pattern in Column B. See Chapter 7 for information about patterns of organization.

Column A: Paragraph	Column B: Organizational Pattern
_____ paragraph 9	a. illustration
_____ paragraph 11	b. cause and effect
_____ paragraph 24	c. definition

Select the best answer.

_____ The word or phrase that points to the pattern in paragraph 24 is

   a. *analyzed.*

   b. *personalize.*

   c. *popularity.*

   d. *determined.*

E. FIGURING OUT IMPLIED MEANINGS

Indicate whether each statement is true (T) or false (F).

_____ 1. In both the real world and the online world, we tend to seek out people who are similar to us.

_____ 2. In Japan, people are more likely to focus on individualistic efforts rather than group needs.

_____ 3. In the decision to quit smoking, spouses have a stronger influence than friends.

_____ 4. Consumers are more likely to take other people's preferences into account when they are buying products with a low perceived value.

_____ 5. A role-relaxed woman does not care much about what people think of her.

F. THINKING CRITICALLY ABOUT THE READING

Select the best answer. See Chapter 9 for information about thinking critically about a reading.

_____ 1. The author's purpose in "Groups and Conformity" is to

   a. provide an overview of the influence of reference groups and conformity on consumers' buying decisions, while providing key definitions, examples, and research findings.

   b. make students aware of the unseen forces at work in advertising, on the Internet, and in public gathering places like malls and coffeehouses.

   c. explain the differences between specific reference groups and specific conformist groups, while showing readers how to make better purchasing decisions.

   d. expose the unethical practices of companies like Harley-Davidson and Tupperware, which take advantage of people's desires to be part of a group or community.

_____ 2. In "Groups and Conformity," the author often uses informal language. Which of the following is *not* an example of informal language?

    a. "perfect for his buddy Dan's new crib" (paragraph 2)

    b. "they link these people to brands" (paragraph 15)

    c. "sounds a bit like some frats we've visited" (paragraph 21)

    d. "remember that on your next date" (paragraph 25)

_____ 3. In paragraph 10, "death sticks" is figurative language whose literal meaning is

    a. baseball bats.

    b. falling branches.

    c. swords.

    d. cigarettes.

_____ 4. What is the connotation of the phrase "freedom statements" that is used on Harley-Davidson's social media? (paragraph 1)

    a. important business documents, such as spreadsheets and corporate mission statements

    b. historical records of freed slaves, such as Harriet Tubman

    c. sense of freedom from responsibilities and the demands of one's job

    d. Twitter updates by political prisoners in countries like Russia and China

_____ 5. Paragraph 24 uses the term "popularity feedback." Which of the following is the best example of popularity feedback?

    a. A singer's album is #1 on the charts, so more people buy a copy of that album.

    b. The most attractive people tend to be the most popular in social situations.

    c. A first-year college student from out of state attempts to make as many friends as possible during his first year on campus.

    d. A young woman who works for a political action committee avoids buying goods in stores that make use of underpaid overseas child labor.

_____ 6. The term "mob mentality" in paragraph 25 refers to

    a. people who see the Mafia as an aspirational reference group.

    b. the tendency for large groups of people to exert powerful influence over the individuals in that group.

    c. the belief that most people prefer the company of others rather than being alone.

    d. the large number of psychological or mental disorders in urban areas with large populations.

Answer the following open ended questions in complete sentence format.

7. An aspiring young athlete purchases basketball shoes that are advertised by a professional basketball player such as Michael Jordan or Kobe Bryant. Using Table 16-1on page 564, identify the type of influence this is. Explain your answer.

8. A female employee at a local flower shop decides to wear the same brand of perfume favored by the shop's other female employees. Using Table 16-1on page 564, identify the type of influence this is. Explain your answer.

9. A recent college graduate buys a car that is recommended as a "best buy" by *Consumer Reports*, an unbiased consumer-advocacy magazine. Using Table 16-1on page 564, identify the type of influence this is. Explain your answer.

10. From Table 16-1on page 564, choose a type of influence and create a scenario from **your** buying behaviors that illustrates that type of influence (see questions 7, 8, and 9 for examples). Also, provide an explanation of how the scenario illustrates the type of influence.

WRITING IN RESPONSE TO THE READING

G. REVIEWING AND ORGANIZING IDEAS WITH A SUMMARY

Write a clear and concise summary of paragraphs 1–11 of the reading. See page 31 for information about writing a summary.

H. ANALYZING THE ISSUE

1. The theme of this chapter is "conformity and nonconformity: following and breaking the rules." Analyze the reading by addressing the following questions:

    a. What examples of conformity has the author provided?

    b. What examples of nonconformity has the author provided?

    c. In what small, everyday ways do you conform to the expectations of others?

    d. Considering your answer in question 1c, what would happen if you chose not to conform to some of those small, everyday expectations?

2. How does the information about the source of the reading and the author provide a hint regarding its overall reliability?

3. Does the author provide adequate background information about the topic of groups and conformity? Explain your answer.

4. What assumptions does the author make about his readers?

5. Do you find any evidence of bias in the reading? Explain.

I. WRITING PARAGRAPHS AND ESSAYS

Write a paragraph or essay in response to the following writing prompts.

1. The reading begins with the example of Zachary, who uses his motorcycle as a way of getting away from his everyday life. What hobby do you engage in when you want to forget about your problems or have a sense of freedom? (For example, do you surf the Web or rent movies?) Write a paragraph about your favorite get-away-from-it-all pastime.

2. The reading discusses the way people can influence one another to quit smoking. Write a paragraph in which you explore some of the ways people can help friends or family members achieve a goal (for instance, getting more exercise, applying for a job, or getting a good grade on an exam).

3. Write an essay in which you explore three groups to which you aspire (that is, three groups you would like to belong to).

4. Think about a celebrity who endorses a particular product. Why do you think the company chose that spokesperson? To whom is the company trying to appeal? Do you think that celebrity endorsements help sell products? Do such techniques work on you? Why or why not? Write an essay in which you explore these questions.

5. Are you a rule keeper or a rebel? Do you march in step with others, or do you "march to the beat of a different drummer"? Write an essay in which you answer this question by providing three examples that support your thesis. You should also talk about why you behave as you do and how you feel when you behave as you do.

ACTIVITIES: EXPLORING CONFORMITY AND NONCONFORMITY

On your own or with a group of classmates, complete two of the following four activities.

1. In Reading Selection 17, Elizabeth Weil talks about how American schools treat children who do not conform to certain behavioral standards in the classroom. Think about your current college experience. What are the norms for behavior in the college classroom and on campus? What are the sanctions for deviating from these norms? Compile a list of at least five in each category.

2. Celebrity magazines (like *Us* and *People*) are filled with photos of glamorous Hollywood stars and musicians. What norms are dominant in Hollywood? How do you think the lives of celebrities are fundamentally different from those of the typical American? Provide at least three examples of the ways in which celebrities' lives differ from that of the "average" person. For instance, some celebrities have hundreds of thousands of followers on their Twitter accounts. Does the average person have that many followers? Why would so many people choose to follow a celebrity's "tweets"?

3. The readings in this chapter discussed just a few aspects of conformity and nonconformity. Other issues related to this topic include:

   - **Dress codes:** What is appropriate to wear in different situations? Do men's dress codes differ from women's? If so, how and why? How have dress codes changed over the years?

   - **Hairstyles:** If you are going for a job interview, what are the expectations for how you should wear your hair? What are the "do's" and the "don'ts" for both women and men?

   - **Body adornment:** How does society view piercings, tattoos, and other body adornments? How have these perceptions changed over the years? For example, what did a tattoo signal in 1950, and what does it signal today?

   - **Political protest:** The United States protects freedoms of speech and demonstration. How is political protest a form of nonconformity, and what types of new tools for political protest or political change are now available (that were not available 20 years ago)?

   - **Life on and off the grid:** "The grid" refers to the system by which companies and the government track you and your activities: your Social Security number, your address, your place of employment, and so forth. Some people, the ultimate nonconformists, choose to live "off the grid." What motivates these people, and why?

   Write an essay or prepare a class presentation about any of these topics, or any other topic regarding conformity or nonconformity.

4. As mentioned in the introduction to this chapter, different sets of norms apply to different groups of people. Write an essay or prepare a presentation in which you compare and contrast two sets of norms. Choose from the list below, or choose two other groups you find particularly interesting.

- Team athletes (for example, baseball and football players) versus individual athletes (for example, gymnasts and ice skaters)
- Upperclassmen (juniors and seniors) versus underclassmen (freshmen and sophomores)
- Students in introductory courses (for example, introduction to psychology) versus students in a discipline's upper-level courses (for example, psychological statistics or abnormal psychology)
- Adolescents/teenagers versus senior citizens

MAKING CONNECTIONS: THINKING WITHIN THE ISSUES

In many college courses, instructors will expect you to read and evaluate a wide variety of materials. This section requires you to draw connections between the readings on this issue explored within the chapter. The activities and assignments below will give you practice in synthesizing information and thinking critically about the relationship of the chapter readings.

1. "Groups and Conformity" (Selection 18, p. 561) ends a chapter devoted to conformity and nonconformity, or people's decisions to follow or break society's rules. How do the parents of "little Sarah Silverman" in "American Schools Are Failing Nonconformist Kids" (Selection 17, p. 549) conform to society's rules? Do they conform to the "rules of parenting" that are more common in the United States? How do their thoughts and behaviors affect their relationships with others?

2. Jay in "A Brother Lost" (Selection 16, p. 538) and "little Sarah Silverman" in "American Schools Are Failing Nonconformist Kids" (Selection 17, p. 549) are both misunderstood by the worlds in which they live, but their loved ones seem to have come to understand them and perceive them in a different light. Your task is to compose an essay in which you discuss the similarities and differences in the two characters. Before you begin writing your essay, brainstorm your ideas and organize them by using a graphic organizer or an outline.

17 Personal Freedoms and Limitations: Lifestyle Choices

How do you define the word freedom?
When you hear the word, do you think about societal freedoms, like freedom of speech and freedom of the press? Or do you think about more personal freedoms, such as the freedom to make the right choices for your life and your family?

People in the United States enjoy some of the greatest personal freedoms in the world, and Americans have become used to living in a free society. But such freedoms are not found around the world. In some Middle Eastern countries, for example, women must have the permission of a male relative to travel, marry, study, or work. Some countries, such as China and Russia, try to control information by censoring the Internet and throwing journalists into jail. Here are some examples of the personal decisions most Americans are free to make:

- They can decide to remain single (rather than get married) and to remain childless (instead of having children).

- They can choose to join groups and organizations that reflect their beliefs and values. For example, the NRA (National Rifle Association) has a very strong membership composed of people who believe that Americans have the right to bear arms. However, the millions of Americans who believe in gun control would never join the NRA.

- They can decide how much education to get (college or trade school?), where to live (city, suburb, or rural area?), and where to work.

But even the freest of societies place some limitations on their people. Laws prevent people from hurting others or society, and illnesses or other factors can limit a person's choices. All the readings in this chapter focus on personal freedoms and/or limitations. For example, how does a mental illness, such as bipolar disorder, limit a person's choices, activities, and relationships? How do public universities allow or limit freedom of speech? What is trafficking in persons (TIP), and what is being done to arrest this form of exploitation and enslavement?

WHY IS FREEDOM SUCH AN IMPORTANT CONTEMPORARY ISSUE?

The United States was founded on the principle of freedom—specifically, freedom of worship. The Puritans who first came to North America were fleeing religious persecution in England. Key documents in the history of the United

States, such as the Bill of Rights written by the Founding Fathers, are very specific about the freedoms permitted to citizens. As a country, we have always been concerned with our freedoms, and these concerns have become more pressing in the twenty-first century, when Americans are having more limitations placed on them. For example, air travel now requires personal searches and body X-rays. Many see these searches as an invasion of privacy, while others argue that such rules are required to prevent terrorist attacks. Recent news reports have also pointed to other limitations that are being proposed or put into place. For example, in 2012 the mayor of New York City proposed banning sugary soft drinks of more than 16 ounces as a way of combating the health problems that go with obesity. Does the government really have the right to tell us how much soda and juice we can drink? This is a question that many people are asking.

How Do Personal Freedoms and Limitations Tie in to My College Courses?

History and political science courses almost always trace the history of groups who are looking for freedom. Psychology courses often discuss decision making and offer tips for analyzing a situation and choosing the best course of action. Sociology courses look at the freedoms and limitations placed on people around the world. And, of course, simply by attending college and choosing a major, you have made personal choices about your education and the path you want your life to take.

TIPS FOR READING ABOUT PERSONAL FREEDOMS AND LIMITATIONS

Here are some tips for reading not only the selections in this chapter, but any reading about personal freedoms and limitations.

- **Look for and analyze opposing viewpoints.** Many of today's most controversial issues regarding personal freedoms revolve around a "benefit analysis." That is, do laws that restrict personal freedoms do more good for society as a whole than they do harm to individuals? Try to understand both sides of the argument to develop a deeper understanding of the topic you are reading about. For example, those who believe in the right to bear arms see this right as essential to defending themselves and their families against people who would hurt them. Meanwhile, those who believe in gun control believe that the murder rate would decrease drastically if guns were not available.

- **Look for indications of bias.** Closely consider the author's thesis and look for signs of bias. Remember that bias is not necessarily negative; a writer may be biased *in favor of* something or *against* something. Understanding the sources of bias will help you better evaluate the reading and its main ideas.

- **Tie the reading to your life and experiences.** Put yourself in the author's position. How would you feel? Would you make the same choices or different choices? How would you react to having limitations placed on your choices?

SELECTION 19
Personal Essay

Bipolar Disorder: The Agony and the Ecstasy

Thomas Wheaton

The author of "Bipolar Disorder: The Agony and the Ecstasy" is a freelance journalist who chose to publish this personal essay under a pseudonym (a false name) to protect his privacy.

GETTING READY TO READ

PREVIEW IT

Preview the reading using the guidelines on page 6. When you have finished, complete the following items:

1. Indicate whether each statement is true (T) or false (F).

_____ Bipolar disorder affects many Americans.

_____ Bipolar disorder is not a medical condition.

LOOK IT UP

Thomas Wheaton suffers with bipolar disorder. Before you read his story, spend some time on the Internet researching this mental health condition and its effects on those who live with it. Take notes on your findings so that you can share with your discussion group.

DISCUSS IT

In a group with three or four of your classmates, discuss the findings of your research on the issue of bipolar disorder. Broaden your discussion to include other mental health conditions and the resulting challenges that affect one of your friends or acquaintances.

WRITE ABOUT IT

Connect the reading to your own experience by writing about your own familiarity with depression. Have you or someone you know ever experienced a period of depression? How long did it last? How did it make you feel? What helped to lift you out of a depressive state?

READ IT

Understanding word parts can help you better understand the author's definition of bipolar disorder. *Bi-* means "two," and bipolar disease means alternating between two "poles": depression and euphoria. In the past, people who suffered with bipolar disorder were called "manic-depressives," but psychologists no longer use that term.

As you read the selection, highlight and annotate the text so that you can answer the detailed questions that follow the reading. Take a look at these questions before reading so that you can understand the level of recall that is expected.

Bipolar Disorder: The Agony and the Ecstasy

Thomas Wheaton

1   Bipolar disorder (BP) is a mental health condition typified by mood swings between gushing euphoria and draining depression. Out of the 26.2 percent of Americans over age 18 with a form of mental illness, BP affects 5.7 million ("Numbers"). Bipolar disorder is a medical condition like heart disease or arthritis. It doesn't have anything to do with someone being weak or lazy. Living with bipolar disorder requires more personal strength and hard work than the non-bipolar can imagine.

2   There are three types of bipolar disorder, as defined in the *Diagnostic and Statistical Manual: IV*, the current reference manual for psychiatric diagnosis. Bipolar 1 requires at least one episode of **mania** or a mixed episode in a person's lifetime. (A mixed episode is an epic freak-out where mania and depression coexist. They're awful.) Bipolar 2 describes patients who alternate mood states between severe depression and a milder form of mania. Bipolar 2 often looks like high functionality. The intense mood intervals, or cycles, last a few days each. Cyclothymic disorder is very much like BP, but with less severe mood swings happening more frequently ("Bipolar Disorder").

mania a period of intense, robust activity accompanied by euphoria

3   Bipolar disorder requires multidisciplinary treatment. Medication alone isn't enough. In addition to writing in my journal daily, I have biweekly appointments with my therapist to talk about feelings and bimonthly appointments with my psychiatrist to make sure the meds are working. I'm prescribed 1500 mg of Depakote daily, 100 mg of Zoloft, and the occasional Xanax for panic attacks. 50 mg of Trazodone makes sure I sleep all night. If I take my meds exactly on time every day, stability's easier. If I'm off a few hours one day, I can feel the difference. If I miss a dose, I'm not suitable for the general public. I need them for stability, but the meds have side effects.

4   Dealing with the side effects requires more than just taking medication on time. Because pills are broken down in the stomach and intestines before being filtered through the liver and kidneys, I must drink uncomfortable amounts of water to avoid organ damage. The medications make me heat-sensitive. My mouth is always dry. Sometimes my head buzzes when I stand up. Everything I take has a warning label for dizziness. Being without medication, though, is far worse than taking it. That's because my specific type of bipolar disorder is unusually challenging.

5   Based on the current definitions, my diagnosis is "Bipolar–Not Otherwise Specified, with ultra-ultra rapid cycling." That means I experience significant mood swings from mania to depression more than once daily, but my symptoms don't meet the strict criteria for Bipolar 1, 2, or cyclothymic disorder ("Bipolar Disorder"). Cycles this short are rare and very challenging, because I have to deal with both depression and mania, sometimes less than minutes apart. What are those states like? Here's a brief primer for those not lucky enough to know firsthand.

6   Depression is soul-wrenchingly awful. If you've never been depressed, imagine being sad, except the saddest you've ever been and all the time. When my meds are working, I get an occasional horrible thought, but it goes no further. Before doctors got my medications balanced, thinking about suicide to the point of holding a knife to my wrist was familiar territory. I tried to kill myself twice, at age six and early freshman year. I finally got the help I needed in an **inpatient facility** where trained professionals could watch and medicate me. Not everyone with BP needs that level of help, but I did. I was lucky to have access to inpatient care—the number of available beds has been shrinking nationwide (Daviss). Unfortunately, depression is only half of the bipolar experience.

7   Manic mood states lead to impulsivity, hypersexuality, and rash decisions. Untreated bipolar disorder is the reason I bought 29 pairs of sneakers and nearly had to buy a friend an $80 drinking glass from a Web site. (I'm glad they were out of stock.) Manic or elevated moods can also involve high energy, rapid speech, and the ability to take care of what's been neglected while depressed. As long as I'm not overly agitated, manic focus rivals the feelings described by students who utilize **amphetamines** as study drugs. Mania is an elevated state of mood that, for me, feels very much like being "in the zone." I enjoy being manic. Previously, that led me away from taking my meds.

8   Going on and off meds can wreak havoc on a class schedule. I barely showed up to college classes, but when I did I was annoyingly attentive. I didn't have my diagnosis yet, so professors thought I was high all the time. This did not go over well. Bipolar disorder usually develops in one's twenties—having mental health care available on campus is crucial. Waiting only means things get worse.

9   Bipolar has a "kindling effect"—it gets worse the longer it's not dealt with (Purse). My symptoms appeared early—I can remember BP moments in preschool. Later in life, it manifested itself in spending a large percentage of my income on recreational drugs. I was the guy who'd do and say the stuff you wanted to but knew societal rules meant you shouldn't. Every day without mood stabilizers was another twig thrown on the growing fire of my instability. Every day I regret not getting a diagnosis and proper medication sooner.

10   There's speculation that the kindling effect can increase the cycling speed of mood swings, one of the most **confounding** aspects of bipolar disorder. It's like being *both* Dr. Jekyll and Mr. Hyde, but without the ability to choose when. I'd drive girlfriends to tears, and then switch moods and try to cuddle. It's harder to fix tears you brought on. I've learned to recognize when I'm not in control of my mood by the reactions of others—and how to give myself a minute outside. These skills help keep my actions from getting too much in the way of relationships, but at the cost of having to constantly watch everything I do, everything I say, and everyone's reaction to it.

11   Having to pay constant attention is a theme for anyone with BP who wants to thrive, not just survive. Sleeping enough, eating healthy, and managing my **electrolyte** levels can buy me enough time not to yell at the police. Nutrition and self-care aren't fixes any more than

inpatient facility a medical building in which patients stay for a period of time (often several days or weeks) to help get their illness under control

amphetamines drugs that stimulate the central nervous system, such as caffeine; "uppers"

confounding causing surprise or confusion in someone, often by acting against their expectations

electrolytes chemicals in the body that regulate nerves, muscles, blood pressure, and other important functions

meds are, though. I can eat and sleep and take meds and rehydrate perfectly but still be talking a mile a minute or be totally uninterested in playing with kittens. Times like that are when I rely on my safety net or learn how strong I really am.

12   ⟍Family and friends make the bipolar life much, much easier. When you're all wrapped up in your own head, calm outside input can make all the difference. I can always depend on my mom to focus on the actual problem instead of my emotional response. My girlfriend knows that occasionally I need to hide under a blanket in the dark until the depression fades. If it weren't for Nikki gently reminding me that I'm talking a little too fast, I might not notice. She's good at spotting when I need alone time. Her and others' perception is very helpful. But I still can't let my guard down. This constant internal struggle is one of my least favorite parts of living with BP.

13   Being bipolar doesn't just suck on the inside. The world thinks it's acceptable to insult people by calling them crazy. That word hurts a lot more when you have a diagnosis. When I leave my therapist's office, I make sure to fold the yellow full-page receipt and get it out of view so people won't treat me differently. As much as I've wanted to write this essay, I wouldn't dare do it under my real name.

14   Living with bipolar disorder requires a terribly intimate knowledge of yourself. Maintaining stability requires maintaining all aspects of regular health plus the ability to find strength when moods cycle anyway. I need a thick skin to deal with the challenges BP brings, especially taking meds on time. It'd be much harder without my safety net of family, friends, and doctors. I must fight every single frustrating day to be good to and for myself. Living with bipolar, however, is far better than the alternative.

Works Cited

"Bipolar Disorder." National Alliance on Mental Illness, www.nami.org/Learn-More /Mental-Health-Conditions/Bipolar-Disorder.

Daviss, Steven Roy. "Running Out of Psychiatric Beds." *Psychology Today*, 8 Mar. 2011, www. psychologytoday.com/blog/shrink-rap-today/201103/running-out-psychiatric-beds.

"The Numbers Count: Mental Disorders in America." National Institute of Mental Health, www.nimh.nih.gov/health/publications/the-numbers-count-mental-disorders-in-america/index.shtml . Accessed 3 Aug. 2012.

Purse, Marcia. "The Kindling Effect and Theory in Bipolar Disorder." *VeryWell*, About, 15 May 2012, www.verywell.com/the-kindling-model-in-bipolar-disorder-378713.

UNDERSTANDING AND ANALYZING THE READING

A. BUILDING VOCABULARY

Context

Using context and a dictionary, if necessary, determine the meaning of each word as it is used in the selection.

_____ 1. epic (paragraph 2)
   a. classic
   b. expensive
   c. large-scale
   d. wonderful

_____ 2. primer (paragraph 5)
   a. first in a series
   b. liquid used to prepare wood for finishing
   c. instruction in the basics
   d. most exciting event of a lifetime

_____ 3. rash (paragraph 7)
   a. impulsive and hasty
   b. red and irritated
   c. expensive and unnecessary
   d. emotionally draining

_____ 4. havoc (paragraph 8)
   a. unpredictability
   b. swing made from cloth
   c. complete destruction
   d. attendance problem

_____ 5. manifested (paragraph 9)
   a. showed
   b. prepared
   c. energized
   d. created

_____ 6. speculation (paragraph 10)
   a. disagreement
   b. anger
   c. guessing
   d. research

Word Parts

A REVIEW OF PREFIXES, ROOTS, AND SUFFIXES	
CO-	means *joint, mutual,* or *together*.
RE-	means *back* or *again*.
HYPER-	means *over* or *excessive*.
HYDRO	means *water*.
MULTI-	means *many*.
-ITY	refers to a *state, condition,* or *quality*.

Use your knowledge of word parts and the review above to fill in the blanks in the following sentences.

1. When two groups of people *coexist* (paragraph 2), they live _____, or side by side, in peace.

2. When used to describe college studies, *multidisciplinary* refers to courses that use information from _____ different disciplines. As used in paragraph 3, *multidisciplinary* refers to treatment for mental illness that requires _____ different specialties to be involved.

3. Someone who engages in a period of *hypersexuality* (paragraph 7) has an _____ amount of sex.

4. To *rehydrate* (paragraph 11) means to add _____ back into the body.

B. UNDERSTANDING THE THESIS AND MAIN IDEAS

Select the best answer.

_____ 1. The thesis statement for "Bipolar Disorder: The Agony and the Ecstasy" is
   a. the first sentence of paragraph 2.
   b. the last sentence of paragraph 1.
   c. the first sentence of paragraph 5.
   d. the third sentence of paragraph 14.

_____ 2. The topic of paragraph 6 is
   a. suicide.
   b. medication.
   c. inpatient care.
   d. depression.

_____ 3. The main idea of paragraph 9 is found in the
   a. first sentence.
   b. second sentence.
   c. fourth sentence.
   d. fifth sentence.

C. INTERPRETING SUPPORTING DETAILS

Select the best answer.

_____ 1. Depression is all of the following *except*
   a. a soul-wrenching mental health disorder.
   b. one "pole" of bipolar disorder.
   c. another name for bipolar disorder.
   d. one of the causes of suicide.

_____ 2. Which of the following does *not* characterize the manic state?
   a. paranoia
   b. impulsiveness
   c. rapid speech
   d. high energy

_____ 3. When the author refers to his "safety net," he means
   a. the medications prescribed for him.
   b. his doctors, friends, and family.

      c. the college counseling center.

      d. his own feelings of self-esteem and worthiness.

_____ 4. The author supports his thesis primarily with

      a. research, statistics, and personal experience.

      b. case studies of anonymous people who suffer from BP.

      c. an explanation of the different types of bipolar disorder.

      d. expert opinions and quotations from doctors.

D. RECOGNIZING METHODS OF ORGANIZATION AND TRANSITIONS

Select the best answer. See Chapter 7 for information on patterns of organization.

_____ 1. Which paragraph makes use of the definition pattern of organization?

      a. paragraph 5

      b. paragraph 8

      c. paragraph 11

      d. paragraph 13

_____ 2. Which paragraph makes use of the classification organizational pattern?

      a. paragraph 2

      b. paragraph 4

      c. paragraph 7

      d. paragraph 9

_____ 3. The sentences 5–8 of paragraph 3 all use the _____ pattern.

      a. comparison and contrast

      b. process

      c. cause and effect

      d. chronological order

_____ 4. Two transitional phrases that signal the cause and effect pattern in paragraph 7 are

      a. *can also involve, the ability to.*

      b. *lead to, the reason.*

      c. *manic focus, elevated state.*

      d. *high energy, rapid speech.*

E. FIGURING OUT IMPLIED MEANINGS

Indicate whether each statement is true (T) or false (F).

_____ 1. Medications are broken down in the stomach and intestines.

_____ 2. The amount of inpatient care for those suffering from BP is increasing in the United States.

_____ 3. Trazodone functions as a type of sleeping pill.

_____ 4. The author attempted to commit suicide three times.

_____ 5. The author's BP diagnosis clearly falls into the "Bipolar 2" category.

F. THINKING CRITICALLY ABOUT THE READING

Select the best answer. See Chapter 9 for information about thinking critically about a reading.

_____ 1. The author's purpose in "Bipolar Disorder: The Agony and the Ecstasy" is to

    a. encourage readers to engage in self-reflection and self-evaluation.

    b. distinguish among the different types of bipolar disorder.

    c. describe his experiences and struggles with bipolar disorder.

    d. criticize the medical system for its tendency to overprescribe drugs.

_____ 2. The tone of the selection can accurately be described as all of the following *except*

    a. personal.

    b. removed.

    c. revealing.

    d. informative.

_____ 3. Often, a photo of the author accompanies a personal essay. Why do you think no author photo is included with "Bipolar Disorder: The Agony and the Ecstasy"?

    a. The author is not young and handsome.

    b. The author does not want to imply that bipolar disorder affects only men.

    c. The author's girlfriend asked him not to include a photo of himself.

    d. The author wishes to remain anonymous.

_____ 4. The phrase "high functionality" in paragraph 2 refers to

    a. a type of high brought on by large doses of medication.

    b. the positive effects of seeing a therapist and discussing one's personal issues.

    c. a state in which a person performs well in his or her personal life and at work.

    d. the mathematics and statistics required to understand psychological diagnoses.

_____ 5. In paragraph 14, the author states, "Living with bipolar, however, is far better than the alternative." What does he mean?

    a. Medications have made living with bipolar disorder much easier on those who are affected by it.

    b. BP people generally prefer to have other BP people as roommates.

    c. Living with a mental illness is better than being dead.

    d. His girlfriend would rather have him (and his accompanying BP) than a different boyfriend who does not have a psychological illness.

_____ 6. When the author says "I'm not suitable for the general public" in paragraph 3, he means

    a. he has not washed his hair or taken a shower for several weeks.

    b. his BP makes it likely that he will behave inappropriately around other people.

    c. his employer has asked him to take sick leave to care for his illness.

    d. he avoids crowded areas, such as movie theaters, restaurants, and shopping malls.

Answer the following open-ended questions in complete sentence format.

7. Explain how Wheaton's bipolar disorder affected his relationships with others.

8. In paragraph 1, Wheaton says, "Living with bipolar disorder requires more personal strength and hard work than the non-bipolar can imagine." Give three details from the reading that support this statement.

9. What does the author imply about society's assumptions regarding mental illness?

10. What type of photo (or other visual aid) might the author use to illustrate the main points raised in his essay? Describe the visual and explain why you chose that particular one.

WRITING IN RESPONSE TO THE READING

G. REVIEWING AND ORGANIZING IDEAS WITH A PARAPHRASE

Complete the following paraphrase of paragraphs 1–3. Begin your paraphrase with the following sentence.

Bipolar disorder, or BP, is a psychological illness characterized by two extreme emotional states: euphoria (or mania) and depression.

_____

_____

_____

_____

_____

_____

_____

_____

_____

_____

For paragraph 4 of the reading, write your own two-sentence paraphrase.

_____

_____

_____

_____

H. ANALYZING THE ISSUE

Discuss in class or write in your journal a response to the following questions.

1. What contemporary issue is the author discussing in this reading? Write a one- or two-sentence paraphrase of the author's thesis.

2. Is the author making an argument in "Bipolar Disorder: The Agony and the Ecstasy," or is his primary goal to provide information? Explain your answer.

3. Has the author provided sufficient evidence to support his thesis? What other types of evidence might he provide to strengthen the reading's main ideas?

4. Do you find any evidence of bias in the reading? Explain.

5. The theme of this chapter is "personal freedoms and limitations: lifestyle choices." Analyze the reading by addressing the following questions:

   a. What examples of limitations has the author presented?

   b. How is the theme of freedom presented in this reading?

   c. What lifestyle choices does the author make? Explain your answer.

   d. How does the author feel about the limitations he lives with?

   e. How is the author treated by those he encounters?

I. WRITING PARAGRAPHS AND ESSAYS

Write a paragraph or essay in response to the following writing prompts.

1. Write a paragraph summarizing the three major types of bipolar disorder.

2. Suppose a friend asks you, "What does a person with bipolar disorder typically experience?" Write a paragraph explaining the disorder to your friend.

3. The author says that manic moods lead to "impulsivity." Have you ever made an impulsive decision? What were the effects of that decision? Write an essay describing your experience.

4. What types of mental health care are available on your campus? Write an essay providing information about the available options.

5. People who are diagnosed with bipolar disorder are sometimes called crazy, according to the author. Write an essay in which you explore the differences between being "called crazy" and being diagnosed with bipolar disorder.

SELECTION 20
Digital News Article

Hate Speech Is Protected Free Speech, Even on College Campuses

Erwin Chemerinsky

This entry appeared on Vox, a digital news site. The author, Erwin Chemerinsky, is dean and professor of law at the University of California Berkeley School of Law. He also is the co-author of a book, along with Howard Gillman, entitled *Free Speech on Campus* (Yale University Press, 2017).

GETTING READING TO READ

PREVIEW IT

Preview the reading using the guidelines on page 6. When you have finished, complete the following items.

1. This reading is about the issue of freedom of _____.

2. List three questions that you expect to find answered in this reading.

   a. _____

   b. _____

   c. _____

LOOK IT UP

Before you read this essay, spend some time on the Internet researching the free speech movement of the 1960s. Read about some of the historical events that were a part of this movement. Take notes on your findings so that you can share with your discussion group.

DISCUSS IT

In a group with three or four of your classmates, discuss the findings of your research on the free speech movement of the 1960s. Be prepared to share the highlights of your discussion with the class.

WRITE ABOUT IT

Connect the reading to your own experience as you consider the following questions: What does freedom of speech mean to you? Have you ever felt that you were not free to speak out on a controversial issue? Do you know of any instances when someone's speech caused him or her to be arrested? Did you agree or disagree with the individual's actions or his/her punishment? Is there any issue that you feel so strongly about that you would speak out or risk arrest?

READ IT

In this essay, the author speaks from his perspective and shares his personal experience. How does this technique contribute to his argument and your willingness to listen to what he has to say?

As you read the selection, highlight and annotate the text so that you can answer the detailed questions that follow the reading. Take a look at the questions before reading so that you can understand the level of recall that is expected.

Hate Speech Is Protected Free Speech, Even on College Campuses

My students trust colleges to control offensive speech. They shouldn't.

Erwin Chemerinsky

Paul Hennessy/Alamy Stock Photo

Protesters confront each other while white nationalist Richard Spencer, president of the National Policy Institute, a white supremacist think tank, speaks at the University of Florida in Gainsville, Florida.

1   "We should refuse to allow hateful speakers on campus," a campus faculty member said. The statement was met with resounding applause. I mentally prepared for the response to what I was going to say next. It was September, and I was at a forum at which several professors, including me, discussed free speech issues before a large audience of students at the University of California Berkeley. Several faculty and students had already implored Chancellor Carol Christ to revoke the invitations of conservative provocateurs Milo Yiannopoulos and Ann Coulter to speak on campus, and their declarations were met with enthusiasm.

2   Finally I spoke up. "Be clear that if Chancellor Christ were to exclude speakers based on their viewpoint, she would get sued and lose," I said. "The speakers would get an injunction and be allowed to speak. They would recover attorneys' fees and maybe money damages. They would be portrayed as victims. And since they would get to speak anyway, nothing would be gained." No one applauded.

3   I have been dean of Berkeley's law school for several months. But before I arrived at campus, the university, home of the free speech movement of the 1960s, had become a battleground for a new kind of campus speech debate. In late September, elaborate security precautions were taken when conservative commentator Ben Shapiro spoke at Berkeley; $600,000 had to be spent so he could deliver his remarks without disruption. When conservative student groups attempted to host a "Free Speech Week," and invited conservative speakers like Coulter and Steve Bannon, the campus steeled itself to spend in excess of $1 million to allow them to speak while ensuring safety on the campus. (In the end, "Free Speech Week" was canceled by the student group that had organized it.)

4   I have been teaching First Amendment law to law students and undergraduates for more than 37 years. I have also litigated free speech cases, including at the Supreme Court. I believe that Chancellor Christ and the campus have done a superb job of adhering to the First Amendment, protecting free speech while ensuring the safety of students, staff, and faculty. But it's also become clear to me that current college students are often ambivalent, or even hostile, to the idea of free speech on campus.

Students Today Are Driven by a Desire to Protect Their Classmates from Hate Speech

5   Disputes over free speech on campus have long occurred, but today is different. Usually in the past, it was students who wanted to speak out and campus administrators who tried to stop demonstrations. Now it often is about outside speakers and outside disruptors, like the radical leftist protest group Antifa. The campus is just the place for their battle.

6   At Berkeley and elsewhere, it is now often students and faculty calling for preventing the speakers while campus officials are steadfastly protecting freedom of expression. In my seminars the past two years (before Berkeley, I was at UC Irvine's law school), I was surprised by how much the students wanted campuses to stop offensive speech—and the degree to which they trusted campus officials to have the power to do so. A 2015 survey by the Pew Research Institute said that four in 10 college students believe the government should be able to prevent people from publicly making statements that are offensive to minority groups.

7   While teaching our class on free speech on campus at UC Irvine, Chancellor Howard Gillman and I realized that the students' desire to restrict hurtful speech came from laudable instincts. This is the first generation of college students to be taught from a young age that bullying is wrong; they have internalized this message. Many spoke powerfully of instances in which they or their friends had suffered from hurtful speech. They want to make campuses inclusive for all, and they know that hate speech causes great harm, especially among those who have been traditionally underrepresented in higher education.

8   But I worry, too, that students do not realize the degree to which free speech has been essential for the advancement of rights and equality. There would not have been a 19th Amendment, which gave women the right to vote, without the women's suffrage movement

and its widespread demonstrations. The civil rights protests of the 1960s—lunch counter sit-ins, the march on Selma, demonstrations on campuses—were essential to bringing about the end of segregation.

9   Those events, though, are ancient history for my students. I worry that they equate freedom of speech more with the vitriol of the anonymous messaging app Yik Yak than the anti-Vietnam War protests I participated in when I was in college. I was surprised by how little our students knew about the history of free speech, including the outbreak of McCarthyism, when faculty and students suffered greatly from the lack of legal protection for expression and academic freedom.

10   Although all of this makes the context different today, the law of the First Amendment and the principles of academic freedom are clear and long established. The Supreme Court repeatedly has said that the First Amendment means public institutions cannot punish speech, or exclude speakers, on the grounds that it is hateful or deeply offensive. This includes public colleges and universities.

Hate Speech Is Protected by the First Amendment

11   Every effort by the government to regulate hate speech has been declared unconstitutional. Over 25 years ago, more than 350 colleges and universities adopted hate speech codes. But every court to consider such a hate speech code declared it to be unconstitutional. The codes inevitably were far too vague in terms of what speech was permitted and what was prohibited. Of course, free speech is not absolute and can be punished when it incites illegal activity, constitutes a "true threat" that causes a person to fear imminent harm to his or her physical safety, or rises to the level of prohibited harassment.

12   This does not mean that campuses are powerless in the face of disruptive or hateful speech. Even though there is a First Amendment right to speak, that does not mean that protesters have the right to demonstrate in the middle of a freeway at rush hour. A campus surely could prohibit a large demonstration in a classroom building while classes are in session. Campuses can regulate when and where speech takes place in order to prevent disruption of school activities. Controversial speakers can be placed in auditoriums where it is easier to assure safety and prevent disruptions. Demonstrations can be placed in areas away from where classes are in session. Although the First Amendment applies only to the government, including public universities, private universities should follow these same principles. They are essential to academic freedom, which is at the very core of a university's mission.

13   There might be a point at which it is impossible to simultaneously protect public safety and allow controversial speech to occur. Then campus officials have no choice but to prevent the speech, given that they must provide for the safety of students, staff, and faculty. But canceling a speaker should truly be a last resort and never based on the viewpoint expressed.

14   At what point should a campus cancel a speaker because it cannot afford to ensure the safety of students, staff, and faculty? Chancellor Christ has estimated that already this semester, the campus has spent more than $2 million to protect free speech. I believe Berkeley campus officials made the right choice in protecting these speakers from harm, but I also know that such expenditures are not sustainable.

15   Although speakers have a right to express hateful messages on campus, that does not mean that campus officials should silently tolerate such speech. It is important that campus officials denounce hate when it occurs and explain why it is inconsistent with the type of community we desire.

Education Is Enhanced When There Is More Speech, not When Speech Is Regulated by Campus Officials

16   The law is clear that a public university may not exclude a speaker based on his or her views, nor may students or faculty be punished for the views they express. In a separate piece for Vox, professor Robert Post challenges this by suggesting that usual free speech principles should not apply on campus. He argues that campuses must of course engage in content-based judgments in evaluating a faculty member's scholarship or a student's work. From this, he concludes that universities are justified in excluding outside speakers that do not serve the educational mission of the campus.

17   Post's premise is undoubtedly correct: universities must evaluate the content of faculty and student work. But it does not follow that outside of this realm, free speech principles do not apply on campus. It is a logical fallacy to say that because basic free speech principles sometimes do not apply on campus, they must never apply.

18   First, it is important to distinguish what the law is from what Post thinks the law should be. Under current First Amendment law, a public university clearly would be acting unconstitutionally if it excluded a speaker from campus based on his or her viewpoint. When Auburn University attempted to prevent white supremacist Richard Spencer from speaking, a federal court ruled against the university. Second, Post ignores the distinction between the university's ability to regulate speech in professional settings (such as in grading students' papers or in evaluating teaching and scholarship) and its ability to regulate speech in other contexts. The former does not justify a university's ability to restrict campus speakers based on viewpoint or to punish student or faculty speech in a nonprofessional setting.

19   Professor Post also argues that a primary purpose of a university is to educate students—so a campus would be justified in excluding speakers that it perceives as interfering with this mission. But the law says quite the contrary. It does not allow a public university to exclude a speaker by claiming that the viewpoint expressed would be so offensive to students that it would interfere with their education. Also, this would seem to give unlimited discretion to campus officials to exclude or punish any speaker that they deemed to be inconsistent with students' education. The assumption of freedom of speech, and of academic freedom, is that education is enhanced when there is more speech, not when government officials have the power to censor and punish speech they don't like.

20   Having seen the enormous amount of time and money invested by the Berkeley campus to deal with the appearances of Ben Shapiro and Milo Yiannopoulos, I cannot help but wish this had happened someplace else. But I know that Berkeley, especially because of its history with the free speech movement of the 1960s, is a unique place for expression. This is why it is so important that the campus did all it could to ensure freedom of speech. It is also why this campus has the chance to be a model for other schools in upholding the principle that all ideas and views can be expressed at colleges and universities.

UNDERSTANDING AND ANALYZING THE READING

A. BUILDING VOCABULARY

Context

Using context and a dictionary, if necessary, determine the meaning of each word as it is used in the selection.

_____ 1. injunction (paragraph 2)
   a. order
   b. invitation
   c. engagement
   d. opinion

_____ 2. steeled (paragraph 3)
   a. positioned
   b. prepared
   c. insured
   d. decided

_____ 3. ambivalent (paragraph 4)
   a. decisive
   b. puzzled
   c. uncertain
   d. critical

_____ 4. laudable (paragraph 7)
   a. natural
   b. basic
   c. praiseworthy
   d. learned

_____ 5. vitriol (paragraph 9)
   a. bullying behavior
   b. personal comments
   c. cruel criticism
   d. confrontational remarks

_____ 6. incites (paragraph 11)
   a. encourages
   b. opposes
   c. mimics
   d. affects

Word Parts

> ### A REVIEW OF PREFIXES AND SUFFIXES
>
> | | |
> |---|---|
> | **UN-** | means *not.* |
> | **IL-** | means *not.* |
> | **-IAL** or **-AL** | refer to *a state* or *condition*. |

Use your knowledge of word parts and the review above to fill in the blanks in the following sentences.

1. An *unconstitutional* act (paragraph 11) is one that does _____ uphold the Constitution of the United States.

2. *Illegal* activities (paragraph 11) refer to those that have the condition of being _____.

B. UNDERSTANDING THE THESIS AND MAIN IDEAS

Select the best answer.

_____ 1. Which of the following best states the thesis or central idea of the reading?

    a. The issue of free speech on college campuses has a long history, especially on the Berkeley campus, and is not as cut and dried as students and administrators would like for it to be.

    b. An educated individual is one who has been exposed to many different ideas and established his or her own belief system after deliberately examining the ideas of others.

    c. While many college students oppose hate speech, university officials must respect free speech principles and allow hate speech, while ensuring the safety of university faculty, students, and staff.

    d. Based on their feelings about bullying and harming others with their speech, today's students are vehemently opposed to free speech.

_____ 2. The topic of paragraph 19 is

    a. public universities

    b. education

    c. academic freedom.

    d. censorship

_____ 3. Which of the following is true of the main idea in paragraph 7?

    a. The main idea is stated directly in the first sentence.

    b. The main idea is stated directly in the second sentence.

    c. The main idea is stated directly in the last sentence.

    d. The main idea of this paragraph must be inferred from context.

C. INTERPRETING SUPPORTING DETAILS

Select the best answer.

_____ 1. Which of the following historical events is *not* associated with freedom of speech?

    a. McCarthyism

    b. the Vietnam War protests

    c. the march on Selma

    d. the death of Rev. Martin Luther King

_____ 2. The author believes that some of today's students are in favor of restricting hurtful speech because of their

    a. prolonged exposure to conservative ideologies.

    b. deep religious beliefs about treating everyone as an equal.

    c. belief that hurting others is wrong.

    d. overly-protective upbringing.

_____ 3. The author uses all of the following types of evidence _except_

    a. personal experience.

    b. quotes from students.

    c. historical evidence.

    d. research and statistics.

D. RECOGNIZING METHODS OF ORGANIZATION AND TRANSITIONS

Select the best answer. See Chapter 7 for information on patterns of organization.

_____ 1. The dominant organizational pattern in paragraph 5 is

    a. classification.

    b. comparison and contrast.

    c. definition.

    d. process.

_____ 2. The dominant organizational pattern in paragraph 7 is

    a. cause and effect.

    b. comparison and contrast.

    c. order of importance.

    d. spatial order.

_____ 3. The transitional word or phrase that signals the organizational pattern of paragraph 7 is

    a. _while._

    b. _came from._

    c. _in which._

    d. _and._

E. FIGURING OUT IMPLIED MEANINGS

Indicate whether each statement is true (T) or false (F).

_____ 1. Although he favors freedom of speech on college campuses, the author does not support the idea that college officials should tolerate hateful and damaging messages.

_____ 2. The author believes that colleges should not refuse any requests by controversial speakers because they will get sued for doing so.

_____ 3. The author asserts that although college administrators understand the issue of freedom of speech, they are still not open to demonstrations, whether peaceful or not.

_____ 4. The author thinks that college officials have no constitutional right to ban controversial speakers solely because of their viewpoint.

_____ 5. The author believes that freedom of speech contributes positively to one's education.

F. THINKING CRITICALLY ABOUT THE READING

Select the best answer. See Chapter 9 for information about thinking critically about a reading.

_____ 1. The author's primary purpose in "Hate Speech Is Protected Free Speech, Even on College Campuses" is to

  a. offer his perspective on the constitutionality of freedom of speech on college campuses.

  b. compare and contrast students' feelings about having controversial speakers on college campuses in the '60s and now.

  c. explore differences in attitudes toward freedom of speech in college students and administrators.

  d. inform those who are opposed to free speech on college campuses of the historical significance of the First Amendment.

_____ 2. The author's tone in this selection is best described as

  a. objective.

  b. earnest.

  c. pessimistic.

  d. mocking.

_____ 3. What right do college administrators have when it comes to having a controversial speaker on campus?

a. They can request a preview of the speech before it is given.

b. They can conduct a thorough background check of the speaker.

c. They can dictate where the speech will take place.

d. They can deny a speaker access to its students in the days leading up to and following the speech.

_____ 4. In paragraph 11, when the author says, "free speech is not absolute," he means that

a. hate speech codes can prevent controversial speakers from freely speaking their convictions.

b. free speech cannot be monitored or regulated closely.

c. having the right to free speech does not protect one from punishment.

d. there are exceptions to the freedom one has to speak one's convictions.

_____ 5. The First Amendment applies to all entities *except* for

a. private colleges and universities.

b. state-supported colleges and universities.

c. state governments.

d. federal governments.

_____ 6. Which of the following excerpts from the reading is a fact?

a. "I believe that Chancellor Christ and the campus have done a superb job of adhering to the First Amendment, protecting free speech while ensuring the safety of students, staff, and faculty." (paragraph 4)

b. "But every court to consider such a hate speech code declared it to be unconstitutional." (paragraph 11)

c. "But canceling a speaker should truly be a last resort and never based on the viewpoint expressed." (paragraph 13)

d. "It is important that campus officials denounce hate when it occurs and explain why it is inconsistent with the type of community we desire." (paragraph 15)

Answer the following open-ended questions in complete sentence format.

7. What is a logical fallacy? Explain the one that the author mentions n paragraph 17.

8. How has the First Amendment contributed to the advancement of rights and equality in the United States? Explain in your own words.

9. If you were to choose a visual to accompany this reading, what would it be? Describe the visual, explain how it supports the author's message, and propose a caption for the visual.

10. What is Yik Yak? You may look up this term if you do not know what it means. Why does the author include a reference to Yik Yak in paragraph 9?

WRITING IN RESPONSE TO THE READING

G. REVIEWING AND ORGANIZING IDEAS WITH A MAP

Create a conceptual map of the reading selection. See page 29 for information about mapping.

H. ANALYZING THE ISSUE AND THE ARGUMENT

1. What contemporary issue is discussed in this reading? Phrase this issue in the form of a question.

2. The theme of this chapter is "personal freedoms and limitations: lifestyle choices." Analyze the reading by addressing the following questions:
   a. What freedoms and limitations has the author presented?
   b. What lifestyle choices has the author presented?
   c. What misconceptions about the First Amendment has the author presented?

3. What is the author's background, and is he qualified to write about the topic? Why or why not? (Be sure to take note of the various references to the author's work that are mentioned in the reading.)

4. Would you describe the author's approach to the issue as "pro" or "con"?

5. Evaluate the reading on the following criteria:
   a. Is the reading timely?
   b. Does the author offer any opposing viewpoints? If so, does he refute them? If not, what might some opposing viewpoints be?
   c. What assumptions (either stated or implied) do you find in the reading?
   d. Does the article offer any emotional appeals? If so, identify them and evaluate their fairness.
   e. Do you find any bias in the selection? Explain.

I. WRITING PARAGRAPHS AND ESSAYS

Write a paragraph or essay in response to the following writing prompts.

1. Write a paragraph in which you explain how you, personally, have exercised your right to speak freely on a college campus or in a public place.

2. "A 2015 survey by the Pew Research Institute said that four in 10 college students believe the government should be able to prevent people from publicly making statements that are offensive to minority groups" (paragraph 6). Write a paragraph response to this statement.

3. In paragraph 9, the author writes about the outbreak of McCarthyism. Research this topic and then write a paragraph or essay explaining why this event is a critical piece of the history of free speech in the United States.

4. In paragraph 18, the author asserts that "education is enhanced when there is more speech, not when government officials have the power to censor and punish speech they don't like." In an essay, discuss what you see as being the purpose of education and then explain how free speech contributes to or detracts from that purpose.

5. "Hate Speech Is Protected Free Speech, Even on College Campuses" presents both a pro and con argument on the right to free speech. With which viewpoint do you agree? Write an essay in which you answer this question. Be sure to use both personal experience and points from the reading as support for your thesis.

SELECTION
21
Textbook Reading

Human Smuggling and Trafficking

Frank Schmalleger

Frank Schmalleger has both a master's and doctorate degree in sociology and is a distinguished professor emeritus at the University of North Carolina at Pembroke, where he taught criminology and criminal justice courses from 1976 to 1994 and was chair of the Department of Sociology, Social Work, and Criminal Justice for 16 years. He is the author of a textbook titled *Criminology Today: An Integrative Introduction*. Criminology is the scientific study of the causes and prevention of crime and the rehabilitation and punishment of offenders. The selection that follows is an excerpt from his book.

GETTING READY TO READ

PREVIEW IT

Preview the reading using the guidelines on page 6. When you have finished, complete the following items:

1. This reading will define the terms _____ and _____
   _____.

2. List three aspects of human smuggling and trafficking that you expect the reading will discuss. _____
   _____
   _____

3. Determine whether each statement is true (T) or false (F).

   _____ a. There are important differences between smuggling and trafficking.

   _____ b. Human trafficking takes place only outside of the United States.

LOOK IT UP

In this reading, Frank Schmalleger writes about two of the fastest-growing international criminal activities today—human smuggling and human trafficking. Before you read this selection, spend some time on the Internet researching the two criminal activities. Take notes on your findings so that you can share with your discussion group.

DISCUSS IT

In a group with three or four of your classmates, discuss the findings of your research on the illegal activities of human smuggling and human trafficking. If time permits, broaden your discussion to include misconceptions you had about the two activities and what you found most surprising in your research. Be prepared to share the highlights of your discussion with the class.

WRITE ABOUT IT

Connect the reading to your own experience by writing a paragraph about the victims and perpetrators of human smuggling and trafficking. What types of people do you picture? Think of news reports you have read about people involved in smuggling and trafficking. How have these stories formed your mental image of both victims and smugglers/traffickers?

READ IT

This reading contains detailed information about the government agencies and federal legislation that relate to human smuggling and trafficking. You may want to create a study sheet so you can keep track of this information as you read.

As you read the selection, highlight and annotate the text so that you can answer the detailed questions that follow the reading. Take a look at these questions before reading so that you can understand the level of recall that is expected.

Human Smuggling and Trafficking

Frank Schmalleger

1   According to the United Nations, trafficking in persons and human smuggling are some of the fastest-growing areas of international criminal activity today. There are important distinctions between the two. The U.S. State Department defines **human smuggling** as "the facilitation, transportation, attempted transportation or illegal entry of a person(s) across an international border, in violation of one or more country's laws, either clandestinely or through deception, such as the use of fraudulent documents." In other words, human smuggling refers to illegal immigration in which an agent is involved for payment to help a person cross a border clandestinely. Human smuggling may be conducted to obtain financial or other benefits for the smuggler, although sometimes people smuggle others to reunite their families. Human smuggling generally occurs with the consent of the people being smuggled, who often pay for the services. Once in the country they've paid to enter, they usually are no longer in contact with the smuggler. The State Department notes that the vast majority of people who are assisted in illegally entering the United States annually are smuggled rather than trafficked.

2   Although smuggling might not involve active coercion, it can be deadly. In January 2007, for example, truck driver Tyrone Williams, 36, a Jamaican citizen living in Schenectady, New York, was sentenced to life in prison for causing the deaths of 19 illegal immigrants in the nation's deadliest known human smuggling attempt.

3   The Intelligence Reform and Terrorism Prevention Act of 2004 established the Human Smuggling and Trafficking Center (HSTC) within the Department of Homeland Security (DHS). U.S. Immigration and Customs Enforcement (ICE), the largest investigative agency within the DHS, has primary responsibility for enforcing laws related to human smuggling and trafficking. As a result, ICE plays a leading role in the fight against human smuggling and trafficking.

4   In contrast to smuggling, **trafficking in persons (TIP)** can be compared to a modern-day form of slavery. Trafficking involves the exploitation of unwilling people through force, coercion, threat, or deception and includes human rights abuses such as debt bondage, deprivation of liberty, or lack of control over freedom and labor. Trafficking is often undertaken for purposes of sexual exploitation or labor exploitation. The Global Fast Fund, a nonprofit international charity that tracks TIP incidents, says that "the primary countries of destination for victims of trafficking are the United States, Italy, Japan, Canada, Australia, and other 'advanced nations.'"

5   A 2011 report by the United Nations Office on Drugs and Crime says that "The term trafficking in persons can be misleading [because] it places emphasis on the transaction aspects of a crime that is more accurately described as enslavement. Exploitation of people, day after day. For years on end."

6   Practically speaking, it is sometimes difficult to distinguish between a smuggling case and a trafficking case because trafficking often includes an element of smuggling (that is, the illegal crossing of a national border.) Some trafficking victims may believe they are being smuggled when they are really being trafficked but are unaware of their eventual fate. This happens, for example, when women trafficked for sexual exploitation may have thought they were agreeing to work in legitimate industries for decent wages—part of which they may have agreed to pay to the trafficker who smuggled them. They didn't know that upon arrival, the traffickers would keep them in bondage, subject them to physical force or sexual violence, force them to work in the sex trade, and take most or all of their income. Table 17-1 draws some important distinctions between human trafficking and smuggling.

Human Trafficking

7   U.S. government officials estimate that 800,000 to 900,000 victims are trafficked globally each year and that 17,500 to 18,500 are trafficked into the United States. Women and children comprise the largest group of victims, and they are often physically and emotionally abused. Although TIP is often an international crime that involves the crossing of borders, it is important to note that TIP victims can be trafficked within their own country and community. Traffickers can move victims between locations within the same country and often sell them to other trafficking organizations.

8   A few years ago, the Department of Justice funded the creation of the Human Trafficking Reporting System (HTRS) to report on human trafficking within the United States. The most recent HTRS report provides data on human trafficking incidents that were investigated between January 2008 and June 2010.

TABLE 17-1 DISTINGUISHING BETWEEN HUMAN TRAFFICKING AND SMUGGLING

TRAFFICKING	SMUGGLING
Must contain an element of force, fraud, or coercion (actual, perceived, or implied), unless the victim is under 18 years of age and is involved in commercial sex acts.	The person being smuggled is generally cooperating.
Forced labor and/or exploitation.	No forced labor or other exploitation.
Persons trafficked are victims.	Persons smuggled are violating the law. They are not victims.
Enslaved, subjected to limited movement or isolation, or had documents confiscated.	Persons are free to leave, change jobs, and so forth.
Need not involve the actual movement of the victim.	Facilitates the illegal entry of person(s) from one country into another.
No requirement to cross an international border.	Smuggling always crosses an international border.
Person must be involved in labor/services or commercial sex acts (that is, must be "working").	Person must only be in the country or attempting entry illegally.

Note: This table is meant to be conceptual and is not intended to provide precise legal distinctions between smuggling and trafficking.

Source: Adapted from U.S. Department of State, Bureau for International Narcotics and Law Enforcement Affairs, Human Smuggling and Trafficking Center, *Distinctions between Human Smuggling and Human Trafficking* (Washington, DC: January 1, 2005).

9   Seen globally, the International Labour Organization (ILO), the United Nations agency charged with addressing labor standards, employment, and social protection issues, estimates that 12.3 million people are in forced labor, bonded labor, forced child labor, and sexual servitude throughout the world today. Other estimates range as high as 27 million.

INTERNATIONAL SEX TRAFFICKERS TURN GIRLS INTO SLAVES

10   According to wide-ranging estimates from the United Nations (UN) and the FBI, hundreds of thousands of girls around the world are in bondage to sex traffickers, and the numbers are rising. The victims are typically aged 8 to 18, and some are as young as 4 or 5.

11   In poor countries like Cambodia, families reportedly sell a young daughter to sex traffickers for the equivalent of $10. Some of these girls are later rescued and sent to shelters. Then–Secretary of State Hillary Clinton visited one such shelter in Cambodia in 2010. "I met with dozens of girls, most of them very young, who had been sexually exploited and abused," she recalled. "They had been given refuge at the shelter and they were learning valuable skills to help them reenter society."

12   Sex traffickers are most active within their own countries, but many of them cross borders and even enter the United States. In some cases, they lure their victims with promises of a legitimate job, and then keep them in bondage until they pay off excessively high debts for their transportation. The Department of Justice reported 1,220 sex trafficking incidents in the United States from January 2007 to September 2008. These girls are often afraid to contact authorities for fear of being

identified as illegal immigrants, the State Department reports. They have justification, the department explained in a 2012 report. When they are found out, they are often arrested, incarcerated, and deported, rather than given shelter.

13   To address this rising international crime, Congress in 2000 passed the Trafficking Victims Protection Act, which also addresses indentured laborers. On the international level, the law authorizes the State Department to create public awareness programs, assess trafficking in each foreign country, and develop sanctions against countries that fail to take action. Within the United States, the law steps up prosecution of traffickers based on new federal crimes and heightened penalties. The U.S. Immigration and Customs Enforcement unit oversees prosecution, and victims are protected from deportation through a new T visa. Although no more than 5,000 T visas are allowed per year, less than half that amount is granted, but the number is growing.

14   In a related action in 2003, the FBI launched the U.S. Innocence Lost National Initiative, in conjunction with other federal agencies. In June 2012, the FBI reported that the initiative had rescued almost 900 children and helped secure the convictions of more than 500 sex traffickers.

Federal Immigration and Trafficking Legislation

15   The United States had open national borders until the 1880s, when limited federal controls on immigration began. One of the nation's first immigration laws was the Chinese Exclusion Act, which became law in 1882 and was enforced for ten years; it was enacted in response to large numbers of Chinese male laborers who had immigrated to the western United States in the mid-1800s looking for work and often took jobs on railroads and in the mining industry.

16   A more comprehensive piece of federal immigration legislation was the 1924 Immigration Act limiting the number of immigrants who could be admitted from any one country to 2% of the number of people from that country who were already living here (calculated using the Census of 1890). The law also barred immigration from specific parts of the Asia-Pacific Triangle, including Cambodia, China, Japan, Korea, Laos, the Philippines, and Thailand. The Immigration and Nationality Act (INA) of 1952, establishing the Immigration and Naturalization Service (INS) while continuing numerical ethnic quotas, provided criminal penalties for anyone bringing or attempting to bring unauthorized aliens into the United States; years later, the INA amendments of 1965 abolished quotas based on ethnicity. The Homeland Security Act of 2002 (HSA) dissolved the INS and transferred most of its functions to three branches of the DHS: Citizenship and Immigration Services (CIS), Customs and Border Protection (CBP), and ICE.

17   Recognizing that human smuggling and TIP were serious social issues, Congress passed the Trafficking Victims Protection Act of 2000 (TVPA), which addressed the significant problem of TIP for the purposes of having people commit commercial sex acts (termed sex trafficking) and of subjecting them to involuntary servitude, **peonage**, or debt bondage, and increased the protections afforded victims of trafficking. The TVPA specified severe forms of trafficking: "a.) sex trafficking in which a commercial sex act is induced by force, fraud, or coercion, or in which the person induced to perform such an act has not attained 18 years of age; or b.) the recruitment, harboring, transportation, provision, or obtaining of a person for labor or services, through the use of force, fraud, or coercion for the purpose of subjection to involuntary servitude, peonage, debt bondage, or slavery."

peonage
a type of involuntary servitude where laborers are bound to work until their debts are paid

18   Under the TVPA, human trafficking does not require the crossing of an international border or even the transportation of victims from one locale to another because victims of certain forms of trafficking are not just illegal aliens, but also U.S. citizens, legal residents, or visitors. Victims do not have to be women or children; they may also be adult males.

19   The Trafficking Victims Protection Reauthorization Act (TVPRA) of 2003 added a new initiative to the original law to collect foreign data on trafficking investigations, prosecutions, convictions, and sentences. Its 2006 data showed that reporting **jurisdictions** prosecuted 5,808 people for trafficking-related offenses and secured 3,160 convictions, the lowest number of reported foreign prosecutions since reporting began in 2003. TVPA was again reauthorized in 2005 and 2008. As this text goes to press, a 2013 congressional reauthorization is pending.[1] The reauthorization would improve the original legislation by, among other things, authorizing the TIP Office to negotiate child protection compacts with designated focus countries to increase resources to eradicate child trafficking.

jurisdictions
areas within which a particular system of laws is used

20   Section 7202 of the Intelligence Reform and Terrorism Prevention Act of 2004 established the HSTC within the U.S. State Department, and the secretary of state, the secretary of the DHS, the attorney general, and members of the National Intelligence Community oversee it. The center was created to achieve greater integration and overall effectiveness in the U.S. government's enforcement of issues related to human smuggling, TIP, and criminal support of clandestine terrorist travel.

[1] The 2013 reauthorization passed. Congress also passed the Justice for Victims of Trafficking Act in 2015.

UNDERSTANDING AND ANALYZING THE READING

A. BUILDING VOCABULARY

Context

Using context and a dictionary, if necessary, determine the meaning of each word as it is used in the selection.

_____ 1. clandestinely (paragraph 1)
    a. securely
    b. transparently
    c. secretly
    d. carefully

_____ 2. fraudulent (paragraph 1)
    a. harmful
    b. false
    c. unfortunate
    d. restricted

_____ 3. coercion (paragraph 2)
    a. cooperation
    b. prevention
    c. progress
    d. intimidation

_____ 4. exploitation (paragraph 4)
    a. unfair manipulation
    b. mutual agreement
    c. constant escalation
    d. informal regulation

_____ 5. sanctions (paragraph 13)

    a. payments

    b. decisions

    c. authorizations

    d. penalties

_____ 6. launched (paragraph 14)

    a. began

    b. seized

    c. required

    d. changed

Word Parts

> **A REVIEW OF PREFIXES AND ROOTS**
>
> | | |
> |---|---|
> | **DE-** | means *away* or *from*. |
> | **UN-** | means *not*. |
> | **PORT** | means *carry*. |

Use your knowledge of word parts and the review above to fill in the blanks in the following sentences.

1. When a person is *deported* (paragraph 12), he or she is _____ away or sent _____ a country.

2. An *unauthorized* (paragraph 16) person is someone who has _____ been given permission or authority to do something.

B. UNDERSTANDING THE THESIS AND MAIN IDEAS

Select the best answer.

_____ 1. Which of the following best states the thesis or central thought of the reading?

    a. Human smuggling is often intended to benefit the smuggler, but sometimes people smuggle others to reunite their families.

    b. Although there are similarities between trafficking in persons and human smuggling, these are complex crimes with distinct differences.

    c. Trafficking in persons and human smuggling are two of the fastest growing areas of international criminal activity.

    d. Federal legislation addressing trafficking in persons and human smuggling has changed significantly over the years.

_____ 2. The topic of paragraph 1 is

    a. the United Nations.

    b. illegal immigration.

    c. human smuggling.

    d. the U.S. State Department.

_____ 3. The main idea of paragraph 6 is found in the
   a. first sentence.
   b. second sentence.
   c. third sentence.
   d. fourth sentence.

_____ 4. The topic of paragraph 12 is
   a. where sex trafficking takes place.
   b. how sex traffickers operate.
   c. why sex trafficking is increasing.
   d. who is targeted for sex trafficking.

C. INTERPRETING SUPPORTING DETAILS

Select the best answer.

_____ 1. The organization that has primary responsibility for enforcing laws related to human smuggling and trafficking is the
   a. United Nations Office on Drugs and Crime.
   b. Human Rights Center.
   c. United States Immigration and Customs Enforcement agency.

_____ 2. According to paragraphs 1–4, the most prominent characteristic used to differentiate between human smuggling and human trafficking is
   a. the manner in which the individuals are removed from the country.
   b. the distance that the individuals travel from their country of origin.
   c. the degree of coercion imposed on the individual.
   d. the age of the individual.

_____ 3. The author supports his ideas primarily with
   a. opinions.
   b. facts and statistics.
   c. case studies.
   d. personal experience.

_____ 4. The author includes the example of Tyrone Williams in paragraph 2 to illustrate the fact that

    a. many smugglers are trying to help others improve their lives.

    b. smuggling occurs with the consent of the people being smuggled.

    c. victims usually do not remain in contact with their smuggler.

    d. even when victims are not coerced, smuggling is dangerous.

_____ 5. The federal legislation that limited the number of immigrants from any one country to 2 percent of the people from that country already living here was the

    a. Chinese Exclusion Act of 1882.

    b. Immigration Act of 1924.

    c. Immigration and Nationality Act of 1952.

    d. Homeland Security Act of 2002.

D. RECOGNIZING METHODS OF ORGANIZATION AND TRANSITIONS

Select the best answer. See Chapter 7 for information on patterns of organization.

_____ 1. The pattern of organization used in paragraph 1 is

    a. process.

    b. classification.

    c. definition.

    d. chronological order.

_____ 2. The transitional phrase that provides a clue to the organizational pattern used in paragraph 4 is

    a. _in contrast to._

    b. _such as._

    c. _for purposes of._

    d. _the primary countries._

_____ 3. The organizational pattern used in paragraphs 15–20 is

    a. cause and effect.

    b. chronological order.

    c. comparison and contrast.

    d. definition.

E. FIGURING OUT IMPLIED MEANINGS

Indicate whether each statement is true (T) or false (F).

_____ 1. The author believes that trafficking in persons is a worse crime than human smuggling.

_____ 2. The author believes that trafficking victims often begin as willing participants in an act of smuggling.

_____ 3. The author implies that the number of people in forced labor, bonded labor, forced child labor, and sexual servitude throughout the world is greater than the International Labour Organization's estimates.

_____ 4. The author believes that the U.S. Immigration and Customs Enforcement unit should grant fewer T visas.

_____ 5. The author implies that people do not realize that men can be victims of human trafficking as well as women and children.

F. THINKING CRITICALLY ABOUT THE READING

Select the best answer. See Chapter 9 for information about thinking critically about a reading.

_____ 1. The author's primary purpose in "Human Smuggling and Trafficking" is to

   a. discuss key elements of human smuggling and trafficking as well as the U.S. government's response to these crimes.

   b. persuade Congress to enact stricter laws and develop sanctions against countries that permit trafficking.

   c. describe the issues surrounding illegal immigration in the United States as it relates to human smuggling.

   d. explain the way government agencies function in support of the fight against international crime.

_____ 2. Overall, the author's tone in this selection can best be described as

   a. passionate and outraged.

   b. indifferent and detached.

   c. informative and objective.

   d. pessimistic and hopeless.

_____ 3. The purpose of Table 17-1 is to

   a. describe basic distinctions between human smuggling and trafficking.

   b. provide precise legal definitions of smuggling and trafficking.

c. summarize key legislation related to smuggling and trafficking.

d. provide a snapshot of fast-growing areas of international criminal activity.

_____ 4. The report by the United Nations Office on Drugs and Crime describes the term *trafficking in persons* as "misleading" because the term

a. minimizes or understates the severity of the crime.

b. does not recognize that a transaction is taking place.

c. has been defined differently in countries outside the United States.

d. leaves out any reference to the illegal crossing of national borders.

_____ 5. The author describes Hillary Clinton's visit to a Cambodian shelter to show

a. how politicians can make a difference in other countries.

b. what causes families to sell their daughters to traffickers.

c. what can happen to child victims of sex traffickers.

d. why girls are often afraid to contact authorities.

_____ 6. The author concludes the reading by describing the details of recent legislation in order to

a. emphasize the need for better laws addressing human smuggling and trafficking.

b. point out the lack of similar legislation in other countries affected by human smuggling and trafficking.

c. illustrate that progress is being made in the fight against human smuggling and trafficking.

d. highlight the differences between penalties for human smuggling and for human trafficking.

Answer the following open-ended questions in complete sentence format.

7. According to Table 17-1, what are the key differences between human trafficking and human smuggling?

8. In your own words, compare young girls involved in sex trafficking to slaves. What characteristics do the two groups have in common?

9. Trafficking in persons and human smuggling are considered to be serious social issues (paragraph 17). What does this mean to you? What is a social issue?

WRITING IN RESPONSE TO THE READING

G. REVIEWING AND ORGANIZING IDEAS WITH A SUMMARY

Write a clear and concise summary of the section of the reading titled "Human Trafficking" (paragraphs 7–9). See page 31 for information about writing a summary.

H. ANALYZING THE ISSUE

Discuss in class or write in your journal a response to the following questions.

1. What contemporary issue is the author discussing in this reading? Phrase the issue as a question. Is there a "pro" or "con" side of this issue?

2. What is the author's background? Is he qualified to write about the topic? Why or why not?

3. Does the source from which this reading is taken help you determine the credibility of the information presented? Do you find any bias in the selection? Please explain both of your answers.

4. Evaluate the reading on the following criteria:

   a. Is the information timely? What trends does the author identify?

   b. Has the author provided sufficient evidence to support his main ideas? What other types of evidence would have been compelling?

   c. What assumptions (either stated or implied) do you find in the reading?

5. The theme of this chapter is "personal freedoms and limitations: lifestyle choices." Analyze the reading by addressing the following questions:

   a. Why do you think the author of this textbook chose to put this reading in this chapter?

   b. What personal freedoms are addressed in this reading?

   c. What personal limitations are discussed in this reading?

   d. Are any lifestyle choices presented in the reading? Please explain your answer.

I. WRITING PARAGRAPHS AND ESSAYS

Write a paragraph or an essay in response to the following writing prompts.

1. What are the key differences between "trafficking" and "smuggling"? Write a paragraph giving a definition of each term in your own words and making the distinction between the two terms clear to someone who knows little about the subject.

2. Which fact or statistic in this reading did you find most shocking? Write a paragraph explaining why.

3. How has legislation relevant to human smuggling and trafficking changed over the years? Write a paragraph or essay summarizing the legislation described in this reading and exploring how laws regulating immigration issues have changed. Predict how laws might change in the future and give your opinion of how you think they *should* change to reflect modern realities.

4. Research one of the agencies or initiatives discussed in this reading (e.g., the U.S. Innocence Lost National Initiative). Use the information you find to write a persuasive essay explaining the goals and accomplishments of the initiative and arguing for support for the initiative.

5. What do you think is the most effective deterrent to criminal activity such as human smuggling or trafficking? Should penalties or sanctions be more severe? Should assistance to victims be emphasized? Should victims receive restitution? In what ways should the issue be addressed locally, nationally, and internationally? Write an essay exploring these questions and examining the factors surrounding the fight against human smuggling and trafficking.

ACTIVITIES: EXPLORING PERSONAL FREEDOMS AND LIMITATIONS

On your own or with a group of classmates, complete two of the following three activities.

1. Reading Selection 19, "Bipolar Disorder: The Agony and the Ecstasy," discusses one common type of mental disorder. Research another mental disorder and write an essay or prepare a class presentation explaining it. Choose from the following list:

   - anxiety disorders
   - autism
   - schizophrenia
   - major depression
   - dementia

2. In Reading Selection 20, Edwin Chemerinsky talks about the First Amendment that guarantees the freedom of speech. Spend some time reading the actual First Amendment document, and make a list of the other issues that are addressed in the amendment. After you have made the list, write an essay or prepare a class presentation explaining these rights and how they are exercised in our society.

3. In Reading Selection 21, the author states that human trafficking is a worldwide problem that affects 12.3 million people in the world today, according to the International Labour Organization. Conduct research on this international issue, explore the forms it takes in various countries around the world, and prepare a class presentation on your findings.

Integrating the Readings

The readings in this chapter discussed just a few aspects of the broad topic of personal freedoms and limitations. Other issues related to personal freedoms include the following:

- *Technological surveillance:* Is it acceptable to place video cameras at intersections to catch people who run red lights? Should stores be allowed to monitor the store, including dressing rooms, with video cameras?

- *Database compilation and sales:* Do companies have the right to sell your personal information to other companies who are looking to advertise their products to you?

- *Social media:* How do your posts on Facebook, or your tweets on Twitter, affect the way possible employers will view you?

- *"Gag rules":* Many companies prevent their employees from discussing company business with the media. Yet, at the same time, the United States has laws to protect "whistle blowers" who expose a company's dangerous practices. Do businesses have the right to tell employees how they should behave in their private lives?

- *Gender roles:* Today, there are more female firefighters than ever before, as well as more male nurses. Should both men and women have to pass the same physical tests to become firefighters and police officers? Why or why not?

- *Sports teams:* Some schools' sports teams have begun allowing girls to play on otherwise all-male teams, while other activities (such as cheerleading) have begun allowing boys to take part in otherwise all-female activities. What are the pros and cons of these developments?

Write an essay or prepare a class presentation about any of these topics, or any other topic concerning personal freedoms or limitations.

MAKING CONNECTIONS: THINKING WITHIN THE ISSUES

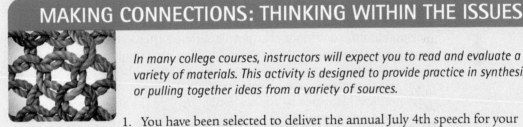

In many college courses, instructors will expect you to read and evaluate a wide variety of materials. This activity is designed to provide practice in synthesizing or pulling together ideas from a variety of sources.

1. You have been selected to deliver the annual July 4th speech for your community, and the title of the speech is "What Freedom Means to Me." The organizer of the event has encouraged you to think outside the box and present examples of personal freedoms that a diverse audience can relate to and appreciate. After researching contemporary examples of freedom and bondage, you settle on using the three selections in this chapter as your sources. Compose your speech and present it to your classmates.

2. Although the issue of human smuggling and trafficking (Selection 21, p. 604) is obviously a limitation of freedom, the issue of mental illness (Selection 19, p. 581) is often overlooked when it comes to thinking about personal freedom, and when considering freedom of speech, we often fail to consider the exceptions to that freedom (Selection 20, p. 592). In your sociology course, you have been assigned an essay that addresses the limitations of personal freedom. You may use these three readings as well as other examples from contemporary society as sources to support your main ideas.

MAKING CONNECTIONS: THINKING ACROSS THE ISSUES

In many college courses, instructors will expect you to read and evaluate a wide variety of materials. This section requires you to draw connections between the readings on various issues explored within Part Two. The activities and assignments below will give you practice in synthesizing information and thinking critically about the relationship of the chapter readings.

1. "'Hurtful and Beautiful': Life with Multiple Sclerosis" (Selection 2, p. 353) and "Bipolar Disorder: The Agony and the Ecstasy" (Selection 19, p. 580) are both personal essays. What types of details do the authors provide to help readers understand their experiences? How are the authors' experiences fundamentally different? How are they similar?

2. *Social justice* refers to the idea that society should be based on principles of fairness and equality, with all people having a reasonable standard of living and equal access to opportunities. For example, "'Katrina Brain': The Invisible Long-term Toll of Megastorms" (Selection 4, p. 380) explores the mental health conditions that people suffered after a traumatic weather event and the strain it put on the mental health systems and those who were not able to access its resources. Identify at least two other readings in this text that are concerned with social justice. In each reading, what is the key problem identified by the author(s)? How do the authors suggest these problems may be remedied?

3. Two readings in this text are focused on parents and children: "Eggs for Sale" (Selection 10, p. 459) and "American Schools Are Failing Nonconformist Kids" (Selection 17, p. 549). In the United States, what is the traditional role of the family? What are the expectations regarding marriage and family for young unmarried people? How are these expectations changing or evolving, and how does each of these readings either support or challenge traditional ideas of marriage and family?

4. Many college campuses are a microcosm of the larger society. In other words, the college campus often reflects what is happening in the larger society. In some cases, campus trends follow trends in society; in other cases, colleges are at the forefront of research, technology, and other movements that will later find their way into the surrounding communities (and the nation and the world). Identify three readings that are likely to be of interest to college students. For example, you might choose "Are You 'Phubbing' Right Now?" (Selection 8, p. 432), "Hooking Up" (Selection 7, p. 421), and "Hate Speech Is Protected Free Speech, Even on College Campuses" (Selection 20, p. 591). Now suppose that you are counseling a high school senior about the college experience. Based on these readings, what five pieces of advice would you give him or her?

5. The goal of many textbook writers is to define key terms that will help students understand the world better. Each textbook chapter (or textbook section) usually offers further details about those key terms, providing richer information about them. Consider three readings that are primarily definitional: "Poison in the Bottle: How Safe Is Bisphenol A?" (Selection 6, p. 405), "Technology in the Fight Against Crime" (Selection 15, p. 522), and "Human Smuggling and Trafficking" (Selection 21, p. 603). What do these three readings have in common? How are they different? Do the authors focus primarily on the United States, or do they discuss other countries as well? What are the authors' purposes for writing?

A Multi-Disciplinary Casebook on Globalization

PART THREE

magadesigns/123rf.com

Rawpixel.com / Shutterstock

EXAMINING ONE ISSUE IN DEPTH

Throughout this text, you've read many selections that consider various aspects of contemporary issues. As you pursue your college studies, you will often be asked to study one topic in more depth, consulting multiple sources to gain a deeper understanding of it. In research papers and on written exams, you will need to synthesize all of these sources to demonstrate your mastery of the topic. This casebook will give you an opportunity to explore one issue in depth, synthesize ideas, and write about the issue.

In this casebook, we take a closer look at a contemporary issue—**globalization**—with readings that examine its development and impact. Because the topic is rapidly developing and its impact is of growing importance, globalization is studied across a variety of academic disciplines. You may think that students who take courses in economics and political science are concerned with globalization, and you would be correct. However, globalization has a wide-ranging impact in a variety of disciplines and is also a part of many other college courses. For example,

- **Sociology** courses may examine how globalization impacts societies and group behavior.
- **Criminal Justice** courses may look at the impact of globalization on crime, law enforcement, and public safety.
- **Psychology** courses may examine the effects of globalization on human behavior and motivation.
- **Allied Health** courses may look at the impact of globalization on the spread and control of infectious diseases.
- **History** courses may track the evolution of globalization and its impact on various countries.

The following six readings present a variety of perspectives on the impact of globalization within six disciplines: **geography, biology, business and marketing, cultural anthropology, communication, and economics.** Your instructor may assign all of the readings or select specific readings. Each reading is followed by critical-thinking questions specific to the reading. At the end of the casebook, you will find synthesis and integration questions that draw upon two or more of the readings contained here, as well as both high and low stakes writing assignments.

Preview the Readings

An important part of working with multiple readings from various academic disciplines is the ability to find the information you are looking for. Previewing (see page 6) can be extremely helpful.

Look Up Globalization

The field of globalization changes rapidly. There are likely to be numerous new developments since this casebook was published. Conduct an Internet search to discover what recent developments have taken place in the field of globalization. Take notes on what you learn and be prepared to share this information with your discussion group.

Discuss Globalization

In a group with three or four of your classmates, discuss the findings of your research on the recent impacts of globalization. In addition, broaden your discussion to include how these impacts might affect the well-being of world citizens' privacy, safety, or security. Be prepared to share the highlights of your discussion with the class.

Write About Globalization

Write a list of questions you expect to find answers to in this casebook. Connect the reading to your own experience by writing a list of people, places, or things from countries other than your native country that have affected your life. (Hint: think of products you buy that are produced in other countries or how events in other countries affect your own life.)

Read About Globalization

Here are some tips for reading not only the selections in this casebook, but any reading about globalization. As you read, highlight and annotate. You can later use your highlights and annotations to help you create an outline, map, or summary of the reading. As you read, be sure to

- **Get an overview of the topic.** The first reading in this casebook presents three extended examples of the impact of globalization, explaining what it is and how it works. This will serve as helpful background information as you read the other selections in this section.

- **Understand the history and world geography as best you can.** It is helpful to know more about countries, policies, or products discussed in the reading. You may need to stop and look up information during or after reading.

- **Focus on the impact of globalization.** For example, how does globalization impact the availability of health care for people in the United States? How is that impact similar or different for people living in India or China?

- **Be aware of underlying ethical concerns.** Globalization is an expanding and developing field. As you read the selections in this casebook, you will see that the topic is sometimes controversial and raises many questions and issues. Be sensitive and alert to these concerns. Write annotations to record your thinking.

Synthesize Sources

As you consult many sources to learn more about specific topics introduced in the casebook readings, you will need to *synthesize* this information into a coherent, useful whole. Here are some tips to help you work with and synthesize multiple sources.

1. **Choose sources that are trustworthy and reliable.** Carefully examine the results of your Internet search. For example, suppose you conduct a Google search on lead in drinking water. Do not assume that the first ten "hits" are the best sources of information. Always examine the "About Us" section of a Web site for more information about its sponsor. Do not assume that nonprofit organizations (denoted by .org in their Web addresses) are unbiased.

2. **Read for the "big picture": Identify the thesis or central thought and main ideas.** As you set out to learn more about a particular topic, you should first establish a broad base of knowledge. The first time you read each source, look for the key ideas. What argument is the author making? What are the author's main points? You can go back and learn the details later.

3. **Use electronic search tools if you are working with electronic documents.** Suppose you are working with ten documents and you are researching the topic of robotics. Conduct a search for the word *robotics* to help you find information about that topic within each document. In printed books, consult the index.

4. **Look for areas of common agreement.** As you read multiple sources, you may encounter the same information several times. Make note of the facts on which most reliable, credible people agree. Having a solid understanding of these facts can help you evaluate an author's claims and determine whether the author is biased.

5. **Be suspicious of highly emotional language.** As you read multiple sources, you may find yourself favoring readings that are colorful and intense while paying less attention to sources that seem more "dry" or dull. Avoid this tendency and seek objective sources as you begin your research. As you learn more about the topic, you will be better able to evaluate and synthesize sources in which the author offers strong opinions or exhibits strong bias.

READING 1
Geography

The Impact of Globalization

Les Rowntree, Martin Lewis, Marie Price, and William Wyckoff

The following selection is taken from a textbook entitled Globalization and Diversity: Geography of a Changing World, *fifth edition. The authors of this selection think it is essential for readers to understand and critique two themes in relation to globalization: 1. the consequences of converging environmental, cultural, political, and economic systems that are a part of globalization and 2. the persistence and expansion of geographic diversity and differences in the face of globalization.*

1   **Globalization**—the connecting of people and places through converging economic, political, and cultural activities—is one of the most important forces shaping the world today. Let's examine the history and global impact of three everyday items that connect you to globalization—jeans, engagement rings, and chocolate.

S_E/Shutterstock

ssavic8/123rf.com

Anna_Pustynnikova / Shutterstock

Denim jeans, engagement rings, and chocolate are just a few of the everyday items that connect you to globalization.

The History and Symbolic Meaning of Denim Jeans

2   Denim jeans are an iconic American cultural symbol found all over the world—yet very few jeans are made in the United States anymore. The story of the humble blue work pants created for gold miners in 1850s California, but later reimagined by high-end design houses in Europe and assembled in sweatshops in China and Mexico, is indicative of the long-term and uneven workings of globalization. We can think of jeans as an assemblage of materials and processes. Cotton grown in the United States, India, Uzbekistan, or Australia makes its way to textile houses in Turkey and Pakistan that convert it into denim. The bolts of denim are shipped to scores of countries for cutting and sewing; usually places where labor costs are low or trade agreements give preference to particular markets. One of the largest producers of blue jeans is China. In places such as Shenzhen in southern China, men and women toil in large factories sewing pant legs or putting in rivets. The long hours of work with this dyed fabric stain the workers' fingers blue. The finished products are then packaged and shipped all over the world or sold to Chinese consumers. After years of wear, a pair of jeans may even end up in the recycled clothing market or sold in bundles to hawkers in African cities such as Lusaka or Accra. Such global patterns of production and trade are increasingly the norm.

3   Blue jeans are also a cultural product, which can be a comfortable work pant or a high-end status symbol. In some cultures, mostly men wear jeans, which are associated with modern Western values; meanwhile women might wear more traditional attire. Styles and colors of jeans vary from place to place. The meaning people give to the blue jeans, and the decisions about who can wear them and when, underscore the diverse cultural practices at play with this ordinary garment. A single pair of blue jeans has environmental impacts as well. A study of Levi Strauss & Co. determined that 3,000 liters of water were consumed during the life of one pair of 501 jeans: half of the water went to growing the cotton, less than half went to customers washing jeans, and a small fraction was used to manufacture them.

The African Origins of the Diamond Engagement Ring

4   The tradition of a diamond engagement ring stems from the remarkable advertising efforts of DeBeers, a South African firm that dominated southern Africa's enormous diamond market throughout the 20th century. DeBeers Consolidated Mines was established in 1888 and steadily expanded to include diamond mines in Botswana, Namibia, and Canada, eventually controlling 90 percent of the global diamond trade. DeBeers' genius was threefold: it expanded the supply of quality diamonds, controlled the global market, and convinced a growing middle class that diamonds were proof of love. After sales to Europe slowed in the 1920s, DeBeers began marketing in the United States, convincing American suitors to spend a month's wages on a diamond ring.

5   DeBeers' lock on diamonds unraveled in the 1990s when Russia became a major diamond producer, marketing outside of the DeBeers commodity chain. The idea of "conflict diamonds" or "blood diamonds"—uncut diamonds mined in a war zone and sold to finance the conflict—also emerged at that time, tainting the image of African diamonds. A certification process makes blood diamonds less of a concern today, but DeBeers' dominance has also slipped; the company now accounts for 40 percent of diamond sales, although southern Africa is still a major producer.

The Rainforest and Your Chocolate Fix

6   Your chocolate bar comes from the tropical rainforest, and satisfying your sweet tooth could be either destroying or saving the rainforest, depending on how the cocoa was grown. Cocoa, chocolate's main ingredient, comes from cacao trees, which grow exclusively in equatorial rainforests—mainly in Ghana and other African countries, but also in the Amazon Basin of South America. Cacao trees prefer the shade of higher rainforest trees, which is good news. But to meet the ever-increasing demand for chocolate, cacao is also cultivated for short periods of time in the full sunlight of newly cleared rainforest plots. That's the bad news—because this method of cacao farming is a major factor in the destruction of African rainforests.

7   So what's a rainforest-loving chocolate lover to do? Easy: take an extra 30 seconds and read the candy bar label to see whether there's any mention of shade-grown and/or sustainably farmed cacao trees. After that, it's up to you.

8   These three examples—denim jeans, diamond engagement rings, and chocolate—together demonstrate that globalization has a long-term effect on business, cultural, political, and environmental problems the world faces.

ORGANIZING IDEAS ABOUT THE READING

Create a study sheet that features the main points and supporting details of the reading.

THINKING CRITICALLY ABOUT THE READING

Your answers to the questions below should be in complete sentences and may require more than one sentence.

1. The authors choose three examples to illustrate the concept of globalization. Evaluate how helpful each example is in defining globalization and discussing its impact. Which example was most helpful? Which was least helpful? Justify your answers.
2. What types of details and evidence do the authors use to explain the three examples?
3. What are the authors implying about the working conditions in the Shenzhen jeans factory described in paragraph 2?
4. Identify at least three facts and three opinions found in the reading.
5. In paragraph 7, the authors ask the question, "So what's a rainforest-loving chocolate lover to do?" Personally, how would you respond to this question?

READING 2
Biology

World Overpopulation and Resource Management

Teresa Audesirk, Gerald Audesirk, and Bruce E. Byers

The following selection is from a textbook entitled Biology: Life on Earth, *eleventh edition. Amongst the authors' goals in writing this book is to give readers the scientific information and framework necessary to develop scientific literacy so that they can make informed choices in both their personal lives and the political arena.*

1

squatter
a person who settles on land or property without legal authority to do so

In Côte d'Ivoire, a country in western Africa, the government is waging a battle to protect some of its rapidly dwindling tropical rain forest from illegal hunters, farmers, and loggers. Officials destroy the shelters of the **squatters**, who immediately return and rebuild. One such squatter, Sep Djekoule, explained, "I have ten children and we must eat. The forest is where I can provide for my family, and everybody has that right." His words exemplify the conflict between population growth and wise management of Earth's finite resources.

2

How many people can Earth sustain? The Global Footprint Network, consisting of an international group of scientists and professionals from many fields, is attempting to assess humanity's *ecological footprint*. This project compares human demand for resources to Earth's capacity to supply these resources in a sustainable manner. "Sustainable" means that the resources can be renewed indefinitely and that the ability of the biosphere to supply them is not diminished over time. Is humanity living on the "interest" produced

As of 2018, the Earth's population is approximately 7.6 billion. Much of this population is concentrated in cities.

by our global endowment, or are we eating into the "principal"? The Global Footprint Network concluded that, in 2010 (the most recent year for which complete data are available), humanity consumed more than 150% of the resources that were sustainably available. In other words, to avoid damaging Earth's resources (thus reducing Earth's carrying capacity), our population in 2010 would require more than one and a half Earths. But by 2015, we had added about 400 million more people. Because people have used their technological prowess to overcome environmental resistance, our collective ecological footprint now dwarfs Earth's sustainable resource base, reducing Earth's future capacity to support us.

3   For example, the human population now uses almost 40% of Earth's productive land for crops and livestock. Despite this, the United Nations estimates that more than 800 million people are undernourished, including an estimated 25% of the population of sub-Saharan Africa. Erosion reduces the ability of land to support both crops and grazing livestock. The quest for farmland drives people to clear-cut forests in places where the soil is poorly suited for agriculture. The demand for wood also causes large areas to be deforested annually, causing the runoff of much-needed fresh water, the erosion of topsoil, the pollution of rivers and oceans, and an overall reduction in the ability of the land and water to support not only future crops and livestock, but also the fish and other wild animals that people harvest for food. Human consumption of food, wood, and, more recently, biofuels (crops that provide fuel) drives the destruction of tens of millions of acres of rain forest annually.

4   The United Nations estimates that about 60% of commercial ocean fish populations are being harvested at their maximum sustainable yield, and another 30% are being overfished. In parts of India, China, Africa, and the United States, underground water stores are being depleted to irrigate cropland far faster than they are being refilled by rain and snow. Because irrigated land supplies about 40% of human food crops, water shortages can rapidly lead to food shortages.

5   Our present population, at its present level of technology, is clearly "overgrazing" the biosphere. As the 6 billion people in less developed countries strive to raise their standard of living and the billion people in more developed countries continue to increase theirs, the damage to Earth's ecosystems accelerates. We all want to enjoy luxuries far beyond bare survival, but unfortunately, the resources currently demanded to support the high standard of living in developed countries are unattainable for most of Earth's inhabitants. For example, supporting the world population sustainably at the average standard of living in the United States would require about four and a half Earths. Technology can help us improve agricultural efficiency, conserve energy and water, reduce pollutants, and recycle far more of what we use. In the long run, however, it is extremely unlikely that technological innovation can compensate for continued population growth.

6   Inevitably, the human population will stop growing. Hope for the future lies in recognizing the signs of human overgrazing and responding by reducing our population before we cause further damage to the biosphere, diminishing its ability to support people and the other precious and irreplaceable forms of life on Earth.

ORGANIZING IDEAS ABOUT THE READING

Write a clear and concise summary of the reading. See page 31 for information about writing a summary.

THINKING CRITICALLY ABOUT THE READING

Your answers to the questions below should be in complete sentences and may require more than one sentence.

1. Do the authors seem to be biased toward the issue of global consumption?
2. Are the authors optimistic or pessimistic about the future? Supply evidence from the reading to support your answer.
3. What types of evidence do the authors use to support their thesis?
4. What attitude do the authors express toward luxuries and a high standard of living?
5. What is the meaning of "ecological footprint" in paragraph 2? If needed, you may research the topic for help with defining the term.

READING 3
Business and
Marketing

Marketing on the Global Stage

Michael R. Solomon, Greg W. Marshall, and Elnora W. Stuart

The following selection is taken from a textbook entitled Marketing: Real People, Real Choices, *eighth edition. In this reading and throughout the book, the authors look at the value, ethics, and effectiveness of different marketing strategies and tactics in the U.S. and throughout the world.*

1   Here's an important question: Do you primarily see yourself only as a resident of Small-town, USA, or as a member of a global community? The reality is that you and all your classmates are citizens of the world and participants in a global marketplace. It is likely that you eat bananas from Ecuador, drink beer from Mexico, and sip wine from Australia, South Africa, or Chile. When you come home, you may take off your shoes that were made in Thailand, put your feet up on the cocktail table imported from Indonesia, and watch the World Cup football (soccer) match being played in Brazil or Canada on your smart TV while checking your Facebook page on your smartphone, both made in China. Hopefully, you also have some knowledge and concern for important world events such as the recent Ebola epidemic in Africa, terrorist attacks in Europe, and recent developments in North Korea and Syria. And you may even be looking for an exciting career with a firm that does business around the globe.

2   Firms doing business in this global economy face uncertainty in the future of the global marketplace. For a number of years, consumers and world leaders have argued that the development of free trade and a single global marketplace will benefit us all because it allows people who live in developing countries to enjoy the same economic benefits as citizens of more developed countries.

3   There are other reasons that many leaders want a single marketplace. One important reason comes from fears that the **Greenhouse Effect** may threaten the future of the planet. What is the Greenhouse Effect? In simple terms, our factories and automobiles continue to pump more and more carbon dioxide (the most important of the greenhouse gasses) into our atmosphere while at the same time we cut down the rain forests and reduce the amount of oxygen the trees add to the atmosphere. This increase in greenhouse gasses causes the earth to get warmer, just like a greenhouse provides a warm place for tender plants. The result, many believe, is global warming, a warming of the earth which will have disastrous effects on the planet. These fears have caused many to demand international agreements that would force industries and governments to develop and adhere to the same environmental standards to protect the future of the planet.

4   Of course, there is another side to the issue of a single marketplace. The **Arab Spring,** a series of anti-government protests and uprisings in a number of Arab countries that were largely aided by new social media tools available to people in the region, gave hope to many that dictatorships in countries in the Middle East would become democracies and bring a better life to peoples of the countries. Instead, new violent radical groups such as ISIS took over large portions of these countries. This was accompanied by a growing number of terrorist attacks in other parts of the world, causing citizens and country leaders to propose greater restrictions on immigration and on trade with countries that aid or harbor terrorists. At the same time, the decrease in the price of oil has increased concerns about a downturn in the global economy where each individual country will want to protect its own industries.

5   You may be asking, "What do these current events have to do with marketing?" Whether we like it or not, we are a global community. Everything that happens in any part of the world has a potential to influence what marketers need to do to be successful at home and around the globe.

6   The global marketing game is exciting, the stakes are high, and it's easy to lose your shirt. Competition comes from both local and foreign firms, and differences in national laws, customs, and consumer preferences can make your head spin.

World Trade

7   **World trade** refers to the flow of goods and services among different countries—the total value of all the exports and imports of the world's nations. In 2009, the world suffered a global economic crisis that resulted in dramatic decreases in worldwide exports. Today, we see increasing growth in world trade with world exports of merchandise increasing from $12 trillion in 2009 to nearly $19 trillion in 2014. Just how much is $19 trillion? Think about it this way: A recent lottery prize grew to a whopping $1 billion. If a lottery awarded a $1 billion prize every day, it would take more than 50 years to equal $19 trillion. Of course, not all countries participate equally in the trade flows among nations. Understanding the "big picture" of who does business with whom is important to marketers when they devise global trade strategies.

8   It's often a good thing to have customers in remote markets, but to serve their needs well requires flexibility and the ability to adapt to local social and economic conditions. For example, you may have to adapt to the needs of foreign trading partners when those firms can't pay cash for the products they want to purchase. Believe it or not, the currencies of as many as 100 countries—from the Albanian "lek" to the Uzbekistan "sum"—are not *convertible;* you can't spend or exchange them outside the country's borders. In other countries,

because sufficient cash or credit simply is not available, trading firms work out elaborate deals in which they trade (or barter) their products with each other or even supply goods in return for tax breaks from the local government. This countertrade accounts for as much as 25 percent of all world trade.

9   Our ever-increasing access to products from around the world does have a dark side: the growth in world trade in recent years has been accompanied by a glut of unsafe products—toys with lead paint, toothpaste containing poisonous diethylene glycol, and more recently, crayons laced with cancer-causing asbestos—many of which have come from China. In 2014, the European Commission's early warning system for dangerous products (RAPEX) reported a notable increase in alerts of unsafe products; of the more than 2,000 alert issues the commission received, almost two-thirds of the unsafe products came from China. Although most Chinese manufacturers make quality products, some unscrupulous producers have damaged the reputation of Chinese manufacturers and prompted U.S. and European officials to increase their inspections of Chinese imports.

The United States imports many quality products from China; however, there has been an increase in unsafe products, prompting U.S. and European officials to increase inspections of Chinese imports.

Should We Go Global?

10   When firms consider going global they must think about this in four steps:

Step 1. "Go" or "no go"—is it in our best interest to focus exclusively on our home market, or should we cast our net elsewhere as well?

Step 2. If the decision is "go," which global markets are most attractive? Which country or countries offer the greatest opportunity for us?

Step 3. What market-entry strategy, or rather, what level of commitment is best? It is pretty low risk to simply export products to overseas markets. On the other hand, although the commitment and the risk are substantial if the firm decides to build and run manufacturing facilities in other countries, the potentially greater payoff may be worth the extra risk.

Step 4. How do we develop successful marketing mix strategies in these foreign markets—should we standardize what we do across all the countries where we operate or develop a unique localized marketing strategy for each country?

The Globalization Decision

11   Although the prospect of millions—or even billions—of consumers salivating for your goods in other countries is tempting, not all firms can or should go global. When they make these decisions, marketers need to consider a number of factors that may enhance or detract from their success abroad.

ORGANIZING IDEAS ABOUT THE READING

Create a conceptual map of the reading. See page 29 for information about mapping.

THINKING CRITICALLY ABOUT THE READING

Your answers to the questions below should be in complete sentences and may require more than one sentence.

1. What is the authors' purpose for writing this textbook selection?
2. With which countries does the U.S. trade most heavily? You may use research to answer the question. Using evidence from the reading, why do you think the U.S. has chosen to trade with these specific countries?
3. The authors present both the pros and cons of a single global marketplace. Which set of reasons were more convincing? Explain your answer.
4. Describe the authors' attitude toward marketing on the global stage. Supply evidence from the reading to support your answers.
5. What techniques do the authors use to make their subject interesting and understandable?

READING 4
Cultural
Anthropology

Globalization and Health

Barbara Miller

The following selection is taken from a textbook entitled Cultural Anthropology in a Globalizing World, *fourth edition. The author, Dr. Barbara Miller, is a Professor of Anthropology and International Affairs. One of her areas of expertise is health and demography, and she has conducted concentrated research on gender and health issues in Southeast Asia, specifically India.*

1   With globalization, health problems move around the world and into remote locations and cultures more rapidly than ever before. At the same time, Western culture, including biomedicine, is on the move. Perhaps no other aspect of Western culture, except for the capitalist market system and the English language, has so permeated the rest of the world as **Western Biomedicine (WBM)**—a healing approach to medicine based on modern Western science that emphasizes technology for diagnosing and treating health problems related to the human body. But the cultural flow is not one-way: many people in North America

and Europe are turning to forms of non-Western and nonbiomedical healing, such as acupuncture and massage therapy. Let's now consider some new and emerging health challenges and changes in healing.

Infectious Diseases

2   In the mid-twentieth century, scientific advances such as antibiotic drugs, vaccines against childhood diseases, and improved technology for sanitation dramatically reduced the threat from infectious disease. The 1980s, however, brought an era of shaken confidence, with the onset and rapid spread of the HIV / AIDS epidemic.

3   New contexts for exposure and contagion are created through increased international travel and migration, deforestation, and development projects, among others. Increased travel and migration have contributed to the spread of HIV / AIDS, SARS, Ebola, and other new infectious diseases. A subcategory of infectious diseases is zoonotic diseases. A zoonotic disease is a disease that is spread from animals to people. Two examples are malaria and Lyme disease.

4   Deforestation is related to higher rates of malaria, which is spread by mosquitoes; mosquitoes thrive in pools of water in open, sunlit areas, as opposed to forests. Development projects such as constructing dams and clearing forests create unintended health problems for local people.

Diseases of Development

5   A disease of development is a health problem caused or increased by economic development projects. For example, the construction of dams and irrigation systems throughout the tropical world has brought dramatically increased rates of schistosomiasis (shish-to-suh-MY-a-sis), a disease caused by the presence of a parasitic worm in the blood system. Over 200 million people suffer from this debilitating disease, with prevalence rates the highest in sub-Saharan countries in Africa (Michaud, Gordon, and Reich 2005). The larvae hatch from eggs and mature in slow-moving water such as lakes and rivers. When mature, they can penetrate the human (or other animal) skin with which they come into contact. Once inside the human body, the adult schistosomes breed in the veins around the human bladder and bowel. They send fertilized eggs into the environment through urine and feces. These eggs then contaminate water, in which they hatch into larvae.

6   Anthropological research has documented steep increases in the rates of schistosomiasis at large dam sites in tropical countries (Scudder 1973). The risk is caused by the dams slowing the rate of water flow. Stagnant water systems offer an ideal environment for development of the larvae. Opponents of the construction of large dams have used this information in support of their position.

7   Increased obesity in many countries can also be viewed as a disease of development, somewhat ironically. In high-income countries around the world, rising rates of childhood obesity have generated concern about the children's health and the toll they will take on public health systems as they age. The so-called child obesity epidemic surely has health implications, but its causes are not first and foremost medical and the most effective steps to its prevention are also outside the medical domain (Moffat 2010). In general, prevention has to do with changing the child's diet and activity patterns.

Medical pluralism—the presence of several health systems within a society—offers a range of choices and enhanced quality of health, but it sometimes presents conflicting models of illness and healing practices.

Ezz Mika Elya/Shutterstock

Medical Pluralism

8   Contact between cultures often leads to a situation in which aspects of both cultures coexist: two (or more) different languages, religions, systems of law, or health systems, for example. The term medical pluralism refers to the presence of several, separate health systems within a society. The coexistence of many forms of healing provides clients a range of choices and enhances the quality of health. While medical pluralism offers the advantage of choice, it also presents people with conflicting models of illness and healing, which can result in misunderstandings between healers and clients and in unhappy outcomes.

Separate Medical Systems Can Coexist: The Sherpas

9   The Sherpa of Nepal are an unusual example of a culture in which the preference for traditional healing systems remains strong and is combined with the selective use of WBM (Adams 1988). Healing therapists available in the Upper Khumbu (khoom-boo) region in northeastern Nepal fit into three categories:

- Orthodox Buddhist practitioners, including *lamas,* whom Khumbu people consult for prevention and cure through their blessings, and *amchis,* who practice Tibetan medicine, a humoral healing system.
- Unorthodox religious or shamanic practitioners, who perform divination ceremonies for diagnosis.
- Biomedical practitioners who work in a clinic that was first established to serve tourists. The clinic was established as a permanent medical facility in 1967, and many Sherpa selectively use it.

10   Thus, three varieties of health care exist in the region. Traditional healers are thriving, unthreatened by changes brought by the tourist trade, the influx of new wealth, and notions of modernity. The question of why WBM has not completely taken over other healing practices requires a complicated answer. One part of the answer is that high-mountain tourism does not deeply affect local production and social relations. Although it brings in new wealth, it does not require large-scale capital investment from outside as, for example, mega-hotel tourist developments have elsewhere. So far, the Sherpa maintain control of their productive resources, including trekking knowledge and skills.

11   In many other contexts, however, anthropologists have documented conflicts and misunderstandings between WBM and local health systems. Miscommunication often occurs

between biomedical doctors and patients in matters seemingly as simple as a prescription that should be taken with every meal. The Western biomedical doctor assumes that this means three times a day. But some people do not eat three meals a day and thus unwittingly fail to follow the doctor's instructions.

12   One anthropological study of a case in which death resulted from cross-cultural differences demonstrates the complex issue of communication across medical cultures. The "F family" were immigrants from American Samoa living in Honolulu, Hawaii (Krantzler 1987). Neither parent spoke English. Their children were "moderately literate" in English but spoke a mixture of English and Samoan at home. Mr. F was trained as a traditional Samoan healer. Mary, a daughter, was first stricken with diabetes at age 16. She was taken to the hospital by ambulance after collapsing, half-conscious, on the sidewalk near her home in a Honolulu housing project. After several months of irregular contact with medical staff, she was again brought to the hospital in an ambulance, unconscious, and she died there. Her father was charged with causing Mary's death through medical neglect.

13   In the biomedical view, her parents failed to give Mary adequate care, even though the hospital staff took pains to instruct her family about how to give insulin injections, and Mary was shown how to test her urine for glucose and acetone and counseled about her diet. She was to be followed up with visits to the outpatient clinic, and, according to the clinic's unofficial policy of linking patients with physicians from their own ethnic group, she was assigned to see the sole Samoan pediatric resident. Over the next few months, Mary was seen once in the clinic by a different resident, missed her next three appointments, came in once without an appointment, and was readmitted to the hospital on the basis of test results from that visit. At that time, she, her parents, and her older sister were once again advised about the importance of compliance with the medical advice they were receiving. Four months later, she returned to the clinic with blindness in one eye and diminished vision in the other. She was diagnosed with cataracts, and the Samoan physician again advised Mary about the seriousness of her illness and the need for compliance. The medical experts increasingly judged that "cultural differences" were the basic problem and that, in spite of all their attempts to communicate with the F family, they were basically incapable of caring for Mary.

14   The family's perspective, in contrast, was grounded in *fa'a Samoa*, the Samoan way. Their experiences in the hospital were not positive from the start. When Mr. F arrived at the hospital with Mary the first time, he spoke with several hospital staff, through a daughter as translator. It was a teaching hospital, so various residents and attending physicians had examined Mary. Mr. F was concerned that there was no single physician caring for Mary, and he was concerned that her care was inconsistent. The family observed a child die while Mary was in the intensive care unit, reinforcing the perception of inadequate care and instilling fear over Mary's chance of surviving in the hospital.

15   Language differences between Mary's family and the hospital staff added to the problem. Some hospital staff told Mary's family that her problem was "sugar," using a folk term in English for diabetes (1987:330). Mary's mother thought that meant she needed more sugar in her diet. Miscommunications led to lack of trust in Mary's family of the hospital staff, and they began to resort more to their traditional resources including relying on Mary's father, a traditional Samoan healer.

16   From the Samoan perspective, the F family behaved logically and appropriately. The father, as household head and healer in his own right, felt he had authority. Dr. A, though

Samoan, had been resocialized by the Western medical system and alienated from his Samoan background. He did not offer the personal touch that the F family expected. Samoans believe that children above the age of 12 are no longer children and can be expected to behave responsibly, so the family's assigning of Mary's 12-year-old sister to assist with her insulin injections and in recording results made sense to them. Also, the hospital in American Samoa does not require appointments. Cultural misunderstanding was the ultimate cause of Mary's death.

ORGANIZING IDEAS ABOUT THE READING

Write a list of five questions that could be used to test your classmates' understanding of the main points of the reading.

THINKING CRITICALLY ABOUT THE READING

Your answers to the questions below should be in complete sentences and may require more than one sentence.

1. The author presents information on both biomedical and nonbiomedical healing. Do you detect any bias in her presentation? Explain your answer completely using evidence from the reading.
2. What is the author implying about the prevention of childhood obesity as presented in paragraph 7?
3. In your opinion, how could the situation with Mary (described in paragraphs 12–16) have been handled differently so as to insure a better outcome?
4. The author devotes more coverage to the "F family" than she does to the Sherpa. Why do you think she does this, and what does it suggest about the relative importance of the ideas each group represents?
5. What is the most important fact you have learned from this reading? How has this piece of information impacted your perspective on globalization and health?

READING 5
Communication

Globalization and Intercultural Communication

Joseph A. DeVito

This reading is an excerpt from a textbook entitled Interpersonal Messages, *fourth edition. The author, Joseph DeVito, is Professor Emeritus at Hunter College of the City University of New York. He is recognized as a scholar in the field of communication and has written numerous scholarly articles and textbooks on the subject.*

1   At the heart of globalization is the connecting of people from different cultures; communication plays a significant role. **Intercultural communication** is communication between persons who have different cultural beliefs, values, or ways of behaving. You com-

municate as you do largely as a result of your culture. Culture influences every aspect of your communication experience. And, of course, you receive messages through the filters imposed by a unique culture. Cultural filters, like filters on a camera, color the messages you receive. They influence what you receive and how you receive it. For example, some cultures rely heavily on television or newspapers for their news and trust them implicitly. Others rely on face-to-face interpersonal interactions, distrusting any of the mass communication systems. Some look to religious leaders as guides to behavior; others generally ignore them.

2   Above all, intercultural communication depends on the cultural sensitivity of both individuals. **Cultural sensitivity** is an attitude and way of behaving in which you're aware of and acknowledge cultural differences. Cultural sensitivity is crucial on a global scale, as in efforts toward world peace and economic growth; it's also essential for effective interpersonal communication and for general success in life (Franklin & Mizell, 1995). Without cultural sensitivity, there can be no effective interpersonal communication between people who are different in gender or race or nationality or affectional orientation. So be mindful of the cultural differences between yourself and others. For example, the close physical distance that is normal in Arab cultures may prove too familiar or too intrusive in much of the United States and northern Europe. The empathy that most Americans welcome may be uncomfortable for most Koreans (Yun, 1976).

3   The following guidelines can help you achieve cultural sensitivity: (1) prepare yourself, (2) reduce your ethnocentrism, (3) confront your stereotypes, (4) recognize differences, (5) adjust your communication, and (6) recognize culture shock—its inevitability and its symptoms.

Prepare Yourself

4   There's no better preparation for intercultural communication than learning about the other culture. This will help to reduce your uncertainty, which is present in all interpersonal situations, but generally greater in intercultural situations.

5   Fortunately, there are numerous sources to draw on. View a video or film that presents a realistic view of the culture that is new to you. Read what members of the culture, as well as "outsiders," write about the culture. Scan magazines and websites from the culture. Talk with members of the culture. Chat on international Internet Relay Chat (IRC) channels. Read materials addressed to people who need to communicate with those from other cultures. The easiest way to do this is to search the online bookstores (for example, Barnes and Noble and Amazon) for such keywords as *culture, international,* and *foreign travel.*

6   Another part of this preparation is to recognize and face fears that may stand in the way of effective intercultural communication. For example, you may fear for your self-esteem. You may be anxious about your ability to control the intercultural situation, or you may worry about your own level of discomfort. You may fear saying something that will be considered politically incorrect or culturally insensitive and thereby losing face.

7   Some fears, of course, are reasonable. In many cases, however, fears are groundless. Either way, you need to assess your concerns logically and weigh their consequences carefully. Then you'll be able to make informed choices about your communications.

Cultural sensitivity is at the heart of intercultural communication.

Reduce Your Ethnocentrism

8   **Ethnocentrism** is the tendency to see others and their behaviors through your own cultural filters, often as distortions of your own behaviors. It's the tendency to evaluate the values, beliefs, and behaviors of your own culture as superior—as more positive, logical, and natural than those of other cultures. For example, highly ethnocentric individuals would think that other cultures should be more like theirs, that people from other cultures often don't know what's good for them, that the lifestyles of people in other countries are not as good as theirs, and that people from other cultures are not as smart or trustworthy as people from their own culture. To achieve effective intercultural communication, it helps to see yourself and others as different but as neither inferior nor superior. And, try to become aware of the potential blinders that ethnocentrism might impose on you—admittedly, not a very easily accomplished task.

9   Ethnocentrism exists on a continuum. People are not either ethnocentric or non-ethnocentric; rather, most people are somewhere between the extremes. We're all ethnocentric to at least some degree. The most important thing to see here is that your degree of ethnocentrism will influence your interpersonal (intercultural) communications, as both sender and receiver.

Confront Your Stereotypes

10   Originally, the word *stereotype* was a printing term that referred to a plate that printed the same image over and over. A sociological or psychological **stereotype** is a fixed impression of a group of people. Everyone has attitudinal stereotypes—of national groups, religious groups, or racial groups, or perhaps of criminals, prostitutes, teachers, or plumbers. Consider, for example, if you have any stereotypes of, say, bodybuilders, the opposite sex, a racial group different from your own, members of a religion very different from your own, hard drug users, or college professors. It is very likely that you have stereotypes of several, or perhaps all, of these groups. Although we often think of stereotypes as negative ("They're lazy, dirty, and only interested in getting high"), they may also be positive ("They're smart, hard-working, and extremely loyal").

11   If you have these fixed impressions, you may, on meeting a member of a particular group, see that person primarily as a member of that group. Initially this may provide you with some helpful orientation. However, it creates problems when you apply to the person all the characteristics you assign to members of that group without examining the unique individual. If you meet a politician, for example, you may have a host of characteristics for politicians that you can readily apply to this person. To complicate matters further, you may see in this person's behavior the manifestation of various characteristics that you would not see if you did not know that this person was a politician. Because there are few visual and auditory cues in online communication, it's not surprising to find that people form impressions of their online communication partners with a heavy reliance on stereotypes (Jacobson, 1999).

Recognize Differences

12   To communicate interculturally, you need to recognize the differences between yourself and people who are culturally different, the differences within the culturally different group, and the numerous differences in meaning that arise from cultural differences.

13   **DIFFERENCES BETWEEN YOURSELF AND CULTURALLY DIFFERENT PEOPLE** A common barrier to intercultural communication is the assumption that similarities exist but that differences do not. For example, though you may easily accept different hairstyles, clothing, and foods, you may assume that, in basic values and beliefs, everyone is really alike. But that's not necessarily true. When you assume similarities and ignore differences, you'll fail to notice important distinctions. As a result, you'll risk communicating to others that your ways are the right ways and that their ways are not important to you. Consider: An American invites a Filipino coworker to dinner. The Filipino politely refuses. The American is hurt, feels that the Filipino does not want to be friendly, and does not repeat the invitation. The Filipino is hurt and concludes that the invitation was not extended sincerely. Here, it seems, both the American and the Filipino assume that their customs for inviting

people to dinner are the same—when, in fact, they aren't. A Filipino expects to be invited several times before accepting a dinner invitation. In the Philippines, an invitation given only once is viewed as insincere.

14   **DIFFERENCES WITHIN THE CULTURALLY DIFFERENT GROUP** Within every cultural group, there are wide and important differences. Just as all Americans are not alike, neither are all Indonesians, Greeks, Mexicans, and so on. When you ignore these differences—when you assume that all persons covered by the same label (in this case, a national or racial label) are the same—you're guilty of stereotyping. A good example of this is the use of the term "African American." The term stresses the unity of Africa and those who are of African descent and is analogous to "Asian American" or "European American." At the same time, if the term is used in the same sense as "German American" or "Japanese American," it ignores the great diversity within the African continent. More accurate terms would be "Nigerian American" or "Ethiopian American."

Adjust Your Communication

15   Adjusting your communication is especially import ant in intercultural situations, largely because people from different cultures use different signals or sometimes use the same signals to signify quite different things. For example, focused eye contact means honesty and openness in much of the United States. But in Japan and in many Hispanic cultures, that same behavior may signify arrogance or disrespect, particularly if engaged in by a youngster with someone significantly older.

16   As you adjust your messages, recognize that each culture has its own rules and customs for communication. These roles identify what is appropriate and what is inappropriate. Thus, for example, in U.S. culture, you would call a person you wished to date three or four days in advance. In certain Asian cultures, you might call the person's parents weeks or even months in advance. In U.S. culture, you say, as a general friendly gesture and not as a specific invitation, "Come over and pay us a visit sometime." To members of other cultures, this comment is sufficient to prompt the listeners to actually visit at their convenience. A good example of a set of cultural rules are the guidelines for communicating with people with disabilities, an extremely large and important culture that many people don't understand.

Recognize Culture Shock

17   **Culture shock** is the psychological reaction you experience when you encounter a culture very different from your own. Culture shock is normal; most people experience it when entering a new and different culture. Going away to college, moving in with a significant other, or joining the military, for example, can also result in culture shock. Nevertheless, it can be unpleasant and frustrating. Entering a new culture often engenders feelings of alienation, conspicuousness, and difference from everyone else. When you lack knowledge of the rules and customs of a new society, you cannot communicate effectively. You' re apt to blunder frequently and seriously. In your culture shock, you may not know basic things: how to ask someone for a favor or pay someone a compliment; how to extend or accept an invitation; how early or how late to arrive for an appointment, or how long to stay; how to distinguish seriousness from playfulness and politeness from indifference; how to dress for an informal, formal, or business function; how to order a meal in a restaurant, or how to summon a waiter.

18   People also may experience a kind of reverse culture shock when they return to their original culture after living in a foreign culture. Consider, for example, Peace Corps volunteers who work in economically deprived rural areas around the world. On returning to Las Vegas or Beverly Hills, they too may experience culture shock. Sailors who serve long periods aboard ships and then return to, for example, isolated farming communities may also experience culture shock.

19   Intercultural communication may be challenging, but these suggestions make it possible to communicate effectively with our diverse global community.

ORGANIZING IDEAS ABOUT THE READING

Create an outline that features the main points and supporting details of the reading. See page 26 for information about creating an outline.

THINKING CRITICALLY ABOUT THE READING

Your answers to the questions below should be in complete sentences and may require more than one sentence.

1. What types of evidence does the author use to support his thesis? Are there other types of evidence he could have used to strengthen his support?
2. On a scale of 1 to 10, how would you rate your level of ethnocentrism? Using personal examples, explain your answer.
3. How much did you know about intercultural communication before you read this selection? How has the reading changed your ideas about the topic or a specific aspect of the topic?
4. Do you detect any bias in the reading? Explain your answer.
5. Overall, what was the author's purpose in writing this excerpt, and for what specific audience is the reading most suited?

READING 6
Economics

The Global Economy

Robin Bade and Michael Parkin

This reading is an excerpt from a textbook entitled Essential Foundations of Economics, *eighth edition. Robin Bade and Michael Parkin are Professors of Economics at the University of Western Ontario. Dr. Bade graduated with a Ph.D. in Economics from Australian National University and taught in Australia and Scotland before settling in Canada. Dr. Parkin studied economics at Leister College in England, and shortly after graduating, he moved to Canada to teach at the University of Western Ontario. This husband and wife team have conducted joint research projects and published numerous scholarly articles and textbooks.*

global economy 1
The international
exchange of
goods and
services between
countries around 2
the world.

To examine the **global economy**, we must first look at the people and countries that form it.

The People

Visit the Web site of the U.S. Census Bureau and go to the population clocks to find out how many people there are today in both the United States and the entire world. On the day these words were written, November 8, 2015, the U.S. clock recorded a population of 322,115,000. The world clock recorded a global population of 7,284,290,000. The U.S. clock ticks along showing a population increase of one person every 15 seconds. The world clock spins faster, adding 30 people in the same 15 seconds.

The Economies

3   The world's 7.3 billion (and rising) population lives in 176 economies, which the International Monetary Fund classifies into two broad groups:

- Advanced economies
- Emerging market and developing economies

Advanced Economies

4   Advanced economies are the richest 29 countries (or areas). The United States, Japan, Italy, Germany, France, the United Kingdom, and Canada belong to this group. So do four new industrial Asian economies: Hong Kong, South Korea, Singapore, and Taiwan. The other advanced economies include Australia, New Zealand, and most of the rest of Western Europe. Almost 1 billion people (15 percent of the world's population) live in the advanced economies.

Emerging Market and Developing Economies

5   Emerging market economies are 28 countries in Central and Eastern Europe and Asia. Almost 500 million people live in these countries—about half of the number in the advanced economies. These countries are important because they are emerging (hence the name) from a system of state-owned production, central economic planning, and heavily regulated markets moving toward a system of free enterprise and unregulated markets.

6   Developing economies are the remaining 119 countries in Africa, Asia, the Middle East, Europe, and Central and South America. More than 5.5 billion people—almost four out of every five people—live in the developing economies.

7   Developing economies vary enormously in size, the level of average income, and the rate of growth of production and incomes. But in all the developing economies, average incomes are much lower than those in the advanced economies, and in some cases, they are extremely low.

8   Five emerging market and developing economies, representing 3 billion people or 42 percent of the world's population and known as BRICS (Brazil, Russia, India, China, and South Africa), hold regular meetings to advance the interests of these nations and draw attention to their development problems.

What in the Global Economy

9   First, let's look at the big picture. Imagine that each year the global economy produces an enormous pie. In 2015, the pie was worth about $113 trillion! To give this number some

China represents 17 percent of the economic output of the global economy.

kadmy/123rf.com

meaning, if the pie were shared equally among the world's 7.3 billion people, each of us would get a slice worth a bit less than $15,500.

Where Is the Global Pie Baked?

10   The advanced economies produce 43 percent—16 percent in the United States, 17 percent in the European Union, and 10 percent in the other advanced economies. This 43 percent of global output (by value) is produced by 15 percent of the world's population.

11   The BRICS economies together produce 31 percent of the world's output. China, with 17 percent of world production, dominates this group, and South Africa, the group's smallest member, produces barely 1 percent of global output. This 31 percent of the global pie is baked by 42 percent of the world's population.

12   The remaining 26 percent of the global pie comes from other emerging market and developing economies and is baked by 43 percent of the world's people.

13   Unlike the slices of an apple pie, those of the global pie have different fillings. Some slices have more oil, some more food, some more clothing, some more housing services, some more autos, and so on. Let's look at some of these different fillings and at some similarities too.

Some Differences in What Is Produced

14   What is produced in the developing economies contrasts sharply with that of the advanced economies. Manufacturing is the big story. Developing economies have large and growing industries, which produce textiles, footwear, sports gear, toys, electronic goods, furniture, steel, and even automobiles and airplanes.

15   Food production is a small part of the U.S. and other advanced economies and a large part of the developing economies such as Brazil, China, and India. But the advanced economies produce about one third of the world's food. How can this be? *Total* production is much larger in the advanced economies than in the developing economies, but a small percentage of a big number can be a *greater amount* than a large percentage of a small number!

Some Similarities in What Is Produced

16   If you were to visit a shopping mall in Canada, England, Australia, Japan, or any of the other advanced economies, you would wonder whether you had left the United States. You

would see Starbucks, Burger King, Pizza Hut, Domino's Pizza, KFC, Kmart, Wal-Mart, Target, Gap, Tommy Hilfiger, Lululemon, Banana Republic, the upscale Louis Vuitton and Burberry, and a host of other familiar names. And, of course, you would see McDonald's golden arches. You would see them in any of the 119 countries in which one or more of McDonald's 30,000 restaurants are located.

17   The similarities among the advanced economies go beyond the view from main street and the shopping mall. The structure of *what* is produced is similar in these economies. As percentages of the total economy, agriculture and manufacturing are small and shrinking whereas services are large and expanding.

How in the Global Economy

18   Goods and services are produced using land, labor, capital, and entrepreneurial resources, and the combinations of these resources used are chosen to produce at the lowest possible cost. Each country or region has its own blend of factors of production, but there are some interesting common patterns and crucial differences between the advanced and developing economies that we'll now examine.

Human Capital Differences

19   One of the biggest distinguishing features of an advanced economy from an emerging market or developing economy is its quantity of *human capital*. Advanced economies have much higher levels of human capital.

20   Education levels are the handiest measure of human capital. In an advanced economy such as the United States, almost everyone has completed high school. And 30 percent of the U.S. population has completed four years or more of college.

21   In contrast, in developing economies, the proportion of the population who has completed high school or has a college degree is small. In the poorest of the developing economies, many children even miss out on basic primary education—they just don't go to school at all.

22   On-the-job training and experience are also much less extensive in the developing economies than in the advanced economies.

Physical Capital Differences

23   Another major feature of an advanced economy that differentiates it from a developing economy is the amount of capital available for producing goods and services. The differences begin with the basic transportation systems. In the advanced economies, a well-developed highway system connects all the major cities and points of production. Open a map app on your phone. Contrast the U.S. interstate highway system in Texas with the sparse highways of Mexico. You would see a similar contrast if you swiped across the Atlantic Ocean and checked out the highway structures in Western Europe and Africa.

24   But it isn't the case that the developing economies have no highways and no modern trucks and cars. In fact, some of them have the newest and the best, but the new and best are usually inside and around the major cities.

25   The contrasts in the transportation system are matched by those on farms and in factories. In general, the more advanced the economy, the greater are the amount and sophistication of the capital equipment used in production. But again, the contrast is not all or nothing. Some factories in India, China, and other parts of Asia use the very latest technolo-

gies. Furniture manufacturing is an example. To make furniture of a quality that Americans are willing to buy, firms in Asia use machines like those in the furniture factories of North Carolina.

26   The differences in human capital and physical capital between advanced and developing economies have a big effect on *who* gets the goods and services, which we'll now examine.

For Whom in the Global Economy

27   Who gets the world's goods and services depends on the incomes that people earn. We're now going to see how incomes are distributed within economies and across the world.

Personal Distribution of Income

28   In the United States, the lowest-paid 20 percent of the population receives 3 percent of total income and the highest-paid 20 percent receives 50 percent of total income. The personal distribution of income in the world economy is much more unequal. According to World Bank data, the lowest-paid 20 percent of the world's population receives 2 percent of world income and the highest-paid 20 percent receives about 70 percent of world income.

International Distribution

29   Much of the greater inequality at the global level arises from differences in average incomes and the dollar value of what people can afford each day. In the United States, that number is $153 a day—an average person in the United States can buy goods and services that cost $153. This amount is around five times the world average. The European Union has an average income of around two-thirds that of the United States at $104 per day, Russia at $65 a day, China $39 a day, India $17 a day, and Africa only $11 a day.

30   As people have lost well-paid manufacturing jobs and found lower-paid service jobs, inequality has increased in the United States and in most other advanced economies. Inequality is also increasing in the developing economies. People with skills enjoy rapidly rising incomes but the incomes of the unskilled are falling.

A Happy Paradox and a Huge Challenge

31   Despite the increase in inequality inside most countries, inequality across the entire world has decreased during the past 20 years. And most important, according to Xavier Sala-i-Martin, an economics professor at Columbia University, extreme poverty has declined. Professor Sala-i-Martin estimates that between 1976 and 1998, the number of people who earn $1 a day or less fell by 235 million and the number who earn $2 a day or less fell by 450 million. This positive situation arises because in China, the largest nation, incomes have increased rapidly and lifted millions from extreme poverty. Incomes are growing quickly in India too.

32   Lifting Africa from poverty is today's big challenge. In 1960, 11 percent of the world's poor lived in Africa, but in 1998, 66 percent did. Between 1976 and 1998, the number of people in Africa who earn $1 a day or less rose by 175 million, and the number who earn $2 a day or less rose by 227 million.

The U.S. and Global Economies in Your Life

33   You've encountered a lot of facts and trends about what, how, and for whom goods and services are produced in the U.S. economy and the global economy. How can you use this information? You can use it in two ways:

1. To inform your choice of career
2. To inform your stand on the politics of protecting jobs

Making Career Choices

34   As you think about your future career, you are now better informed about some of the key trends. You know that manufacturing is shrinking.

35   The U.S. economy is what is sometimes called a post-industrial economy. Industries that provided the backbone of the economy in previous generations have fallen to barely a fifth of the economy today, and the trend continues. It is possible that by the middle of the current century, manufacturing will be as small a source of jobs as agriculture is today.

36   So, a job in a manufacturing business is likely to lead to some tough situations and possibly the need for several job changes over a working life.

37   As manufacturing shrinks, so services expand, and this expansion will continue. The provision of health-care, education, communication, wholesale and retail trades, and entertainment are all likely to expand in the future and be sources of increasing employment and rising wages. A job in a service-oriented business is more likely to lead to steady advances in income.

Taking a Political Stand on Job Protection

38   As you think about the stand you will take on the political question of protecting U.S. jobs, you are better informed about the basic facts and trends.

39   When you hear that manufacturing jobs are disappearing to China, you will be able to place that news in historical perspective. You might reasonably be concerned, especially if you or a member of your family has lost a job. But you know that trying to reverse or even halt this process is flying in the face of stubborn historical trends.

ORGANIZING IDEAS ABOUT THE READING

Write an informal response (in the form of a journal entry) to Reading #6. See page 33 for information on how to write an informal response.

THINKING CRITICALLY ABOUT THE READING

Your answers to the questions below should be in complete sentences and may require more than one sentence.

1. Why do you think the authors chose to include the visual in the reading? What message does it convey?

2. Much of the evidence included by the authors is statistical data. What statistic do you find most interesting, and how has it changed your perspective on the global economy?

3. The author uses an apple pie as a vehicle to explain the global economy. Why did the author use this comparison? Evaluate its effectiveness.

4. Do you perceive bias in paragraphs 38 and 39, or do these two paragraphs represent an attempt to present multiple sides of the issue? Explain your answer.

5. In paragraph 37, the authors state, "As manufacturing shrinks, so services expand..." Explain how and why this shift occurs.

SYNTHESIS AND INTEGRATION QUESTIONS AND ACTIVITIES

The following questions and activities ask you to synthesize information from two or more readings.

1. **Comparing Tone and Author's Purpose.** Compare the tone of Reading 1 and Reading 6. How does the writers' purpose in Reading 1 differ from the writers' purpose in Reading 6?

2. **Summarizing Readings.** Summarize what you have learned about the cultural aspects of globalization. Use information from Reading 4 and Reading 5.

3. **Explaining Relationships.** Explain the relationship of wealth to health in a globalizing world as presented in Readings 2 and 4.

4. **Comparing Sources.** In Reading 2, the authors contend that global consumption is extremely uneven and inefficient. Explain the similarities and differences in how the authors of Reading 3 and Reading 6 address the problem of wealth vs. poverty in a globalized world.

5. **Determining Agreement and Disagreement Between Readings.** On what points related to global marketing would the authors of Reading 3 and Reading 6 agree and disagree?

6. **Creating a Visual Summary.** Create a graphic or visual aid to summarize the ethical concerns of globalization found in Readings 1 and 4.

7. **Finding Agreement Among Readings.** From Readings, 1, 3, and 6, what facts do most people agree on with regard to a single global marketplace?

8. **Finding Disagreement Among Readings.** In Readings 1, 3, and 6, what facts about a single global marketplace do most people disagree about?

9. **Identifying Statements of Opinion.** Using three or more readings, underline at least five statements of opinion.

10. **Preparing a Fact Sheet.** Prepare a list of ten facts regarding globalization that would be useful in writing a response paper on the issue of globalization and diversity.

WRITING ABOUT THE READINGS

Low Stakes Writing Assignments

1. What issue related to globalization concerns you the most—a geographical, biological, business, health, communication, or economic issue? Review the readings to help you decide on the ONE issue that you would like to see addressed by policy makers. Then, in a letter to your U.S. congressional representatives, express your concerns about the issue and suggest ways that policymakers can help to address this issue.

2. In Reading 3, the authors pose this question: "Do you primarily see yourself only as a resident of Smalltown, USA, or as a member of a global community?" Write a paragraph in which you answer this question. Be sure to support it with evidence from the readings.

High Stakes Writing Assignments

3. Globalization can be of great economic, political, and cultural benefit to our world. Using the casebook readings and outside sources, write an essay on one or more positive effects of globalization. Format your essay and document your sources according to MLA standards.

4. The readings in this casebook identify numerous world problems. Choose one problem and write an essay exploring the problem and identifying possible solutions. Use the readings in this casebook as a starting point, but use other print or digital sources as well. Format your essay and document your sources according to MLA standards.

Grammar and Correctness Skill Refreshers

Writing clear, error-free sentences is an important part of the writing process. Grammatical errors can cause confusion, even misinterpretation of your ideas. Errors also create the impression that you are careless or are unconcerned about your audience and the impression you make on them.

The following section provides a brief review of common grammatical errors and explains how to correct them:

If you need further information on or practice with any of these errors, consult an online grammar help center such as https://owl.english.purdue.edu/ or use the MyLabs associated with this book.

goodluz/Shutterstock

SKILL REFRESHER #1: SENTENCE FRAGMENTS

A **sentence fragment** is a group of words that (1) lacks a subject, (2) lacks a verb, or (3) is a dependent (subordinate) clause unattached to a complete sentence. It therefore fails to express a complete thought. NOTE: A **subject** is the noun or pronoun that performs the action of the sentence. A **verb** is a word that conveys the action or state of being of the subject. A **dependent clause** is a group of words beginning with a subordinating conjunction like *although, because, if, since, unless, wherever,* or *while* or with a relative pronoun like *which, that, what, who,* or *whoever.*

How to Spot Sentence Fragments

To identify fragments in your writing, ask the following questions of each sentence.

1. **Is there a subject?** To find the subject, ask who or what is performing the action of the sentence.

   FRAGMENT: Asked Professor Gomez how long he had been teaching at Ohio State. [Who asked Professor Gomez?]

   CORRECT: Gail asked Professor Gomez how long he had been teaching at Ohio State.

2. **Is there a verb?** To find the verb, look for a word that conveys what is happening, what has happened, or what will happen. Do not confuse a verb with verbals (*-ing, -ed,* or infinitive *"to"* forms of verbs that are used as nouns or modifiers). A true verb changes form to communicate a time change. A verbal does not.

   FRAGMENT: A nervous, pressured feeling and a headache.

   CORRECT: A nervous, pressured feeling and a headache struck me.

   FRAGMENT: The express train leaving the station at four.

   CORRECT: The express train will leave the station at four.

   FRAGMENT: To get a taxi and hurry downtown.

   CORRECT: I need to get a taxi and hurry downtown.

3. **Is the dependent clause—a group of words starting with a subordinating conjunction or relative pronoun—attached to a complete sentence?** A dependent clause cannot stand alone.

   FRAGMENT: Although we wanted to go to the softball game.

   CORRECT: Although we wanted to go to the softball game, we could not find the park.

   FRAGMENT: If we had asked directions or bought a map.

   CORRECT: We might have found the park if we had asked directions or bought a map.

How to Correct Sentence Fragments

1. **Add the missing subject or verb.**

   FRAGMENT: Waiting for my paycheck to be delivered.

   REVISED: I was waiting for my paycheck to be delivered.

2. **Revise by combining the fragment with an appropriate existing complete sentence.**

   FRAGMENT: My sister loved her job at the jewelry store. Until she got a new boss.

   REVISED: Until she got a new boss, my sister loved her job at the jewelry store.

3. **Remove the word or phrase that makes the statement incomplete.**

   FRAGMENT: While I was waiting for class to begin.

   REVISED: I was waiting for class to begin.

SKILL REFRESHER #2: RUN-ON SENTENCES

A **run-on sentence** (also known as a fused sentence) consists of two complete thoughts within the same sentence, without the necessary punctuation to separate them. Each thought could stand alone as a separate sentence.

RUN-ON: Political science is a difficult course I am thinking of dropping it and taking it next semester.

RUN-ON: My younger sister will visit next weekend I probably will not have much time to study.

How to Spot Run-Ons

You can often spot run-ons by reading them aloud. Listen for a break or change in your voice midway through the sentence. Read aloud the two examples above to see if you can hear the break.

How to Correct Run-Ons

Simply adding a comma to correct a run-on sentence does not work. Doing so leads to an error known as a *comma splice*. There are four basic ways to correct a run-on sentence.

1. **Create two separate sentences**. End the first thought with a period and begin the next with a capital letter.

   My younger sister will visit next weekend. I probably will not have much time to study.

2. **Connect the two thoughts by using a semicolon**. My younger sister will visit next weekend; I probably will not have much time to study.

3. **Join the two thoughts by using a comma and a coordinating conjunction** (*and, or, but, for, nor, so,* or *yet*).

   My younger sister will visit next weekend, so I probably will not have much time to study.

4. **Subordinate one thought to the other**. To do this, make one thought into a dependent clause (a subordinate clause) by adding a subordinating conjunction (such as *although, because, since,* or *unless*) or a relative pronoun (such as *which, that, what, who,* or *whoever*). Then connect the dependent clause to an independent clause (a group of words with a subject and a verb that expresses a complete thought and that can stand alone as a complete sentence).

   Since my young sister will visit next weekend, I probably will not have much time to study.

SKILL REFRESHER #3: SUBJECT-VERB AGREEMENT

A verb must agree with its subject in number. A subject that refers to one person, place, or thing is called a *singular subject*. A subject that refers to more than one is called a *plural subject*.

Guidelines

1. A singular subject must be used with a singular verb. The <u>dog wants</u> to go jogging with me.

2. A plural subject must be used with a plural verb. The <u>dogs want</u> to go jogging with me.

Mistakes to Watch For

Subject-verb agreement errors often occur in the following situations:

1. **With compound subjects (two or more subjects)**.

   INCORRECT: <u>Yolanda</u> and <u>Lion wants</u> to lead the way.

   CORRECT: <u>Yolanda</u> and <u>Lion want</u> to lead the way.

2. **When the verb comes before the subject**.

   INCORRECT: There <u>is</u> four gas <u>stations</u> on Main Street.

   CORRECT: There <u>are</u> four gas <u>stations</u> on Main Street.

3. **When a word or phrase comes between the subject and the verb**.

   INCORRECT: The <u>woman</u> standing in the waves with the other swimmers <u>win</u> a prize for her endurance.

   CORRECT: The <u>woman</u> standing in the waves with the other swimmers <u>wins</u> a prize for her endurance.

4. **With indefinite pronouns (pronouns like *someone* or *everybody*, which do not refer to a specific person)**. Some indefinite pronouns (*everyone, each, neither, such as*) take a singular verb; others (both or many) always take a plural verb. Some indefinite pronouns may take either a singular or a plural verb (all, any, none). Treat the pronoun as singular if it refers to something that cannot be counted. Treat the pronoun as plural if it refers to more than one of something that can be counted.

   INCORRECT: <u>Everybody wish</u> to become a millionaire.

   CORRECT: <u>Everybody wishes</u> to become a millionaire.

SKILL REFRESHER #4: PRONOUN-ANTECEDENT AGREEMENT

A **pronoun** (*he, she, it*) substitutes for a noun and must agree in person, number, and gender (male, female) with its **antecedent** (the word it replaces).

Rules to Follow

1. **If the noun is singular, the pronoun replacing it must also be singular.**

   <u>Robert</u> wanted to lend me <u>his</u> class notes.

2. **If the noun is plural, the pronoun substitute must be plural.**

   Mark wrote <u>lyrics</u> for songs; <u>many</u> were depressing and sad.

3. **Some indefinite pronouns are singular; others are plural.** Use a singular pronoun to replace a singular noun and a plural pronoun to replace a plural noun.

   <u>One</u> of the team members could not find <u>his</u> keys.

   <u>Both</u> of the instructors said <u>they</u> planned to vacation in Maine.

4. **Some indefinite pronouns are either singular or plural, depending on how they are used.** If the pronoun refers to something that cannot be counted, use a singular pronoun to refer to it. If the pronoun refers to something that can be counted, use a plural pronoun to refer to it.

   Too much <u>ice</u> on airplane wings is dangerous, so <u>it</u> is removed before takeoff.

   Many <u>students</u> think <u>they</u> will register for an economics course.

5. **Use a plural pronoun to refer to two or more nouns linked by** *and.*

Sam and Mark lost their keys.

6. **If a pronoun substitutes for two or more nouns joined by** *or* **or** *nor,* **the pronoun agrees with the noun it is nearer to.**

Either Mrs. Marcus or her sons will drive their car.

SKILL REFRESHER #5: PRONOUN REFERENCE

A **pronoun** refers to a specific noun and is used to replace that noun. It must always refer clearly to the noun or pronoun intended.

Rules to Follow

1. **A pronoun must refer to a specific word or words.** Avoid vague or unclear references.

   INCORRECT: They said on the evening news that the President would visit France. [Who said this?]

   CORRECT: The evening news commentator reported that the President would visit France.

2. **If more than one noun is present, it must be clear to which noun the pronoun refers.**

   INCORRECT: Jackie told Amber that she passed the exam. [Did Jackie pass, or did Amber pass?]

   CORRECT: Jackie told Amber, "You passed the exam."

3. **Use the relative pronouns** *who, whom, which,* **and** *that* **with the appropriate antecedent.**

   INCORRECT: Sam, whom is the captain of the team, accepted the award.

   CORRECT: Sam, who is the captain of the team, accepted the award. [Sam is the subject, so the correct pronoun is who.]

SKILL REFRESHER #6: DANGLING MODIFIERS

A **modifier** is a word or group of words that describes another word or qualifies or limits the meaning of another word. When a modifier appears at the beginning of the sentence, it must be followed immediately by the word it describes. Dangling modifiers are *not* followed by the word they describe. Dangling modifiers either modify nothing or do not clearly refer to the correct word or word group.

   DANGLING: After getting off the bus, the driver pulled away.

   CORRECT: After I got off the bus, the driver pulled away.

How to Correct Dangling Modifiers

There are two ways to correct dangling modifiers:

1. **Add a word or words so that the modifier describes the word or words it is intended to describe.** Place the new word(s) just after the modifier.

   DANGLING: While sitting under the maple tree, ants started to attack.

   CORRECT: While sitting under the maple tree, I was attacked by ants.

2. **Change the modifier to a dependent clause.** (You may need to change the verb in the modifier.)

   DANGLING: After giving the dog a flea bath, the dog hid under the bed.

   CORRECT: After I gave the dog a flea bath, she hid under the bed.

SKILL REFRESHER #7: MISPLACED MODIFIERS

Misplaced modifiers are words or phrases that do not modify or explain other words the way the writer intended.

MISPLACED: Crisp and spicy, the waitress served the chicken wings to our table. [Was the waitress crisp and spicy, or were the wings?]

CORRECT: The waitress served the crisp, spicy chicken wings to our table.

MISPLACED: I saw a dress in a magazine that cost $1200. [Did the magazine or the dress cost $1200?]

CORRECT: In a magazine, I saw a dress that cost $1200.

MISPLACED: Already late for class, the red light delayed Joe even longer. [Was the light or Joe late for class?]

CORRECT: The red light delayed Joe, already late for class, even longer.

How to Avoid Misplaced Modifiers

To avoid misplaced modifiers, place the modifier immediately before or after the word or words it modifies.

SKILL REFRESHER #8: PARALLELISM

Parallelism means that words, phrases, or clauses in a series have similar grammatical form. Making corresponding parts of a sentence parallel in structure and length makes your writing clearer and easier to read.

What Should Parallel?

1. **Words in Series.** When two or more nouns, verbs, or adjectives appear together in a sentence, they should be parallel in grammatical form. Verbs should be in the same tense.

   INCORRECT: All day long the workers on the construction project next door were banging, thumping, and pounded so loudly I couldn't concentrate on my job.

   CORRECT: All day long, the workers on the construction project next door banged, thumped, and pounded so loudly that I couldn't concentrate on my job.

2. **Phrases.**

   INCORRECT: My sister likes wearing crazy hats, dressing in funky clothes, and to go to classic movies.

   CORRECT: My sister likes wearing crazy hats, dressing in funky clothes, and going to classic movies.

3. **Clauses**.

   INCORRECT: While Marita worked on her history paper, her husband was watching the baby.

   CORRECT: While Marita worked on her history paper, her husband watched the baby.

SKILL REFRESHER #9: COMMA USAGE

Commas separate parts of a sentence from one another. Commas most often separate

1. **items in a list or series**

   I need to buy jeans, socks, T-shirts, and a new tie.

2. **introductory phrases**

   After a cup of coffee, I was awake enough to read the paper.

3. **information that interrupts the sentence**

   The president of our chamber of commerce, Lucy Skarda, arranged the meeting.

4. **direct quotations**

   Barbara Walters always says, "We're in touch, so you'll be in touch."

5. **two independent clauses joined by a conjunction**

   We bill on a 60-day cycle, and we expect payment within 30 days.

6. **a dependent clause from an independent clause when the dependent clause comes first in the sentence.**

   Because I enjoy watching animals, I visit the zoo often.

Commas are also used in dates, addresses, numbers, and openings and closings of letters.

SKILL REFRESHER #10: USING COLONS AND SEMICOLONS

When to Use Colons

Colons are most commonly used

1. **after an independent clause to introduce a concluding explanation**

   Use the right tool: if you want to drive a nail, use a hammer, not your shoe.

2. **after an independent clause to introduce a list or series**

   The American poetry class surveyed a wide range of poets: Whitman, Dickinson, Ashbery, and Pound.

3. **after an independent clause to introduce a long or formal quotation**

   Mark Twain commented on human behavior: "Man is the only animal that blushes—or needs to."

When to Use Semicolons

Semicolons are most commonly used

1. **between two independent clauses not connected by a coordinating conjunction** (*and, but, for, nor, or, so, yet*)

   Each state has equal representation in the Senate; representation in the House of Representatives is based on population.

2. **to separate items in a list when they themselves contain commas**

   The library bulletin board has a display of "Pioneers in Thought," which includes Freud, the creator of psychoanalysis; Marx, the famous communist writer; Copernicus, the father of modern astronomy; and Watson and Crick, the discoverers of DNA.

Text Credits

Chapter 1

pp. 8–10: Henslin, James M., *Sociology: A Down–to–Earth Approach.* 11th ed., pp. 261-264, 403, © 2012. Reprinted and electronically reproduced by permission of Pearson Education, Inc. New York, NY; **p. 19:** Suppes, Mary Ann and Carolyn Cressey Wells, *The Social Work Experience: An Introduction to Social Work and Social Welfare*, 6th ed., © Pearson Education, Inc., 2013; **p. 20:** Seiler, William J., Melissa L. Beall, and Joseph P. Mazer, *Communication,* 10th ed., © Pearson Education, Inc., 2017. **pp. 25–26:** Thompson, William E. and Joseph V. Hickey, *Society in Focus, 2010 Census Update,* 7th ed., © Pearson Education, Inc., 2012; **pp. 27–28:** Keegan, Warren J. and Mark C. Green, *Global Marketing*, 7th ed., © 2012. Reprinted and electronically reproduced by permission of Pearson Education, Inc., New York, NY.

Chapter 2

pp. 41–42: Garcia, Santiago Quintana, Student Essay, "The Space In-Between." Reprinted with permission; **pp. 44–45:** Garcia, Santiago Quintana, Student Essay, "The Space In-Between." Reprinted with permission; **pp. 50–51:** Garcia, Santiago Quintana, Student Essay, Identity – Mexican? White?" Reprinted with permission; **pp. 63–64:** Garcia, Santiago Quintana, Student Essay, "Living in Two Worlds." Reprinted with permission.

Chapter 3

p. 74: Keegan, Warren J. and Mark C. Green, *Global Marketing*, 7th ed., © 2012. Reprinted and electronically reproduced by permission of Pearson Education, Inc., New York, NY; **p. 75:** Rubenstein, James, *Contemporary Human Geography*, 2nd ed., © Pearson Education, Inc., 2013; **p. 76:** Carnes, Mark C. and John A. Garraty, *The American Nation*, 11th ed., © Pearson Education, Inc., 2003; **pp. 76–77:** Keegan, Warren J. and Mark C. Green, *Global Marketing*, 7th ed., © 2012. Reprinted and electronically reproduced by permission of Pearson Education, Inc., New York, NY; **p. 81:** Ciccarelli, Saundra K. and J. Noland White, *Psychology*, 3rd ed., © Pearson Education, Inc., 2012; **p. 83:** Donatelle, Rebecca, *Health: The Basics, Green Edition*, 9th ed., © Pearson Education, Inc., 2012; **p. 86:** Ebert, Ronald J. and Ricky W. Griffin, *Business Essentials*, 8th ed., © Pearson Education, Inc., 2011; **p. 87:** © Merriam-Webster. Used with Permission.

Chapter 4

p. 99: Devito, Joseph A., *Human Communication: The Basic Course*, 12th ed., © Pearson Education, Inc., 2012; **pp. 100–101:** Hubbard, R. Glenn and Anthony Patrick O'Brien, *Essentials of Economics*, 3rd ed., © Pearson Education, Inc., 2013; **p. 101:** Krause, Mark and Daniel Corts, *Psychological Science: Modeling Scientific Literacy*, © Pearson Education, Inc., 2012; **pp. 101–102:** Schwartz, Mary Ann and Barbara Marliene Scott, *Marriages and Families: Diversity and Change,* 7th ed., © Pearson Education, Inc., 2012; **p. 102:** Goodenough, Judith and Betty A. McGuire, *Biology of Humans*, 6th ed., p. 233, © Pearson Education, Inc., 2017; **p. 105:** Kotler, Phillip and Gary Armstrong, *Principles of Marketing*, 11th ed., © Pearson Education, Inc., 2013; **p. 106:** Kunz, Jennifer, *THINK Marriages and Families,* 1st ed., © Pearson Education, Inc., 2011; **p. 106:** Benokraitis, Nicole V., *Marriages and Families*, 8th ed., © Pearson Education Inc., 2015; **p. 107:** Clow, Kenneth E. and Donald Baack, *Integrated Advertising, Promotion, and Marketing Communications*, 7th ed., p. 208, © Pearson Education, Inc., 2016; **p. 107:** Belk, Colleen and Virginia Borden Maier, *Biology: Science For Life With Physiology, Books A La Carte Edition,* 4th ed., © 2013. Reprinted and electronically reproduced by permission of Pearson Education, Inc., New York, NY; **pp. 107–108:** Feldman, Robert, *Development Across the Life Span*, 8th ed., p. 173, © Pearson, Inc., 2017 **p. 108:** Goldman, Thomas F. and Henry R. Cheeseman, *The Paralegal Professional*, 3rd ed., © Pearson Education, Inc., 2011; **p. 108:** Marshall, Suzanne G., Hazel O. Jackson, and M. Sue Stanley, *Individuality in Clothing Selection and Personal Appearance,* 7th ed., © Pearson Education, Inc., 2012;

Wilcox, Dennis L., Glen T. Cameron, and Bryan H. Reber, *Public Relations: Strategies and Tactics*, 11th ed., p. 291, © Pearson Education, Inc., 2016; **p. 109:** Solomon, Michael R., *Consumer Behavior*, 10th ed., © 2011. Reprinted and electronically reproduced by permission of Pearson Education, Inc., New York, NY; **pp. 109–110:** Blake, Joan Salge, *Nutrition and You, My Plate Edition*, 2nd ed., © 2012. Reprinted and electronically reproduced by permission of Pearson Education, Inc., New York, NY.

Chapter 5

pp. 119–120: Donatelle, Rebecca J., *My Health: An Outcomes Approach*, 2nd ed., © Pearson Education, Inc., 2013; **p. 120:** Powers, Scott K. and Stephen L. Dodd, *Total Fitness and Wellness*, 7th ed., © Pearson Education, Inc., 2017; **p. 120:** Barlow, Hugh D., *Criminal Justice in America*, © Pearson Education, Inc., 2000; **p. 135:** Hill, John W., Terry W. McCreary, and Doris K. Kolb, *Chemistry for Changing Times*, 13th ed., © 2013. Reprinted and electronically reproduced by permission of Pearson Education, Inc., New York, NY; **p. 136:** DeVito, Joseph A., *Messages: Building Interpersonal Communication Skills*, 5th ed., Pearson Education, Inc., 2002; **p. 136:** Solomon, Michael, *Consumer Behavior*, 5th ed., © Pearson Education, Inc., 2002; **p. 137:** Ebert, Ronald J. and Ricky W. Griffin, *Business Essentials*, 7th ed., © Pearson Education, Inc., 2009; **p. 138:** Keegan, Warren J. and Mark C. Green, *Global Marketing*, 7th ed., © 2012. Reprinted and electronically reproduced by permission of Pearson Education, Inc., New York, NY; **p. 139:** Bonvillain, Nancy, *Cultural Anthropology*, 3rd ed., © Pearson Education, Inc., New York, NY; **p.140:** Adapted from Stanford, Craig, John S. Allen, and Susan C. Anton, *Exploring Biological Anthropology: The Essentials*, 4th ed., © Pearson Education, Inc., 2017; **pp. 140–141:** Sayre, Henry M., *Discovering the Humanities*, 2nd ed., © Pearson Education, Inc., 2013; **p. 141:** Donatelle, Rebecca J., *Health: The Basics*, 10th ed., © Pearson Education, Inc., 2013.

Chapter 6

pp. 145–146: Stroup, Claire, Student Essay, "The Woes of Internet Dating." Used with permission.

Chapter 7

p. 164: Newell, Lyman Churchill, *Descriptive Chemistry*, © DC Heath, 1909; **p. 169:** Donatelle, Rebecca J., *Access to Health*, 12th ed., © Pearson Education, Inc., 2012; **p. 170:** Limmer, Daniel and Michael F. O'Keefe, *Emergency Care*, 12th ed., © Pearson Education, Inc., 2012; **pp. 171–172:** Belk, Colleen and Virginia Borden Maier, *Biology: Science For Life With Physiology, Books A La Carte Edition*, 4th ed., © 2013. Reprinted and electronically reproduced by permission of Pearson Education, Inc., New York, NY; **p. 178:** Rowntree, Les, Martin Lewis, Marie Price, and William Wyckoff, *Diversity Amid Globalization: World Regions, Environment, Development*, 5th ed., © Pearson Education, Inc., 2012; **p. 179:** Miller, Barbara, *Cultural Anthropology in a Globalizing World*, 3rd ed., © Pearson Education, Inc., 2011; **p. 179:** Donatelle, Rebecca J., *Health: The Basics*, 10th ed., © Pearson Education, Inc., 2013; **p. 184:** Krogh, David, *Biology: A Guide to the Natural World*, 4th ed., © Pearson Education, Inc., 2009; **p. 184:** Tortora, Gerald J. and Sandra Reynolds Grabowski, *Introduction to the Human Body*, 9th ed., © John Wiley, 2012; **p. 184:** Frank Schmalleger, *Criminology Today, An Integrative Introduction*, 8th ed., © Pearson Education, Inc., 2017; **p. 187:** Thio, Alex, *Sociology: A Brief Introduction*, 7th ed., © Pearson Education, Inc., 2009; **pp. 188–189:** Lynch, April, Barry Elmore, and Tanya Morgan, *Choosing Health*, 1st ed., © Pearson Education, Inc., 2012; **p. 189:** Carl H. Dahlman, *Introduction to Geography: People, Places & Environment*, 6th edition, Pearson; **p. 194:** Krogh, David, *Biology: A Guide to the Natural World*, 4th ed., © Pearson Education, Inc., 2009; **p. 196:** Christensen, Norm, *The Environment and You*, © Pearson Education, Inc., 2013.

Chapter 8

pp. 210–214: Matsui, David Student Essay, "The iAm: How Certain Brands Inspire the Most Loyal Consumers Ever." Used with Permission; **pp. 237–240:** Simmons, Adam. "Weighing the Consequences of Censorship in Media." Used with Permission. **pp. 243–244:** Kotler, Phillip and Gary Armstrong, *Principles of Marketing*, 11th ed., © Pearson Education, Inc., 2013; **pp. 247–248:** Brehm, Sharon S., Saul M. Kassin, and Steven Fein, *Social Psychology*, 5th ed., © Houghton Mifflin, 2002; **p. 248:** Weaver II, Richard, *Understanding Interpersonal Communication*, 7th ed., © Pearson Education, Inc., 1997; **pp. 249–250:** Audesirk, Teresa, Gerald Audesirk, and Bruce E. Byers, *Biology: Life on Earth*, 10th ed., © Pearson Education, Inc., 2014; **p. 250:** Wright, Richard T. and Dorothy O. Boorse, *Environmental Science: Toward a Sustainable Future*, 11th ed., © Pearson Education, Inc., 2011.

Chapter 9

p. 265: Batstone, David, excerpt from "Katja's Story: Human Trafficking Thrives in the New Global Economy," *Sojourners Magazine*, June 2006, © 2006 David Batstone. Reprinted by permission of the author; **p. 268:** Thompson, William E. and

Joseph V. Hickey, *Society in Focus, 2010 Census Update,* 7th ed., © Pearson Education, Inc., 2012; **p. 268:** Schwartz, Mary Ann and Barbara Marliene, Scott, *Marriages and Families: Diversity and Change,* 7th ed., © Pearson Education, Inc., 2012; **p. 269:** Fagin, James A., *Criminal Justice,* 2nd ed., © 2007. Reprinted and electronically reproduced by permission of Pearson Education, Inc., New York, NY; **pp. 278–279:** Solomon, Michael R., *Consumer Behavior,* 10th ed., © 2011. Reprinted and electronically reproduced by permission of Pearson Education, Inc., New York, NY; **p. 279:** Edwards, George C., Martin P. Wattenberg, and Robert L. Lineberry, *Government in America: People, Politics, and Policy,* 4th ed., © Pearson Education, Inc., 1989; **p. 280:** Donatelle, Rebecca J. and Patricia Ketcham, *Access to Health,* 12th ed., © 2012. Reprinted and electronically reproduced by permission of Pearson Education, Inc., New York, NY; **p. 281:** Thompson, William E. and Joseph V. Hickey, *Society in Focus, 2010 Census Update,* 7th ed., © Pearson Education, Inc., 2012; **pp. 290–291:** Hill, John W., Terry W. McCreary, and Doris K. Kolb, *Chemistry for Changing Times,* 13th ed., © Pearson Education, Inc., 2013; **pp. 291–292:** Hill, John W., Terry W. McCreary, and Doris K. Kolb, *Chemistry for Changing Times,* 13th ed., © 2013. Reprinted and electronically reproduced by permission of Pearson Education, Inc., New York, NY; **p. 292:** Yudkin, Jeremy, *Understanding Music,* 6th ed., © Pearson Education, Inc., 2010; **p. 297:** Henslin, James M., *Sociology: A Down-to-Earth Approach,* 10th ed., pp. 39, 109, 111, 317, © 2010. Reprinted and electronically reproduced by permission of Pearson Education, Inc., New York, NY; **p. 299:** Henslin, James M., *Sociology: A Down-to-Earth Approach,* 10th ed., pp. 39, 109, 111, 317, © 2010. Reprinted and electronically reproduced by permission of Pearson Education, Inc., New York, NY.

Chapter 10

p. 307: Carl, John, *Think Social Problems,* 1st ed., © Pearson Education, Inc., 2011; **pp. 311–313:** Akhtar, Aysha. "Who Are the Animals in Animal Experiments?" Originally published in *The Huffington Post,* January 12, 2014. Used by permission of the author; **p. 317:** Faragher, John Mack, Mari Jo Buhle, Daniel Czitrom, and Susan H. Armitage, *Out of Many: A History of the American People,* 7th ed., © Pearson Education, Inc., 2010; **pp. 324–328:** Frey, Sarah. "Standardized Testing: An Argument for Abolishment," Used by permission.

Chapter 11

pp. 341–346: Donatelle, Rebecca J. and Patricia Ketchum, *Access to Health,* 12th ed., pp. 282-83, 386, 646-647, © 2012. Reprinted and electronically reproduced by permission of Pearson Education, Inc., New York, NY; **pp. 354–357:** Walton, Alice, "Hurtful and Beautiful: Life with Multiple Sclerosis," *The Atlantic,* August 30, 2012. Used with permission; **pp. 364–367:** Ginty, Molly M., "Military Women: All Guts, No Glory." *Ms.* Magazine, Fall 2011. As appeared in *Utne Reader,* March/April 2012. Reprinted by permission of *Ms.* Magazine, © 2011.

Chapter 12

pp. 381–385: Vestal, Christine, "'Katrina Brain': The Invisible Long-Term Toll of Megastorms," *Politico,* October 12, 2017. Christine Vestal, Politico, and Pew Charitable Trusts. Used by permission; **pp. 395–398:** Bonnington, Christina, "Our E-Waste Problem Is Ridiculous and Gadget Makers Aren't Helping," *Wired,* December 8, 2014. Christina Bonnington/*Wired* © Conde Nast. Used with permission; **p. 406–409:** Withgott, Jay H. and Matthew Laposata, *Environment: The Science Behind the Stories,* 5th ed., pp.135–139, 655-665, © 2014. Reprinted and electronically reproduced by permission of Pearson Education, Inc., New York, NY; **p. 408:** Withgott, Jay H. and Matthew Laposata, *Environment: The Science Behind the Stories,* 6th ed., © 2018. Reprinted and electronically reproduced by permission of Pearson Education, Inc., New York, NY.

Chapter 13

pp. 422–424: Kunz, Jenifer, *Think Marriages and Families,* 1st ed., pp. 83-84, © 2011. Reprinted and electronically reproduced by permission of Pearson Education, Inc., New York, NY; **pp. 433–435:** Seppala, Emma, "Are You 'Phubbing' Right Now?" This article was originally published in *Greater Good,* the online magazine of the Greater Good Science Center at UC Berkeley. Reprinted with permission. For more articles like this, visit greatergood.berkeley.edu.

Chapter 14

pp. 460–436: Garcia, M.A., "Eggs for Sale." Used with permission; **pp. 472–474:** Ray, Keisha, "Why the Right to Die Movement Needed Brittany Manyard," Bioethics.net, November 12, 2014. Reprinted with permission; **pp. 484–487:** Berman, Audrey T., Shirlee Snyder, and Geralyn Frandsen, *Kozier & Erb's Fundamentals of Nursing,* 10th ed., © 2016. Reprinted and electronically reproduced by permission of Pearson Education, Inc., New York, NY.

Chapter 15

pp. 500–503: Hinman, Ed, "How to Protect Yourself During a Mass Shooting," *The Washington Post*, November 6, 2017. Used by permission; **pp. 512–515:** Mitchell, Anna and Larry Diamond, "China's Surveillance State Should Scare Everyone," © 2018, The Atlantic Media Co., as first published in *The Atlantic* Magazine. All rights reserved. Distributed by Tribune Content Agency, LLC. Used with permission; **pp. 523–526:** Schmalleger, Frank, *Criminology Today: An Integrative Introduction*, 7th ed., © 2015. Reprinted and electronically reproduced by permission of Pearson Education, Inc., New York, NY.

Chapter 16

pp. 539–551: Womble, Ashley, "A Brother Lost." This article first appeared in Salon.com, July 27, 2010 at https://www.Salon.com. An online version remains in the Salon archives. Reprinted with permission; **pp. 550–553:** Weil, Elizabeth, "American Schools are Failing Nonconformist Kids. Here's How," *The New Republic*, September 2, 2013, © 2013. Used by permission; **pp. 562–568:** Solomon, Michael R., *Consumer Behavior*, 10th ed., © 2011. Reprinted and electronically reproduced by permission of Pearson Education, Inc, New York, NY.

Chapter 17

pp. 581–583: Wheaton, Thomas, "Bipolar Disorder: The Agony and the Ecstasy." Used with permission; **pp. 592–595:** Chemerinsky, Erwin, "Hate Speech Is Protected Free Speech, Even on College Campuses," Vox Media, Inc., December 26, 2017. https://www.vox.com/the-big-idea/2017/10/25/16524832/campus-free-speech-firstamendment-protest\. Used by permission; **pp. 604–608:** Schmalleger, Frank J., *Criminology Today: An Integrative Introduction*, 6th ed., pp.397–400, © 2012. Reprinted and electronically reproduced by permission of Pearson Education, Inc., New York, NY.

Part 3

pp. 625–627: Rowntree, Lester, Martin Lewis, Marie Price, and William Wyckoff, *Globalization and Diversity: Geography of a Changing World*, 5th ed., © 2017. Reprinted and electronically reproduced by permission of Pearson Education, Inc., New York, NY; **pp. 628–629:** Audesirk, Gerald, Teresa Audesirk, and Bruce E. Byers, *Biology: Life on Earth with Physiology*, 11th ed., © 2017. Reprinted and electronically reproduced by permission of Pearson Education, Inc., New York, NY; **pp. 630–633:** Solomon, Michael R., Greg W. Marshall, and Elnora W. Stuart, *Marketing: Real People, Real Choices*, 9th ed., © 2018. Reprinted and electronically reproduced by permission of Pearson Education, Inc., New York, NY; **pp. 633–637:** Miller, Barbara, *Cultural Anthropology in a Globalizing World*, 4th ed., © 2017. Reprinted and electronically reproduced by permission of Pearson Education, Inc., New York, NY; **pp. 637–642:** Devito, Joseph A., *Interpersonal Messages*, 4th ed., © 2017. Reprinted and electronically reproduced by permission of Pearson Education, Inc., New York, NY; **pp. 642–647:** Bade, Robin and Michael Parkin, *Essential Foundations of Economics*, 8th ed., © 2018. Reprinted and electronically reproduced by permission of Pearson Education, Inc., New York, NY.

Index